IBM® WebSphere®
Application Server
Programming

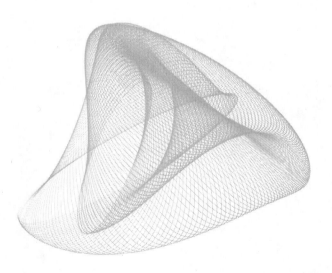

About the Author

Bassem (Max) Jamaleddine is a Web Systems Engineer with five years of diversified contractual experience with IBM. He administered and orchestrated the development of several main projects at IBM's T.J.Watson Research Center, from the Java-based network computer to the new generation of IBM's WAS technology.

A strong mathematical background has helped foster his belief that the soul of understanding new computer technology lies in disciplined coding coupled with proper system administration.

His UNIX knowledge dates from the early stages of PDP-11 system programming to the IBM SuperPower Parallel machines geared by newer AIX technologies. He has lectured at the City University of New York on advanced system programming, and on compiler and assembler construction. During the dot.com explosion, he was a major Object Oriented developer for Wall Street e-businesses, building user registration, authentication, shopping carts, and tracking and debugging routines. His forte is the development of algorithms for pattern recognition and calligraphy, such as the grammar to recognize chromosomes and digital signatures.

He earned an M.S. in Computer Science from the City University of New York, a B.S. in Computer Mathematics from Lebanese American University, and a mathematics diploma from International College in Lebanon.

He started development of Project-9 at Total Computing & Network Design, Inc. He is actively consulting on the East Coast for WebSphere deployment.

IBM® WebSphere®
Application Server
Programming

Bassem W. Jamaleddine

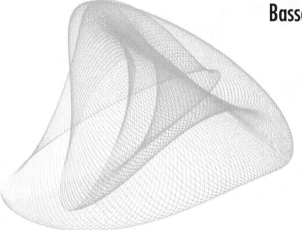

McGraw-Hill/Osborne

New York   Chicago   San Francisco
Lisbon   London   Madrid   Mexico City   Milan
New Delhi   San Juan   Seoul   Singapore   Sydney   Toronto

The McGraw·Hill Companies

McGraw-Hill/Osborne
2600 Tenth Street
Berkeley, California 94710
U.S.A.

To arrange bulk purchase discounts for sales promotions, premiums, or fund-raisers, please contact **McGraw-Hill**/Osborne at the above address. For information on translations or book distributors outside the U.S.A., please see the International Contact Information page immediately following the index of this book.

IBM® WebSphere® Application Server Programming

1234567890 CUS CUS 0198765432

ISBN 0-07-222459-2

Publisher	Brandon A. Nordin
Vice President & Associate Publisher	Scott Rogers
Editorial Director	Wendy Rinaldi
Project Editor	Elizabeth Seymour
Technical Editor	Chris Moss
Copy Editor	Chrisa Hotchkiss
Proofreader	Paul Medoff
Indexer	Valerie Perry
Computer Designers	Carie Abrew, Lucie Ericksen, Apollo Publishing Services
Illustrators	Michael Mueller, Lyssa Wald
Series Designer	Roberta Steele
Cover Series Designer	Greg Scott
Cover Illustration	Akira Inoue/Photonica

This book was composed with Corel VENTURA™ Publisher.

This book is dedicated in loving memory to my sister,
Dima Jamaleddine

Contents at a Glance

Part IV   **Stress-Testing, Tracing, and Debugging**

Part V   **Monitoring, Tuning, and Risk Management**

Part VI   **Appendixes**

Contents

Part V   **Monitoring, Tuning, and Risk Management**

Acknowledgments

My thanks are extended to all those who stood by me during the writing and editing of this work; to those who exercised patience at my obstinacy in re-working the text for greater clarity, and to those who, sometimes, lost patience with me. I am particularly grateful to Chris Moss who, all the way from Down Under, carefully checked my ramblings for clarity and correctness, and even found WASMON a ripper. I am deeply indebted to Elizabeth Seymour and Chrisa Hotchkiss, as well, for having glanced fair enough at each and every letter in this manuscript.

Foreword

This text explains the fundamentals of the functionality and programming of WebSphere Application Server (WAS) that are essential for readers whose aim is programming or administering the product. The text is intended to give the reader an understanding of the basic functions of WAS from the computer system perspective. The explanation follows a practical approach to understanding WAS independently of a specific version. Therefore, the text shows a (programming) methodology that is applicable to WAS v3.5, v4, and to the upcoming release of WAS v5.

As necessary background, the reader should possess programming ability in some high-level language. One full course in Java programming and some rudimentary knowledge of Perl and shell script programming constitute the level of competence required for all parts of this text. Programming for WAS is not confined solely to Java. Because J2EE application servers and J2EE application programming demand the editing of many metafiles and descriptor files, we have chosen to use Perl, shell, the UNIX make utility, and other UNIX tools, to do the text preprocessing, compilation, and deployment of code. The choice of UNIX as a development environment is justified since it is the only system that promotes application development in enterprises.

Basic application server programming is taught in the context of distributed systems that vary in platforms; therefore, various operating systems were considered. Although the Java machine is common to all platforms, threads management is operating system dependent and greatly impacts the performance of the application server. Here we have chosen AIX and Linux as platforms to highlight this difference.

Explanation of the structure of WebSphere Application Server has been made generic for the most part, without targeting any specific version of the product. The text addresses the fundamentals of WAS programming and integration, and offers many utility scripts that can be used regardless of the specific version of the product. WAS AE stands for WAS Advanced Edition. The version implied by the term WAS AE refers to either v3.5 or v4. WAS AEs stands for Advanced Edition Single Server v4. The code and utility scripts represented herein are backward compatible with WAS v5.

The reader will use WAS AEs in most of the programming (Part III), because this version is the most adequate (and is free of charge) for writing J2EE applications based on the IBM J2EE application server.

J2EE is not treated as a separate topic; rather, it is introduced in the context of web application programming and deployment under WAS. This is done very specifically, based on the assumption that most readers will probably receive a complete treatment of J2EE in another course or on their own by consulting online documentation.

The reader who would like to write web application programs and test them with WAS may begin with Part III of this book. The only requirement is a Linux sandbox with a connection to the Internet to download the WAS AEs trial version, the IBM UDB v7.2 trial version, and the code distribution of this text. No other third party software is required.

Part III can be used on its own, provided a system administrator has prepared the development environment to be used by the reader, as explained in chapters 3 and 4, or alternatively, as it is explained in Appendix A.

Material has been sequenced scrupulously to avoid forward references and to present sufficient steps that allow the reader to program with WAS AEs' free trial (but fully functional) version on a home computer. The approach taken here is to present the reader with some mechanisms to build web applications using IBM's J2EE application server—WebSphere Application Server—without the interference of any other WebSphere product. In this way, the reader will gain a clear understanding of WAS, making the IBM application server an openly available product that can, for example, be taught in a college course.

The text also breaks the dependency on using a graphical interface for programming, debugging, deployment, and administration. This is achieved by applying Perl scripts, and by using applications such as Lynx and the WebSphere Control Language (known as WSCP, and replaced by wsadmin in WAS v5). In addition, many other standard UNIX commands are used, which should be at the fingertips of any competent programmer. Using Lynx is appropriate because it provides an instantaneous view to the HTML header. Perl is an easy language that permits the automation of text processing, and therefore fits to generate the deployment descriptor of J2EE applications automatically.

The material has been classified into six parts so the text can be used in a university for two full courses as an introduction to WAS. Part I targets the preparation of the development environment; Part II supplies the requisite knowledge to administer WAS; Part III teaches programming for WAS; Part IV teaches stress-testing and debugging; Part V examines WAS monitoring, tuning, and risk management; finally, Part VI forms the appendixes.

The manuscript was written at Total Computing & Network Design, Inc. (TCND), in New York City, and was carefully reviewed by several IT professionals at IBM. TCND provided the computing facilities on which programming and testing took place. It also provided the tools and applications that helped generate the code listings.

The Gramercy Toolkit and the WASLED/WASMON application are the result of Project-9, likewise conducted at TCND. The toolkit and the application are freely distributed with the purchase of this text, and licensing is waived solely for educational use (non-commercial use): that is, specifically to accredited Computer Science departments and/or readers who will use the product on their home computers.

The most recent update of Gramercy Toolkit and WASLED/WASMON may be obtained from the website www.tcnd.com. The author welcomes readers' comments and critiques about the project, and asks that they be sent to wasbook@tcnd.com.

Bassem W. Jamaleddine
Total Computing & Network Design, Inc.
New York, New York
November 2002

PART

1

Getting Started

OBJECTIVES

► Installing WAS

► Setting the WASDG Programming Environment

► Defining a WebSphere Domain

► Defining a WebSphere Region

► Learning WAS tools

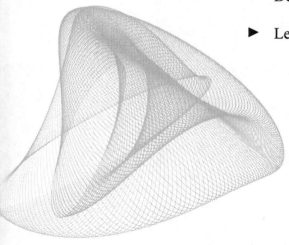

Introduction to IBM WAS Programming

IN THIS CHAPTER:

The Simplest WAS View

IBM's Offering for the WebSphere Application Server

What's In the Five Parts of the Book

Special Consideration of WAS v5

Utility Scripts

Printing Unicode, Localization, and Internationalization

UNIX Commands, Shell, Perl, and Lynx

Applications Used in This Book

WebSphere Application Server (WAS) is IBM's Java 2 Enterprise Edition application server. WAS is in its fifth year of development, with four official releases and an upcoming fifth release in 2003. WAS is a deployment environment for J2EE enterprise applications implemented on the server side. A J2EE application server defines a platform where HTTP servlets, Java ServerPages, and Enterprise JavaBeans (EJBs) can coexist; it also outlines the framework of how these technologies work together.

After you have installed WAS, you will learn about the scripts that comprise the programmer development environment. These scripts form a group of basic shell programs that are to be included in the user profile. This ensures compatibility between the code developed and the WAS run-time environment on which the code is tested. You will also learn the essential details about the internal structure of WAS and explore the basic system commands to control WAS processes.

Most J2EE application server vendors provide customers with a J2EE Application Assembly Tool and many other (graphical-based) tools that facilitate the process of describing, assembling, (de)archiving, and deploying J2EE applications. The Application Assembly Tool (AAT) that is provided with WAS is graphical and mirrors the internal structure of a J2EE application.

Although the WebSphere AAT is a useful vehicle for generating the details of J2EE applications, it is not convenient for writing and testing web applications in a dynamic environment. Once you understand the essential elements involved in describing a J2EE web application, using alternative text preprocessing with the power of interpreted scripts becomes essential.

Perl is more appropriate for writing simple scripts that automate the process of text preprocessing and replace the lengthy procedure of using a graphical-based tool such as the AAT.

As you study WAS programming, you will learn about the system's capability to handle processes and threads needed by WAS containers. This book explains the underlying features of WebSphere by examining WAS from the outside in—that is, from the system perspective. You will be exposed to many utilities that facilitate your understanding of WAS' systematic consumption to the system resources.

This book discusses WAS generically; therefore, if you are familiar with any version, you will be able to relate to the text because it uses nomenclature common to all versions of WAS to explain the WAS run-time environment. It also describes many UNIX commands and scripts that have been tested on WAS v4, which are backward compatible with WAS v5.

This first chapter introduces the different WAS versions, describes the contents of each chapter and appendix, and discusses the approach taken in the book.

The Simplest WAS View

A client browser uses the HTTP protocol to perform I/O with an Internet server. The Internet server is an HTTP server that is patched with WAS' vendor plug-in: WS-plug-in. Requests from the HTTP server are then forwarded—by means of the plug-in—to the WAS server. The WAS plug-in intercepts these requests intended for WebSphere and forwards them to the application server. The WAS server consists of a WAS engine whose functionality is rendered by an initial

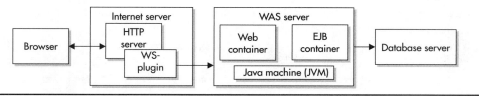

Figure 1-1   *Simple view of WebSphere Application Server*

Java machine; the WAS engine is therefore said to be bootstrapped by such an initial Java machine. The WAS server holds two containers: a web container and an EJB container. WAS communicates with the database server using Java APIs.

IBM's Offering for the WebSphere Application Server

IBM packaged WAS v4 into five deliverable products. The release of WAS v5 is expected to be packaged into three categories. The following two sections list the deliverable products of WAS v4, and (unofficially) of WAS v5.

WebSphere Application Server v4

IBM packages the latest official releases of WAS v4 into five commercial products:

- ▶ **WebSphere Application Server Advanced Edition (WAS AE)**   Provides the application server that is scalable with distributed security and command-line-based administration via the WebSphere Control Program (WSCP). This version is used to group a cluster of machines (called *nodes* in WAS v4 and *cells* in WAS v5) in a logical group, hence providing scalability, failover, and high performance. This book refers to WAS AE v3.5 and WAS AE v4 simply as WAS AE. Because WAS AE is used on production computer systems to run the final web application code, it is not suited for your programming needs. WAS AE is used in a production environment after the programmers' code has been tested on the smaller version, WAS AEs.

- ▶ **WebSphere Application Server Advanced Edition Single Server (WAS AEs)**   Provides an application server that is easily manageable, with all the features you need to get started programming for WAS. It is easy to install, administer, and test code with. You can test code quickly using this version because it stops and restarts WAS much faster than any other version. If you are using Linux, you can get started by downloading a free, fully functional trial version of WAS. The code developed in this book runs on both versions of WAS: WAS AE and WAS AEs. (Part III uses WAS AEs.)

- ▶ **WebSphere Application Server Advanced Edition Developer (WAS AEd)**   Provides the application server with many other IBM applications and tools to write applications that run under WAS. WAS AEd is an expensive solution, and its dependency on other IBM tools hides many development aspects that a beginner needs to be aware of. Use WAS AEs instead, so that you will have a productive environment that is cheaper and more solid than the one WAS AEd offers.

▶ **WebSphere Application Server Enterprise Edition (WAS EE)**   Provides application servers that run on many platforms. The functionality of WAS EE is similar to WAS AE, with some extras at an extra cost. This product is intended for enterprises with a variety of platforms.

▶ **WebSphere Application Server for IBM z/OS and IBM OS/390**   Provides a scalable, high-performance, highly available architecture with workload management for IBM zSeries and IBM S/390. This application server is also used for production environments, and if you test code using WAS AEs, you should be able to port the code to this application server.

WebSphere Application Server v5

IBM has recently announced the upcoming release of WebSphere Application Server version 5.0. As of this writing, the packaging of the new product is targeted as follows:

▶ **IBM WebSphere Application Server**   Equivalent to WAS AEs, this product is to be used as a single-server development environment that runs on a programmer desktop. It supports standards-based programming of web, EJB, and other components, including web services.

▶ **WebSphere Application Server Network Deployment**   Equivalent to WAS AE, this product fits into departmental computing scenarios. It supports clustering, caching, and a centralized administration for multiple application servers.

▶ **WebSphere Application Server Enterprise**   Equivalent to WAS EE, this product is similar to the one described in the previous bullet, but it also provides additional administrative accessories—content distribution and dynamic workload management—which makes it fit in a large production environment.

What's In the Five Parts of the Book

This book consists of five parts and six appendixes. In Part I, you will learn about the WASDG environment and the many systems involved in a WebSphere region. Part II introduces a quick and essential administrative guide that you can use to understand and control the processes involved in WAS. In Part III, you will use the WASDG environment to program the WASDG application. In the process, you will learn about WAS session management, its startup classloader, its containers, and its support to Apache SOAP (Simple Object Access Protocol) programming and to JAAS (Java Authentication and Authorization Service) programming. In Part IV, you will stress-test the WASDG application and add the WASDG exception handler to the application. And in Part V, you will use WASLED/WASMON to monitor WAS and use many utilities to collect statistics that assist you in tuning WAS performance.

Part I

In Part I, you will learn how to install WAS, how to write effective scripts for a cost-effective enterprise development environment, and how to test the functionality of WAS.

The development environment used in Part I is WASDG. This environment is sufficient for enterprise development at colleges and small or large businesses that use primarily UNIX and Windows NT systems. Although the cost of the WASDG environment is minimal, it is solid, portable, and manageable because of the use the Korn shell, Perl, Makefile utilities, and other UNIX commands. If you decide to learn programming for WAS and to start directly with Part III, you do *not* need to learn about the complexity of setting the WASDG environment. A system administrator can setup the environment as described in Part I by altering the user login profile.

Of course, WAS is not a programming language; the phrase *WAS programming* refers to the many system commands, scripts, and programs and the configuration and programming of many other applications that are used in a WAS region. Only a subset of Java programming is required, and employing complex Java programs in WAS programming can drastically inhibit the performance of WAS. Chapter 5 introduces the WebSphere domain and defines its constituent elements. You will understand the benefits of a WebSphere domain and the WebSphere nodes that can participate in it.

Chapter 5 also takes a broader look at the systems and services involved in rendering a WebSphere domain usable; as a result, the WebSphere region is also defined. This chapter concludes with a comparison between WAS v3.5 and WAS v4.

Chapter 6 discusses WAS tools and sample Web applications that you will learn to deploy to test the functionality of WAS.

Part II

In Part II, you will learn the fundamentals about the processes and the many systemic and network resources used by WAS; you will learn the effective commands to administer WAS; and you will learn to extrapolate WAS configuration data with automation tools. Chapter 7 introduces the basic programs and scripts that automatically generate administrative reports about the WAS domain. The technique is called WAS *report extrapolation*. Such a technique is generic, and you can use it with WAS v3.5 and v4, in which the WSCP is distributed. You can also adapt it to WAS v5 by writing similar scripts to wrap the `wsadmin` command, which replaced the `wscp` command of prior versions.

Chapter 8 is a quick but efficient chapter filled with commands to administer and look closely at the processes of WAS. A distinction is drawn between AIX threads and Linux threads (which are really forked processes). The chapter also introduces the essential administrative commands to quickly troubleshoot WAS in a multiplatform environment.

Part III

Part III discusses programming J2EE web applications specifically targeted to be deployed and tested on WAS. The web application developed is called the WASDG application: a simple bank application in which an employee of a bank, known as a teller, acts on the bankers' or clients' accounts. Based on the WASDG application, you will learn how to quickly develop a J2EE application.

In Chapter 9, you will create the database for the WASDG application. The chapter also addresses Java Database Connectivity (JDBC) programming to manipulate the database and to get the database's metadata. Using the Perl Database independent (DBI) module shows the efficiency of simple scripts to populate the database and fetch data from it. You will use such scripts during the course of Part III to quickly rebuild the database and to monitor the subsequent inserts, updates, and deletions of its records. For instance, in Chapter 17 you will use qry_session, a Perl script that uses DBI, to get a quick snapshot of the SESSION database.

Chapter 10 progressively shows how to build a data access component (DAC) to transparently manipulate the records in a database. This data access component is called the DataAccessComponent class. You can set the JDBC driver type of this component through a properties file so that you will be able to practice with the JDBC drivers of type 2 and type 3, which are discussed in Chapter 2. The data access component has been carefully designed so that it can be turned into an Enterprise JavaBean in Chapter 18. This EJB forms the essential interface to the database and will be used in implementing the business logic by many other EJBs.

Chapter 11 discusses a development approach for web applications based on J2EE that apply specifically to WAS. The approach taken here is based on Perl and shell scripts to create and deploy a web application with a single command: `svlbuild`. As an example, you will use this method to build the WASDG application that is used throughout this text.

Chapter 12 uses the DataAccessComponent (of Chapter 11) within the J2EE web application (of Chapter 11) to write servlet programs that access the database. As servlets are loaded in the WAS web container, the servlets directly use the data access component module to fetch and store data in the database. Merging the data access component with the J2EE application is a simple operation: just add the com/tcnd/wasdg tree to the development tree, and the package is available to the WASDG application.

Chapter 14 gives a more detailed view about the elements describing a J2EE application, and the additional elements introduced by IBM as an extension to these descriptors. You will learn how to obtain these descriptors and how to (de)archive enterprise and web applications through the use of simple customized scripts. Such scripts allow you to effectively and quickly control J2EE application during the development process.

Once you have established the method to quickly write servlets and test them, you will be comfortable writing specific code to explore with WAS: JSP programming and JSP tag libraries programming are the subjects of Chapter 13, and WAS bootstrap classloader is discussed in Chapter 15.

In Chapter 15, the classes' loading order versus their visibility order is justified using a simulation process.

Chapters 16 and 17 provide a solid foundation in programming session management and configuring IBM session persistence; this is validated by using very short programs and testing techniques by tapping into the communication between WAS and the client browser. This is made possible by using Lynx and the scripts developed in Chapter 9.

In Chapter 18, the data access component of Chapter 10 is turned into an Enterprise JavaBean: DataAccessComponentBean. This EJB forms the essential interface to the database, and it will be used in implementing the business logic (separately from the servlets) through many other EJBs. Using the web application development tree from Chapter 16, you will merge to it the business logic development tree either by using an explicit copy of the EJB development tree or by establishing a symbolic link to the EJB development tree.

In Chapter 19 you will learn how to use Apache SOAP with WAS to turn the EJBs in Chapter 18 into Web services. The discussion is specific to SOAP programming for WAS. The chapter discusses the technique of parameter passing between the SOAP client program and the SOAP server. You will learn how to edit the SOAP deployment descriptor and how to programmatically use qualified parameters names (QNames), the SOAP mapping registry (SOAPMappingRegistry) and mapTypes() method, and the SOAP org.apache.soap.util.xml. Serializer and org.apache.soap.util.xml.Deserializer.

Java Authentication and Authorization Service (JAAS) programming is not addressed by WAS v4, but because it is part of Java 2 v1.3 and will be supported by WAS v5, JAAS is covered in Chapter 20. Applying JAAS programming to the servlets in the context of WAS v4 has proven that WAS technology is totally coupled to the Java Virtual Machine API. Chapter 20 shows how to add JAAS authentication to the same data access component developed in Chapter 10. The programming shows how only privileged servlets can access the database to modify the timestamp of a teller logout. Chapter 20 concludes by showing how to use Cipher in the context of a servlet writer to protect signed HTML pages such as a registration page.

Finally, Chapter 21 shows how to run multiple WAS instances on a single server and how to apply source control commands to the development tree that is shared by many developers. The method uses the make utility and is adequate for developing web applications in enterprises and colleges.

Whereas Chapter 5 defines the WebSphere *domain,* Chapter 21 proves the looseness of the nomination of the WebSphere domain. WAS v5 does not use the word "domain" in the context of WebSphere clustering. However, the same information is communicated to you when drawing the similarity between a WebSphere domain that spans many nodes (WAS v4) and a WebSphere cluster that spans many cells (WAS v5).

Part IV

Part IV consists of two chapters: Chapter 22 presents a stress tester for web applications, and Chapter 23 presents the programming of a logger and an exception handler.

Chapter 22 focuses on how to fork multiple processes, each of which generates a set of web hits. Such understanding is used in programming a stress tester, an application that is used to measure web application performance. In addition, this chapter shows the significance of using a network analyzer (similar to Sniffer) to analyze the performance of the web application.

Chapter 23 shows the programming of a log writer, a bundle manager, and an exception handler that can be added to any web application. This exception handler—called the WASDG exception handler: WasdgException—writes messages similar to the messages that WAS writes to its standard output.

Part V

In Part V, Chapters 24 through 26 form an essential basis from which to monitor WAS and its containers, web applications and the exceptions thrown by these applications, and the systems in a WebSphere region. Performance tuning is also briefly considered but supported with efficacious scripts to monitor network resources, system resources, and threads.

Chapter 24 introduces a new lightweight application to monitor WAS, called WASLED/ WASMON. The application allows the WASMON console to monitor WAS' web container, EJB container, and run-time components. WASLED shows WAS run-time severity errors in green, orange, and red.

Chapter 25 offers a few scripts to monitor the system and network resources during WAS run time. In particular, because WAS is a thread-intensive application, you will learn how to gather threading information on AIX and Linux systems. Two exclusive scripts called MrThread and MrTop are explained and used. MrThread runs on UNIX systems where the `pstat` command is available and generates an output similar to the `pstat` command found on AIX. When MrThread runs on AIX, it shows the creation of new threads and how they are allocated to a specific CPU on Symmetric Multiprocessing (SMP) systems. Any change in a thread is also detected between different instances. MrTop monitors threads on a Linux system. (The distinction between AIX and Linux threads is outlined in Chapter 8.) Chapter 25 also discusses EJB caching and offers a method for parametric tuning of the database used in session persistence.

Chapter 26 demonstrates how to use WASMON to switch into supervisor mode so that a roaming operator can supervise and remotely control (via e-mail) the systems in a WebSphere region. WASMON can also supervise web applications that use the WASDG exception handler implemented in Chapter 23.

Appendixes

There are six appendixes that complement the material in the chapters. These appendixes elaborate on material and the usage of tools and commands that might have been a disruption to the reader if included in the chapters.

Appendix A lets you know where to find and download the distribution code and documentation for the applications and programs in this book. Assuming the reader has an internet connection, he will be able to get up-to-date distribution code and last-minute information on errata whenever it is made available on the Web.

Appendix B shows you how to back up and restore WAS. Back up and restore rely on the use of UNIX archiving commands and WAS' XMLConfig.

In Appendix C, you will get your hands on a powerful tool, MrUnicode, and you will learn how to generate servlets that maps the Unicode as provided by the Unicode Consortium. This appendix replaces the discussion of localization and internationalization in a separate chapter and provides a clear understanding of the differences between Sun Microsystems and IBM in their supports to character sets.

Appendix D complements Chapters 3 and 4 to show you how to print the environment variables as set by WASDG environment. In addition, it presents the syntax for a few of the tools that have been used in the chapters.

Appendix E complements Chapter 24 and 26 and provides a guideline on WAS monitoring using WASLED/WASMON.

Appendix F details the differences between WAS v4 and WAS v5 in their support to the Java APIs and shows you how to change the scripts explained in this book so that they run on WAS v5.

Special Consideration of WAS v5

The programming approach used in this text is also applicable to WAS v5. Appendix F outlines the differences between WAS v4 and WAS v5 in their level of support for the Java 2 API, JSP, and EJB.

Although this book specifically uses WAS AEs v4 in the programming chapters, WAS v5 has been given special consideration:

- ▶ As programming is explained, the text takes WAS v5 into account so that deprecated methods and classes are not used, and deployment specific to a particular J2EE component version or level is contrasted.

- ▶ To eliminate confusion, this book does not discuss communication between servlets that live in different web containers because this subject is obsolete.

- ▶ This book does not discuss subjects that might be irrelevant in a future release of WAS. For example, IBM supports servlet chaining in WAS v3.5 and v4 (many servlets being dispatched to generate a final output to be shipped to a browser—known since JDK v1); however, this topic is not discussed because Java 2 v1.3 supports a more efficient approach using <filter>. Although WAS v4 uses IBM Java 2 v1.3, <filter> is not supported. Servlet filtering is now possible with WAS v5, which uses IBM Java 2 v1.3.1.

- ▶ JAAS programming is not addressed by WAS v4 but because JAAS is part of Java 2 v1.3, it is possible to add JAAS APIs to the WAS v4 startup classloader (the subject of Chapter 15). Although JAAS is used in light of Java 2 v1.3, the text mentions JAAS support with Java 2 v1.4.[1]

- ▶ Before exploring WAS v5, you must understand the definition of a WebSphere domain. Although the word "domain" is no longer used in WAS v5, the explanation provided specifically in Chapters 2, 5, 8, and 21 is the main information you need to understand.

---

[1]   WAS v4 uses IBM Java 2 v1.3, which is limited and does not include the JAAS API. WAS v5 uses IBM Java 2 v1.3.1, which includes the JAAS API. However, none of the WAS versions yet support Java 2 v1.4.

The method discussed in Chapter 7 to extrapolate WAS reports using Perl and WSCP can also be modified and applied in light of Perl and wsadmin. In WAS v5, wsadmin replaced WSCP, but the JACL API is still the means of programming for both wsadmin and WSCP.

Utility Scripts

This book includes sufficient tools and utilities that help you absorb the material efficiently. You can download the Gramercy Toolkit and WASLED/WASMON[2] as explained in Appendix A, so that the following utilities are available on your system:

► Utilities to stress-test web applications

► Utilities to monitor WAS

► Utilities to monitor WAS threads consumption

► Miscellaneous utilities to complement WAS programming environment

Stress Testing

The time it takes for a number of clients to access the web application(s) concurrently—with each client placing a number of hits—represents a realistic measurement for the performance of WAS. Chapter 22 shows how to use the SharkUrl tool to simulate multiple client browsers by forking multiple processes and to place a sequence of hits per each client.

Monitoring WAS

This book considers WAS monitoring by using WASLED/WASMON, a monitoring application developed at Total Computing & Network Design, Inc. WASMON provides WAS monitoring for the standard output and standard error of the application server. It also provides a smart supervisor to monitor a WebSphere region and engage in a secure e-mail conversation with a roaming operator.

The application allows you to monitor the WAS components and its containers' activities. WASMON is configurable to filter specific events from WAS' log file; consequently, it triggers corrective administrative scripts, sends e-mail as alerts, and enters into a remote conversation with an operator. Chapters 24 and 26 explain how to use WASMON for risk management of WAS.

Monitoring WAS Threads

Because WAS is a thread-intensive application, MrThread is presented as the unique tool to monitor the kernel thread table and the variation in the activity of a specific thread during WAS run time.

---

[2]   Refer to Appendix A on downloading the Grammercy Toolkit and WASLED/WASMON. You must read the license agreement before using the toolkit or the monitoring application.

Miscellaneous Utilities

In addition, the text introduces many utility scripts that facilitate the generation of J2EE applications and their deployment.

Printing Unicode, Localization, and Internationalization

The text does not include a separate chapter on localization and internationalization, but it focuses on the servlet writer and on its printing for the Unicode, as provided by the Unicode Consortium. Appendix C shows how to use MrUnicode to generate servlets and search converters and charsets.[3] for specific encoding that is supported in Java 2. MrUnicode clarifies the differences in nomenclature between IBM and Sun Microsystems and their support for converters in their many releases of Java 2 versions.

For example, to reveal these character sets for which a Unicode mapping for the Euro sign has been defined, use this command:

```
# MrUnicode -info -desc euro
```

or to view its representation as it is printed in a browser, use MrUnicode to generate the servlet whose output can be viewed in a browser:

```
# MrUnicode -t cp1250.txt -s Uni_Eng.java -c windows-1250
```

By requesting the Uni_Eng servlet, you can view the Unicode mapping for the Euro sign of the Unicode mapping found in the cp1250 converter.

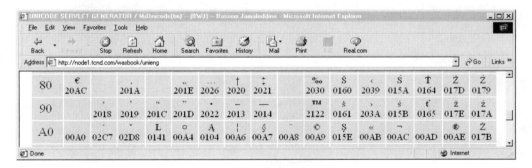

UNIX Commands, Shell, Perl, and Lynx

This book uses UNIX commands and shell scripts, Perl scripts, and the Lynx textual browser. Whereas the Perl interpreter and Lynx are available for many UNIX operating systems and Windows NT, the UNIX commands and the UNIX shell interpreter are available on all UNIX systems and only on Windows NT where the MKS Toolkit has been installed.

---

[3]   Appendix C defines converters, charsets, and canonical names (used by Sun Microsystems).

The MKS Toolkit is available for DOS and Windows with tools that give you the ability to execute UNIX commands and shell scripts from the command prompt. Yet, it is always less expensive and more resourceful to use Linux than to use Windows NT and the MKS Toolkit.

By convention we will use the hash (#) to represent the command prompt, and a computer command will be printed following the hash. We will also use a few verbs that are derived from UNIX commands: to *head* a file and to *tail* a file refer to the execution of the `head` command and the `tail` command against a file, respectively. In addition, we will often use environment variables (as set by the WASDG environment) to refer to specific files; for instance, the $WASCFG refers to WAS server configuration file, and `$STOPWAS; $STARTWAS`, when typed on the command prompt, will restart WAS.

WAS Programming on the UNIX Platform

Due to its native scripting ability, UNIX offers the only development platform for enterprise Java applications. Many of the UNIX commands can simplify the build process of a web application. For instance, Chapter 18 shows how one programmer can develop, compile, and test the business logic as a set of Enterprise JavaBeans in a separate directory (such as /BOOK/18/DevSess), and another programmer can use these EJBs in his or her own web application development tree (such as /BOOK/18/Code) simply by establishing a symbolic link to the development tree of the first programmer.

If you are using Linux or AIX, you can bring together all the JVM processes started by WAS with a simple command:

```
# ps  -A -o "%p  %a" | grep java | awk '/AppServer/ {system("kill -9 "$1)}'
```

To compile all source .java files in the development tree of a Java package, consider the following three lines of script to be executed in the parent directory of the Java package:

```
#!/bin/sh
find . -follow -name "*.java" > javafiles.list
cat javafiles.list | xargs javac -deprecation
```

You will learn more about such handy commands and scripts throughout this book.

Using Lynx

This book often uses Lynx as the browsing agent for two reasons: first, so that you can clearly see what is being sent and received in the HTML headers; second, to break the dependency on a graphical interface and allow the programmer to issue instantaneous bulk requests to the web application. Using textual commands is a valid strategy that enhances knowledge and quick programming and testing, which we will follow in this book.

For instance, to provide a clear explanation of the creation and deletion of session persistence data, Chapter 17 uses Lynx followed by a subsequent query to the SESSIONS table to prove that the record is in accordance with what is returned in the HTTP header of a Lynx command. As a practical example, Listing 1-1 shows the response of the servlet TellerLogged when logging in teller1. The header shows a session id that is similar to the one written to the SESSIONS table when IBM session persistence is enabled.

Listing 1-1   *Issuing a Lynx command to log in teller1*

```
# echo "userid=teller1&password=secret1&---" | lynx
      -accept_all_cookies -post_data -mime_header
        http://node2.tcnd.com/wasbook/tellerlogged | grep Set-Cookie
Set-Cookie: JSESSIONID=0001BL13IMQRF5R2LBOOPTJ1M1Q:-1;Path=/
```

Listing 1-2 is the output of the Perl/DBI script qry_session that reveals the content of the SESSIONS table.

Listing 1-2   *Output result when issuing qry_session to query the SESSIONS table*

```
Connected.
Row 0 ------
...
Row 1 ------
0 ID -- BL13IMQRF5R2LBOOPTJ1M1Q
1 PROPID -- BL13IMQRF5R2LBOOPTJ1M1Q
2 APPNAME -- default_host/wasbook
3 LISTENERCNT -- 0
4 LASTACCESS -- 1019550936764
5 CREATIONTIME -- 1019550936764
6 MAXINACTIVETIME -- 1800
7 USERNAME -- anonymous
8 SMALL -- (object as stream of bytes)
9 MEDIUM --
10 LARGE --
```

Perl Scripts in Enterprise WAS Programming

Perl is an essential interpreter that is included as a standard interpreter on UNIX systems like AIX and Linux. Because a Perl interpreter exists for almost every platform, the interpretation of Perl scripts is platform-independent. As a result, Perl scripts written on UNIX can also be interpreted by Perl on Windows NT or IBM OS/390.

Perl is an extremely simple and powerful interpreter. Its use in this book is justified for the following reasons:

▶   To offer a limited introduction on using Perl/CGI scripts that is essential to the understanding of session management. Perl/CGI is briefly used in Chapters 12 and 16.

▶   To quickly format and print database records, like the example shown in the previous section.

▶   To extrapolate WAS reports. Chapter 7 uses the Perl interpreter in conjunction with WSCP to carry out such an extrapolation.

▶ To automate text processing and to facilitate the build process of an enterprise application. Specifying web application properties and descriptive values using graphical applications is tedious and time consuming.

▶ To clarify the meaning of a language processor such as JSP. In this context, the Perl interpreter is used for pedagogical reasons to show you the connection between text preprocessing and the language processors used in conjunction with application server programming such as JSP. Chapters 16 and 17 present the SessionFairy servlet that automatically introspects sessions and generates a JSP file. Chapter 22 shows how to preprocess anonymous Perl subroutines to stress-test a web application.

Finally, besides the traditional thrust of WebSphere marketing concerned with eliminating bad CGI to replace it with good Java-based servlets and JSPs, Perl/CGI is apparently still in existence. Some major web sites still favor the power of Perl to parse regular expressions.

Even on the WebSphere web site, http://www-4.ibm.com/software, you'll find a few important references to Perl scripts. On a Linux system, a quick dump exercised on the page seen in Figure 1-2 can be realized using this simple command:

```
# GET -e 'www-4.ibm.com/software' | grep "\.pl"
```

The content of the page can also be revealed using the browser's view source capability, as shown in the following illustration.

Applications Used in This Book

Besides the WebSphere Application Server software product, this book also uses the following software:

▶ IBM Universal Database (UDB).

▶ Standard UNIX interpreters and commands, such as `Perl`, `awk`, `sed`, and `ksh`.

▶ Perl, Perl/CGI, and Perl modules.

▶ MKS ToolKit from Mortice Kern Systems, Inc. When this toolkit is installed on Windows NT workstations, UNIX commands and shell scripts can be executed;

consequently, such a workstation can then be merged to a heterogeneous distributed environment. We will use Samba to mount the NFS-exported directory.

▶ Exceed for Windows NT. Install Exceed if you would like to export your X Window display to a Windows NT workstation.

▶ Internet browsers: Lynx, Netscape, and Microsoft Internet Explorer.

▶ IBM Dataglance, the network analyzer that is similar to Sniffer and that runs on IBM OS/2. Used in Chapter 22.

▶ The AIX performance-monitoring agent package. Used in Chapter 25.

▶ WASLED and WASMON from Total Computing & Network Design, Inc. A monitoring and supervising application that can monitor WAS v4 and v5. Used in Chapters 24 and 26.

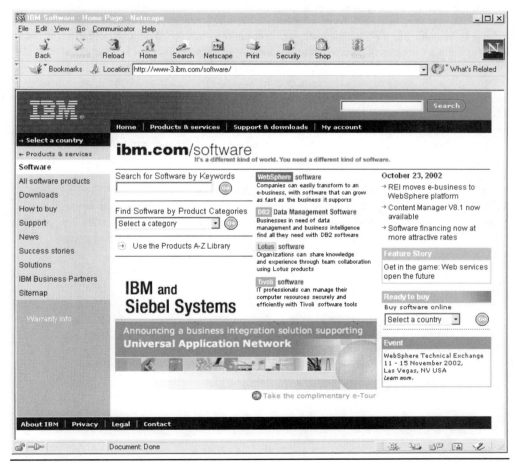

Figure 1-2 *IBM corporate web site*

▶ The Gramercy Toolkit from Total Computing & Network Design, Inc. This toolkit provides many of the utility scripts and necessary libraries to run system management commands used in this book.

▶ A text editor such as emacs or vi, which are freely distributed with any version of Linux.

In addition to these products, some add-on components to WAS v3.5 (that are now included with v4.0.3 and v5) are used:

▶ WebSphere Resource Analyzer

▶ WebSphere Log Analyzer

This text does not use WebSphere Studio Application Developer (WSAD) or any of the Visual Age products that are available from IBM to provide a front end for developing code for WebSphere Application Server. Our enterprise development environment will be realized with a system startup profile that is derived from and parallel to WAS configuration. It is a development environment, where, upon user login, the environment is set and you are ready to start programming.

Using Visual Age products does not provide a cost-effective development environment administratively, financially, or educationally. In fact, using such products diverts you from the specific applications of WebSphere Application Server and makes the material seem to be more complicated than it should be.

The focus is on the application server processes, and anyone can get started by supplementing the material in this book with a $600 PC to run Linux and an Internet connection to download the code.

We will tackle the installation, usage, programming, and tuning of WAS like any other UNIX-distributed application, by using simple commands and an integration strategy that is nothing but a classical approach in any enterprise computing environment. It is classical in the sense that it s not specific to a particular version of WAS or any of its components, but it can be adapted to future versions of the product.

Installing the WAS Repository

IN THIS CHAPTER:

Rationales to Install a Database

WAS Compatibility with UDB

Binary Distribution and Basic Installation of UDB

Installing the Components of the Universal Database (UDB)

UDB Installation on AIX

Classifying the Universal Database JDBC Driver Types

Threads database used in this book is the IBM universal database (UDB). This chapter starts by introducing the rationale behind installing a database as a first step to fulfill the WebSphere Application Server (WAS) installation requirement. It then addresses the installation of the UDB server and client components, and discusses Java support using two types of JDBC drivers. Testing local and remote connectivity to the UDB in a TCP/IP distributed environment is briefly mentioned here with references to the appropriate chapters in this text.

Although the WAS database configuration repository can be set up on a variety of databases, UDB is used because of its powerful, simple, and clear system management control, and its flexible parametric tuning that fits the requirement of WebSphere distributed computing. Refer to Appendix A for directions on downloading the UDB trial version from IBM's web site. Chapter 8 briefly mentions the property definitions of other databases that can be used with WAS Advanced Edition (AE).

Rationales to Install a Database

A database needs to be installed in a WebSphere computing environment for two basic reasons. First of all, a distributed WAS that spans several nodes' machines needs to store common data in a sharable and unified database repository. Such distributed capability of WAS is available in the products' advanced or enterprise editions.

The second reason to install a database is to use it as a data source to store web application data.

A Database Used as an Administrative Repository

For each WebSphere domain,[1] a database repository is defined to store the application server's *configuration data*. This database is referred to as the WAS repository. Because the configuration data is manipulated through an administrative agent, referred to as the *administrative console*, this configuration data is also called *administrative data*; consequently, the WAS repository is also called the *administrative repository*. Therefore, configuration data and administrative data can be used interchangeably to refer to the classified objects and attributes that are stored in the WAS repository.

The WAS repository is needed only for the WAS Advanced Edition (AE) or the WAS Enterprise Edition (EE). The WAS Advanced Edition Single Server (AEs) defines its domain on a single machine, and it uses a textual XML file to store its administrative data: server-cfg.xml.

A good percentage of a web application is based on a transactional mechanism that is perpetually active, or lives between an engine that runs and implements web applications' business logic and a remote database. The administrative and configuration aspects of WAS

---

[1] For now, consider a WebSphere domain as the grouping of server machines, each of which is running an administrative server and is sharing the same configuration data of the domain. Chapter 5 provides a more detailed explanation of a WebSphere domain.

AE's business logic by itself can be classified within this category when we look at a WebSphere domain as a bunch of nodes running on several machines and trying to scrutinize the application servers' *administrative data.* (See the following illustration.)

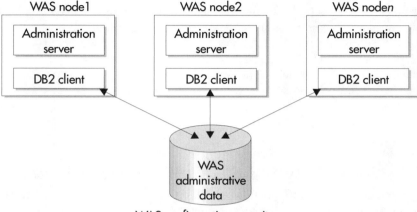

WAS configuration repository

This scrutinizing is possible only if all nodes can look up the common data cooperatively. The database is the common way to let all nodes share the administrative data defining a WebSphere domain. Therefore, the database acts as a postboard, where nodes defined in a WebSphere domain can communicate and synchronize the data change(s) of their underlying application servers. The WebSphere domain and its constituents are explained in Chapter 5.

A Database Used as a Data Source

Regardless of the version of WAS you will be using, there is another reason to have a database server available: to store the data of your web application, such as the user session, the user profile, bank transactions, and so on. Such a database can be manipulated either directly through your web application, for example, by writing a data access component library that you will then use in your servlets programming; or via the intermediary procedures of the WAS Enterprise JavaBeans container. WAS treats such a database as a data source and allows you to manipulate its properties as a DataSource object. For now, you should not focus on the specifications of a data source; this will become clearer in Chapter 7. Also, note that WAS AEs v4 is shipped with samples that require the availability of a UDB server to run them. These samples are discussed in Chapter 6.

WAS Compatibility with UDB

To avoid compatibility problems between a specific WAS version and a UDB version, follow the IBM guidelines about version compatibility that are released with each WAS version and with each of its service packs.

The version and release level of the UDB is a prerequisite for the installation of a specific WAS version and its service pack. WAS v3.5 requires DB2 v6.1, but applying service pack 5 to this specific version brings it to WAS v3.5.5 so that it is compatible with DB2 v7.1. The current version of DB2 is v7.2 and is the one required by WAS v4.0.2.

Version compatibility is important due to a dependency file that is delivered by a UDB client component and that provides JDBC connectivity through the JDBC driver provided as a Java package: db2java.zip. WAS AE needs this file to properly connect to (or create when first run) the WAS repository. Several JDBC drivers are available, and all share the same filename, db2java.zip, which confuses many administrators and developers. Later in this chapter, in the section "Classifying the Universal Database JDBC Driver Types," you will learn about two of them so that you will set up your development environment properly before starting to write programs for WAS.

Binary Distribution and Basic Installation of UDB

For AIX systems, the UDB distribution is a set of .bff files. These are called file sets that are presented to and processed by the AIX command `installp`. For Linux, the UDB distribution is a set of .rpm files that are installed with the `rpm` command.

Regardless of the UNIX platform you are on, the UDB classic installation is performed by executing the db2setup script that is available in its base product directory. The requirements for db2setup to run properly are the availability of the curses C library, which provides character-based windowing on a terminal, and enough allocated disk space on the computer system. If you get strange characters on the terminal upon invoking db2setup.sh, make sure the curses C library is available on the system.

When you run the db2setup script using the `root` userid, you will be presented with a window, as shown in Figure 2-1.

You interact with the text-based window using the TAB key to move from one element to another, and the SPACE key to select an element; and finally, to process the selected elements, you TAB to the [OK] in the lower-left corner of the window and press ENTER. If a product is customizable, then you can TAB to the [Customize] following the product name and press ENTER to further refine your selection from the product. Similar to the customization just discussed, the properties of some elements are settable when the [Properties] follow the element.

As shown in Figure 2-1, the db2setup screen allows you to select from three customizable products:

► DB2 client components

► DB2 server components

► DB2 application development client

The UDB installation creates three UNIX usernames with their corresponding three groups on your system, but you can elect to create them yourself manually prior to installing the UDB and going further with the db2setup installation. Table 2-1 shows each user and its

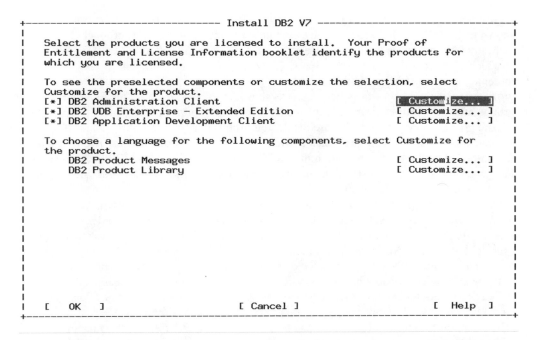

```
+------------------------------- Install DB2 V7 -------------------------------+
| Select the products you are licensed to install.  Your Proof of             |
| Entitlement and License Information booklet identify the products for       |
| which you are licensed.                                                     |
|                                                                            |
| To see the preselected components or customize the selection, select        |
| Customize for the product.                                                 |
| [*] DB2 Administration Client                       [ Customize... ]       |
| [*] DB2 UDB Enterprise - Extended Edition           [ Customize... ]       |
| [*] DB2 Application Development Client               [ Customize... ]       |
|                                                                            |
| To choose a language for the following components, select Customize for    |
| the product.                                                               |
|     DB2 Product Messages                            [ Customize... ]       |
|     DB2 Product Library                             [ Customize... ]       |
|                                                                            |
|                                                                            |
|                                                                            |
|                                                                            |
|                                                                            |
|                                                                            |
|                                                                            |
|                                                                            |
|                                                                            |
| [   OK   ]                  [ Cancel ]                   [  Help  ]         |
+----------------------------------------------------------------------------+
```

Figure 2-1   *The default text-based window started by db2setup for a first-time installation*

User	Group	Home	Important Directories
db2as	db2asgrp	/home/db2as	/home/db2as/sqllib contains the binary executable. Many symbolic links point to subdirectories in the DB2 install base directory (e.g., /usr/IBMdb2/Vn.n where n.n depicts the version number) and are owned by user.group=db2as.db2asgrp.
db2fenc1	db2fadm1	/home/db2fenc1	Empty directory. The user db2fenc1 is called the fenced. This user and his group are used when executing user defined functions (UDFs) and their stored procedure.
db2inst1	db2iadm1	/home/db2inst1	/home/db2inst1/sqllib contains the binary executable. Many symbolic links point to subdirectories in the DB2 install base directory (e.g., /usr/IBMdb2/Vn.n where n.n depicts the version number) and are owned by user.group=db2inst1.db2iadm1. /home/db2inst1/db2inst1 contains the repository data that is managed by the DB2 engine.

Table 2-1   *UDB Usernames and Groups Created on a UNIX System*

corresponding group to be created on the system. The important directories for each user shown in Table 2-1 will be created after the final installation of the UDB product.

Many DB2 instances and fenced users can share the same installation of a UDB server, in which case, the usual way to handle such a number of instances and fencers is through an incremental number that is shown as the last digit(s) in their corresponding usernames. The group names do not necessarily need to be as shown in Table 2-1; you can choose your own group name or put these usernames in an already created group name.

The groups shown in Table 2-1 are the default groups that are created by db2setup. It is recommended that you keep the db2as username in a separate group because this user has full authority on the UDB installation in terms of directories, files, and UDB authorization. Further administrative configuration and authorization is drawn from UNIX security, which is beyond the scope of this chapter.[2]

A Windows NT install is done through its setup.exe program. Before installing the product on Windows NT, you need to create a DB2 username that is eight characters or less, and make it belong to the Administrators group with the Act As Part Of The Operating System advanced user right. A valid username that is commonly used is DB2ADMIN.

Because Windows NT is not considered an enterprise server, you should consider installing only the DB2 client product on such a system. Installing the DB2 run-time client allows you to merge a Windows NT host machine to a WebSphere domain on which a developer can have his or her own WebSphere Application Server. Due to the simplicity of installing the DB2 client on Windows NT, such an installation will not be discussed in this chapter.

Installing the Components of the Universal Database (UDB)

UDB components are grouped into three products, as seen in Figure 2-1. You will be customizing each of the three products to select and configure only the part required to test code written in this book.

From the DB2 Administration Client, you will select only the Java Support, as shown in the following illustration.

```
+--- DB2 Administration Client ---------------------------------------------+
|                                                                           |
|    Required:      DB2 Client                                              |
|    Optional:      [*] Java Support                                        |
|                   : : DFS Client Enabler                                  |
|                   : : Information Catalog for the Web                     |
|                   : : Light-weight Directory Access Protocol             |
|                   [ ] Control Center                                      |
|                                                                           |
|    [ Select All ]              [ Deselect All ]          [ Default ]      |
|    [   OK   ]                    [ Cancel ]              [  Help  ]       |
+---------------------------------------------------------------------------+
```

---

[2]   We address UNIX security in Chapter 20 in conjunction with Java security. At this juncture, the reader
      is advised to ignore such a forward reference because of the confusion that might arise, as Chapter 20
      depends on many other preceding chapters.

From the DB2 Universal Database Enterprise Extended Edition, select the default excluding the Control Center, as shown in this illustration.

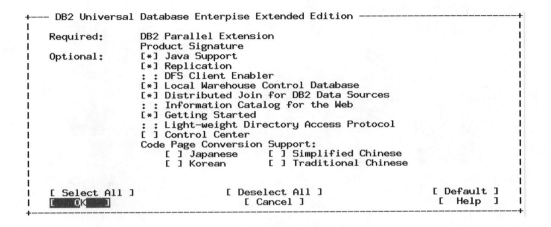

```
+--- DB2 Universal Database Enterpise Extended Edition ----------------------+
|                                                                           |
|   Required:        DB2 Parallel Extension                                 |
|                    Product Signature                                      |
|   Optional:        [*] Java Support                                       |
|                    [*] Replication                                        |
|                    : : DFS Client Enabler                                 |
|                    [*] Local Warehouse Control Database                   |
|                    [*] Distributed Join for DB2 Data Sources             |
|                    : : Information Catalog for the Web                    |
|                    [*] Getting Started                                    |
|                    : : Light-weight Directory Access Protocol            |
|                    [ ] Control Center                                     |
|                    Code Page Conversion Support:                          |
|                        [ ] Japanese      [ ] Simplified Chinese          |
|                        [ ] Korean        [ ] Traditional Chinese         |
|                                                                           |
|   [ Select All ]                 [ Deselect All ]          [ Default ]    |
|   [    OK    ]                    [ Cancel ]               [ Help ]       |
+---------------------------------------------------------------------------+
```

The installation requires setting a username for the instance, if not already created, and setting the TCP/IP properties for the connectivity of the instance to the remote database, as shown in the following illustrations.

```
+---- DB2 Instance ----------------------------------------------------------+
|                                                                           |
|   Authentication:                                                         |
|        Enter User ID, Group ID, Home Directory and Password that will be  |
|        used for the DB2 Instance.                                         |
|                                                                           |
|        User Name         [db2inst1]                                       |
|        User ID           [531    ]                [ ] Use default UID     |
|        Group Name        [db2iadm1]                                       |
|        Group ID          [107    ]                [ ] Use default GID     |
|        Home Directory    [/home/db2inst1  ]                               |
|        Password          [            ]                                   |
|        Verify Password   [            ]                                   |
|                                                                           |
|   Select Properties to view or change more           [ Properties... ]    |
|   options.                                                                |
|                                                                           |
|   Select Default to restore all default             [ Default ]          |
|   settings.                                                               |
|   [   OK   ]                      [ Cancel ]         [  Help  ]           |
+---------------------------------------------------------------------------+
```

```
+--- DB2 Instance Properties -----------------------------------------------+
I                                                                          I-
I   Authentication Type:                                                   I
I      Select one of the following types of authentication for            I
I      the DB2 Instance.                                                   I
I      (*) Server                                                          I
I      ( ) Client                                                          I
I      ( ) DCS                                                             I
I      ( ) DCE                                                             I
I      ( ) Server Encrypt                                                  I
I      ( ) DCS Encrypt                                                     I
I      ( ) DCE Server Encrypt                                              I
I                                                                          I
I   Communication Protocols:                                              I
I      Select protocols and then select Properties to modify             I
I      the protocol values.                                               I
I      [*] TCP/IP    Detected                          [ Properties... ]  I
I                                                                          I
I   [*] Auto start DB2 Instance at system boot.                          I
I   [*] Create a sample database for DB2 Instance.                       I
I                                                                          I
I   [   OK   ]                 [ Cancel ]              [  Help  ]          I
+--------------------------------------------------------------------------+
```

Edit the /etc/services and make sure that port 50000 is not in the services database. This situation could happen because of a failed installation of the UDB. If port 50000 is in use, select a different port than the default set by db2setup. The following illustration shows the default port selected for the TCP/IP connection.

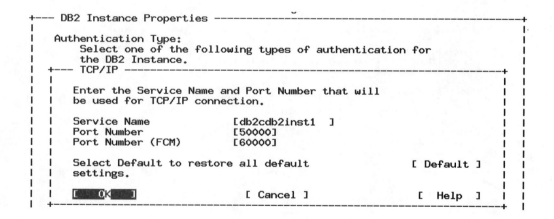

A fenced user is then selected so stored procedures will execute under this user and group. For this step, take the default if the username and group have not already been created on the system.

```
+--- Fenced User -------------------------------------------------------------+
|                                                                             |
|   Fenced user defined functions (UDFs) and stored procedures will           |
|   execute under this user and group.                                        |
|                                                                             |
|                                                                             |
|   Authentication:                                                           |
|       Enter User ID, Group ID, Home Directory and Password that will be     |
|       used for the Fenced User.                                             |
|                                                                             |
|       User Name          [db2fenc1]                                         |
|       User ID            [530    ]              [ ] Use default UID          |
|       Group Name         [db2fadm1]                                         |
|       Group ID           [108    ]              [ ] Use default GID          |
|       Home Directory     [/home/db2fenc1 ]                                  |
|       Password           [           ]                                      |
|       Verify Password    [           ]                                      |
|                                                                             |
|   Select Default to restore all default                    [ Default ]      |
|   settings.                                                                 |
|                                                                             |
|   [   OK   ]                    [ Cancel ]                 [  Help  ]        |
+-----------------------------------------------------------------------------+
```

Because you have selected to install the UDB server, you need to customize the Create the Administration Server, as shown in the next illustration. The DB2 server has two essential components: a DB2 run-time environment, and the DB2 engine. These two components contain the application binary files and libraries to manage the relational database and authenticate requests from remote DB2 hosts.

```
+------------------------- Create DB2 Services ------------------------------+
|  Select the items you want to create, and select OK when finished.         |
|                                                                            |
|  A DB2 Instance is an environment where you store data and run             |
|  applications.  An instance can contain multiple databases.                |
|                                                                            |
|  (*) Create a DB2 Instance.                        [ Customize... ]        |
|  ( ) Do not create a DB2 Instance.                                         |
|                                                                            |
|  An Administration Server provides services to support client tools that   |
|  automate the configuration of connections to DB2 databases.               |
|                                                                            |
|  (*) Create the Administration Server.             [ Customize... ]        |
|  ( ) Do not create the Administration Server.                              |
|                                                                            |
|                                                                            |
|                                                                            |
|                                                                            |
|                                                                            |
|                                                                            |
|                                                                            |
|                                                                            |
|                                                                            |
|                                                                            |
|  [    OK    ]                     [ Cancel ]            [  Help  ]          |
+----------------------------------------------------------------------------+
```

Create the db2as username as the account to be used for the UDB administration server, as shown in the following illustration. Set the db2as.db2asgrp to allow the administration of the DB2 server locally or remotely (set TCP/IP port) from a host running the Control Center.

```
+--- Administration Server --------------------------------------------------+
I                                                                            I
I   Authentication:                                                          I
I       Enter User ID, Group ID, Home Directory and Password that will be    I
I       used for the Administration Server.                                  I
I       User Name          [db2as  ]                                         I
I       User ID            [532    ]                    [ ] Use default UID   I
I       Group Name         [db2asgrp]                                        I
I       Group ID           [109    ]                    [ ] Use default GID   I
I       Home Directory     [/home/db2as  ]                                   I
I       Password           [          ]                                      I
I       Verify Password    [          ]                                      I
I                                                                            I
I   Select Properties to view or change more          [ Properties... ]      I
I   options.                                                                 I
I                                                                            I
I   Select Default to restore all default             [ Default ]           I
I   settings.                                                                I
I                                                                            I
I                                                                            I
I   Note: It is not recommended to use the DB2 Instance user ID for         I
I         security reasons.                                                  I
I   [   OK   ]                    [ Cancel ]                   [  Help  ]     I
+----------------------------------------------------------------------------+
```

Finally, the last screen shows all the components to be installed. Select [Continue] by pressing the ENTER key. This completes the UDB installation.

Restart your system, and look at the DB2 processes in the kernel table. Figure 2-2 shows the tree hierarchy of the DB2 processes.

As shown in Figure 2-2, two db2wdog processes are started with root UID, called the db2 watchdog processes. One db2 watchdog process for the db2 engine can be administered by the user db2as, and another db2 watchdog process for the db2 instance is started and administered by db2inst1.

The lengthy installation described in this section deposited and configured all the components for the UDB server and client at once. You do not need to install both of these

```
root       18819     1   db2wdog
db2inst1   18820 18819   \_ db2sysc
root       18821 18820      \_ db2gds
db2inst1   18824 18821      |   \_ db2resyn
db2inst1   18825 18821      |   \_ db2srvlst
db2inst1   18822 18820      \_ db2ipccm
db2inst1   18823 18820      \_ db2tcpcm
root       18952     1   db2wdog
db2as      18953 18952   \_ db2sysc
root       18954 18953      \_ db2gds
db2as      18956 18954      |   \_ Scheduler
db2as      18955 18953      \_ db2ipccm
db2as      18957 18953      \_ db2tcpcm
db2as      18958 18953      \_ db2tcpdm
```

Figure 2-2 *db2 processes tree hierarchy*

products on every system where you install WAS unless you intend to use the same computer system for both WAS AE and its database repository. Only the components of the DB2 client and the DB2 application development client with Java are required to be installed on a machine on which WAS AE or WAS EE is to be installed. This requirement is justified in the section "JDBC Type 2: The app Driver" later in this chapter.

Finally, to test your installation, log in as db2inst1, or alternatively, if you are `root`:

```
# su - db2inst1
```

Set the UDB environment and start db2:

```
# cd /home/db2inst1/sqllib; . ./db2profile;  db2
```

At the db2 command prompt, issue a simple DB2 command like the following:

```
LIST DATABASE DIRECTORY
```

UDB Installation on AIX

This section explains how to install the UDB specifically on AIX using the `smitty` and `installp` commands. To install the UDB on AIX, follows these steps:

1.   Locate the product installation directory and head the .toc file, as shown in the following illustration, to reveal which Java machine version is required for the DB2 installation.

```
X DB2 Server Install                                                    _ □ ✕
 # pwd
 /vol/node2-06/WAS_2001/aix_db2_ee_72_SBCS_GTK3T-5224-00/023_EE_AIX32_SBCS
 #
 # head .toc
 0 041717430301 2
 ./db2/Java.adt.src.1.1.8.6.bff 4 R S Java.adt {
 Java.adt.src 01.01.0008.0006 1 N U en_US Java Class Source Code
 [
 *ifreq Java.rte.bin (1.1.0.0) 1.1.8.6
 *prereq Java.adt.src 1.1.8.0
 %
 /usr/jdk_base 2984
 /usr/lpp/SAVESPACE 2984
 /usr/lib/objrepos 8
 #
 # ls -l
 total 200
 -rw-r--r--    1 11744     imnadm       54324 Apr 19 07:55 .toc
 drwxr-sr-x    2 11744     imnadm        4096 Apr 17 17:44 NetQ
 drwxr-sr-x    6 11744     imnadm        4096 Jun 08 15:52 db2
 -rwxr-xr-x    1 11744     imnadm        5407 Apr 17 17:43 db2setup
 drwxr-sr-x    6 11744     imnadm        4096 Jun 08 15:52 doc
 drwxr-sr-x    3 11744     imnadm        4096 Apr 17 10:47 doc.cmn
 -rw-r--r--    1 11744     imnadm       12563 Apr 17 18:21 readme.txt
 #
 # ▓
```

This is an important step to resolve the issue of the product's compatibility with a particular WAS version and release. The head of the .toc file shows the UDB version and release number, along with the Java run-time environment required for the installation.

2. Invoke `smitty` to install the product and enter the directory where the distribution binary of the software can be found, as shown here.

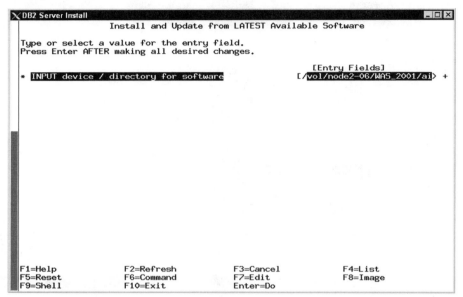

3. TAB to the SOFTWARE to install, press F4 to list all available packages, and then select the product you want to install, as shown in the following illustration.

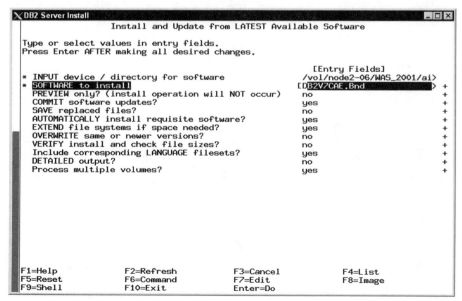

4. Press ENTER to do the installation. After the product installs, you will see the following screen, indicating a successful installation.

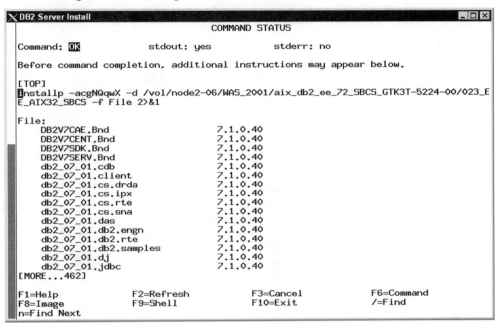

5. Make sure the binary of the UDB product has been successfully installed using the `lslpp` command, as shown in the following illustration.

Also, as shown at the bottom of the previous illustration, make sure you have created the db2as, db2fenc1, and db2inst1 users and their respective groups. (Refer to the section "Binary Distribution and Basic Installation of UDB.")

On AIX, if you added these usernames and groups, you need to make sure the password is not checked for a change. To do so, edit the /etc/security/passwd and /etc/security/opasswd and set the attribute flags = NOCHECK for all three usernames. Also edit the /etc/security/group and /etc/security/ogroup and make sure that all three groups created have the attribute admin = false.

6. To complete the installation, invoke the db2setup (the curses C library-based script) and follow the instructions as explained in the section "Installing the Components of the Universal Database."

Before running the db2setup on AIX, make sure you have enough disk space allocated on the logical partition where the /home and /usr directories are mounted; otherwise, the install will abort. The df command returns the disk space available, and the chfs command can be used to allocate more free disk space, as shown in Listing 2-1.

Listing 2-1   *Using the* df *and* chfs *commands to reveal and increase the size of a filesystem on AIX*

```
# df -k
Filesystem      1024-blocks      Free %Used     Iused %Iused Mounted on
/dev/hd4              8192       2784   67%       1062    26% /
/dev/hd2            413696       1660  100%      16384    16% /usr
/dev/hd9var           4096       2528   39%        192    19% /var
/dev/hd3             24576      23392    5%         55     1% /tmp
/dev/hd1            258048     249776    4%         26     1% /home
# chfs -a size=+500000 /usr
Filesystem size changed to 1335296
# df   -k
Filesystem      1024-blocks      Free %Used     Iused %Iused Mounted on
/dev/hd4              8192       2784   67%       1062    26% /
/dev/hd2            667648     247644   63%      16384    10% /usr
/dev/hd9var           4096       2528   39%        192    19% /var
/dev/hd3             24576      23392    5%         55     1% /tmp
/dev/hd1            258048     249776    4%         26     1% /home
```

In Listing 2-1, the df -k command reveals that the /usr free disk space is 1660 free 1024-byte blocks. The chfs command allocated 500,000 extra 512-byte blocks. It is recommended that you read the man pages for the df and chfs commands.

A failed UDB install through the db2setup may create a locked file in /tmp/.db2inst.lck that needs to be removed to continue the installation.

Classifying the Universal Database JDBC Driver Types

IBM UDB v7.2 used in this book supports JDBC versions 1.2, 2.0, and 2.1.[3] Different Java distributions use different JDBC versions. IBM UDB v7.2 provides certifiable support for different versions of JDBC. We will use the JDBC drivers that are provided with the UDB v7.2 distribution, specifically JDBC version 2.0, and that are packaged in two different files coincidentally named by the same name, db2java.zip.

The UDB JDBC drivers consist of four types, two of which are important to us. These are naturally numbered in sequence: type 1, type 2, type 3, and type 4. We will discuss type 2 and type 3 because they are the ones we need to use when installing WAS and when programming for WAS in this book.

JDBC Type 2: The app Driver

The UDB JDBC type 2 driver is referred to as the app driver and is supported by UDB v7.2 used in this book. The Java package name for this driver is COM.ibm.db2.jdbc.app.*, from which the app driver name is derived. Because this driver performs a native connect through a local DB2 client to a remote database, the DB2 client must be installed on the machine where the application that is making the JDBC calls runs. Because WAS AE requires such an app driver (or type 2 driver), you need to install the DB2 client on each machine that will participate as a node to a WAS AE installation. J2EE application servers use this driver for programming SQL on a Web application server.

NOTE

WAS AE installation uses the type 2 driver, which means you need to install the DB2 client on each node or machine on which you will install an application server. However, you do not need to install such a client if you intend to install only the WebSphere Control Program (WSCP is discussed in Chapter 7) on a workstation. Although WSCP will access the WAS repository, this is done through the administrative server with which WSCP is connected.

The next illustration shows how a Java application such as WAS' Java machine uses the JDBC type 2 driver.

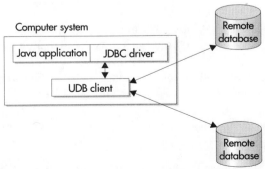

---

[3]   JDBC versions 2.0 and 2.1 are similar with respect to a UDB environment. Specifications for JDBC version 3.0 are under way at Sun Microsystems.

The JDBC type 2 driver uses a Java layer that is bound to the native platform C libraries. This driver functionality relies on a combination of Java and native code, which makes it a better performing driver than the JDBC type 3 driver discussed in the following section.

Before testing code using the app driver, make sure you have installed the proper UDB client and you have a privileged connection from the remote machine. The simplest way to perform such a test is by connecting to the database from the local machine and cataloging a database that is available on the remote database server. Chapter 4 discusses how to catalog a database. Chapter 12 shows how to use the app driver in your web application.

When using JDBC type 2 (the app driver), a local UDB client must be installed on each machine so that application software can connect to a remote database. For example, an application's software can be a WAS AE or a web application that you will write and deploy under WAS. Because this type of connection requires that you install the UDB application client locally, it is referred to as an app driver. Java programs use this driver to make a native connection through the UDB client installed locally to the remote database.

JDBC Type 3: The net Driver

The UDB JDBC type 3 is referred to as the net driver and is a pure Java implementation whose functionality requires a middleware (or proxy) that provides a JDBC applet server. Often, Java applets that access UDB data sources use this driver.

The following illustration shows the use of the JDBC type 3 driver.

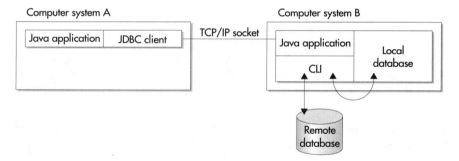

The Java package name for this driver is COM.ibm.db2.jdbc.net.*, from which the net driver name is derived. The UDBC JDBC type 3 driver is supported with UDB v7.2 and can be used with JDBC 1.2, 2.0, and 2.1.

In Chapter 3, the section "Testing Remote Database Connection with the JDBC Driver" shows you how to test database connectivity using the net driver.

Wrapping Up

This chapter discussed the rationale behind installing databases in a WebSphere computing environment. In particular, the database is needed to save WAS AE configuration data and to save web application data for all other purposes.

The database used in this book is UDB v7.2, yet the method presented in this chapter can be used to install any version of UDB. This is possible because the UNIX installation is based on db2setup, a text window application based on the curses C library.

This chapter also discussed two JDBC driver types: JDBC type 2, or the app driver, and JDBC type 3, or the net driver. WAS AE v4 requires the JDBC type 2 driver. The programming examples in this book use both driver types.

# CHAPTER 3

Setting Development Environment Prerequisites

IN THIS CHAPTER:

The HTTP Server

The Java Machine

The Windows NT User Environment

Working with the Java Machine

Testing Remote Database Connection with the JDBC Driver

This chapter explains how to install and test the prerequisite applications that WAS needs within a WebSphere Domain development environment. Among these applications are the HTTP server, the Java machine, and JDBC connectivity. This chapter and Chapter 4 tackle commonly used scripts to set up the development environment in a mixed distributed platform which we will refer to as *The WASDG Environment*. The WebSphere Domain, mentioned here, is further defined in Chapter 5.

Nowadays, you don't have to install a JDK before installing WAS because WAS v3.5 and v4 both come with Java distribution. Since this book addresses advanced WAS installation within a distributed environment, you must plan a proper customized installation where selective components of WAS can be made available on workstations. You will learn about the necessity of having developers compile and run their code with a Java machine that is at the same level as the one used by WAS and its application servers.

The HTTP Server

You can install the HTTP Server independently of a WebSphere Application Server. IBM refers to the HTTP server as the *web server*. However, this book uses HTTP server and web server interchangeably, although HTTP server is preferred.

This section discusses the basic tasks for installing the IBM HTTP Server on three platforms: AIX, Linux, and Windows NT. It then describes the operations to start, stop, and check the status of the HTTP server.

Installing the HTTP Server

Although you can install WAS v4 and make it functional without an HTTP server, such a default installation (based on the proprietary HTTP transport built within WAS) is not recommended. An HTTP server is mandatory in a normal WAS environment. Because the proprietary HTTP transport is installed by default during the product installation, it is not discussed here. The transport listening on port 9080, however, will be used later, in Chapters 6 and 8, when troubleshooting WAS.

The IBM HTTP Server (IHS), used in this book, is a hybrid of the Apache HTTP Server. IBM ships IHS with its WebSphere Application Server, but you can download a copy of it from IBM's web site for free. IHS is also available in the custom installation of WAS v4. You can install it at this time without going through the installation of WAS.

On each of the three platforms, the default install of the IHS product is placed into a different directory. Table 3-1 provides the commands to install IHS on AIX, Linux, and Windows NT, and the default directory in which it is installed. This information assumes, of course, that you have extracted the WAS binary distributions into the /tmp/was4distribution directory.

Product Installation Method	Binary Location with WAS v4 Distribution	ihs_home after Product Installation
AIX: use smitty or installp	/tmp/was4distribution/usr/sys/inst.images/his	/usr/HTTPServer
Linux: use rpm installation: `rpm -i`	/tmp/was4distribution/ihs_128	/opt/IBMHTTPServer
Windows NT: `run setup.exe`	drive:/was4distribution/httpd	drive:/IBMHTTP Server

Table 3-1   *IHS Installation Directory for AIX, Linux, and Windows NT*

In this book, *ihs_home* is used as an alias that refers to the product installation directory commonly found on any of the platforms, as depicted in Table 3-1. All IHS configuration files reside in the ihs_home/conf directory. Once in that directory, you should edit the httpd.conf file and make sure that you have the proper setup for the document root directory and the cgi-bin directory aliases. These directories are necessary to understand the examples in this book. On a Linux platform, the httpd.conf file should have the entries in Listing 3-1.

Listing 3-1   *httpd.conf DocumentRoot, and cgi-bin setup*

```
DocumentRoot "/opt/IBMHTTPServer/htdocs"
<Directory "/opt/IBMHTTPServer/htdocs">
ScriptAlias /cgi-bin/ "/opt/IBMHTTPServer/cgi-bin/"
```

Although the default installation of IHS might reflect a different directory for the document root, e.g., /opt/IBMHTTPServer/htdocs/en_US, you need to change the entries in the httpd.conf file, as seen in Listing 3-1.

IHS serves documents from its document root directory, located by default one level up from the ihs_home directory: ihs_home/htdocs. This directory is henceforth referred to with the alias *ihs_docroot.* This directory usually contains static .html pages and .jsp files, and its subdirectories contain images, voice files, and style sheets for a server-side include.

At this point, it will help you to understand the following references: the IHS installation directory is referred to as ihs_home, the document root is referred to as ihs_docroot, and the IHS configuration directory is *ihs_home/conf.*

To install IHS, log in as root, change to the installation directory corresponding to your product distribution, (as listed in Table 3-1), and carefully follow these steps:

▶   **AIX**   Locate the table of contents .toc file in your installation images directory. Use an editor to view the .toc file. If the file describes the HTTP server, then you are in the correct directory. Invoke smitty with install_latest.

```
# smitty install_latest
```

This command starts the curses-based window tool (based on the curses C library), which will subsequently ask you to enter the input directory of your software. Enter the full path specification for the directory that contains the .toc file. Proceed with the installation. Alternatively, you can invoke the X-based `smit install_latest` to start the graphical user interface, as seen here.

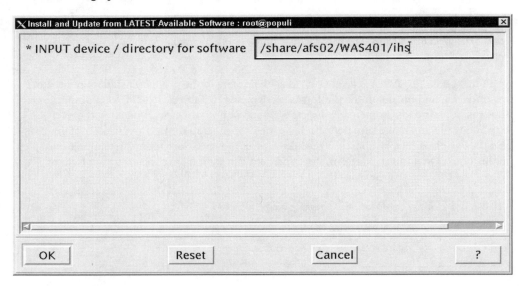

▶   **Linux**   Use the rpm installation tool to install the product.

```
# rpm -i IBM_HTTPServer-1.3.19-0.i386.rpm
```

You can use the wildcard with the `rpm` command, as in

```
# rpm -i *.rpm
```

This command installs all .rpm file sets available in the current directory. With this wildcard installation, rpm will manage to resolve the dependency between file sets when dependent files are available in the current directory. If you need to gather information about an .rpm package, use the -qip options:

```
# rpm -qip  IBM_HTTP_Server-1.3.12-2.i386 .rpm
```

Sometimes you need to extract an .rpm package so that you can manually install one or more of its components without registering it in the RPM database. For example, to extract the IHS package contents from an .rpm package, change to the directory where you want to extract the package, and then use the `rpm2cpio` command to extract the .rpm file:

```
# rpm2cpio  /tmp/IBM_HTTP_Server-1.3.12-2.i386.rpm  |  cpio  -ivd
```

This will extract the contents of the package IBM_HTTP_Server-1.3.12-2.i386.rpm into the current directory. The `cpio` command preserves the tree structure of the directories when extracting the archive.

► **Windows NT**   Run the classical setup.exe and select the appropriate language for your install procedure. From the Select Components dialog box (see the following illustration), select HTTPServer Base and Base Extensions. Click Next, and the next screen will prompt you to enter the user ID and password of a valid username on the local machine.

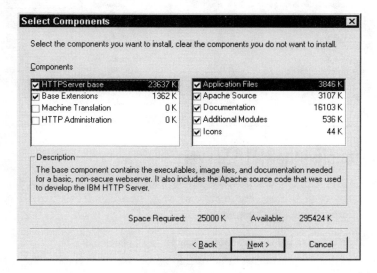

For any of the platforms, if your installation was successful, you should have the ihs_home and the ihs_home/conf directories created. To further confirm the success of your installation, issue the following commands according to your platform:

► **AIX**   Use the `lslpp` command:

```
# lslpp -L | grep HTTP
```

This command should reveal at least three filesets, as in the following:

```
Fileset                  Level   State  Description
---------------------------------------------------------
http_server.admin      1.3.19.0    C    HTTP Server Administration
http_server.base.rte   1.3.19.0    C    HTTP Server Base Run-Time
http_server.html.en_US 1.3.19.0    C    HTTP Server Documentation
1                      1.3.19.0    C    HTTP Server Admin Messages
```

► **Linux**   The following command returns all installed RPM-based packages in which the IBM_HTTP string appears:

```
# rpm -qa | grep IBM_HTTP
```

▶ **Windows NT** The IBM HTTP Server should be registered in the operating system's services. When you select Start | Control Panel | Services, IBM HTTP Server should be listed, as in this illustration.

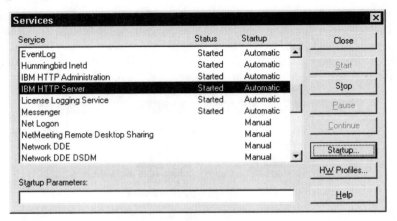

Starting/Stopping the HTTP Server

On both the AIX and Linux platforms, the program apachectl (located in ihs_home/bin) may be followed by any of these three arguments: `start`, `stop`, and `status`. To start the IBM HTTP Server, simply issue this command:

```
# apachectl start
```

This command will start a couple of httpd daemon processes that you can list with the `ps -ef | grep http` command. On Linux, the IBM HTTP Server then writes its parent's process ID in the default log directory /opt/IBMHTTPServer/logs/httpd.pid, and you can check on the process ID of the HTTP server to confirm whether it is operational or not:

```
# ps -ef | grep cat '/opt/IBMHTTPServer/logs/httpd.pid'
```

On Windows NT, use the `net START` and `net STOP` commands to start and stop the server. For example, the following command will start the IBM HTTP Server when issued at a DOS command prompt:

```
# net START "IBM HTTP Server"
```

The system will reply back with this:

```
The IBM HTTP Server service is starting.
The IBM HTTP Server service was started successfully.
```

HTTP Server Log Files

The HTTP server log files are quite possibly the most important resources in the whole web development chain. In every deployment scenario, they are the undisputed key to understanding and troubleshooting web server problems. Obviously, it is the HTTP server that first receives clients' URL requests, and it is the last to reply back to these requests.

To enable logging of information, edit the httpd.conf file and make sure that the CustomLog and ErrorLog directives have been defined:

```
CustomLog  /opt/IBMHTTPServer/logs/referer_log  "%t \"%{Referer}i\"  \"%{User-agent}i\""
TransferLog  /opt/IBMHTTPServer/logs/access_log
AgentLog  /opt/IBMHTTPServer/logs/agent_log

ErrorLog   /opt/IBMHTTPServer/logs/error_log
```

Log formats can also be given nicknames to be used with a CustomLog directive. For example, the following defines the combined nicknames to be used with CustomLog to log detailed information in each record of the access_log file:

```
LogFormat "%h %l %u %t \"%r\" %s %b \"%{Referer}i\" \"%{User-agent}i\"" combined
CustomLog  /opt/IBMHTTPServer/logs/access_log combined
```

The preceding format results in logging records of the following format:

```
desk4.tcnd.com - -  11/Nov/2001  00:42:56  -0800  "GET / HTTP/1.0" 200 1653
"http://www.altavista.com/cgi-bin/query?pg=q&what=web&q=websphirian+nights"
"Mozilla/2.0 (compatible; MSIE 3.02; AK; Windows 95; T2 Win95 9701)"
```

In a production environment, optimally, try to minimize the information logged to the files, and do not use DNS for the client IP name resolution. Also, keep the log files within a certain limit because logging information to a huge file can render your application hopelessly slow.

CAUTION

If your log files are huge and you want to delete them while your HTTP server is running, do not use the remove (rm) command to unlink them, but use the null device to truncate them to zero length, as in cat /dev/null > access_log.

On Linux, you must rotate log files by writing a log-rotation informational script to the directory /etc/logrotate.d. A daily cron job runs the `logrotate /etc/logrotate.conf` command to rotate the log files. For the syntax of the `logrotate` command, consult the manual pages, i.e., `man logrotate`. A typical script to rotate the IHS log files is usually copied to the directory /etc/logrotate, and is shown here:

```
/opt/IBMHTTPServer/logs/access_log {
    missingok
    postrotate
      /bin/kill -HUP 'cat /opt/IBMHTTPServer/logs/httpd.pid 2>/dev/null' 2>
/dev/null || true
    endscript
}
/opt/IBMHTTPServer/logs/error_log {
```

```
    missingok
    postrotate
        /bin/kill -HUP 'cat /opt/IBMHTTPServer/logs/httpd.pid 2>/dev/null' 2>
/dev/null || true
    endscript
}
/opt/IBMHTTPServer/logs/referer_log {
    missingok
    postrotate
        /bin/kill -HUP 'cat /opt/IBMHTTPServer/logs/httpd.pid 2>/dev/null' 2>
/dev/null || true
    endscript
}
```

The Java Machine

The WebSphere Application Server components are, in general, Java applications, each of which runs inside a run-time instance of a Java (virtual) machine.

In the past four years, IBM has released four distinct versions of WebSphere Application Server. Each version uses the next-higher version of Java machine than the last. The Java machine is simply the *java* program (or application-launcher program) that is shipped with the Java distribution. WAS v1, v2, and v3 used JDKs that are downloaded and installed separately from the product. Starting with WAS v3.5, IBM shipped the product with an IBM Java 2 technology that provides the Java machine, along with library packages that are specifically useful for the WAS programming environment. In the earlier versions of WAS, it is confusing to determine which JDK is appropriate to use. Each new release was—and continues to be—highly co-related to the release of the newest JDK, or what the marketing flyers continue to label Java technologies.

The following table summarizes each WAS version, along with the Java distribution on which the specified default WAS depends.

WAS Version	Java Machine
v1	JDK 1.1.6
v2	JDK 1.1.6
v2.02	JDK 1.1.7
v3	JDK 1.1.7 and 1.1.8
v3.02	JDK 1.1.8
v3.5	JDK 1.2.2
v4	JDK 1.3

In this book, *Java machine* refers to any Java Virtual Machine that is either used by the application server or started by a developer. The Java machine is simply started by the binary executable program named Java. The Java machines for different distributions might have a different parametric set of options that can be passed to the java program on the command line. Also, the java program does not need to be located in the bin directory of a Java distribution, but it may be in java_home/jre/sh/, or, in some instances, may be only a symbolic link in /usr/bin.

This book does not distinguish between a Java startup program that is part of a Java runtime environment and one that is part of a JDK. The Java machines used here are those IBM offers for the WAS v3.5 and WAS v4 releases. This section walks you through the installation of the Java machine and guides you through using a script to set up the user and administrative environments.

The release of not only a new Java distribution affects the WAS, but also the release of a new HTTP server. IBM calls the HTTP server a *web server* to untie the product from its dependency on HTTP protocols as the sole protocols for this web server. In reality, all web servers are primarily based on the HTTP protocol, in which one or more plug-ins are possibly added by a third-party application, such as WebSphere Application Server.

As you saw earlier in this chapter, IHS is the HTTP server used in this book. Again, IHS is a hybrid of the Apache Server that IBM delivered loaded with WAS v2.02.

Table 3-2 summarizes the different releases of WAS, along with their Java machine launchers and IHSs. The shaded cells indicate that security has been enhanced for these elements.

Installing the Java Machine

The IBM Java machine is either bundled as a part of the WAS product or is downloaded separately. Locating the product and installing it for each platform is similar to the process used for the IBM HTTP Server described previously. The installation of the IBM Java machine is not described in detail here; however, Table 3-3 explains how to install the product on three different platforms and summarizes the location for each one. Remember that you need to be root user to install the base Java binary. Of paramount importance is setting the system environment for the Java machine, as you will see next.

WAS Version	Java Machine	IHS
WAS v1	JDK 1.1.6	Apache 1.2.x, Netscape Enterprise 2.01
WAS v2	JDK 1.1.6	ibid.
WAS v2.02	JDK 1.1.7	IHS 1.3.3
WAS v3	JDK1.1.7 and 1.1.8	IHS 1.3.6.4 (56- and 128-bit encryption)
WAS v3.02	JDK 1.1.8	IHS 1.3.12
WAS v3.5	IBM Java2 1.2.2	IHS 1.3.12
WAS v3.5.4	IBM Java2 1.2.2	IHS 1.3.12.4
WAS v4	IBM Java2 1.3	IHS 1.3.19
WAS v5	IBM Java2 1.3.1	IHS 1.3.24

Table 3-2   *WAS Releases and Their Corresponding Java Machines and HTTP Servers*

Product Installation Method	Binary Location with WAS v4 Distribution and Installation Commands	JAVA_HOME after Product Installation
AIX: Use the `tar` command to replicate the tree.	mkdir /usr/java_dev2 cd /usr/java_dev2 tar cvf - -C. /tmp/was4distribution/aix/java/ . | tar xvf – (Make sure you have the recommended PTFs applied to your AIX system before executing the Java machine commands.)	/usr/java_dev2
AIX: Use `smitty` or `installp`.	Directory where you downloaded the product. `gzip -d` to decompress the files, `tar -xf` to dearchive the files. The files are file sets that can be installed with `smitty install_latest`. Usually, you need to download the Java130 or SDK130, the jre130 J2EE RunTime Environment, and the AIX 4.3.3 PTFs.	/usr/java_dev2
Linux: If the rpm installation is not available, use the `tar` command.	mkdir /opt/IBMJava2-130 cd /opt/IBMJava2-130; tar cvf - -C /tmp/was4distribution/java/ . | tar xvf - Make the /opt/java symbolic link: ln -s /opt/IBMJava2-130 /opt/java.	/opt/IBMJava2-130 /opt/java

Table 3-3   *Java Machine Installation Directory for AIX, Linux, and Windows NT*

Table 3-4 summarizes the commands that are available with each Java distribution.

You don't need to know how to use all these commands to be able to work with and program for WAS because WAS is intended to make Java coding and deployment easier. At the very least, you need to be familiar with two basic commands to get you started with Java programming for WAS: `javac` and `java`. The first one compiles your Java program, and the second one runs a Java machine to execute your program.

Setting Up the Java Computing System Environment

Your local computing environment should use a standard that conforms to the usability of the commands or tools that are available with WAS. It should also provide a nonconflicting development environment that can promote the deployment of Java code under WAS— nonconflicting in the sense of having control over the tools and classes that the developers use. Such control over the system environment can be realized with the aid of shell scripts where system environment variables are being set at, or before, the users log in. These shell scripts should be mounted on a shared directory between all systems in the network so that central control can be administratively realized.

Your aim is to control the WAS system environment so that, while promoting the portability of the developer's code, it is possible to expand it and keep it under the administrator's control. In a UNIX environment, the system environment for the WAS deployment consists of five basic building blocks:

▶ **Scripts**   Allow you to set the developer environment with the Java machine and its libraries.

▶ **Version control commands (or scripts)**   Allow you to check in/check out of programs or pieces of programs (discussed in Chapter 21).

▶ **Created files**   Allow you to compile and test specific programs.

▶ **Set of make files**   Allow you to manage, process, move, and distribute files (such as configuration files or code archives): JAR/Zip/EAR files within a (r-exec-enabled) trusted environment, for example, like on a bunch of UNIX servers where WAS nodes are distributed and NIS+ and YP are enabled.

▶ **Performance-tuning tools**   Give the manager of the development team some control. These tools can be either platform-dependent commands that are installed as an extra package (as is the case with AIX performance-monitoring agent tools) or generic commands that are available on all UNIX and Windows NT servers (some of which we will explore over the course of this book and discuss in depth in Chapter 25).

Command	Function
appletviewer	Reads HTML documents specified by filename or URL on the command line.
jarsigner	Signs Java Archives (JAR), and verifies the signature and integrity of the signed JAR archives. (Java Archives are formed from a compressed Zip file with a manifest file.)
jar	Creates or operates on JAR files. This command has nothing to do with the UNIX tar command, although its options are similar.
java	Functions as the Java byte-code interpreter. It runs a classname that is specified with its fully qualified name. The file extension .class should not be specified.
java_g	Functions the same as the java command but with debugging and tracing features.
javac	Compiles a Java source-code file (with extension .java) into a Java byte-code file (with extension .class). The extension of the Java source code must be specified.
javadoc	Generates API documentation in HTML format. The Java documentation generator.
javah	Produces C header (.h) and source files (.c) that describe the specified class. The native method C file generator.
javap	Disassembles the class files specified by the class names on the command line. The Java class disassembler.
native2ascii	Converts Java source code to ASCII.
rmic	Generates skeleton, stubs, and ties for remote objects using the IIOP protocols (option -iiop).
rmid	Starts the activation system daemon to register and activate objects in the Java machine.
rmiregistry	Starts a remote registry on a host machine.
serialver	Displays the unique version number identifier for a named class or classes. The class version number generator.

Table 3-4   *Typical Commands Available with the Java Distribution*

NOTE

This book discusses some of the building blocks that manage the WebSphere Application Server development environment. The work has been performed on a variety of platforms: Linux, AIX, and Windows NT. However, the scripts have been carefully written and designed in a generic way, so that they can be run on other UNIX platforms, such as Sun Solaris and HP-UNIX.

Java Environment Variables

Probably one of the most notorious shell variables that everyone is familiar with is the PATH variable, which defines the search path for the shell to look for a command. This variable is defined in the system profile and in the user profile. This section talks about how to set up these profiles and how to build three basic shell scripts to preserve the uniformity of your WAS environment.

Table 3-5 shows the environment variables that can be affected by installing a Java machine.

To compound the difficulty, the values of the environment variables differ not only from one platform to another, but also between different versions of the Java machine.

The CLASSPATH Environment Variable

The Java machine, via its class loader, loads the specific classes that an application needs. The class loader looks into the environment variable CLASSPATH to find the needed classes.

NOTE

It is possible to override the classpath specified by the environment variable CLASSPATH, by specifying it on the command line of the Java machine. The Java machine takes -classpath as a command-line argument, making it possible to specify a classpath as per the application basis.

Environment Variable	Description
JAVA_HOME	Used as the home directory of the Java machine.
CLASSPATH	Used to specify the path to the library packages that the Java machine can load to resolve the names of the symbols within a Java program.
J2EE_CLASSPATH	Used as the classpath referenced by the J2EE server. Not needed for WAS.
JAVA_COMPILER	Used to enable or disable the JIT.
PATH	Used to append the directory where the java program of your Java machine distribution is located. The search path is where the shell looks for commands.
LD_LIBRARY_PATH LIBPATH (on Sun Solaris)	Used as the path for the dynamically linked libraries.
JAVA_EXE	Used in the WAS shell or batcj scripts. This variable is not Java specific, but worth mentioning because it refers to the Java program to run the Java machine.
THREADS_FLAGS	Used prior to JDK 1.1.7. No longer used.

Table 3-5   *Java Environment Variables*

The classpath specifies the following:

▶ Package root directory for classes in a package. Notably the dot (.), which depicts the current directory as the root directory for the classes.

▶ JAR and ZIP archive files containing classes: these are files that end with the extension .jar and .zip.

▶ Directories that contain class files for class files not in a package.

The order of the classes specified in the classpath is important because the class loader searches for the needed class by following that order until the specified class is found; then it will ignore the rest of the classpath entries. In UNIX, the classpath is separated by a colon (:); on Windows NT, it is separated by a semicolon (;). It is customary to include the current directory in the classpath to let the Java run-time environment find these classes relative to the current working directory. The current directory is added to the classpath by appending a period followed by a slash (/) to it. In each directory, the special directory dot (.) specifies the current directory.

NOTE

CLASSPATH is the only environment variable still used, and it can be overridden by using the java command-line options -classpath and -cp. The -cp option is identical to -classpath in the new `java` *command.*

A Java package or a class name is mapped using the hierarchy of the directories on every system. In every case, the fully specified directory name and filename of such a package or class has all its slashes replaced by dots. The illustration shows a tree of directories and how the Java program locates a class file.

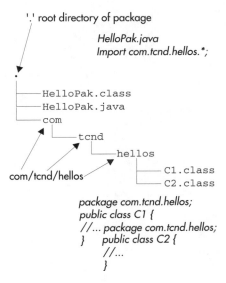

Systemwide profile and User .profile (bash_profile)

On a UNIX platform, the systemwide profile /etc/profile is executed initially upon each user login; then the user profile, located in the user home directory, is executed subsequently. This means the user profile takes precedence over the system profile because it is the last to be executed. Users can put any command in their user profile so that they can customize their system's environment to suit their personal tastes.

On AIX, the system profile is /etc/profile; the user profile is the hidden .profile file located in the user home directory (which can be obtained by echoing the variable $HOME).

On Linux, RedHat 7.x, in addition to the global system profile /etc/profile, a set of files located in the /etc/profile.d/ directory are executed through a loop invoked in the /etc/profile script. Also, the Linux user profile is the hidden file .bash_profile located in the home directory.

When a user logs in, before the command prompt appears, every command in the systemwide profile files is executed first, and then the user profile is executed second.

If you decide to set up a systemwide Java environment on a UNIX platform, edit the /etc/profile, add the appropriate variable, and export them. For instance, Listing 3-2 demonstrates a suitable profile for a Linux platform.

Listing 3-2   */etc/profile on Linux*

```
# /etc/profile
# System wide environment and startup programs
# Functions and aliases go in /etc/bashrc
PATH="$PATH:/usr/X11R6/bin:/tools"
ulimit -S -c 1000000 > /dev/null 2>&1
if [ 'id -gn' = 'id -un' -a 'id -u' -gt 14 ]; then
      umask 002
else
      umask 022
fi
USER='id -un'
LOGNAME=$USER
MAIL="/var/spool/mail/$USER"
HOSTNAME='/bin/hostname'
HISTSIZE=1000
export PATH USER LOGNAME MAIL HOSTNAME HISTSIZE INPUTRC
for i in /etc/profile.d/*.sh ; do
      if [ -x $i ]; then
            . $i
      fi
done
unset i
#PROJECT12-JAVA-SYSTEMWIDE-ENVIRONMENT-001
JAVA_HOME=/opt/java
```

```
JRE_HOME=$JAVA_HOME/jre
LD_LIBRARY_PATH=$JAVA_HOME/jre/bin:$JAVA_HOME/jre/bin/classic:$LD_LIBRARY_PATH
PATH=$JAVA_HOME/sh:$JAVA_HOME/jre/sh:$PATH
CLASSPATH=.:$CLASSPATH:/common/classes/db2java.zip
export JAVA_HOME LD_LIBRARY_PATH CLASSPATH PATH
```

The comment #PROJECT12-JAVA-SYSTEMWIDE-ENVIRONMENT-001 is used as a marker for an automatic script that can do the cut and paste programmatically. Listing 3-3 shows the emitproject12profile.sh that can regenerate the /etc/profile with a new setting of our common Java environment.

Listing 3-3   *emitproject12profile.sh*

```
1.    #!/bin/ksh
2.
3.    # modify the /etc/profile
4.    cd /etc
5.    marker="#PROJECT12-JAVA-SYSTEMWIDE-ENVIRONMENT-001"
6.    if [ -f profile ]
7.    then
8.    awk < profile ""BEGIN {m="""$marker"""; skip=0;}
9.    {
10.   if ( skip == 1 ) next;
11.   if ( index($0, m) == 1 )
12.   {
13.      skip = 1;
14.      next;
15.   }
16.   print $0;
17.   }"" > tmp.$$
18.   fi
19.
20.
21.   cat >> tmp.$$ <<EOF
22.   $marker
23.   JAVA_HOME=/opt/java
24.   CLASSPATH=.
25.   CLASSPATH=\$CLASSPATH:/opt/jsdk/servlet.jar
26.   CLASSPATH=\$CLASSPATH:/opt/jsdk/server.jar
27.   PATH=\$PATH:/tools
28.   export PATH JAVA_HOME CLASSPATH
29.   EOF
30.
```

```
31.   # Backup the profile and move the updated one to it
32.   cp profile profile.$$
33.   mv tmp $$ profile
34.
35.
```

Lines 5 to 18 do the cut and paste of the /etc/profile throughout the marker mentioned in the preceding paragraph. The content is temporarily written to tmp.$$ file, where $$ stands for the unique process number executing the shell script. Lines 23 to 28 are the content that is appended to the profile file, replacing the previous one shown in Listing 3-2.

It is possible to have a unique script to set up the environment on a mix of platforms. The following section discusses the major script, *setj.sh*, that we will use in this book to set our development environment. Almost every chapter in this book refers to environment variables that have been set by setj.sh. We will call the development environment used in this book *The WASDG Environment.*

Setting the WAS/Java Development Environment: The WASDG Environment

The development environment is one of the most important factors in any Java computing that dictates the success and the smooth flow of any WebSphere development project. IBM has a tendency to sell visual-based applications[1] to simplify the task of development. Not to mention the cascading cost of such products, these applications are graphical based and suffer from command-based automation. In addition, they hide the real computational aspects from the developer, often making them seem more complicated than they are. This could result in ambiguous reasoning by the developer.

Here, we embark on a risky path by discussing the setj.sh script that sets up some of the WAS environment variable, before discussing WAS installation. The WASDG development environment is set accordingly with a set of scripts that can be hierarchically organized in a tree, as shown in the chart in Figure 3-1. The chart also shows the flow of the scripts as they are being called from one to another. The root of the tree shows that setj.sh is the first to be called with an argument that decides on setting your environment.

The script setj.sh (Listing 3-4) reads in and identifies the platform by issuing the uname command and branches to the appropriate section to set up the environment. The script can be executed from within the system profile by adding the following line to the /etc/profile:

```
#   /etc/profile
# ...
. /tools/env/setj.sh w130
```

Windows NT users will have to mount the tools directory using Samba. For example, if your tools directory is located on the file server fs under the exported file system fs04, then the command NET USE T: \\fs\fs04\ will make your tools directory accessible from

---

[1]   These are known as the Visual Age series of products from IBM.

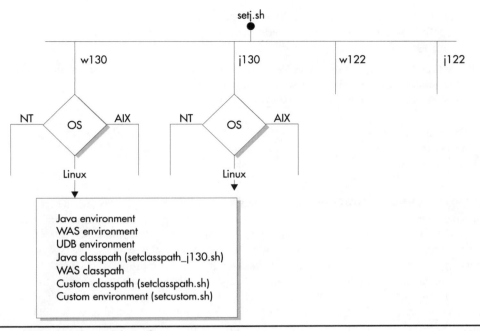

Figure 3-1   *setj.sh script branches*

Windows NT. You can run setj.sh with `T:/tools/env/setj.sh w130` command, or you can set this command in every user profile (discussed at the end of this chapter).

The script setj.sh can also be executed explicitly by users later on to refresh their system environment variables with another setup. For example, to set up their environment for the IBM Java machine 1.2.2 distribution, users execute the script by issuing the following command:

```
# .   /tools/env/setj.sh   j122
```

Notice the dot (.) followed by a space at the beginning of the command. This is important because it causes the commands in the /tools/setj.sh script to be read as if you typed them in. The standard input of the command `/tools/seth.sh j122` is still connected to the terminal, unlike the command `</tools/setj.sh j122`. There is also a difference between this command's function and that achieved by typing the following:

```
# sh  /tools/env/setj.sh   j122
```

This is a child shell or subshell, invoked by your current shell.

From within setj.sh script, after identifying the platform (with `uname`) and branching to the right segment of the setup (due to the parameter specified, i.e., w122), three scripts are executed:

▶   **setclasspath.sh**   Sets the CLASSPATH environment variables. Windows NT uses setclasspath.sh. For example, this script is located in the /tools/project12 directory.

▶ **setw(v)(os).sh**   Sets up the WAS environment variables. It is WAS-version and platform specific. It is executed only when the parameters specified are either w122 or w130.

▶ **setclasspath_(p)(v).sh**   Sets the CLASSPATH of the Java machine for the particular product (p) and the corresponding version (v). The (p) can be either j for Java or w for WAS. The (v) can be 122 or 130 for the level of the Java machine.

You can write the setj.sh script in a more compact way; however, the point here is not to digress to the art of shell programming, but to write a clear program that can be understood by most readers.

Globally Setting the CLASSPATH Environment Variable: setclasspath.sh   In the setj.sh script, the classpath setting of the classpath is being segregated between different scripts. For instance, when invoking the setj.sh on Linux with the w130 option, the classpath is set in the following order: the Java classpath (setclasspath_j130.sh, called from setclasspath_w130.sh); the WSCP classpath (setclasspath_wscp4.sh, from setclasspath_w130.sh); the WAS classpath (from within setclasspath_w130.sh.); and, finally, the custom classpath (setclasspath.sh in the project environment directory is, called from setj.sh). The setj.sh will try to accommodate most of the environment variables for each version of WAS without distinguishing between a version having extra commands from another lacking these commands.[2]

On the other hand, because the basic classpath is held in the environment variable BASE_CLASSPATH, you can add to your classpath by editing the setclasspath.sh in the project environment directory (e.g., /tools/project12/setclasspath.sh) and adding the selected class libraries to it, and then invoking setj.sh once again for the change to take effect. The directory /tools/project12 mentioned in the previous example also contains a script setcustom.sh that holds all extra environment variables that are needed for our project. We will be editing the setcustom.sh script in Part III of this book when we set up our base development environment to build a J2EE application.Windows NT needs a different set of scripts. Remember that the Windows NT directory specification uses a colon (:) for the drive letter and a semicolon (;) in the PATH as a directory separator.

By setting the classpath in this way, you will make sure that it is set equally for all developers; however, you must pay attention to the lax way in which it is being called. Because it is being invoked as a shell script following the dot (.) without enforcing a pathname, the setclasspath.sh file will be looked at in the search path if it is not located

---

[2]   For instance, if a command such as `wscp.sh` is available in WAS Advanced Edition v4 and is not available in WAS Advanced Edition Single Server v4, it will be set anyway to accommodate the former. Otherwise, you need to modify the setj.sh script to take care of such a distinction between both versions. The idea will become clearer after you read the section "Globally Setting the WAS Environment Variables: setw(v)(os).sh," next in this chapter.

in the current directory. This confusion might cause a different setclasspath.sh to be loaded for each user, yet it can be resolved simply by specifying a pathname to the setclasspath.sh:

```
#  .  /tools/project12/setclasspath.sh
```

On UNIX, the setclasspath.sh is as follows:

```
CLASSPATHMORE=$COMMON_CLASSES/whatever.jar
CLASSPATH=$BASE_CLASSPATH:$CLASSPATHMORE
export CLASSPATH CLASSPATHMORE
```

On Windows NT, the ntclasspath.sh should reflect the escaped semicolon (;) for the MKS toolkit shell to interpret it properly as a path separator:

```
CLASSPATHMORE=$NT_COMMON_CLASSES/whatever.jar
CLASSPATH=$BASE_CLASSPATH\;$CLASSPATHMORE
export CLASSPATH CLASSPATHMORE
```

The CLASSPATH consists of a BASE_CLASSPATH and a user-defined CLASSPATHMORE. The first has been already set as the essential classpath for the Java environment, and it is set when invoking the setj.sh script (see Listing 3-4).

The dot (.) is the current directory, and it is also where the java command looks for its classes when expanding a package. It is customary to use it for everyone who would like to run Java programs that import classes from packages. The $JAVA_HOME environment variable has already been set in the calling shell script setj.sh to point to the selected directory where Java has been installed on your platform. Both the run-time library (rt.jar) and the internationalization library (i18n.jar) are set relative to $JAVA_HOME. The UDB library has been added in a commonly mounted directory, /common/classes, which is shared by several machines. This is to eliminate confusion between developers and make them use the same JDBC library. The rest of the libraries in the setclasspath.sh script are Java security libraries that are used in Chapter 20.

NOTE

If you expand all the packages that a Java program needs relative to the current directory where the program itself is located, then you can compile and run this Java program without specifying the classpath. The HelloPak example in the later section "Working with the Java Machine" summarizes this point.

Globally Setting the WAS Environment Variables: setw(v)(os).sh   Remember, setj.sh sets the environment variable for more purposes than discussed so far in this book. Specifically, setj.sh executes the setw(v)(os).sh script to set the WAS-specific environment name mapping that is used in this book. The command shell dot (.) in the following line executes the commands in a file in the current shell rather than in a subshell. Because the WAS installation is platform specific, you need to write the appropriate setw(v)(os).sh script for each version of WAS on each platform. The "v" stands for the version number of the WAS, and the "os" stands for the platform name. Chapter 4 explains the content of setw(v)(os).sh, after you install the WAS product.

Globally Setting the Java Environment Variables: setj.sh (Listing 3-4) The shell scripts used in this book are employed for the Korn shell, which is available on Linux, AIX, and MKS-enabled Windows NT platforms. If you are using the Bourne shell, you must edit and modify the shell scripts to properly set the environment variables. One major difference between the Korn and Bourne shell environment variable is summarized here:

Korn Shell	Bourne Shell
export JAVA_HOME=/usr/java	JAVA_HOME=/usr/java
	export JAVA_HOME

NOTE

When setting the Windows NT environment variable PATH, the value of PATH is separated with "escaped" semicolons (\;) because the classic DOS PATH setup uses semicolons as separators, and the escape is to force the shell interpreter not to interpret the semicolon symbol and to keep it as it is. The next section, "The Windows NT Set User Environment," addresses the Windows NT environment setup and how this book uses it.

Listing 3-4   *setj.sh.script*

```
1.    #!/bin/sh
2.
3.    os='uname'
4.
5.
6.    set_jre()
7.    {
8.    if [ -f "$JRE_HOME/bin/libjava.so" ]; then
9.       jre="$JRE_HOME"
10.   fi
11.   if [ -f "$JAVA_HOME/bin/libjava.so" ]; then
12.      jre="$JAVA_HOME"
13.   fi
14.   }
15.
16.   COMMON_CLASSES=/opt/classes
17.   NT_COMMON_CLASSES=U:/opt/classes
18.
19.   PROJECT_ENV_DIR=/tools/project12
20.   NT_PROJECT_ENV_DIR=T:/tools/project12
21.
22.   COMMON_ENV_DIR=/tools/env
23.   NT_COMMON_ENV_DIR=T:/tools/env
24.
25.   if [ $# -eq 0 ]
```

```
26.  then
27.  echo NONE
28.  elif [ $1 = "j122" ]
29.  then
30.     if [ $os = "AIX" ]
31.     then
32.        echo ""Setting the Java machine 1.2.2 environment on AIX.""
33.        JAVA_HOME=/usr/java_dev2
34.        JAVA_EXE=$JAVA_HOME/jre/sh/java
35.        JRE_HOME=$JAVA_HOME/jre
36.        set_jre
37.        LD_LIBRARY_PATH=$jre/bin:$jre/bin/classic:$LD_LIBRARY_PATH
38.        PATH=$JAVA_HOME/sh:$JAVA_HOME/jre/sh:$PATH
39.        .  $COMMON_ENV_DIR/db2env.sh
40.        .  $COMMON_ENV_DIR/setclasspath_j122.sh
41.        .  $PROJECT_ENV_DIR/setclasspath.sh
42.        .  $PROJECT_ENV_DIR/setcustom.sh
43.        $JAVA_HOME/jre/sh/java -fullversion
44.        export JAVA_EXE JAVA_HOME LD_LIBRARY_PATH PATH COMMON_CLASSES
45.     elif [ $os = "Linux" ]
46.     then
47.        echo 'Setting the Java machine 1.2.2 environment on Linux.'
48.        JAVA_HOME=/opt/IBMJava2-122
49.        JAVA_EXE=$JAVA_HOME/bin/java
50.        JRE_HOME=$JAVA_HOME/jre
51.        set_jre
52.        LD_LIBRARY_PATH=$jre/bin:$jre/bin/classic:$LD_LIBRARY_PATH
53.        PATH=$JAVA_HOME/bin:$JAVA_HOME/jre/bin:$PATH
54.        .  $COMMON_ENV_DIR/db2env.sh
55.        .  $COMMON_ENV_DIR/setclasspath_j122.sh
56.        .  $PROJECT_ENV_DIR/setclasspath.sh
57.        .  $PROJECT_ENV_DIR/setcustom.sh
58.        $JAVA_HOME/bin/java -fullversion
59.        export JAVA_EXE JAVA_HOME LD_LIBRARY_PATH PATH COMMON_CLASSES
60.     elif [ $os = "Windows_NT" ]
61.     then
62.        echo 'Setting the Java machine 1.2.2 environment on Windows NT.'
63.        JAVA_HOME=C:/java
64.        JAVA_EXE=$JAVA_HOME/bin/java
65.        JRE_HOME=$JAVA_HOME/jre
66.        set_jre
67.        LD_LIBRARY_PATH=$jre/bin:$jre/bin/classic:$LD_LIBRARY_PATH
68.        PATH=$JAVA_HOME/bin\;$JAVA_HOME/jre/bin\;$PATH
69.        .  $NT_COMMON_ENV_DIR/ntclasspath_j122.sh
70.        .  $NT_PROJECT_ENV_DIR/ntclasspath.sh
71.        $JAVA_HOME/bin/java -fullversion
72.        export JAVA_EXE JAVA_HOME PATH NT_COMMON_CLASSES
```

```
73.     fi
74.  elif [ $1 = "w122" ]
75.  then
76.     if [ $os = "AIX" ]
77.     then
78.        echo 'Setting the WebSphere / Java machine 1.2.2 environment on AIX.'
79.        JAVA_HOME=/usr/WebSphere/AppServer/java
80.        JAVA_EXE=$JAVA_HOME/jre/sh/java
81.        JRE_HOME=$JAVA_HOME/jre
82.        set_jre
83.        LD_LIBRARY_PATH=$jre/bin:$jre/bin/classic:$LD_LIBRARY_PATH
84.        PATH=$JAVA_HOME/sh:$JAVA_HOME/jre/sh:$PATH
85.        .  $COMMON_ENV_DIR/setw355aix.sh
86.        .  $COMMON_ENV_DIR/db2env.sh
87.        .  $COMMON_ENV_DIR/setclasspath_w122.sh
88.        .  $PROJECT_ENV_DIR/setclasspath.sh
89.        .  $PROJECT_ENV_DIR/setcustom.sh
90.        $JAVA_HOME/jre/sh/java -fullversion
91.         export JAVA_EXE JAVA_HOME LD_LIBRARY_PATH PATH COMMON_CLASSES
92.     elif [ "$os" = "Linux" ]
93.     then
94.        echo 'Setting the WebSphere / Java machine 1.2.2 environment on Linux.'
95.        JAVA_HOME=/opt/IBMJava2-122
96.        JAVA_EXE=$JAVA_HOME/bin/java
97.        JRE_HOME=$JAVA_HOME/jre
98.        set_jre
99.        LD_LIBRARY_PATH=$jre/bin:$jre/bin/classic:$LD_LIBRARY_PATH
100.       PATH=$JAVA_HOME/bin:$JAVA_HOME/jre/bin:$PATH
101.       .  $COMMON_ENV_DIR/setw355lin.sh
102.       .  $COMMON_ENV_DIR/db2env.sh
103.       .  $COMMON_ENV_DIR/setclasspath_w122.sh
104.       .  $PROJECT_ENV_DIR/setclasspath.sh
105.       .  $PROJECT_ENV_DIR/setcustom.sh
106.       $JAVA_HOME/bin/java -fullversion
107.       export JAVA_EXE JAVA_HOME PATH COMMON_CLASSES
108.    elif [ $os = "Windows_NT" ]
109.    then
110.       echo 'Setting the Java machine 1.2.2 environment on Windows NT.'
111.       JAVA_HOME=C:/WebSphere/AppServer/jdk
112.       JAVA_EXE=$JAVA_HOME/jre/bin/java
113.       PATH=$JAVA_HOME/bin\;$JAVA_HOME/jre/bin\;$PATH
114.       .  $COMMON_ENV_DIR/setw355nt.sh
115.       .  $PROJECT_ENV_DIR/ntclasspath122.sh
116.       $JAVA_HOME/jre/bin/java -fullversion
117.       export JAVA_EXE JAVA_HOME PATH COMMON_CLASSES
118.    fi
119. elif [ $1 = "j130" ]
```

```
120. then
121.    if [ $os = "AIX" ]
122.    then
123.       echo 'Setting the Java machine 1.3.0 environment on AIX.'
124.       JAVA_HOME=/usr/WebSphere/AppServer/java
125.       JAVA_EXE=$JAVA_HOME/jre/sh/java
126.       JRE_HOME=$JAVA_HOME/jre
127.       set_jre
128.       LD_LIBRARY_PATH=$jre/bin:$jre/bin/classic:$LD_LIBRARY_PATH
129.       PATH=$JAVA_HOME/sh:$JAVA_HOME/jre/sh:$PATH
130.       . $COMMON_ENV_DIR/db2env.sh
131.       . $COMMON_ENV_DIR/setclasspath_j130.sh
132.       . $PROJECT_ENV_DIR/setclasspath.sh
133.       . $PROJECT_ENV_DIR/setcustom.sh
134.       $JAVA_HOME/jre/sh/java -fullversion
135.        export JAVA_EXE JAVA_HOME LD_LIBRARY_PATH PATH COMMON_CLASSES
136.    elif [ $os = Linux ]
137.    then
138.       echo 'Setting the Java machine 1.3.0 environment on Linux.'
139.       JAVA_HOME=/opt/IBMJava2-130
140.       JAVA_EXE=/opt/IBMJava2-130/bin/java
141.       JRE_HOME=$JAVA_HOME/jre
142.       set_jre
143.       LD_LIBRARY_PATH=$jre/bin:$jre/bin/classic:$LD_LIBRARY_PATH
144.       PATH=$JAVA_HOME/bin:$PATH
145.       . $COMMON_ENV_DIR/db2env.sh
146.       . $COMMON_ENV_DIR/setclasspath_j130.sh
147.       . $PROJECT_ENV_DIR/setclasspath.sh
148.       . $PROJECT_ENV_DIR/setcustom.sh
149.       $JAVA_HOME/bin/java -fullversion
150.       export JAVA_EXE JAVA_HOME PATH COMMON_CLASSES
151.    elif [ $os = "Windows_NT" ]
152.    then
153.       echo 'Setting the Java machine 1.3.0 environment on Windows NT.'
154.       JAVA_HOME=C:/WebSphere/AppServer/jdk
155.       JAVA_EXE=C:/WebSphere/AppServer/jdk/jre/bin/java
156.       PATH=$JAVA_HOME/bin\;$JAVA_HOME/jre/bin\;$PATH
157.       $JAVA_HOME/jre/bin/java -fullversion
158.       . $COMMON_ENV_DIR/ntclasspath_j130.sh
159.       . $PROJECT_ENV_DIR/ntclasspath.sh
160.       export JAVA_EXE JAVA_HOME PATH COMMON_CLASSES
161.
162.    fi
163. elif  [ $1 = "w130" ]
164. then
165.    if [ $os = "AIX" ]
166.    then
167.       echo 'Setting the WebSphere / Java machine 1.3.0 environment on AIX.'
```

```
168.        JAVA_HOME=/usr/WebSphere/AppServer/java
169.        JAVA_EXE=/usr/WebSphere/AppServer/java/jre/sh/java
170.        JRE_HOME=$JAVA_HOME/jre
171.        set_jre
172.        LD_LIBRARY_PATH=$jre/bin:$jre/bin/classic:$LD_LIBRARY_PATH
173.        PATH=$JAVA_HOME/sh:$JAVA_HOME/jre/sh:$PATH
174.        .  $COMMON_ENV_DIR/setw4aix.sh
175.        .  $COMMON_ENV_DIR/db2env.sh
176.        .  $COMMON_ENV_DIR/setclasspath_w130.sh
177.        .  $PROJECT_ENV_DIR/setclasspath.sh
178.        .  $PROJECT_ENV_DIR/setcustom.sh
179.        $JAVA_HOME/jre/sh/java -fullversion
180.         export JAVA_EXE JAVA_HOME LD_LIBRARY_PATH PATH COMMON_CLASSES
181.    elif [ $os = Linux ]
182.    then
183.        echo 'Setting the WebSphere / Java machine 1.3.0 environment on Linux.'
184.        JAVA_HOME=/opt/IBMJava2-130
185.        JAVA_EXE=/opt/IBMJava2-130/bin/java
186.        JRE_HOME=$JAVA_HOME/jre
187.        set_jre
188.        LD_LIBRARY_PATH=$jre/bin:$jre/bin/classic:$LD_LIBRARY_PATH
189.        PATH=$JAVA_HOME/bin:$JAVA_HOME/jre/bin:$PATH
190.        $JAVA_HOME/bin/java -fullversion
191.        .  $COMMON_ENV_DIR/setw4lin.sh
192.        .  $COMMON_ENV_DIR/db2env.sh
193.        .  $COMMON_ENV_DIR/setclasspath_w130.sh
194.        .  $PROJECT_ENV_DIR/setclasspath.sh
195.        .  $PROJECT_ENV_DIR/setcustom.sh
196.        export JAVA_EXE JAVA_HOME PATH COMMON_CLASSES
197.    elif [ $os = "Windows_NT" ]
198.    then
199.        echo 'Setting the WebSphere / Java machine 1.3.0 environment on Windows NT.'
200.        JAVA_HOME=C:/WebSphere/AppServer/jdk
201.        JAVA_EXE=C:/WebSphere/AppServer/jdk/jre/bin/java
202.        PATH=$JAVA_HOME/bin\;$JAVA_HOME/jre/bin\;$PATH
203.        $JAVA_HOME/jre/bin/java -fullversion
204.        .  $NT_COMMON_ENV_DIR/setw4nt.sh
205.        .  $NT_COMMON_ENV_DIR/ntclasspath_w130.sh
206.        .  $NT_PROJECT_ENV_DIR/ntclasspath.sh
207.        export JAVA_EXE JAVA_HOME PATH NT_COMMON_CLASSES
208.    fi
209. fi
```

A script like this is handy when it is made available on a shared file system. For example, it can be made available to all users by placing it in the /tools/env directory, where the /tools directory itself is NFS-mounted on all workstations. This /tools/env directory, however, may be added to the PATH of the user or developer. Use NFS to export the /tools directory from a shared fileserver so that it can be mounted by other servers and workstations. You don't need to use a more sophisticated shared file system such as AFS or DFS because the /tools directory contains a minimal number of files (usually, small scripts) that are read—and even occasionally executed—by users (without any user modification involved). The following list describes the four options that can be passed to setj.sh for setting various development environments.

- ▶ **j122**   To set a Java machine based on IBM Java 2 Technology distribution 1.2.2

- ▶ **j130**   To set a Java machine based on IBM Java 2 Technology distribution 1.3.0

- ▶ **w122**   To set the environment for a Java machine shipped and installed by WAS v3.5.5 distribution

- ▶ **w130**   To set the environment for a Java machine shipped and installed by WAS v4.0.2 distribution

Although the options j122 and w122 seem to be identical, they may have different builds for the Java machine that can be revealed when issuing this command: `java -fullversion`. In fact, when you invoke setj.sh with any one of the options mentioned in the preceding list, the environment is initialized, and the build number is printed as setj.sh initializes your environment, as shown in this illustration.

```
[root@node2 root]# . /tools/env/setj.sh
NONE
[root@node2 root]# . /tools/env/setj.sh w122
Setting the WebSphere / Java machine 1.2.2 environment on Linux.
java full version "J2RE 1.2.2 IBM build cx122-20010308"
[root@node2 root]#
[root@node2 root]# . /tools/env/setj.sh w130
Setting the WebSphere / Java machine 1.3.0 environment on Linux.
java full version "J2RE 1.3.0 IBM build cx130-20010626"
[root@node2 root]# []
```

The first command (in the preceding illustration) called setj.sh without any option—in which case, a NONE is returned since setj.sh exited without doing anything. The second command invoked setj.sh with the option j130 to plainly set up the Java environment, and the third command invoked setj.sh with the option w130 to set up the Java environment and the WAS environment, respectively. The *chekenv*, introduced in Appendix D, can be used to check whether or not the WASDG environment variables have been set properly. You will use chekenv any time you want to check that the setj.sh has properly set up your environment.

The reason to separate the Java environment setup from the profile and put it in a script on its own is to make it easier to change and have centralized control over the Java machine that gears WAS to the developer's application testing. For example, when you upgrade to a newer Java machine and you apply a fixpack to the WAS installation, the developer's system environment can simply be changed to fit the new product by editing and making changes in the setj.sh file and its associated scripts.

The Windows NT User Environment

This section provides a refresher about the Windows NT batch commands that have been inherited from DOS. You will learn how to set up the Windows NT user environment, and how to achieve a UNIX-like computing environment on this platform.

A Refresher on Windows NT's Batch Commands

The MS-DOS command prompt on Windows NT is based on DOS batch commands. You can supply parameters following a batch file as additional information that is supplied on the command line. These parameters are substituted within the batch process with their equivalent numbered variables: %0, %1, %2, and so on. The %0 stands for the batch filename itself, and the %1 stands for the first parameter entered at the command prompt following the batch filename. A simple batch file, such as SHOW.BAT, echoes back to you the first three parameters you entered after the batch file:

```
ECHO OFF
ECHO NAME OF THIS BATCH FILE %0
IF "%1"=="" GOTO HELP
ECHO %1 %2 %3
GOTO EXIT
:HELP
ECHO ENTER SOMETHING AFTER THE BATCH FILE NAME
:EXIT
```

In DOS batch file programming, you must always remember two commands: set and call. In a batch file, call does what the dot (.) does in a UNIX shell—it invokes another batch script and then executes it. The set command creates a system environment variable and assigns a value to it, similar to what the export command does. For example, SETJAVA.BAT calls on the batch file SETCLASS.BAT to set the CLASSPATH:

```
ECHO OFF
REM SETJAVA.BAT
CALL SETCLASS.BAT
ECHO CLASSPATH IS SET TO:
echo %CLASSPATH%
SET PATH=C:\JAVA\BIN:%PATH%
ECHO OFF
REM SETCLASS.BAT
SET CLASSPATH=C:\DB2SQL\DB2JAVA.ZIP
```

You can manipulate DOS variables from the command prompt. They are invoked by their name surrounded with percent signs. For example, to append C:\BIN to your PATH variable, issue the following at a command prompt:

```
C:\> SET PATH=C:\BIN;%PATH%
```

Setting the User Environment on Windows NT

There are two steps in setting up the user environment variables on Windows NT. The first is global and resides in the system properties of the system; the second is local and personal to the user, and it is defined in the user login script (executed each time the user logs in).

Generic Variables Set Up with System Properties

System properties define system variables and user variables. To edit these properties, select Start | Settings | Control Panel. Then double-click System, and click the Environment tab, shown here:

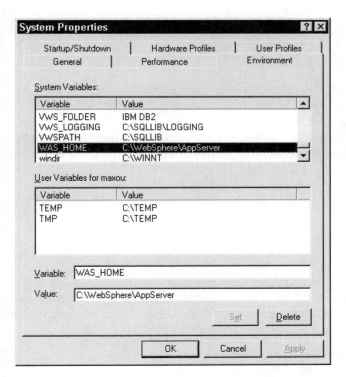

A Personalized Profile with the Login Script

You can provide persistent connection and primary user environment setup by writing login scripts under NT. To set up the login script, follow these steps:

1. Start the User Manager by selecting Start | Programs | Administrative Tools | User Manager For Domains.
2. Double-click the username to open the User Properties window.

3. Click Profile to open the User Environment Profile dialog box.

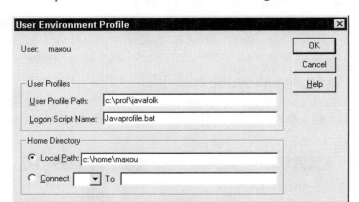

4. In the User Profile Path text box, enter the name of the profile if you have already created one. Consult your Windows NT documentation to learn how to create one.

5. In the Logon Script Name text box, enter the batch file that you created as the startup login script for the user. This script resides in the %WindowRoot%\SYSTEM32\ REPL\ IMPORT\SCRIPTS directory, because this directory automatically shares as NETLOGON. The following is an example of the login script for the user "maxou" on my system:

```
ECHO OFF
REM Ensure the tools is Samba mounted and acessible with T:/tools
NET USE T:  \\fs\fs04
CLEAR
REM Get a shell prompt and setup the environment
C:\MKSNT\sh.exe C:\profile.ksh
```

NET USE mounts the Samba shared directory on the T: drive, and then the sh.exe is executed to turn the DOS command prompt into a shell interpreter to be shown upon user login. The profile.ksh is invoked and typically should have two entries:

```
. T:/tools/env/setj.sh w130
C:/MKSNT/sh.exe
```

6. In the Local Path text box, enter the path of the user home directory.

7. Click OK to close the User Environment Profile dialog box and save the changes.

8. Log off Windows NT, and then log in as the user whose login script you just enforced.

The Shell Interpreter on Windows NT

The Windows NT command processor used in this book has been enabled with the Korn shell. The advantages of doing this are the following:

►   When you want to refer to the environment variable, say PATH, you will use $PATH instead of %PATH%.

►   You can run the Korn shell script on the Windows NT platform.

►   You can use shell loop control in conjunction with UNIX system commands and utilities on Windows NT.

The next illustration shows the DOS prompt being turned into a shell command processor by typing the `sh` command (installed by the MKS Toolkit).

```
MKS Korn Shell - C:/home/maxou/waswork/zoo                              _ □ ×

C:\home\maxou\waswork>sh
$ ls -l
total 1
-rwxrwxrwa   1 Everyone        Everyone            124 Sep 28 10:02 ntjava.sh
$ cat ntjava.sh
#!/usr/bin/sh

JAVA_HOME=C:/java
JAVA_EXE=C:/java/bin/java
PATH=C:/java/bin\;$PATH
export JAVA_HOME  JAVA_EXE  PATH

$ . ./ntjava.sh
$ java -fullversion
java full version "J2RE 1.3.0 IBM build cn130-20010502w"
$
$ echo $PATH
C:/java/bin;C:\Program Files\ibm\gsk5\lib;C:\mksnt;C:\WINNT\system32;C:\WINNT;C:\WebSphere\A
ppServein;C:\SQLLIB\BIN;C:\SQLLIB\SAMPLES\REPL;C:\SQLLIB\HELP;C:\IBM\IMNNQ
$
$ history
72      ls -l
73      set
74      echo $PATH
75      exit
76      echo $PATH
77      . ./ntjava.sh
78      echo $PATH
79      vi nt*
80      . ./ntjava.sh
81      exit
82      ls -l
83      cat ntjava.sh
84      . ./ntjava.sh
85      java -fullversion
86      echo $PATH
87      history
$ mkdir zoo
$ cd zoo
$ find C:/WebSphere/AppServer/bin -name *.xml -exec cp {} . \;
$ ■
```

However, if the MKS Toolkit is not available on your system, you will need to deal with the classical DOS batch commands.

Working with the Java Machine

This section reviews some simple "Hello" programs that you can use to test the efficacy of the installation so far. The following examples provide you with a concise reference for saying "Hello, World!"

Hello World

Let's start at the very beginning (a very good place to start). The HelloWorld.java program is a handy program to test your Java machine's prowess. Edit and write the program HelloWorld.java, shown in Listing 3-5.

Listing 3-5 *HelloWorld.java*

```
class HelloWorld {
   public static void main (String args[]) {
      System.out.println("Hello, World!");
   }
}
```

This program will start a Java machine by itself. To test it, follow these steps:

1. Edit and save the program.
2. Compile it with javac `HelloWorld.java`
3. Run it by invoking the Java program: `java HelloWorld`

The output should be simple: Hello, World!

Working with Java Packages: A Simple View

This section introduces you to Java packages and shows you how to do batch processing on them and their directory hierarchies. An example is provided to rename a package and modify all related programs by using a few lines of Korn shell with a script editor (sed). Similar techniques can be applied in an application upgrade/migration with the aid of UNIX system tools.

The HelloPak Program

Listing 3-6 shows how the program HelloPak.java resolves the names of the symbols by importing the classes within the com.tcnd.hellos package. As you can see, the path com/tcnd/hellos is the same as the package name with the slash (/) separator translated to a dot (.).

In your work directory, create the directory tree with the `mkdir` command:

```
# mkdir -p com/tcnd/hellos
```

Listings 3-6 and 3-7 show the C1.java and C2.java class files of the com.tcnd.hellos package. Copy these two files to com/tcnd./hellos, and HelloPak.java to the root directory of the package (the current directory in this situation). Using the `javac` command, compile all programs in the tree (mirroring the package) with the `javac` command:

```
# find com -name "*.java" -exec javac {} \;
```

Next, compile the source program:

```
# javac HelloPak.java
# java HelloPak
```

Package com.tcnd.hellos with the `jar` command:

```
# jar cvf  pak.jar  com;  rm -rf  com
```

This command creates a package called pak.jar, and then it removes the directory tree com/tcnd/hellos recursively. You can compile and run your HelloPak.java program, this time by specifying the package pak.jar in the classpath:

```
# javac -classpath ./pak.jar HelloPak.java
# java -classpath .:./pak.jar HelloPak
```

On Windows NT, the semicolon (;) must be used instead of the colon (:) to separate the elements of the class path. The HelloPak.java program follows:

Listing 3-6   *HelloPak .java program*

```
import com.tcnd.hellos.*;
class HelloPak {
    public static void main(String args[]) {
        C1 hi = new C1();
        hi.sayHello();
        C2 ho = new C2();
        ho.sayHello();
        System.out.println(hi.S1);
        System.out.println(ho.S1);
        System.out.println(C1.S1);
        System.out.println(com.tcnd.hellos.C1.S1);
        System.out.println(com.tcnd.hellos.C2.S1);
    }
}
```

Listing 3-7   *classes com/tcnd/hellos/C1.java*

```
package com.tcnd.hellos;
public class C1 {
    public static final String S1 = "Snow White in C1";
    public void sayHello() {
        System.out.println("Hello World (C1) !");
    }
}
```

Listing 3-8   *com/tcnd/hellos/C2.java*

```
package com.tcnd.hellos;
public class C2 {
    public static final String S1 = "Snow White in C2";
    public void sayHello() {
        System.out.println("Hello World (C2) !");
    }
}
```

Batch Processing with Shell/Sed

When you decide to change the package name from com.tcnd.hellos to com.ibmsos.hellos, you carry out this shift by administering the following programming changes:

1. Change the directory name from com/tcnd to com/ibmsos.
2. Edit every program (at least Java source code programs) in the directory tree and make the change for the newly created package.
3. Recompile the classes in the directory tree with `javac`.
4. Package the new tree in a .jar archive, and recompile the HelloPak.java with the new package.

This kind of work is commonly known in an enterprise environment when a specific management plan mandates a migration from one product to another, but may also result from myriad other reasons.

The tediousness of making these changes manually from within a GUI environment—although it happens in a lot of places in this time of visual-age products—dictates the necessity of UNIX-based batch processing.

To address the problem, you first create the sed script, as in Listing 3-9. This script simply says, "Globally substitute any occurrence of com.tcnd.hellos with com.ibmsos.com." A slash before each dot (\.) is used to escape this special character.

Listing 3-9   *map.sed script*

```
s/com\.tcnd\.hellos/com\.ibmsos\.com/g
```

The map.sed script is called from the shell script map.sh shown in Listing 3-10. A sed script is presented as an input to be processed by the `sed` command after the option -f. This substitution takes place on the input file presented by the variable $1; and the output of the processed file is directed to the /tmp/map.$$ file, where *$$* is the unique number of the process. The processed file is then deleted after copying it to the original.

Listing 3-10   *map.sh script*

```
#!/usr/bin/ksh
echo "map $1"
sed -f ./map.sed $1  > /tmp/map.$$
cp /tmp/map.$$   $1
rm /tmp/map.$$
```

Both the map.sed and map.sh files should reside in the root directory of your package. The map.sh file is made executable with chmod 755 map.sh. Then, in the root directory of the package, you issue this series of commands to recompile your program:

1. Make the string substitution changes in every .java file:

   ```
   # find ./ -name  "*.java"  -type f -exec map.sh {} \;
   ```

2. Rename the directory com/tcnd to com/ibmsos:

   ```
   # mv com/tcnd com/ibmsos
   ```

3. Recompile every .java program located in the com/* directory:

   ```
   # find com -name "*.java" -exec javac {} \;
   ```

4. Compile the program in the current directory and/or rebuild the .jar archive:

   ```
   # javac HelloPak.java
   ```

   Alternatively,

   ```
   # jar cvf pak.jar
   # javac -classpath ./pak.jar HelloPak.java
   ```

5. Execute the program:

   ```
   # java -classpath .:./pak.jar HelloPak
   ```

Batch processing is an adequate way to write compact, simple scripts to use migration scripts. It can also facilitate the installation of multiple WebSphere Domains on the same machine, because you can automatically process the server configuration file to map to a different set of ports for each of these WebSphere Domains. Chapter 21 shows you a simple way to preprocess such configuration files in a multidomain deployment.

HelloURL Example

For this second example, let's create a handy Java program that ensures that the HTTP Server is running by returning your request. You run this program on any machine connected to the same network as your HTTP server.

Using Netscape Composer or a similar web page editor, create a blank page by selecting File | New | Blank Page. Then type **Hello World!** in a 4+ font size. Select File | Save As and type *ihs_docroot*/**HelloWorld.html**, where *ihs_docroot* is the document root directory for your IBM HTTP server; for example, on Linux, it is /opt/IBMHTTPServer/htdocs. The HelloWorld.html can also be manually edited, as in Listing 3-11.

Listing 3-11   *HelloWorld.html*

```
<html>
<head>
<title>Hello World Test</title>
<meta http-equiv="Content-Type" content="text/html; charset=iso-8859-1">
<meta name="Manually Generated" content="P/5.xx [en] (X11; U; Linux 2.4.3-12 i686) [Perl CGI]">
</head>
<body>
    <b><font size=+4>Hello World!</font></b>
</body>
</html>
```

Make sure that your HTTP server is running (i.e., look for a few httpd daemons by *grepping* your workstation processes list: ps -ef | grep http). If it is not running, change directory to ihs_home/bin and start it with the command apachectl start.

Now edit and save the HelloURL.java program shown in Listing 3-12. Also note that you need to make the URL point to the server where you installed your HTTP server (instead of the my.http.server). Compile the program with javac and run it to get a textual output of your request, as shown in the illustration that follows the listing.

Listing 3-12   *HelloURL.java*

```
import java.net.*;
import java.io.*;
public class HelloURL
{
     public HelloURL()
     {
          super();
     }
     public void printHelloURL( String helloUrlStr )
     {
          URL url = null;
          BufferedReader reader = null;
          String data = null;
          try {
               url = new URL(helloUrlStr);
```

```
                    reader = new BufferedReader(new InputStreamReader(url.openStream()) );
                    while ((data = reader.readLine()) != null )
                    {
                            System.out.println(data);
                    }
            }
            catch (MalformedURLException e) {
                    e.printStackTrace();
            }
            catch (IOException e) {
                    e.printStackTrace();
            }
    }
    // start the Java machine here with main()
    public static void main(String args[]) {
            String url = "http://http.server.name/HelloWorld.html";
            HelloURL o = new HelloURL();
            o.printHelloURL(url);
    }
}
```

The illustration shows the HelloURL output. It is simple to check this program to see if the HTTP server is replying to URL requests properly from its document root. Checking on the HTTP server is important because it is the first agent in the row to forward requests to WAS for application servers, as you will see in Chapter 8.

```
X root@node1: /BOOK/33/url                                              _ □ X
# ls -l *.class
-rw-r--r--    1 root      root          1052 Sep 20 16:29 HelloURL.class
-rw-r--r--    1 root      root           427 Sep 20 23:09 HelloWorld.class
# java HelloWorld
Hello, World!
#
# java HelloURL
<html>
<head>
<title>Hello World Test</title>
<meta http-equiv="Content-Type" content="text/html; charset=iso-8859-1">
<meta name="Manually Generated" content="Perl/5.xx [en] (X11; U; Linux 2.4.3-12
i686) [Perl CGI]">
</head>
<body>
   <b><font size=+4>Hello World!</font></b>
</body>
</html>

#
```

The CGI Version of Hello World: HelloWorld.cgi

CGI programming is addressed in this book because it is the foundation of web programming. The CGI environment variables are also the subject of discussion when going from the generic programming of client-server conversation to the specific servlet. Among other things, CGI programming can be used to develop debugging and stress-testing tools for web application servers.

Listing 3-13 shows the Perl/CGI script for Hello World! The first line specifies the location of the Perl interpreter, followed by the Perl CGI module that directs the I/O to be handled by the HTTP protocol. Copy the script to the document root of your HTTP server and make sure its executable bits are set before requesting it from a browser:

```
# chmod 755 HelloWorld.cgi
```

This script uses the *here string* to embed the document to be printed within the Perl script. A here-string starts at a particular line following an identifier and continues until the identifier appears on a line by itself. A here-string can also be used similarly to a here-document in a Korn shell script, where you can specify batch input to be presented to programs. You can use this technique when wrapping commands in Perl scripts.

Listing 3-13   *HelloWorld.cgi*

```
#!/usr/bin/perl
use CGI qw(:standard);
$s = << "EOF";
<html>
<head>
   <title>Hello World Test</title>
   <meta http-equiv="Content-Type" content="text/html; charset=iso-8859-1">
      <meta name="Manually Generated" content="Perl/5.xx [en] (X11; U; Linux
 2.4.3-12 i686) [Perl CGI]">
      </head>
      <body>
      <b><font size=+4>Hello World!</font></b>
      </body>
</html>
EOF

print "Content-type: text/html
      Pragma:no-cache\n\n";
print "$s";
```

Testing Remote Database Connection with the JDBC Driver

This chapter closes with a simple program that ensures that your database server is functioning properly and can connect properly to remote clients. The program connect.java is shown in Listing 3-14. This is the first program to test with your remote client database connectivity. You can use it to test your UDB remote client connection from any host machine, provided that you have a Java machine available on it and the UDB JDBC driver db2java.zip properly set in your classpath.[3] Earlier in this chapter, on line 7 of the setclasspath.sh script (see Listing 3-4), the JDBC driver is set to /common/classes/db2java.zip. The remote machine that you intend to connect to its database should have either the DB2 UDB server or the DB2 UDB client components running on it.[4]

Listing 3-14   *Connecting to UDB using JDBC: connect.java*

```
1.   import java.sql.*;
2.   public class connect {
3.       public static void main( String argv[] ) {
4.           if (argv.length < 1) {
5.               System.out.println("Usage:\njava connect URL [USERID PASSWRD]");
6.               System.exit(0);
7.           }
8.           String url, userid, passwrd;
9.           url = argv[0];
10.          userid = argv.length > 1 ? argv[1] : "";
11.          passwrd = argv.length > 2 ? argv[2] : "";
12.          try {
13.              Class.forName("COM.ibm.db2.jdbc.net.DB2Driver");
14.          } catch (ClassNotFoundException e) {
15.              e.printStackTrace();
16.              System.exit(0);
17.          }
18.          try {
19.              Connection conn = DriverManager.getConnection(url, userid, passwrd);
20.          } catch (SQLException e) {
21.              e.printStackTrace();
22.              System.exit(0);
```

---

[3]   The host machine is the machine on which you intend to install the WAS product.

[4]   A remote machine with the UDB client components can catalog a database defined on another machine, and it appears like any other UDB server. Chapter 4 has an example showing you how to catalog a database.

```
23.            }
24.            System.out.println("Got Connection to " + url);
25.    }
26. }
```

You should run the connect.java program on the server on which you intend to install the WAS. Its connectivity success ensures that you can remotely connect to the database server.

NOTE

If you intend to use this book with WebSphere Advanced Edition Single Server (AEs,) then you do not need to install the UDB Server. However, some of the sample programs in Part III of this book may require you to have a database available. On the other hand, the petstore sample application discussed in Chapter 6 requires you to have a database server, such as UDB or Oracle.

To test the connect.java program, copy it and compile it on the host machine with the `javac` command. Next, try to connect to the SAMPLE database simply by requesting a connection to your database UDB node:

```
# java connect jdbc:db2://node2:50068/SAMPLE db2inst1 pwd
```

This command connects to the server whose hostname is node2, on which a UDB instance has been defined for the user db2inst1. The "pwd" is the password for the db2inst1 user. Prior to running the previous command, db2inst1 must have explicitly started db2jstrt (/home/db2inst1/sqllib/bin/db2jstrt 50068) on node2.

A successful connection returns the following:

```
Got Connection to jdbc:db2://node2:50068/SAMPLE
```

You can test the connection to the SAMPLE database, provided that you have installed it during the default installation of UDB.

The program connect.java, on line 19 of Listing 3-14, uses the DriverManager to connect to the database.

Figure 3-2 shows how the JDBC driver works: it consists of a JDBC client and a JDBC server (db2jstrt.) The JDBC client driver is loaded by the connect.java program. When the program requests a connection to a UDB database through the DriverManager, the client opens a TCP/IP socket to the JDBC server listening on the specified port. The JDBC server can be either a server on which a UDB server has been installed, or a server on which the UDB client components have been installed and a database has been cataloged on it.

The string that forms the address of a JDBC call is referred to as the JDBC URL. It has three parts: the protocol, the subprotocol, and the data source identifier.

The JDBC URL is one of the few protocol-based URLs discussed in this book.

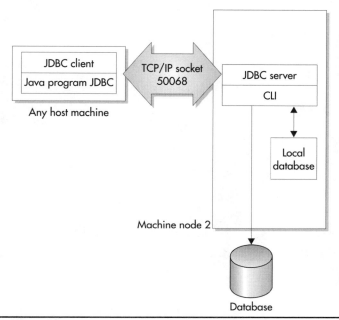

Figure 3-2   *The JDBC driver*

Wrapping Up

Let's review this chapter's salient points:

▶   It addressed the installation and basic configuration of the IBM HTTP Server, the Java machine. The administrative consideration in a WAS development environment was discussed solely on three different platforms: AIX, Linux, and Windows NT.

▶   It presented a set of simple programs to test whether your HTTP server and the Java machine were properly installed. The HelloPak program introduced you to Java packages and archives.

▶   Short UNIX scripts with Shell/SED proved the efficacy of the UNIX computing environment to manage, maintain, and migrate applications.

▶   The chapter concluded by testing the JDBC connectivity.

Installing WAS on Linux, Windows NT, and AIX

T his chapter acts as the manual with which to install the WebSphere Application Server on your platform. The installation instructions provided are for a mix of platforms. You will learn how to install two WAS versions: v3.5 and v4. Regardless of which version you install, WAS needs an administrative or configuration repository in which to store its administrative data. For the WAS Advanced Edition (v3.5 or v4), we will use the UDB (discussed in Chapter 2) as a database repository; for the WAS Advanced Edition Single Server (AEs) v4, the configuration data is flattened in XML files. In Chapter 2 and in the last section of Chapter 3, you were introduced to the fundamentals of UDB installation, and to the verification of a successful JDBC connection.

Installing WAS is straightforward. To install the product, this chapter follows the same approach as Chapter 3 to complete the setting of the developer's system environment. We call such a development environment *The WASDG Environment*.

Conventions Used in This Book

Chapter 2 addressed the installation of the WAS repository; this chapter addresses WAS installation on three different operating systems (OS): AIX, Linux, and Windows NT. For this reason, you need to learn about the common aliases used as naming conventions to refer to important directories on the file system.

Home Directory Conventions

You must decide on a directory nomination to designate the home directory for each product. The *home directory* of a product refers to the base installation directory of the product on the file system. By knowing the path of a product's home directory, you can gain access to its binary, configuration, and data files. Table 4-1 summarizes the home and commonly known directories designation used in this book.

The setj.sh script, introduced in Chapter 3, prematurely sets the home directories of various application components, some of which will be introduced and installed in this chapter.

Home Directory Designation	Product [A]
was_home	WebSphere Application Server installation root
	AIX: /usr/WebSphere/AppServer
	Linux: /opt/IBMWebAS (WAS v3.5)
	Linux: /opt/WebSphere/AppServer (WAS v4)
	Windows NT: drive:\WebSphere/AppServer (2)
ihs_home	IBM HTTP Server home directory
	AIX: /usr/HTTPServer
	Linux: /opt/IBMHTTPServer
	Windows NT: drive:\IBM HTTP Server

Table 4-1 *Defining the Commonly Known Directories*

Home Directory Designation	Product [A]
ihs_docroot	IHS document root directory
	AIX: /usr/HTTPServer/htdocs
	Linux: /opt/IBMHTTPServer/htdocs
	Windows NT: drive:\IBM HTTP Server/htdocs
java_home	IBM Developer Kit, Java 2 Technology Edition home directory
	AIX: /usr/java_dev2
	Linux: /opt/IBMJava2-122 or /opt/IBMJava2-130, depending on the WAS version
	Windows NT: *was_home*/jdk (WAS v3.5)
	Windows NT: *was_home*/java/bin (WAS v4)
db2_home	UDB or DB2 Instance home directory for db2inst1 user [B], which is on the UNIX system
	/home/db2inst1
wscp_home	WebSphere Control Program (WSCP) home directory
	Although WSCP is available as a script located in was_home/bin, in this book, WSCP can be installed on a separate workstation or server, in which case, wscp_home refers to the home directory where WSCP script (i.e., wscp.sh) is started.
shared_tools	In a multiplatform distributed environment, shared_tools is the directory that is mounted by all machines to find utility scripts to set up a developer environment, or to communicate scripts to be used jointly by all users on a mixture of machines. For example, */tools* can be such a shared directory, and a script such as setj.sh is a common script to set up the *java_home* environment of a user will be placed in this shared directory.
~	The tilde refers to the home directory of the user. As an example, on UNIX, when user dave logs in to the system, his home directory is /home/dave, and the command `cd ~` is equivalent to cd /home/ dave. There is no restriction on where the home directory of a user is defined as long as it is defined on a live file system. For example, it is also possible to create a user wasadm and set her home directory to *was_home/bin*. The /etc/passwd file contains the UNIX user accounts and their home directories mapping.

[A] A platform might have two different directories specified for the same product when such a product has more than one version. In particular, WAS v3.5 and WAS v4 use different Java machines that reside in different locations on the file system.

[B] The UDB instance db2inst1 is the default user created by UDB for a first-time installation of the product. You can have more than one UDB instance, or you can create your own user instance; however, keep in mind that UDB user accounts should be eight characters long.

Table 4-1 *Defining the Commonly Known Directories* (continued)

This book uses four software products: the WebSphere Application Server, the UDB repository, the IBM HTTP Server (IHS), and the IBM Developer Kit, Java 2 Technology Edition.

NOTE

The designation of the Windows NT PATH is traditionally inherited from MS-DOS, and it uses the backslash (\) as a separator to describe the PATH of a directory or to a file. In this book, we installed the MKS Toolkit to make Windows NT somehow similar to UNIX in terms of running commonly shared shell scripts that are mounted on a shareable directory and made available for the UNIX and Windows NT platforms. In particular, the path specification under Windows NT uses the forward slash (/) like in UNIX. For example, on a Windows NT platform, was_home refers to C:/WebSphere/AppServer.

Conventions of WAS Processes

At any given time on a UNIX platform, the IBM WebSphere Application Server has four distinct Java machine processes (or groups of processes) running:

▶   The administrative server

▶   An administrative client, such as WSCP or the administrative console (also known as web console under the single version edition of WAS v4). Running one or more of these processes is optional and is not required for the functionality of the application server.

▶   One or more application server processes

▶   A nanny process running as a watchdog for the administrative server

In general, you should favor the server resources to be used by the application server (and its associated administrative server or servers), and run the administrative client on a separate workstation.

In this book, *WAS* refers to the WebSphere Application Server in its generality as a product installed on a server or servers. When WAS is installed on a UNIX platform, all four groups of processes mentioned previously are available. WAS processes are usually started by preconfigured shell or batch scripts in which the `java` command is invoked to start one or more Java machines. Starting one Java machine may fire hundred of threads at a time. As a reminder, the author uses *Java machine* to express the Java virtual machine that is started by the `java` command.

Conventions of the WebSphere Domain

Throughout this book, WebSphere Domain is used interchangeably with WebSphere Administrative Domain; although the former is less confusing, the latter is IBM's choice as the default name given in any installation of WAS v3 and later, for the root directory of the product and for the root directory of the topology tree representing the product.

Products Dependency

Although you can customize a WAS installation to use different Java machines, web servers, and databases than the ones it is shipped with, you should use IBM guidelines in selecting the right version of these other components.

WAS v3.5 Components	WAS v4 Components
IBM Developer Kit, Java 2 Tech Ed 1.2.2	IBM Developer Kit, Java 2 Tech Ed 1.3.0
IBM HTTP Server 1.3.12	IBM HTTP Server 1.3.19
InstantDB	InstantDB (sample support only)
UDB v7.1 (with WAS Service Pack 4)	UDB v7.2 (WAS AEs does now ship with UDB, but trail code can be downloaded)

Table 4-2   *WAS v3.5 Versus WAS v4 Software Components*

The WAS trial versions that you can download from the IBM site usually come bundled with three components:

► IBM Developer Kit, Java 2 Technology

► IBM HTTP Server, a hybrid of the HTTP server build based on Apache HTTP Server

► InstantDB

If you are using WAS v3.5 or v4, these three components are bundled with the WAS trial version, and they can be automatically installed during WAS custom installation. However, there are differences between the bundled software in v3.5 and v4, as shown in Table 4-2.

InstantDB is used in a quick install, when installing WAS on the same server. The WAS AEs v4 trials don't give you the option to use UDB as a repository. You can download UDB from the IBM site. The UDB versions come with a different db2java.zip library to provide JDBC connectivity. Having the correct UDB version for each WAS version and release is crucial; otherwise, the product won't operate.

Requirements

The WebSphere Application Server requirements are classified into four categories: hardware, operating-system level, GUI interface dependency, and database.

Hardware Requirements

The hardware requirements for the installations in this book are the following:

► **Memory**   396MB of RAM. You will need more memory if you intend to run the Administrative Console of WAS v3.*x* (see the upcoming section "GUI Interface Dependency") or WSCP (see Chapter 7) on the same server.

► **Disk space**   240MB to 400MB of free disk space to install WAS and JDK, and an extra 30MB to install the HTTP server. With WAS v4, application servers can run without an HTTP server through the use of an internal preconfigured HTTP transport [1]; however, it is best to install the IBM HTTP Server for the examples in this book.

---

[1]   The use of a WAS internal HTTP transport is adequate only for testing, and should be disabled in a production environment. The WAS HTTP transport uses the default port 9080, as you will see in Chapters 5 and 6.

▶ **Swap space**   (1.8) * (amount of RAM) of free swap space allocated on a separate disk. The swap space is usually calculated as 1.6 to 1.8 multiplied by the amount of RAM available in your system.

▶ **Drive**   A CD-ROM drive if available; otherwise, 600MB extra to copy a disk image for AIX, and twice the free space of 140MB to download and extract a Linux or WinNT trial version image.

▶ **Network hardware**   A network adapter or a token ring card.

▶ **CPU**   Pentium II 300 MHz or above for Linux and Windows NT; RS/6000 for AIX.

Operating System–Level Requirements

For a Linux install, make sure you have the correct level for the Kernel. The installation and testing of WAS v3.5 on a Linux Kernel 2.2.16-22 and WAS v4 on a Linux Kernel 2.4.9-13 went pretty well. The Linux was a RedHat Linux v7.*x*.

For AIX, you need AIX 4.3.3 4330-07(or 08) maintenance level plus APAR IY19277 or AIX 5.1.

For Windows NT Server 4.0, you need to install Service Pack SP6a, and Windows 2000 requires Service Pack SP1 or SP2.

GUI Interface Dependency

WebSphere Application Server is usually administered from a GUI-dependent interface, known as the *administrative console,* and is started differently when using WAS AE v3.5 or v4 than when using WAS AEs v4. It is also possible to administer WAS AE using WSCP from a simple text-based console (or simple telnet session), which is discussed in Chapter 7.

The administrative console has several expanded panes that display different views related to your WebSphere administrative domain. The layout of the WAS AE v3.5 administrative console is similar to WAS AE v4. Despite the same window views in the administrative console for both versions, WAS AE v4 has major differences from v3.5 in organizing the tree topology of the product and in the nomenclature (see Figure 4-1). This reorganization is due to the support of J2EE applications in the new WAS product.

The WAS AE v3.5 and v4 Administrative Console

To start the administrative console for WAS AE v3.5 and v4, your workstation needs to have a graphical user interface (GUI). On UNIX, WAS AE uses its own X Windows–based console that is started with the command `adminclient.sh`; in other words, your workstation should be X Window capable. For example, a Linux machine should be installed as a workstation and not as a server simply so that the XFree86 base package is installed.

If the host machine does not have X Window components installed, you can still start the administrative console by exporting the display from the console where it was started to an authorized X Window–capable machine. You need to either have an X Window–compliant

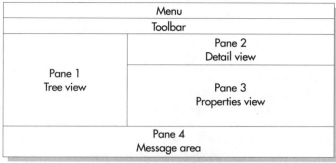

WAS Advanced Edition v4

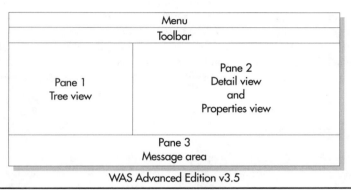

WAS Advanced Edition v3.5

Figure 4-1   *Layout of WAS AE v3.5 and v4 administrative console*

application that enables you to export the display to your workstation (e.g., for Windows NT, Exceed from Hummingbird Communications) or have the Administrative Console installed on your workstation.

In the first case, the administrative console is started on a host machine (which can be the server by itself) with its own Java machines running on the server, but the graphics for the console are rendered on a host workstation. In the second case, the administrative console with its own Java machine(s) along with the X-Window–based console are started on the workstation, hence releasing the CPU and memory resources of the WAS server for the application servers.

On UNIX, when invoking the shell script was_home/bin/adminclient.sh, first the administrative client tries to connect (via the default port 900) to the administrative server that has already been started on a host machine. If the connection is successful, then the administrative client opens the administrative console. On Windows NT, the equivalent script is adminclient.bat, which can also be started by selecting Start | Programs | IBM WebSphere | ApplicationServer V4.0 | Administrator's Console.

The WAS AEs v4 Administrative Console

WAS AEs v4 uses an Internet browser, such as Netscape Navigator 4.7, to administer WAS. The URL to start the administrative console points to the host where WAS is started, and is listening to port 9090 by default. The following is a valid URL to start the administrative console for WAS running on machine populi.tcnd.com:http://populi.tcnd.com:9090/admin.

Port 9090 is the default port for WAS v4 (the same port the earlier version WAS v2.02 [2] used for its administrative console), and can be administratively changed to another value.

Because the administrative console in WAS AEs is started within a browser, it is also referred to as a web console. The administrative console layout for WAS AEs v4 is different than WAS AE v3.5 and v4 seen earlier, and is shown in Figure 4-2.

Use the Tree view to navigate the resources and the components of the WebSphere Domain. Clicking an item in the tree allows you to see the detailed view of the item and to expose its properties when available in the right pane of the console. In WAS v3.5 and WAS AEs v4, when you right-click an item, a drop-down menu appears, in which you can select further action. Of course, the Tree view follows the hierarchy of folders and their associated items. You expand and collapse the tree of each folder by clicking the plus (+) and minus (–) signs preceding each item. The message area in the WAS AE administrative console has no counterpart in WAS AEs v4. However, all messages can usually be read from the log files, as you will see in Chapter 8.

Database Requirements

In the installation of the WebSphere Application Server Advanced Edition, a database is required to manage the tables of WAS administrative data. In this book, such a database is referred to as the WAS configuration repository or the WAS administrative repository, or simply the WAS repository. In Chapter 5, the definition of a WebSphere Domain is coupled with the

Figure 4-2   *Layout of the WAS AEs v4 administrative console*

---

[2]   Unlike WAS v2, the HTTP server does not need to be installed or be running on the same server that is running WAS to be able to administer WAS. In other words, the administrative console does not depend on an HTTP server instance to start up.

WAS configuration repository. Do not confuse the WAS repository with a DataSource defined within WAS configuration. As a reminder from Chapter 2, any database that WAS connects to for any purpose other than saving its administrative data can be configured as a DataSource.

Usually, DataSources are used to maintain web *applications data* (and not WAS administrative data)—for example, sessions, persistent EJBs, and so on. Although the WebSphere Advanced Edition stores its administrative data in the database using a number of EJBs, such a database is neither considered to be a DataSource, nor considered to be treated as a DataSource object. Therefore, tuning the database properties of the WAS administrative repository and tuning the database properties of a DataSource configured within WAS resources are unrelated. The illustration shows an administrative repository and application data both defined on the server machine populi.

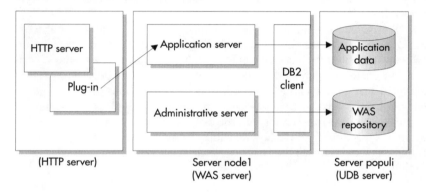

Chapter 7 shows you how to fetch the properties of a DataSource. If you plan to use a database other than UDB, refer to Chapter 8 for the properties of the different database brands.

Preinstallation Verification

If you are installing the trial version of WAS, known as WebSphere Advanced Edition Single Server (AEs), then you can skip this section and the next one. The trial version of WAS AEs automatically installs the HTTP server, and does not need a database server for its configuration repository because it uses a local flat XML file instead. However, because this section addresses the advanced installation of WebSphere Application Server, it is useful to read anyway. Also, the trial version of WAS v3.5 Advanced Edition allows you to experiment with this advanced installation because it is not limited to using a database repository such as Oracle or UDB.

Before installing WAS, three prerequisites must be checked and satisfied:

▶ Database connectivity between the UDB client and the UDB server must be successful.

▶ An HTTP web server must be available to be plugged in with a loadable module to the WAS installation. Although this situation is the normal installation in a WebSphere Domain installation, WAS has an internal HTTP transport (that is configured by default to use port 9080) to provide the basic serving functionality of a URL in the absence of an HTTP web server.

▶ A Java machine must be available, such as IBM Developers Kit, Java 2 Technology Edition. (See Chapter 3.)

Successful Database Connectivity

Running WebSphere Application Server Advanced Edition on multiple servers requires database connectivity to store configuration data for its WebSphere Domain configuration. Usually, such connectivity is established through a URI locator such as jdbc:was:wasdb_ name for UDB, and jdbc:oracle:thin:@dbhostname:port:sid for Oracle. However, this is not required for the WAS AEs v4.

In a WAS production deployment scenario, it is good to separate the database repository and install it on a separate server for the following reasons: to separate the administration of the WAS repository from the rest of the product; to replicate and back up the WAS repository; to allow a comprehensive tuning due to such segregation; and to put a failover mechanism in place. In Chapter 2, you learned how to install the UDB client, which is required to be installed on the same server where WAS is being installed; needless to say that is because WAS requires a UDB driver support of type 2. Now, all you need to do is verify that the connectivity is successful from the host machine on which you will install WAS. In Chapter 3, the program connect.java used the DriverManager to show you how to verify the success of a connection.

Availability of an HTTP Web Server to be Plugged Into the WAS Installation

The plug-in allows the communication between the web server and the application server to handle requests for web applications. Adding the plug-in to your HTTP server is usually handled automatically by the WAS install (except when using the Domino Server). However, when using the IBM HTTP Server, it is worth noting the little changes done to ihs_home/conf/httpd.conf, which is plugged in with the loadable module mod_app_server_http.c. The plug-in configuration for WAS v3.5 is different than for WAS v4.

For WAS v3.5, add the following lines to your httpd.conf:

```
# WAS V3.5
AddModule mod_app_server.c
NcfAppServerConfig BootFile /opt/IBMWebAS/properties/bootstrap.properties
```

The configuration that holds the properties for the transport between the HTTP server and the application server is mainly bootstrap.properties. The transport is set by default to the IBM proprietary protocol Open Servlet Engine (OSE) (mentioned briefly in the Chapter 5). Because IBM has replaced the OSE protocol with the HTTP protocol in its new releases of WAS v4, delving into the details of this property file is useless and not recommended.

For WAS v4, the installation program should append the following lines to the httpd.conf file:

```
Alias /WSsamples   /opt/WebSphere/AppServer/WSamples
Alias /IBMWebAS/   /opt/WebSphere/AppServer/web/
AddModule mod_app_server_http.c
LoadModule ibm_app_server_http_module
/opt/WebSphere/AppServer/bin/mod_ibm_app_server_http.so
WebSpherePluginConfig   /opt/WebSphere/AppServer/config/plugin-cfg.xml
```

On the other hand, if you are using the Apache HTTP Server, both the httpd.conf and srm.conf files should be modified. In the httpd.conf of the Apache HTTP Server, append the following lines:

```
AddModule mod_app_server_http.c
LoadModule ibm_app_server_http_module
/opt/WebSphere/AppServer/bin/mod_ibm_app_server_http.so
```

And, in the srm.conf file of the Apache server, add these lines:

```
Alias /WSsamples   /opt/WebSphere/AppServer/WSamples
Alias /IBMWebAS/   /opt/WebSphere/AppServer/web/
WebSpherePluginConfig   /opt/WebSphere/AppServer/config/plugin-cfg.xml
```

In this plug-in configuration, notice the locations of the library mod_ibm_app_server_http and of the configuration file plugin-cfg.xml, which happen to be in the was_home/bin and was_home/config directories, respectively. Although the installation root directory of WAS is reflected in the plug-in of the HTTP server, this does not imply that the HTTP server should reside on the same machine as WAS. In fact, you can place the plug-in–dependent files anywhere on the file system and have an HTTP server running on a separate machine than the one on which you installed WAS.

The Alias directive has also been used to point to the sample and web directories of WAS. These aliases are optional and have nothing to do with the HTTP server plug-in.

Java Machine Availability

Usually, a Java machine is shipped with every distribution of WAS; however, if you will be using a different Java machine to power the WAS engine, you need to check with IBM for its compatibility with the WAS product.

On the Linux platform, the Java machine shipped with WAS is installed in /opt/ IBMJava2-*nnn*, where *nnn* refers to the version of the Java machine, or JDK[3]: 122 for WAS v3.5, and 130 for WAS v4. On AIX, the default install for the JDKs of version 1.2.2 and version 1.3.0 go into /usr/java_dev2 as the home directory of the Java machine. Most AIX 4.3.3 servers that are shipped come with a default install of Java machine version 1.1.8 that is installed in /usr/jdk_base as the Java home directory. Also, on such AIX-ready systems, be aware of any

---

[3]   The Developer Kit 1.1.6 on AIX is no longer supported as of May 1, 2000; its last update was the IBM fix PTF 12.

java-executable program that takes precedence over your installed java command. You can detect this situation by looking into your search PATH and issuing either the command whence or the command which, as in which directory the java command is executed from (i.e., which java).

Installing WAS with a UDB Configuration Repository

If you are installing the WebSphere Advanced Edition Single Server v4, you might want to skip this part. However, this section shows you how to catalog a UDB node so that you connect to a UDB server from a client workstation.

In this installation, the UDB repository that is hosted on a separate UDB server is used. WAS is installed on a separate machine on which you have already installed the proper UDB client component to access and manage a UDB instance database remotely over TCP/IP, as explained in Chapter 2. Table 4-3 summarizes the steps for this installation.

While Table 4-3 shows you clearly the stepwise installation and the order in which it should be done on each machine. Let's go over each step once again and show the corresponding commands that you need to issue accordingly.

1. Make sure that you are logged in to the correct server where the UDB server engine is running. Log in as db2inst1, and set up your UDB environment by executing this command:

```
# . /home/db2inst1/sqllib/db2profile
```

Step	Machine A	Machine B
1	---	Install the UDB server engine.
2	---	Create the database repository WAS01.
3	---	Increase the heap size of WAS01.
4	Install the UDB client components.	---
5	Edit /etc/services and add the TCP/IP port on which the UDB server is listening.	----
6	Catalog the TCP/IP node to the remote UDB server.	----
7	Catalog the database WAS01 and alias it as WAS01.	----
8	Connect to WAS01 to test whether the communication is successful.	----
9	Install WAS and select jdbc:db2:WAS01.	----
10	Start WAS as a first startup. Wait two minutes. Stop WAS. Start WAS again.	----
11	----	db2 connect to WAS01 and list the tables. WAS tables should be created.

Table 4-3 *Steps for WAS Advanced Edition Installation*

2. Create the database repository WAS01. Use the `db2` command to create this database:

   ```
   # db2 create database WAS01
   ```

3. Blast up the Heap Size of WAS01 with the following command:

   ```
   # db2 "update DB CFG for WAS01 using APPLHEAPSZ 256"
   ```

4. Install the UDB client components, as discussed in Chapter 3.

5. Edit /etc/services and add the TCP/IP port on which Machine DB2 Server is listening:

   ```
   db2cdb2inst1       50000/tcp
   db2jdbcconn        50068/tcp
   ```

   The first line shows the standard port used for a UDB instance connection. The second line shows an optional port that will be set to test with the wasconnect.java program mentioned later in this chapter.

6. Catalog the node:

   ```
   db2 catalog tcpip node REPNODE remote WASDB.TCND.COM server db2cdb2inst1
   ```

7. Catalog the database WAS01 and alias it as WASREP:

   ```
   db2 catalog database WAS01 at node REPNODE
   db2 catalog db WAS01 as WASREP at node REPNODE
   ```

8. Connect to WAS01 to test whether the communication is successful:

   ```
   db2 connect to WAS01 user db2inst1 using pwd123
   ```

9. Install WAS and select jdbc:db2:WASREP as the configuration repository when prompted.

10. Start WAS as a first-time startup. Wait a few minutes. Stop WAS and then start it again. Executing this step ensures that the WAS database tables are created.

    ```
    # startupServer.sh
    ```

11. Check whether the WAS database tables have been created. `db2 connect` to WAS01 and list the tables:

    ```
    # db2 connect to WAS01 user db2inst1 using pwd123
    # db2 list tables
    ```

Suppressing the prereq_checker

If you are installing WAS against a newer version of the UDB database, the GUI installation may fail. Tailor the configuration prerequisite file to bypass any version dependency before installing the product. To locate the configuration prerequisite file, use the `find` command to locate the file prereq.properties in the product directory:

```
# find <your-product-binaries-directory> -name prereq.properties -print
```

This command locates the prereq.properties file in the product distribution directory /products/wasbinaries. Next, you need to edit the file and turn off the prereq_checker in the [WAS] section by setting its value to 0, as follows:

```
[WAS]
prereq_checker=0
```

The WAS install.sh takes the -prereqfile option to explicitly read a prerequisite file:

```
# ./install.sh  -prereqfile  /tmp/myprereq.properties
```

Also, this option allows you to explicitly specify the prereq.properties file if an updated version is available from the Internet.

It is possible to install WAS in a noninteractive mode known as a *silent installation*. On AIX, customize a response file by copying and editing the response_aix.res file from the image directory of the product. On Windows NT, ensure that the software prerequisites are met, and provide valid authentication (through szUser and szPassword) before running the setup against `setup.iss -s`.

Installing WAS v4 Advanced Edition Single Server

Installing WebSphere AEs v4 is straightforward. It does not require any database to render it functional. The only requirement for an easy install is a machine with a graphical user interface. Start the installation by invoking the installation script from the directory containing the distribution image, such as install.sh or setup.exe. Select the components to be installed, as shown here.

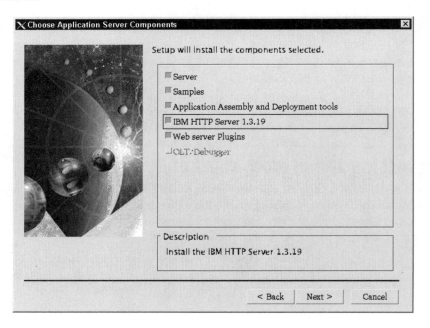

Take the default PATH to install the product because this is what is assumed in this book.

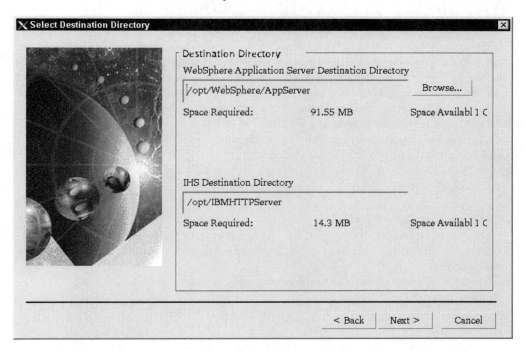

In most cases, the installation will apply all required components and present you with the Where Do I Start? opening screen.

WAS Startup and First-Time Configuration

Now it is time to start the application server so that you can look into its structured organization via the administrative console. This sequence of operations—starting the administrative server first, and then launching the administrative console—should not imply that there is a dependency on the administrative server (kind of a prerequisite) to have the console operational. However, whether you are using WAS v3.5 or v4, the administrative console needs to connect to an administrative server process so that it can gain access to the administrative data. The administrative server is started by the WAS startup script.

Start the application server by changing the directory to the WAS binary directory (was_home/bin) and by executing the startup script.

For WAS AE (v3.5 or v4), the script is startupServer.sh, which you need to run as a background process:

```
# startupServer.sh &
```

The command ends with an ampersand (&) to put the process in the background. On Windows NT, the script is the batch file startupServer.bat, which is usually associated with a shortcut.

For WAS AEs v4, the script is startServer.sh and can simply be executed at the command prompt:

```
# startServer.sh
```

While the script startServer.sh is starting the WAS AE's application server, some descriptive messages are printed to the console:

```
1.  [root@node1 bin]# ./startServer.sh
2.  WebSphere Application Server, Advanced Single Server Edition V4.0
3.  Application Server Launcher
4.  Copyright (C) IBM Corporation, 2001
5.  The configuration file was defaulted to:
6.  /opt/WebSphere/AppServer/config/server-cfg.xml
7.  Using the single available node or the localhost node.
8.  Using the single available server.
9.  Initiating server launch.
10. Loaded domain "WebSphere Administrative Domain".
11. Selected node "node1".
12. Selected server "Default Server".
13. WSPL0065I: Initiated server launch with process id 23048.
14. Time mark: Wednesday, February 6, 2002 4:02:53 AM EST
15. Waiting for the server to be initialized.
16. Time mark: Wednesday, February 6, 2002 4:02:57 AM EST
17. Initialized server.
18. Waiting for applications to be started.
```

```
19. Time mark: Wednesday, February 6, 2002 4:03:17 AM EST
20. Started applications.
21. WSPL0057I: The server Default Server is open for e-business.
22. Please review the server log files for additional information.
23. Standard output: /opt/WebSphere/AppServer/logs/default_server_stdout.log
24. Standard error: /opt/WebSphere/AppServer/logs/default_server_stderr.log
```

Usually, the application server is successfully started if you get the message shown on line 21. Furthermore, line 9 says that this application server consists of one node machine, which is the localhost. However, because this machine's hostname is node1.tcnd.com as registered in the /etc/hosts or in the DNS registry, line 11 shows that the WebSphere node name has been set by default to node1.

The administrative console of WAS AE is started with the shell script was_home/bin/adminclient.sh, which has no equivalence in WAS AEs. The later administrative console is started by typing the address http://was.host.name:9090/admin in an Internet browser such as Netscape. In the left pane of the administrative console. For WAS v4, the root of the topological tree reflects the name of the loaded domain on line 10.

At least one application server is installed and preconfigured by WAS for the first-time installation. The server is named "default server," and it is also started when invoking the startServer.sh script on line 12. While starting this default server, WAS prints messages to the log file "as_home/logs/default_server_stdout.log" (line 23) to show the progress of starting its containers. The default server has also been configured to use some default hosts (default_hosts), which are explained next.

Configuring the Common Resources

Now that WAS is running and the administrative console is ready, you need to configure a few of the common resources of your WebSphere Domain: namely, the JDBC driver and the Virtual Hosts. Resources that are machine (or node[4]) specific are called *common resources*. They are common because they are global to the WebSphere Domain. In addition, they are static data, and not live objects that can be programmatically refreshed, but currently you need toWAS for them to take effect. (Like when you change the IP address of your workstation, you need to reboot your workstation.)

Keep in mind that these resources have nothing to do with the functionality of WAS, and they are not integral to the viability of WAS itself. You can wipe them all out and still have

---

[4]   In this book, the hostnames of the machines were configured as node1, node2, node3, and so on, to use these machines as WebSphere nodes. Therefore, a physical machine is also called a node, and node1.tcnd .com is the machine whose hostname is node1. When installing WAS on node1.tcnd.com, the WebSphere node is called node1, and it happens to be coincidentally reflected by the hostname node1.tcnd.com.

WAS running, like a running server without a network interface. Resources are used further by WAS when configuring the web applications under a WebSphere node.

There are two ways to modify resources. The simpler and more coherent way is through the administrative console, but you can edit the configuration files directly (for those resources whose data is not saved in the administrative repository, as is the case with WAS AEs).

In WAS v3.5, to create a Virtual Host or a JDBC Driver/DataSource, right-click the WebSphere Domain name in the administrative console and select Create. "Model" is no longer supported by IBM, and you should not pay attention to it.

Setting the JDBC Driver

When connecting to a database, [5] WAS follows the standard practice of J2EE applications in using the DataSource Java class. The database connection properties of a DataSource are facilitated through the use of a DataSource object. Because the DataSource is an extension based on the JDBC2.0 standard, you need to set up the JDBC driver and make it known to your WAS administrative configuration. Like in a virtual hosting setup, which is discussed in the following section, the JDBC drivers are first set within the resources of your WebSphere Domain before they can be used and logically mapped [6] per application server on each node.

To set up a JDBC driver to be used within a WebSphere Domain, follow these steps:

1. Identify the JDBC driver that you want to use. This book uses the UDB JDBC driver db2java.zip.

2. Identify a common directory location to put in the JDBC driver. Keep it in a common directory such as the COMMON_CLASSES directory so that you isolate developers from using different releases of the same driver that may be problematic during deployment.

3. **For WAS AEs v4:** Start the Administrative Console, and, in the left pane, select WebSphere Domain | Resources | JDBC Drivers | Db2JdbcDriver to get the property of the driver in the right pane. Modify the properties by typing in the correct path of your driver, e.g., /common/classes/db2java.zip. Confirm the change by clicking OK. The Db2JdbcDriver is added as a resource during the product default installation; however, you need to edit its property and make the change mentioned here.

4. If you want to use a different driver than the UDB JDBC driver, you must add the driver name yourself under WebSphere Domain Resources–JDBC Drivers.

---

[5]   This is not for the WAS configuration repository, but to store, retrieve, and change what would otherwise be client data, such as employee records.

[6]   Such a logical mapping is discussed in Chapter 17.

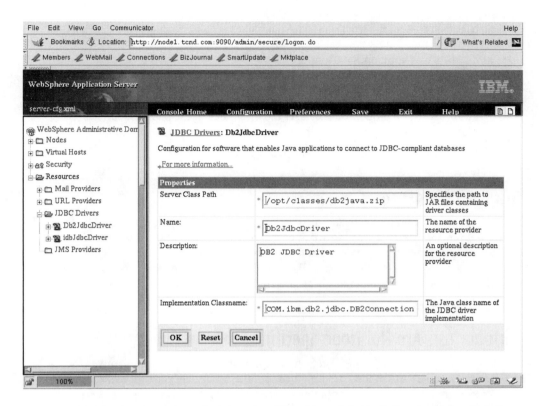

5. **For WAS v3.5:** Start the Administrative Console, and, in the left pane, right-click the WebSphere Domain name, and then select create-JDBC Driver. Alternatively, you can just modify the already configured JDBC Driver, Admin DB Driver, that the WAS installation sets by default. Unlike WAS v4, the JDBC driver pathname is not entered explicitly, but you can select it from the Class Name drop-down menu:

6. Save your configuration and then exit the administrative console. Restart WAS.

The benefits of using the DataSource to manipulate a database include the following:

► **Portability of your application**

► **Ease of programming**   The programmer can follow simple guidelines to get a connection with the getConnection() method.

► **Tunability**   The programmer can set the properties of the database through the DataSource object (for example, by using WSCP to administer and to manipulate such an object, as you will see in Chapter 7).

Virtual Hosting

By setting virtual hosting, you make sure that URL requests that are first received by the HTTP server plug-in are then forwarded to WAS, or that they are directly placed into the WAS built-in HTTP transport and can be resolved and dereferenced properly by the application server. Also note that setting virtual hosting in WAS v3.5 is different than in WAS v4. In WAS v4, an administrative host grouping has been preconfigured under its Virtual Hosts, known as admin_host.

Virtual Hosts Are Not Node Specific

If you look at the left pane of the WebSphere Application Server Administrative Console, you realize that the virtual hosts are not node specific; rather, they are globally set under the WebSphere Domain, and therefore made global to any WAS node running on the same physical machine. Consequently, you cannot stop and restart the virtual hosting as a resource. If you make a change in the virtual hosts, you must stop and restart WAS because the changes are saved in the WAS server configuration data, and restarting WAS is the only way to have them in effect after modification. The following illustration shows you the Virtual Host in the left pane of the Administrative Console for WAS AE v3.5 (far left), WAS AEs v4 (middle), and WAS AE v4 (right).

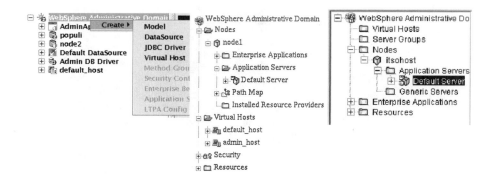

Having virtual hosting independent of the node on which a web application is defined requires a binding rule. You need to bind the web application to a virtual host to enable it to execute on the specified virtual host. This binding process is done through the application property *Virtual hostname* of the web application, and it is discussed more thoroughly later in this chapter when discussing the assembly properties of a web module.

Reasons for Setting the Virtual Hosts

After a successful WAS installation, you need to configure virtual hosting in the following situations:

► If you want to protect the administrative data of your WAS AEs v4 and you want to administer WAS solely from the local (localhost) machine.

► If you have installed WAS v3.5 on a machine that is attached to the network. By setting the virtual host, you will make the web resources known to their associated hostname (the machine name, in this case). The WAS v3.5 default installation includes the localhost (but not the machine name) in mapping the default_host name.

► If you want to have multiple nodes to participate in a server group.[7]

There are other reasons to have virtual hosting properly set up; for example, as you will see in Part III, it is important to the functionality of a cookie-based web application.

Setting the admin_host to "localhost" to Protect WAS AEs v4

When installing WAS on a machine that is available on the Internet, WAS v4 initially creates an admin_host with the wildcard general alias (*), which can cause a security risk.

If you want to protect the WAS administrative configuration data, you can prevent anyone from starting an administrative console except on the same machine on which the application server is running (see Figure 4-3). Configure the admin_host of your application server. Select WebSphere Administrative Domain- Virtual Hosts-|Admin_host-|Aliases, and delete any entry in the hostname column. Add the following entry: 127.0.0.1. Keep the default port 9090 unless you want to change it.

Save the change, exit the administrative console, and then restart WAS. With this change, you cannot invoke the administrative console from any browser except the one that is installed on the same machine that is running the administrative server.

Do not enter "localhost" instead of 127.0.0.1 because anyone can alias the IP of your machine with a localhost and start an administrative console on his or her machine. For example, a user on a workstation attached to the same network as the WAS machine can edit the host file (i.e., /etc/hosts) and make the following changes:

```
127.0.0.1          localwhatever
110.120.130.140    wastarget    localhost
```

---

[7]   For the definition of server group, refer to Chapter 5.

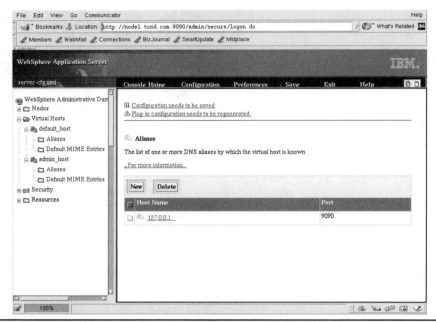

Figure 4-3 *The left pane of the administrative console for WAS AEs v4*

Such a user has altered the first line, changing the commonly known alias localhost that points to his or her local workstation, and then used the localhost to alias the target machine that is running the application server. Obviously, this user will be able to start a remote administrative session by typing http://localhost:9090/admin in his or her browser.

Setting Virtual Hosting in WAS v3.5

You can create a new virtual host by right-clicking the WebSphere Domain name in the appropriate pane (see the illustration): from left to right, for WAS AE v3.5, WAS AEs v4, WAS AE v4, and WAS v5.

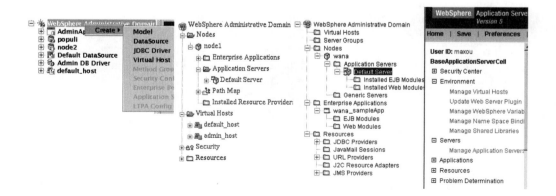

The aim here is not to create a new virtual host, but to modify the default_host that has been preconfigured by the WAS v3.5 default installation so that you render it functional and you use the URL to place requests to the servlets that are hosted by the WAS.

In the left pane of the administrative console, locate the default_host and click it. The default_host is the virtual host name that has been configured during your WAS first-time install. The right pane shows you the property of the default_host; you then click the Advanced property to get to the Host Aliases dialog box as shown in Figure 4-4.

Enter the hostnames of your machine, and then click Apply. For example, for the machine named populi at domain tcnd.com, the following host aliases should be added to the list: populi, populi.tcnd.com, and the machine numerical IP address *nnn.nnn.nnn*. Each of these is entered at a separate line in the Host Aliases dialog box. If no port number is specified, then port 80 is assumed as the default; otherwise, to specify a port, follow the alias with a colon and then the port number (e.g., populi.tcnd.com:8082).

Now that you are setting the virtual host, it is worth mentioning the Web Resources that are grouped under the virtual host, specifically under WAS v3.5.

Web Resources with WAS v3.5   The Web Resources in WAS v3.5 are typically grouped under a virtual hostname, such as default_host. In Figure 4-4, the left pane of the administrative console shows a list of what is called Web Resources that are associated with default_host.

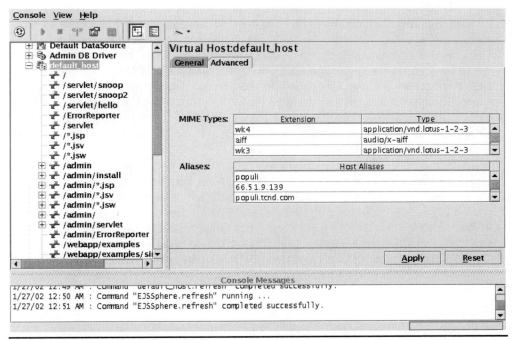

Figure 4-4   *Protecting WAS configuration data*

While the term *Web Resources* is widely used with WAS v3.5, it totally vanished in WAS v4. To view the Web Resources in WAS v3.5, select the View | Type from the administrative console, expand the Virtual Hosts in the left pane, and click on Web Resources, as seen here:

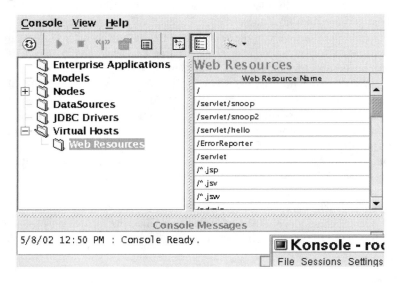

WAS v3.5 uses the term Web Resources in its administrative console to depict a URIs grouping. These Web Resources, or URIs, are components that can be accessed only from web clients. Such components are physical resources like servlets, JSP files, and HTML files, which are to be mapped into a logical representation of what would make the URI part of the address to access the resource. For example, consider this URL: http://was.host.name/servlet/snoop. To satisfy such a request, the WAS virtual host should have an entry to reflect the URI part of this URL address, specifically, the /servlet/snoop part. Therefore, Web Resources are strings that are matched first, and then concatenated to the URI of a URIs group such as default_host to form the final URI.

Deprecating Web Resources in WAS v4   On the other hand, because WAS v4 is J2EE compliant, and an application server context root can be specified through a descriptor, this URIs grouping, which is known as Web Resources in WAS v3.5, is no longer known by this name in WAS v4. However, securing Web resources through a URIs grouping in WAS v4 is reflected in two different locations. The first is web application specific and is managed by the Application Assembly Tool (AAT), and the second is application server specific and is managed through the URIs grouping in the plug-in configuration (e.g., the plugin-cfg.xml) of the HTTP server. At least in WAS AEs, you can manually edit the plugin-cfg.xml, but you must restart the HTTP server for the changes to take effect. Furthermore, the plugin-cfg.xml can be regenerated through the administrative console.

Setting the Virtual Hosts default_host Aliases in WAS v4

WAS v4 is also preconfigured with a Virtual Host named default_host. You can change the aliases of the default_host by selecting in the left pane of the administrative console WebSphere Domain | Virtual Hosts | default_host | Aliases (see Figure 4-5). You change an alias name by clicking it. You can also delete and add an alias name and its associated port number. For example, wwwsrv.tcnd.com to be set as an alias associated with port 80 (assuming that wwwsrv.tcnd.com is the hostname of the machine that has the HTTP server

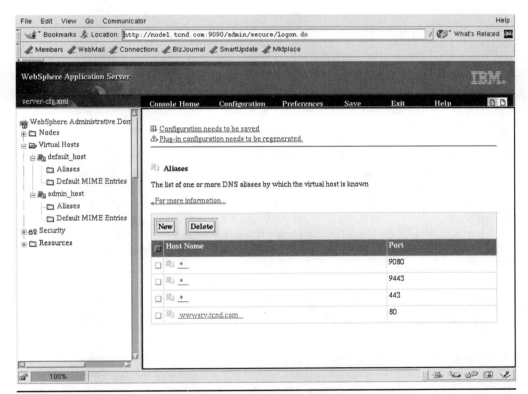

Figure 4-5   *Setting aliases for the virtual host default_host in WAS AEs v4*

running, and is plugged into the WAS module to forward the request to the application server). This does not mean that WAS is using port 80 in any way; it is just being set to tell you that an incoming request *to* the application server *from* host wwwsrc.tcnd.com—and which has been set initially by a client browser to wwwsrc.tcnd.com:80—is an acceptable request and can be satisfied by the application server.

Virtual Hosts Name Resolvability

The mapping of the names in virtual hosting is not case-sensitive; therefore, the user requests http://plugged.http.server/webapp/examples/showCfg and http://plugged.http.server/webapp/examples/showCfg are equivalent. But keep in mind that the client host machine and the server machine on which WAS is running should be able to resolve the hostname and its aliases. The resolvability of a hostname is independently handled from WAS.

The following list summarize how you can check whether a hostname and its aliases can be resolved on a workstation or server attached to the network:

▶ From the client machine, issue the `ping` command, e.g., `ping was.host.name`. It does not really matter if you get your data sent, but at least a hostname should be resolved into its IP address.

▶ From the client machine, use `nslookup` or `dig` on a Linux machine.

These methods ensure that the client machine on which a user is issuing an HTTP request can reach the server machine on which the HTTP server is running. The name can be resolved if it is registered in a Domain Name Server (DNS) or it is mapped in the host's file that is located in the /etc directory on UNIX, or in $WINDIR/system32/drivers/etc/hosts on Windows NT.

After setting up your virtual hosts, restart WAS, and then test with the snoop servlet, explained in the next section, to ensure that WAS and its web container (discussed in Chapter 5) are functioning properly.

Serving the Test Servlet: snoop

WAS automatically installs the snoop servlet to let you check whether the WAS HTTP transport is properly configured. In your browser, enter this URL: http://plugged.http.server/servlet/snoop.

This should echo back information about the HTTP request sent by the client and the initialization parameters of the servlet. The request returned from the snoop test servlet is shown next.

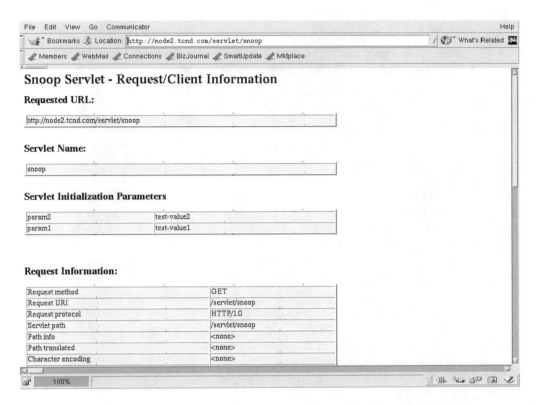

If the snoop servlet fails, then try to access it through the WAS internal HTTP transport listening on the default port 9080: http://was.host.name:9080/servlet/snoop.

If this passed the test, then the problem resides in the HTTP server or in its plug-in. However, if the pervious URL is still failing, then log in to the server on which WAS is running and invoke `netstat` with `netstat -na | grep 9080` to find out if there is a TCP-based application listening to that port. A typical output should show you a line with the following entry, provided you installed WAS with its default configuration: 0.0.0.0:9080.

Use this general guideline to troubleshoot the failure of the http://plugged.http.server/servlet/snoop URL:

1. Ensure that the plugged HTTP server is running and accepting requests. Use `ps -ef | grep httpd` to list the httpd daemons. Check the log files of the HTTP server: access_log and error_log. Then reload the servlet and see whether anything is written in the log files. If nothing is written, then it is a problem with your HTTP server.

NOTE

Make sure that logging is enabled for your HTTP server. Check the httpd.conf configuration file in the ihs_home/conf/ directory. On Linux, it should contain these two entries:

```
CustomLog  /opt/IBMHTTPServer/logs/access_log common
ErrorLog  /opt/IBMHTTPServer/logs/error_log
```

2. Reload the servlet, and on the server on which the HTTP server is running, issue `netstat -e` and try to determine if the `http socket` establishes a connection with your client machine (where the web browser is running). If no connection is established, then the problem is probably with the sockets.

3. Edit the HTTP server configuration file httpd.conf and check whether the plug-in has been added to it.

4. See whether the WAS Java machines are running. Locate the Nanny process and the associated application server that is started for the node you are trying to access (i.e., `ps -ef | grep -i websphere`).

5. If you are using a WAS database repository, make sure you can connect to it from the server on which WAS is running. To do this, use wasconnect.java, mentioned later in this chapter in the section "An Undocumented Shortcut to Test WAS Installation."

6. On WAS v3.5, try to ping the snoop servlet from within the administrative console. You do this by right-clicking the servlet and selecting Ping.

File Locations

File extensions have meaning, and so do their location(s) on the file system. The directory structure is important for two reasons. First, the directory structure is inherently important in Java applications (and in WAS) because of the nature of the application objects that are hierarchically structured within their archives. Second, WAS initial server configuration is saved on such a file system.

Table 4-4 shows the different file types and their associated location(s).

Description	Directory Location	Other Location Affected
HTML documents (.html)	ihs_root.	.html files can also be extracted by SEAppInstall.sh when they are part of an installed web application.
JavaServer Page (.jsp)	HTTP server document root.	JSP processor generates .java and .class files from JSP and places those files in the was_home/temp directory.was_home/temp/node1/Default_Server/Server_Administration_Application/admin.war/secure/ directory.

Table 4-4 *Important File Types and File Types in WAS v4*

Description	Directory Location	Other Location Affected
Servlet (.class, .jar)	was_servlet directory or reloadable servlet directory.	Classes of a package must be placed into a directory whose name is created where the servlets can be located.
.ear	An application.ear is set by default in the installableApps.	.ear files are usually extracted by default in was_home/installedApps by the EAR installer SEAppInstall.sh script.
.war	A webmodule .war is a web archive that is usually a subfolder of application.ear.	
.log	Usually was_home/logs unless it has been specified otherwise.	It can be reconfigured to any other directory using the administrative console, as discussed in Chapter 8.
server-cfg.xml	was_home/config (WAS AEs only).	It can placed anywhere on the file system, but you need to specify its location using the -configFile option of the startServer.sh script.
plugin-cfg.xml	was_home/config.	It can be placed anywhere on the file system of the server running the plugged in HTTP server.
application.xml	In the META-INF of an application.ear folder.	This is relative to the enterprise application as a whole, as defined in J2EE.
web.xml	In the WEB-INF of a webmodule.war folder.	This cannot be changed and is relative to the web module as defined by J2EE.

Table 4-4   *Important File Types and File Types in WAS v4* (continued)

Setting the WAS Development Environment

In Chapter 3, you learned how to set up the user environment for a community of developers using a mixture of platforms. Now that you have WAS installed on your file system, this section explores how to set up the development environment with the WAS system tools.

Setting the Commands

The setj.sh script in Chapter 3 set up the Java environment, or the Java and the WAS environments. When setj.sh script is invoked with either option w122 or w130, the setw(V) (os).sh script is executed within it. The *V* stands for the WAS version number, e.g., 354 or 4, and the *os* stands for the platform name, e.g., aix, nt, or lin. For example, setw4lin.sh shown in Listing 4-1 is executed when setj.sh w130 is invoked. The script sets the environment variables to substitute for having to type in the lengthy WAS commands and to isolate the PATH dependency. Such substitution makes it easy to manage and deploy the code using shell scripts and macros in the Make file; to set up properties of shortcut icons on desktops for a mix of platforms; and to communicate commands and file names independently of the WAS version in the rest of the book. For example, $STARTWAS to start the WAS, $WASCFG to refer to the server-cfg.xml file of WAS AEs, and $WASLOG_STDOUT to refer to the standard output where WAS logs its messages.

Listing 4-1   *setw4lin.sh set up the environment variable for WAS v4 on Linux platform*

```
1.   #!/usr/bin/sh
2.
3.   WASDOMAIN="Total Computing Domain"
4.   WAS_HOME=/opt/WebSphere/AppServer
5.   WAS_CLASSPATH=$WAS_HOME/properties:$WAS_HOME/lib/bootstrap.jar
6.
7.   # WAS commands
8.   STARTWAS=/opt/WebSphere/AppServer/bin/startServer.sh
9.   STOPWAS=/opt/WebSphere/AppServer/bin/stopServer.sh
10.  WSCP=/opt/WebSphere/AppServer/bin/wscp.sh
11.  ASSEMBLY=/opt/WebSphere/AppServer/bin/assembly.sh
12.  EAREXPANDER=/opt/WebSphere/AppServer/bin/EARExpander.sh
13.  SEAPPINSTALL=/opt/WebSphere/AppServer/bin/SEAppInstall.sh
14.  SOAPENABLER=/opt/WebSphere/AppServer/bin/SoapEarEnabler.sh
15.  CLIENTCONFIG=/opt/WebSphere/AppServer/bin/clientConfig.sh
16.  DRADMIN=/opt/WebSphere/AppServer/bin/DrAdmin.sh
17.  DUMPNAMESPACE=/opt/WebSphere/AppServer/bin/dumpNameSpace.sh
18.  JSPCOMPILER=/opt/WebSphere/AppServer/bin/JspBatchCompiler.sh
19.  LAUNCHCLIENT=/opt/WebSphere/AppServer/bin/launchClient.sh
20.  LOGANALYZER=/opt/WebSphere/AppServer/bin/waslogbr
21.
22.  # WAS AEs
23.  WASCFG=/opt/WebSphere/AppServer/config/server-cfg.xml
24.  WASLOG_STDOUT=/opt/WebSphere/AppServer/logs/default_server_stdout.log
25.  WASLOG_STDERR=/opt/WebSphere/AppServer/logs/default_server_stderr.log
26.  WASLOG_ACTIVITY=/opt/WebSphere/AppServer/logs/activity.log
27.
28.  # A list of all the Commands set above
29.  WASCOMMANDS="STARTWAS(startServer.sh) STOPWAS(stopServer.sh)
        WSCP(wscp.sh) ASSEMBLY(assembly.sh) EAREXPANDER(EARExpander.sh)
        SEAPPINSTALL(SEAppInstall.sh) SOAPENABLER(SoapEarEnabler.sh)
        CLIENTCONFIG(clientConfig.sh) DRADMIN(DrAdmin.sh)
        DUMPNAMESPACE(dumpNameSpace.sh) JSPCOMPILER(JspBatchCompiler.sh)
        LAUNCHCLIENT(launchClient.sh) LOGANALYZER(waslogbr)"
30.
31.  # WAS Installed/Installable directory
32.  INSTALLEDAPPS=/opt/WebSphere/AppServer/installedApps
33.  INSTALLABLEAPPS=/opt/WebSphere/AppServer/installableApps
```

```
34.
35.    # Port assignments
36.    ADMINPORT=9090
37.    DRADMINPORT=7000
38.
39.    PATH=/opt/WebSphere/AppServer/bin:$PATH
40.    LD_LIBRARY_PATH=$WAS_HOME/lib/odbc/lib:$LD_LIBRARY_PATH
41.    LD_LIBRARY_PATH=$WAS_HOME/bin:$WAS_HOME/lib:$LD_LIBRARY_PATH
42.
43.    export PATH LD_LIBRARY_PATH
44.    export WASDOMAIN WAS_HOME INSTALLEDAPPS INSTALLABLEAPPS ADMINPORT
          DRADMINPORT WASCOMMANDS
45.    export STARTWAS STOPWAS WSCP ASSEMBLY EAREXPANDER SEAPPINSTALL
          SOAPENABLER CLIENTCONFIG DRADMIN DUMPNAMESPACE JSPCOMPILER LAUNCHCLIENT
46.
```

Such a script resides in the same directory as setj.sh, for example, the shared directory /tools/env that is NFS mounted on every system.

In a mixed-platform environment, where you are running multiple versions of WAS, you need to have as many setw(v)(os).sh scripts as the number of WAS versions multiplied by the number of platforms. A good way to do this is to tabulate them, as shown in Table 4-5.

To test your setup at this time, assuming you have WAS v4 installed on Linux, enter the following:

```
# .  /tools/setj.sh  w130
```

This command executes setj.sh and setw4lin.sh. Next, type the following at the command prompt:

```
# $CLIENTCONFIG  &
```

This command starts the graphical user interface of the Application Client Resource Configuration Tool. To remember your WAS Commands list, type this command:

```
# echo  $WASCOMMANDS
```

This will list all the commands and their aliases. For later versions of WAS, you can modify these setup scripts to add in or remove aliases. You can also use the command chekenv to list your environment variables set by setj.sh (refer to Appendix D for this command).

	Linux	AIX	Windows NT
v3.5.5	setw355lin.sh	setw355aix.sh	setw355nt.sh
v4.0.1	setw4lin.sh	setw4aix.sh	setw4nt.sh

Table 4-5 *setw(v)(os).sh*

Remembering aliases as such might not be an efficient way to work with WAS binary tools; however, they can facilitate managing and setting up your desktop. These aliases can also make the current setup of WAS components visible to the developer, who can also use these aliases in shell scripts and Make files that can run successfully regardless of the platform setup.

Setting the Desktop

There are two reasons to alias the WAS commands just listed. The first reason is to simplify the process of making global changes from a common script when upgrading or configuring multiple WebSphere Application Servers on the same machine. Installing multiple WASs on the same server for multiple programmers working together is the subject of Chapter 21. The second reason is to have a common setup in a mixed environment on which an enterprise (multiplatform) version of WAS, or different versions of WAS, have been put in place. In either case, on a UNIX platform, it is possible to have icons (similar to a Windows shortcut) whose execute command properties are set to the programs to which the aliases are pointing.

For instance, consider creating an icon labeled AAT with an execute command property set to $ASSEMBLY.

You will have an icon available on your desktop that you click to start the Application Assembly Tool.

Whether this icon is defined on Linux, AIX, or any other UNIX platform, it will start the binary program to which the variable $ASSEMBLY is pointing (in this case, it is the Application Assembly Tool). Obviously, when a new version of WAS is available, or if you want to distribute the WAS components on different remote machines, you may need to make changes to the common script, while the user desktop environment is not affected.

An Undocumented Shortcut to Test WAS Installation

When you start WAS for the first time, it remote-connects to a repository and populates the database with first-run information. To pretest if this really took place, compile and run the wasconnect.java program from any remote host. The program in Listing 4-2 has been tested for the WAS v3.5.4 Advanced Edition. It queries the node name from the database table EJSADMIN.NODE_TABLE. Testing the connection with wasconnect .java ensures the following:

▶ The first run of WAS was successful because it connected to the database and created the table NODE_TABLE in which a first node was created. The node name has the same name as the hostname of the server on which you installed WAS. Remember that at least one node is created after a WebSphere Application Server installation.

▶ You can successfully connect to the data server from a remote host, and you have the correct authentication to do so.

▶ Your JDBC driver is at the same level as the data server, and it is the same driver to be used with WAS to connect to the data server. Therefore, this eliminates the possibility that the failure of WAS data source configuration has nothing to do with the JDBC driver. WAS uses the object DataSource to set up its data server (or data source) connectivity, as you will see in Chapter 7. Notice that this last point is valid only when you are using the same database server as a WAS configuration repository, and as a data source. This is true in most cases.

Listing 4-2   *wasconnect.java*

```java
import java.sql.*;
public class wasconnect {
    public static void main( String argv[] ) {
        if (argv.length < 1) {
            System.out.println("Usage:\njava wasconnect URL [UID PWD]");
            System.exit(0);
        }
        String url, userid, passwrd;
        url = argv[0];
        userid = argv.length > 1 ? argv[1] : "";
        passwrd = argv.length > 2 ? argv[2] : "";
        try {
            Class.forName("COM.ibm.db2.jdbc.net.DB2Driver");
        } catch (ClassNotFoundException e) {
            e.printStackTrace();
            System.exit(0);
        }
        try {
            Connection conn = DriverManager.getConnection(url, userid,
passwrd);
            System.out.println("Retrieving the NODE NAME from the WAS
Repository");
            Statement stmt = conn.createStatement();
            try {
                ResultSet rs = stmt.executeQuery("SELECT * FROM
EJSADMIN.NODE_TABLE");
                rs.next();
                String nodename = rs.getString(3);
                System.out.println("NODE NAME = "+nodename);
                rs.close();
            } catch (SQLException e) {
                e.printStackTrace();
                System.exit(0);
            }
            stmt.close();
        } catch (SQLException e) {
            e.printStackTrace();
            System.exit(0);
        }
    }
}
```

To test the connection to the newly created WAS01 database, first make sure that db2jstrt is running on port 50068 of the host machine where the WAS repository has been created; then, run wasconnect.java from any remote client:

```
# java wasconnect jdbc:db2://node1.tcnd.com:50068/WAS01 db2inst1 password
```

This command executes the wasconnect program with three arguments: the first is the JDBC URL of the database you are trying to connect to, the second and third are the login and password, respectively, of the UDB instance user. A successful connection returns the following:

```
Retrieving the NODE NAME from the WAS Repository:
NODE NAME = node1
```

If for any reason the connection fails, an exception is returned. For instance, if the WAS01 table has not been created, an exception is returned like this:

```
COM.ibm.db2.jdbc.DB2Exception:[IBM][CLI Driver] SQL 1013N
The database alias name or database name "WAS01" could not be found. SQLSTATE=42705
```

Make sure that the db2java.zip placed in your classpath is the same as the one that has been installed on the DB2 server. For example, assuming the default install of UDB, the db2java.zip resides in /home/db2inst1/sqllib/java[8] and should be copied to the host machine on which the wasconnect program is executed. Refer to Chapter 3 on setting your development environment.

Uninstalling the Product

Uninstalling the product on Linux is easy: with WAS v3.5, use the `rpm` command with the -e option; for WAS v4, use the UNIX command `rm -rf/opt/WebSphere/AppServer` to force the removal of the WAS directory recursively.

To uninstall on AIX, use the command `installp`.

Uninstall the product on Windows NT by clicking the Uninstall icon when available; otherwise, remove the product directory, and then start regedit and delete the registry hive that corresponds to your WebSphere Application Server version. For example, walk down the registry tree My Computer | HKEY_LOCAL_MACHINE | SOFTWARE | IBM | WebSphere Application Server | 4.0 and right-click the hive to select Delete.

---

[8]   The app-driver is contained in /home/db2instl/sqllib/java12. Selecting the appropriate driver will become clearer in Part III of this book.

Replicating an Installation on Several Machines

A base installation can be replicated on more than one machine, yet you must remember that this is done only when you customize the response file.

On AIX, if you are using the `smit` or `smitty` command to install the product, it is possible to duplicate the base installation of the product by using the smit.script. First, make sure that you delete the smit.script from your home directory before starting smitty. Second, install your product using smitty. After you exit smitty, you can copy the shell script smit.script from your home directory ($HOME/smit.script) and execute it on another AIX machine for a similar base installation. Specify the -s option with smitty to deposit the smit.script file in a specific directory.

Wrapping Up

This chapter described the system requirements to install WAS. We took a stepwise approach in installing WAS Advanced Edition (AE) and WAS Advanced Edition Single Server (AEs). The administration of WAS is done through its GUI administrative console. While WAS AE uses an X Windows–based application to administer WAS, WAS AEs uses an Internet browser.

You also learned about the common resources that need to be configured after the first-time installation of the product, in particular, the JDBC driver and virtual hosting.

The chapter walked you through the set up of the WAS development environment that was discussed in Chapter 3 (script.setj.sh). The development environment considered is for mixed platforms and mixed versions of WAS. We call the environment *The WASDG Environment* and we will use it in Part III.

Defining a WebSphere Domain

IN THIS CHAPTER:

Understanding the WebSphere Region

Understanding the WebSphere Domain

Comparing WAS v3.5 and v4

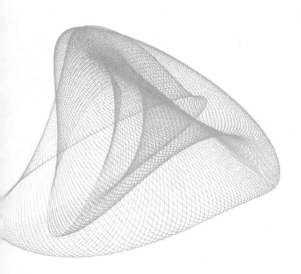

W ebSphere Application Server is comprised of a set of Java machine processes (known as Java virtual machines or JVM) that act together to manage web-specific data. In each WAS installation, at least one WebSphere domain is defined and identified by its name. The WebSphere domain name can be set selectively through the WAS administrative console.

The notion of a WebSphere domain is loosely described in the literature. However, this book defines it from the system point of view, in terms of processes, threads, and their dependencies. The basic reason for defining a WebSphere domain is to make a *scalable* WebSphere Application Server easily manageable in a distributed environment where one or many application servers' Java machines (or Java processes and threads) are started under the same bailiwick: the WebSphere domain.

To define a region that encompasses a WebSphere domain and its requisite applications (which are not part of its topology), you need to understand the WebSphere region. The WebSphere region is made up of the WebSphere domain and the many parts that are needed to render it functional.

This chapter defines the constituents of the WebSphere region, the WebSphere domain, and the WebSphere node. It also introduces you to the basics of administering such a domain. The major differences between WAS v3.5 and WAS v4 are also outlined.

Understanding the WebSphere Region

A typical WAS installation can span several networked servers in a region. The WebSphere region designates the grouping of several servers that are topologically intradependent in their *outermost* WAS layers. As seen in this illustration, a WebSphere region can consist of servers that are running the following:

► WAS processes

► A plugged-in HTTP server

► One or more database servers

► Miscellaneous monitoring applications to monitor WAS and server dependencies

WebSphere Region

WSCP-enabled
workstation

WASLED™/
WASMON™

WAS
config
repository

Administrative console

HTTP
server

Admin
server
(WAS node)

Application
database

The servers that are running WAS processes in a WebSphere region are grouped under a WebSphere domain. These servers are running WAS processes for one or more of the following reasons:

► To store in and retrieve information from the WAS configuration repository

► To manage and serve the requests redirected by the plugged in HTTP server

► To service and organize workload distribution for several mechanisms, such as Open Servlet Engine (OSE), Remote, Workload Management (WLM), and Servlet Redirector

► To supervise WAS containment and cache cleanup (for the Enterprise JavaBeans container and the servlets container)

A WebSphere domain makes the topology manageable in a tree-structured way, called the WebSphere configuration tree (see the illustration), such that each server running WAS can be part of that domain. Each server is referred to as a node.

From the topological point of view, all nodes are treated *equally* in a WebSphere domain. Also notice that the WebSphere domain topology includes neither the web server application nor the database application on which the configuration repository is saved.

All components that constitute a WebSphere region can also be set up on a single server. In such a strategy, the WebSphere region comprises the WebSphere domain configured as a single node, the server itself on which both an HTTP server and the database configuration repository are installed. This is the case in which you install WAS v4 Advanced Single Server Edition.

Understanding the WebSphere Domain

The WebSphere configuration repository, also known as the WebSphere administrative repository, defines a WebSphere domain. In other words, it is the persistent configuration database that defines the WebSphere domain. It is not any of the WAS Java machines that are running on any of the servers. However, a Java machine[1] acts like an interface to communicate and to manage this persistent repository. For example, an administrative client can start a Java machine process to grant you access to the WebSphere configuration repository, and thus to the defined WebSphere domain itself.

Background About the WebSphere Domain

The literature has not clearly defined a WebSphere domain. However, one approach is to look at it as a general model in which distributed processes are grouped under a topology. A WebSphere domain contains access rights that allow the Java machine processes within the domain to perform privileged operations on the objects in the distributed systems. The WebSphere domain by itself defines the access rights of Java machine processes that are localized in its topology.

---

[1]   Actually, this is the administrative server process.

IBM really started to define the WebSphere Domain with WAS v3. Little is known about this whole business of WebSphere domain topology. However, an analogy can be made between the WebSphere domain and IBM system management components, such as the Scalable POWERparallel (SP)^2 system's nodes management and the Tivoli Management Environment (TME).

On one hand, IBM has been using a general model based on objects and attributes that are stored in a repository to manage its large SP multinodes systems. For instance, to store operational information for the entire SP system, a system data repository (SDR) is used. Data information is categorized and stored in classes, which, in turn, contain instances of data called objects. The objects store numerous attributes. Similar to the WebSphere Control Program (WSCP)^3, the SDR objects can be managed with Tcl/Tk.

On the other hand, both WAS and TME applications use a database repository to store object data that can be administered as a whole through their attributes. Listing 5-1 shows a similarity between WAS and TME in modeling their systemic object data.

Tivoli TME uses a series of commands (starting with the prefix "od") to manipulate objects in its repository. TME uses the word Region instead of domain, and nodes can be added to a Region. The following TME command lists all nodes in every Region.

Listing 5-1   *Comparing the WAS nodes model to the TME nodes model*

```
root@vnode5 </usr/Tivoli>: odadmin odlist
Region  Disp  Flags  Port         IPaddr   Hostname(s)
300408  1     ct-    94        66.51.9.151 node1.tcnd.com
        2     ct-    94        66.51.9.155 node5.tcnd.com
300410  1     ct-    94       162.34.20.35 central.tcnd.com

WebSphere Control Program (WSCP): To list all nodes defined in a WebSphere
Domain, use the ApplicationServer object with the list attribute.
# wscp.sh -p dom01.properties
wscp> ApplicationServer list
   {/Node:populi/ApplicationServer:Default Server/}
   {/Node:node2/ApplicationServer:Default Server/}
```

WebSphere AEs defines the notion of WebSphere domain. This is true for the grouping of the nodes running on the same single server. In this particular case, the WebSphere domain is defined in the server-cfg.xml file, which acts as the configuration repository for WAS.

WebSphere AE uses a database to store the configuration data, which raises this question: Why not use an XML flat file to save the configuration data, as is the case with the single

---

[2]   This IBM-scalable UNIX system known as the SP system consists of many thin nodes that are networked together through a high-speed switch. A thin node is just a server machine stripped down to its minimal functional serving components, such as excluding any graphic interface, and the word "node" has nothing to do with a WAS node, although it is possible to define a WAS node on each SP thin node. Usually these thin nodes are 8 to 16 drawers stacked in a tower. Informally speaking, towers are grouped together to form a frame.

[3]   WSCP is discussed more in detail in Chapter 7.

server WebSphere AEs? It is true that the configuration data can be minimal in most cases and is unchanged in a production environment. You would think that using a master/slave strategy[4] of file replication might be a better answer to eliminate the repository and gain performance by not accessing a database. This is not true, however, because nodes within a WebSphere domain are live entities and their status is registered in the repository.

In Listing 5-1, the WSCP command `ApplicationServer list` revealed each node (that can be running on its own machine) within the WebSphere domain. As you will see in Chapter 7, the `monitorNode` action can be used to get the status of these nodes. Finally, the configuration data defining the nodes within a WebSphere domain needs to be shared and localized in a common repository and cannot be replaced with the master/slave strategy of file replication for the administrative data.

Now that IBM is using the database as an administrative repository for its advanced edition versions, WAS AE has been improved to cache the configuration data (ideally replicated) after fetching it from the database. Caching is possible because the administrative data is stored as EJBs.

By using a database, IBM is also offering a secure WebSphere Advanced Edition, whose configuration data is not laid in a flat editable file. On the other hand, the database is managed via an administrative server running on each node (a physical machine on which WAS has been installed). Therefore, such administrative servers inherit all the security of Java and add to this the possibility of serializing administrative objects and making them persistent.

It is up to IBM to use the specification of WAS business logic to program and to interface with the administrative repository. Your role is to manage it through the administrative console or WSCP, as explained in Chapter 7.

Benefits of a WebSphere Domain

Despite the complexity of laying down, maintaining, and administering the topology of a WebSphere domain, using it results in several benefits.

Distributing WAS Processes

One benefit of having a WebSphere domain is to have Java machine processes distributed on several machines, as well as scheduling threads for WAS clones to different processors on Symmetric Multiprocessing (SMP) machines. While such a topological approach gives you the feasibility to deploy WebSphere in different scenarios, you must consider two points in such Java machines' distribution:

▶   Eliminating interprocess communication

▶   Distributing the Java machines on multiple servers instead of using an SMP machine

---

[4]   This technique is used in a distributed system to reduce network traffic and improve response time by providing host machines with a local representative of the replicated file. Tools are available on UNIX to distribute files. For example, the NIS+/YP (Sun Yellow Pages) service is based on the master/slave strategy.

Eliminating Interprocess Communication   First, it is desirable to eliminate interprocess communication in a single computer between processes. Although it is using pipes and sockets, a considerable performance penalty occurs due to the two-stage memory copying within the UNIX kernel buffers. In general, communication between processes is more efficient when using multiple computers because such communication between kernels occurs through the network transport layer.

However, sometimes local calls are preferred over network calls, especially if the implementation of an application, such as the WAS engine, has not been carefully designed to take advantage of kernel communication. This is true, in particular, when you realize that WAS offers the option to use some stub programming to avoid network calls between its containers. For example, it is desirable to have local calls instead of network calls between the web container and the EJB container (both discussed later in this chapter). This is made possible by co-locating the web container and the EJB container to the same Java machine.

Starting with WAS v4, a new feature allows you to start an application server on UNIX as a user process with an UMASK, as shown in Figure 5-1.

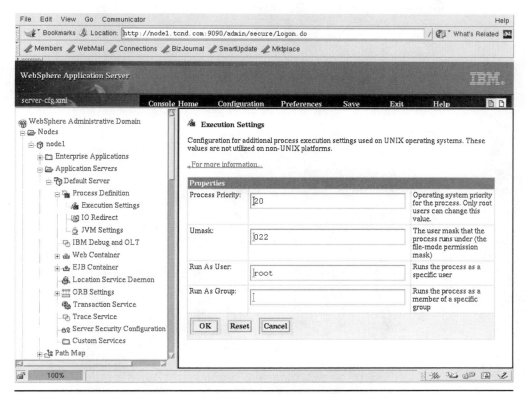

Figure 5-1   *Setting the execution property of the application server process*

Remember that interprocess communication between processes running at the user level can suffer a penalty in performance. To see how this applies to WAS, you need to test your application using both modes (system level versus user level) and capture systemic data.

Distributing the Java Machines on Several Machines   Second, it is better to distribute WAS Java machines over several machines than on a single multiprocessor SMP system.[5] This is due to the single-threaded nature of the modern Java machine, which can be a killer for an SMP system during garbage collection (GC). Although IBM documentation claims to add multithreaded garbage collection support in JVM v1.3, it remains to be seen how this new GC tactic works on SMP machines.

Gaining More Performance

There is another benefit in separating the administrative data configuration defining WAS topology from the nodes running the application servers. This separation makes it possible for workstations or thin servers acting as nodes to join the domain, adding more granularity to the performance of the application servers. For example, a bunch of SP thin nodes can be configured as WAS nodes to participate in a WebSphere domain, as seen in the illustration. Also, it is possible to have a mix of different platform machines participate in the WebSphere domain.

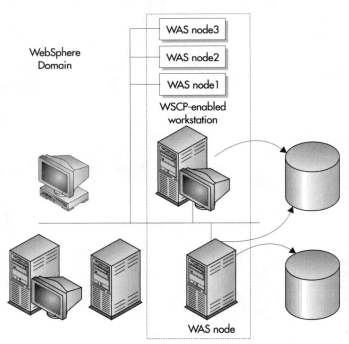

---

[5]   In other words, don't rely on threads scheduling over several CPUs to give you better performance. Application server clones use Java machines that need to be halted at once during garbage collection, but you can use SMP for many other reasons.

Securing the WebSphere Domain

Separating WAS topology from node machines makes it possible to have a universal database (UDB) server on which the configuration data of the WebSphere domain is stored; hence, the WebSphere domain itself is highly available. This high availability can be implemented by using clustering and takeover with IBM's High Availability Cluster Multi-Processing (HACMP) for AIX for this particular UDB server.

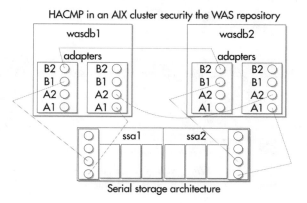

The high availability of UDB where WAS configuration data is stored is important because a WebSphere region can be rendered useless in the absence of UDB.

Defining the Name for the WebSphere Domain

In WAS AE, the WebSphere domain name is stored as a 256-character string in the table EJSADMIN.APPL_TABLE of the configuration repository database, as shown in the following illustration.

```
X xterm                                                                _ □ X
db2 => describe table EJSADMIN.APPL_TABLE

Column                          Type        Type
name                            schema      name              Length  Scale Nulls
------------------------------  ----------  ------------------ -------- ----- -----
INSTANCE_ID                     SYSIBM      VARCHAR                 64      0 No
TYPE_ID                         SYSIBM      VARCHAR                 64      0 No
NAME                            SYSIBM      VARCHAR                256      0 No

  3 record(s) selected.

db2 => select name from ejsadmin.appl_table

NAME

---------------------
AdminApplication

  1 record(s) selected.

db2 =>█
```

The default install sets up the name *WebSphere Administrative Domain* (WAS AE v3.5) or the name *WebSphere Application Server* (WAS v4), which is defined at the root tree of the administrative console.

When using WAS AE v3.5, to change the name of the WebSphere domain, click it and type in the desired name in the left pane, as shown in Figure 5-2. Choose a descriptive name such as the name of the company or the developers' group that will use the domain.

For WAS AEs v4 Advanced Single Server Edition, the default name is *WebSphere Administrative Domain*, and it is stored in the file was_home/config/server-cfg.xml or $WASCFG, as shown in Listing 5-2.

Listing 5-2   *A WebSphere domain name as defined in server-cfg.xml of WAS AEs*

```
<applicationserver:Domain xmi:version="2.0" xmlns:xmi="http://www.omg.org/XMI"
xmlns:applicationserver="applicationserver.xmi" xmlns:security="security.xmi"
xmlns:resources="resources.xmi" xmlns:server="server.xmi" xmi:id="Domain_1"
name="Total Computing Domain">
```

Redefining the domain name in WAS AEs is quite easy. At the web console, click the name and enter the desired name in the left pane, as shown in Figure 5-3. Confirm the name

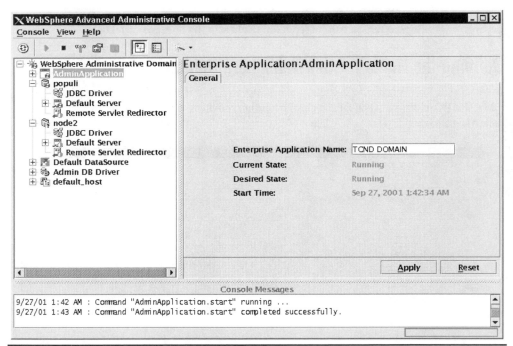

Figure 5-2   *Defining the name of a WebSphere domain in WAS AE v3.5*

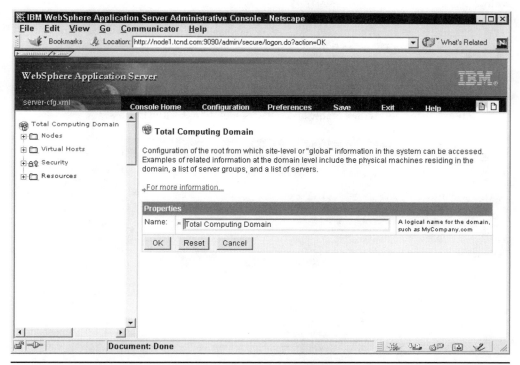

Figure 5-3   *Defining the name of the WebSphere domain in WAS AEs v4*

by clicking OK, and remember to save permanently before you exit; the setting should be reflected in the server-cfg.xml file but will not take effect until you restart WAS.

Administering a WebSphere Domain

You can administer a WebSphere domain through an administrative agent: either the GUI administrative console or WSCP. In either case, the administrative agent interfaces with the administrative server (a multithreaded Java machine that is running on each node) to change and update administrative data in the configuration repository.

The WAS administrative client is launched by one of the following methods:

▶   In WAS AE v3.5 and v4, start the administrative console on UNIX via the shell script adminclient.sh, and on Windows NT by either running the batch file adminclient.bat or by selecting the shortcut Start | Programs | IBM WebSphere Admin Console | Administrative Console. The adminclient syntax is

```
adminclient [was.host.name | IP_Address]  [port]
```

where was.host.name is the hostname (or IP address) of the remote machine on which a WebSphere administrative server has been started, and port is the bootstrap port number (default to 900).

If you are using the shortcut, be cautious about its properties. The link will work as long as WAS is installed on the same machine (localhost) as the adminclient and is listening on port 900. Otherwise, you need to modify the shortcut property and make it point to the correct hostname and port, as shown in the illustration.

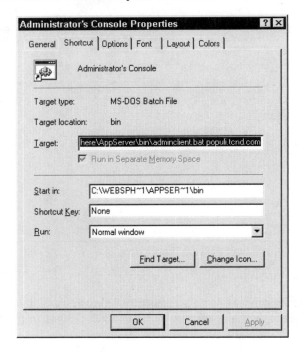

▶ In WAS AEs v4, start the web administrative console, also known as the web console, by entering the following URL in a web browser,

```
http://was.host.name:9090/admin
```

where was.host.name is the hostname of the machine running WAS. You can also start it from the shortcut that is created at installation: Start | Programs | IBM WebSphere | Application Server V4.0 | Administrative Console. Again, the shortcut properties need to be edited to make any change for the was.host.name and/or port if different than the default.

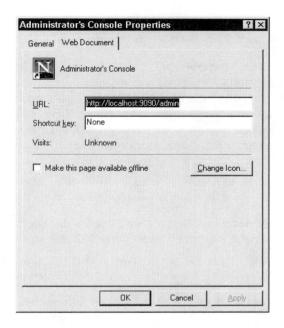

In WAS AE you can also use the WebSphere Control Program (WSCP) to administer WAS, Chapter 7 discusses administering WAS using WSCP

Although you can manipulate configuration data through an administrative client or by directly editing the configuration files (to be done with care), note that you can also manipulate the administrative configuration data programmatically through an XML file. WAS uses an XML grammar that allows you to take action on the named attributes (or resources) of specific objects. As an example, the following object tag in an XML configuration file <application-server name="node4" action="update"> is available for an import, and it says to take an update action on the application server object node4.

Such a programmatic XML configuration is useful during migration from WAS v3.5 to WAS v4, or for an import from a partial export between WAS configuration. Also, be aware of the limitations when using the XML programmatic export/import. The related file that lists the objects and their associated actions (after WAS v4 installation) is was_home/bin/xmlconfig35.dtd.

The XMLConfig.sh script is run as a command, which uses the following syntax:

```
{ ( -import xml_data_file ) ||
 [ ( -export xml_output_file [-partial xml_data_file] )
 -adminNodeName primary_node_name
 [-nameServiceHost host_name [ -nameServicePort port_number ]]
 [-traceString trace_spec [-traceFile file_name]]
```

```
[-generatePluginCfg true | false]
[-substitute "key1=value1[;key2=value2;[...]]"]
}
```

Usually the $XMLCONFIG is exercised at two consecutive instances. In the first instance, an export is realized on a source node; then it is followed by an import on a target node. This is like copying a file from one computer to another using a floppy medium. The following example exports the configuration file from a source node1 and imports it to a target machine node2. The example assumes that r'commands (that is, rsh) have been enabled in the WebSphere region:[6]

```
rsh node1 "/tools/env/setj.sh w122; cd $WAS_HOME/bin; $XMLCONFIG
-adminNodeName node1 -export /common/junk/exportedfrom_node1.xml"
```

Edit the exportedfrom_node1.xml file to define the action that you desire (update or create) in each action tag. Next, rsh to the target node2 and import the configuration file:

```
rsh node2  "/tools/env/setj.sh w122; cd $WAS_HOME/bin; $XMLCONFIG
-adminNodeName node2 -import /common/junk/exportedfrom_node1.xml"
```

At the root of a WebSphere domain is the main WAS Java machine that is pointed to by the plugged-in HTTP server. This main administrative server and every additional administration server defined under the same domain are referred to as nodes.

Having several managing clients managing the WAS repository explains one of the dilemmas that IBM faces in separating WAS administration from WAS development. The problem is due to the concurrent access of managing clients trying to pull and push information into the common WAS repository. You need to use manual refresh to know about the latest state of the domain.

The Structure of a WebSphere Domain

A WebSphere domain is a set of nodes that shares a common administrative repository. For tuning purposes, it is recommended that you use UDB as a database repository. Nodes can be run on any platform, as long as they have the same level of WAS installed (the same version and patch level of WAS with the same Java machine release).

The WebSphere Node

A WebSphere node is a server machine that is identified by its network hostname or IP address and running one or more Java machine processes, which are managed by WebSphere. For example, Figure 5-4 shows the server whose hostname is node1.tcnd.com as a WebSphere Node node1. defined in the domain Total Computing Domain.

---

[6]   The r'commands refer these commands that can be executed on a remote computer. rcp and rsh. You need to have an account on the remote computer; that account must have an .rhosts file in its home directory containing the name of the computer from which you are connecting (unless the /etc/hosts.equiv file contains such a mapping). You also need to have the rexec service (or subsystem on AIX) running; for example on Linux, the extended Internet services daemon (xinetd) needs to have started the rexecd server for the rexec routine.

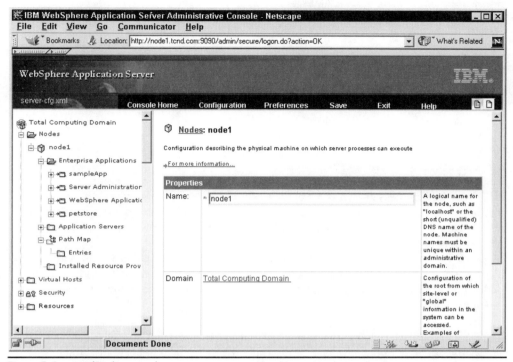

Figure 5-4   *WebSphere node*

WebSphere Advanced Edition v3.5 tabulates its nodes in the WAS repository. For instance, the following illustration shows two nodes, `populi` and `node2`, as they are saved in the WAS repository.

```
X xterm                                                                    _ □ X
db2 => describe table EJSADMIN.NODE_TABLE

Column                            Type        Type
name                              schema      name          Length  Scale Nulls
------------------------------    --------    ------------  ------  ----- -----
INSTANCE_ID                       SYSIBM      VARCHAR           64      0 No
TYPE_ID                           SYSIBM      VARCHAR           64      0 No
NAME                              SYSIBM      VARCHAR          256      0 No
DEPLOYEDJARDIR                    SYSIBM      VARCHAR          256      0 Yes

  4 record(s) selected.

db2 => select NAME from EJSADMIN.NODE_TABLE

NAME
------------------------
populi

node2


  2 record(s) selected.

db2 => █
```

The Java machine processes running under the node are server processes that can be classified into three categories:

► Generic servers

► Enterprise application servers

► Application servers, where each contains a web container (also known as a servlet engine prior to WAS v4) and an EJB container

Because a node can run several JVMs as application servers, it can be said that a node is a machine that can run several machines.

Usually, in a WebSphere domain, each node has an administration server that is started by a Java machine process known as a Nanny process.[7] The Nanny process makes sure that the administration server process (or processes, since it is possible to run more than one on a node machine) is running in perpetuity. If an application server process dies, the Nanny process restarts it.

In a WebSphere domain, resources are defined and categorized either for the domain as a whole or per each node. While every resource in the WebSphere domain resides on one node or another, the following resources make an exception and are neither node specific nor application-server specific:

► **Virtual hosts**   Each virtual host has a logical name associated with one or more name aliases that are either mapped in the DNS aliases or the /etc/hosts file on the local machine. A virtual host cannot share resources with another virtual host, even if they reside on the same server.

► **Security services**   An example is local security, which is associated with the operating system of the local machine on which your application server is running.

► **Resource providers**   These providers are specific to the operating system, such as Mail providers, JDBC providers, URL providers, and JMS providers.[8]

Web Container   The WebSphere application domain contains one or more application servers, which can contain no more than one web container to handle server-side requests, including coding such as servlets and JSP files. Sitting at the top of the application servers hierarchy, WebSphere Application Server manages requests forwarded by an HTTP server (plugged in with the modules provided by WAS) and passes them to the web containers defined in its hierarchy.

---

[7]   The Nanny process exists only on the UNIX platform.

[8]   With WAS v4, J2EE, resource providers can be associated with each node (for example, a UDB JDBC driver). These are listed under WebSphere Domain- | nodes- | Node Name- | Installed Resource Providers. However, a resource should be added to the WebSphere domain first so it can go into its providing functionality.

The web container's basic operation is to manage servlets effectively as it performs these tasks:

- ▶ Creates servlet instances
- ▶ Creates and manages request and response objects
- ▶ Loads and unloads servlets

The web container is the latest IBM nomenclature for what used to be known as the Servlet Engine (SE) in WebSphere v3.5.

Web Container or Servlet Engine   A web container as defined by J2EE manages web modules. It creates servlets instances and loads and unloads them. It manages objects' requests and responses. In WAS v3.5, the web container is often referred to as Servlet Engine (SE).

EJB Container   Within an application server, the EJB container acts as an interface between the enterprise beans and the server by managing data storage (data source) and retrieval of data for the beans within the application server. Therefore, the application server and the EJB container provide the bean run-time environment.

An EJB container as defined by J2EE provides run-time services to the EJB modules deployed within it.

The Nanny Process

The Nanny process is known to be started in WAS Advanced Edition for UNIX. This watchdog run by a Java machine makes sure the Java machines (of the application servers that have been started in a WebSphere domain) are up and running. The illustration shows the Nanny process on an AIX server.

```
X xterm                                                                    _ □ ✕
# ps -ef | grep Nanny
    root 17674  3002    0 06:40:41  pts/6  0:17 /usr/WebSphere/AppServer/java/jre/s
h/../bin/java -classpath /home/db2inst1/sqllib/java12/db2java.zip:/usr/WebSphere/
AppServer/lib/ibmwebas.jar:/usr/WebSphere/AppServer/properties:/usr/WebSphere/AppS
erver/lib/servlet.jar:/usr/WebSphere/AppServer/lib/webtlsrn.jar:/usr/WebSphere/App
Server/lib/lotusxsl.jar:/usr/WebSphere/AppServer/lib/compat.jar:/usr/WebSphere/App
Server/lib/xalan.jar:/usr/WebSphere/AppServer/lib/ns.jar:/usr/WebSphere/AppServer/
lib/ejs.jar:/usr/WebSphere/AppServer/lib/ujc.jar:/usr/WebSphere/AppServer/lib/repo
sitory.jar:/usr/WebSphere/AppServer/lib/admin.jar:/usr/WebSphere/AppServer/lib/con
sole.jar:/usr/WebSphere/AppServer/lib/was20cm.jar:/usr/WebSphere/AppServer/lib/tas
ks.jar:/usr/WebSphere/AppServer/lib/xml4j.jar:/usr/WebSphere/AppServer/lib/vaprt.j
ar:/usr/WebSphere/AppServer/lib/dertrjrt.jar:/usr/WebSphere/AppServer/lib/sslight.
jar:/usr/WebSphere/AppServer/lib/ibmjndi.jar:/usr/WebSphere/AppServer/lib/deployTo
ol.jar:/usr/WebSphere/AppServer/lib/epmJvmpi.jar:/usr/WebSphere/AppServer/java/lib
/tools.jar -DDER_DRIVER_PATH= com.ibm.ejs.sm.util.process.Nanny admin.config
    root 20526 17570    1 13:45:34  pts/7  0:00 grep Nanny
# █
```

Running the Nanny process does not guarantee that WAS is functioning properly. You can have the Nanny process running while your application server database repository and the data source used by the EJB container are inaccessible. This means if you are configuring or setting a monitoring agent event to monitor the Nanny process and to send you a page or an alarm upon failure, it won't ensure that WAS is up and running properly.

The Nanny process is available only on UNIX and has no equivalent process on Windows NT. On the latter platform, WAS is registered with the operating system services that are listed in the Control Panel | Services.

Ports Used by WAS

Throughout its processing cycle, WAS uses a set of ports to accommodate communication with its active protocols. Because each WebSphere domain is started as a Java machine process, multiple WebSphere domains can be defined on a single server as long as each of them is using a disjoint set of ports. This approach is discussed in Chapter 21.

Table 5-1 summarizes the default ports that may be active while running WAS.

Notice that these default ports are used by an active WebSphere domain and not by a WebSphere region. For instance, in an active WebSphere region, in addition to these ports, the following are also used:

▶ The default port 80 used by the HTTP server

▶ The ports that are used to connect to the UDB instance, such as the following: db2cdb2inst1 50000/tcp # Interrupt port for DB2 instance db2inst1 db2idb2inst1 50001/tcp # Interrupt port for DB2 instance db2inst1

▶ The selected port on which the db2jstrt has been started, such as 50068. The db2jstrt is needed when using the JDBC type 3 or net-driver, as explained in chapters 2 and 3.

Default Port	Usage
900	Bootstrap
9000	Location service daemon
9080	Internal HTTP transport
9443	Internal secured HTTP transport
9090	Internal HTTP transport for the web console of WAS AEs
7000	Dynamically assigned port for DrAdmin
Randomly assigned	ORB listener port for RMI-IIOP
2012	Object-level trace and debugger

Table 5-1   *Default Ports Used by an Active WebSphere Domain*

Comparing WAS v3.5 and v4

Changes within WAS v4 can affect an environment running a previous version of WAS. These changes affect WAS at the system-installation level and at the development level. These changes can also affect scalability scenarios when deploying WAS. If you're using WAS v4 and not migrating from WAS v3.5, you can skip this section.

Suppressing the Servlet Redirector

As with WAS prior to v4, the OSE is an IBM proprietary protocol that has been used as a plug-in between the web server and the application server to forward the former requests. It acts like a processor to associate URLs requested by the web server's clients, with a data queue connected to the application server. The queue can be any of the types shown in Figure 5-5.

Because an application server can be cloned (or mirror-imaged) to another server in WAS v3.*x*, OSE has been extended to a remote OSE that uses only TCP/IP to communicate between the web server and the application server clones.

While the WAS v3.*x* servlet engine uses OSE as a default transport, WAS v4 uses solely HTTP transports. OSE is not supported in WAS v4; thus, the Servlet Redirector has been eliminated from this latest version. This is good because servers can be freed from loading

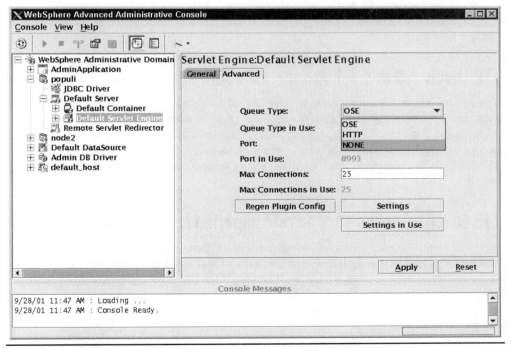

Figure 5-5 *Types of data queues*

an unnecessary transport layer and all its associated threads. Another reason IBM eliminated OSE is because it does not support data encryption between the web server and the application server. Also, having the HTTP protocol as a transport enables generic support in a networked environment where firewalls and proxies have been enabled.

Suppressing the Servlet Redirector in WAS v4 also eliminated OSE Queue, or HTTP Queue. WAS v3.5 users are advised to change the queue type from OSE to NONE (as shown in Figure 5-5) to gain remarkable performance improvement (that may range between nine percent and 22 percent in some situations!). It took IBM two versions to throw this killer protocol away, and WAS v2 users would say it's about time.

In any case, the use of Remote OSE is superfluous. When configuring an HTTP server on a separate machine from the application server(s), all servlet requests are placed over RMI-IIOP.

NOTE

The OSE plug-in of WAS v3.x can be kept operative with the HTTP plug-in of WAS v4. This is true as long as both plug-ins do not share the same properties for the port number and the URI. Therefore, a cluster of machines on which OSE has been configured can be migrated progressively with one machine at a time.

Suppressing Augmented datasources.xml Configuration

WAS v3.x used the optional configuration file datasources.xml in its configuration directory to allow initialization of a data source. This optional file is no longer used in WAS v4. If any data source has been set in this file, you need to add it to the JDBC provider resources, as we did in Chapter 4.

JSP Levels 1.0 and 1.1 Are the JSPs Supported in WAS v4

The JSP objects that are configured to run JSP 0.91 need to be rewritten. WAS v4 neither provides support to JSP level 0.91 nor migrates these objects. WAS v3.5 can be patched with the fixpack PTF 5 to bring it to the later release level of WAS v3.5.5, in which case, the servlet engine (or web container) can be run in WAS v3.5 Compatibility Mode or Servlet 2.2/ JSP 1.1 Full Compliance Mode. Figure 5-6 shows the mode-switching of the servlet engine in WAS v3.5.5.

EJB Level 1.1 Is the Only Level Supported in v4

WAS v3.5 supports solely EJB 1.0, while WAS v4 supports EJB 1.1. Usually, most EJB 1.0 beans can be ported to EJB 1.1. You should inspect and make the appropriate changes to these enterprise beans before redeployment under WAS v4.

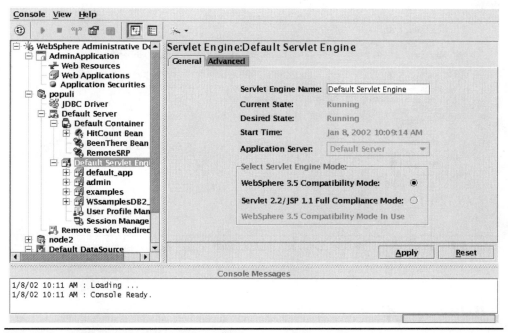

Figure 5-6   *Mode-switching the servlet engine*

Models and Clones Are Only for Application Servers in WAS v4

WAS v3.5 offers the ability to create models and clones for many objects (see Figure 5-7), which can be confusing and add complexity; in contrast, WAS v4 is more simplistic and straightforward in this aspect because none of these models and clones are supported.

Instead of using the cloning nomenclature, WAS v4 introduces the server grouping concept, where an original server can be replicated into an identical image by means of a template called *server group*. These identical images are called *clones* and are used for workload management (WLM). Usually, you start building an enterprise application and define it on an application server constrained to a single administrative node in your WebSphere domain. Later, if you decide to augment the performance and availability of your enterprise application, you can add another remote node to your WebSphere domain and then copy the enterprise application folder[9] from the administrative directory of the source node to the target node. You also need to configure the virtual host alias to associate with a separate port by editing the HTTP transport properties of each server in the server group.

---

[9]   As you will see in Chapter 6, the enterprise application is a J2EE .ear file that has been extracted in the installedApps directory of WAS. It is good to mount the source node administrative directory and export to the target node machines by using Network File System (NFS) or Andrew File System (AFS.) Then an easy way to perform this task on AIX is by using `backup` and `restore` commands, or on Linux, by using `cpio` or `tar`. Chapter 21 demonstrates how to move directory tree structures across machines.

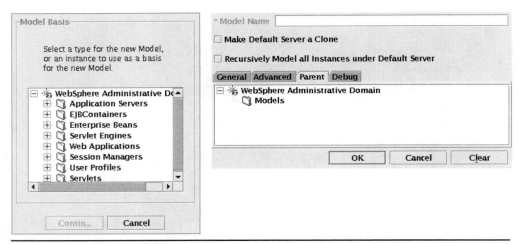

Figure 5-7   *WAS v3.5 offers the ability to create models and clones for many objects.*

Wrapping Up

The WAS repository is the essential means to define the relationship hierarchy of WebSphere Application Servers within its bailiwick. While these processes are primarily Java machine processes, their existence does not define the WebSphere domain. The WAS repository acts as a postboard on which the WAS nodes' Java machine write to communicate their persistent data between themselves.

You can define the name of your WebSphere domain and add nodes to it. All nodes are treated equally in WAS v4, and each of them contains and EJS container and a web container (known as the servlet engine in previous versions of WAS).

You can have one or more WebSphere domains configured on your server machine. Each of them should be configured to use a different set of ports to establish nonconflicting socket-based communication. Chapter 21 shows you how to install multiple WAS domains on the same server.

CHAPTER

6

Testing Your Installation: WAS Tools and Examples

IN THIS CHAPTER:

WAS Systemwide Tools

WAS Testing Tools

Sectioning an EAR Sample File: sampleApp.ear

The Petstore Sample

Miscellaneous WAS Tools

A fter installing WAS, you can use the examples provided with WAS and discussed in this chapter to test and practice with the product. Even though the examples provide a good starting point for new WAS users, advanced users might also find them good exercises for exploring the product—especially the examples that verify that WAS is configured correctly and operating properly.

This chapter introduces you to the many archives that are known to WAS. It also shows you the WAS way of deploying installable EAR applications, and therefore marking them as installed applications.

Some of the examples, provided as a tutorial to test with Enterprise JavaBeans (EJB,) require a data source (that is, an authorized connection to a database server). You can download the IBM Universal Database DB2 from the Internet, and for all practical purposes, install it on the same server. Chapters 2 and 3 cover installing and connecting to the DB2 server in more detail.

This chapter concludes with the installation and use of two WAS tools: the Log Analyzer and the Resource Analyzer.

WAS Systemwide Tools

This section introduces the WAS tools that are available with the product distribution of WAS v4 (and v3.5.5 when available). These tools are started as shell scripts on a UNIX system or as batch files on Windows NT. Each tool is briefly described, and an example is provided.

The Application Server Start/Stop Commands

Two scripts come with WAS AEs v4 to start and to terminate a WebSphere domain's Java processes: the first is startServer.sh (startServer.bat), which starts the server, and the second is stopServer.sh (stopServer.bat), which stops the server. WAS AE uses the startup Server.sh script to start the application server; stopping it is done interactively through the administrative console or by using the WebSphere Control Program (WSCP) command.

When a WebSphere domain is started, one or many Java machines are started all together, depending on the running state of the nodes and its web container. When a WebSphere domain is stopped, all the Java machines of the specific server (started with the startServer.sh script) are brought down.

To gather the status of the WAS, on UNIX use the ps command, or on Windows NT, look into the services registered by the operating system and the associated events log. Chapter 8 discusses how to manage WAS Java processes. Chapter 7 introduces the WSCP, which can be used effectively to monitor WAS.

Each WebSphere Application Server directs its standard input, output, and error to log files. These WAS log files can be a valuable resource to inform you about the status of the virtual servers. They are located in was_home/logs, or they can be selectively defined in your administrative console. Chapter 24 introduces the WASLED and WASMON utility software, which can extensively facilitate the monitoring of WAS.

The WebSphere Administrative Console

The WebSphere administrative console is the GUI interface used to modify the configuration data of the WebSphere domain. It replaces the manual editing of the many configuration scripts that were necessary with the earlier versions of WAS. However, some of the script must still be edited manually under the current version of WAS.

The WAS Advanced Edition (AE) administrative console is a GUI application that runs as an interface to modify the configuration database repository. While the configuration data is stored in a database, the backend of the administrative console of v3.5.5 is an application that stores the application server configuration in 34 entity EJBs in a database.

On the other hand, the WAS AEs v4 administrative console[1] (see Figure 6-1) is started within an Internet browser by entering the URL http://*was.host.name*:9090/admin, where *was.host.name* is the server on which WAS is installed—or to be more precise, the server on which WAS is running the Java machine to define a WebSphere domain that is listening on port 9090. Such a definition implies that you can have more than one WebSphere domain running on a server, as long as you disjointedly map their ports so they do not collide. Chapter 21 discusses how to install multiple WAS domains on the same server.

The WebSphere Control Program: WSCP

The WebSphere Control Program allows you to administer WAS textually from the command prompt, and to write administrative procedures (in Tcl) to run within the WSCP shell. Java packages can be called from within these procedures. WSCP of WAS v4 comes with the WscpCommand interface that allows you to program WSCP in Java. In Chapter 7, you will learn how to use WSCP with another programming language such as Perl to generate reports about your WebSphere domain, and distribute these reports via e-mail to your group.

WSCP is based on the Java implementation of Tcl (known as JACL) and is launched by a Java machine. Because this tool runs a Java machine by itself and consumes quite a bit of memory and CPU time, you should install it on a separate workstation by itself or on a developer desktop (since it runs on a number of platforms such as Linux and NT). However, expect a lot from it in terms of exposing and managing the WAS environment. Be careful, though: some commands can recursively remove objects (such as an application server or a node) and its dependencies. Therefore, you should practice with it on a separate machine on which you have installed WAS along with a database repository. WSCP is secure because its connectivity is based on the Secure Association Service (SAS.) However, keep in mind that someone who can authenticate a WSCP session has direct access to the WAS configuration repository.

WSCP is available with WAS AE v3.5 or v4 (not with the v4 Advanced Single Server Edition). You can download WAS v3.5 Advanced Edition from the Internet; WAS

---

[1] WAS v2 introduced the Application Server Manager, which runs as an applet that needs an applet viewer or a browser that supports JDK1.1. This Manager is started through an applet viewer or within a browser that supports JDK1.1 by requesting the URL http://*was.host.name*:9090/. Because the Application Server Manager for WAS v2 is slow and may corrupt your installation, manual editing is the only way to configure and test code under that version.

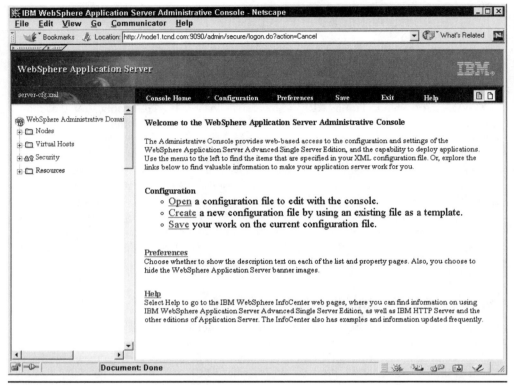

Figure 6-1   *WAS AEs v4 administrative console*

administrators and many developers should take advantage of this tool. Chapter 7 has a complete discussion about using WSCP.

DrAdmin: Generating Thread Dumps

DrAdmin is a utility that assists you in detecting problems in an application server that is idle or not responding, because this utility continues to run in the background and to generate a javacore file of the format javacore(*ProcessNumber*).(*Number*).txt, where the *ProcessNumber* is the process of the Nanny process on UNIX, or the main service process that started the WebSphere Application Server on Windows NT.

For the default install of WAS v4, set port 7000 for DrAdmin; otherwise, when the port is not specified, it is dynamically assigned and can be obtained from the was_home/logs/default_server_stdout.log or by looking into the activity.log. For example, the following command looks for all DrAdmin ports assigned in the activity.log file:

```
# showlog  activity.log  |  grep DrAdmin
```

You should get the last DrAdmin port reported. Next, invoke DrAdmin as follows:

```
# DrAdmin.sh  serverport  7000  -dumpThreads
```

This command assumes that the DrAdmin port is listening on port 7000. You can also use it to test and retrieve the state of a running application server.

Enterprise Application Archive (EAR)

You will find files with the .ear extension, which are called Enterprise Application Archive files. So-designated files are subsequently subdivided into other archive files, each having its own configuration (sub-sub) files that describe the mapping in these archives. WAS uses the specified Application Assembly Tool (AAT), started with the assembly.sh script, to create, manage, and alter the content of the EAR files (*.ear).

In WAS AEs v4 terminology and its explicit deployment strategy, an EAR file is usually placed in the $INSTALLABLEAPPS directory. It is not considered an installed application unless the WebSphere J2EE Application Installation tool (SEAppInstall) has installed it under its $INSTALLEDAPPS directory. The installation extracts the file into a directory that is named after the very same filename. The $INSTALLABLEAPPS and $INSTALLEDAPPS directory stand for the directory locations that were was_home/installableApps and was_home/installedApps, respectively. These two environment variables were illustrated in Chapter 4.

Next, you will be guided through the many definitions of the file archive types and the WAS tools that, no doubt, will help you manage and deploy EAR files.

The Application Assembly Tool (AAT)

The Application Assembly Tool creates the WAR, EAR, and JAR files. It assembles application components into web modules. EAR files can be created with either the Application Assembly Tool or with the EAR-compliant J2EE. AAT is started as a graphic interface with the script assembly.sh (or assembly.bat on Windows NT), or simply by typing **$ASSEMBLY** at the command prompt. The illustration shows the startup screen of the AAT wizard.

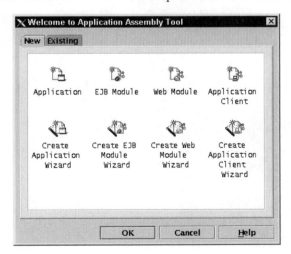

Web Archive files, or WAR files

Files with the .war extension are Java archives used as web modules representing standalone web applications. They can be used in conjunction with EJB modules to form a J2EE application that can, in turn, be deployed and run in your WAS web container.

Typically, a .war file contains one or more of these web application elements: servlets, JavaServer Pages, utility classes, HTML files and images, client-side applets, beans classes, and descriptive meta-information (also known as a deployment descriptors). A deployment descriptor is an XML file web.xml that declares the contents of the module, resolves the external dependencies of the web components, and describes how the components are to be used at run time.

The JAR Archives

Files with the .jar extension are Java archives used to package EJB modules and application client modules. Therefore, in a .jar archive, you can bundle .class files, .jsp files, .war files, .html files, .gif files, and so on. JAR archives are created with either the use of the ATT or with the `jar` command. A typical .jar file that you can take a look at is the SoapEnabler.jar in the was_home/lib directory. The following illustration shows the contents of the SoapEnabler.jar that you can extract by issuing this command:

```
# jar  -xvf  SoapEnabler.jar
```

If you plan to extract .jar files, you should do that in your work directory.

Traditionally, .jar files are archived of Java packages that hold the same representation of the directory structure as the original package. It is then presented in the classpath (or after the option -classpath) of the javac archives command and of the java interpreter command to resolve symbols that are used in a target program. Chapter 3 shows an example that explains the mapping between the directory tree structure and a Java package name.

The jar command has been merged with the java command and is given as the option -jar to follow the later command (java). Adding the -jar option to the java application-launcher command allows you to run applications packages in .jar files. When you run the java command with the -jar option, the java.class.path property is set to the JAR file or files executed, and it overrides any classpath defined with the -classpath or -cp options.

The EARExpander

The EARExpander expands the EAR files into or collapses the expanded EAR format back to JAR or ZIP file format. The tool is executed by invoking the script was_home/bin/EARExpander.sh (or EARExpander.bat on Windows NT). For example, to expand the file.ear into the directory /tmp/fileEAR; then to reciprocate by collapsing the expanded directory into the file.ear, you will issue these two commands respectively:

```
# cd $WAS_HOME# $EAREXPANDER -ear file.ear -expandDir /tmp/fileEAR -operation
expand
# $EAREXPANDER -ear file.ear -expandDir /tmp/fileEAR -operation collapse
```

Think of EAR as in the equation Enterprise application ARchive = enterprise beans + web applications.

SEAppInstall

This is the J2EE Application Installation Tool of WAS v4. On UNIX, it is invoked as the shell script SEAppInstall.sh (or SEAppInstall.bet on Windows NT) located in was_home/bin. To check the version of the Application Installation Tool, just invoke the script at the command line.

The SEAppInstall.sh activity is triggered exclusively with one of the following six options, where each of these options can be followed selectively by a set of arguments:

- ▶ -install *<ear file or directory>*
- ▶ -uninstall *<application name>*
- ▶ -export *<application name>*
- ▶ -list <apps | wars | ejbjars | all>
- ▶ -extractDDL *<application name>*
- ▶ -validate <app | server | both | NONE>

All of these options share one common argument (-configFile) to specify the server configuration file. When this option is ignored, the SEAppInstall defaults to the was_home/config/server-cfg.xml file. The file is backed up before being modified.

The -install and -uninstall options are the most commonly used, and they can be specified with arguments to point to a particular server (-serverName) and/or node (-nodeName).

To list all installed applications on your WAS, use this command:

```
# $SEAPPINSTALL  -list  apps
```

The illustration shows the typical output of such a command, which shows the web archives that are deployed under WAS. The output of the `SEAppInstall -list wars` shows the installed web applications.

```
root@node1: /opt/WebSphere/AppServer/bin
[root@node1 bin]# SEAppInstall.sh -list wars -configFile ../config/server-cfg.xml
IBM WebSphere Application Server Release 4, AEs
J2EE Application Installation Tool, Version 1.0
Copyright IBM Corp., 1997-2001

Loading Server Configuration from /opt/WebSphere/AppServer/config/server-cfg.xml
Server Configuration Loaded Successfully

Installed Web Applications
--------------------------------------------------------------------
1) sampleApp:Examples Application [WebModuleRef_2]: WebSphere Application Server Ex
ample Servlets
2) sampleApp:Default Application [WebModuleRef_1]: WebSphere's Default Application
Example
3) Server Administration Application:admin [WebModuleRef_3]: Admin servlets
4) WebSphere Application Server Samples:Samples Web Application [WebModuleRef_5]: M
isc Samples Web App
5) WebSphere Application Server Samples:YourCo Web Application [WebModuleRef_4]: Yo
urCo is the best
6) WebSphere Application Server Samples:theme Web Application [WebModuleRef_6]: the
me
7) petstore:WebTier [WebModuleRef_7]: Web Tier DD for the PetStore application
[root@node1 bin]#
[root@node1 bin]#
[root@node1 bin]#
```

When installing an EAR file, SEAppInstall may prompt you with the security message CHKW6595W of the IBM WebSphere validation; deny this message because for the time being, you don't want to have any user or group assigned to the security role.

The Application Client Resource Configuration Tool: clientConfig

This graphical interface is started with the command `clientConfig`. It allows you to open, view, manipulate, and save an EAR file. The illustration shows the Client Resource Configuration graphical interface.

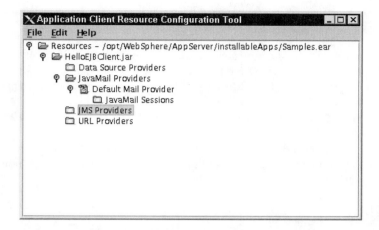

SoapEarEnabler: Enabling SOAP Services in the EAR File

This tool enables a set of Simple Object Access Protocol (SOAP) services within an EAR archive. WAS v4 provides services for standard Java classes and enterprise beans. You start the tool from the command line as the shell script was_home/bin/SoapEarEnabler.sh (or on Windows NT as the batch file SoapEarEnabler.bat). This tool runs either in silent mode or in an interactive mode, where you must have an EAR archive that has already been created with the AAT tool or a J2EE-compliant EAR file. In either case, the original EAR archive that you are starting with should not be originally "SOAP-enabled" outside of this tool. Once you enable the web services for the EAR archive, you can install it in your WAS.

Applet Clients (Only for Windows NT/2000)

WebSphere Application Server comes with its specific and singular applets configuration called WebSphere Applet clients. These applets are different than the regular applets known to other developers in their capability to communicate over RMI-IIOP. Because using the extra features of these applets requires a particular setup in reconfiguring and plugging in the client browser, you should use them only within an intranet application for specific purposes.

Don't use the WebSphere Applet clients as the basis of your application because first, these applets have nothing to do with the application server, and second, they require special setup for the client machine where the browser is installed. After all, users are already hesitant to accept cookies in their browsers. So it would be hard to make them accept turning their client browser into a little WebSphere server!

WAS Testing Tools

After installing WAS successfully, you can use a set of tools that are internally installed by default with the product. Prior to WAS v4, some of these tools needed to be installed manually after downloading them from the IBM web site; however, in the new version, some of these tools have been integrated with the product.

The tools can be divided into two sets. The first, as shown in Table 6-1, is a set of URLs for WAS v3.5 and v4.

Table 6-2 lists a second set of miscellaneous tools included in WAS v4. It is recommended that you check from time to time on the WebSphere Problem Determination Tools web site maintained by IBM.

Servlet	Description
Been There v3.5	URL: http://machine/webapp/examples/BeenThere Tests session persistence. In WAS v4, it is a bean linked to in the EJB1.1 deployment descriptor.
Hit Count v3.5 and v4	URL: http://machine/webapp/examples/HitCount Tests HTTP session requests, enterprise beans, and JSP files.
HelloPervasive v3.5 and v4	URL: http://was.host.name/webapp/examples/HelloPervasive Tests pervasive computing capability by calling it from different clients such as HTML, VXML (speech), and WML (wireless). On WAS v4, it is part of the examples.war file located in was_home/installedApps/sampleApp.ear/examples.war. The source code is in was_home//installedApps/sampleApp.ear/examples.ear/WEB-INF/classes.
ShowCfg v3.5 and v4	The Configuration Display Servlet tests the configuration of the system. URL: http://machine/webapp/examples/showCfg In WAS v4, it is the class com/ibm/websphere/examples/ServletEngineConfigDumper.class in the JAR file was_home/lib/websphere.jar. Its context is defined in the EAR: sampleApp.ear (context: /webapp/examples/), and the servlet name mapping is on the WAR: examples.war/WEB-INF/web.xml (servlet-name:showCfg url-pattern:/showCfg).
StockQuote StockQuoteServlet HelloPervasive v3.5 and v4	URL in v4: http://was.host.name/WebSphereSamples/SingleSamples/StockQuoteServlet http:/was.host.name/WebSphereSamples/SingleSamples/StockQuote Location: $INSTALLED/Samples.ear/Samples.war/WEB-INF/classes/StockQuote URL in v3.5: http://was.host.name/webapp/examples/StockQuote URL: http://machine/webapp/examples/HelloPervasive Tests pervasive computing capability by calling it from different clients such as HTML, VXML (speech), and WML (wireless).
Snoop servlet v3.5 and v4	URL: http://was.host.name/servlet/snoop Location: was_home/InstalledApps/sampleApp.ear/default_app.war/WEB-INF/classes/SnoopServlet.java Tests the servlet engine and the client request submitted via the browser. For example, invokes the snoop servlet with some query string. URL: http://machine/servlet/snoop?x=120&y=a

Table 6-1   *Servlets Used as Debug Tools*

Problem Type	Tool	Description
Administration server seems to be dead, but its processes are running	DrAdmin trace function	Dumps the thread stacks in an application server
Servlets, EJB problems	Distributed Debugger	Works in conjunction with the HitCount and Snoop servlet. Directs trace to WAS-specific stderr/stdout (was_home/logs)
Servlets, EJB, and JSP problems	Object Level Trace (OLT)	Debugs and traces for servlets and EJB
Name space problems	Java Name Tree Browser	Displays elements in a WAS name space
ORB communication problems	Java Socket Level Trace	Describes ORB communication problems via IIOP in a multiplatform distributed environment
Run-time errors of the application server(s)	Log Analyzer	Graphical interface that displays the run-time records captured in a WAS log file
Performance problems and Java garbage collection	Resource Analyzer	Monitors WAS resources for tuning reasons. Monitors garbage collection of the Java machine
Startup failure due to database connectivity	Jdbctest.java	Tests JDK settings and database connectivity

Table 6-2   *Tools for Trace, Log, and Problem Determination*

Bookmark the URLs shown in Table 6-1 so you can easily check on the functionality of your WAS installation. The illustration shows the output when requesting HitCount servlet.

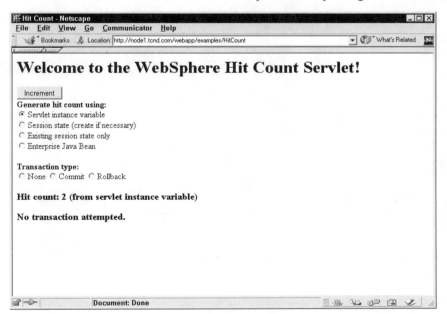

Sectioning an EAR Sample File: sampleApp.ear

We will make good use of the WAS examples in the previous section to make a URL request for the showCfg servlet and to get a response back from the server. How does the URL get resolved? And where does WAS get the servlet from? The answers will become clear after walking through this example.

Start the administrative console and browse through the Enterprise Applications: Node1 | Enterprise Application, as you see in Figure 6-2. You should see at least three applications installed:

▶ sampleApp

▶ Server Administration Application

▶ WebSphere Application Server Samples

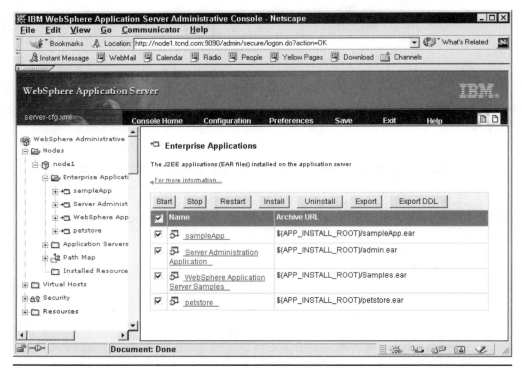

Figure 6-2   *The enterprise application in the administrative console*

These three applications are EAR files that have been installed automatically during the first-time installation of your WAS v4.

Focusing on the sampleApp, three files are of interest to us:

▶ sampleApp.ear, which in reality is a directory, but in the UNIX world anything is a file, and the directory sampleApp.ear is no exception

▶ application.xml

▶ web.xml

Change the directory to $INSTALLEDAPPS (was_home/installedApps) and walk through the tree structure of the sampleApp.ear directory. the hierarchy of the directory. is shown here.

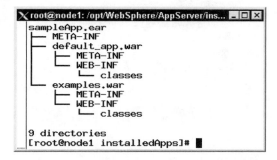

What you are looking at is the result of the installation of the sampleApp.ear file. This file is located in $INSTALLABLEAPPS (was_home/installableApps), and you can use the AAT tool to skim over it.

The sampleApp.ear file was installed during the first-time WAS installation, and it is called an installed-ear file because in WAS terminology, anything that goes in the $INSTALLEDAPPS directory is considered an installed application that is managed by WebSphere Application Server. Using the administrative console, Figure 6-3 shows the definition of the META file (deployment descriptor) that describes the layout of the directory structure of the sampleApp.ear shown in the preceding illustration: the sample application (sampleApp) definition as seen through the administrative console.

The META file named application.xml is a deployment descriptor that is stored in XML format, and it is located in the META-INF of the sampleApp.ear directory. Once it is deployed, each .ear file must have an application.xml deployment descriptor file. This file declares the contents of the module and contains information used to set up security and to look up references to enterprise beans needed by the application. Figure 6-3 shows the content of the application.xml file for the sampleApp enterprise application.

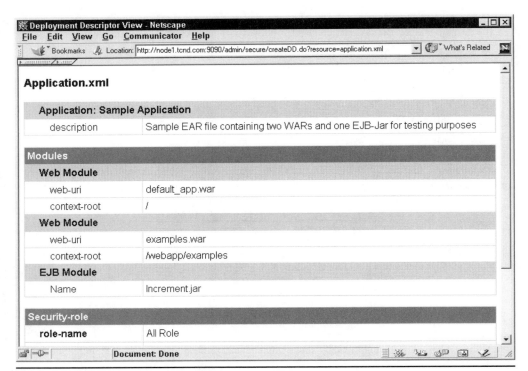

Figure 6-3 *sampleApp as seen through the administrative console*

Figure 6-4 more clearly shows the mapping of the deployment descriptor to the layout of the directory.

The explanation for the mapping shown in Figure 6-4 is as follows:

▶ The application descriptor contains two web modules (with ids WebModule_1 and WebModule_2) and an EJB module (with id EjbModule_1).

▶ Focusing on WebModule_1, this module directory location (that is, its web-uri as going up the tree hierarchy predefined by WAS's $INSTALLEDAPPS/sampleApp.ear directory) is default_app.war. This segregation of directory names when specifying a web-uri explains the mobility of the web application. In other words, a web application is uncoupled from the server on which it is being deployed. The web-uri is also mapped to a root described between the tag context-root. This mapping shows how the web module's physical name is mapped to (or fit in the context of) the client browser's logical name.

▶ In the sampleApp.ear directory, go up one level to defaultApp.war and locate the web.xml file in the WEB-INF directory. The web.xml file is the deployment descriptor that declares the contents of the module, resolves the external dependencies of the web

```
sampleApp.ear
├── Increment.jar
├── META-INF
│       └── application.xml          (1- application.xml)
├── default_app.war
│       ├── META-INF
│       └── WEB-INF
│               ├── classes
│               └── web.xml          (2- web.xml)
└── examples.war
        ├── META-INF
        └── WEB-INF
                ├── classes
                └── web.xml
```

Web Module 1
```
<module id="WebModule_1">
    <web>
        <web-uri>default_app.war</web-uri>
        <context-root>/</context-root>
    </web>
</module>
</module>
```
Web Module 2
```
<module id="WebModule_2">
    <web>
        <web-uri>examples.war</web-uri>
        <context-root>/webapp/examples</context-root>
    </web>
</module>
```
EJB Module
```
<module id="EjbModule_1">
    <ejb>Increment.jar</ejb>
</module>
```

Figure 6-4   *Dissecting the sampleApp.ear*

components, and describes how the components are to be used at run time. As an example, look at how the snoop servlet is defined:

```
<servlet id="Servlet_1">
        <servlet-name>snoop</servlet-name>
        <description>snoop servlet</description>
        <servlet-class>SnoopServlet</servlet-class>
        <init-param id="InitParam_1">
            <param-name>param1</param-name>
            <param-value>test-value1</param-value>
        </init-param>
        <init-param id="InitParam_2">
            <param-name>param2</param-name>
            <param-value>test-value2</param-value>
        </init-param>
    </servlet>
    <security-constraint id="SecurityConstraint_3">
        <web-resource-collection id="WebResourceCollection_3">
```

```
        <web-resource-name>Snoop Servlet Protected Area</web-resource-name>
        <url-pattern>/servlet/snoop/*</url-pattern>
        <http-method>DELETE</http-method>
        <http-method>GET</http-method>
        <http-method>POST</http-method>
        <http-method>PUT</http-method>
    </web-resource-collection>
    <auth-constraint id="AuthConstraint_3">
        <description>All Role - snoop:+:</description>
        <role-name>All Role</role-name>
    </auth-constraint>
    <user-data-constraint id="UserDataConstraint_3">
        <transport-guarantee>NONE</transport-guarantee>
    </user-data-constraint>
  </security-constraint>
```

▶ The snoop url-pattern is once again concatenated to the root-context mapping, to result in the URI: /servlet/snoop. Place this URL request:

http://*was.host.name*/servlet/snoop

was.host.name is the hostname where your WAS-enabled HTTP server is running, and you will get the request back with the default parameters as described previously in the init-param of the snoop servlet.

The Petstore Sample

If you installed the WAS sample programs, the EAR file petstore.ear is available to you. It is important to have the petstore.ear file that is available with WAS v4 (from IBM) for this sample application to be functional. The following section describes the steps for a successful Petstore installation.

Installing the Petstore Sample

Unlike the previous sample programs, the Petstore sample is not automatically enabled after your first-time WAS installation. You need to install and deploy the application on your own. Petstore is marked as an installable application and is located in the was_home/installableApps directory. A tree view of the Petstore application is shown in Figure 6-5.

You should install the Petstore application to explore the basic tools of WAS v4, in particular:

▶ AAT invoked with was_home/bin/assembly.sh

▶ The SEAppInstall script

▶ The WebSphere administrative console to define the application resources

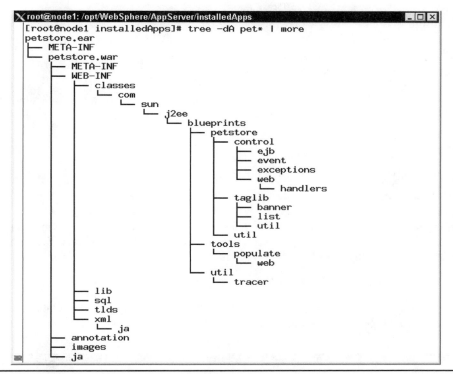

Figure 6-5 *Tree view of the Petstore application*

Petstore requires a database. You can download a DB2 version from the web and install it either on a separate machine that you can connect to remotely, or on the local machine on which you have WAS installed.

Preinstallation Verification

▶ Verify your authorization credentials on the DB2 server: check that you can log in to the server running DB2 with the db2'instance account. For example, you need to use the db2inst1 account and its password, because this is the account that you will be using to connect successfully from a remote DB2 node.

▶ Verify your authorization credential on the DB2 node: check that you can log in to the server running WAS with the db2 instance account; this is not the same account as the one defined on the DB2 server mentioned previously. However, the same login name (that is, db2inst1) can occasionally be given. This machine should have the DB2 client components, and it should be the same machine that is running WebSphere Application Server.

▶ Locate the db2java.zip file in your db2 instance directory, that is, /home/db2inst1/sqllib/java/db2java.zip.

▶ Locate the ps_db2.sql file in your Petstore directory.

Installation Steps for Petstore

The installation scenario described in this section uses a WAS/HTTP server running on node1.tcnd.com and a DB2 database server running on node2.tcnd.com.

Follow these steps to install Petstore on the aforementioned machines:

1. Create the database and connect to tables from the node on which the application server is running.
2. Use AAT to modify the petstore.ear file.
3. Configure resources from the administrative console.
4. Run $SEAPPINSTALL to install the application.
5. Set the context root of the web application in the default_host URI group.

Creating the Database   Table 6-3 summarizes the steps needed to create the database used by the Petstore application. Log in to the server on which you have the DB2 server running with your db2's instance login, and issue this command:

```
# . ./sqllib/db2profile; db2 create database PETSTORE
```

Figure 6-6 labels the steps in creating PETSTORE on a DB2 server. These labels are being further referred to in the steps summarized in Table 6-3.

```
X xterm                                                             _ □ ✕
1 bash-2.04$ . ./db2profile
  bash-2.04$ db2 catalog tcpip node TONODE2 remote NODE2.TCND.COM server db2cdb2inst1
2 DB20000I   The CATALOG TCPIP NODE command completed successfully.
  DB21056W   Directory changes may not be effective until the directory cache is
  refreshed.
  bash-2.04$ db2 catalog database PETSTORE at node TONODE2
3 DB20000I   The CATALOG DATABASE command completed successfully.
  DB21056W   Directory changes may not be effective until the directory cache is
  refreshed.
  bash-2.04$ db2 catalog db PETSTORE as PETSDB at node TONODE2
4 DB20000I   The CATALOG DATABASE command completed successfully.
  DB21056W   Directory changes may not be effective until the directory cache is
  refreshed.
  bash-2.04$ db2 connect to PETSDB user db2inst1 using pwd123
5
     Database Connection Information

   Database server        = DB2/LINUX 7.2.0
   SQL authorization ID   = DB2INST1
   Local database alias   = PETSDB

  bash-2.04$ db2 list node directory

   Node Directory

   Number of entries in the directory = 2

  Node 1 entry:

   Node name              = NODE1
   Comment                =
   Protocol               = TCPIP
   Hostname               = wasdb.tcnd.com
   Service name           = db2cdb2inst1
```

Figure 6-6   *Creating PETSDB on server node1.tcnd.com that is running WAS. This server can act as a DB2 node because it has all DB2 client components installed.*

Steps	Steps on the DB2 Node Server Running WAS: node1.tcnd.com	Steps on the DB2 Server: node2.tcnd.com
1		Log in as db2inst1 (or with your db2 instance login name) and create the PETSTORE database: # db2 create database PETSTORE
2	Log in with your db2 instance (i.e., db2inst1) and catalog the node if not already done. See Figure 6-6, label 2.	
3	Catalog the database PETSTORE (of node2.tcnd.com) at the node defined in step 2. See Figure 6-6, label 3.	
4	Alias the PETSTORE database as PETSDB, as you see in Figure 6-6, label 4.	
5	Connect to the PETSDB store using the credentials of the DB2 instance defined on sever node2.tcnd.com. See Figure 6-6, label 5.	
6	As the DB2 user, populate the database by running the SQL script ps_db2.sql: db2 -f $INSTALLABLEAPPS/petstore/ps_db2.sql. The first time you run this script, you might get errors that you can disregard. Run the script a second time.	
7		Connect to the PETSTORE database and check if the tables have been created. If not, repeat the previous steps; otherwise, proceed: # db2 connect to PETSTORE # db2 list tables The tables created are shown in Listing 6-1.

Table 6-3 *Steps to Create the PETSTORE Database*

After having completed the steps shown in Table 6-3, you need to define the properties of the petstore data source that will be used in WAS. From the administrative console, locate the Resources underneath the WebSphere Domain, then add the data source for the Petstore application: WebSphere Domain | Resources | JDBC Drivers | Db2JdbcDriver | Data Sources. You will add the data source by clicking on new and filling in the properties and the appropriate database authentication as shown in Figure 6-7.

Listing 6-1 *Tables in the PETSTORE database*

```
 Database Connection Information
Database server        = DB2/LINUX 7.2.0
```

```
SQL authorization ID   = DB2INST1
Local database alias   = PETSTORE

db2 => list tables
```

Table/View	Schema	Type	Creation time
ACCOUNT	DB2INST1	T	2001-10-01-00.49.35.376693
BANNERDATA	DB2INST1	T	2001-10-01-00.49.35.918943
CATEGORY	DB2INST1	T	2001-10-01-00.49.36.798131
INVENTORY	DB2INST1	T	2001-10-01-00.49.37.640536
ITEM	DB2INST1	T	2001-10-01-00.49.37.265816
LINEITEM	DB2INST1	T	2001-10-01-00.49.37.711277
ORDERS	DB2INST1	T	2001-10-01-00.49.36.163995
ORDERSTATUS	DB2INST1	T	2001-10-01-00.49.36.498891
PRODUCT	DB2INST1	T	2001-10-01-00.49.37.038731
PROFILE	DB2INST1	T	2001-10-01-00.49.35.667451
SEQUENCE	DB2INST1	T	2001-10-01-00.49.37.941275
SIGNON	DB2INST1	T	2001-10-01-00.49.35.141819
SUPPLIER	DB2INST1	T	2001-10-01-00.49.34.812994

```
  13 record(s) selected.
```

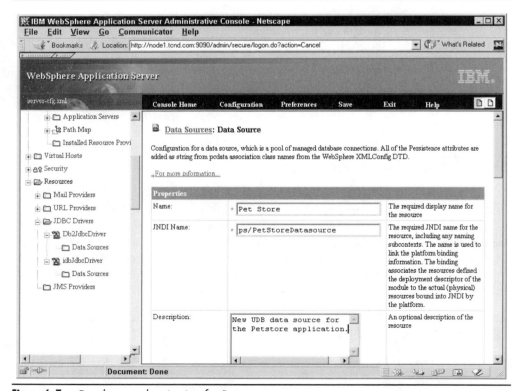

Figure 6-7   *Database authentication for Petstore*

Modifying the petstore.ear File Using AAT   Use the Application Assembly Tool to make two changes to the petstore.ear file before installing it:

1. Start AAT by invoking it with its alias $ASSEMBLY.

2. Select File | Open, and go to the $INSTALLABLEAPPS and select the petstore.ear file, as shown here.

3. Expand petstore | EJB Modules | Customer Component | Entity Beans | TheOrder | Environment Entries. Highlight the ejb/order/OrderDAOClass and set its properties to the following:

   ▶ **Name**   ejb/order/OrderDAOClass

   ▶ **Value**   com.ibm.j2ee.blueprints.customer.order.dao.OrderDAODB2.

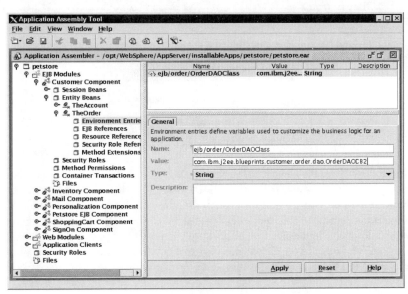

4. Expand petstore | EJB Modules | Petstore EJB Component | Session Beans | TheShoppingClientConfirmationMail | Environment Entries. Highlight the ejb/mail/SendConfirmationMail and set its properties to the following:

   ▶ **Name**   ejb/mail/SendConfirmationMail
   ▶ **Value**   true

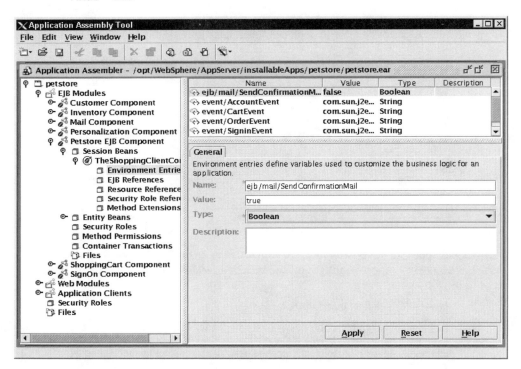

5. Save the archive, and make sure that AAT has saved it successfully Exit AAT.

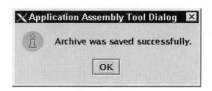

Configuring Resources from the Administrative Console   If your Petstore has already been configured by default to use the InstantDB (IDB) after the first-time installation, then you need to remove the Petstore application from your application server. To do this, in the left pane of your administrative console, click Resources | JDBC Drivers | idbJdbcDriver | Datasources, and if you find a Petstore data source, delete it and save your changes.

Furthermore, you need to configure two resources in the administrative console: the Datasource and Mail Session configuration data, respectively.

Set the properties of the JDBC driver for the connection pool that relates to the Name PetStore Datasource with the JNDI name: ps/PetStore Datasource. In the left pane of the administrative console, click Resources | JDBC Drivers | Db2JdbcDriver and fill in these fields:

Name	PetStoreDatasource
JNDI Name	ps/PetStoreDatasource
Description	-
Category	-
Database Name	PETSDB
Default User ID	db2inst1 (your db2's instance login)
Default Password	****** (your db2's instance password)
Minimum Pool Size	-
Maximum Pool Size	-
Connection Timeout	-
Idle Timeout	-
Orphan Timeout	-
Statement Cache Size	-

Set the properties of the mail transport for all outgoing mail that relates to the Name PetStoreMail with JNDI Name: ps/PetStoreMailSession.

Name	PetStoreMail
JNDI Name	ps/PetStoreMailSession
Description	-
Category	-
Mail From	dave@tibmsos.com (your From e-mail signature)
Mail Transport Host	dave
Mail Transport Protocol	smtp
Mail Transport User	dave
Mail Transport Password	dave
Mail Store Host	-
Mail Store User	-
Mail Store Password	-
Mail Store Protocol	-

In the left pane of the administrative console, click Save The Changes, stop WAS, and start it again.

To reiterate from Chapter 5, resources are not node-specific; rather, they relate to the WebSphere domain as a whole. You modify these domainwide resources of the WebSphere domain by clicking Resources in the left pane of the administrative console.

Making the Changes Manually

If you are using the trial WAS AEs that you downloaded from the Web, you can edit the server-cfg.xml file located in was_home/config and make the changes manually for the XML-formatted tags that define the JDBC Datasource configuration and Mail Session configuration:

JDBC changes:

```
<factorie xmi:type="resources:DataSource" xmi:id="DataSource_5"
name="PetStoreDatasource" jndiName="ps/PetStoreDatasource" description="New
DB2 Data source" jtaEnabled="false" databaseName="PETSDB"
minimumPoolSize="1" maximumPoolSize="30" connectionTimeout="180"
idleTimeout="1800" orphanTimeout="1800" statementCacheSize="100"
defaultUser="db2inst1" defaultPassword="{xor}Lyg7bm1s"
disableAutoConnectionCleanup="false"> <propertySet
xmi:id="J2EEResourcePropertySet_2"/> </factories>
```

Mail changes:

```
<resourceProviders xmi:type="resources:MailProvider" xmi:id="MailProvider_1"
name="Default Mail Provider" description="The default internal Mail Provider that
may be used to create Mail Sessions"> <factories xmi:type="resources:MailSession"
xmi:id="MailSession_1" name="PetStoreMail" jndiName="ps/PetStoreMailSession"
jtaEnabled="false" mailTransportHost="mail.tcnd.com" mailTransportProtocol="smtp"
mailTransportUser="dave" mailTransportPassword="{xor}PTBuZjM6Pg=="
mailFrom="dave@ibmsos.com"> <description xsi:nil="true"/> <category
xsi:nil="true"/> <mailStoreHost xsi:nil="true"/> <mailStoreUser xsi:nil="true"/>
<mailStorePassword xsi:nil="true"/> <mailStoreProtocol xsi:nil="true"/>
<propertySet xmi:id="J2EEResourcePropertySet_3"/> </factories> <propertySet
xmi:id="MailProvider_1_ps"/>
</resourceProviders>
```

Installing the Application   Follow these steps to install the application:

1. Remove the InstantDB (IDB) preconfiguration from the petstore.ear by running the SEAppInstall with the uninstall option:

   ```
   # $SEAPPINSTALL  -uninstall petstore -delete true
   ```

2. Install the newly created petstore.ear file by issuing this command:

   ```
   # SEAppInstall.sh -install
   $WAS_HOME/installableApps/petstore/petstore.ear -ejbdeploy false
   -precompileJsp false -interactive false
   ```

Setting the Context Root of the Petstore Web Application   To set the context root of the Petstore application, follow these steps:

1. Stop the HTTP server.

2. Edit the plugin-cfg.xml file located in the WAS config directory, i.e., was_home/ config/plugin-cfg.xml, and add the entry <Uri Name="/estore"/> to the default_host URI group.

3. Start the HTTP server.

4. Stop WAS and restart it.

5. From a browser, request the URL: http://was.host.name/estore.

You will be presented with the Java Pet Store Demo page. Click the link Enter The Store. Your request will take few seconds to be fulfilled as the database is populated for the first time. If your database server is located underneath your desk, you will hear the hard disk at work! (See Figure 6-8.)

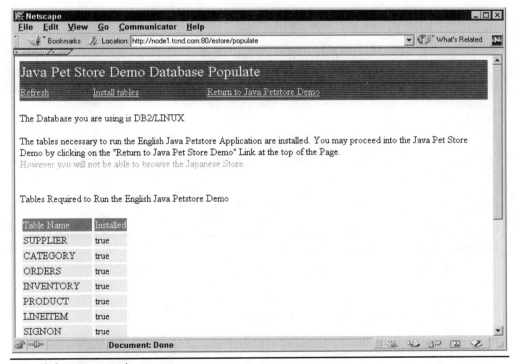

Figure 6-8   *Entering the Petstore*

Miscellaneous WAS Tools

This section discusses some of the many extra tools that are available to help developers analyze data. Data to be analyzed can be either collected by dumping it to a file, or it can be analyzed and charted while being processed, which is the case with the Resource Analyzer.

The Log Analyzer

This tool is available for Windows NT, AIX, and Sun Solaris. The Log Analyzer opens the activity.log file that is collected while WAS is running and deposited into the was_home/ logs directory.

Download the archive or copy it from your product media. The Log Analyzer is usually a package file named with the suffix logbr. To see whether it is available on your media, use the `find` command, as in `find /mnt/cdrom -print | grep logbr`. To install it, you need close to 5MB of disk space. The product installation is an add-on to the WAS installation directory; in particular, it installs into was_home by adding files to the was_home/bin, was_home/ lib directory. It may also create one or more directories into the was_home directory (such as dtd, and symptoms directories). To install it, follow these steps:

1. Stop all Java machines started by your WAS. You can use the `stopServer` command when available, or use the `kill` command on the group of Java processes (see Chapter 8).

2. Change the directory to was_home/bin, and back up the showlog file. The showlog file is usually the only file that might be overwritten by the installation process. To rename the file, use this command:

    ```
    # mv  showlog  showlog.bk
    ```

3. Change the directory to your was_home installation and dearchive the product in it.

4. Restart WAS.

5. The `waslogbr` command should be available now in your was_home/bin directory.

To start the Log Analyzer, go to the was_home/bin directory and execute the `waslogbr` command, followed by the activity.log file:

```
# waslogbr  /usr/WebSphere/AppServer/logs/activity.log
```

The documentation of the Log Analyzer is available in was_home/doc as a set of HTML formatted files. The Log Analyzer is shown in the following illustration.

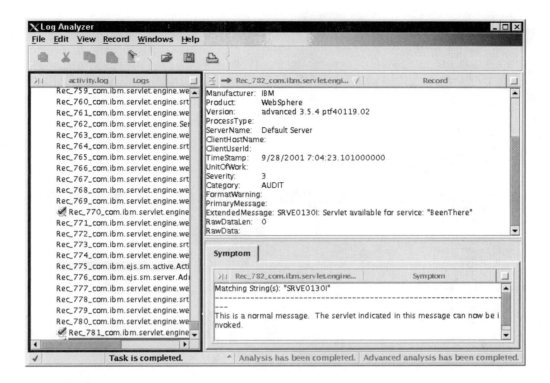

The Resource Analyzer

The Resource Analyzer (ra) is shipped with WAS v4 Advanced Edition, but it is an additional application for WAS v3.5 that you can download from the web. The web site maintained for this book points you to the URL where you can download the Resource Analyzer package. As a prerequisite, this utility requires the WAS library files, the same level of Java machine that your WAS is using, and the JCChart that is included with your WebSphere Application Server product.

Use the Resource Analyzer to collect and analyze run-time data (claimed to be real time) of your WAS resources. The analysis can be based on saved (or previously recorded) performance data in a log, to be replayed from previous sessions. Because this is a statistical tool, you can specify collection time intervals (1, 5, 10, or 20 minutes) and view the data in a chart. The WAS resources being treated include the following: web containers, database connection pools, object request broker thread pools, and enterprise bean methods and object pools.

Its installation is straightforward and does not affect any of your WAS directories:

1. Create a directory /usr/ra, copy the Resource Analyzer archive in it, and unzip this archive file in it. After extraction, the directories /usr/ra/bin, /usr/ra/lib, and /usr/ra/doc are created.

2. Edit the file /usr/ra/bin/ra.sh (or ra.bat on Windows NT) and set up the WAS_HOME to the location of the Java machine home directory. If you used the setj.sh script discussed

in Chapter 3, your was_home is already set up in $JAVA_HOME and can be echoed with echo $JAVA_HOME. Otherwise, set it up, like this:

```
# export WAS_HOME=/usr/WebSphere/AppServer/java
```

3. Invoke the Resource Analyzer by executing the ra.sh script (or the batch file ra.bat on Windows NT). The syntax of the command is `ra.sh [host [port]]`, where the host is the machine on which you have WAS installed, and the port number is the lsdPort default 900:

```
# ra.sh  populi 900
```

The Resource Analyzer is shown here:

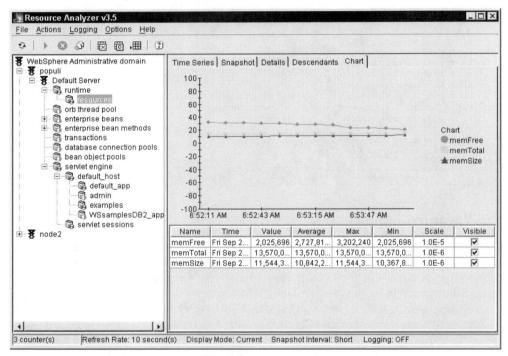

Because this utility is based on the Java machine to measure performance, you shouldn't make it the cornerstone of your benchmark analysis. Its availability is good as a tutorial (or as a teaching tool) to understand WAS resources.

Because the Resource Analyzer command can specify a host machine to connect to, you can install this utility on a separate machine by copying the appropriate library files from the WAS install directory and by replicating the same Java machine install directory on the target machine. You need to edit and make changes to the ra.sh script. This script also points you to the library files that need to be replicated. It comes with the epmJvmpi package, which is discussed next.

Profiling the Java Machine GC with epmJvmpi

The epmJvmpi is not really a tool, but a library; however, because it is part of the Resource Analyzer, it is worth mentioning here. This package is included with Resource Analyzer v3.5.2 or later. Use this package to collect data about the garbage collection (GC) of the Java machine. Follow these steps to install it:

1. Locate the directory where you dearchived the Resource Analyzer file. For this installation, assume it is this directory: /usr/ra.

2. Copy the library libepmJvmpiProfiler.a (or libepmJvmpiProfiler.dll for Windows NT) to the was_home/bin:

   ```
   # cp  /usr/ra/bin/libepmJvmpiProfiler.a $WAS_HOME/bin
   ```

3. Copy its JAR archive epmJvmpi.jar to the was_home/lib:

   ```
   # cp  /usr/ra/bin/epmJvmpi.jar   $WAS_HOME/lib
   ```

4. Edit the startup server script and add in the epmJvmpi.jar file to the application server startup CLASSPATH. You do this by adding this line to the was_home/bin/startServer.sh:

   ```
   CLASSPATH=$CLASSPATH:$WAS_HOME/epmJvmpi.jar
   ```

5. Modify the command-line option of the application server you want to profile by adding the switch -XrunepmJvmpiProfiler to its command-line arguments. You do this through the administrative console.

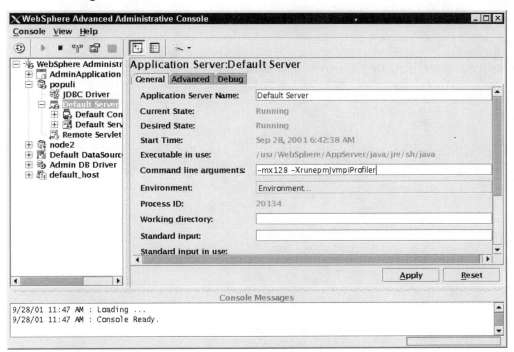

6. Restart WAS: stop the Java machines of WAS, and restart the it again.

You can capture the time interval between each GC event and gather the average duration of the GC events.

NOTE

To measure performance within a WebSphere domain, you can apply a set of APIs available within the packages of the Performance Monitoring Infrastructure, also known as the PMI API. PMI is a set of packages and libraries that you can use within your client code to collect performance data from the servers. The PMI API provides two sets of interfaces: the first set is to be exported by the PMI PerfServer providing performance data to the interested clients, and the second set is used by the clients to receive the performance data from the PMI-enabled server. In addition to these interfaces, PMI allows you to monitor changes of data on the server through its event-and-listener interfaces.

Wrapping Up

This chapter showed you how to test WAS by running the examples available to you with the first-time installation of WebSphere Application Server. It also introduced a few of the available tools that you can add to your WAS installation: The Log Analyzer and the Resource Analyzer.

As for the examples, the chapter focused on two directories in the tree structure of the WAS installation. These have already been set in the environment variables $WAS_INSTALLED and $WAS_INSTALLABLE of the setj.sh script discussed in Chapter 3. The two directories are was_home/installedApps andwas_home/installableApps.

In the first directory, WAS offers you examples that are ready to test with after the first-time installation. The examples are useful to test whether WAS is operating properly. Some of the source code for these examples is available to you in the same directory. The second directory, was_home/installableApps, houses files with .ear extensions that are available to be installed, but which need specific actions to render them usable before installing them.

The Essential Administrative Guide for WAS Developers

OBJECTIVES

► Extrapolating WAS Configuration

► Administering WAS

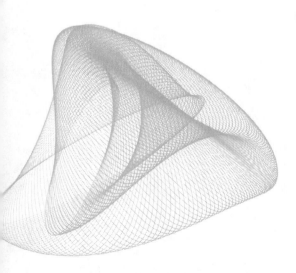

WAS Report Extrapolation with Perl/WSCP

O ne of the major concerns WAS designers have is how to interact with the configuration repository and control the WebSphere Domain in the absence of a GUI interface. Starting with WAS v3.5, the designers made the WebSphere Control Program (WSCP) available as the interface to control WAS systemic data, superceding previous command-line interfaces that started with earlier versions, such as the com.ibm.servlet .cmdline.wascmd interface known in WAS v2.02.

This chapter describes how to set up `wscp` as a command, how to administer WAS from the command prompt, how to practically automate reports extraction, and how to monitor WAS status. The discussion proceeds from a general description of WSCP and its interactive functionality to specific details about certain WAS objects and concludes with Perl-based programming examples to generate formatted reports from WSCP output.

Introduction to WSCP

WSCP is based on a tool command language (Tcl), which controls application software from the command line. IBM chose Tcl because of its ability to interact with programs through simple textual commands, and because of its portability. Tcl's list-processing capability and its procedural ability allows users to write commands that suit their needs. Tcl is a primitive language best suited to control jobs that are carried out from the command prompt. Only global variables can be shared between pieces of code that are evaluated dynamically.

Although commands under Tcl can be associated with a GUI-based application user interface (programmed with the Tk GUI toolkit), there is no reason to build such a graphical interface because WAS provides a powerful administrative console (as seen in Chapter 4).

WSCP extends Tcl to provide a set of commands to manage WAS objects from the command line. Choosing open-source Tcl has three advantages:

► It releases the administration of WAS from third-party components that need licensing at an extra cost.

► Tcl is platform independent.

► It makes the WSCP Java language programmable because it is based on JACL (Java Tcl, a Java implementation of Tcl).

This chapter does not discuss Tcl, but you can install it and practice with it. For the latest release of Tcl for Linux, look in your RPMS directory for the rpm files: itcl-*.rpm, tcl-*.rpm, tcllib-*.rpm, and tclx-*.rpm. (The wildcard stands for the version number and platform name of the Tcl binaries.)

The wscp Command

As a matter of fact, the `wscp` command does not exist, but on Windows NT, because the execution of a batch file does not require you to specify the file extension (.bat), wscp.bat is executed simply by issuing `wscp` at the command prompt, which is where the `wscp` command name comes from. In reality, WSCP is started by the script was_home/bin/wscp.sh (or its batch file counterpart on Windows NT). Nonetheless, on UNIX, you can make WSCP available as a command to your WAS users by including a link to wscp.sh (i.e., ln -s was_home/bin/wascp.sh /usr/bin/wscp), and it will start by itself because WSCP configuration is in its own script. However, you need to edit and modify the original wscp.sh that is shipped with WAS to make sure that it can find its command-line setup script.

WAS commands are usually shell scripts (or batch files on Windows NT) whose environments are set up from the file setupCmdLine.sh (or setupCmdLine.bat on Windows NT). One of the environment variables used by wscp.sh is the WAS_HOME variable, which points to the was_home directory. You can tailor a wscp.sh script by rewriting it and making it available on a sharable directory (e.g., shared home) so that it runs on any platform.

Starting WSCP

WSCP is started as a script that runs a Java machine with a classpath that includes JACL, which allows you to invoke Java methods in Tcl scripts using the java::package.For the simplest startup case, change the directory to was_home/bin and invoke wscp.sh (or wscp.bat on Windows NT) by issuing this command:

```
# wscp.sh
```

If the current directory (.) is not in your PATH environment variable, then issue ./wscp.sh instead. If the wscp.sh executable flag is not set, then set it with `chmod 755 wscp.sh`.

After loading and starting its Java machine, this script presents you with the WSCP prompt:

```
wscp>
```

Following this prompt, you will issue specific WSCP commands. At any time, you can type **Help** (with an uppercase *H*) to get the Help menu. The illustration shows the reply of WSCP after typing in the Help command.

```
wscp> Help

The general format of all wscp actions is:
        <object-type> <action> [name] [options]

The following is a list of the supported objects:

        ApplicationServer
        Context
        DataSource
        DrAdmin
        EJBContainer
        EnterpriseApplication
        EnterpriseBean
        GenericServer
        Help
        JDBCDriver
        Model
        Node
        Remote
        Servlet
        ServletEngine
        ServletRedirector
        SessionManager
        UserProfile
        VirtualHost
        WebApplication
        WebResource
        XMLConfig

To list all actions an object supports: <object> help
To list all the options for an action:  <object> help <action>
For verbose information on an action:    <object> help <action> -verbose

wscp>
```

WSCP works on objects, where each object can be followed by an action to be taken on the object. The actions that can be selected are create, modify, show, and start. You obtain information about the actions that can be taken on an object by typing the object name followed by **help**. For example, to get the actions that can be taken on the DataSource object, type the following:

```
wscp> DataSource help
```

Also, with the use of help, WSCP provides you with the syntax to be used when applying an action on an object. For instance, to get the syntax of the action to be taken on a servlet, issue this command:

```
wscp> Servlet help show
```

The syntax of the show action is printed:

```
Servlet show <name> [-all] [-attribute <attribute list>]
```

The WSCP Property File

When WSCP starts, it reads the property file specified after the -p flag; if none is specified, it defaults to the file .wscprc in the user home directory (~/.wscprc). On UNIX, the user home directory is the value set to the HOME environment variable, and if the default .wscprc file is present in there, it can be typed to standard output by issuing this command: cat $HOME/.wscprc.

A typical property file contains information about the node and the port to be accessed where a WebSphere Application Server is running, as in Listing 7-1.

Listing 7-1 *WSCP's typical property configuration file*

```
wscp.hostName=node2
wscp.hostPort=900
```

This property file, manage-node2.properties, is specified after the option -p of the `wscp.sh` command:

```
# wscp.sh  -p  manage-node2.properties
```

This command directs WSCP to manage the administrative server running on node2 and listening on port 900. A workstation on which the WSCP components have been installed can manage all these nodes that pertain to a particular WebSphere Domain. Be sure WSCP is the same version and fixpack level as its WAS counterpart; otherwise, exception errors will be printed. Typically, these errors can be WAS repository incompatibility errors or run-time errors such as these:

- ▶ com.ibm.ejs.sm.client.RepositoryOpException: Failed to create InitialContext: Error during resolve at com.ibm.ejs.sm.client.RepositoryOpException.<init> (RepositoryOpException.java:47)

- ▶ Exception in thread "P=706578:O=0:CT" org.omg.CORBA.MARSHAL: Unable to read value from underlying bridge: Unable to read value from underlying bridge: Mismatched serialization UIDs: Source (Rep. IDRMI:com.ibm.ejs .sm.beans.ServletEngineAttributes:C48A3091DF373F26:5CEA0548C3A84882) = 5CEA0548C3A84882 whereas Target (Rep. ID RMI:com.ibm.ejs.sm.beans .ServletEngineAttributes:C48A3091DF373F26:1F71EDEC49CDFA39) = 1F71EDEC49CDFA39 minor code: 0 completed: No at java.lang.RuntimeException. <init>(RuntimeException.java:49)

NOTE

Concurrent use of WSCP and the administrative console requires real-time refresh to reflect the current state of the objects' repository. In such a situation, you may need to refresh the administrative console and use the `wscp list` *command to update the WSCP cache. If you are using security objects, you need to use the administrative console because neither XMLConfig export/import nor WSCP support security objects at this time.*

Table 7-1 summarizes the WSCP properties that can be set up in a user's property files or in the $HOME/.wscprc directory.

A Conversation with WSCP

As an example, here is a simple conversation between a user and WSCP. The user starts by requesting the application server name to make sure that he or she is gaining access to the right node and not tampering with another one:

```
wscp> ApplicationServer list
```

WSCP replies with the node name. For our example:

```
{/Node:populi/ApplicationServer:Default Server/}
```

The curly braces come from the fact that WSCP is built upon Tcl, which is syntactically a list processing language. Later in this chapter, in the section "Formatting Output with Nested Braces," you will see how to parse WSCP output by applying recursion in a Perl program.

To know which JDBC your application server is using, use this command:

```
wscp> JDBCDriver show "/JDBCDriver:Admin DB Driver/"
```

This command returns the following:

{FullName {/JDBCDriver:Admin DB Driver/}} {Name {Admin DB Driver}} {ImplClass COM.ibm.db2.jdbc.app.DB2Driver} {JTAEnabled False} {UrlPrefix jdbc:db2}

Property	Explanation
wscp.hostName	Points to the host to administer. This entry is used with com.ibm.CORBA.BootstrapHost.
wscp.hostPort	Refers to the ORB port number on which the application server is listening. The default is 900. This entry is used with com.ibm.CORBA.BootstrapPort.
wscp.primaryNode	Used with qualifyHomeNames.
wscp.remoteConnectionAllowed	Defaults to false.
wscp.remoteConnectionTimeout	Defaults to 300 seconds.
wscp.remoteHostListAccept	Defaults to none. The list of hosts is colon-separated.
wscp.remoteHostListReject	Defaults to none. The list of hosts is colon-separated.
wscp.remotePasswordFile	Is the full path to the password file.
wscp.traceString	Enables tracing. Can be specified multiple times, each followed by a package name, and an asterisk can be used to specify all classes of a specific package. For example, com.ibm.ejs.sm.*=all=enabled.

Table 7-1   *WSCP Properties*

You can obtain the data source parametric setting with this command:

```
wscp> DataSource show "/DataSource:Default DataSource/"
```

In this case, WSCP returns the setting, such as this:

> {FullName {/DataSource:Default DataSource/}} {Name {Default DataSource}}
> {ConnTimeout 120000} {DatabaseName WAS} {IdleTimeout 180000}
> {JDBCDriver {/JDBCDriver:Admin DB Driver/}} {MaxPoolSize 10}
> {MinPoolSize 1} {OrphanTimeout 1800000}

Of course, you can obtain these parameters by querying the database repository setting; however, for the sake of compatibility with future versions of WAS, follow the IBM documentation when querying and setting the values of the configuration repository. If you prefer text-based administration, use WSCP to change WAS' configuration data.

Finally, to exit the WSCP session, type **exit**.

WSCP and Tcl

Tcl can be represented as a script to the `wscp` command. First, you write and save a script as a file; then you invoke `wscp` and represent the script as its argument. You need to use only a subset of the Tcl language to write specific scripts for WSCP. Basically, the Tcl commands that you need to be familiar with are `proc`, `eval`, and `catch`, in addition to the iteration command for each to enable looping over a list of elements.

Say you would like to monitor (or check on the status of) the nodes within a WebSphere Application Server. Going interactively with WSCP, you will first issue a command to list the nodes (`Node list`), followed by as many `Node show` commands as the number of nodes that have been listed in first. You can write a procedure to perform the task all at once by using a loop, as Listing 7-2 does. When typing it, take care to include the spaces between each token.

Listing 7-2   *monitorNode*

```
proc monitorNode1 {} {
puts "\nStatus of nodes in the WAS domain:\n"
foreach node [Node list] {
set nodeInfo($node) [Node show $node -attribute {Name CurrentState}]
puts $nodeInfo($node)
}
}
```

You invoke monitorNode within WSCP, and you should get the status of every node within your WAS domain. the following illustration shows sample output of such a comm and on the populi.tcnd.com system; the output reveals that node "node2" cannot be located.

```
X xterm                                                              _ | □ | ×
# wscp.sh
wscp> Node list
/Node:populi/ /Node:node2/
wscp> proc monitorNode {} {
puts "\nStatus of nodes in the WAS domain:\n"
foreach node [Node list] {
set nodeInfo($node) [Node show $node -attribute {Name CurrentState}]
puts $nodeInfo($node)
}
}

?
?
?
?
?
? wscp> monitorNode

Status of nodes in the WAS domain:

{Name populi} {CurrentState Running}
{Name node2} {CurrentState {Lost Contact}}
wscp> █
```

It is possible to remove the object (the node object, in this case) and all references to this object recursively. To do so, check the state of the object first and stop it if it is a live object; next, issue this command:

```
Node remove <nodename> -recursive
```

If you don't put the recursive option after the `remove` command, the command may fail because other objects containing references to this object must also be removed. The recursive option makes sure that the command acts on the dependent objects as well.

The Tcl/Java integration allows you to access the Java packages from within WSCP. In the Tcl procedures, you can issue commands such as java::call, java::info, and java::field on a particular package. Listing 7-3 summarizes the use of such commands to list and to map the WscpStatus fields by symbol, by number, and by an explanatory string.

Listing 7-3   *wscpMsg*

```
proc wscpMsg {} {
foreach s [java::info fields -static com.ibm.ejs.sm.ejscp.WscpStatus] {
set s [string trimleft $s]
if [string match {[A-Z]*} $s] {
set v [java::field com.ibm.ejs.sm.ejscp.WscpStatus $s]
set m [java::call com.ibm.ejs.sm.ejscp.WscpStatus statusToString $v]
puts "$s $v: $m";
```

```
}
}
}
```

The illustration shows the output of wscpMsg.

```
X xterm                                                              _ □ ×
wscp> wscpMsg
SUCCESS 0: Success
ACTION_TIMEOUT 1: Timeout occurred before task completed
CAUGHT_EXCEPTION 2: An Exception was caught during command processing
CONTEXT_NOT_EMPTY 3: The specified Context was not empty
INTERNAL_ERROR 4: An internal error occurred
INVALID_ACTION 5: An invalid action was specified
INVALID_ATTRIBUTE 6: An invalid attribute was specified
INVALID_ATTRIBUTE_FORMAT 7: An invalid attribute format string was specified
INVALID_CONTEXT 8: An invalid Context was specified
INVALID_NODE_NAME 9: An invalid Node name was specified
INVALID_OBJECT_NAME 10: An invalid object name was specified
INVALID_OPTION 11: An invalid option was specified
INVALID_PROPERTIES_FORMAT 12: An invalid properties format string was specified
INVALID_SEARCH_FILTER 13: An invalid search filter was specified
MISSING_ACTION 14: An action must be specified
MISSING_ARGUMENT 15: A required argument was not specified
MISSING_OPTION 16: A required option was not specified
MISSING_OPTION_ARGUMENT 17: An option was specified that requires an argument
NAME_ALREADY_BOUND 18: The specified name is already bound
NO_CURRENT_CONTEXT 19: No current context
OPERATION_NOT_SUPPORTED 20: Operation not supported
PERMISSION_DENIED 21: Permission denied
SOCKET_ERROR 22: Socket error
OBJECT_GROUP_NOT_EMPTY 23: Object group is not empty
wscp> █
```

Sole Installation of WSCP on a Workstation

WSCP is started as a Java machine by itself, just like the application server. If you look closely at the processes started on a UNIX machine when WSCP is running, you find out that this utility consumes CPU and memory that you should save for the application server. Install WSCP on a separate machine and set up a property file that points to the machine hosting the WebSphere Application Server. You can make WSCP available on a machine without going through the WAS installation procedure.

To do this, first install the components of the WAS administrative client on a machine that will participate in your WebSphere Domain. Second, use the `tar` command to archive the Java machine home directory used by WSCP and the WAS subdirectories that WSCP uses (mainly the directory containing the library files for WSCP). Third, untar the file on the workstation to be used as the WSCP managing agent. Basically, WSCP uses the library files that are in was_home and the Java machine that WAS is using (i.e., java_home).

In Chapter 22, you will learn how to customize your installation to bring WSCP to a workstation or a server in a distributed environment.

The WscpCommand Interface

You can embed WSCP commands in Java programs through the com.ibm.ejs.sm.ejscp.wscpcommand.WscpCommand interface. However, you can do this only with WAS Adanced Edition v4, where the wscp.jar file is included in the was_home/lib/ directory. Basically, you need to include the wscp.jar file in your CLASSPATH to use the WscpCommand interface. The package provides you with the methods, objects, and a utility class:

▶ **WscpResult evalCommand(`String` command)** This method returns a result that can be extracted from the com.ibm.ejs.sm.ejscp.wscpcommand.WscpResult object.

▶ **String getErrorInfo()** This method returns the exception information if the previous method fails.

▶ **WscpCommand(`String n`, `String p`)** This constructor that takes a node and a port number; it defaults to localhost node listening on port 900.

▶ **WscpQualifiedName()** This class allows you to act on WSCP objects. The class has a set of constants defining the containment levels of various components that are passed to the two methods: the first to get the object name, *getName(level)*, the second to get the object type, *getObject(level)*.

Listing 7-4 is a simple program that uses the WscpCommand interface.

Listing 7-4 *WscpNodeList.java*

```
import com.ibm.ejs.sm.ejscp.wscpcommand.WscpCommand;
class WscpNodeList {
    public static void main (String args[]) {
        String c = "Node list";
        WscpResult r = WscpCommand.evalCommand(c);
        if (!r.success()) {
            System.out.println("Command failed: " + r.getErrorInfo());
        }
    }
}
```

To compile this program, issue these commands,

```
# javac -classpath $WAS_HOME/lib/wscp.jar WscpNodeList.java
```

where $WAS_HOME is set to the was_home directory on your system. Alternatively, if you set up the environment using this script discussed in Chapter 3,

```
# .   /tools/setc.sh   w130
```

you can use the environment variable $WSCP_CL as the classpath when compiling the program:

```
# javac -classpath  $WSCP_CL  WscpNodeList.java
```

Using WSCP in Java programs is one option offered with the new release of WAS v4. However, Java does not offer you the power of reports formatting and generation that Perl does. Next, you will see how to run WSCP within Perl and generate formatted reports.

Practical Reports Extraction with Perl/WSCP

Practically extracting the WAS configuration couldn't be more easy than using Perl and WSCP. To do this, you need to have the Perl interpreter (version 5 or later) installed on your machine. To check for the availability of Perl on your system, simply run

```
# perl  -V
```

at the command prompt. This prints the version of Perl along with other messages, including the compilation time and date.

Running WSCP from Perl

UNIX commands and shell scripts can be executed from within a Perl script. Simply execute the command binary file and redirect its output to be processed as an open file by Perl. The redirection is similar to what is known under UNIX as *pipe*.

As a first example, Listing 7-5 shows how you can run the WSCP command to list the servlets. The WSCP command equivalent to this program is the following:

```
wscp> Servlet list
```

Listing 7-5   *wscp_Servlet-list.pl*

```
$WAS_HOME="/usr/WebSphere/AppServer";
$JAVA_HOME="/usr/WebSphere/AppServer/java";
$JAVA_EXE="$JAVA_HOME/jre/sh/java";
$WAS_CP="$WAS_HOME/lib/jacl.jar";
$WAS_CP="$WAS_CP:$WAS_HOME/lib/tcljava.jar";
$WAS_CP="$WAS_CP:$WAS_HOME/lib/ibmwebas.jar";
$WAS_CP="$WAS_CP:$WAS_HOME/lib/ejscp.jar";
$WAS_CP="$WAS_CP:$WAS_HOME/lib/xml4j.jar";
$WAS_CP="$WAS_CP:$WAS_HOME/lib/ujc.jar";
$WAS_CP="$WAS_CP:$WAS_HOME/lib/ejs.jar";
$WAS_CP="$WAS_CP:$WAS_HOME/lib/console.jar";
$WAS_CP="$WAS_CP:$WAS_HOME/lib/admin.jar";
```

```
$WAS_CP="$WAS_CP:$WAS_HOME/lib/repository.jar";
$WAS_CP="$WAS_CP:$WAS_HOME/lib/tasks.jar";
$WAS_CP="$WAS_CP:$WAS_HOME/lib/servlet.jar";
$WAS_CP="$WAS_CP:$WAS_HOME/lib/sslight.jar";
$WAS_CP="$WAS_CP:$WAS_HOME/properties";
$WAS_CP="$WAS_CP:$JAVA_HOME/lib/classes.zip";
$WAS_CP="$WAS_CP:$JAVA_HOME/lib/tools.jar";
$SHELL="com.ibm.ejs.sm.ejscp.WscpShell";
$EXT =  " -x com.ibm.ejs.sm.ejscp.RemoteExtension";
$EXT .= " -x com.ibm.ejs.sm.ejscp.ContextExtension";
$EXT .= " -x com.ibm.ejs.sm.ejscp.DrAdminExtension";
$EXT .= " -x com.ibm.ejs.sm.ejscp.EjscpExtension";
open(WSCP, "$JAVA_EXE -classpath $WAS_CP -Dserver.root=$WAS_HOME $SHELL $EXT -c
'Servlet list' |");
while (<WSCP>) {
$v = $_;
print ">>>> $v\n";
}
```

When wscp_Servlet-list.pl is executed by invoking the Perl interpreter,

```
# perl  wscp_Servlet-list.pl
```

it returns a long list of the servlets hosted by the node. The output is of the form {...}{...}{...} ...{...}, where the ellipsis points (...) represent strings. Each servlet is given with its fully qualified name between two braces. You can get a servlet's full information by using the Servlet show {...} -all command. The illustration shows the reply of WSCP to the snoop servlet on node populi in the example.

Parsing the WSCP Output

The aim is to get the output of WSCP into a file, parse it, and then restructure it into Perl hashes so that Perl generates a formatted report out of it. The next illustration shows a simple report.

```
X PERL-WSCP                                                              _ □ ×
# perl format-ServletList-aix.pl
Appl Server     Servlet Engine                Location                 Servlet Name
------------    -------------------------     -----------------------  ------------

populi/Appl   Default Server/ServletEngine  default_app/Servlet  snoop/
populi/Appl   Default Server/ServletEngine  default_app/Servlet  hello/
populi/Appl   Default Server/ServletEngine  default_app/Servlet  ErrorReporter/
populi/Appl   Default Server/ServletEngine  default_app/Servlet  invoker/
populi/Appl   Default Server/ServletEngine  default_app/Servlet  jsp10/
populi/Appl   Default Server/ServletEngine  admin/Servlet        install/
populi/Appl   Default Server/ServletEngine  admin/Servlet        jsp10/
populi/Appl   Default Server/ServletEngine  admin/Servlet        file/
populi/Appl   Default Server/ServletEngine  admin/Servlet        invoker/
populi/Appl   Default Server/ServletEngine  admin/Servlet        ErrorReporter/
populi/Appl   Default Server/ServletEngine  examples/Servlet     simpleJSP/
populi/Appl   Default Server/ServletEngine  examples/Servlet     error/
populi/Appl   Default Server/ServletEngine  examples/Servlet     ping/
# █
```

To parse the output of WSCP, you should consider two cases. The first is a straight forward parsing of a bracketed list of tokens of the form: {...}{...}...{...}. The second require a recursive parsing because the brackets can be nested into each other.

Formatting Output with Simple Bracketing

In the first case, the output is of the format {...}{...}...{...}. This is simple, and you can use a Perl regular expression to split it. In the other case, where the output is formed of nested braces, you should write a recursive parsing routine to reformat the output. At any time, you need to understand the output of the WSCP commands and tailor your Perl program to manage its final output. This seems time-consuming, but once it is in place, you will save a tremendous amount of time by having ready-to-go reports about your WebSphere Domain that you can e-mail to developers and managers.

Listing 7-6 shows the Perl program format-ServletList-aix that can format the WSCP command `Servlet list` whose output is given in Figure 7-5. The output of WSCP `Servlet list` is assigned to the $s variable and has been truncated in the listing to save space.

Listing 7-6   *format-ServletList-aix formats the servlet list*

```
1.    #!/usr/bin/perl
2.
3.    format top =
4.    Appl Server    Servlet Engine                    Location
      Servlet Name
5.    -----------    ------------------------------    -----------------------
      --------------
6.
7.    .
8.
9.    format =
10.   @<<<<<<<<<   @<<<<<<<<<<<<<<<<<<<<<<<<<<<   @<<<<<<<<<<<<<<<<<<<<<<<
      @<<<<<<<<<<<
11.   $u2, $u3, $u5, $u6
```

```
12.  .
13.
14.  $s = " {/Node:populi/ApplicationServer:Default
     Server/ServletEngine:Default Servlet
     Engine/WebApplication:default_app/Servlet:snoop/} ... /}";
15.
16.  while (length($s) > 0) {
17.      $s =~ s/^\s+//;
18.      $left = index($s,"\{");
19.      $tall = index(substr($s,$left,length($s)),"\}",1);
20.      $f = substr($s,$left+1,$tall-1);
21.      $s1 = substr($s,0,$left);
22.      $s2 = substr($s,$left+$tall+1,length($record)-$left-$tall);
23.      $s = $s1 . $s2;
24.      # Node(1), Appl Server(2), Default SE (3), Default WebApp(4),
     Locatin(5), Servlet name(6)
25.      ($u1,$u2,$u3,$u4,$u5,$u6) = split(":",$f);
26.      write;
27.  }}
```

Formatting Output with Nested Braces

In the other case, WSCP output can be formed of bracketed keywords followed by nested braces. Parsing nested braces within an expression is classically done by applying recursion. ParseWscp, shown in Listing 7-7, is a Perl program that parses the WSCP command `Servlet show {some_servlet_name_Uri} -all` and breaks its output intoying recursion. multiple strings to be formatted further by Perl.

Listing 7-7   *ParseWscp to recursively parse the WSCP output*

```
1.   #!/usr/bin/perl
2.
3.   $debug=0;
4.
5.   format top =
6.   SERVLET NAME        STATE               CODE
     DESCRIPTION
7.   ---------------   ---------  -------------------------------
     ------------------------
8.   .
9.
10.  format =
11.  @<<<<<<<<<<<<<<< @<<<<<<<<   @<<<<<<<<<<<<<<<<<<<<<<<<<<<<<<<
     @<<<<<<<<<<<<<<<<<<<<<<<<
12.  $svlt_name, $svlt_state, $svlt_code, $svlt_desc
13.  .
14.
```

```
15.   my $s = &strpool(2);
16.
17.   # Attribute names for a servlet
18.   $ServletAttributes = 'FullName Name CurrentState DesiredState StartTime
      Code CodeActive DebugMode Description DescriptionActive Enabled
      EnabledActive InitParams InitParamsActive LoadAtStartup
      LoadAtStartupActive URIPaths URIPathsActive UserServlet
      UserServletActive';
19.
20.   # Attribute names that we seek to capture
21.   $ServletAttr = 'Name CurrentState Code Description';
22.
23.   my @ServletAttributes = split(/\s/,$ServletAttributes);
24.   my @ServletAttr = split(/\s/,$ServletAttr);
25.
26.   $_ = $s;
27.
28.   my($count,$hold,$reset);
29.   $count = $hold = $reset = 0;
30.   my $key = '';
31.   my $flag = 0;
32.   my %hash = ();
33.
34.
35.   do { doexpression(); }  while $_;
36.
37.   if ($debug) { foreach $key (sort keys %hash) { print ">>> $key ++
      $hash{$key} \n"; } }
38.   $svlt_name = $hash{Name};
39.   $svlt_state = $hash{CurrentState};
40.   $svlt_code = $hash{Code};
41.   $svlt_desc = $hash{Description};
42.   write;
43.
44.   if ($debug) { foreach $e (@L) { print ">>> $e\n"; } }
45.
46.   sub literal ($) {
47.       my $lit = $_[0];
48.       my $r = s/^\s*\Q$lit\E(\s*[\w\:\-\*\.\/]*\s*){0,}//;
49.       my $m;
50.       $m = $&; $m =~ s/^\s*\Q$lit\E\s*//; $m =~ s/\s*$//;
51.       if ($hold == $count) { $bingo = 1; } elsif (!($m eq '')) { $bingo =
      2; } else { $bingo = 0; }
52.       $hold = -1;
53.
54.       if ($bingo == 1) {
55.           if ($m =~ /\s/) { ($key,$rest) = split(/\s/,$m,2); } else { $key
      = $m; undef($rest); }
56.           if (in_list($key,\@ServletAttr)) {
57.               $hash{$key} = (defined($rest)) ? $rest :  '' ;
```

```perl
58.                $flag = 1;
59.            } else {
60.                $flag = 0;
61.            }
62.        }
63.        elsif ( ($bingo == 2) && ($flag == 1) ) { $hash{$key} = $m; }
64.        print "[$count][$r][$m][$bingo] ++ [$flag][$key][$hash{$key}]\n" if
       $debug;
65.        return $r
66.    }
67.
68.    sub doliteral ($) {
69.        my $lit = $_[0];
70.        my $r = s/^\s*\Q$lit\E(\s*[\w\:\-\*\.\/]*\s*){0,}//;
71.        my $m;
72.        $m = $&; $m =~ s/^\s*\Q$lit\E\s*//; $m =~ s/\s*$//;
73.        if ($hold == $count) { $bingo = 1; } elsif (!($m eq '')) { $bingo =
       2; } else { $bingo = 0; }
74.        $hold = -1;
75.        if ($bingo == 1) {
76.            push(@L,$m);
77.            if ($m =~ /\s/) { ($key,$rest) = split(/\s/,$m,2); } else { $key
       = $m; undef($rest); }
78.            if (in_list($key,\@ServletAttr)) {
79.                $hash{$key} = (defined($rest)) ? $rest :  '' ;
80.            }
81.        }
82.        print "==========[$count][$r][$m][$bingo]==\n" if $debug;
83.        return $r
84.    }
85.
86.
87.    sub in_list {
88.    local $temp = shift;
89.    local *list = shift;
90.    my $e;
91.    foreach $e (@list) { if ($temp eq $e) { return 1; } }
92.    return 0;
93.    }
94.
95.    sub error ($) {
96.    my $msg = $_[0];
97.    warn "error: $msg: $_\n";
98.    }
99.
100.
101. sub doexpression {
102. do {
```

```
103.     if ($reset == 0) { $count++; $hold = $count; }
104.        do {
105.            if (doliteral '{') {
106.                $reset++;
107.                expression();
108.                $reset--;
109.                error "********* missing }" unless literal '}';
110.            }
111.        }
112. } while (/^\{/);
113. }
114.
115. sub expression {
116. do {
117.     if ($reset == 0) { $count++; $hold = $count; }
118.        do {
119.            if (literal '{') {
120.                $reset++;
121.                expression();
122.                $reset--;
123.                error "********* missing }" unless literal '}';
124.            }
125.        }
126. } while (/^\{/);
127. }
128.
129.
130.
131. sub strpool {  # Sample string pool of WSCP output to test ParseWscp
132. my $i = $_[0];
133. my @s;
134. ...
135. return $s[$i];
136. }
```

The ParseWscp provides you with a method to recursively parse WSCP output. The program has been targeted to parse the servlet information with the attributes shown on line 18. Of all of these attributes, we are most interested with a subset of them, shown on line 21. While the attributes are specific to a WSCP command, the parsing routine is generic and can be adapted to other outputs of WSCP.

Automating the Process

On the workstation where you installed WSCP to monitor your WebSphere Domain, you can set your script to automatically run on a daily basis by adding it to the daily cron job that runs every night. To do this on a UNIX system, use the crontab command. Consult your UNIX system documentation about how to add `cron` jobs. If you are using a current version of Linux, you can do this by adding a `cron` script (as in Listing 7-8) to the /etc/cron.daily/ directory.

Listing 7-8 *wasreport.cron*

```
#!/usr/bin/sh
renice +15 $$ > /dev/null 2>&1
/tools/wasreport.pl
```

Line 1 is a preprocessor that indicates that this is a shell script that is run with the /usr/bin/sh program. Line 2 makes the process get less priority while running on the system, and line 3 is the Perl program itself that is to be executed within the context of this shell. The first line of the Perl program wasreport.pl should be #!/usr/bin/perl, specifying that the program is to be processed with the /usr/bin/perl program. Of course, you assume that the Prl interpreter and the shell interpreter sh are located in /usr/bin/perl and /usr/bin/sh on your system, respectively.

E-Mailing the Reports

Having generated the reports as described previously, you can automatically send them out as e-mail attachments by using a Perl e-mailing program. The easiest way to perform this task is to install the Perl module MIME::Lite on your workstation. Listing 7-9 is a simple Perl script that reads a list of e-mails from a text file wasdomain.email and sends the report wasreport.txt as an attachment to the listed e-mail addresses.

Listing 7-9 *Automating e-mail with Perl/MIME::Lite*

```
#!/usr/bin/perl
use MIME::Lite;
open(FILE,"<wasdomain.email");
while ($line = <FILE>) {
    ($fname,$title,$email) = split(/,/,$line);
    chomp($email);
    email_out($email,$jobid);
}
sub email_out {
my  ($to_address) = $_[0];
my  ($jobid) = $_[1];
my $from_address = 'root';
$subject = "WAS DOMAIN Report: ";
$subject .= date;
$body = 'Please find attached WAS DOMAIN Report for: ';
```

```
$body .= date;
$body .= "\n";
#
# Create a multi-part message.
#
$msg = MIME::Lite->new(
        From => $from_address,
        To   => $to_address,
        Subject => $subject,
        Type => 'multipart/mixed' );
#
# Attach the main part of the message.
$msg->attach(
    Type => 'TEXT',
    Encoding => '7bit',
    Data => $body);
#
# Attach the report
#
$msg->attach(
    Type => 'application/text',
    Encoding => 'base64',
    Path => 'wasreport.txt',
    Filename => 'wasreport.txt');
# Convert message to text string.
$string = $msg->as_string();
# Send the message.
$msg->send();
}
```

You may need to add this program to the crontab, to run after the program that generates the wasreport.txt finishes running.

WSCP Message Codes

While executing a WSCP command, messages can be printed in the log files or on your terminal following a WSCP command. A WSCP message starts with code of the form WSCP*NNNN*[*s*], where *NNNN* is a number, and [*s*] is a severity one letter code. Such code is followed by a description causing a message to be printed. For example, the code WSCP0007E means "Editor not defined for this property," and WSCP0046' means "Invalid combination of options. Only one search method can be specified," and so on. For a list of the code and its specific meaning, consult the IBM info pages about WSCP messages. Chapter 23 gives you a thorough understanding of WAS components message codes.

Wrapping Up

The WebSphere Control Program (WSCP) provides a way to control WAS using textual commands. At the time of this writing, no further information was available on WSCP for WAS v4 besides which objects it is about to support.

Installing WSCP is fairly simple, and you are advised to install it on a separate workstation. Once installed, you can run WSCP from a command prompt or from within a UNIX script that you can tailor to your own needs.

No matter which version you are using, because WSCP is based on JACL, you can take advantage of WSCP to invoke Java methods to program WSCP in Java. However, in this chapter, you learned how to use WSCP with Perl to generate reports about your WAS configuration. You also learned how to use a wrapper to automate the process of periodically submitting these reports as e-mail attachments to a list of e-mail addresses.

A Quick and Essential Guide to Administering WAS

T his chapter is a lesson in administering WAS. It explains how to start, stop, and test its proper systemic functionality. Because WAS processes are based on one or more Java machines that are started at once, you will learn how to work with a group of processes. In addition, this chapter describes how to rebuild the WAS repository. Such an action is needed in a situation where the WAS repository is corrupt or if you wish to work with a different configuration repository than the one you have already created and configured in a first installation.

Chapters 3, 4, 7, and 8 provide the fundamentals to administering and setting up a successful environment for the WebSphere Application Server. As a reminder, WAS AE is WAS Advanced Edition v3.5 or v4, and WAS AEs is WAS Advanced Edition Single Server v4. When it is important in specific situations, the WAS edition or version is explicitly mentioned.

Starting, Stopping, and Testing WAS

With the new version of WAS AEs, you can easily start and stop WAS from the command prompt with a shell script (or a batch file on the NT platform). WAS AE does not offer a script such as stopServer.sh to halt WAS, but you can either use the administrative console to stop (and to start) an application server by right-clicking it and then clicking the Stop button, or the WSCP command prompt as in: wscp> Node stop /Node:node1/. However, in WAS AE v3.5 and v4, like any previous versions of WAS prior to v3.x, you may need to use the kill command to stop WAS Java machines running on a UNIX system. Generally, terminating the process in such an ungraceful way should not be a problem if you have configured WAS to save its data in a persistent database repository. Be aware that connected clients might lose their sessions if you have not configured database persistence for performance reasons.

Starting WAS

The WAS startup script is located in was_home/bin in the WebSphere installation directory. The script for WAS AE is startupServer.sh/bat; for WAS AEs, it's startServer.sh. Change to the WAS binary directory was_home/bin and execute the corresponding script for your WAS product. For example, if you installed WAS AEs, invoke the startServer.sh script at the command prompt:

```
# startServer.sh
```

You can also start WAS generically by issuing the command $STARTWAS, which is the environment variable that was introduced in chapters 3 and 4.

Figure 8-1 shows the WAS AEs startup messages that result from executing this command. The product starts with its default setup configuration preset in server-cfg.xml file.

You can override the startup behavior of this script by following the command with predefined options; edit the startServer.sh to view the list of options for this command. Chapter 23 shows you how to start this script with arguments to enable the debugging mode.

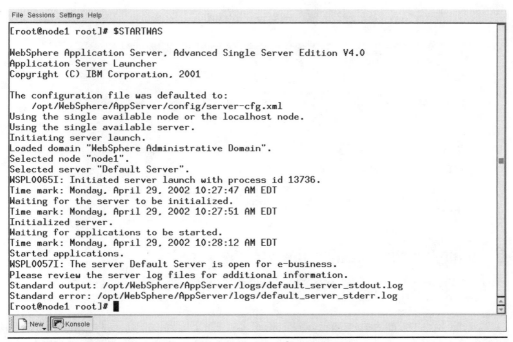

```
File  Sessions  Settings  Help
[root@node1 root]# $STARTWAS

WebSphere Application Server, Advanced Single Server Edition V4.0
Application Server Launcher
Copyright (C) IBM Corporation, 2001

The configuration file was defaulted to:
    /opt/WebSphere/AppServer/config/server-cfg.xml
Using the single available node or the localhost node.
Using the single available server.
Initiating server launch.
Loaded domain "WebSphere Administrative Domain".
Selected node "node1".
Selected server "Default Server".
WSPL0065I: Initiated server launch with process id 13736.
Time mark: Monday, April 29, 2002 10:27:47 AM EDT
Waiting for the server to be initialized.
Time mark: Monday, April 29, 2002 10:27:51 AM EDT
Initialized server.
Waiting for applications to be started.
Time mark: Monday, April 29, 2002 10:28:12 AM EDT
Started applications.
WSPL0057I: The server Default Server is open for e-business.
Please review the server log files for additional information.
Standard output: /opt/WebSphere/AppServer/logs/default_server_stdout.log
Standard error: /opt/WebSphere/AppServer/logs/default_server_stderr.log
[root@node1 root]# █

  New    Konsole
```

Figure 8-1   *Descriptive messages printed on startup of WAS AEs*

Stopping WAS

You stop WAS by stopping its Java machines. On UNIX prior to WAS v4, there is no single command or script that halts WAS from running; the only way to halt WAS processes is usually by killing its Java machines. WAS AEs offers the script stopServer.sh (or stopServer.bat on Windows NT) to halt WAS processes.

On WAS AE, use the `kill` command to kill all Java machines that are started by WAS. The section "Working with WAS Processes" later in this chapter shows you how to halt half of these processes.

On WAS AEs, issue the command $STOPWAS or simply change the directory to was_home/bin and invoke the stopServer.sh script:

```
# stopServer.sh
```

Upon completion of this command, messages are printed, as shown here.

```
X root@node1: /opt/WebSphere/AppServer/bin                    _ □ ×
[root@node1 bin]# stopServer.sh

WebSphere Application Server, Advanced Single Server Edition V4.0
WebSphere Application Server, Advanced Developer Edition V4.0
WebSphere Application Server, Advanced Edition V4.0
Runtime Utility Program
Copyright (C) IBM Corporation, 1997-2001

WSRU0025I: Loading configuration from file.
WSRU0028I: Using the specified configuration file:
     /opt/WebSphere/AppServer/config/server-cfg.xml
WSRU0029I: The diagnostic host name read as localhost.
WSRU0030I: The diagnostic port was read as 7000.
Stopping server.
The server was successfully stopped.
[root@node1 bin]# ▊
```

Stopping/Starting/Testing the HTTP Server

You can start or stop the HTTP server independently of WAS because it is not coupled with the WAS processes. Although WAS AEs is administered via an Internet browser (such as Netscape), it is possible to administer it without starting the HTTP Server.

For the IBM HTTP Server used in this book, you can start it, stop it, and monitor its status simply by changing to the ihs_home/bin directory and invoking the following command:

```
# apachectl [ start  |  stop  |   status ]
```

You have to choose one argument at a time. You can always find out if the HTTP server is running by looking at its processes with the ps command:

```
# ps -ef  |  grep  http
```

Finally, check if the plug-in for WAS is in place. To find the loadable module configuration in the file ihs_home/conf/httpd.conf, locate the identifier *ibm_app_server_http*. Usually, you should find a segment of lines similar to this:

```
LoadModule ibm_app_server_http_module
 /opt/WebSphere/AppServer/bin/mod_ibm_app_server_http.so
WebSpherePluginConfig /opt/WebSphere/AppServer/config/plugin-cfg.xml
AddModule mod_app_server_http
```

Testing WAS

You can use two quick methods to test whether WAS is operational:

▶ Put a request to a servlet through an Internet browser such as Netscape.

▶ Gather information via the WebSphere Control Program (WSCP). (See Chapter 7 for complete details on using WSCP.)

Testing by Invoking Servlet URLs

The first method requires that the HTTP Server be running. Invoke one of the sample servlets discussed in Chapter 6; for example, invoke the snoop servlet by typing its URL in the Netscape browser:

http://was.host.name/servlet/snoop

http://was.host.name/webapp/examples/showCfg

Figure 8-2 shows the output of the showCfg request using WAS v4. Because this testing method requires that the HTTP Server process be running, it tests whether client requests are being forwarded properly to WAS. Notice also that the output may be slightly different between WAS v3.5.5 and v4.

Using WAS v4, if a URL request fails for any reason, you can try to place the URL address to the HTTP transport port (9080 by default.) For example:

http://was.host.name:9080/servlet/snoop

If such a request is successful, then your WAS is operational and the problem may be either in the HTTP Server or in its plug-in.

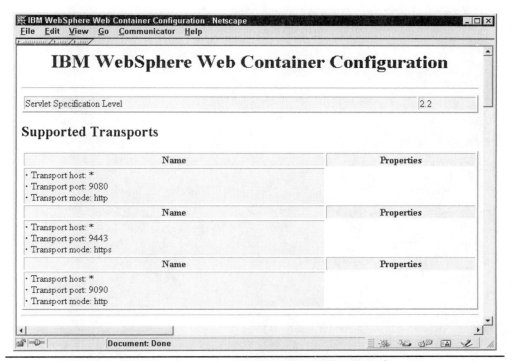

Figure 8-2   *Checking whether WAS is operational by invoking the showCfg request*

Testing by Gathering Information via WSCP

The second method does not require that the HTTP Server be running. Invoke the WSCP program to check on the integrity of the WebSphere Application Server and its database repository. Change the directory to was_home/bin and invoke the `wscp` command (on Windows NT, `wscp.bat`) as follows:

```
# wscp.sh
```

This invokes the WSCP interpreter to start a session.

Checking the Application Server and Its Data Source   Once the WSCP interpreter has been invoked, you will be presented with the command line of the interpreter, always starting with "wscp >". To list the nodes that are defined within the application server, issue the following WSCP command:

```
wscp>   ApplicationServer list
```

WSCP should reply by listing the nodes that are within the WAS Domain. (See Chapter 5 for the definition of WebSphere Domain.) A reply looks like this:

```
{/Node:populi/ApplicationServer:Default Server/}
{/Node:node2/ApplicationServer:Default Server/}
```

Next, check the integrity of the DataSource used as the WAS configuration repository:

```
wscp> DataSource list
```

WSCP replies with the DataSource name:

```
{/DataSource:Default DataSource/}
```

To get the information about the DataSource just retrieved, issue a `show` on the DataSource object:

```
wscp>DataSource show "/DataSource:Default DataSource/"
```

The command shows the default values set by WAS installation for the UDB DataSource:

```
{FullName {/DataSource:Default DataSource/}} {Name {Default
DataSource}} {ConnTimeout 120000} {DatabaseName WAS} {IdleTimeout
180000} {JDBCDriver {/JDBCDriver:Admin DB Driver/}} {MaxPoolSize 10}
{MinPoolSize 1} {OrphanTimeout 1800000}
```

This exactly reflects the DATASOURCE_TABLE as defined in the db2390.sql file located in the was_home/bin directory and as used by the WAS Advanced Edition v3.5.5 initial installation:

```
CREATE TABLE EJSADMIN.DATASOURCE_TABLE (
INSTANCE_ID                         VARCHAR(64) NOT NULL,
TYPE_ID                             VARCHAR(64) NOT NULL,
NAME                                VARCHAR(255) NOT NULL,
DB_NAME                             VARCHAR(255) NOT NULL,
MINPOOLSIZE                         INTEGER NOT NULL,
MAXPOOLSIZE                         INTEGER NOT NULL,
CONNTIMEOUT                         INTEGER NOT NULL,
IDLETIMEOUT                         INTEGER NOT NULL,
ORPHANTIMEOUT                       INTEGER NOT NULL,
PRIMARY KEY (INSTANCE_ID)) IN wasdb.EJSTB007;
```

Retrieving such information is important when tuning the WAS configuration database. Tuning a database is an administrative task and is mentioned in Chapter 25.

At this juncture, let's clarify the meaning of a data source and the way it is defined by its representative object: DataSource. In WAS v3 and later, the databases used for user applications are referred to as data sources and are mapped to DataSource objects, which make it possible to easily look them up and manage them atomically through the use of an application such as WSCP.

The database used by a WebSphere Domain to store the administrative repository is not considered a data source and therefore has no DataSource object, because WAS is not considered a user application. However, if you do not plan to have the administrative repository and the data source (or data sources) co-located to the same UDB server, then it is recommended that you create and add a dummy database on the same UDB server on which the administrative repository has been hosted. Such a dummy database allows you to add a DataSource object that you can monitor to check on the connectivity between the administrative server and the UDB server by using WSCP. The *Default DataSource* in the previous example can play such a role.

Checking on the Nodes That Are Defined in Your Domain   At least one node is defined in a WebSphere Domain. Use the WSCP Node object to list and gather information about the status of your node. For example, list the nodes defined in your WebSphere Domain,

```
wscp> Node list
```

which returns a list of all your nodes; then issue Node show <nodename> -all on each node:

```
wscp> Node show /Node:nodename/ -all
```

The illustration shows such an action taken on two nodes, and it reveals that one of the nodes lost contact.

```
X xterm                                                              _□×
# wscp.sh
wscp> Node list
/Node:populi/ /Node:node2/
wscp> Node show /Node:populi/ -all
{FullName /Node:populi/} {Name populi} {CurrentState Running} {DesiredState Runn
ing} {StartTime 10013517179917} {DependentClasspath {}} {DeployedJarDirectory /us
r/WebSphere/AppServer/deployedEJBs} {HostName populi} {HostSystemType ppc} {Inst
allRoot /usr/WebSphere/AppServer} {ProcessId 2954}
wscp>
wscp> Node show /Node:node2/ -all
{FullName /Node:node2/} {Name node2} {CurrentState {Lost Contact}} {DesiredState
 Running} {StartTime 0} {DependentClasspath {}} {DeployedJarDirectory /opt/IBMWe
bAS/deployedEJBs} {HostName Unknown} {HostSystemType Unknown} {InstallRoot Attri
buteNotSet} {ProcessId 0}
wscp> █
```

Checking for WAS Version and Release Level/Date

You can check for the WAS version and release date in a couple of ways. Identifying the WAS product release is crucial when communicating problems to IBM or your vendor. It is also important for the interoperability within a distributed environment when the WAS components are not localized on a single server. These are the three ways to check for the WAS version and release level:

▶ On WAS v3.5.x, use the well-known Help | About drop-down menu.

▶ On WAS v3.5.x or v4, use the product.xml file.

▶ Browse the activity.log file using the Log Analyzer.

To check the version/release on WAS v3.5, you simply select Administrative Console | Help | About. Figure 8-3 shows WAS v3.5 on AIX before and after applying Service Pack 4.

On WAS AEs v4, check the messages printed to your console upon invoking the startServer.sh or startServer.bat script. Refer to Figure 8-1 to see the startup messages of WAS AEs v4 on a Linux system.

If you want to get more accurate information about the WAS version, its build number, and date, you can edit the XML file was_home/properties/com/ibm/websphere/product.xml, as shown in Figure 8-4.

This information is important when you want to package and propagate WAS components in your distributed environment. Although the interoperability between the WAS components

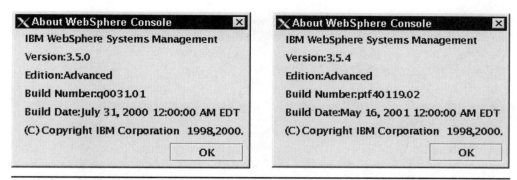

Figure 8-3   *Verifying the WAS version and patch level before and after patching the product*

is platform independent, it is highly dependent on the release (patches) and build date. In other words, there is no guarantee that a WAS v3.5 WSCP will operate against the repository of WAS v3.5.5, and vice versa.

```
File Sessions Settings Help
[root@node1 root]# cat $WAS_HOME/properties/com/ibm/websphere/product.xml
<?xml version="1.0" encoding="UTF-8"?>

<!DOCTYPE websphere SYSTEM "product.dtd">
<websphere>
        <appserver>
                <name>IBM WebSphere Application Server</name>
                <edition>
                        <value>AEs</value>
                        <name>Advanced Single Server Edition for Multiplatforms</name>
                </edition>

                <version>4.0.2</version>

                <extensions>
                </extensions>

                <build>
                        <number>a0150.05</number>
                        <date>12/18/2001</date>
                </build>

    <history>
        <event>
            <sqlTime>2002/03/14 18:17:11</sqlTime>
            <description/>
            <type>PTF</type>
            <containerType>Plugins,Console,Tools_Common,Client,Server_Common,Samples,J2EEClie
nt,Server,Deploytools,Samples_Common,Common,JTCClient</containerType>
            <installPath>/opt/WebSphere/AppServer/</installPath>
            <unInstallScript>/opt/WebSphere/AppServer/was40_ptf_2_backup.jar</unInstallScript
>
            <activityLog>/opt/WebSphere/AppServer/logs/was40_ptf_2.log</activityLog>
            <startingVersion>4.0.1</startingVersion>
            <endingVersion>4.0.2</endingVersion>
            <source>/tmp/was402/was40_aes_ptf_2.jar</source>
            <status>Successful</status>
            <errorMessage>0 errors were noted</errorMessage>
            <apar/>
            <pmr/>
            <developer/>
        </event>
```

New   Konsole

Figure 8-4   *Getting the product build and release date from the product.xml file*

Finally, the third way to check your WAS version is by using the Log Analyzer. You already installed it in Chapter 6. When you invoke the Log Analyzer and open the activity.log file, the record window in the right pane reveals the product version for some of the records, as you will see in Figure 8-7, later in the chapter.

Keeping Track of the Version of Your WAS Java Machine

Keep track of the Java machine version that WAS is using and let every developer working in your environment know about it. If possible, you should test developers' code with the same version and level of Java machine as the one used by WAS. To get the version of the Java machine that WAS is using, edit the script that sets up the WAS startup command line:

```
was_home/bin/setupCmdLine.sh
```

or for Windows NT:

```
was_home/bin/setupCmdLine.bat
```

Then locate the JAVA_HOME environment variable. This variable contains the location of the Java machine home directory used by WAS, and the Java machine is located in its bin directory. The version of the Java machine can be obtained by running the java command:

```
# java  -fullversion
```

Log Files and Startup Messages

Every time you start the WebSphere Application Server, information about the startup and the activity of its processes is logged in a set of files located in was_home/logs. The information in these log files might be valuable for troubleshooting and monitoring your WAS activities. The log files are of two kinds: a text file that is ASCII readable, and a binary file that needs to be viewed with a tool (showlog or Log Analyzer).

If WAS Fails to Start

If WAS does not start, check the reason for its startup failure in the log files, located by default in was_home/logs. Usually the standard output (stdout) and standard (stdrr) files are redirected to the log files. The following are the known files that can help you detect the reason for the WAS startup failure:

▶ **nanny.trace file**   Shows messages about starting the nanny process Java machine. This file might get through even though your database repository might be corrupt or inaccessible. If this file shows no symptoms, then look into the tracefile log.

▶ **tracefile log**   Shows the exceptions in case WAS cannot communicate with its UDB repository.

▶ **default_server_stderr.log file**   Is where the stderr file is directed with WAS v4. Recall that the setj.sh script (see Chapter 3) sets the environment variable WASLOG_STDOUT to point to this file.

▶ **default_server_stdout.log file**   Is where the stdout file is directed with WAS v4. For example, if the administrative session console times out, then a message is printed into this file. The setj.sh points to this file with the environment variable WASLOG_STDERR.

The startServer.sh script (startServer.bat on Windows NT) of WAS AEs v4 prints out message codes that you can cross-reference and better understand after reading Chapter 24. These messages have a mnemonic formed of four character prefixes followed by four to five alphanumeric characters, as you saw in Figure 8-1.

WAS v3.5 specifies the location and name of the standard error and I/O files (stdout, stdin, stderr) in its general server's property file of the administrative console: WebSphere Administrative Domain | Your Node Name | Default Server (top of Figure 8-5). As for WAS v4, the redirection of stderr and stdin/stdout is performed through the administrative console: WebSphere Administrative Domain | Nodes | *your-node-name* | Application Servers | Default Server | Process Definition | IO Redirect (bottom of Figure 8-5 for WAS AEs). The *default server* is the application server that is installed by default during your first-time WAS installation.

On the other hand, with WAS v4, a trace service is associated with each application server that you can enable or disable using the administrative console: WebSphere Administrative Domain | your_node_name | Application Servers | Default Server | Trace Service. As you can see, once a J2EE-compliant application server has been deployed under a WAS node, it can have its own tracing service enabled or disabled.

Formatting of the Log File

The information logged in a log file adheres to a specific format. For example, the entries in Listing 8-1 have been selected from the default_server_stdout.log file.

Listing 8-1   *stdout.log*

```
[01.08.21 18:42:56:214 EDT] 55465433 Server       A WSVR0025I: Creating temporary product license
[01.08.21 18:43:00:117 EDT] 55465433 DrAdminServer I WSVR0053I: DrAdmin available on port 7000
[01.08.21 18:43:00:204 EDT] 55465433 ResourceBinde I WSVR0049I: Binding Session Persistence datasource
as jdbc/Session
[01.08.21 18:43:08:901 EDT] 55465433 EJBEngine     I WSVR0037I: Starting EJB jar: Increment EJB Module
[01.08.21 18:43:09:049 EDT] 55465433 EJBEngine     I WSVR0037I: Starting EJB jar: Hello EJB Module
[01.08.21 18:43:09:217 EDT] 55465433 EJBEngine     I WSVR0037I: Starting EJB jar: Account And Transfer
EJB Module
[01.08.21 18:43:10:051 EDT] 55465433 EJBEngine     I WSVR0037I: Starting EJB jar: Customer Component
[01.08.21 18:43:11:395 EDT] 55465433 EJBEngine     I WSVR0037I: Starting EJB jar: Mail Component
```

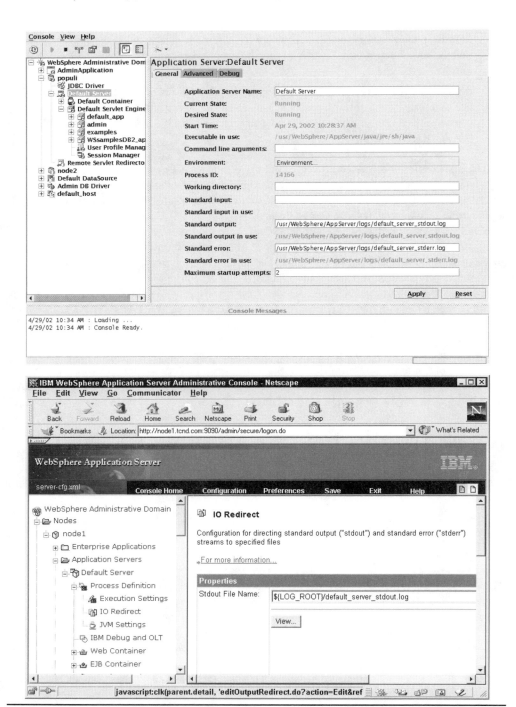

Figure 8-5 *Redirecting the standard I/O files to be used in WAS v3.5.5 (top) and AEs v4 (bottom)*

Each entry can be viewed as a record with the following information:

▶ **[Time Stamp]**   The full date and time zone given in millisecond precision

▶ **Thread ID**   The hash code of the thread issuing this message

▶ **Component**   An abbreviated name of the component issuing this message

▶ **Level**   A one-character symbol designating the level of the message.
   The level is one of the following symbols:

   ▶ > Entry to a method

   ▶ < Exit a method

   ▶ A Audit

   ▶ W Warning

   ▶ X Error

   ▶ E Event

   ▶ D Debug

   ▶ T Terminate exiting the process

   ▶ F Fatal termination, exiting the process

   ▶ I Information

▶ **Symbolic Message**   A message formed by a four-character acronym followed by four digits number and a severity character. Chapter 24 discusses how to interpret and capture the symbolic messages in the graphical console of WASLED™/WASMON™.

The first entry in Listing 8-1 is an audit message issued by the thread 55465433 of the WebSphere Application Server run-time component. The AIX command to list statistics on processes and their threads is `pstat`. On another UNIX platform, use the `top` command if available, which gives you a less detailed view of processes and threads. Chapter 25 discusses threads in more detail, including their systemic consumption and how to count them.

The activity.log File

Because activity.log is a binary file, it cannot be viewed with an ASCII editor. Its default size is 1MB, but it can be changed by editing its properties file: `was_home/properties/logging.properties`.

Rotating the activity.log File

When the activity.log file reaches its maximum size, it wraps around. If you decide to keep every single log, you should rotate the file periodically. Generally, you achieve this log rotation on UNIX by setting a cron job. On Linux you use `logrotate`, which is run normally

---

Be Cautious When Editing Properties Files

When editing properties files, be careful not to add spaces between an entry and the equal sign. For instance, examine the following two lines:

```
com.ibm.ws.ras.ActivityLogSize=3096
com.ibm.ws.ras.ActivityLogSize= 3096
```

The first line is a valid entry, but the second line is not.

---

as a daily cron job. The `logrotate` command allows automatic rotation, removal, and mailing of log files. Edit the /etc/logrotate.conf and make sure that the directory /etc/logrotate.d has been included. To use an alternate directory, refer to the manual pages of the logrotate command. Edit and save the following waslogrotate configuration file to the directory /etc/logrotate.d:

```
"/opt/WebSphere/AppServer/logs/activity.log" /opt ... {
   rotate 5
   mail wasgroup1@ibmsos.com
   size=500k
   sharedscripts
   postrotate
      /sbin/killall  -HUP   java
   endscript
```

Deleting the activity.log File

If you need to delete a log file while the application server is running, never remove (unlink) its associated log files with the `rm` command. Use the null device to empty the file. This deletion method must be applied to all WAS log files. For example, to empty the activity.log file, issue this command:

```
# cat /dev/null  >  /opt/WebSphere/AppServer/logs/activity.log
```

Using such a command is important in case you don't want to interrupt the logging process that is appended to the open file activity.log.

Using the showlog Script to Browse Through the activity.log File

To view the file, invoke the showlog script (or showlog.bat on Windows NT) and follow it with the name of the log file. The showlog script is located in the was_home/bin directory.

For example, the following command uses the UNIX pipe to direct the activity log contents
to the file /tmp/was-activity.txt:

```
# showlog    /opt/WebSphere/AppServer/logs/activity.log > /tmp/was-activity.txt
```

Figure 8-6 shows showlog/usr/WebSphere/AppServer/logs/
activity.log | more when directed to the standard output (or your console.)

Using waslogbr to Analyze the activity.log File

The Log Analyzer is now shipped with WAS v4.0.2. Users of WAS v3.5.5 can download
the WebSphere Log Analyzer from the IBM site (refer to Chapter 6 for its installation) and

Figure 8-6   *The showlog script of the activity.log file directed to STDOUT*

install it on AIX, Windows NT, or Sun Solaris. Invoke it by issuing was_home/bin/waslogbr. From the drop-down menu, select File | Open and open the activity.log file.

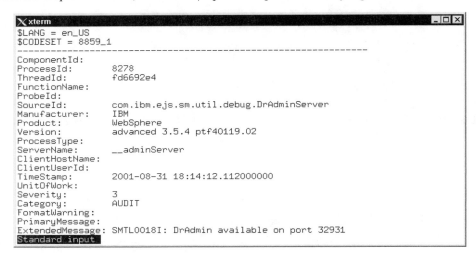

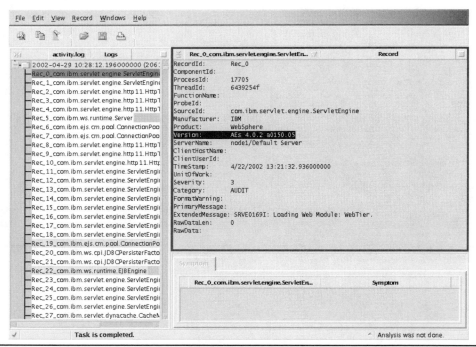

Figure 8-7   *Viewing the records of the activity.log file in the Log Analyzer*

Figure 8-7 shows the activity log records as seen in the Log Analyze that is shipped with WAS AEs v4.0.2.

Working with WAS Processes

As a WAS developer, you should be aware of the hierarchical structure of the processes the WebSphere Application Server starts. Usually, these are Java processes or Java threads that can be identified by their number. You may be writing and testing code on your WAS workstation and need to monitor these processes and threads started by WAS. The following sections briefly explain how to work with these processes.

Demystifying WAS Processes

WAS programmers should be aware that when WAS AE starts on UNIX, a watchdog process—accurately named the *Nanny process*—is started. The Nanny is a Java machine by itself that is started by the startup script to launch an application server.

Use the `ps` command to dump the state of all Java machine processes:

```
# ps -ef | grep WebSp
```

The hierarchy of the Java machine processes started by WAS is best seen when presented as a tree. On Linux, there are two ways to list the processes as a tree representation: by using the `pstree` command: `# pstree -p processnumber`; or by using the `ps` command with the option --forest, and the -t option to specify the pts where WAS started: `# ps -t pts/ 14 --columns=4092 --forest`.

Because the output of the `ps` command is limited to the terminal width, you can override this with the use of the --columns option; this is the case only for Linux. On AIX, pipe the output and `grep` it to overcome this limitation *(ps -ef | grep WebS)*.

For example, having started the WAS Java machine process with startupServer.sh process 12143, use the `pstree` command to reveal the processes and threads tree hierarchy of the Java machine(s) that are snowballed by the startupServer.sh process. Listing 8-2 is the result of running the `pstree` command.

Listing 8-2   *Reply of the command* `pstree -p 12143`

```
startupServer.sh(12143)---java(12147)---java(12151)-+-java(12152)
The tree has been truncated and continued on the next line to make it visible
for the processes cascading down the processes 12152 and 12161.
...---java(12151)-+-java(12152)
                  |-java(12153)
                  |-java(12154)
                  `-java(12155)---java(12156)---java(12160)-+-java(12161)
                                                            |-java(12162)
                                                            |-java(12163)
```

```
                                         |-java(12164)
                                         |-java(12165)
                                         |-java(12166)
                                         |-java(12167)
                                         |-java(12168)
                                         |-java(12170)
                                         |-java(12172)
                                         |-java(12173)
                                         |-java(12174)
                                         |-java(12175)
                                         |-java(12176)
                                         |-java(12178)
                                         |-java(12179)
                                         |-java(12180)
                                         |-java(12181)
                                         `-java(12182)
```

end of pstree listing

To understand what these processes are for and how they depend on each other, think in terms of how a WebSphere Domain starts up and operates its Java machines. In Chapter 5, the WebSphere Domain was defined as a bunch of nodes operating together, where each node has at least one application server. At the root of each WebSphere Domain, there is a Nanny process that is keeping the application server Java process in perpetuity.

The acronym *AS* stands for application server, and the term *lightweight process* depicts a thread. Listing 8-2 is read: startupServer.sh process 12143 started the Nanny process 12147, which started the Nanny lightweight process 12151, which started the Nanny lightweight processes (or the four threads) 12152, 12153, 12154, and 12155. Next, process 12155 is the last Nanny lightweight process in the chain that is watching the Application Server (AS) started with process 12156. AS 12156 starts AS 12160. AS 12160 starts the threads for AS 12161 through 12182.

While the analysis of these processes is taking place on Linux, you might wonder what is happening here. To find out, you need to understand how IBM manages the threading of the Java machine on Linux. In implementing Java threads, IBM has shifted from supporting the green threads approach[1] to using the native thread that is tied to the underlying kernel thread. This way, Java Virtual Machine (JVM) code initially written for the AIX platform can be shared and made available on Linux.

There are several advantages of having Java threads implemented this way: Multiple kernel threads can be executing concurrently in a Java machine, hence taking advantage of an SMP system; It is possible to adjust the efficiency of thread execution by using system commands that act at the OS level (when available); The set of OS thread-enabled libraries can be used directly without any extra layer to wrap calls into the library; Each Java thread appears to the OS as a separate kernel thread, making it possible to map per-thread system

---

[1] The green threads are defined at the user-level and are not mapped to multiple kernel threads by the operating system. Therefore parallel architecture machines cannot take advantage of using them.

objects for each Java thread (a one-to-one mapping). Therefore, it is possible to have multiple instances (such as connections to a data source) of per-Java-threads system objects.

While AIX allows several kernel threads to be packaged inside a process, Linux uses the system call clone() (a special fork()) to start a child process in the same address space as its parent. The Linux threading library uses the system call to present an abstract threading interface for the Linux user. Therefore, the Java threads in the IBM Java machine for Linux are implemented as user processes, and you use the ps command to list the process ID and the status of such threads.

Acting on a Group of Processes

To control a group of Java machines with a single command from the prompt, UNIX provides the xargs command, which can automate an action to be taken on a group of objects. Use xargs as a final component of a pipe to append each item that it reads from standard input to the UNIX command given as its argument.

Renicing the WAS Java Machines

Now that you know that xargs can be tailored with grep to act on a group of items, you can use it to renice the WAS Java processes:

```
# ps -ef | grep "WebSphere\/AppServer\/java" | awk '{ print $2 }' | xargs renice +5
```

The meaning of *renice* is in the word itself: to make a more or less nice process. A nice process has a positive number, and it is said to be nice because it runs with less importance than another and requires less attention from the operating system. It can also run less nicely with a negative number, increasing its importance higher in the processes chain. Dedicating the whole CPU time for WAS Java machine processes does not make WAS run faster. Other subsystem processes need to be satisfied that WAS processes might be waiting for.

Killing the WAS Java Machines

Sometimes the WAS AEs v4 stop script does not terminate all Java machines gracefully. Also, WAS Advanced Edition does not have a stop script to terminate WAS processes. To terminate all Java machines on UNIX, use the xargs command to redirect all processes' numbers to the kill command:

```
# ps -ef | grep "WebSphere\/AppServer\/java" | awk '{print $2}' | xargs kill -9
```

The /etc/services Ports

Port numbers range from 1024 to 64,000 and are usually maintained in a flat text file (as the services database), located in /etc/services on UNIX or in nt_home\winnt\system32\drivers\etc\services on WinNT. If a service is listed in the /etc/services file, that does not mean that the server will activate such a service. On UNIX, services are defined in their inetd.conf configuration file. On AIX, the file is /etc/inetd.conf, and on the current version of Linux used in this book, the file is /etc/xinetd.conf.

NOTE

Once you decide on a set of ports to be used with your application server, edit the services file and add in these ports. This file is a useful reference for troubleshooting the network.

You can monitor and report the network status of ports pertaining to a server in a number of ways. The simplest method, no doubt, is to use the `netstat` command. The netstat client places a request to inetd (listening on port 15), which in turn invokes the netstat server to query the server network status and ship the output to the requesting client.

The Default Ports Used by WAS

At any time, a number of ports are used by each application server: the bootstrap port 900, a randomly assigned port for the ORB listener port for RMI-IIOP, the Location Service Daemon (LSD) port 9000, the HTTP transport port 9080, the internal HTTP transport secure port 9443, the dynamically assigned port 7000 for the DrAdmin, and port 2012 for the Object Level Trace (OLT) and Debugger.

Use the `netstat` command to determine if your server is listening to any particular port. For example, port 9090 is the default port for the administrative server AEs, and to determine if this is the port it is listening on, issue this command:

```
# netstat -nae | grep 9090
```

In the section "Monitoring the Ports" later in this chapter, you will learn how to monitor this port. However, if you run `netstat` and find out that the port is listening, this ensures that the port is configured properly but does not guarantee that it is accessible. Therefore, you need to use more than `netstat` to check on a port's accessibility.

Sometimes, developers have trouble testing their code due to a port configuration problem; in this case, a system administrator should ask developers to test the accessibility of the port. A quick and simple way to check on port accessibility is by using `telnet`. For example, when an enterprise bean servlet (acting as a client application) fails with a generated exception *COMM_FAILURE,* the developer has to make sure the administrative server host is running and accessible through the bootstrap port. If the port is kept to its default setting of 900 and the application server is running on node1.tcnd.com, the following command should return a successful *Connected to node1.tcnd.com.* Press CTRL and type] to get the telnet prompt:

```
# telnet node1.tcnd.com 900
```

Enter **quit** to end the session.

Chapter 26 introduces, through the use of a supervisor, a more administrative way to monitor whether or not a port or a set of ports are active on a server.

Debugging Default Ports

Port 2102 is the default Object Level Debugger (OLT) port, and port 7777 is the default Java Debug Wire Protocol (JDWP) port. These two ports can be overridden at the command prompt of the startServer.sh script (or startServer.bat for Windows NT). The administrator can change these default ports to accommodate developers who use the default command without any arguments, by editing the WAS startup script and changing the default ports to whichever free port is desired:

```
DEFAULT_OLT_PORT=2102
DEFAULT_JDWP_PORT=7777
```

Monitoring the Ports

Use the `netstat` command to monitor the activity of a port on your system. But before using this utility, read the documentation or man pages on how to use this command on your system. The `netstat` options vary between different platforms; for example, the option -c is used for continuous show on Linux, it used is to show the statistics of the network buffer cache on AIX 4.3.2 or later, and it is not available on Windows NT. Chapter 25 discusses in depth how to interpret the `netstat` output and how to use the `netstat` command by wrapping it in a Perl script to collect network statistics. For now, consider this command:

```
# netstat -naec  |  grep 9090
```

When run on Linux, such a command gathers continuous information on port 9090. In the command output, the hostname's IP addresses are numeric (not being resolved because of the -n option). Listing 8-3 shows the output of the command when a Netscape browser (installed on a client machine with IP address 66.51.9.149) requested to start the administrative console of a WAS v4 machine running on server 66.51.9.151.

In this example, the command reveals that port 9090 on server 66.51.9.151 is changing states while connected to the foreign addresses.

Initially, WAS is started with a configuration for the administrative port listening on port 9090 as it is defined in the was_home/config/server-cfg.xml configuration file. The following snippet of the server-cfg.xml file shows the many ports preallocated by the default WAS AEs v4 installation:

Listing 8-3   *HTTP transport port in server-cfg.xml*

```
<virtualHosts xmi:id="VirtualHost_1" name="default_host">
    <aliases xmi:id="HostAlias_1" hostname="*" port="9080"/>
    <aliases xmi:id="HostAlias_2" hostname="*" port="9443"/>
    <aliases xmi:id="HostAlias_3" hostname="*" port="80"/>
```

```
      <aliases xmi:id="HostAlias_4" hostname="*" port="443"/>
...
  </virtualHosts>
  <virtualHosts xmi:id="VirtualHost_2" name="admin_host">
    <aliases xmi:id="HostAlias_5" hostname="*" port="9090"/>
  </virtualHosts>
...
  <transports xmi:type="applicationserver:HTTPTransport" xmi:id="HttpTransport_3"
hostname="*" port="9090" external="false">
    <properties xmi:id="SystemProperty_6" name="MaxConnectBacklog" value="511"/>
...
  </transports>
```

It is usually good practice to show developers how to monitor ports this simple way, especially when it comes to testing code that allocates dynamic ports; such is the case with RMI-IIOP.

Consider Listing 8-4 which shows the output of the netstat command revealing all these lines where port 9090 appear.

Listing 8-4   *port 9090 activity*

```
[root@node1 /root]# netstat -naec | grep 9090
        LocalAddress           Foreign Address      State         User Inode
tcp 0 0 0.0.0.0:9090           0.0.0.0:*            LISTEN        0    28388
tcp 0 0 0.0.0.0:9090           0.0.0.0:*            LISTEN        0    28388
tcp 0 0 0.0.0.0:9090           0.0.0.0:*            LISTEN        0    28388
tcp 0 0 66.51.9.151:9090       66.51.9.149:4805     ESTABLISHED 0    180747
tcp 0 0 0.0.0.0:9090           0.0.0.0:*            LISTEN        0    28388
tcp 0 0 66.51.9.151:9090       66.51.9.149:4805     FIN_WAIT2     0    0
tcp 0 0 66.51.9.151:9090       66.51.9.149:4807     TIME_WAIT     0    0
tcp 0 0 66.51.9.151:9090       66.51.9.149:4806     FIN_WAIT2     0    0
tcp 0 0 66.51.9.151:9090       66.51.9.149:4808     FIN_WAIT2     0    0
tcp 0 0 66.51.9.151:9090       66.51.9.149:4810     ESTABLISHED 0    180925
tcp 0 0 0.0.0.0:9090           0.0.0.0:*            LISTEN        0    28388
tcp 0 0 66.51.9.151:9090       66.51.9.149:4805     TIME_WAIT     0    0
tcp 0 0 66.51.9.151:9090       66.51.9.149:4807     TIME_WAIT     0    0
tcp 0 0 66.51.9.151:9090       66.51.9.149:4806     FIN_WAIT2     0    0
tcp 0 0 66.51.9.151:9090       66.51.9.149:4808     FIN_WAIT2     0    0
tcp 0 0 66.51.9.151:9090       66.51.9.149:4810     FIN_WAIT2     0    0
tcp 0 0 0.0.0.0:9090           0.0.0.0:*            LISTEN        0    28388
tcp 0 0 66.51.9.151:9090       66.51.9.149:4805     TIME_WAIT     0    0
tcp 0 0 66.51.9.151:9090       66.51.9.149:4807     TIME_WAIT     0    0
tcp 0 0 66.51.9.151:9090       66.51.9.149:4806     TIME_WAIT     0    0
```

```
tcp 0 0 66.51.9.151:9090    66.51.9.149:4808 TIME_WAIT    0    0
tcp 0 0 66.51.9.151:9090    66.51.9.149:4810 FIN_WAIT2    0    0
tcp 0 0 0.0.0.0:9090        0.0.0.0:*        LISTEN       0    28388
tcp 0 0 66.51.9.151:9090    66.51.9.149:4805 TIME_WAIT    0    0
tcp 0 0 66.51.9.151:9090    66.51.9.149:4807 TIME_WAIT    0    0
```

Use `netstat` before and after you take an action that would activate or change the status of a port; then you can differentiate between the outputs of your `netstat` command to understand what has happened. For example, to find out what is happening portwise when you put a request in for the showCfg servlet or snoop servlet (refer to Chapter 6 for these examples), follow these steps:

1. At a first instance, run `netstat -e`.

2. From the browser, put a request in for the URL, http://was.host.name/servlet/snoop.

3. Subsequently, run the `netstat -e` command again.

Differentiating between the outputs of the `netstat` command in steps 1 and 3, which is summarized in Listing 8-5, reveals the following port activities for WAS v4 running on the server node1.tcnd.com:

▶ When the browser running on *jade* put the request to showCfg to node1, node1 opened an HTTP connection to the foreign host *jade* on port 3752.

▶ The HTTP transport port 9080 on node1 established a local connection to itself (node1) on port 34547.

▶ At its turn, port 34547 established a connection to node1 to return the request.

This simple analysis reveals that WAS and the HTTP servers are running on the same machine. Having multiple requests on a server on which WAS and the HTTP Server are installed will stress out the server with socket connections, because each request consumes at least three connections. If you move the HTTP Server to another server, you will save at least one connection per request.

Listing 8-5   `netstat -e` *output before and after invoking showCfg*

```
Before invoking the showCfg URL
Pr Rcv Snd Local Address  Foreign Address State      User   Inode
tcp 0  0  localhost:33490 localhost:900   ESTABLISHED root   28285
tcp 57 0  hacmp1:34519    service2:eye    CLOSE_WAIT  root   178732
tcp 3  0  node1:900       node1:34226     CLOSE_WAIT  root   163104
tcp 0  0  node1:9090      jade:3741       TIME_WAIT   root   0
tcp 0  0  localhost:900   localhost:33490 ESTABLISHED root   28282
```

Upon the invocation of the URL

```
Pr Rcv Snd Local Address   Foreign Address   State        User    Inode
tcp 0   0   localhost:33490 localhost:900     ESTABLISHED  root    28285
tcp 57  0   hacmp1:34519    service2:eye      CLOSE_WAIT   root    178732
tcp 0   0   node1:http      jade:3752         TIME_WAIT    root    0
tcp 3   0   node1:900       node1:34226       CLOSE_WAIT   root    163104
tcp 0   0   node1:9090      jade:3741         TIME_WAIT    root    0
tcp 0   0   localhost:9080  localhost:34547   ESTABLISHED  root    185874
tcp 0   0   localhost:900   localhost:33490   ESTABLISHED  root    28282
tcp 0   0   localhost:34547 localhost:9080    ESTABLISHED  nobody  186156
```

The Administrative Configuration Files

In this section, for the sake of explanation, WAS AE will refer to any of WAS Advanced Edition v3.5 and v4, and WAS AEs will refer to WAS Advanced Edition Single Server v4. Also, the administrative console is used to describe the graphical console of any of these WAS versions, whether it is started through a separate graphical application or through a web browser.

Starting WAS invokes the Java machine with an initial configuration that is dictated in its own configuration files. These files differ between WAS AE and WAS AEs. At any time, you can locate these files in one of these directories:

▶ **was_home/bin for admin.config**   Typically for WAS AE only

▶ **was_home/config for server-cfg.xml, admin-server-cfg.xml, and template-server-cfg.xml**   Typically for WAS AEs

The *.xml configuration files are usually updated using the WAS administrative console (also known as web console) from the browser by pointing to the server that is running WAS, e.g., http://node1.tcnd.com:9090/admin. When a user logs in to the administrative console and makes a change, WAS creates a home directory in a temp directory (e.g., was_home/temp), where it maintains backup and timeout copies of the changed administrative *.xml files.

Although it is possible to use the administrative console to make the changes in the admin.config file, it is good practice to edit it and browse over it. Such manual editing will become necessary in some situations, as you will learn in Chapter 17 when configuring the IBM Session Persistence.

To invoke the WAS AE Administrative Console, either change the directory to was_home/bin and run adminclient.sh, or invoke the startup script by typing the preset environment variable $ADMINCLIENT on the command prompt; this starts a console, as shown in Figure 8-8. As for WAS AEs v4, you start the console through Netscape by using this URL: http://was.serve.name:9090/ admin.

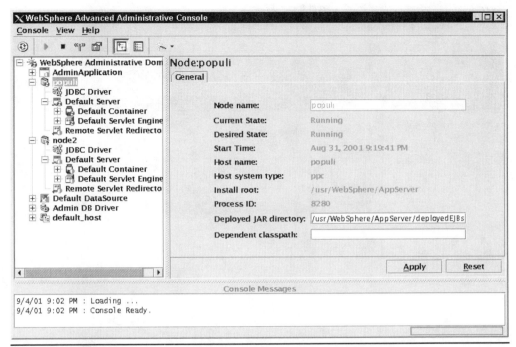

Figure 8-8   *The WAS AE v3.5 Administrative Console*

After checking your credentials, the browser displays the WAS AEs Administrative Console (see Figure 8-9.) Remember that port 9090 is the default port preset by the WAS first-time installation. This port can be changed.

The WAS Startup Java Machine

Chapter 3 discussed the setj.sh script that sets up the developer environment. Once again, the aim is to have control over the Java machine that gears the WAS components and the development environment. Most of the WAS commands are script files that execute as a first command the setupCmdLine.sh script (or call setupCmdLine.bat batch file) to properly set up the environment. It is this setupCmdLine file that sets up the environment for the Java machine to the WAS scripts or commands. Therefore, if you plan to point to another Java machine distribution, back up and

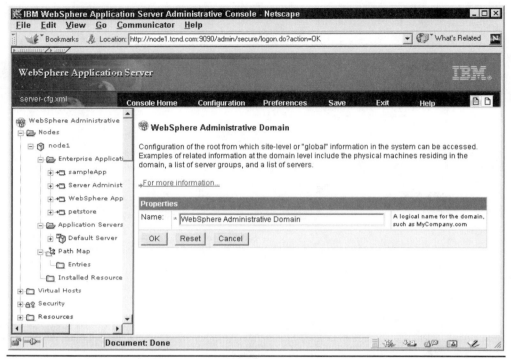

Figure 8-9   *The WAS AEs Adminstrative Consloe*

then edit the setupCmdLine.sh script (or setupCmdLine.bat) and make the appropriate changes. In addition, with WAS v3.5.5, you may need to edit the startupServer.sh file (or startupServer.bat) to modify the entries that point to the Java machine.

Java Machine Parametric Tune-Up

The WAS Java machine can be tuned by editing the was_home/bin/admin.config file. When WAS starts, the Java machine is invoked with a set of arguments that define the behavior and performance of the JVM. These arguments define the heap size, the garbage-collection behavior, the Java stack size, the native thread stack size, and the enabling of the Just-In-Time (JIT) compiler. To find a list of these arguments available on your operating system, invoke java at the command prompt with the -X option:

```
# java  -X
```

Table 8-1 shows the arguments that can be passed to a Java machine.

NOTE

The -nojit argument is for the Java 1.1 run-time command. The Java 2 run-time command takes -Djava.compiler=NONE or the exported environment variable JAVA_COMPILER=NONE. For example, to turn JIT off on the Linux platform, export the JAVA_COMPILER=NONE, and then issue `java -fullversion` *to check whether the JIT option is on or off. In your code, use java.lang.Compiler.disable() and java.lang.Comiler.enable().*

Disabling the Just-In-Time Compiler

Sometimes you need to disable the Just-In-Time (JIT) compiler. Turning it off may solve a number of problems.

To perform this task, first disable JIT from the WebSphere Application Server startup configuration by appending the property java.compiler=NONE to the arguments of the Nanny process. Remember, the Nanny process is started as a Java machine, and its argument list is in the admin.config file. For example, the following line of the admin.config file shows how you can disable the Nanny process's JIT:

```
com.ibm.ejs.sm.util.process.Nanny.adminServerJvmArgs= -mx128m
        -Djava.compiler=NONE
```

Next, disable JIT for every application server that is listed in the administrative console. The command-line argument passed to the Java machine of *each* application server should be appended with -Djava.compiler=NONE.

Because the administrative console runs independently from the Nanny process and its application servers, you do not need to disable JIT for the administrative console.

Argument	Notes
-ms	Memory allocated for the heap as the JVM starts. Defaults to 32MB, set it within the range [0.10 * mx, 0.25 mx].
-mx	Maximum memory allocated for the heap by the JVM for dynamically allocated objects and arrays. Usually 0.25 * physical memory.
-oss	Size of the stack allocated for each Java thread.
-ss	Size of the native code stack allocated for each thread.
-noasyncgc	
-noclassgc	Enables more class reuse by turning off the class garbage collection. The default for classgc is on.
-verbose	The Java machine prints a message each time it loads a class.
-nojit	Disables the JIT compiler. This is not available on AIX, Solaris, and Linux. However, for the UNIX platform, use the method described in the following note to disable it.

Table 8-1   *Arguments That Can Be Passed to a Java Machine*

Select a Heap Size That Fits Within the Physical Memory Constraint

Try to select a size for the heap that fits in the physical memory. When all the real memory has been consumed, the operating system starts to swap pages to the hard disk: a costly operation. You can get the physical memory on your machine by issuing the appropriate command:

▶ On Linux, issue the `free` command.

▶ On AIX, use the `lsattr` command. For example, first get the memory device name with `lsdev -C -c memory` and then issue `lsattr -E -lmem0`, assuming the memory device is mem0. Alternatively, you can issue the command `lsattr -E -l sys0 -a realmem`.

▶ On NT, choose this option: CTRL-ALT-DELETE | Task Manager | Performance. Alternatively (assuming you have the MKS Toolkit installed), you can issue the command: `sysinf memory`.

Managing the WAS Repository

Using WAS AEs, you can alter the server configuration data simply by first stopping the application server, altering the server-cfg.xml file with another copy, and then restarting the application server. While this is true for this single-server version of the product, it does not hold for its advanced edition.

After starting WAS AE for the first time, the configuration repository (or administrative repository) is created. This is a set of tables that is managed by a Universal Database (UDB) server, as seen in Chapter 4. You may want to recreate the configuration repository, or you may want to switch to another repository when working with WAS. This section briefly shows you how to recreate the WAS repository.

Dropping and Recreating the WAS Repository

If you want to recreate from scratch the database tables of the administrative repository, you need to reconfigure some of the properties of the WAS admin.config file. If you are practicing with WAS on your workstation, it is worth playing around to recreate the database.

CAUTION

Recreating the database as described in the following steps will delete your previous data in the database unless you choose to replicate it or rebuild a database administrative repository by another name.

Follow these steps to recreate a new administrative repository on a DB2 server:

1. Shut down the administrative server.

2. Drop the database. Be careful: all data will be lost here, so you may need to do a backup. On machine B, db2inst1 performs the step: *# db2 drop database WAS02.*

3. Recreate a new database. It is best to use the same name for your database as the previous one that you dropped, because this will save you tweaking time with the WAS property files. However, if you change the database name, you need to make the change in the dbUrl property as well. Remember to increase the APPLHEAPSZ for a DB2 database. For example, log on to machine B as the db2inst1 account and do the following:

```
# db2 create database WASDATA
# db2 update db cfg for WAS02 using APPLHEAPSZ 256
```

4. Edit and make changes in the was_home/bin/admin.config property file. For WAS v3.5, make the following changes in the admin.config file:

```
install.initial.config=true
com.ibm.ejs.sm.adminServer.dbInitialized=false
```

For WAS v4, make the following change in the admin.config file:

```
com.ibm.ejs.sm.adminServer.createTables=true
```

5. Restart WAS.

Once you restart WAS, the administrative repository database will be recreated, and the value of the Boolean flag that you set in the fourth step will be reverted.

Properties of the Repository

Because WAS v4 supports a variety of database brands, the dbUrl (com.ibm.ejs.sm .adminServer.dbUrl) settable property in the admin.config file has been replaced with a more extended data source property that varies with each database brand. Table 8-2 summarizes the properties by database brand.

WAS v3.5 uses this property to specify the database URL of the repository. You can alternate between databases by specifying different URLs of databases. For instance, a valid DB2 URL is of the form jdbc:db2:dbname_repository.

Dealing with the Sybase UNICODE Character Set

When using Sybase as the administrative database repository, the setConnectionProperties() for the WAS Java machine can access property names listed in the form PROPERTY_NAME=value;PROPERTY_NAME=value by getting them from the admin.config property directive:

```
com.ibm.ejs.sm.adminServer.connectionProperties
```

Database Brand	Settable Properties
DB2	serverName (only for iSeries toolbox driver; otherwise, not required)
Informix	ifxIFXHOST serverName portNumber informixLockModeWait
Merant	serverName portNumber disable2Phase
Oracle	url
Sybase	serverName connectionProperties

Table 8-2   *Data Source Properties by Database Brand*

You need to set up the connectionProperties to point to the appropriate character set; otherwise, annoying exception messages will be printed.

For example, by supplying the following entry,

```
com.ibm.ejs.sm.adminServer.connectionProperties=CHARSET_CONVERTER_
CLASS=com.sybase.jdbc2.utils.TruncationConverter.
```

the exception messages are suppressed when dataSource.getConnection() is executed.

Common Administrative Practices

There are couple of administrative tasks that are handy and should be easily realized by any reader running WAS on his workstation. They are common because they can be applied to any WAS versions. You can quickly perform the following handy administrative practices in a couple of minutes: perform a diagnostic with showConfig, check the configuration repository, monitor the size and checksum of deployable .jar files, and finally, back up the WAS tree.

NOTE

So far all WAS versions, including the latest v4, are not tightly bound to the strict IBM registration, known as IBM License Use Management (LUM); this is good because it frees you from the complexity of managing the product.

A Quick WAS Diagnostic: Invoking showCfg

One of the quickest ways to check if your WAS Web Container (or Servlet Engine) is functional is by invoking the showCfg servlet. This servlet is known as the IBM WebSphere

Servlet Engine Configuration and is automatically installed and configured during the first-time installation of both WAS v3.5 and WAS v4. This servlet does not check whether the WAS data sources are accessible, but it ensures that your servlet engine is running. You invoke this servlet through its URL: http://*was.host.name/webapp/examples*/showCfg where *was.host.name* is the machine on which the application server is running, *webapp* is the virtual directory of the web application loader, and *examples* is the application web path.

Finally, *showCfg* is the servlet itself (sometimes referred to as the servlet URL) whose actual byte code name is *ServletEngineConfigDumper.class.* This class is defined in the web module examples.war that is part of the EAR sampleApp.ear preinstalled by WAS. The URI of the web module examples.war has a context root /webapp/examples,[2] which should also be a part of the URIs grouping in the plugin-cfg.xml file.

Checking on the WAS Database Repository

A quick way to check if WAS can connect to the database repository is through connect.java and wasconnect.java, which have been discussed in previous chapters. In some cases, a WebSphere Application Server has been started—or at least its (Nanny) Java machine was launched—without having connected to its database repository. In other words, having the WAS Nanny process running does not guarantee that WAS is properly functioning.

Monitoring the Application Archives

Be sure to do the housekeeping of the files that go into your WAS installation directories. Whether they're EAR, JAR, or ZIP archives, you should periodically run the *find* command to find out if any suspected application archives have been modified or added in the WAS directories:

```
# find $WAS_HOME \( -name '*.class' -o -name '*.jar' -o -name
'web.xml' \) -type f -atime +5 -print
```

This command finds all .class files, .jar files, and web.xml files that have not been accessed in the last five days. Of course, you need to run this command against the directory where you have the application installed, such as the default was_home/installedApps directory. The manager should be aware of every servlet placed in the classpath of an application, or that can be invoked by its classname.

Use the find command to quickly search the configuration files that contain a classpath definition:

```
# find $WAS_HOME  -type f -name "*.config" -exec  grep -l  classpath {}  \;
```

---

[2]   The context root is defined in the XML deployment descriptor of the EAR sampleApp.ear. For instance, using the WAS v4 default install, the was_home/installedApps/sampleApp.ear/META-INF/ application.xml contains the description of the context root of the examples.war web module.

Be aware that configuration files used by WAS startup scripts can be custom named and placed in different directories than the conventional location. If this is the case, you need to walk through the configuration startup script yourself to know which configuration files are being read so as not to be eluded.

You may also need to scan the HTML files looking for malicious constructs that can cause security risks. For instance, a security breach can be caused by calling a class name directly from within an HTML file by embedding it within the <SCRIPT> ... </SCRIPT> tag:

```
# find /usr/HTTPServer/htdocs -type f -name "*.html" -exec  grep -l  "SCRIPT>" {}  \;
```

You can block the serving of servlets by their class names by disabling the *Serve Servlets by Classname* in the assembly properties of the web module.[3]

Archiving the WAS Directory

It is possible to store the WAS installation by archiving it with the *tar* command. First, stop all WAS processes and then issue the *tar* command:

```
# tar  cf  /dump/wasbk.tar   /usr/WebSphere/AppServer
```

This command creates the wasbk.tar archive for the directory /usr/WebSphere/AppServer and deposits it in the /dump directory. To restore it, change to the root directory and use the `tar xf   /dump/wasbk.tar` command. For WebSphere Advanced Edition, because the WAS data source repository is a database itself that is managed by a database engine, you need to back up the database separately (except for with the WAS v4 Advanced Single Server Edition, which has its configuration data in an XML file located in the was_home/config directory).

You can use the commands `dump` or `cpio` to back up the WAS installation. The `tar` command allows you to replicate your installation to do more testing. For example, to replicate the installation to the directories /opt/was1, /opt/was2, and /opt/was3:

```
# cd  /opt/was1
# tar  -cvf  -  -C  /usr/WebSphere/AppServer/  .  |  tar xvf  -
```

This will replicate the contents of /usr/WebSphere/AppServer into /opt/was1 and keep the directory structure intact. Repeat the command by subsequently changing to /opt/was2 and /opt/was3. You need to change the name of AppServer to something else:

```
# mv /usr/WebSphere/AppServer  /usr/WebSphere/AppServer.BK
```

Next, establish the symbolic link to /opt/was1:

```
# ln  -s  /opt/was1  /usr/WebSphere/AppServer
```

---

[3] You perform this task either by using the Application Assembly Tool (AAT) or by directly editing the ibm-web-ext.xmi file (located in the WEB-INF directory of the web module) and by setting the flag of serveServletsByClassnameEnabled to true.

This way, you have three original installs of WAS that you can point to by deleting the link for one and recreating it for another to test with WAS. You can also have more than one WebSphere Domain installed on a single server, as you will see in Chapter 21.

Archiving the WAS directory on Windows NT

On Windows NT, since you do not have the capability of using symbolic links, such as ln, you must resort to using the move or rename command to change the name of the directory containing an image of the product. However, make sure that you stop the Application Server before starting the product with another image. For example, here is the series of commands to issue on Windows NT (assume that the directory c:\WebSphere\AppServer\AppServer.img1 contains an image of the original installation of the product):

```
c:\WebSphere\AppServer\bin\stopserver.bat
cd c:\WebSphere
rename AppServer  AppServer.old
rename AppServer.img1 AppServer
c:\WebSphere\AppServer\bin\startserver.bat
```

It is necessary to restore a copy of the registry tree structure (hive) of the original install of WAS (see the following illustration). This hive should have originally been copied after starting and then stopping WAS for the first time.

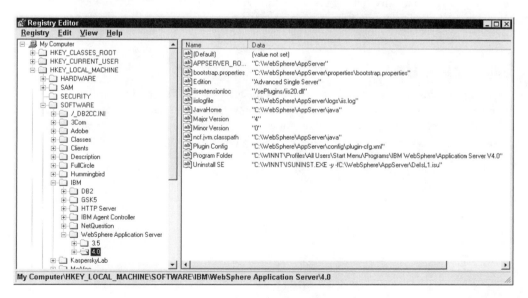

From the Windows NT registry editor (command regedit), browse through the registry and locate the HKEY_LOCAL_MACHINE\SOFTWARE\IBM\WebSphere Application Server branch. Select File | Export Registry File and make sure Selected Branch is selected at the bottom of the dialog box. Enter a filename to save the branch into the .reg file. You can use this exported file to revert the branch to the original install of WAS by selecting File | Import Registry File.

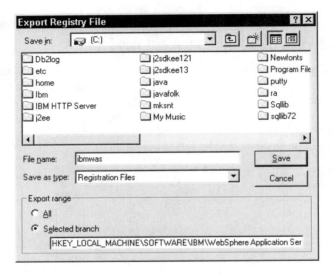

Perl for Win32 has a set of modules that allows you to manipulate the Windows NT registry programmatically. The MKS Toolkit provides the `registry` command, which allows textual manipulation of the registry as well.

Wrapping Up

This chapter demonstrated a quick way to administer WebSphere Application Server. It covered the essential points that you need to know after the first installation of WAS. You learned how to retrieve information about the WAS version and how to release at an instant. You were also introduced to log files and shown where to locate them and how to read them.

PART III

Programming for WAS

OBJECTIVES

► Programming the Data Access Component

► Defining J2EE Web Applications

► Learning about Servlets and JSP

► Understanding the WAS' Classloader

► Defining Session Management and IBM Session Management

► Understanding EJB, SOAP, and JAAS Programming

► Setting the Environment for Enterprise Programming

Preparing the Database

IN THIS CHAPTER:

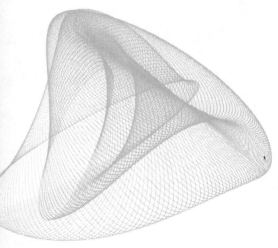

I n Part I, Chapter 2 addressed the installation of the IBM Universal Database (UDB). The installation of the database is mostly required to install the WAS Advanced Edition or Enterprise Edition. However, as mentioned in Chapter 6, there is another reason to have a database when using any of the WAS versions: to use it as a data source. This chapter shows you how to programmatically manage and populate the database example used in Parts III and IV. Chapter 10 addresses developing a Java data-access component and its interface.

Ideally, a web application developer needs to exercise code in a dynamic web environment where client-browsers make requests to create, delete, and change information in a data source. Because this might be feasible only in a production environment, which should not be compromised for experimentation, a set of tools is required to imitate the dynamism of a real web environment. This chapter describes these tools that permit you to populate a database, to retrieve a database, and to change information in a database in a batch mode. Tools for stress-testing and monitoring system threads are also discussed in chapters 22 and 25 of this book.

Introduction

You should be able to make transactions to a data source regardless of the brand of the database. You usually accomplish this task by having a common language and command syntax that offer the flexibility to program and manage databases regardless of their brands. SQL is a commonly portable language for database brands such as Oracle and UDB. Disregarding the algebraic foundation and the administrative aspects of the database, the discussion here focuses on the necessary elements for a developer to write two types of code: first, generic scripts to randomly populate and query a database; and second, Java code good enough to be part of a web application. Such Java code should be secure, modular, and sharable by the other applications' components.

UDB Authority on UNIX

To be able to access information saved in a database table in UDB, you need to have the password of an authorized user who has been granted access to the table. For instance, the user db2inst1 (usually created by default in UDB) can create a database and its table and then grant the user dbuser selective access to the database and its table. The account dbuser is just a regular UNIX account. Granting selective access to a database table allows you to design a structured application that is secure even among the developers.

For instance, it is customary to create a separate account to access the registration table. Such an account, for example dbreg, will be used by a developer implementing the registration module of the web application that can have sole authority to access the employee password table (EMPPWD.) While it is possible to implement a secure web application by adequately distributing roles and authorities to different developers (and their pieces of code), this chapter addresses a simple situation in which all database tables have been granted access to the user dbuser.

Creating the Database

The database used in this book is named DBGUIDE and can be created with the simple UDB script shown in Listing 9-1. This database is used in conjunction with simple programs that allow you to exercise basic codes with WAS. The database consists of these four tables:

Table	Description
EMPPWD	Stores the employee password, time entry created, and time employee login and logout.
EMPACCNT	Stores the information about the employees.
CLIPWD	Stores the client passwords, time entry created, and time client login and logout.
CLIACCNT	Stores the client information. Of interest is the balance field that can be credited or debited by the bank employee.

The employees of a banking company have their passwords saved in EMPPWD, and their account information is saved in EMPACCNT. These bank employees are known as *tellers*. The bank has many customers, known as *clients*, who can remotely log in from their browsers to look up their checking balances. A client's password and profile information are saved in the CLIPWD and CLIACCNT tables, respectively. A teller can credit and debit a client's balance. Every time the client's balance is credited or debited, the fields CCREDITS or CDEBITS (defined in the CLIACCNT table) are incremented correspondingly. The client bank accounts are categorized (CATEGORY) within one of the following lists: A, B, or C. Furthermore, each client's account has a primary contact with a teller who is specified in the REMPID field.

Listing 9-1 *dbguide.sql*

```
--
-- Create the DBGUIDE db
--
-- CREATE DATABASE DBGUIDE on server.name in DB instance /home/db2inst1
--
CONNECT TO DBGUIDE
GRANT CONNECT ON DATABASE TO USER DBUSER
--
-- Define the EMPPWD table
--
DROP TABLE EMPPWD
```

```
CREATE TABLE EMPPWD (
USERID    VARCHAR(12) NOT NULL,
PRIMARY   KEY ( USERID ),
PASSWORD VARCHAR(38) NOT NULL,
CREATED TIMESTAMP NOT NULL WITH DEFAULT,
TMLOGIN   TIMESTAMP NOT NULL WITH DEFAULT,
TMLOGOUT TIMESTAMP NOT NULL WITH DEFAULT,
NDX DECIMAL(15,0) GENERATED BY DEFAULT AS IDENTITY(START WITH 1)
)
GRANT SELECT, INSERT, UPDATE (USERID) ON TABLE EMPPWD TO USER DBUSER
--
-- Define the EMPACCNT table
--
DROP TABLE EMPACCNT
CREATE TABLE EMPACCNT (
USERID VARCHAR(12) NOT NULL,
PRIMARY   KEY ( USERID ),
FRSTNAME VARCHAR(16) NOT NULL,
LASTNAME VARCHAR(32) NOT NULL,
IMAGE     VARCHAR(255),
SSN       VARCHAR(9),
EMPNO     CHAR(7)   NOT NULL,
EMAIL     VARCHAR(32),
CONTACT   VARCHAR(32) NOT NULL,
COUNTER   INTEGER NOT NULL WITH DEFAULT 0,
NDX DECIMAL(15,0) GENERATED BY DEFAULT AS IDENTITY(START WITH 1)
)
GRANT ALL PRIVILEGES ON TABLE EMPACCNT TO USER DBUSER
--
-- Define the CLIPWD table
--
DROP TABLE CLIPWD
CREATE TABLE CLIPWD (
CLIENTID VARCHAR(12) NOT NULL,
PRIMARY   KEY ( CLIENTID ),
PASSWORD VARCHAR(38) NOT NULL,
CREATED   TIMESTAMP NOT NULL WITH DEFAULT,
TMLOGIN   TIMESTAMP NOT NULL WITH DEFAULT,
TMLOGOUT TIMESTAMP NOT NULL WITH DEFAULT,
NDX DECIMAL(15,0) GENERATED BY DEFAULT AS IDENTITY(START WITH 1)
)
GRANT ALL PRIVILEGES ON TABLE CLIPWD TO USER DBUSER
--
-- Define the CLIACCNT table
```

```
--
DROP TABLE CLIACCNT
CREATE TABLE CLIACCNT (
CLIENTID VARCHAR(12) NOT NULL,
PRIMARY  KEY ( CLIENTID ),
BANKID   VARCHAR(9) NOT NULL,
CATEGORY VARCHAR(1) NOT NULL,
REMPID   VARCHAR(12) NOT NULL,
FRSTNAME VARCHAR(16) NOT NULL,
LASTNAME VARCHAR(32) NOT NULL,
IMAGE    VARCHAR(255),
EMAIL    VARCHAR(32),
CDEBITS  INTEGER NOT NULL WITH DEFAULT 0,
CCREDITS INTEGER NOT NULL WITH DEFAULT 0,
BALANCE  INTEGER NOT NULL WITH DEFAULT 0,
NDX DECIMAL(15,0) GENERATED BY DEFAULT AS IDENTITY(START WITH 1)
)
GRANT ALL PRIVILEGES ON TABLE CLIACCNT TO USER DBUSER
---
DISCONNECT ALL
```

The tables use the identity feature that is available with UDB v7. If you are using WAS v3.5 and its associated UDB v6.1, then you need to take off the NDX field from each table before running the script. To create the DBGUIDE database and its tables, follow these four steps:

1. With the db2inst1 account, log in to the server where you have installed the UDB server. Set up your environment by executing

   ```
   # . $HOME/sqllib/db2profile
   ```

2. As db2inst1, create the database:

   ```
   # db2 create database DBGUIDE
   ```

3. Create the dbuser account. This is the user who will be granted access to the table of the DBGUIDE database.

4. As db2inst1, execute the script dbguide:

   ```
   # db2 -f  dbguide.sql
   ```

   Note that you may need to run this command twice in a row each time you want to recreate the DBGUIDE tables after dropping the DBGUIDE database.

The dbguide.sql script will drop all previously created tables before creating the DBGUIDE database and its tables, therefore freeing the contents of the EMPPWD, EMPACCNT, CLIPWD, and CLIACCNT tables successively. You can run the db2 -f dbguide.sql command every time you want to recreate the tables and empty their contents.

The DBGUIDE database is simple to comprehend; just keep these tips in mind:

► The identity is a new feature of UDB that automatically generates sequential values for primary keys. You should use this feature instead of using the timestamp as a primary key.

► Use the TIMESTAMP with the specification NOT NULL WITH DEFAULT to assign a value equal to the current time when the row is inserted. The TIMESTAMP has a precision down to the microsecond and is of the following format: YYYY-MM-DD hh.mm.ss.zzzzzz. The USERID is the unique key in the EMPPWD and EMPACCNT tables.

► The CLIENTID is the unique key in the CLIPWD and CLIACCNT tables.

► The REMPID field in the client record refers to the USERID of the teller who is a primary contact to the client. In other words, each teller is a primary contact for one or more clients.

Populating the Database

The following sections discuss two approaches to populate the DBGUIDE database tables. The first approach is based on Java and uses the JDBC driver; the second approach is based on Perl and uses the Perl Database independent (DBI) module. Although Perl and DBI seem to be irrelevant to mention in a WAS book, they can be adequately used (but totally insecure) in the process of writing handy scripts to manipulate the database tables in these lessons.

Java and JDBC

Java programs can use the JDBC driver to connect to a live database and make changes to its content. Such Java programs can be run on any host machine on which the JDBC driver is available, such as the db2java.zip library used in Chapter 3. The machine on which the database instance is defined with its database(s), and to which you want to connect, must be running db2jstrt on a predefined port: db2jstrt 50068. You can log in as the db2inst1 user, set your environment with the db2profile, and then run db2jstrt 50068. This type of connectivity discussed here is based on a JDBC driver known as type 3 driver.[1] Java programs can connect to the UDB server database by identifying it through the URL jdbc:db2://node2:50068/DBGUIDE, and by providing the authentication of the user who has been granted access to the database and its tables:

```
String url = "jdbc:db2://node2:50068/DBGUIDE";
Connection conn = DriverManager.getConnection(url,"dbuser","pwd123");
```

---

[1]   There are four types of JDBC drivers of which type 2 and type 3 are of importance to us. Chapter 2 discusses each type of driver. The code in this book has been tested using both types of drivers (type 2 and type 3.) In Chapter 12 we will use the JDBC type 2 driver to access the DBGUIDE tables from the servlets.

The first line is a string that identifies the URL of the data source you want to access, and that is passed (second line) to the DriverManager with the credential to get a connection. Once you get a successful connection, you can prepare a statement and execute it. If the statement is successfully executed, you can get the result set and the metadata (or detailed information) about the database, as you will see in the next examples.

Java/JDBC: A Simple Insert Statement

Listing 9-2 shows the complete program to insert a record in the EMPPWD table. The program InsertEmpPwd takes two arguments: the first is the value of the USERID, and the second is the value of the PASSWORD. It then inserts a record in the DB2INST1.EMPPWD table. Based on this program, you can write the code with an iteration to populate the DBGUIDE tables.

Listing 9-2   *InsertEmpPwd.java*

```
import java.sql.*;

class InsertEmpPwd {
  static {
    try {
      Class.forName("COM.ibm.db2.jdbc.net.DB2Driver");
    } catch (Exception e) {
      e.printStackTrace();
    }
  }

  public static void main(String argv[]) {
    try {
      Connection conn;
      Connection local;
      String url = "jdbc:db2://node2:50068/DBGUIDE";

      System.out.println("Trying to connect");
      // connect
      conn = DriverManager.getConnection(url, "dbuser", "pwd123");

      // Use the java.sql.Statement class to execute the SQL statement
      Statement stmt = conn.createStatement();

      String updateStmt = "INSERT INTO DB2INST1.EMPPWD
      (USERID,PASSWORD,CREATED,TMLOGIN,TMLOGOUT) VALUES ('" + argv[0] + "','"
      + argv[1] + "', CURRENT TIMESTAMP, CURRENT TIMESTAMP, CURRENT
      TIMESTAMP)";
      stmt.executeUpdate(updateStmt);
```

```
        stmt.close();
        conn.close();
    } catch( Exception e ) {
        e.printStackTrace();
    }
  }
}
```

Because the InsertEmpPwd program takes command-line arguments, you can use it to batch-process a list of passwords. For instance, say that you want to add a record in the EMPPWD table for each UNIX user who got an account mapped in /etc/passwd. Recall that, on a standard UNIX box, /etc/passwd[2] is a flat file database that holds the user accounts in a colon- (:) delimited format.[3] Here is an example showing the record as saved on one line in the /etc/passwd for the user john:

john:Fo5580WFySPqE:508:102:John Doe:/home/john:/bin/bash

To map each entry in the /etc/passwd file to a record in the EMPPWD table, you first copy the /etc/passwd file into your current directory and delete the records that are not needed, such as the daemons and system users. Then, in a single command, you can invoke Perl to read and split each record and then execute InsertEmpPwd for each account:

```
# perl -e 'open(F,"passwd");while(<F>){@p=split(/:/); `java
InsertEmpPwd $p[0] \"$p[1]\"`;}'
```

This example shows that UNIX commands can help you to achieve tasks in a simple way, and they can be programmatically overwhelming otherwise.

Sometimes, it is desirable to keep the integrity in user authentication between the system accounts and the application accounts. Mapping the /etc/passwd file can be a quick solution; however, Java offers a more dynamic solution that can integrate with system authentication on UNIX NIS+ and Windows NT: Java JAAS. (Programming with Java JAAS security is the topic of Chapter 20.)

Java/JDBC: Getting the Metadata

You can use the Connection class used in Listing 9-2 to get detailed information about the database to which it is connecting. This class implements the interface java.sql.DatabaseMeta Data, which defines several methods that allow you to retrieve all kinds of information about the database. The StructureEmpPwd.java program in Listing 9-3 allows you to retrieve the structure of the database table EMPPWD created previously. On line 22, there's a connection to the database, which is followed by executing any valid query statement against the table whose structure you seek (lines 23 and 24). On line 26, getMetaData is called on the connection object to get the metadata for the database to which the connection is made.

---

[2]   YP/NIS+ authentication requires that you fetch the passwords list with the `ypcat` or similar commands.

[3]   The colon (:) is a character used in this book to mark and identify special strings to be substituted in a query. Because we won't consider a colon to be part of the value of a database field, it won't manifest any ambiguity when marking special strings to be replaced by another.

Listing 9-3 *StructureEmpPwd program to retrieve the structure of the EMPPWD table*

```
1.    import java.sql.*;
2.    import java.io.*;
3.
4.    class StructureEmpPwd {
5.
6.        static {
7.            try {
8.                Class.forName("COM.ibm.db2.jdbc.net.DB2Driver");
9.            } catch (Exception e) {
10.               e.printStackTrace();
11.           }
12.       }
13.
14.       public static void main(String argv[]) {
15.           try {
16.               Connection conn;
17.               Connection local;
18.               String url = "jdbc:db2://node2.tcnd.com:50068/DBGUIDE";
19.
20.               System.out.println("Trying to connect.");
21.               // connect
22.               conn = DriverManager.getConnection(url, "dbuser", "pwd007");
23.               Statement stmt = conn.createStatement();
24.               ResultSet rs = stmt.executeQuery("SELECT * FROM
          DB2INST1.EMPPWD");
25.               String createstring = "CREATE TABLE DB2INST1.EMPPWD (";
26.               ResultSetMetaData md = rs.getMetaData();
27.               int n = md.getColumnCount();
28.               int k = 0;
29.               for (int i = 1; i <= n; i++) {
30.                   createstring += md.getColumnName(i) + " ";
31.                   switch (md.getColumnType(i)) {
32.                   case 1:
33.                       createstring += "CHAR(" + md.getPrecision(i) + ")";
34.                       k = md.getPrecision(i);
35.                       break;
36.                   case 2:
37.                       createstring += "INTEGER";
38.                       k = md.getPrecision(i);
39.                       break;
40.                   case 3:
41.                       createstring += "DECIMAL(" + md.getPrecision(i) + ",
          " + md.getScale(i) + ")";
42.                       if (md.getScale(i) != 0) {
43.                           k = md.getPrecision(i) + 1 + md.getScale(i);
```

```
44.                         } else {
45.                             k = md.getPrecision(i);
46.                         }
47.                         break;
48.                     case 4:
49.                         createstring += "DATE";
50.                         k = md.getPrecision(i);
51.                         break;
52.                     case 5:
53.                         createstring += "LOGICAL";
54.                         k = md.getPrecision(i);
55.                         break;
56.                     case 12:
57.                         createstring += "VARCHAR(" + md.getPrecision(i) +
         ")";
58.                         if (md.getScale(i) != 0) {
59.                             k = md.getPrecision(i) + 1 + md.getScale(i);
60.                         } else {
61.                             k = md.getPrecision(i);
62.                         }
63.                         break;
64.                     case 91:
65.                         createstring += "CHAR(10)";
66.                         k = 10;
67.                         break;
68.                     case 93:
69.                         createstring += "TIMESTAMP NOT NULL WITH DEFAULT";
70.                         break;
71.                     default:
72.                         System.err.println("Unknown type : " +
         md.getColumnType(i));
73.                         k = 0;
74.                         break;
75.                     }
76.                     if (i < n) {
77.                         createstring += ",";
78.                     }
79.                 }
80.             createstring += ")";
81.
82.             System.out.println(createstring);
83.
84.             stmt.close();
85.             conn.close();
86.         } catch ( Exception e ) {
87.             e.printStackTrace();
88.         }
89.     }
90. }
```

To run the program, make sure you have replaced the parameters on lines 18, 22, 24, and 26 to match your setup for the database URL, its instance creator, and the correct credential to access it. A typical output is shown here:

```
Trying to connect.
CREATE TABLE DB2INST1.EMPPWD (USERID VARCHAR(12),PASSWORD VARCHAR(38),
CREATED TIMESTAMP NOT NULL WITH DEFAULT,TMLOGIN TIMESTAMP NOT NULL WITH
DEFAULT,TMLOGOUT TIMESTAMP NOT NULL WITH DEFAULT,NDX DECIMAL(15, 0))
```

Using the DBD::DB2 Module

Often, you need to quickly write some customized scripts to manipulate data in your database. The Perl Database Independent (DBI) is quite useful in such a situation. Also remember that the regular expression, hashes, list processing, and type glob in Perl allow you to write inductively powerful and compact programs. Although the Perl DBI is widely used for mediocre CGI programming, the intention is different in this book—here, it is used to write easy enough scripts to populate the database in the process of doing stress-testing, as seen in Part IV. It is never used in conjunction with WAS or Java programming otherwise.

You can quickly install the DBD::DB2 module in a single step, assuming your machine is connected to the Internet and you have installed the CPAN module. Start a CPAN shell (as root, issue the `cpan` command), and install the DBD::DB2 module simply by issuing the following command:

```
cpan > i   DBD::DB2
cpan > i   DBI
```

These commands will install Bundle::DBD::DB2 and the module DBD::DB2; and Bundle::DBI and the module DBI. If any prerequisite module is missing from your system, it is also installed. You can then log in to the server machine on which you have created the database and run Perl programs to access the UDB database. Remember to export DB2_HOME in your environment before installing the DBD::DB2 module; this is certainly true when you are building the package yourself (using Make) on the machine on which you have UDB installed. Typically you need to export the DB2_HOME variable as follows:

```
# export DB2_HOME=/usr/IBMdb2/V7.1
```

(Appendix A explains how to install Perl modules.)

Populating the Database with Perl DBI

Any user can run DBI scripts and query a database because the authorization on the database is passed in the object-based call to the connect method (subroutine) DBI->connect(). For example, the following shows how to connect the DBGUIDE using the credential of the dbuser account:

```
DBI->connect("DBI:DB2:DBGUIDE","dbuser","pwd123")
```

However, for these users, you need to set up their environment with the db2profile script. For example, copy the /home/db2inst1/sqllib/db2profile file to the commonly mounted directory /tools and add the following line to the /etc/profile (of the machine on which the UDB client or server has been installed):

```
.   /tools/db2profile
```

Alternatively, the user can set his or her DB2 environment by executing a similar command at the shell prompt:

```
#  .   /tools/db2profile
```

Also notice that users who got their environment setup using the setj.sh script discussed in Chapter 3 will have their environment setup with all UDB necessary variables, and calling the db2pfolile as seen in the above step is not necessary in this case.

As a first example, consider the following dbieg program in Listing 9-4:

Listing 9-4   *dbieg program uses the Perl DBI to access UDB*

```
1.    #!/usr/bin/perl
2.
3.    use strict;
4.    use DBI;
5.    require "dbguide.pl";
6.
7.    my($dbuname)="dbuser";
8.    my($dbpw)="pwd123";
9.    my($dbname)="DBGUIDE";
10.   my($dbinstance)="DB2INST1";
11.
12.   my($emppwd)="EMPPWD";
13.
14.   my ($conn,$cursor,@values);
15.
16.   $conn = DBI->connect("DBI:DB2:$dbname",$dbuname,$dbpw);
17.
18.   die "Cannot connect to conn: $DBI::errstr\n" unless $conn;
19.
20.   print "Connected.\n";
21.
22.   # Prepare an SQL query.
23.   $cursor = $conn->prepare("INSERT INTO $dbinstance.$emppwd
        (USERID,PASSWORD,CREATED,TMLOGIN,TMLOGOUT) VALUES ('dave1','apple1',
        CURRENT TIMESTAMP, CURRENT TIMESTAMP, CURRENT TIMESTAMP)");
24.
25.   $cursor->execute(); # Execute the query.
26.   die "Insert failed: $DBI::errstr\n" unless !($cursor->err());
27.
```

```
28.   $cursor->finish(); # We are done with the cursor.
29.
30.   $conn->disconnect or warn "Disconnection failed: $DBI::errstr\n";
31.
```

Line 16 initializes the connection to the database; then a statement is prepared on line 23 to insert into the DB2INST1.EMPPWD database table the password *apple1* for the user whose userid is *dave1*. The prepared statement is pointed to by a cursor that is then executed on line 25.

In Perl, it is possible to write a package (which has nothing to do with Java packages) in which you can define all sensitive variables that you need to pass to a program. For example, the dbguide.pl package in Listing 9-5 defines the parameters to access the database:

Listing 9-5   *dbguide.pl package*

```
#!/usr/local/bin/perl
package dbguide;
$dbuname="dbuser";
$dbpw="pwd123";
$dbinstance="db2inst1";
$dbname="DBGUIDE";
$emppwd="EMPPWD";        # employee passwords and time login/logout table
$empaccnt="EMPACCNT";  # employee accounts table
$clipwd="CLIPWD";        # client passwords and time login/logout table
$cliaccnt="CLIACCNT";       # client accounts table

$totemp=4; # total number of employees
$totcli=20; # total number of clients
```

To query the EMPPWD table, consider the query program qry_emppwd in Listing 9-6:

Listing 9-6   *qry_emppwd to query the EMPPWD table*

```
#!/usr/bin/perl

use strict;
use DBI;
require "dbguide.pl";

$SIG{`INT`} = sub { die };  # Enable Control-C to terminate the program

my($dbuname)=$dbguide::dbuname;
my($dbpw)=$dbguide::dbpw;
```

```perl
my($dbname)=$dbguide::dbname;
my($dbinstance)=$dbguide::dbinstance;

my($emppwd)=$dbguide::emppwd;

my ($conn,$cursor,@values);

$conn = DBI->connect("DBI:DB2:$dbname",$dbuname,$dbpw);
#$conn = DBI->connect("DBI:DB2:$dbname",$dbuname,$dbpw,, {RaiseError => 0,
      PrintError => 1,  ChopBlanks => 0 , AutoCommit => 0}) || die
      print"$DBI::errstr";
#$conn = DBI->connect("DBI:DB2:$dbname");

die "Cannot connect to conn: $DBI::errstr\n" unless ($conn);

print "Connected.\n";

#
# Prepare an SQL query.
#
$cursor = $conn->prepare("SELECT * FROM $dbinstance.$emppwd");

#
# Execute the query.
#

$cursor->execute();

#if ($DBI::err) {
if ($cursor->err()) {
    die "Cannot query conn: $DBI::errstr\n";
}

#
# Extract the data.
#
while (@values = $cursor->fetchrow() ) {
    print "@values\n";
}
# We are done with the cursor.
$cursor->finish();

$conn->disconnect or warn "Disconnection failed: $DBI::errstr\n";
```

Now let's extend the dbieg program into the ins_dbguide program shown in Listing 9-7, to populate the DBGUIDE database.

Most of the ins_dbguide script is self-explanatory. A bank employee USERID is typically formed by the string *teller*, to which an incremented number is appended (lines 24 and 39), and a bank client CLIENTID is formed by the string *client*, to which an incremented number is appended (lines 57 and 71). The category for each client has been randomly chosen from the set [A, B, C] (lines 75 and 78); also, the REMPID has been randomly assigned one of the many employees or tellers (lines 73 and 79). The number of employees and clients can be adjusted by editing the dbguide.pl package and setting the number for totemp and totcli, respectively.

Listing 9-7   *ins_dbguide, a Perl program that populates the DBGUIDE tables*

```
1.    #!/usr/bin/perl
2.
3.    use strict;
4.    use DBI;
5.    require "dbguide.pl";
6.
7.    my($dbuname)=$dbguide::dbuname;
8.    my($dbpw)=$dbguide::dbpw;
9.    my($dbname)=$dbguide::dbname;
10.   my($dbinstance)=$dbguide::dbinstance;
11.
12.   my($conn,$cursor,@values);
13.   my($emppwd,$empaccnt,$clipwd,$cliaccnt)=($dbguide::emppwd,
         $dbguide::empaccnt, $dbguide::clipwd, $dbguide::cliaccnt);
14.   my($totemp,$totcli)=($dbguide::totemp,$dbguide::totcli);
15.
16.   srand;
17.
18.   $conn = DBI->connect("DBI:DB2:$dbname",$dbuname,$dbpw);
19.   die "Cannot connect to conn: $DBI::errstr\n" unless $conn;
20.   print "Connected.\n";
21.
22.   print "Populating the table: $emppwd.\n";
23.   for (my $i=1; $i<=$totemp; $i++) {
24.       my($userid) ='teller' . $i;
25.       my($password) = 'secret' . $i;
26.       # Prepare an SQL statement
27.       $cursor = $conn->prepare("INSERT INTO $dbinstance.$emppwd
        (USERID,PASSWORD,CREATED,TMLOGIN,TMLOGOUT) VALUES
        ('$userid','$password', CURRENT TIMESTAMP, CURRENT TIMESTAMP, CURRENT
        TIMESTAMP)");
```

```
28.
29.     $cursor->execute(); # Execute the query.
30.
31.     die "Insert failed: $DBI::errstr\n" unless !($cursor->err());
32.     # print "Inserted in table $emppwd: USERID=$userid
        PASSWORD=$password\n";
33.
34.     $cursor->finish(); # We are done with the cursor.
35.  }
36.
37.  print "Populating the table: $empaccnt.\n";
38.  for (my $i=1; $i<=$totemp; $i++) {
39.     my($userid) ='teller' . $i;
40.     my($frstname) ='Jane' . $i;
41.     my($lastname) ='Doe' . $i;
42.     my($image) ='../images/teller' . $i;
43.     my($ssn) = '000000000';
44.     my($empno) = $i;
45.     my($email) ='teller' . $i . '@wasette.com';
46.
47.     # Prepare an SQL statement
48.     $cursor = $conn->prepare("INSERT INTO $dbinstance.$empaccnt
        (USERID,FRSTNAME,LASTNAME,IMAGE,SSN,EMPNO,EMAIL,CONTACT) VALUES

('$userid','$frstname','$lastname','$image','$ssn','$empno','$email','somecontact')");
49.
50.     $cursor->execute(); # Execute the query.
51.     die "Insert failed: $DBI::errstr\n" unless !($cursor->err());
52.     $cursor->finish(); # We are done with the cursor.
53.  }
54.
55.  print "Populating the table: $clipwd.\n";
56.  for (my $i=1; $i<=$totcli; $i++) {
57.     my($clientid) ='client' . $i;
58.     my($password) = 'mystery' . $i;
59.     # Prepare an SQL statement
60.     $cursor = $conn->prepare("INSERT INTO $dbinstance.$clipwd
        (CLIENTID,PASSWORD,CREATED,TMLOGIN,TMLOGOUT) VALUES
        ('$clientid','$password', CURRENT TIMESTAMP, CURRENT TIMESTAMP, CURRENT
        TIMESTAMP)");
61.
62.     $cursor->execute(); # Execute the query.
63.
64.     die "Insert failed: $DBI::errstr\n" unless !($cursor->err());
65.
```

```
66.        $cursor->finish(); # We are done with the cursor.
67.    }
68.
69.    print "Populating the table: $cliaccnt.\n";
70.    for (my $i=1; $i<=$totcli; $i++) {
71.        my($clientid) ='client' . $i;
72.        my(@refemp);
73.        for (my $k=1; $k<=$totemp; $k++) { push(@refemp,$k); }
74.
75.        my(@a) = ('A','B','C'); my($t)=int(rand(3));
76.        my($bankid)=$a[$t] . '000';
77.        if ($i < 10) { $bankid .= "00" . $i; } elsif ($i < 100) { $bankid .=
       "0" . $i; } else { $bankid .=  $i; }
78.        my($category)=$a[$t];
79.        my($rempid) = 'teller' . $refemp[rand($totemp)];
80.        my($frstname) ='Dave' . $i;
81.        my($lastname) ='Spender' . $i;
82.        my($image) ='../images/client' . $i;
83.        my($email) ='client' . $i . '@wasette.com';
84.        # Prepare an SQL statement
85.        $cursor = $conn->prepare("INSERT INTO $dbinstance.$cliaccnt
       (CLIENTID, BANKID, CATEGORY, REMPID, FRSTNAME,LASTNAME,IMAGE,EMAIL,
       CDEBITS,CCREDITS,BALANCE) VALUES
       ('$clientid','$bankid','$category','$rempid',
       '$frstname','$lastname','$image','$email',0,0,0)");
86.        $cursor->execute(); # Execute the query.
87.        die "Insert failed: $DBI::errstr\n" unless !($cursor->err());
88.        $cursor->finish(); # We are done with the cursor.
89.    }
90.
91.    $conn->disconnect or warn "Disconnection failed: $DBI::errstr\n";
```

After executing the script for 4 tellers and 20 clients, you can inspect the DBGUIDE tables. Log in as db2inst1 or dbuser and then start a DB2 session by issuing the db2 command at the command prompt. Try the following db2 commands:

▶ List all records in the EMPACCNT table: SELECT * FROM EMPACCNT.

▶ List the CLIENTIDs in CLIACCNT: SELECT CLIENTID FROM CLIACCNT.

▶ List the USERID and FRSTNAME of each bank employee, along with the CLIENTID and CATEGORY of the clients she has been assigned as a primary contact. For this, you need to use a JOIN: db2 => select userid, empaccnt.frstname, clientid, category from empaccnt left outer join cliaccnt on (userid=rempid) order by empaccnt.userid

► USERID   FRSTNAME   CLIENTID CATEGORY

USERID	FRSTNAME	CLIENTID	CATEGORY
teller1	Jane1	client2	B
teller1	Jane1	client8	C
teller2	Jane2	client3	A
teller2	Jane2	client4	B
teller2	Jane2	client7	A
teller2	Jane2	client11	C
teller2	Jane2	client12	B
teller2	Jane2	client20	B
teller3	Jane3	client1	C
teller3	Jane3	client5	A
teller3	Jane3	client6	C
teller3	Jane3	client9	C
teller3	Jane3	client14	A
teller3	Jane3	client15	C
teller3	Jane3	client16	C
teller3	Jane3	client19	B
teller4	Jane4	client10	C
teller4	Jane4	client13	A
teller4	Jane4	client17	B
teller4	Jane4	client18	C

The output of the last db2 command may vary on your system because the CATEGORY has been randomly selected when populating the database with ins_dbguide.

Closing Note on DBD::DB2

The current version of DBI for DB2 requires that you install the UDB client or server on the machine on which you have compiled the DBD::DB2 module and on which you want to run Perl scripts that will use this module.

Another good reason to mention Perl DBD programming in a WAS book is to alert you of the possibility of easing database portals between different database brands with simple Perl programs. For example, you can install from CPAN the DBI driver DBD::CSV to write a program to import a generic comma-separated values flat file from Microsoft Access to UDB.

Wrapping Up

This chapter discussed how to create and populate the DBGUIDE database used for the examples in this book. There are many ways you can populate a database, two of which were discussed in this chapter: Java programs using the JDBC API, and Perl programs using the DBI driver. The Perl DBI programs allow you to work with your database with a lot of flexibility. This is true especially when you need to exercise your code on a database that is often regenerated due to simulation patterns.

Now that you have learned how to populate the database with efficient scripts, in Chapter 10, you will learn how to build the Java components to access the DBGUIDE database. These Java classes are referred to as the Java data-access component and its interface.

Accessing the Database in Java: DataAccessComponent

IN THIS CHAPTER:

Defining the DataAccessComponent

Examining Characteristics of the
DataAccessComponent

Understanding the Build Process

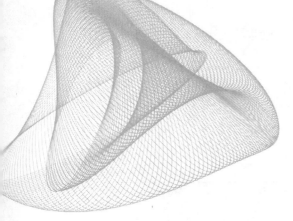

T here are two ways to prepare your code to access the database. The first way is through the standard JDBC library and its DriverManager class. Specifying the database location URL and its corresponding authentication (login and password) is required. The second way is through a Java Naming and Directory Interface (JNDI) call (as specified in Java 2 Enterprise Edition) to obtain a DataSource object. The DriverManager configuration is saved in the web application deployment descriptor.

This chapter considers the former, while the latter is discussed in Chapter 18. We will progressively build a generic model to access the records from the DBGUIDE database that we populated in Chapter 9. A record will be mapped into a Java object or class. We will (ideally) map each field of the record to an attribute in that class.

You should have basic knowledge of how to work with the JDBC API. Therefore, this chapter does not discuss the many methods found in JDBC and its interface. The approach for discussing this component (DataAccessComponent) is top down: we will start with a discussion of the component itself, and then discuss its constituent parts and interfaces.

The chapter concludes by putting together a simple script to build or to compile the DataAccessComponent package. This package will be imported into the servlets program to access the database in chapters 12, 16, 17, 18, and 20.

Defining the DataAccessComponent

A DataAccessComponent is a Java library package that can be imported into a program to effectively access the database tables and carry out simple operations such as inserting, updating, and retrieving data from the tables. Figure 10-1 shows an example of a main program that is using this library package.

The use of the library will hide the initialization[1] of the database driver and the authentication to the database by encapsulating these two into an object. This basic initialization is straightforward: the first time, the DataAccessComponent is instantiated with the use of the

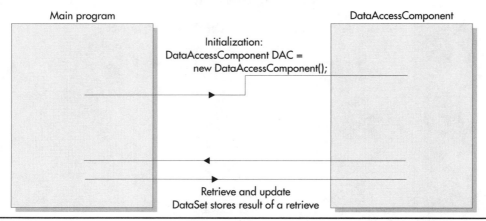

Figure 10-1 *A main program accessing the database through a DataAccessComponent*

[1] The term *initialization* is used here to stress the fact that this library call will also be initiated in the init() method of the servlet later in the book.

new operator followed by the signature of the constructor DataAccessComponent(), as shown in the following Java code example:

```
// Main program code
DataAccessComponent DAC = new DataAccessComponent();
```

The new operator returns a reference to the newly created DataAccessComponent that is returned to the DAC variable. Listing 10-1 shows the initial part of the DataAccessComponent package. From lines 9 to 18, all of the package variables are declared as private, particularly those that pertain to the database connection setting.

Listing 10-1   *DataAccessComponent initialization part*

```
1.    package com.tcnd.wasdg.dataaccess;2.
3.    import java.util.*;
4.    import java.sql.*;
5.    import java.io.*;
6.    import com.tcnd.wasdg.common.*;
7.
8.    public class DataAccessComponent
9.    {
10.       private java.sql.Connection conn;
11.       private static final boolean SUCCESS = true;
12.       private static final boolean FAILURE = false;
13.       private boolean someData;
14.       private static final String
      dbguidePropertiesFileName="/BOOK/10/Code/dbguide.properties";
15.       private String dbDriver;
16.       private String dbUrl;
17.       private String dbUser;
18.       private String dbPassword;
19.
20.
21.       public DataAccessComponent()
22.       {
23.          super();
24.          loadDefaultConnectionSettings();
25.       }
26.
27.       private void loadDefaultConnectionSettings()
28.       {
29.          java.util.Properties prop;
30.          prop = new Properties();
```

```
31.          try
32.          {
33.              prop.load(new
FileInputStream(dbguidePropertiesFileName));
34.          } catch (Exception e)
35.          {
36.              e.printStackTrace();
37.          }
38.
39.          dbDriver = prop.getProperty("dbdriver");
40.          dbUrl = prop.getProperty("dburl");
41.          dbUser = prop.getProperty("dbuser");
42.          dbPassword = prop.getProperty("dbpassword");
43.      }
44.
```

The DataAccessComponent defines its own constructor, shown on line 21. It also loads the default connection settings (line 24) from the properties file specified on the file system /BOOK/ 10/Code/dbguide.properties (line 14). The file dbguide.properties is shown in Listing 10-2. The dbdriver shows that we are using the DB2 net driver, known as type 3 driver. You can change the dbdriver from COM.ibm.db2.jdbc.net.DB2Driver to the app driver COM.ibm.db2.jdbc.app.DB2Driver instead, but you also need to change the dburl (shown in Listing 10-2) to jdbc:db2:DBGUIDE. Chapter 2 discusses the difference between type 2 and type 3 database drivers.

Listing 10-2   *dbguide.properties*

```
dbdriver=COM.ibm.db2.jdbc.net.DB2Driver
dburl=jdbc:db2://node2:50068/DBGUIDE
dbuser=dbuser
dbpassword=pwd123
dbinstance=DB2INST1
```

These properties are read and assigned to the private variable of the package on lines 39 to 42. Eventually, this causes a problem if a program using this package needs to modify the values of these variables. To solve this problem, you need to define "setter" and "getter" methods to access these variables. These data access methods are defined in the interface: IDataAccessComponent class. Your main program, as well as the DataAccessComponent class, will use this interface class to set and get specific data.

The DataAccessComponent will further set the database setting variables through an initDefaultConnectionSettings() method:

```
private void initDefaultConnectionSettings (IDataAccessObject iDAO)
    {
```

```
    iDAO.setDBdriver(dbDriver);
    iDAO.setDBurl(dbUrl);
    iDAO.setDBuser(dbUser);
    iDAO.setDBpassword(dbPassword);

    String dbu = iDAO.getDBuser();
    String dbpasswd = iDAO.getDBpassword();

    if (dbUser != null && (dbUser.equals("null") || dbUser.equals("")))
  iDAO.setDBuser(null);
    if (dbPassword != null && (dbPassword.equals("null") ||
  dbPassword.equals(""))) iDAO.setDBpassword(null);
  }
```

In your main program, you can change the settings to connect to a database either by editing the dbguide.properties file, or programmatically through the IDataAccessObject object.

```
// Main program code
DataAccessComponent DAC = new DataAccessComponent();
IDataAccessObject iDAO = DAC.createDAObject();
```

The second line creates an instance of the IDataAccessObject and returns a reference to the instance. This reference can be used to update the settings to connect to a database. Keep in mind that the code shown here does not connect or initialize the connection to the database, but it sets the default values to be used in the database connection.

The createDAObject() method is also defined in the DataAccessComponent package:

```
public IDataAccessObject createDAObject()
{
        IDataAccessObject iDAO = new IDataAccessObject();
        return iDAO;
}
```

The IDataAccessComponent interface is shown in its entirety in Listing 10-3. The interface has many getter/setter methods, which are summarized in Table 10-1.

Variable and Its Data Type	Additional information	Setter/Getter Methods
String dbUrl	JDBC thin driver URL	setDBurl getDBurl
String dbInstance	UDB instance	setDBinstance getDBinstance
String dbDriver	Driver by name	setDBdriver getDBdriver

Table 10-1   *The Getter/Setter as Defined in the Interface IDataAccessObject*

Variable and Its Data Type	Additional information	Setter/Getter Methods
String dbUser	User granted access to the database	setDBuser getDBuser
String dbPassword	Database user password	setDBpassword getDBpassword
nt maxRows	Maximum number of rows to store in the resultSet	setMaxRows getMaxRows
String commandString	SQL command to be processed	setCommandString getCommandString
java.util.Hashtable parameters	List of name-value pairs to be substituted in the commandString	setCommandString getCommandString
DataSet resultSet	Holds the result of a successfully executed SQL query	getDataSet setDataSet
boolean result	True if the executed statement is successful and data is available to you in the resultSet	setCommandResult getCommandResult
EmpAccnt empAcc	Mapping an employee record account into an EmpAccnt object	getEmpAccnt setEmpAccnt
CliAccnt cliAcc	Mapping a client record account into a CliAccnt object	getCliAccnt setCliAccnt

Table 10-1   *The Getter/Setter as Defined in the Interface IDataAccessObject* (continued)

The DataAccessComponent and your main program communicate data through the methods of the interface defined in Table 10-1.

Listing 10-3   *IDataAccessObject interface*

```
package com.tcnd.wasdg.common;

import java.io.*;
import java.util.*;

public class IDataAccessObject
{
    private java.lang.String dbUrl;
    private java.lang.String dbInstance;
    private java.lang.String dbDriver;
    private java.lang.String dbUser;
    private java.lang.String dbPassword;
    private java.lang.String commandName;
    private java.lang.String commandString;
    private java.util.Hashtable parameters;
    private int maxRows;
```

```java
private DataSet resultSet;
private boolean result;
private EmpAccnt empAcc;
private CliAccnt cliAcc;

public IDataAccessObject()
{
    super();
}

public String getDBurl() {return dbUrl;}
public void setDBurl(String s) {dbUrl = s;}
public String getDBinstance() {return dbInstance;}
public void setDBinstance(String s) {dbInstance = s;}
public String getDBdriver() {return dbDriver;}
public void setDBdriver(String s) {dbDriver = s;}
public String getDBuser() {return dbUser;}
public void setDBuser(String s) {dbUser = s;}
public String getDBpassword() {return dbPassword;}
public void setDBpassword(String s) {dbPassword = s;}
public int getMaxRows() {return maxRows;}
public void setMaxRows(int i) {maxRows = i;}
public String getCommandString() {return commandString;}
public void setCommandString(String s) {commandString = s;}
public void setParameters(java.util.Hashtable h) {parameters = h;}
public java.util.Hashtable getParameters() {return parameters;}

public DataSet getDataSet() {return resultSet;}
public void setDataSet(DataSet r) {resultSet = r;}
public boolean getCommandResult() {return result;}
public void setCommandResult(boolean b) {result = b;}

public EmpAccnt getEmpAccnt() {return empAcc;}
public void setEmpAccnt(EmpAccnt r) {empAcc = r;}
public CliAccnt getCliAccnt() {return cliAcc;}
public void setCliAccnt(CliAccnt r) {cliAcc = r;}
}
```

Examining Characteristics of the DataAccessComponent

There are four programmatic characteristics of the DataAccessComponent:

► Substitute text in the SQL command.

► Return the result into a DataSet object that can be cached.

▶   Fetch an employee record and map it into an object EmpAccnt.

▶   Fetch a client record and map it into an object CliAccnt.

Text Substitution in the DataAccessComponent

The DataAccessComponent provides a means of performing text substitution on a SQL command string during program execution. This is done through the use of a hash object that holds the key-value pairs and that are processed within the replacement string routines of the StrTool class file.

For instance, to insert a record for a new employee with userid dave into the EMPPWD table, you simply prepare the name-value pairs of the record fields into a hash, set up the SQL insertion command, and then execute the program, as shown in Listing 10-4.

Listing 10-4   *Ex11Insert inserts a record for userid dave into the EMPPWD table*

```
1.  // Ex11Insert: Insert one record into the EMPPWD table
2.
3.      import com.tcnd.wasdg.dataaccess.*;
4.      import com.tcnd.wasdg.common.*;
5.
6.      class Ex11Insert
7.      {
8.
9.          public static void main(String args[])
10.         {
11.             DataAccessComponent DAC = new DataAccessComponent();
12.             IDataAccessObject iDAO = DAC.createDAObject();
13.
14.             Hashtable hs = new Hashtable();
15.             hs.put("userid","dave");
16.             hs.put("password","dave123");
17.             iDAO.setParameters(hs);
18.
19.             iDAO.setCommandString("INSERT INTO DB2INST1.EMPPWD
        (USERID,PASSWORD,CREATED,TMLOGIN,TMLOGOUT) VALUES
        (':userid',':password', CURRENT TIMESTAMP, CURRENT TIMESTAMP, CURRENT
        TIMESTAMP)");
20.             iDAO = DAC.executeUpdate(iDAO);
21.             boolean result = iDAO.getCommandResult();
22.             System.out.println("Insertion result: " + result);
23.         }
24.     }
```

On lines 15 and 16, the userid and password are set into the Hashtable object, and they are then passed to the DataAccessComponent through the setter method setParameters() of the interface (line 17). The hash will then be used to substitute these parameters of the command string starting with a colon, as shown on line 19. If the command succeeds, then getCommandResult() returns true. When you run this program for the first time, a record for userid = dave is created for the first time. If you run the program a second time, the insertion will fail because USERID is the primary key, and the USERID = dave has already been inserted.

Data Retrieval Using the DataSet

Your main program can also retrieve data records easily. For instance, to retrieve all the records of the user whose userid is teller1, the program Ex10Select shown in Listing 10-5 iterates.

Sometimes, you will want to retrieve the data from a table using the SELECT in a statement, such as SELECT * FROM DB2INST1.EMPPWD. Your main program can retrieve data records easily by making a request using the setCommandString() and then by executing the query through the executeQuery() method. Listing 10-5 shows the Ex10Select code for the program to retrieve the records from the EMPPWD table.

Listing 10-5   *Ex10Select retrieves the USERID and PASSWORD from the EMPPWD table*

```
1.   import com.tcnd.wasdg.dataaccess.*;
2.   import com.tcnd.wasdg.common.*;
3.
4.   class Ex11Select
5.   {
6.
7.       public static void main(String args[])
8.       {
9.           DataAccessComponent DAC = new DataAccessComponent();
10.          IDataAccessObject iDAO = DAC.createDAObject();
11.
12.          iDAO.setCommandString("SELECT * FROM DB2INST1.EMPPWD ");
13.          iDAO = DAC.executeQuery(iDAO);
14.          DataSet dataSet = iDAO.getDataSet();
15.          boolean result = iDAO.getCommandResult();
16.          System.out.println("result= " + result);
17.
18.          if (iDAO.getCommandResult())
19.          {
20.              int rows = dataSet.getRowCount();
21.              dataSet.seekFirstRow();
22.
23.              for (int i=0;i<rows;i++)
24.              {
25.                  System.out.println("userid = " +
         dataSet.getValue("userid"));
```

```
26.                    System.out.println("password = " +
      dataSet.getValue("password"));
27.                    dataSet.seekNextRow();
28.                }
29.            }
30.        }
31.   }
```

After executing the query, the getCommandResult() on line 18 checks whether the command was successfully executed and whether any data is available to you in the dataSet. If data has been returned, then you need to seek to the first row using the seekFirstRow() of the dataSet object (line 21), and then iterate over all the rows (lines 23 and 27).

When you execute the program Ex10Select, you will get an output similar to the following:

```
[root@node1 Code]# java Ex10Select
result = true
userid = teller1
password = secret1
userid = teller2
password = secret2
userid = teller3
password = secret3
userid = teller4
password = secret4
userid = teller5
password = secret5
userid = dave
password = dave123
```

This assumes that you have populated the DBGUIDE database as explained in Chapter 9, and you have also executed the previous program Ex10Insert to insert a record for the user dave into the EMPPWD table.

Retrieving Data for the EmpAccnt and CliAccnt

You retrieve employee and client account information from your main program through the fetchEmpAccount() and fetchCliAccount() methods. The main program Ex10AccountRetrieval in Listing 10-6 shows how to fetch the account for the employee whose userid = teller1. The program uses the fetchEmpAccount() method that is defined in the DataAccessComponent.

Listing 10-6   *Ex10AccountRetrieval*

```
1.    import java.util.Hashtable;
2.
```

```
3.      import com.tcnd.wasdg.dataaccess.*;
4.      import com.tcnd.wasdg.common.*;
5.
6.      class Ex11AccountRetrieval
7.      {
8.
9.          public static void main(String args[])
10.         {
11.             DataAccessComponent DAC = new DataAccessComponent();
12.             IDataAccessObject iDAO = DAC.createDAObject();
13.
14.             Hashtable hs = new Hashtable();
15.
16.             System.out.println("*** 1- Fetching an employee (teller) account
        from EMPACCNT table:");
17.             hs.put("userid","teller1");
18.             iDAO.setParameters(hs);
19.
20.             iDAO.setCommandString("SELECT * FROM DB2INST1.EMPACCNT WHERE
        USERID = ':userid'");
21.             iDAO = DAC.fetchEmpAccount(iDAO);
22.             if (iDAO.getCommandResult()) {
23.                 EmpAccnt aEmp = iDAO.getEmpAccnt();
24.                 aEmp.show();
25.             }
26.
27.
28.             System.out.println("*** 2- Fetching a client account from
        CLIACCNT table:");
29.             hs.put("clientid","client1");
30.             iDAO.setParameters(hs);
31.             iDAO.setCommandString("SELECT * FROM DB2INST1.CLIACCNT WHERE
        CLIENTID = ':clientid'");
32.             iDAO = DAC.fetchCliAccount(iDAO);
33.             if (iDAO.getCommandResult())
34.             {
35.                 CliAccnt aCli = iDAO.getCliAccnt();
36.                 aCli.show();
37.                 System.out.println("The first name of the client with
        cliendid client1: " + aCli.getFrstName());
38.             }
39.
40.             System.out.println("*** 3- Getting an employee (teller)
        password:");
41.             hs.put("userid","teller1");
42.             iDAO.setParameters(hs);
43.
44.             iDAO.setCommandString("SELECT PASSWORD FROM DB2INST1.EMPPWD WHERE
        USERID = ':userid'");
45.             iDAO = DAC.executeQuery(iDAO);
```

```
46.              if (iDAO.getCommandResult()) {
47.                  DataSet dataSet = iDAO.getDataSet();
48.                  dataSet.seekFirstRow();
49.                  System.out.println("The employee teller1 password is :" +
        dataSet.getValue("password"));
50.              }
51.              else {
52.                  System.out.println("The employee teller11 password is:
        AUTHENTICATION FAILED!");
53.              }
54.
55.              System.out.println("*** 4- Getting an employee (teller)
        password:");
56.              hs.put("userid","teller1");
57.              hs.put("password","secret11");
58.              iDAO.setParameters(hs);
59.
60.              iDAO.setCommandString("SELECT * FROM DB2INST1.EMPPWD WHERE
        (USERID = ':userid' AND PASSWORD = ':password')");
61.              iDAO = DAC.executeQuery(iDAO);
62.              if (iDAO.getCommandResult()) {
63.                  DataSet dataSet = iDAO.getDataSet();
64.                  dataSet.seekFirstRow();
65.                  System.out.println("The employee teller1 password is :" +
        dataSet.getValue("password"));
66.              }
67.              else {
68.                  System.out.println("The employee teller1 password is:
        AUTHENTICATION FAILED!");
69.              }
70.
71.          }
72.  }
```

Running the Ex10AccountRetrieval program will produce an output similar to that depicted in Figure 10-2.

The program first creates a reference to the DataAccessComponent; then it does two fetches from the EMPACCNT and CLIACCNT tables, and two data retrievals from the EMPPWD table:

▶ Fetch the employee record for the account with userid = teller1.

▶ Fetch the client record for the account with clientid = client1.

▶ Query the EMPPWD for the userid = teller1.

▶ Query the EMPPWD for the userid = teller1 and password = secret11: this will fail because the teller1 password is secret1.

```
File  Sessions  Settings  Help

[root@node1 Code]# java Ex11AccountRetrieval
*** 1- Fetching an employee (teller) account from EMPACCNT table:
userID: teller1
password: null
frstName: Jane1
lastName: Doe1
image: ../images/teller1
ssn: 000000000
empno: 1
email: teller1@wasette.com
contact: somecontact
counter: 0
*** 2- Fetching a client account from CLIACCNT table:
clientID: client1
password: null
bankID: A000001
category: A
rempID: teller4
frstName: Dave1
lastName: Spender1
image: ../images/client1
email: client1@wasette.com
ccredits: 0
cdebits: 0
balance: 0
The first name of the client with cliendid client1: Dave1
*** 3- Getting an employee (teller) password:
The employee teller1 password is :secret1
*** 4- Getting an employee (teller) password:
The employee teller1 password is: AUTHENTICATION FAILED!
[root@node1 Code]# █

  New    Konsole
```

Figure 10-2   *Output of the Ex10AccountRetrieval program*

The retrieval of an employee (teller) or a client record is done objectively by mapping the record fields into a Java object attribute. The process is a direct mapping and is achieved easily. The following section focuses on the employee records saved in the EMPACCNT table; the same applies for the client records saved in the CLIACCNT table.

Objectifying the Database Records: The Employee Account Object

Each employee record is held in a Java object. This Java object is the class EmpAccnt in which setter/getter methods have been coded. Actually, for each field in the EmpAccnt record, two methods have been defined: the first to set the value and hold it in the object, and the second to retrieve the value from the object. DataAccessComponent makes use of the EmpAccnt class to communicate a retrieved record to your main program. This is done through the IDataAccessObject interface.

Listing 10-7 shows the record of an employee account as defined in the dbguide.sql program (from Chapter 8). Table 10-2 shows each field of the record and the methods defined to set and retrieve its value through the interface IDataAccessObject.

Listing 10-7   *The fields of an employee account as defined in EMPACCNT table*

```
--
-- Define the 'EMPACCNT' table
--
DROP TABLE EMPACCNT
CREATE TABLE EMPACCNT (
USERID VARCHAR(12) NOT NULL,
PRIMARY   KEY ( USERID ),
FRSTNAME VARCHAR(16) NOT NULL,
LASTNAME VARCHAR(32) NOT NULL,
IMAGE    VARCHAR(255),
SSN      VARCHAR(9),
EMPNO    CHAR(7)  NOT NULL,
EMAIL    VARCHAR(32),
CONTACT  VARCHAR(32) NOT NULL,
COUNTER  INTEGER NOT NULL WITH DEFAULT 0,
NDX DECIMAL(15,0) GENERATED BY DEFAULT AS IDENTITY(START WITH 1)
)
GRANT ALL PRIVILEGES ON TABLE EMPACCNT TO USER DBUSER
```

Field	Methods
USERID	getUserID setUserID
FRSTNAME	getFrstName setFrstName
LASTNAME	getLastName setLastName
IMAGE	getImage setImage
SSN	getSsn setSsn
EMPNO	getEmpno setEmpno
EMAIL	getEmail setEmail

Table 10-2   *Fields of an Employee Record and the Getter/Setter Methods Defined in the EmpAccnt Object*

Field	Methods
CONTACT	getContact setContact
COUNTER	getCounter setCounter
NDX	No methods defined here—just used internally

Table 10-2   *Fields of an Employee Record and the Getter/Setter Methods Defined in the EmpAccnt Object* (continued)

Each of the fields of an employee record as defined in the EMPACCNT table has a getter and a setter method, as shown in Listing 10-8 of the EmpAccnt class. This class is also supplemented with a show() method to print the content of each retrieved field to standard output.

Listing 10-8   *EmpAccnt class*

```
package com.tcnd.wasdg.common;

public class EmpAccnt
{
    private String userID;
    private String password;
    private String frstName;
    private String lastName;
    private String image;
    private String ssn;
    private String empno;
    private String email;
    private String contact;
    private int counter;

    public EmpAccnt()
    {
    }

    public String getUserID() {return userID;}
    public void setUserID(String s) {userID = s;}

    public String getPassword() {return password;}
    public void setPassword(String s) {password = s;}

    public String getFrstName() {return frstName;}
    public void setFrstName(String s) {frstName = s;}
```

```
public String getLastName() {return lastName;}
public void setLastName(String s) {lastName = s;}

public String getImage() {return image;}
public void setImage(String s) {image = s;}

public String getSsn() {return ssn;}
public void setSsn(String s) {ssn = s;}

public String getEmpno() {return empno;}
public void setEmpno(String s) {empno = s;}

public String getEmail() {return email;}
public void setEmail(String s) {email = s;}

public String getContact() {return contact;}
public void setContact(String s) {contact = s;}

public int getCounter() {return counter;}
public void setCounter(int i) {counter = i;}

public void show()
{
    System.out.println("userID: " + userID);
    System.out.println("password: " + password);
    System.out.println("frstName: " + frstName);
    System.out.println("lastName: " + lastName);
    System.out.println("image: " + image);
    System.out.println("ssn: " + ssn);
    System.out.println("empno: " + empno);
    System.out.println("email: " + email);
    System.out.println("contact: " + contact);
    System.out.println("counter: " + counter);
}
}
```

Understanding the Build Process

Unlike the design of a package that might be hard to achieve, the build process of a package is simple to realize. However, the design of a package can be impacted by the build process and the discipline of the developer. The discipline is in the way you structure your directory and set up your development environment. This is usually done through the skill of a system integrator.

In Chapter 3, you were introduced to the Java package in a basic way. Now you will see how to compile a Java package in a two-line shell script.

Building a Java package requires basically four steps:

1. Select a base directory where you will build the package.

2. Create the appropriate subdirectories in the base directory. Each subdirectory created must represent the mapping that follows the package statement. Programs that are part of a package usually start with a first line statement starting with the keyword package. Given a set of Java programs in a directory tree, you can get all the package statements with the following command:

```
find . -name "*.java" -exec grep "package" {} \;
```

The command assumes that a package statement is started normally at the beginning of the line, although this is not required.

3. Edit and save the file in the appropriate subdirectories.

4. Run a script that compiles all Java programs in the tree structure collectively.

Creating the Java Package Tree

To build the DataAccessComponent package, you select a base directory in which you will build the directories com/tcnd/wasdg/common and com/tcnd/wasdg/dataaccess:

```
mkdir -p com/tcnd/wasdg/common
mkdir -p com/tcnd/wasdg/dataaccess
```

Each program should be placed in its proper directory, which is specified on the first line of Java code in the package statement.

Mediocre Compilation of the Java Package

A Java program can import one or many packages or class files. Because the standard packages can be found in the CLASSPATH environment variable that should already be set (as discussed in Chapters 3 and 4), you should be concerned to resolve the dependency on only the new class files. The javac command can take a list of interdependent .java files all on the same line to compile them while resolving their dependencies. However, you need to be in the base directory of your development tree when issuing the javac command. For instance, to compile the DataAccessComponent package, from the base directory of the Java package, issue the following command:

```
# javac -classpath $CLASSPATH com/tcnd/wasdg/common/*.java
    com/tcnd/wasdg/dataaccess/*.java
```

This task is easily accomplished for such a small package. Yet this method of explicit compilation is mediocre because it suffers from generality and becomes cumbersome as more classes (from different developers) are added to your development tree. The solution is to batch process the compilation of .java files that form a package, as discussed next.

Compiling .java Programs Collectively: The jall Script

The four commands, `find`, `cat`, `xargs`, and `javac`, can work collectively in a two-line shell script to compile a Java package. Listing 10-9 shows such a shell script.

Listing 10-9   *The jall script compiles all .java programs*

```
#! /bin/sh
find . -name "*.java" > javafiles.list
cat javafiles.list | xargs javac
```

The script finds all these .java programs and dumps them into the file javafiles.list. It then dumps the content of the javafiles.list to be collectively piped and represented to the `javac` command. (Chapter 8 contains a similar technique using `xargs` to work on a collection of processes.) The use of such commands is not restricted to the system administrator; developers should be aware of UNIX commands that put discipline in the development process.

To build a package such as the DataAccessComponent, all you do is run the jall script in the base directory of your package development tree. If you want to recompile the package, you need to remove the .class files from all the subdirectories of the package:

```
# find . -name "*.class" -exec rm -f {} \;
```

This command forces the removal of all the .class files found in the subdirectories relative to the current directory where the command is issued. After removing the .class files, you can recompile the Java package with jall.

Wrapping Up

The DataAccessComponent can be imported into your main program to access the database while hiding the JDBC API calls. The data flowing between the database and your program will be stored in a DataSet object. Because the SQL commands are simple strings where parameters can be selectively set, the DataAccessComponent uses a hash of type java.util.Hashtable to store the parameters to be substituted as key-value pairs.

The data access is generalized through the DataAccessComponent and its interface IDataAccessObject methods—first, by setting the command string with the setCommandString (defined in the interface), and then by executing the command string with executeQuery defined in the DataAccessComponent.

Particular methods are defined in the package to access data from specific tables. To access the DBGUIDE database and fetch records from the EMPACCNT and CLIACCNT table, the DataAccessComponent provides two corresponding methods: fetchEmpAccount() and fetchCliAccount(). You can easily compile the package by using the jall script.

Developing a J2EE Web Application in WAS

IN THIS CHAPTER:

**Loading a J2EE Web Application:
A Simplified View**

**Adding a New Build to an Already Loaded
Web Application**

Understanding the j2tree Script

I n general, WAS contains many interesting features to manage web resources, which makes it an excellent application to study. WAS AEs, however, contains many features found in the larger WAS AE application and is more flexible for a beginning developer to use to manage and test code.

This chapter describes only those features of J2EE that are sufficient for writing reasonably interesting web applications under WAS AEs. Chapter 14 completes the description and deployment of the J2EE application as it is treated by WAS tools (namely the Application Assembly Tool (AAT) and Enterprise ARchive expander).

We refer to the web application that we will build in this chapter with its display name: the WASDG Application. Many of the following chapters will add more programs to the WASDG Application. The reader should not have any difficulty running and testing the code of each chapter, as the method developed here allows a quick deployment of a web application such as the WASDG Application. Note also that the development environment must be set according to the rules set out in chapters 3 and 4, in which we discussed how to prepare the WASDG environment. If readers choose to skip Parts I and II of this book, they will need to go over the README_PART_III.TXT file to quickly set up their development environment.

Loading a J2EE Web Application: A Simplified View

You can program and compile a servlet regardless of the intervention of WAS. You can edit and save a simple JAVA program, and then compile it with the command `javac`. Testing the servlet, however, requires you to lay out the web module directory structure and to fill in the file descriptors as required by J2EE *and* WAS v4.[1]

A J2EE enterprise application in a WAS deployment consists of an EAR archive folder whose contents are laid out to reflect the structure of the web modules and the Enterprise JavaBeans modules. You will learn the simplest way to write and test a web module, which consists of two servlets as required for WAS AEs. In the next chapters, you will expand the web module by adding to it multiple servlets and then study how they interact with each other. As a result, you will understand the loading order versus the visibility order of the classes, as explained in Chapter 15.

Creating the First J2EE Tree

A web module is the basic unit of programming upon which web applications are served. A web application is usually documented at least at two levels, the *intra*module level and the *inter*module level. The first level is described internally to the module within a file, known as the web application deployment descriptor, web.xml. The second level's description is laid in the WAS configuration data when registering the module and is specifically handled by WAS while processing the application specification. The application's specifications are further defined at two levels: within the application server configuration (that is, server-cfg.xml), and within the application configuration file by itself (application.xml and the .xmi IBM extensions files).

---

[1] Usually, that should be "as required solely by J2EE," but WAS v4 adds in some extensions and binding.

In this chapter, you will develop scripts to control the intramodule level of a web application already registered in WAS. These scripts allow you to create and test codes under WAS while gaining a clear understanding of the WAS environment. Although the Application Assembly Tool (AAT) allows you to manipulate the web module at the intramodule level (and will be examined on occasion in later chapters), it is not the subject of its own separate chapter. Using the scripts is better than testing and developing code using any of the supplemental graphical applications.

A programmer should implement web modules according to given specifications and should also provide the intramodule specifications in the deployment descriptor. A web module may contain byte code, data that can be interpreted and compiled as byte code, and such images and text content.

A collection of web modules can be archived and treated as a single unit known as an *enterprise application archive*. In this section, however, we are interested only in building one simple web module into which we will add the servlets' byte code.

Setting Basic EAR Tree Structure

The most basic tree of an enterprise web application consists of two directories: the META-INF directory holding the MANIFEST.MF file, the application.xml file, and the web application directory (webapp), holding the files and the directory structure of the web module.

```
wasdg.ear
|-- wasdg.ear/META-INF/
|     `-- wasdg.ear/META-INF/application.xml
`-- wasdg.ear/webapp/
      `-- wasdg.ear/webapp/WEB-INF/
            |-- wasdg.ear/webapp/WEB-INF/classes/
            |-- wasdg.ear/webapp/WEB-INF/lib/
            `-- wasdg.ear/webapp/WEB-INF/web.xml
```

In reality, this is not the complete tree structure of the J2EE web application. However, for now, we will consider it that simple; rather than allude to unnecessary details about J2EE, we will focus on the basic components of the tree and build simple scripts that allow us to quickly write and test servlets under WAS. We will then emphasize important aspects of WAS such as loading classpath, destroying a servlet, and using the WAS binding and extensions descriptors (see chapters 14 and 15).

Where to Create the EAR Tree Structure

You must choose a base development directory where the enterprise application is to be built. For instance, user dave, whose home directory is $HOME, might choose to have the $HOME/Code directory as his development directory. This user should have an entry in his environment profile that sets and exports BASE_DEV. For example, the Linux user dave would have created the directory Code (`mkdir $HOME/Code chmood 2754`

$HOME/Code) and added the following two lines to the .bash_profile script that resides in his $HOME directory:

```
BASE_DEV=$HOME/Code
export BASE_DEV
```

Because on UNIX, the environment variable HOME reflects the user home directory, you can set the BASE_DEV environment variable globally in the system profile /etc/profile or in the setcustom.sh script (discussed in Chapter 3) so it is set when setj.sh is executed. You can also put the script "thisbase" in your search PATH (e.g./tools directory) to set up the BASE_DEV environment varialble: #!/bin/khk. BASE_DEV="pwol" echo BASE_DEV is now $BASE_DEV export BASE_DEV. You need to change the directory to the location where you have extracted this chapter's code and execute this command:

```
#   .  thisbase
```

Also, be careful not to set BASE_DEV to a commonly mounted directory to be shared by many developers. Sharing a development directory between two or more developers requires the use of a source control application, which is the subject Chapter 21. For now, we'll consider the simplest situation in which you are working on your own development tree that resides in BASE_DEV.

Change the directory to BASE_DEV and create the development tree wasdg.ear. If you downloaded this chapter's code, run the j2tree script to create the basic tree structure. The j2tree script is a Perl program that takes four arguments to build a simple tree structure configured with enough specifications to load a list of servlets:

```
j2tree <earfolder> <web module> <context root> [servlet list]
where [servlet list] is an optional list of servlets of the form:
[[<servlet name>:<servlet classname>:<servlet uri-pattern>][...][
<servlet name>:<servlet classname>:<servlet uri-pattern>]]
```

The tree created will contain the application.xml and web.xml files. If a list of servlets is specified, each servlet is mapped properly in the web.xml file. Finally, the j2tree script inspects the ./Dist directory and if it finds the .tar archive <*web module*>j2tree.tar, it will extract its contents into the classes directory of the web module specified. Obviously, <*web module*>j2tree.tar consists of .java and .class files. Here is an example:

```
# cd $BASE_DEV
# j2tree wasdg.ear webapp /wasbook
dumpenv:DumpEnv:/dumpenv:login:com.tcnd.wasdg.LoginScreen:/login
```

The order of the arguments following the j2tree script is important. Assuming that webappj2tree.tar is available in the $BASE_DEV/Dist directory, the previous command will create the following tree structure.

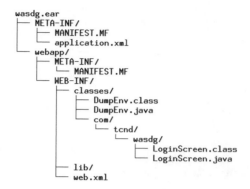

```
wasdg.ear
├── META-INF/
│   ├── MANIFEST.MF
│   └── application.xml
└── webapp/
    ├── META-INF/
    │   └── MANIFEST.MF
    └── WEB-INF/
        ├── classes/
        │   ├── DumpEnv.class
        │   ├── DumpEnv.java
        │   └── com/
        │       └── tcnd/
        │           └── wasdg/
        │               ├── LoginScreen.class
        │               └── LoginScreen.java
        ├── lib/
        └── web.xml
```

Using the Distribution Directory

You need to create a Dist directory in the $BASE_DEV directory. Some of the scripts that we will develop in this book often use this directory as a temporary directory for the `jar` command to store its archives. The location of this directory is important because of the way the `jar` command is exercised when archiving an enterprise application with our scripts. AAT, when used in any future chapter, will also retrieve and store in EAR and WAR archives from the following directory: $BASE_DEV/Dist.

Building the Web Application

The first time you build a web application, you need to follow precise steps so that you register the web application in the WAS administrative repository. This way, WAS will load and manage your web application through its containers.[2]

In this chapter, we will write simple servlet programs without discussing their methodological features, so you won't be distracted by servlet specifications.

Building and Deploying the wasdg.ear Web Application

Table 11-1 shows the steps for creating and installing the enterprise application development tree of wasdg.ear. In fact, steps 1 through 4 are somewhat equivalent to running the `j2tree` command discussed in "Setting the Basic EAR Tree Structure."

The listing of the servlets DumpEnv.java and LoginServlet.java mentioned in step 2 in Table 11-1 aren't discussed until Chapter 12.

Step 6 actually performs two functions: it extracts the wasdg.ear file into the $INSTALLEDAPPS/wasdg.ear directory, and it updates the configuration repository (namely, server-cfg.xml in our WAS AEs) with the new enterprise application wasdg.ear. These two actions are referred to as deploying the archive wasdg.ear into WAS. If you opted to, you certainly could make these changes manually; however, it is recommended that you use the tools provided by IBM to ensure proper compatibility with future product releases.

---

[2]   In this chapter, we are considering only the WAS web container to manage our servlets. The EJB container is the subject of Chapter 18.

Steps	Programmer Actions and Notes
1. Create the tree structure described previously.	```mkdir -p wasdg.ear/META-INF``` ```mkdir -p wasdg.ear/WEB-INF/classes.```

2. Locate the DumpEnv.java servlet and compile it with `javac`.	```cd $BASE_DEV/wasdg.ear/webapp/WEB-INF/classes```
	```javac DumpEnv.java```
	```cd $BASE_DEV/wasdg.ear/webapp/WEB-INF/classes/com/tcnd/```
	```wasdgjavac LoginScreen.java.```

3. Locate the web module deployment descriptor file web.xml in the wasdg.ear/WEB-INF directory. No action is necessary because j2tree will deposit it there.	This step is to describe the web app and defines the configuration and mapping of the servlets, JSPs, and EJBs.
4. Locate the application.xml in the wasdg.ear/META-INF directory. No action is necessary because j2tree will deposit it there.	This step is to describe the web module created in step3 and add it to the web application. It also shows the context root mapping between the module name (physical URI, location on the file system) and the HTTP URI.

5. Archive the application using the `jar` command. The directory Dist that has been created by j2tree is also being used in this archiving operation.	Make sure you are in $BASE_DEV and then issue
	```jar cvf Dist/webapp -C ./wasdg.ear/webapp.```
	```jar cvf Dist/wasdg.ear -C ./wasdg.ear```
	```META-INF -C Dist webapp.```

6. Load the EAR archive in WAS using SEAppInstall.	$SEAPPINSTALL—install Dist/wasdg.ear.
7. Add in the URI /wasbook to the default_host.	Stop the HTTP server: `apachectl stop`. Edit the plugin-cfg.xml file located in the WAS config directory, i.e., was_home/config/plugin-cfg.xml, and add the entry `<Uri Name="/wasbook"/>` to the default_host URI group. Start the HTTP server: `apachectl start`.
8. Stop and restart WAS for the major changes in the administrative repository to take effect.	$STOPWAS; $STARTWAS.

Table 11-1   *Basic Steps to Create, Build, and Deploy a J2EE Application*

If your installation completed properly, then step 9 should show the output of the DumpEnv servlet.

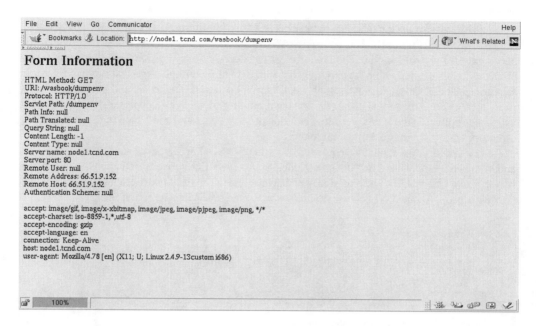

Because SEAppInstall.sh makes a backup copy of server-cfg.xml before making any changes to it, you can differentiate (using the `diff` command) the modified file server-cfg.xml to its backed up copy server-cfg.xml~. The bold font in the following lines reflects the changes:

```
1.<webContainer xmi:id="WebContainer_1"
installedWebModules="WebModuleRef_1 WebModuleRef_2 WebModuleRef_3
WebModuleRef_4 WebModuleRef_5 WebModuleRef_6 WebModuleRef_7
WebModuleRef_8">
2.<installedApps xmi:id="ApplicationRef_5" name="The WASDG
Application" archiveURL="${APP_INSTALL_ROOT}/wasdg.ear">
3.<modules xmi:type="applicationserver:WebModuleRef"
xmi:id="WebModuleRef_8" uri="webapp"/>
```

Line 3 shows that the web application webapp is a web module that is pointed to with a WebModuleRef_8. Line 1 shows that this web module is to be loaded in the servlet container WebContainer_1. For now, we are not concerned with other web modules, but notice that several web modules can be managed or served from within a single web container, as shown in line 1. This point is important for understanding the interoperability between servlets from different web modules.

You should also notice that deploying wasdg.ear did not require any actions to be taken through the web or administrative console of WAS AEs. However, you can certainly look into the administrative console to realize that wasdg.ear has been registered properly with its displayed name, which is set in the application.xml file: /display-name/Sample Application/display-name. Be aware that our simple deployment of this J2EE application is quite basic and has some missing files, such as the .xmi files (IBM extensions and binding files). While deploying the application using SEAppInstall, these missing files are automatically generated and added in the deployment directory (more about these files in Chapter 14).

To browse through the deployed wasdg.ear's the WASDG application, start the web console and in the left pane, walk down the tree: Nodes| *node name*-|Enterprise Applications-| *application server name* (the WASDG application)-|Web Modules; in the right pane, click the web module: ours is webapp. Figure 11-1 shows you that webapp is in a START Execution State.

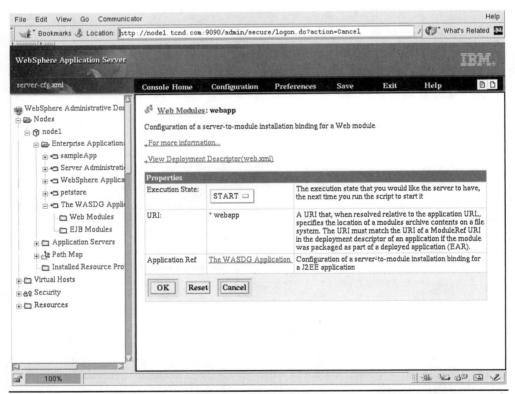

Figure 11-1   *The wasdg.ear file displayed as the WASDG application in the web console*

You can also browse through the web.xml of this web module by clicking View Deployment Descriptor(web.xml). Because the webapp web module is part of the wasdg.ear file installed application, its settings are read-only and cannot be modified from the web console[3] (see Figure 11-2).

The enterprise application descriptor application.xml can also be browsed in read-only by selecting in the left pane.[4] Nodes | *node name* | Enterprise Applications | Sample Application; and clicking View Deployment Descriptor(application.xml) in the right pane (see Figure 11-3).

Refreshing a Deployed EAR: refreshear.sh

Step 6 in Table 11-1 shows the first time you installed the application wasdg.ear on WAS. You need to reinstall wasdg.ear in case you make global changes that can affect the description of the enterprise application as a whole. Such changes include modifying the

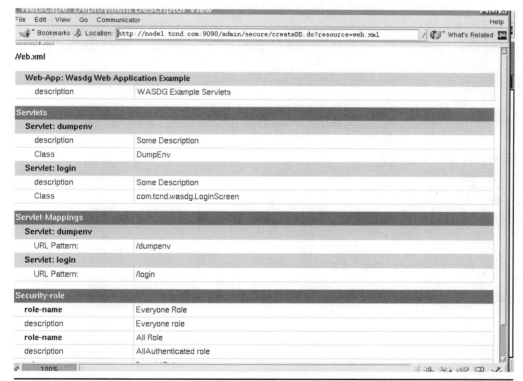

Figure 11-2   *Viewing the deployment descriptor web.xml from the administrative console*

---

[3]   Although the web.xml of a web module cannot be changed from the administrative console, some properties of the EJB modules can be changed from the WAS AEs administrative console.

[4]   A couple of the properties of an enterprise application are not read-only and can be changed from the administrative console. These are known as IBM extensions, that is, IBM application binding properties, which can be edited by selecting Modify Role to User Mappings.

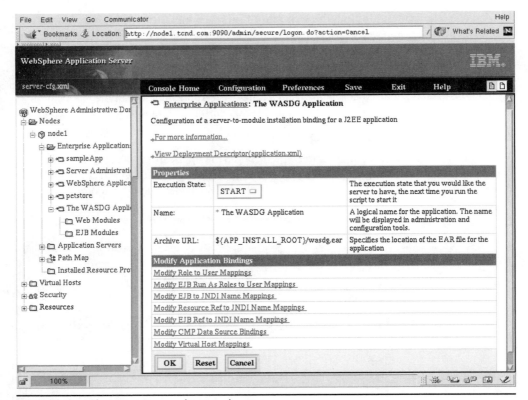

Figure 11-3 *The enterprise application descriptor*

application.xml, the MANIFEST.MF, for example, adding a classpath, and changing the structure of the web application tree.

After installing EAR for the first time, as outlined in Table 11-1, you can use a script such as the refreshear.sh file to refresh the EAR application (see Listing 11-1).

Listing 11-1 *refreshear reinstalls the Entrprise Archive application then restarts WAS*

```
1.  #!/bin/sh
2.
3.  # Uninstall the application and delete it any previous install. Ok with
    WAS AEs
4.  $SEAPPINSTALL -uninstall wasdg.ear -delete true
5.
6.  # First archive the web application, then the enterprise application
7.  jar cvf $BASE_DEV/Dist/webapp -C $BASE_DEV/wasdg.ear/webapp .
8.  jar cvf $BASE_DEV/Dist/wasdg.ear -C $BASE_DEV/wasdg.ear META-INF -C
    $BASE_DEV/Dist webapp
```

```
9.
10.   # Install the application
11.   $SEAPPINSTALL -install Dist/wasdg.ear -ejbdeploy false -precompileJsp
      false -interactive false
12.
13.   # Restart WAS
14.   $STOPWAS
15.   $STARTWAS
```

You usually do not need to deploy an .ear file from the beginning if you make changes to one of its already registered web applications. For instance, you do not need to reinstall the web module or restart WAS if you add a servlet to or delete a servlet from the wasdg.ear/webapp/WEB-INF/classes or wasdg.ear/webapp/WEB-INF/classes/com/tcnd/wasdg directories, if you add a .jar file to the wasdg.ear/webapp/WEB-INF/lib directory, or if you change the content of the web.xml file of the web module. WAS keeps on monitoring the deployed web.xml file and any changes in the servlets or the contents of the lib and classes directories, but keep in mind this is true only for a development environment, because such dynamic loading does not promote stability and security of a production environment.

Generating a Basic Web Application Deployment Descriptor: web.xml

The detailed content of the web application deployment descriptor is the subject of Chapter 14. However, there are a few entries you should be familiar with. In particular, the following tags that pertain to mapping a servlet's byte code into a logical url-pattern name that can be requested by a browser:

```
1. <servlet id="Servlet_NUMBER">
2.         <servlet-name>SERVLETNAME</servlet-name>
3.         <description>Some Description</description>
4.         <servlet-class>SERVLETCLASS</servlet-class>
5. </servlet>
6. <servlet-mapping id="ServletMapping_NUMBER">
7.         <servlet-name>SERVLETNAME</servlet-name>
8.         <url-pattern>URLPATTERN</url-pattern>
9. </servlet-mapping>
```

On lines 1 and 6, NUMBER is a positive integer that is incrementally assigned for each servlet. Line 2 associates an identity name for the servlet class named on line 4. Line 8 shows the mapped *url-pattern* name for this servlet.

Another point you should notice is that the mapping mechanism uses some primitive pointers that can be randomly assigned if you opt to use a descriptive SERVLETNAME on lines 2 and 7. It might be confusing to someone who thinks that this is a descriptive field of the servlet, while in reality, it is just a pointer. You might wonder why you should use an extra pointer such as this one if the mapping can already be realized with the id numbering schema shown on lines 1 and 6. Obviously, this pointer is not a surplus, and it plays a basic role when a servlet participates in a WebGroup. The web container uses this SERVLETNAME when initializing and destroying a servlet.

Every time you create a servlet, or if you need to change the Uri-pattern of a servlet, you need to edit and make changes to the web.xml file. Using our method of deployment does not require manual editing of the web.xml file. We will make changes in the servlets.list, then run resetwebxml to regenerate the web.xml file. The resetwebxml script in Listing 11-2 regenerates the web.xml and deposits it into the corresponding directories.

Listing 11-2 *resetwebxml script*

```
1.   #!/bin/ksh
2.
3.   # genwebxml must be in your PATH, e.g. /tools
4.   genwebxml  >  $BASE_DEV/wasdg.ear/webapp/WEB-INF/web.xml
5.   genwebxml  >  $INSTALLEDAPPS/wasdg.ear/webapp/WEB-INF/web.xml
```

The resetwebxml script calls the genwebxml, a Perl script that generates the web application deployment descriptor. genwebxml (shown in Listing 11-3) opens and reads the file servlets.list, processing each line, to generate a web.xml with a proper servlet mapping. Each line of servlets.list contains three fields separated by a space, and they are described as follows: SERVLETNAME SERVLETCLASS URLPATTERN. The following shows the contents of the servlets.list used in this chapter:

```
login com.tcnd.wasdg.LoginScreen /login
dumpenv DumpEnv /dumpenv
```

Both scripts, genwebxml and resetwebxml, should be located in your search PATH directory so that they can execute properly. You do not need to execute either one of the scripts explicitly. However, if you want to see what is being written to the web.xml file, invoke genwebxml, and it will print the content of the generated file to your screen.

The servlets.list file also resides in the base development directory, and it is the only file that you need to edit in case you need to modify or add a new servlet mapping.

Listing 11-3 *genwebxml script to process servlets.list and generate the web.xml*

```
1.   #!/usr/bin/perl
2.
3.   my $webxml = <WEBXML;
4.   <?xml version="1.0" encoding="UTF-8"?>
5.   <!DOCTYPE web-app PUBLIC "-//Sun Microsystems, Inc.//DTD Web Application
     2.2//EN" "http://java.sun.com/j2ee/dtds/web-app_2_2.dtd">
6.       <web-app id="WebApp_1">
7.          <display-name>Wasdg Web Application Example</display-name>
8.          <description>WASDG Example Servlets</description>
9.   SERVLET_CONTEXT_PARAM
10.  SERVLET_NAMES
11.  SERVLET_MAPPINGS
12.          <security-role id="SecurityRole_1">
```

```perl
13.                <description>Everyone role</description>
14.                <role-name>Everyone Role</role-name>
15.            </security-role>
16.            <security-role id="SecurityRole_2">
17.                <description>AllAuthenticated role</description>
18.                <role-name>All Role</role-name>
19.            </security-role>
20.            <security-role id="SecurityRole_3">
21.                <description>Deny all access role</description>
22.                <role-name>DenyAllRole</role-name>
23.            </security-role>
24.        </web-app>
25.    WEBXML
26.
27.    my $svname = <SVNAME;
28.            <servlet id="Servlet_NUMBER">
29.                <servlet-name>SERVLETNAME</servlet-name>
30.                <description>Some Description</description>
31.                <servlet-class>SERVLETCLASS</servlet-class>
32.            </servlet>
33.    SVNAME
34.
35.    my $svmapping = <SVMAPPING;
36.            <servlet-mapping id="ServletMapping_NUMBER">
37.                <servlet-name>SERVLETNAME</servlet-name>
38.                <url-pattern>URLPATTERN</url-pattern>
39.            </servlet-mapping>
40.    SVMAPPING
41.
42.    my $svcontextparam = <SVCONTEXTPARAM;
43.            <context-param>
44.                <param-name>PARAMNAME</param-name>
45.            <param-value>PARAMVALUE</param-value>
46.            </context-param>
47.    SVCONTEXTPARAM
48.
49.    sub in_list {
50.    my($temp,@list) = @_;
51.    my($e);
52.    foreach $e (@list) {if ($temp eq $e) { return 1; } }
53.    return 0;
54.    }
55.
56.    # srand;
57.    my $stuffer1 = "";
58.    my $stuffer2 = "";
59.    my $stuffer3 = "";
60.    my $fin;
61.    if ( (defined($ENV{BASE_DEV})) && (-d $ENV{BASE_DEV}) ) { $fin =
       "$ENV{BASE_DEV}/servlets.list"; }
62.    else { $fin = "servlets.list"; }
63.    die "It does not seem you have any servlets.list! Set up the BASE_DEV\n"
       unless (-r $fin);
```

```perl
64.  open(FILE,"<$fin");
65.  my $i = 0;
66.  my(@contextlist) = (); # this holds a list of context init parameters
67.  while (<FILE>) {
68.      next unless (!((/^#/) || (/^$/)));
69.      my $s1 = $svname;
70.      my $s2 = $svmapping;
71.
72.      $i++;
73.      my($name,$classname,$urlpattern,$param) = split(/\s/,$_,4);
74.      # $name = 'map' . int(rand(1000000));
75.      $s1 =~ s/Servlet_NUMBER/Servlet_$i/;
76.      $s1 =~ s/SERVLETNAME/$name/;
77.      $s1 =~ s/SERVLETCLASS/$classname/;
78.      $s2 =~ s/ServletMapping_NUMBER/ServletMapping_$i/;
79.      $s2 =~ s/SERVLETNAME/$name/;
80.      $s2 =~ s/URLPATTERN/$urlpattern/;
81.
82.      $stuffer1 .= $s1;
83.      $stuffer2 .= $s2;
84.
85.      if (defined($param) && ($param =~ /\&/)) {
86.          my @param = split(/&/,$param);
87.          my $j = 0;
88.          while ($j <= $#param) {
89.              # if not in the list then add it and prepare the segment for
      web.xml
90.              if (!(in_list($param[$j],@contextlist))) {
91.                  push(@contextlist,$param[$j]);
92.                  my $s3 = $svcontextparam;
93.                  $s3 =~ s/PARAMNAME/$param[$j]/;
94.                  $s3 =~ s/PARAMVALUE/$param[$j+1]/;
95.                  $stuffer3 .= $s3;
96.              }
97.              $j = $j+2;
98.          }
99.      }
100. }
101. close(FILE);
102.
103. $webxml =~ s/SERVLET_NAMES/$stuffer1/;
104. $webxml =~ s/SERVLET_MAPPINGS/$stuffer2/;
105. $webxml =~ s/SERVLET_CONTEXT_PARAM/$stuffer3/;
106. print $webxml;
```

Creating a More Complete J2EE Tree

The previous section showed you the simplest tree for a web application that will pass the test for loading its servlet in WAS. As shown in step 1 of Table 11-1, the tree was made with two mkdir commands. The following script creates a more complete tree:

```
 1. mkdir -p wasdg.ear/META-INF
 2. mkdir -p wasdg.ear/webapp/META-INF
 3. mkdir -p wasdg.ear/webapp/images
 4. mkdir -p wasdg.ear/webapp/classes
 5. mkdir -p wasdg.ear/webapp/WEB-INF/lib
 6. mkdir -p wasdg.ear/webapp/WEB-INF/classes
 7. mkdir -p wasdg.ear/webapp/WEB-INF/classes/com/tcnd/wasdg
 8. mkdir -p wasdg.ear/webapp/WEB-INF/classes/com/tcnd/wasdg/common
 9. mkdir -p wasdg.ear/webapp/WEB-INF/classes/com/tcnd/wasdg/dataaccess
10. mkdir -p wasdg.ear/webapp/WEB-INF/classes/com/tcnd/wasdg/tagbin
11. mkdir -p wasdg.ear/webapp/WEB-INF/classes/com/tcnd/wasdg/lorder
```

On line 5, the lib directory holds the .jar files, which are Java classes library files. The loading order of these .jar files is discussed in Chapter 15. On lines 4 and 6, the classes directory holds the byte code of .class files. Line 7 shows the directory that will hold the com.tcnd.wasdg package that is used in this book. Lines 8 to 11 shows the different directories to hold some components of the package com.tcnd.wasdg that we will introduce in the next chapters.

Because modifying the tree structure of the webapp is a major change in the structure of the web application, you need to run the refreshear script for the changes to take effect. For example, if you decide on adding an additional package com.tcnd.wasdg.security, you will create the directory that will hold the package:

```
# cd $BASE_DEV
# mkdir -p wasdg.ear/webapp/WEB-INF/classes/com/tcnd/wasdg/security
```

After creating the directory, you need to run refreshear for the change to take effect in the $INSTALLEDAPPS directory.

Adding a New Build to an Already Loaded Web Application

A web application that has already been loaded in WAS, such as the webapp of the wasdg.ear discussed in the previous sections, does not need to be redeployed (or expanded again) in WAS if you make changes in it. You also do not need to stop and restart WAS for the changes to take effect. This is adequate for us, for as you progressive through the next chapters, you will be able to add more servlets to your web application without having to restart WAS (which is known as a hot deployment[5]). Therefore, we need to develop a mechanism that allows you to quickly test your servlet under WAS.

---

[5] *Hot deployment* refers to process of changing components or adding new components to a live server without having to stop and start the application server again. Hot deployment and dynamic reloading is discussed in Chapter 15.

This section shows you a final script, svlbuild, which you can use from now on every time you make a change to the web module. It is located in your development directory.

Having built the wasdg.ear and registered it in WAS as discussed in the section "Building the Web Application," use the svlbuild script (Listing 11-4) to quickly compile Java code and to make all appropriate changes both in the development directory $BASE_DEV/wasdg.ear and in the WAS deployment directory $INSTALLEDAPPS/wasdg.ear.

Listing 11-4 *svlbuild script*

```ksh
1.    #!/bin/ksh
2.
3.    deployDir=$INSTALLEDAPPS
4.
5.    find . -name "*.java" > javafiles.list
6.    cat javafiles.list | xargs javac -deprecation
7.
8.
9.    for dir in 'find . -type d -print'
10.   do
11.       ls -l $dir/*.class > /dev/null 2>&1
12.       if [ $? = 0 ] ; then
13.       (
14.         print "copying from $dir to $deployDir/$dir"
15.         cp $dir/*.class $deployDir/$dir
16.       )
17.       fi
18.   done
19.
20.   for dir in 'find . -type d -print'
21.   do
22.       ls -l $dir/*.jsp > /dev/null 2>&1
23.       if [ $? = 0 ] ; then
24.       (
25.         print "copying from $dir to $deployDir/$dir"
26.         cp $dir/*.jsp $deployDir/$dir
27.       )
28.       fi
29.   done
30.
31.   for dir in 'find . -type d -print'
32.   do
33.       ls -l $dir/*.xmi > /dev/null 2>&1
```

```
34.      if [ $? = 0 ] ; then
35.      (
36.        print "copying from $dir to $deployDir/$dir"
37.        cp $dir/*.xmi $deployDir/$dir
38.      )
39.      fi
40.  done
41.
42.  for dir in 'find . -type d -print'
43.  do
44.      ls -l $dir/*.tld > /dev/null 2>&1
45.      if [ $? = 0 ] ; then
46.      (
47.        print "copying from $dir to $deployDir/$dir"
48.        cp $dir/*.tld $deployDir/$dir
49.      )
50.      fi
51.  done
52.
53.  resetwebxml
54.
```

Line 5 makes a collection into a javafiles.list of all the .java files located in any subdirectories located off the current (.) directory; then it iterates all these files collectively to the javac command to be compiled on line 6. Line 9 iterates to visit the directories, looking for .class files (line 11). The .class files are copied from the development directory to the deployment directory (line 15). Line 53 calls the resetwebxml script to make sure that web.xml is up to date both in the development directory and in the deployment directory. Lines 22, 26, 44, and 48 specifically detect these files known as JSP files and tag library respectively, to be copied to the deployment directory (topic of Chapter 13.) Lines 33 and 37 detect the IBM extension files (.xmi extensions files) to be copied from the development tree to the deployment directory (topic of Chapter 14.)

Understanding the j2tree Script

We avoided the explanation and elaboration of the j2tree script until now so that you wouldn't be distracted by its lengthy (but simple) code. The j2tree is a simple Perl program that does nothing but perform some string preprocessing to create a basic tree that conforms to J2EE, which is adequate enough to be successfully deployed under WAS. However, learning how j2tree creates a J2EE tree will prove to you that this technology is quite simple and can be easily mastered without the use of extra expensive software.

Listing 11-5 shows the j2tree Perl script.

Listing 11-5   *j2tree PERL script*

```
1.    #!/usr/bin/perl
2.    $applicationxml = <<APPLICATIONXML;
3.    <?xml version="1.0" encoding="UTF-8"?>
4.    <!DOCTYPE application PUBLIC "-//Sun Microsystems, Inc.//DTD J2EE
      Application 1.2//EN"
      "http://java.sun.com/j2ee/dtds/application_1_2.dtd">
5.      <application id="Application_ID">
6.         <display-name>Sample Application</display-name>
7.         <description>Sample EAR file containing a Login servlet for
      testing</description>
8.         <module id="WebModule_1">
9.            <web>
10.              <web-uri>APPNAME</web-uri>
11.              <context-root>APPCONTEXT</context-root>
12.           </web>
13.        </module>
14.        <security-role id="SecurityRole_1">
15.           <description>Everyone role</description>
16.           <role-name>Everyone Role</role-name>
17.        </security-role>
18.        <security-role id="SecurityRole_2">
19.           <description>AllAuthenticated role</description>
20.           <role-name>All Role</role-name>
21.        </security-role>
22.        <security-role id="SecurityRole_3">
23.           <description>Deny all access role</description>
24.           <role-name>DenyAllRole</role-name>
25.        </security-role>
26.     </application>
27.   APPLICATIONXML
28.
29.   $webxml = <<WEBXML;
30.   <?xml version="1.0" encoding="UTF-8"?>
31.   <!DOCTYPE web-app PUBLIC "-//Sun Microsystems, Inc.//DTD Web Application
      2.2//EN" "http://java.sun.com/j2ee/dtds/web-app_2_2.dtd">
32.     <web-app id="WebApp_1">
33.        <display-name>Wasdg Web Application Example</display-name>
34.        <description>WASDG Example Servlets</description>
35.   SERVLET_NAMES
36.   SERVLET_MAPPINGS
37.        <security-role id="SecurityRole_1">
38.           <description>Everyone role</description>
39.           <role-name>Everyone Role</role-name>
40.        </security-role>
41.        <security-role id="SecurityRole_2">
42.           <description>AllAuthenticated role</description>
```

```
43.              <role-name>All Role</role-name>
44.          </security-role>
45.          <security-role id="SecurityRole_3">
46.              <description>Deny all access role</description>
47.              <role-name>DenyAllRole</role-name>
48.          </security-role>
49.      </web-app>
50.  WEBXML
51.
52.  $svname = <<SVNAME;
53.          <servlet id="Servlet_NUMBER">
54.              <servlet-name>SERVLETNAME</servlet-name>
55.              <description>Some Description</description>
56.              <servlet-class>SERVLETCLASS</servlet-class>
57.          </servlet>
58.  SVNAME
59.
60.  $svmapping = <<SVMAPPING;
61.          <servlet-mapping id="ServletMapping_NUMBER">
62.              <servlet-name>SERVLETNAME</servlet-name>
63.              <url-pattern>URLPATTERN</url-pattern>
64.          </servlet-mapping>
65.  SVMAPPING
66.
67.  # srand;
68.
69.  ($earfolder,$appname,$appcontext,$servletslist) = @ARGV;
70.  (@parts) = split(/:/,$servletslist);
71.  $j = 0;
72.  for ($i=0;$i<$#parts;$i=$i+3) {
73.      $svl[$j]{svlname} = $parts[$i];
74.      $svl[$j]{svlclass} = $parts[$i+1];
75.      $svl[$j]{svlurl} = $parts[$i+2];
76.      $j++;
77.  #    $appname,$appcontext,$classname,$urlpattern) =
     split(/:/,$servletslist);
78.  }
79.  print "$earfolder,$appname,$appcontext,$classname,$urlpattern\n";
80.
81.
82.  `mkdir -p $earfolder/META-INF`;
83.  `mkdir -p $earfolder/$appname/WEB-INF/classes/com/tcnd/wasdg`;
84.  `mkdir -p $earfolder/$appname/WEB-INF/lib`;
85.
86.  $stuffer1 = "";
87.  $stuffer2 = "";
88.
89.  # $j = 0;
90.
91.  if (! defined($servletslist) ) {
92.      print "UNDEFINED: $servletslist\n";
```

```
93.        $stuffer1 = $svname;
94.        $stuffer2 = $svmapping;
95.    }
96.
97.    for ($j=0;$j < ($#parts / 3);$j++) {
98.
99.    local $s1 = $svname;
100.   local $s2 = $svmapping;
101.
102.   # $name = 'map' . int(rand(1000000));
103.   $name = $svl[$j]{svlname};
104.   $classname = $svl[$j]{svlclass};
105.   $urlpattern = $svl[$j]{svlurl};
106.
107.   print "LOOPING[$j]: $name  $classname  $urlpattern\n";
108.
109.   local $i = $j + 1;
110.   $s1 =~ s/Servlet_NUMBER/Servlet_$i/;
111.   $s1 =~ s/SERVLETNAME/$name/;
112.   $s1 =~ s/SERVLETCLASS/$classname/;
113.   $s2 =~ s/ServletMapping_NUMBER/ServletMapping_$i/;
114.   $s2 =~ s/SERVLETNAME/$name/;
115.   $s2 =~ s/URLPATTERN/$urlpattern/;
116.
117.   $stuffer1 .= $s1;
118.   $stuffer2 .= $s2;
119.   }
120.   $webxml =~ s/SERVLET_NAMES/$stuffer1/;
121.   $webxml =~ s/SERVLET_MAPPINGS/$stuffer2/;
122.   open(FILE_WEBXML,">$earfolder/$appname/WEB-INF/web.xml");
123.   print FILE_WEBXML $webxml;
124.   close(FILE_WEBXML);
125.
126.   $applicationxml =~ s/APPNAME/$appname/;
127.   $applicationxml =~ s/APPCONTEXT/$appcontext/;
128.   open(FILE_APPLICATIONXML,">$earfolder/META-INF/application.xml");
129.   print FILE_APPLICATIONXML $applicationxml;
130.   close(FILE_APPLICATIONXML);
131.
132.   $tar = $appname . "j2tree.tar";
133.   'cd $earfolder/$appname/WEB-INF/classes; tar xvf ../../../../Dist/$tar'
134.   if -r "./Dist/$tar";
```

The j2tree script does the following:

▶ It creates a J2EE-compliant tree. Lines 82, 83, and 84 create the J2EE basic tree using the mkdir command.

▶ It generates the web module web.xml file with the basic servlets specification to make them functional.

▶ It generates the application.xml file describing the enterprise application's web modules.

▶ It extracts the content of the web module into the web modules classes directory. Such a web module, if there is one, is contained in a file located in the Dist directory; the file prefix has the web module name itself, suffixed by j2tree.tar. Such extraction is done on line 133 provided the condition set on the existence of the formerly mentioned met (line 134).

The j2tree is just a script, and its behavior fulfills the requirements of an application as specified by J2EE. However, J2EE does not require such a script. The j2tree script, like many others in this book, is written for convenience, to develop and deploy applications under WebSphere Application Server. Additional code will be added to the j2tree in the next chapter, when necessary to further describe the web module.

Wrapping Up

This chapter explained how to build and deploy a J2EE web module as required by WAS AEs v4. First, you set and export the BASE_DEV environment variable to point to the working directory where you will exercise your code. You change the directory to your working directory, cd $BASE_DEV, then follow these four steps:

1. From the scripts listed in Table 11-1, make sure that you have in the BASE_DEV directory the j2tree script, the svlbuild script, and the servlets.list file. The rest of the scripts—namely, refreshear, genwebxml, resetwebxml, and thisbase scripts— are copied to a common directory that has been set in your search PATH, for example /tools directory discussed in Chapter 4. The script thisbase is a convenient script. When it is run from a current directory with the command #.thisbase it will set the BASE_DEV environment variable to the current directory where the command has been issued.

2. Run the j2tree script in the base directory; this creates the wasdg.ear tree structure and prepares the web application configuration file (web.xml) with the servlets that are listed in the servlets.list file. Also note, if a web module j2tree.tar archive is available in the Dist directory, then it is being extracted in the created tree.[6]

3. Run the refreshear to deploy the wasdg.ear into the application server. You need to run refreshear if this is the first time you created the web application and the application is not known to WAS, or if you make global changes in the application beyond the web module.

4. Test whether the deployment is successfully achieved by requesting either http://was.server.name/wasbook/dumpenv or http://was.server.name/wasbook/login.

Table 11-2 summarizes the scripts introduced in this chapter.

---

[6] Supplementing a .tar archive in this way is optional. However, such a .tar file facilitates the code distribution of each chapter.

Script Name	Comment
j2tree	A Perl script that creates a basic EAR tree structure and may deposit some servlets into it.
genwebxml	A Perl script that reads the servlets.list file and generates a basic web.xml file.
resetwebxml	A shell script that deposits the web.xml (generated with genwebxml) in the development and deployment directories, respectively.
refreshear	A shell script to be run when global changes are made in the wasdg.ear. It reinstalls the EAR application and restarts WAS. When running this script, an EAR archive is created in the $BASE_DEV/Dist directory.
svlbuild	A shell script that is run when adding a new servlet. Make sure you add the servlet alias name, the servlet class name, and its url-pattern mapping in the servlets.list file before running this script.

Table 11-2 *Scripts Needed for BASE_DEV Directory*

Although it would have been possible to put the j2tree and svlbuild scripts in the /tools directory, this has been avoided so a developer will not run them incidentally from any directory when his BASE_DEV environment variable has not been set.

You can download this chapter's code by getting the ch11code.tar from www.osborne.com. Extract the archive in a temporary directory and get started by following the instructions in the README file.

HTTP Servlet Programming

IN THIS CHAPTER:

From CGI Programming to Java Servlets

Developer's Tactics While Programming Servlets

Understanding the Need for Servlet
Programming

Using Servlets for the Teller/Client Example

Batch Processing with Lynx

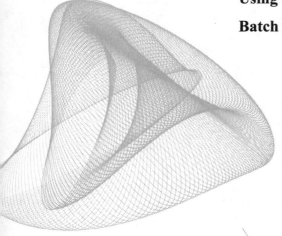

Compiling a servlet is the first step in transforming a Java language program into a form suitable for direct execution by the web container. There are three steps to compile, deploy, and load a servlet in a web container. Compiling is a process of translating from a source program into a bytecode program to be run by any Java machine.

Chapter 11 introduced a simple view of a J2EE application, in which you deployed two HTTP servlets into the web container: DumpEnv and LoginScreen. In Chapter 11, the focus was on creating a methodical process to deploy servlets under WAS, so the servlets' coding was not discussed. This chapter solely discusses the HTTP servlet code structure. Programming under WAS does not require you to know all about *generic* servlets programming, but only about the HTTP-type servlets.

This chapter begins with simple and fundamental CGI programming, and then it explains the flow of HTTP requests between the client browser and the web server. The chapter proceeds to discuss HTTP servlets programming through examples. A few useful scripts are also introduced to assist you in testing your programs. The servlets for the Teller example will be established using Lynx to update client accounts.

From CGI Programming to Java Servlets

Almost any HTTP server is capable of interpreting CGI programs, whether they are compiled programs or scripts. CGI programming using an interpreted language is direct and quick when you need to realize administrative tasks or debug a web application on the fly. The first line of these programs tells the HTTP server which scripting language you are using and provides the directory where the processing agent of your script is located. Typically, CGI scripts are written using the Perl interpreter or the shell script interpreter. Such scripts are quite simple; however, they are the basis for any HTTP programming. Because CGI programming is stateless, it is possible to have both CGI Perl programs and Java servlets seamlessly manipulate the CGI environment variables (also known as attributes).

The program printenv.cgi, shown in Listing 12-1, prints the CGI environment variables. Copy the program into your ihs_home/cgi-bin directory, and make sure its executable bits are set properly (chmod 755 printenv.cgi) before invoking it.

Listing 12-1   *printenv.cgi to dump the CGI environment variables*

```perl
#!/usr/bin/perl
#
# printenv.cgi prints its environment
#

print "Content-type: text/plain\n\n";
foreach $var (sort(keys(%ENV))) {
    $val = $ENV{$var};
    $val =~ s|\n|\\n|g;
```

```
    $val =~ s|"|\\"|g;
print "${var}=\"${val}\"\n";
}
```

The first line tells the server which type of script language you are using and specifies the directory where the interpreter is located. This example uses the Perl interpreter, but you can also use the shell scripting language instead, as shown in Listing 12-2. Also, make sure the program is executable before requesting it.

Listing 12-2   *printenv.sh to dump the CGI environment variables*

```
#!/bin/sh

# disable filename globbing
set -f
echo Content-type: text/plain
echo
echo CGI/1.0 test script report:
echo
echo argc is $#. argv is "$*".
echo
echo SERVER_SOFTWARE = $SERVER_SOFTWARE
echo SERVER_NAME = $SERVER_NAME
echo GATEWAY_INTERFACE = $GATEWAY_INTERFACE
echo SERVER_PROTOCOL = $SERVER_PROTOCOL
echo SERVER_PORT = $SERVER_PORT
echo REQUEST_METHOD = $REQUEST_METHOD
echo HTTP_ACCEPT = "$HTTP_ACCEPT"
echo HTTP_COOKIE = "$HTTP_COOKIE"
echo PATH_INFO = "$PATH_INFO"
echo PATH_TRANSLATED = "$PATH_TRANSLATED"
echo SCRIPT_NAME = "$SCRIPT_NAME"
echo QUERY_STRING = "$QUERY_STRING"
echo REMOTE_HOST = $REMOTE_HOST
echo REMOTE_ADDR = $REMOTE_ADDR
echo REMOTE_USER = $REMOTE_USER
echo AUTH_TYPE = $AUTH_TYPE
echo CONTENT_TYPE = $CONTENT_TYPE
```

This listing is merely a dump of CGI environment variables traditionally dealt with through a programming language, as just demonstrated. These variables are used between the HTTP server and the client browser to describe the state between both parties; hence, the communication between the browser and the web server maintain its state through CGI variables as such. Java servlets are not an exception to this rule. Therefore, they must address these CGI variables exactly the same way as any other CGI program does. The following section discusses the DumpEnv servlet with its subclass javax.servlet.HttpServlet to service the HTTP request.

Using the DumpEnv Servlet to Dump CGI Environment Variables

The DumpEnv.java servlet, shown in Listing 12-3, once compiled and deployed in WAS, prints the CGI environment variables like the previous sample programs did.

Like any other servlet, DumpEnv starts by importing these three packages (lines 1, 3, and 4):

▶ **java.io.*** This package is needed for the ServletOutputStream object, line 11.

▶ **javax.servlet.*** This package is needed to override the javax.servlet.HttpServlet class, line 6. The HttpServlet class contains three methods: init(), service(), and destroy(). The init() and destroy() methods are inherited, while the service() method implementation is specific to HttpServlet.

▶ **javax.servlet.http.*** This package is needed to initialize a servlet, to service requests, and to remove a servlet from the server. Line 8 shows how the service is requested through the HttpServletRequest and HttpServletResponse functions.

Listing 12-3   *DumpEnv.java servlet to dump the CGI environment variables*

```
1.    import java.io.*;
2.    import java.util.*;
3.    import javax.servlet.*;
4.    import javax.servlet.http.*;
5.
6.    public class DumpEnv extends HttpServlet {
7.
8.    public void service(HttpServletRequest request, HttpServletResponse
      response)
9.        throws ServletException, IOException {
10.
11.       ServletOutputStream out = response.getOutputStream();
12.       response.setContentType("text/html");
13.       response.setHeader("Pragma", "no-cache");
14.       response.setHeader("Cache-Control", "no-cache");
15.       response.setDateHeader("Expires", 0);
16.
17.       String content =
18.       "<html><head><title>WASDG - Common Form Information</title></head>"
          +
19.       "<body><h1>Form Information</h1>" +
20.       "HTML Method: " + request.getMethod() + "<br>" +
21.       "URI: " + request.getRequestURI() + "<br>" +
22.       "Protocol: " + request.getProtocol() + "<br>" +
23.       "Servlet Path: " + request.getServletPath() + "<br>" +
```

```
24.          "Path Info: " + request.getPathInfo() + "<br>" +
25.          "Path Translated: "+request.getPathTranslated()+"<br>" +
26.          "Query String: " + request.getQueryString() + "<br>" +
27.          "Content Length: "+request.getContentLength()+"<br>" +
28.          "Content Type: " + request.getContentType() + "<br>" +
29.          "Server name: " + request.getServerName() + "<br>" +
30.          "Server port: " + request.getServerPort() + "<br>" +
31.          "Remote User: " + request.getRemoteUser() + "<br>" +
32.          "Remote Address: "+request.getRemoteAddr()+"<br>" +
33.          "Remote Host: " + request.getRemoteHost() + "<br>" +
34.          "Authentication Scheme: "+request.getAuthType()+"<br>" +
35.          "<hr><p>";
36.
37.          out.println(content);
38.
39.          Enumeration names = request.getHeaderNames();
40.          while (names.hasMoreElements()) {
41.
42.              String header = (String) names.nextElement();
43.              out.println(header + ": " + request.getHeader(header) + "<br>");
44.          }
45.
46.          names = request.getParameterNames();
47.          out.println("<hr><p>");
48.          while (names.hasMoreElements()) {
49.              String key = (String)names.nextElement();
50.              String [] values = (String []) request.getParameterValues(key);
51.              if (values != null) {
52.                  out.println("KEY: " + key + "VALUES: ");
53.                  for (int i = 0; i < values.length; i++)
54.                      out.println(values[i] + " ");
55.                  out.println("<br>");
56.              }
57.          }
58.
59.          out.close();
60.      }
61.
62.  }
```

You already compiled and pushed the DumpEnv servlet to the wasdg.ear application when deploying it in Chapter 11. Recall how much effort you put into preparing the whole J2EE shebang to deploy the servlet in the WAS web container. Fortunately, the rebuild operation is totally facilitated through the use of our scripts, in particular, the svlbuild script—provided you built the J2EE tree by running primarily j2tree and refreshear, as explained in Chapter 11.

Of course it is easier and more straightforward to test with the CGI interpreted versions of our examples, because they use *native* UNIX interpreters (Perl and ksh), and they do not depend on a third-party processing agent to launch them, such as WAS' container Java machine.

The DumpEnv servlet still runs on the server, so it can gather (or request) the CGI environment in replying (or in responding) back. However, it is being processed within a servlet engine—a WAS web container. You can use Java servlets to replace CGI programming but not to replace the CGI protocol or the CGI variables; as you will see in Chapters 16 and 17, Java servlets cannot maintain state information between the client browser and the web container without the CGI variables.

Using the DumpEnv Servlet: The service() Method

The service() method is the center of the servlet. All client requests to a servlet are serviced through it. The method of the HTTP request, whether it is a GET or a POST method, is serviced through it (see the illustration). To better understand this concept, invoke the servlet with both methods using Lynx (explained in the next section):

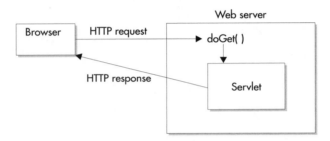

- ▶ **For a GET request:**   # lynx http://node1/wasbook/dumpenv
- ▶ **For a POST request:**   # echo "x=1&---" | lynx -post_data http://node1/wasbook/dumpenv

The x=1 is just a dummy HTTP parameter that is added to pass it along to the POST request. Check the access_log file, and you should see that both GET and POST requests flowed properly for this servlet.

Developer's Tactics While Programming Servlets

You will spend a good deal of time programming and debugging servlets as you start any web project. In particular, if you are exercising servlet programming under WAS, use the following five strategies to get around testing your servlets:

1. Monitor the HTTPD log records to see if your request is passing through the web server.
2. Monitor the WAS log file where standard input/output has occurred. This is typically in the $WAS_HOME/logs/standard_server_stdout.log file.

3. Use Lynx to dump the HTTP request (unless you are working with Unicode and different characters sets).

4. Use svlbuild every time you make a change in your servlet. This will recompile and redeploy, hence making WAS reload the changes in its web container.

5. Use an HTML editor such as Netscape Composer to create the static content of an HTML page. This content can then be filtered with the custom h2j script to generate the Java string to be included in a Java servlet.

Understanding the HTTPD Log Record

Chapter 3 discussed how to enable the logging directive in the httpd.conf file. This example assumes the default setup of the httpd.conf as it is being installed on your system.

When you request the URL http://was.server.host/wasbook/dumpenv from your browser, you place a GET request by default. Usually, the request activities put to an HTTP server are logged to the access_log file in the ihs_home/logs directory; hence, an entry such as

```
66.51.9.151 - - [01/Apr/2002:13:20:06 -0400] "GET /wasbook/dumpenv HTTP/1.0"
200 690 -
```

is logged to your log file, as explained in Table 12-1. Notice that the entry point to a web site is usually through a GET request placed by default to an HTTP server.

WAS Redirection to Standard Input/Output

Chapter 8 discussed how to redirect the standard output to the log file. By default, the WAS AEs v4 default server uses the file $WAS_HOME/logs/default_server_stdout.log. Monitoring this file is very important, and can facilitate your understanding to your servlet *containment* within WAS. For instance, if you monitor this file and you run the svlbuild script, you can realize how the web container re-*init*()ialize your servlets.

On the other hand, you can use System.out.println() in your code to print messages that are written to this log file. Usually, these messages are flagged with the character *U*.

Chapter 24 discusses how you can trap and filter messages written in this log file and trigger associated scripts accordingly. This is with the use of WASLED and WASMON[1], which monitor WAS containment graphically.

---

[1] WASLED™/WASMON™ is a lightweight application that can monitor WebSphere Application Server v4. WASMON™ can also be programmed with logical expressions and triggers so that it can detect a failing WAS server and restart another to replace it.

Component	Example	Description
IP address	66.51.9.151	The IP address of the host putting the request to the HTTP server.
Port	80	The port number on which the request has been placed. The default 80 is not recorded in the log file.
Process ID	(some number)	The process ID of the HTTP daemon servicing the request.
Remote username	-	Not used for a public site.
Remote user	-	Not used for a public site.
Time		The time formatted in the common log format.
Request	GET /wasbook/ dumpenv HTTP/1.0	The first line of the request. Usually it starts with a request method followed by the URI.
Code	200	The status code returned in the response header to tell the client about the state of the URI response. The status falls into one of the following code: 1xx, 2xx, 3xx, 4xx, or 5xx.
Size	690	The size in bytes excluding the HTTP headers.
Referer	-	The component that reveals whether this request is due to a referring page (i.e., an HREF from a previously viewed page).

Table 12-1   *A Typical HTTP Log Record*

Using Lynx to Check on HTTP Requests

As a developer, you need to be able to process HTTP requests quickly and examine the data sent in and out via the HTTP protocol. A browser is quite bulky and requires a graphical interface; in addition, it filters and hides the information sent from the web server. For this reason, you can use Lynx, which is available on the UNIX platform. It is a simple textual browser that can save you (and enterprises) a tremendous amount of time when developing a web application.

The following command is a simple Lynx request to the DumpEnv servlet:

```
# lynx -dump http://node1.tcnd.com/wasbook/dumpenv
```

To log in as the teller with USERID=teller1 through the LoginScreen servlet, because it is a POST method, you issue the following:

```
# echo "userid=client1&password=secret1&---" | lynx -post_data
        http://node1.tcnd.com/wasbook/login
```

In Lynx, when posting data, the last entry must be a triple hyphen (---) followed by a carriage return.

Recompiling Servlets Using the svlbuild Script

The svlbuild script[2] was already explained in Chapter 11. Just recall that, while it is not the most efficient way to recompile a huge web application, it is an excellent tool for any developer to have. The script exposes you to the mechanism required to build and deploy Java code and web data in WAS.

When executing svlbuild in your $BASE_DEV directory, all .java programs are recompiled, then redistributed in the corresponding directory $INSTALLED/wasd.ear. The servlets.list file is also processed to regenerate the web.xml file for your application, which is then redeployed, replacing any previous one.

Turning HTML Content into a Java String

Often, you need to ship out HTML content from a servlet. Whether the HTML content has been prepared by a designer or you have edited it yourself using an HTML editor, to incorporate it in your servlet, you must filter it to make it a valid Java string. The h2j script shown in Listing 12-4 takes one argument as a file, and then it prints to the standard output the preprocessed content as a Java string. You can use it as follows:

```
# h2j somehtmlfile > somejavacontent
```

Just remember to substitute the ending plus sign (+) with a semicolon (;) to terminate the string when incorporating it into a Java servlet program. Copy this tool to your commonly mounted directory and make sure its executable bits are set.

Listing 12-4   *The h2j script turns an HTML file into a Java string*

```
1.    #!/usr/bin/perl
2.
3.    ($fin) = @ARGV;
4.
5.    if (!(defined($fin))) {
6.        print "no file defined!\n";
7.    }
8.    elsif (-r ($fin)) {
9.        open(F,"$fin");
10.   }
11.   else {
12.       print "cannot open file: $fin\n";
13.   }
14.
15.   while (<F>) {
16.       chop; s/^\s*//; s/\"/\\"/g;
17.       print "\"$_\" + \n";
18.   }
19.
20.   close(FILE);
```

The h2j script is fairly simple. The argument is read on line 3, then checked to determine whether it is a valid file that can be read on line 9. An iteration is initiated on line 15, to substitute spaces and escaping quotes on line 16.

Understanding the Need for Servlet Programming

Because a servlet can be programmed, it is possible to make it print layouts of an HTML page differently (for example, use a different color, print different tables, and so on). The flexibility of programming in different pages makes a servlet an adequate tool to generate dynamic page contents on the server side. However, this is just a mediocre reason to use a servlet.

More interestingly, using servlets can be justified for the following reasons:

▶ Although most HTTP servlets usually use string manipulation routines to preprocess the HTTP content before shipping it to an HTTP browser, many interesting methods can filter the content in a uniform and standard way: filtering data by MIME type or using a data bundle for a particular language.

▶ A servlet can use the Java libraries like any other Java program. Consequently, Java security can be imposed on the objects handled within the Java servlet and on classes to be executed from a servlet. For instance, the HTML content can be represented as a signed object that must be requested with a valid signature. A privileged class can be protected and will not be executed by a servlet without passing authentication. Chapter 20 discusses the use of Cipher, and Java Authentication and Authorization Service with Java servlets.

▶ Because a servlet is structurally handled by a processing agent (web container), it can act like a processor that has been initially configured through its init() method, then allocating threads to run the service() method that maps to the request.

▶ An HTTP servlet is a Java program that has been compiled into bytecode and is ready to be executed by a processing agent (web container). Once loaded in the container, the HTTP servlet can be turned into smaller processing units.

▶ A servlet, like all Java code, can be packaged with the `jar` command and therefore distributed to any web container that can process it.

▶ A servlet is managed by a J2EE container that removes many traditional burdens or assists the programmer, such as scalability, security, and failover. Programmers can concentrate on business logic and move the burden of management and execution issues to the container, which may be changed without making any code changes, therefore promoting a more stable environment.

Using a Servlet to Print HTML Content

A servlet is a Java program that is executed on the server to print data or code to an HTTP client browser—but it is much more than that. However, JSPs are preferred over servlets for printing HTML output. Therefore, to be properly handled by the HTTP protocol, the emitted data or code should conform to the rule of the HTTP protocol itself: the HTTP protocol understands HTML, and therefore the HTML code printed by the servlet. The LoginScreen servlet is such an example.

The following illustration shows the flow of generating HTML content and then feeding it to a servlet.

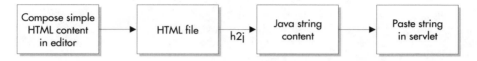

You can generate your own design in an HTML composer such as Netscape and then save the file to be filtered with an h2j script as a Java string.

Using a Servlet to Access the UDB

Like any Java program, servlets can access the database by using the JDBC API library. The following sections demonstrate how to test your connection with a common servlet such as BruteConn, and how to query DBGUIDE tables selectively through servlets. In a later section, you will learn how to use servlets to access the DBGUIDE database to authenticate tellers, and debit/credit client balances.

Using BruteConn to Test a Servlet Connecting to the Database

Before you start coding servlets to access a database, make sure you have the correct DB driver loaded in the WAS classpath (i.e., $WAS_HOME/lib). Chapter 15 discusses how to add libraries to the classpath of WAS and its web applications. For this reason, you must write a simple servlet program in which the driver being used is totally exposed. Such a program should also be neutral and not use any custom library. Simplicity is the key in isolating problems in an interconnected application.

Listing 12-5 shows such a handy program, which makes a simple connection to the DBGUIDE database and retrieves the password USERID=teller1. Running this program reveals whether the connection to the database can be established properly and whether the correct db2java.zip library is being used. On line 21, the servlet uses the type 2 app-driver, but you can also test it with the old and less efficient type 3 net-driver (line 22).

To test with the net-driver, on line 21, change COM.ibm.db2.jdbc.app.DB2Driver to COM.ibm.db2.jdbc.net.DB2Driver; on line 28, change jdbc:db2://node2/DBGUIDE to jdbc:db2://node2:50068/DBGUIDE, assuming you started db2jstrt on port 50068 on hostname node2. (You can specify a different hostname or port than the one mentioned here.) Chapter 2 discusses the difference between the app-driver and the net-driver.

Listing 12-5   *BruteConn.java servlet to test connectivity to our DBGUIDE database*

```
1.    import javax.servlet.*;
2.    import javax.servlet.http.*;
3.    import java.io.IOException;
4.    import java.sql.*;
```

```
5.
6.    public class BruteConn extends HttpServlet
7.    {
8.        public void service(HttpServletRequest request, HttpServletResponse
      response)
9.            throws ServletException, IOException
10.       {
11.           ServletOutputStream out = response.getOutputStream();
12.           response.setContentType("text/html");
13.           response.setHeader("Pragma", "no-cache");
14.           response.setHeader("Cache-Control", "no-cache");
15.           response.setDateHeader("Expires", 0);
16
17.           out.println("<html><head><title>WASDG,
      BRUTE-CONNECTION</title></head>" + "<body><h1>Brute Connection</h1>" +
      "<p>");
18.
19.       try {
20.           // The db2java.zip (V7.1 or V7.2) in UDB_dir/java/db2java.zip
21.           Class.forName("COM.ibm.db2.jdbc.app.DB2Driver");
22.           // Old net driver should also work:
      "COM.ibm.db2.jdbc.net.DB2Driver" Remember to run db2jstrt as well
23.       } catch (ClassNotFoundException e) {
24.           out.println(">>>  DB DRIVER NAME ERROR:" + e.getMessage() + "
      <br>");
25.       }
26.
27.       try {
28.           String url = "jdbc:db2://node2/DBGUIDE";
29.           String username = "dbuser";
30.           String password = "pwd123";
31.
32.           java.sql.Connection conn =
      java.sql.DriverManager.getConnection(url,username,password);
33.           java.sql.Statement stmt = conn.createStatement();
34.
35.           try {
36.               out.println(">>> STARTING QUERY <br>");
37.               java.sql.ResultSet rs = stmt.executeQuery("SELECT PASSWORD
      FROM DB2INST1.EMPPWD WHERE USERID='teller1'");
38.               out.println(">>> ENDING QUERY <br>");
39.               while (rs.next()) {
40.                   String firstname = rs.getString("PASSWORD");
41.                   out.println(">>> PASSWORD: " + firstname);
42.                   out.println("<br>");
43.               }
44.               if (rs != null) rs.close();
45.           } catch (java.sql.SQLException e) {
46.               out.println(">>>  DB ERROR:" + e.getMessage() + " <br>");
47.           }
```

```
48.          if (stmt != null) stmt.close();
49.          if (conn != null) conn.close();
50.       } catch (java.sql.SQLException e) {
51.          out.println(">>>  A DATABASE EXCEPTION:" + e.getMessage() + "
      <br>");
52.       }
53.       out.println(">>> DONE <br>");
54.       out.close();
55.  }
56.  }
```

Recall how to compile this servlet by following these four steps:

1. Change the directory to $BASE_DEV.

2. From the supplied code, edit and change lines 29 and 30 with the correct credential to access the database. Save the program BruteConn.java in the webapp classes directory: $BASE_DEVwasdg.ear/webapp/WEB-INF/classes.

3. Edit the servlets.list and add the following line to it: bruteconn BruteConn /bruteconn.

4. Run the svlbuild: ./svlbuild.

You should be able to put a request to the BruteConn servlet:

```
# lynx -dump http://node1.tcnd.com/wasbook/bruteconn
```

This should return a dump like this:

```
                  Brute Connection

 >>>  STARTING QUERY
 >>>  ENDING QUERY
 >>>  PASSWORD: secret1
 >>>  DONE
```

If the connection fails, then edit the BruteConn.java servlet in your development directory and run svlbuild every time you make a change to the program. However, you need to restart WAS if you change the db2java.zip driver in the $WAS_HOME/lib directory.

Make sure BruteConn is returning the appropriate result before proceeding with the next examples.

Querying the DBGUIDE Table Selectively

Say you need to query the DBGUIDE tables selectively by submitting a table name through the SelectTable servlet, as shown in the next illustration. Listing 12-6 shows such a servlet.

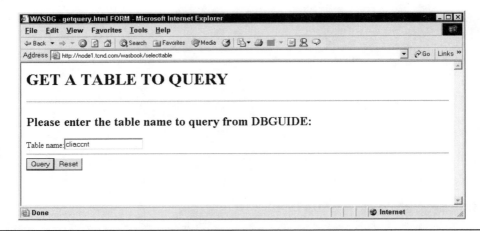

Listing 12-6 *SelectTable servlet to enter a table by name to query*

```
import java.io.*;
import javax.servlet.*;
import javax.servlet.http.*;

public class SelectTable extends javax.servlet.http.HttpServlet {

    String content =
"<HTML>" +
"<HEAD>" +
"<TITLE>WASDG - getquery.html FORM </TITLE>" +
"</HEAD>" +
"<BODY>" +
"<H1>GET A TABLE TO QUERY</H1>" +
"<FORM METHOD=\"POST\" ACTION=\"/wasbook/querytable\">" +
"" +
"<HR>" +
"<H2>Please enter the table name to query from DBGUIDE: </H2>" +
"<P>Table name:<INPUT TYPE=\"text\" NAME=\"table\" SIZE=\"20\">" +
"<HR>" +
"<INPUT TYPE=\"submit\" VALUE=\"Query\"><INPUT TYPE=\"reset\">" +
"</FORM>" +
"</BODY>" +
"</HTML>" ;

public void doGet(HttpServletRequest request, HttpServletResponse response)
        throws IOException{

    ServletOutputStream out = response.getOutputStream();
    response.setContentType("text/html");
    response.setHeader("Pragma", "no-cache");
    response.setHeader("Cache-Control", "no-cache");
```

```
        response.setDateHeader("Expires", 0);
        out.println(content);
}

public void doPost(HttpServletRequest request, HttpServletResponse response)
    throws ServletException, IOException
{
        doGet( request, response);
}
}
```

Figure 12-1 shows the result of requesting to query table. If you enter **CLIACCNT** in the form and you click Submit Query in the browser, the QueryTable servlet (Listing 12-7) is invoked with the attribute table=CLIACCNT (line 19).

0	1	2	3	4	5	6	7	8	9	10	11
client1	B000001	B	teller5	Dave1	Spender1	../images/client1	client1@wasette.com	0	0	0	1
client2	B000002	B	teller5	Dave2	Spender2	../images/client2	client2@wasette.com	0	0	0	2
client3	B000003	B	teller2	Dave3	Spender3	../images/client3	client3@wasette.com	0	0	0	3
client4	B000004	B	teller1	Dave4	Spender4	../images/client4	client4@wasette.com	0	0	0	4
client5	B000005	B	teller5	Dave5	Spender5	../images/client5	client5@wasette.com	0	0	0	5
client6	C000006	C	teller1	Dave6	Spender6	../images/client6	client6@wasette.com	0	0	0	6
client7	C000007	C	teller3	Dave7	Spender7	../images/client7	client7@wasette.com	0	0	0	7
client8	C000008	C	teller1	Dave8	Spender8	../images/client8	client8@wasette.com	0	0	0	8
client9	B000009	B	teller1	Dave9	Spender9	../images/client9	client9@wasette.com	0	0	0	9
client10	A000010	A	teller4	Dave10	Spender10	../images/client10	client10@wasette.com	0	0	0	10
client11	B000011	B	teller1	Dave11	Spender11	../images/client11	client11@wasette.com	0	0	0	11
client12	C000012	C	teller1	Dave12	Spender12	../images/client12	client12@wasette.com	0	0	0	12
client13	B000013	B	teller5	Dave13	Spender13	../images/client13	client13@wasette.com	0	0	0	13
client14	A000014	A	teller2	Dave14	Spender14	../images/client14	client14@wasette.com	0	0	0	14
client15	C000015	C	teller5	Dave15	Spender15	../images/client15	client15@wasette.com	0	0	0	15
client16	B000016	B	teller2	Dave16	Spender16	../images/client16	client16@wasette.com	0	0	0	16
client17	A000017	A	teller1	Dave17	Spender17	../images/client17	client17@wasette.com	0	0	0	17
client18	A000018	A	teller4	Dave18	Spender18	../images/client18	client18@wasette.com	0	0	0	18
client19	B000019	B	teller1	Dave19	Spender19	../images/client19	client19@wasette.com	0	0	0	19
client20	B000020	B	teller4	Dave20	Spender20	../images/client20	client20@wasette.com	0	0	0	20

Figure 12-1   *Result to query table CLIACCNT*

Listing 12-7   *QueryTable servlet to query the selected database table*

```
1.    import java.io.*;
2.    import javax.servlet.*;
3.    import javax.servlet.http.*;
4.    import javax.servlet.http.HttpServlet;
5.
6.    import com.tcnd.wasdg.dataaccess.*;
7.    import com.tcnd.wasdg.common.*;
8.
9.    public class QueryTable extends javax.servlet.http.HttpServlet {
10.       DataAccessComponent DAC;
11.
12.   public void init() throws ServletException {
13.       DAC = new DataAccessComponent();
14.   }
15.
16.   public void doGet(HttpServletRequest request, HttpServletResponse
      response)
17.           throws ServletException, IOException {
18.
19.       String dbTable = request.getParameter("table");
20.       System.out.println(">>>>> " + dbTable);
21.
22.       IDataAccessObject iDAO = DAC.createDAObject();
23.       iDAO.setCommandString("SELECT * FROM DB2INST1." + dbTable);
24.       iDAO = DAC.executeQuery(iDAO);
25.       DataSet dataSet = iDAO.getDataSet();
26.
27.       response.setContentType("text/html");
28.       response.setHeader("Pragma", "no-cache");
29.       response.setHeader("Cache-Control", "no-cache");
30.       response.setDateHeader("Expires", 0);
31.
32.       PrintWriter out = response.getWriter();
33.       out.println("<html><head><title>WASDG Title Page</title></head><body>
       <center><table BORDER=0 CELLPADDING=2 ><tr><td></td>");
34.
35.       if (dataSet.getRowCount() > 0)
36.       {
37.           for (int i = 0; i < dataSet.getColumnCount(); i++)
38.           {
39.               out.println("<td ALIGN=CENTER BGCOLOR=\"#E0D224\"><font
      size=+2>" + i + " </font></td>");
40.           }
41.           out.println("<tr><td></td>");
42.
43.           dataSet.seekFirstRow();
44.           for (int j = 0; j < dataSet.getRowCount(); j++)
45.           {
46.               for (int i = 0; i < dataSet.getColumnCount(); i++)
```

```
47.               {
48.                   out.println("<td ALIGN=CENTER BGCOLOR=\"#E0D1B4\"><font
    size=+1>" + dataSet.getValue(i) + " </font></td>");
49.                 }
50.                 out.println("<tr><td></td>");
51.                 dataSet.seekNextRow();
52.             }
53.         }
54.         else
55.         {
56.             out.println( "</tr>");
57.         }
58.         out.println("</table></body></html>");
59.         out.close();
60.   }
61.
62.   public void doPost(HttpServletRequest request, HttpServletResponse
      response)
63.             throws ServletException, IOException
64.   {
65.                   doGet( request, response);
66.   }
67.   }
68.
```

On line 13, the connection to the database is initiated with an initial instantiation of the DataAccessComponent object. This happens once for the lifetime of the servlet because it is specified in the init() method of the servlet. On line 20, System.out.println() will print the name of the table to the standard output log file every time you request the SelectTable servlet. Browse through the default_stdout.log of your WAS installation, and you should see the table name requested every time you run the servlet. Lines 35 to 57, an iteration over the dataSet of the result, is wrapped with HTML tags to print the table.

Using a Servlet to Print Contents of a File

The FetchFile servlet shown in Listing 12-8 can be called as an entry point with the GET method. It then prompts the user to enter a filename to be printed to his or her browser. When the user enters a filename and submits the form, the servlet calls itself with the POST method, trying to locate the file and print it in the client browser. On line 50, the program calls the getFile() method that is part of the StrTool package, to read file content and return it as a string to be printed.

Listing 12-8   *FetchFile servlet to print the content of a file to the client browser*

```
1.   import java.io.*;
2.   import javax.servlet.*;
3.   import javax.servlet.http.*;
4.
```

```
5.     import com.tcnd.wasdg.common.*;
6.
7.     public class FetchFile extends javax.servlet.http.HttpServlet
8.     {
9.         String step1content =
10.
11.        "<HTML>" +
12.        "<HEAD>" +
13.        "<TITLE>WASDG - Fetch a file and print its content to the
       browser</TITLE>" +
14.        "</HEAD>" +
15.        "<BODY>" +
16.        "<H1>FETCH A FILE AND PRINT IT AS AN HTML CONTENT</H1>" +
17.        "<FORM METHOD=\"POST\" ACTION=\"/wasbook/fetchfile\">" +
18.        "" +
19.        "<HR>" +
20.        "<H2>Enter the file name to read as an HTML content:</H2>" +
21.        "<font size=-1>(this is relative to the base directory specified in
       the context-param)</font>" +
22.        "<P>File name:<INPUT TYPE=\"text\" NAME=\"fname\" SIZE=\"20\">" +
23.        "<HR>" +
24.        "<INPUT TYPE=\"submit\" VALUE=\"Fetch\"><INPUT TYPE=\"reset\">" +
25.        "</FORM>" +
26.        "</BODY>" +
27.        "</HTML>" +
28.        "";
29.
30.        public void doGet(HttpServletRequest request, HttpServletResponse
       response)
31.        throws IOException{
32.
33.            ServletOutputStream out = response.getOutputStream();
34.
35.            response.setContentType("text/html");
36.            response.setHeader("Pragma", "no-cache");
37.            response.setHeader("Cache-Control", "no-cache");
38.            response.setDateHeader("Expires", 0);
39.
40.            out.println(step1content);
41.        }
42.
43.        public void doPost(HttpServletRequest request, HttpServletResponse
       response)
44.        throws IOException{
45.
46.            String fname = request.getParameter("fname");
```

```
47.          ServletContext context = getServletContext();
48.          String fromdir = context.getInitParameter("fromdir");
49.
50.          String content = StrTool.getFile(fromdir + fname);
51.          ServletOutputStream out = response.getOutputStream();
52.
53.          response.setContentType("text/html");
54.          response.setHeader("Pragma", "no-cache");
55.          response.setHeader("Cache-Control", "no-cache");
56.          response.setDateHeader("Expires", 0);
57.
58.          out.println(content);
59.     }
60.  }
```

To locate the directory from which the file will be fetched, on lines 47 and 48, the servlet reads the context init parameter using this method:

```
public String ServletContext.getInitParameter(String name)
```

Context init parameters can be shared by all servlets, and they are specified in the web.xml file of your web application. The following sections describe how to set context init parameters in the deployment descriptor.

Getting the Context init Parameters

The context init parameters are part of the web.xml file. To insert them in the web.xml file, you specify them after the directive :CONTEXTPARAM in the servlets.list file. For example, the following shows such an entry in the servlets.list:

> :CONTEXTPARAM fromdir&/BOOK/12/spool/&a&1&b&2

The previous entry, when processed by svlbuild (actually this is done through the genwebxml script discussed in Chapter 11) creates the following tagged entries in the web.xml file:

```
<context-param>
     <param-name>fromdir</param-name>
     <param-value>/BOOK/12/spool/</param-value>
  </context-param>
  <context-param>
     <param-name>a</param-name>
     <param-value>1</param-value>
  </context-param>
  <context-param>
     <param-name>b</param-name>
     <param-value>2</param-value>
  </context-param>
```

The genwebxml script processes the :CONTEXTPARAM and makes the necessary changes in the web.xml file. Recall that the servlets.list file resides in the $BASE_DEV directory, and each entry in this file goes on a single line.

The changes of the genwebxml Perl script are reflected in Listing 12-9. On line 10, SERVLET_CONTEXT_PARAM was added to be substituted by the XML segment, lines 20–25. The parameter-value pairs are split on line 44, then iterated through each of them on line 47.

Listing 12-9   *Change in the webgenxml script to handle the context init parameter*

```
1.   #!/usr/bin/perl
2.
3.   my $webxml = <<WEBXML;
4.   <?xml version="1.0" encoding="UTF-8"?>
5.   <!DOCTYPE web-app PUBLIC "-//Sun Microsystems, Inc.//DTD Web Application
     2.2//EN" "http://java.sun.com/j2ee/dtds/web-app_2_2.dtd">
6.       <web-app id="WebApp_1">
7.           <display-name>Wasdg Web Application Example</display-name>
8.           <description>WASDG Example Servlets</description>
9.
10.  SERVLET_CONTEXT_PARAM
11.  SERVLET_NAMES
12.  SERVLET_MAPPINGS
13.          <security-role id="SecurityRole_1">
14.  ...
15.
16.  WEBXML
17.
18.  ...
19.
20.  my $svcontextparam = <<SVCONTEXTPARAM;
21.          <context-param>
22.              <param-name>PARAMNAME</param-name>
23.          <param-value>PARAMVALUE</param-value>
24.          </context-param>
25.  SVCONTEXTPARAM
26.
27.  sub in_list {
28.  my($temp,@list) = @_;
29.  my($e);
30.  foreach $e (@list) {if ($temp eq $e) { return 1; } }
31.  return 0;
32.  }
33.
34.  ...
35.
36.  # Second run to process global setting to the web.xml file
```

```
37.   open(FILE,"<servlets.list");
38.   while (<FILE>) {
39.       next unless ((/^\:/));
40.       my($directive,$param) = split(/\s/,$_,2);
41.       if ($directive =~ /^:CONTEXTPARAM/) {
42.           if (defined($param) && ($param =~ /\&/)) {
43.               chop($param);
44.               my @param = split(/&/,$param);
45.               my(@contextlist) = ();
46.               my $j = 0;
47.               while ($j <= $#param) {
48.                   # if not in the list then add it and prepare the segment
      for web.xml
49.                   if (!(in_list($param[$j],@contextlist))) {
50.                       push(@contextlist,$param[$j]);
51.                       my $s = $svcontextparam;
52.                       $s =~ s/PARAMNAME/$param[$j]/;
53.                       $s =~ s/PARAMVALUE/$param[$j+1]/;
54.                       $stuffer4 .= $s;
55.                   }
56.                   $j = $j+2;
57.               }
58.           }
59.       }
60.   }
61.   close(FILE);
62.
63.   $webxml =~ s/SERVLET_NAMES/$stuffer1/;
64.   $webxml =~ s/SERVLET_MAPPINGS/$stuffer2/;
65.   $webxml =~ s/SERVLET_CONTEXT_PARAM/$stuffer4/;
66.   print $webxml;
```

The genwebxml script cheks each parameter name if it is already in a list (line 49) if it is not in the list, then genwebxml pushes the parameter name on the list (line 50) and does the parameter/value pair substitution on lines 52 and 53. When a parameter is redundant, then the first one encountered will take effect. The :CONTEXTPARAM is one of the directive that is used in the servlets.list file, usually directives like one are specified to list parameters and their associated values (if any) that are global to the whole web application.

Getting the File with getFile()

Recall in the FetchFile servlet, on line 50, the getFile() method is called to read a file and to return its content as a string:

```
String content = StrTool.getFile(fromdir + fname);
```

This getFile() method is part of StrTool, which is commonly packaged in the com/tcnd/wasdg/common directory. This method opens the file and random-access reads it one line at a time, appending each line to a string to be returned. Listing 12-10 shows a portion of this file:

Listing 12-10 *getFile() as defined in the StrTool package*

```
1.    package com.tcnd.wasdg.common;
2.
3.    import java.io.*;
4.
5.    public class StrTool
6.    {
7.
8.        public StrTool()
9.        {
10.            super();
11.        }
12.    ...
13.
14.        public static String getFile(String fn)
15.        {
16.            String content = "";
17.            try
18.            {
19.                RandomAccessFile file = new RandomAccessFile(fn,"r");
20.                long seek = 0;
21.                long length = file.length();
22.                while (seek < length)
23.                {
24.                    String s = file.readLine();
25.                    content = content + s;
26.                    seek = file.getFilePointer();
27.                }
28.            } catch (IOException e)
29.            {
30.                e.printStackTrace();
31.            }
32.            return content;
33.        }
34.    ...
35.
36.    }
```

Methods that do string manipulations or are expected to return a Java string[3] will be added to the StrTool package.

---

[3] The power of a language is usually in its string manipulations. A programmer can process strings in any computer language as long as the language has storage capability (stack and queue) and includes conditional statements. Java has numerous methods to perform string processing, but it is quite bulky. Its lack of regular expressions makes it harder to carry out progressive string manipulation tasks because it is not inductive.

Using Servlets for the Teller/Client Example

This section introduces the LoginScreen servlets as an entry point for an employee or teller. Once the teller has been logged in successfully through the TellerLogged servlet, she can start debiting/crediting a client account via the CreditDebit servlet. Therefore, three servlets are required: LoginScreen, TellerLogged, and CreditDebit. Table 12-2 summarizes the steps and the HTTP servlet methods invoked from the time a teller logs in to when it credits an account.

Here is a simple scenario:

▶ The employee with userid=teller1 and password=secret1 logs in successfully. The LoginScreen servlet calls TellerLogged with the POST method.

▶ The teller is authenticated correctly by TellerLogged, and a screen showing the option to credit or debit an account is presented. The teller selects this option, which calls CreditDebit with the GET method.

▶ CreditDebit doGet() shows a screen to the teller, where he or she can input the clientid and the amount to be credited or debited. The teller inputs the information to submit the form. The CreditDebit servlet is called again, this time with the POST method.

▶ CreditDebit doPost() processes the request by accessing the database to fulfill the transaction, and fills in the screen showing the record of the subject (or the client) after the transaction.

The Teller Login Servlet: LoginScreen

The LoginScreen servlet is the entry point for a bank employee or teller. The servlet HTML content is passed as a string in lines 20 to 100 in Listing 12-11. The employee her userid (USERID) and password (PASSWORD) to be input on lines 67 and 72. The form is submitted with a POST action to invoke /wasbook/tellerlogged, as shown on lines 61 and 62. A request to the LoginScreen servlet is shown in the following illustration.

Step	Servlet	Methods	Request Method	URL
1	LoginScreen	doGet() doPost()	GET or POST	http://node1/wasbook/login
2	TellerLogged	init() doGet() doPost()	GET or POST	http://node1/wasbook/tellerlogged
3	CreditDebit	init() doGet() doPost()	GET or POST	http://node1/wasbook/creditdebit

Table 12-2 *Servlets Used in the Teller/Client Example*

Listing 12-11 *LoginScreen servlet*

```
1.    package com.tcnd.wasdg;
2.
3.    import java.io.*;
4.    import javax.servlet.*;
5.    import javax.servlet.http.*;
6.
7.    /**
8.     * The LoginScreen is a simple servlet entry point for our
9.     * bank employee (teller).
10.    * A teller enters his or her userid and the password, then
11.    * clicks Submit to proceed. TellerLogged is then being
12.    * invoked to check on the credential and authorize the teller.
13.    *
14.    */
15.
16.   // public class LoginScreen extends javax.servlet.http.HttpServlet {
17.   public class LoginScreen extends HttpServlet {
18.
19.
20.       String content =
21.       // Write the HTML Header information
22.       "<html>" +
23.       "<head>" +
24.       "<title>WASDG Login</title>" +
25.       "" +
26.       "<meta http-equiv=\"EXPIRES\" content=\"March 2002, 00:00:00 GMT\">"
              +
27.       "<meta http-equiv=\"CHARSET\" content=\"ISO-8859-1\">" +
28.       "<meta http-equiv=\"CONTENT-LANGUAGE\" content=\"English\">" +
29.       "" +
30.       "</head>" +
31.       "<body text=\"#000000\" bgcolor=\"#ffffff\" leftmargin=\"0\"
          marginheight=\"0\" marginwidth=\"0\" rightmargin=\"0\" topmargin=\"0\"
          bottommargin=\"5\">" +
32.       "<table border=\"0\" cellpadding=\"0\" cellspacing=\"0\"
          width=\"760\" align=\"center\">" +
33.       "</table>" +
34.       "" +
35.       "<table border=\"0\" cellpadding=\"0\" cellspacing=\"0\"
          width=\"760\" align=\"center\">" +
36.       "<tr valign=\"top\">" +
37.       "<td width=\"170\"> </td>" +
38.       "<td width=\"590\">" +
39.       "" +
40.       "</td>" +
41.       "</tr>" +
42.       "<tr valign=\"top\">" +
43.       "<td width=\"760\" colspan=\"2\" align=\"center\">" +
```

```
44.      "" +
45.      "<content>" +
46.      "" +
47.      "<table width=\"100%\" border=\"0\"  cellspacing=\"0\"
         cellpadding=\"0\" bgcolor=\"#ffffff\" align=\"center\">" +
48.      "" +
49.      "<tr>" +
50.      "" +
51.      "<td bgcolor=\"#cccccc\" align=\"center\">" +
52.      " <p> <p> " +
53.      "<table cellpadding=\"3\" rules=\"cols\" cellspacing=\"0\"
         width=\"400\"  border=\"1\" bordercolor=\"#000000\"
         bgcolor=\"#eeeeee\">" +
54.      "<tr><td colspan=\"3\" bgcolor=\"#000000\" align=\"center\"
         valign=\"bottom\"> <b><font face=\"arial\" color=\"#ffffff\">" +
55.
56.      "TELLER LOGIN SCREEN</font></b> </td></tr>" +
57.      "<tr>" +
58.      "<td colspan=\"3\" align=\"center\">" +
59.
60.      "<FORM NAME=\"/wasbook/tellerlogged\"" +
61.      " ACTION= \"/wasbook/tellerlogged\" " +
62.      " METHOD=\"POST\">\n" +
63.
64.      "<table cellpadding=\"3\" cellspacing=\"0\" border=\"0\"
         width=\"250\">" +
65.      "<tr>" +
66.      "<td><font face=\"arial\" size=\"-1\">Teller:</font></td>" +
67.      "<td><input type=\"text\" name=\"userid\" ></td>" +
68.      "<td> </td>" +
69.      "</tr>" +
70.      "<tr>" +
71.      "<td><font face=\"arial\" size=\"-1\">Password:</font></td>" +
72.      "<td><input type=\"password\" name=\"password\"></td>" +
73.      "<td><input type=\"submit\" value=\"Login\"></td>" +
74.      "</tr>" +
75.      "<tr><td colspan=\"3\"><font size=\"-3\"> </font></td></tr>" +
76.      "<tr valign=\"top\">" +
77.      "<td colspan=\"2\">" +
78.      "<font face=\"trebuchet ms,arial,helvetica,geneva,sans-serif\"
         size=\"-1\">" +
79.      "</font>" +
80.      "</td>" +
81.      "</tr>" +
82.      "</table>" +
83.      "</form>" +
84.      "" +
85.      "</td>" +
86.      "</tr>" +
87.      "</table>" +
```

```
88.        " <p> <p> " +
89.        "" +
90.        "</td>" +
91.        "</tr>" +
92.        "</table>" +
93.        "" +
94.        "</td>" +
95.        "</tr>" +
96.        "</table>" +
97.        "" +
98.        "</body>" +
99.        "</html>";
100.
101. public void doGet(HttpServletRequest request, HttpServletResponse
     response)
102.         throws IOException{
103.
104.     ServletOutputStream out = response.getOutputStream();
105.
106.     response.setContentType("text/html");
107.     response.setHeader("Pragma", "no-cache");
108.     response.setHeader("Cache-Control", "no-cache");
109.     response.setDateHeader("Expires", 0);
110.     out.println(content);
111.     out.close();
112. }
113.
114. public void doPost(HttpServletRequest request, HttpServletResponse
     response)
115.         throws IOException{
116.     doGet(request,response);
117.
118. }
119. }
120.
121.
```

Teller Authentication: TellerLogged

Once the employee logs in and submits a valid userid and password through the LoginScreen servlet, the TellerLogged servlet is invoked. The next illustration shows the TellerLogged servlet output (active screen) due to the doPost() method.

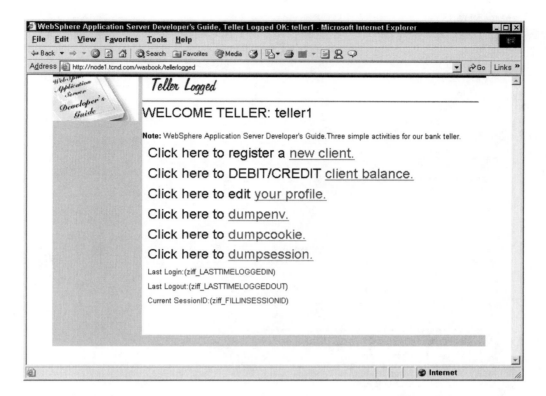

The TellerLogged servlet, shown in Listing 12-12, handles the POST request of LoginScreen and tries to authenticate the employee by checking her userid and password (lines 43–50). The servlet reads the userid and password passed from the LoginScreen servlet on lines 46 and 56. On line 57, the authentication is confirmed if the result of the query is true.

Listing 12-12   *The TellerLogged servlet*

```
1.    import java.io.*;
2.    import javax.servlet.*;
3.    import javax.servlet.http.*;
4.    import java.util.Hashtable;
5.
6.    import com.tcnd.wasdg.dataaccess.*;
7.    import com.tcnd.wasdg.common.*;
8.
9.
10.   public class TellerLogged extends javax.servlet.http.HttpServlet {
```

```
11.        DataAccessComponent DAC;
12.
13.        String pagecontent =
14.
15.  "<html>" +
16.
17.  ...
18.
19.  "</html>";
20.
21.
22.  public void init() throws ServletException {
23.            DAC = new DataAccessComponent();
24.  }
25.
26.
27.  public void doGet(HttpServletRequest request, HttpServletResponse
       response)
28.       throws ServletException, IOException {
29.       response.setContentType("text/html");
30.       response.setHeader("Pragma", "no-cache");
31.       response.setHeader("Cache-Control", "no-cache");
32.       response.setDateHeader("Expires", 0);
33.
34.       PrintWriter out = response.getWriter();
35.
36.       out.println("Hmm!");
37.       out.close();
38.  }
39.
40.
41.  public void doPost(HttpServletRequest request, HttpServletResponse
       response)
42.            throws IOException{
43.
44.       String content = "Hmm!";
45.
46.       String userid = request.getParameter("userid");
47.       String password = request.getParameter("password");
48.
49.       IDataAccessObject iDAO = DAC.createDAObject();
50.
51.       Hashtable hs = new Hashtable();
52.       hs.put("userid",userid);
53.       hs.put("password",password);
54.       iDAO.setParameters(hs);
55.       iDAO.setCommandString("SELECT * FROM DB2INST1.EMPPWD WHERE (USERID =
       ':userid' AND PASSWORD = ':password')");
56.       iDAO = DAC.executeQuery(iDAO);
57.       if (iDAO.getCommandResult())
```

```
58.      {
59.          content = pagecontent;
60.          content = StrTool.replaceUnsensitive( content,
     "ziff_WELCOMETELLER", userid);
61.          content = StrTool.replaceUnsensitive( content, "ziff_SERVERNAME",
     request.getServerName());
62.      }
63.
64.      response.setContentType("text/html");
65.      response.setHeader("Pragma", "no-cache");
66.      response.setHeader("Cache-Control", "no-cache");
67.      response.setDateHeader("Expires", 0);
68.
69.      ServletOutputStream out = response.getOutputStream();
70.      out.println(content);
71.      out.close();
72.  }
73.  }
```

TellerLogged instantiates the DataAccessComponent in its init() method (line 23). This ensures that the servlet can access the DBGUDE database in its doPost() method.

On line 27, TellerLogged handles the GET method request, however, just to print "Hmm!" (line 36) to the intruder.

The active screen of a successful teller login may show many links. Not all links have been activated (except for the dumpenv and Debit/CREDIT client balance). You do not need to be concerned with these links at this time. They have been put in place so that we can proceed and build up the example progressively.

Teller to Credit/Debit a Client Account: CreditDebit

The CreditDebit servlet doGet() shown on line 36 of Listing 12-13 prints the screen that prompts the user to enter the clientid and the amount to be credited or debited.

The servlet also hides the input parameter hiddensessionid on line 20Hidden field parameters are discussed in chapter 16. However, it is possible to hide parameters in an HTTP form like this one. Such a parameter can be read by the doPost() method of the servlet CreditDebit (line 19) once the Submit button is clicked (line 28).

Listing 12-13	*The CreditDebit servlet that the GET request prompts for the CLIENTID and amount to debit or credit*

```
1.    import java.util.Hashtable;
2.    import java.io.*;
3.    import javax.servlet.*;
4.    import javax.servlet.http.*;
5.    import javax.servlet.http.HttpServlet;
6.
7.    import com.tcnd.wasdg.dataaccess.*;
8.    import com.tcnd.wasdg.common.*;
9.
10.   public class CreditDebit extends javax.servlet.http.HttpServlet {
11.       DataAccessComponent DAC;
12.       String step1content =
13.   "<HTML>" +
14.   "<HEAD>" +
15.   "<TITLE>WASDG - Debit/Credit FORM</TITLE>" +
16.   "</HEAD>" +
17.   "<BODY>" +
18.   "<H1>CREDIT/DEBIT a ClientID</H1>" +
19.   "<FORM METHOD=\"POST\" ACTION=\"/wasbook/creditdebit\">" +
20.   "<input type=\"hidden\" name=\"hiddensessionid\"
          value=\"ziff_HIDDENSESSIONID\">" +
21.   "" +
22.   "<HR>" +
23.   "<H2>Please enter the ClientID and the amount to credit/debit: </H2>" +
24.   "<font size=-1>(i.e. to debit $20 you will enter -20)</font>" +
25.   "<P>ClientID:<INPUT TYPE=\"text\" NAME=\"clientid\" SIZE=\"20\">" +
26.   "<P>Amount:<INPUT TYPE=\"text\" NAME=\"amount\" SIZE=\"20\">" +
27.   "<HR>" +
28.   "<INPUT TYPE=\"submit\" VALUE=\"Submit\"><INPUT TYPE=\"reset\">" +
29.   "</FORM>" +
30.   "</BODY>" +
31.   "</HTML>" +
32.   "";
33.
34.   ...
35.
36.   public void doGet(HttpServletRequest request, HttpServletResponse
          response)
37.       throws ServletException, IOException {
38.       response.setContentType("text/html");
```

```
39.         response.setHeader("Pragma", "no-cache");
40.         response.setHeader("Cache-Control", "no-cache");
41.         response.setDateHeader("Expires", 0);
42.
43.         PrintWriter out = response.getWriter();
44.         out.println(step1content);
45.         out.close();
46.     }
47.     ...
48.
49.     }
```

The DebitCredit's doPost() method is shown in Listing 12-14. Knowing that a database connection has already been established the first time the servlet has been loaded (line 32), the doPost() method uses this connection on line 57 to fetch the client account (line 63) and perform the appropriate update. Finally, doPost() performs some string substitution in the content on lines 90 to 99 before printing the client record shown next.

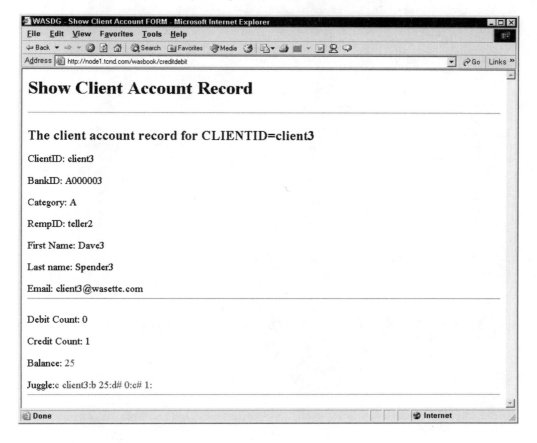

Listing 12-14 *The DebitCredit servlet POST request to access the database and debit or credit the client account*

```
1.   ...
2.       String step2content =
3.   "<HTML>" +
4.   "<HEAD>" +
5.   "<TITLE>WASDG - Show Client Account FORM</TITLE>" +
6.   "</HEAD>" +
7.   "<BODY>" +
8.   "<H1>Show Client Account Record</H1>" +
9.   "<FORM>" +
10.  "" +
11.  "<HR>" +
12.  "<H2>The client account record for CLIENTID=ziff_CLIENTID</H2>" +
13.  "<P><font size=\"+1\">ClientID:  ziff_CLIENTID</font>" +
14.  "<P><font size=\"+1\">BankID:  ziff_BANKID</font>" +
15.  "<P><font size=\"+1\">Category:  ziff_CATEGORY</font>" +
16.  "<P><font size=\"+1\">RempID:  ziff_REMPID</font>" +
17.  "<P><font size=\"+1\">First Name:  ziff_FRSTNAME</font>" +
18.  "<P><font size=\"+1\">Last name:  ziff_LASTNAME</font>" +
19.  "<P><font size=\"+1\">Email:  ziff_EMAIL</font>" +
20.  "<hr>" +
21.  "<P><font size=\"+1\">Debit Count:  ziff_CDEBITS</font>" +
22.  "<P><font size=\"+1\">Credit Count:  ziff_CCREDITS</font>" +
23.  "<P><font size=\"+1\">Balance:   </font><font size=\"+1\"
      color=\"blue\">ziff_BALANCE</font>" +
24.  "<P><font size=\"+1\">Juggle:</font><font size=\"+1\" color=\"blue\">c
      ziff_CLIENTID:b ziff_BALANCE:d# ziff_CDEBITS:c# ziff_CCREDITS:</font>" +

25.  "<HR>" +
26.  "</FORM>" +
27.  "</BODY>" +
28.  "</HTML>" +
29.  "";
30.
31.  public void init() throws ServletException {
32.      DAC = new DataAccessComponent();
33.
34.  }
35.
36.  public void doGet(HttpServletRequest request, HttpServletResponse
     response)
37.      throws ServletException, IOException {
38.      response.setContentType("text/html");
39.      response.setHeader("Pragma", "no-cache");
40.      response.setHeader("Cache-Control", "no-cache");
41.      response.setDateHeader("Expires", 0);
42.
43.      PrintWriter out = response.getWriter();
```

```
44.        out.println(step1content);
45.        out.close();
46.    }
47.
48.
49.    public void doPost(HttpServletRequest resquest, HttpServletResponse
       response)
50.        throws ServletException, IOException {
51.
52.        String content = "Hmmm!";
53.
54.        String clientid = resquest.getParameter("clientid");
55.        String amount = resquest.getParameter("amount");
56.
57.        IDataAccessObject iDAO = DAC.createDAObject();
58.
59.        Hashtable hs = new Hashtable();
60.        hs.put("clientid",clientid);
61.        iDAO.setParameters(hs);
62.        iDAO.setCommandString("SELECT * FROM DB2INST1.CLIACCNT WHERE CLIENTID
       = ':clientid'");
63.        iDAO = DAC.fetchCliAccount(iDAO);
64.        if (iDAO.getCommandResult())
65.        {
66.            // get the client account
67.            CliAccnt aCli = iDAO.getCliAccnt();
68.            // Print the object to standard out, this will go to the
       default_server_stdout.log
69.            aCli.show();
70.            // get the balance, count of credits, count of debits
71.            int balance = aCli.getBalance();
72.            int ccredits = aCli.getCcredits();
73.            int cdebits = aCli.getCdebits();
74.            // add the number of bucks to the balance
75.            balance += Integer.parseInt(amount);
76.            // Increment the credits counter if it is 0 or more, the debits
       counter otherwise
77.            if (Integer.parseInt(amount) >= 0) ccredits += 1; else cdebits +=
       1;
78.
79.            // update the balance, credits and debits counters in the
       database
80.            iDAO.setCommandString("UPDATE DB2INST1.CLIACCNT SET BALANCE = " +
       balance + " , CCREDITS = " + ccredits + " , CDEBITS = " + cdebits + "
       WHERE CLIENTID = ':clientid'");
81.            iDAO = DAC.executeUpdate(iDAO);
82.            if (iDAO.getCommandResult())
83.            {
84.                // update the CliAccnt object if the UPDATE was successful
85.                aCli.setBalance(balance);
```

```
86.                aCli.setCcredits(ccredits);
87.                aCli.setCdebits(cdebits);
88.                // Fill in the HTML presentation
89.                content = step2content;
90.                content = StrTool.replaceUnsensitive(content,
         "ziff_CLIENTID", aCli.getClientID());
91.                content = StrTool.replaceUnsensitive(content, "ziff_BANKID",
         aCli.getBankID());
92.                content = StrTool.replaceUnsensitive(content,
         "ziff_CATEGORY", aCli.getCategory());
93.                content = StrTool.replaceUnsensitive(content, "ziff_REMPID",
         aCli.getRempID());
94.                content = StrTool.replaceUnsensitive(content,
         "ziff_FRSTNAME", aCli.getFrstName());
95.                content = StrTool.replaceUnsensitive(content,
         "ziff_LASTNAME", aCli.getLastName());
96.                content = StrTool.replaceUnsensitive(content, "ziff_EMAIL",
         aCli.getEmail());
97.                content = StrTool.replaceUnsensitive(content, "ziff_CDEBITS",
         String.valueOf(aCli.getCdebits()));
98.                content = StrTool.replaceUnsensitive(content,
         "ziff_CCREDITS", String.valueOf(aCli.getCcredits()));
99.                content = StrTool.replaceUnsensitive(content, "ziff_BALANCE",
         String.valueOf(aCli.getBalance()));
100.           }
101.       }
102.       response.setContentType("text/html");
103.       response.setHeader("Pragma", "no-cache");
104.       response.setHeader("Cache-Control", "no-cache");
105.       response.setDateHeader("Expires", 0);
106.
107.       PrintWriter out = response.getWriter();
108.       out.println(content);
109.       out.close();
110. }
111. }
```

You can always credit a client balance zero dollars. Here is an example to credit client3 with zero dollars:

```
# echo "clientid=client3&amount=0&---" | lynx -post_data
     http://node1/wasbook/creditdebit
Show Client Account Record
```

```
The client account record for CLIENTID=client3
ClientID: client3
BankID: A000003
Category: A
RempID: teller2
```

```
First Name: Dave3
Last name: Spender3
Email: client3@wasette.com
```

```
Debit Count: 0
Credit Count: 1
Balance: 0
Juggle: c client3:b 0:c# 1:d# 0
```

After crediting or debiting a client account, CreditDebit prints the client record as shown previously. The last line shows a `Juggle` used on purpose so that we can use it as a specifier when we grep that line in a batch process. You read this line as follows: client (c) with clientid=client3 has a final balance (b) of zero dollars, and the number of times his or her account has been credited (c#) and debited (d#) are zero times and zero times consecutively.

CreditDebit handles the HTTP POST method to authenticate the teller, and both userid and password must be input to authorize the teller. However, an unauthorized user can enter the CreditDebit servlet with a GET method to credit or debit any client account. For instance, put a request to the servlet in the browser, and you will be presented with a screen in which you can enter the information to debit/credit an account. The servlet must not authorize such a transaction and must check to see whether the teller is in session before prompting for the client entry screen. This is the subject of Chapter 16.

Batch Processing with Lynx

This final section embarks on a risky path. As demonstrated in the example on how to do batch processing on your database via the Teller/Client servlets, you will realize how vulnerable a web application can be. This example uses the technique of simulating database access through the application server. Simulation can also be used by a hacker and can cause damage to an application server.

Consider the following situation in which you want to credit/debit the client1, client2, and client3 accounts with $10, –$2, and $4. The following shows how you can perform this task by using three commands.

```
 [root@node1 12]# for i in 1 2 3;  do echo "clientid=client$i&amount=10&---" |
lynx -post_data http://node1/wasbook/creditdebit | grep Juggle; done
Juggle:c client1:b 10:d# 0:c# 1:
Juggle:c client2:b 10:d# 0:c# 1:
Juggle:c client3:b 10:d# 0:c# 1:
[root@node1 12]# for i in 1 2 3;  do echo "clientid=client$i&amount=-2&---" |
lynx -post_data http://node1/wasbook/creditdebit | grep Juggle; done
Juggle:c client1:b 8:d# 1:c# 1:
Juggle:c client2:b 8:d# 1:c# 1:
Juggle:c client3:b 8:d# 1:c# 1:
[root@node1 12]# for i in 1 2 3;  do echo "clientid=client$i&amount=4&---" |
```

```
lynx -post_data http://node1/wasbook/creditdebit | grep Juggle; done
Juggle:c client1:b 12:d# 1:c# 2:
Juggle:c client2:b 12:d# 1:c# 2:
Juggle:c client3:b 12:d# 1:c# 2:
```

Because it is possible to iterate over HTTP requests, and because each servlet starts a thread to service the request, it is possible to exhaust the system resources of the server on which the web application is running. This is true if the web application is badly designed. On the other hand, let's say someone writes a script that reads a word from the dictionary and tries to log in with someone else's login name. Such a hacker can set up the shell variable $WORD with the target password and try to log in as the user dave.

```
[root@node1 12]# echo "userid=dave&password=$WORD&---" | lynx
-post_data http://node1/wasbook/tellerlogged
```

The reason to use Lynx, Perl, and shell scripts is to perform simulation by batch processing commands against a target web application.

Wrapping Up

This chapter demonstrated many practical ways to program servlets without addressing the broader syllogistics behind them. The chapter showed the essential points required for developing web programs that handle the GET and POST methods to allow the use to interact with the HTTP server. A variety of examples have been offered to show you either how a servlet can be used to print dynamic HTML content or how a servlet can interact with a database server. The examples are simple and straightforward, making them a good example for study or for testing the functionality of WAS and the database server. The building blocks of the Teller/ Client servlets were also put in place. Furthermore, the use of Lynx has proved to be an adequate tool for developers, not only to quickly test their servlets, but also to simulate and batch process bulk HTTP requests.

Java Server Pages (JSP)

his chapter discusses the Java Server Pages (JSP) language,[1] an extremely powerful facility that is usually available in application-server-level programming.

The JSP language provides a way for a programmer to define a code sequence that can be either conveniently dispatched by a Java servlet or can call a Java servlet later. Whereas a Java servlet needs to be compiled before deploying it into the application server, an instruction sequence coded as a JSP program does not need to be compiled explicitly by the programmer. It is called an open Java routine, as compared to a closed (compiled and *secure*) Java servlet. However, using JSP must not replace coding Java servlets.

Programming in a language such as Java is important when it comes to implementing an application specification and its business logic securely. However, Java programming seems to be too bulky to handle the other tasks that a programmer needs to perform quickly. Java is a deeply compiled object-oriented language that does not offer the preprocessing capability that is available with an object-oriented interpreted language such as Perl. JSP processing syntax is carried through a mechanism where user-readable textual files can be submitted to an agent to be preprocessed to generate a .java program: the *JSP processor.*

Prior to JSP 1.1, Sun called the JSP processor the *JSP engine.* Starting with JSP 1.1, Sun gave it an even stronger marketing term: the *JSP container.*[2] We have called the agent that processes .jsp files the *JSP processor* because this is the more factual name. In reality, there is no separate container that handles a .jsp file; instead, a language processor translates such a file into a .java program to be compiled and loaded into the web container.

The combination of .java servlet programs and .jsp files form an entity known as a *web module.* Such a web module is loaded under a web application like the one discussed in Chapter 12: webapp, located in the wasdg.ear/webapp directory. Figure 13-1 shows the steps taken by a WAS JSP processor on the List.jsp file.

Programmatically, handling .jsp pages in a web application is simple: you edit a .jsp file and save it in the $BASE_DEV/wasdg.ear/webapp directory. Then you run svlbuild again to move all .jsp files found in the build tree into their corresponding location in the deployed tree.

These user-readable textual files are called *JSP files.* They have a .jsp extension, and the syntax in these files pertains to a JSP scripting language. A .jsp file, once deployed in WAS, is turned into a Java program first, then compiled into byte code before it is processed internally by a JSP container. The syntax used in a JSP file should match the specification of the JSP container version number. Currently, WAS v4 supports JSP 1.1.

The syntax of the JSP program is quite rudimentary and is easy to program with. This chapter introduces JSP programming.

---

[1]   The word "language" is used loosely here; you will understand this more fully when we consider the formality of a rudimentary language and its grammar. Admittedly, JSP reduces the finesse of Java programming capabilities. I use it here precisely for its simplicity.

[2]   The JSP container is not a separate container, but the web container itself. JSP is not considered a computer language, but a workaround preprocessor that can facilitate servlet testing. The SessionFairy servlet in Chapter 16 shows an alternative method of preprocessing by using Perl.

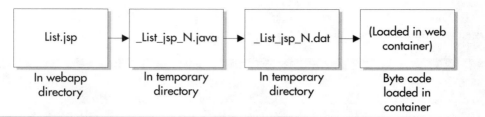

Figure 13-1   *Stages undertaken by a WAS JSP processor on a JSP page*

JSP Programming: A First Example

Consider the JSP file List.jsp, shown in Listing 13-1. Edit and save this file in the BASE_DEV/
wasdg.ear/webapp directory. Then run the svlbuild script to move this file to the deployment tree.

Listing 13-1   *List.jsp*

```
1.    <html>
2.    <head>
3.    </head>
4.    <body>
5.
6.    <p>
7.    <ul>
8.    <%
9.    for (int i = 0; i < 4; i++)
10.   {
11.        out.println ("<li>" + i);
12.   }
13.   %>
14.   </ul>
15.
16.   </body>
17.   </html>
```

In a browser, place a request to the JSP page simply by typing in the URL in a browser, as shown in the following illustration.

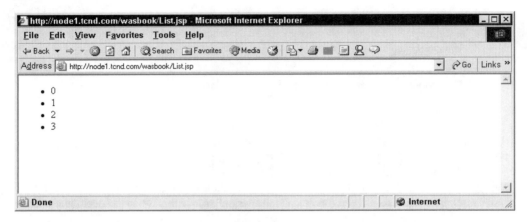

The code shown in Listing 13-1 is a mix of HTML tags and Java code. In fact, the Java code is also being tagged in between angle brackets and percent signs (<% and %>), which denotes the syntax for a Java code fragment called scriplet:

```
<% Java code fragment %>
```

As you will see in the next section, the scriplet is being presented to the _jspService() method. In the $WAS_HOME directory, locate the scratch directory where the JSP processor is performing its compilation:

```
# find $WAS_HOME -name The_WASDG_Application -type d
```

The command prints a directory that you will cd to it:

```
# cd $WAS_HOME/temp/<nodename>/Default_Server/The_WASDG_Application/webapp
```

In this directory, you should be able to locate one or more files that start with the prefix _List_jsp_. WAS uses this directory to compile JSP pages.

Remove all files that start with _List_jsp_ as a prefix (rm -f _List_jsp_*) and rerun svlbuild to refresh the deployed files. This time, before you request the List.jsp file, monitor the $WASLOG_STDOUT, and edit and save the capture script (see Listing 13-2) in the scratch directory just discussed. Run the capture directory with the following command:

```
# perl capture _List_jsp_
```

From a browser, request the List.jsp page. Notice that the JSP processor has been active, as revealed in the $WASLOG_STDOUT file. In the /tmp directory, the file _List_jsp_0.java that once existed has been copied from the scratch directory.

Listing 13-2   *capture*

```perl
1.    #!/usr/bin/perl
2.
3.    while (1) {
4.        @files = glob("*.java");
5.        foreach $f (@files) {
6.            `cp -f $f /tmp` if ($f =~ /^@ARGV/);
7.        }
8.        sleep(2);
9.    }
```

The capture script loops forever looking for all files that start with _List_jsp_*.java in the current directory. Once a file is found, it is copied to the /tmp directory. Because the capture script loop continues forever, you need to break the process by pressing CTRL-C.

View the _List_jsp_.java file that has just been captured (see Listing 13-3) in the /tmp directory. At the head of the file, there is a list of imports.

Listing 13-3   *_List_jsp_0.java*

```java
1.    import javax.servlet.*;
2.    import javax.servlet.http.*;
3.    import javax.servlet.jsp.*;
4.    import javax.servlet.jsp.tagext.*;
5.    import java.io.PrintWriter;
6.    import java.io.IOException;
7.    import java.io.InputStream;
8.    import java.io.ObjectInputStream;
9.    import java.util.Vector;
10.   import org.apache.jasper.runtime.*;
11.   import java.beans.*;
12.   import org.apache.jasper.JasperException;
13.   import java.io.ByteArrayOutputStream;
14.   import org.apache.jasper.compiler.ibmtsx.*;
15.   import org.apache.jasper.compiler.ibmdb.*;
16.   import java.sql.SQLException;
17.
18.
20.
21.       static char[][] _jspx_html_data = null;
```

```
22.
23.       static {
24.       }
25.       public _List_jsp_0( ) {
26.       }
27.
28.   ...
29.
30.       public final void _jspx_init() throws JasperException {
31.   ...
32.       }
33.
34.       public void _jspService(HttpServletRequest request,
      HttpServletResponse  response)
35.           throws IOException, ServletException {
36.
37.           JspFactory _jspxFactory = null;
38.           PageContext pageContext = null;
39.           HttpSession session = null;
40.           ServletContext application = null;
41.           ServletConfig config = null;
42.           JspWriter out = null;
43.           Object page = this;
44.           String  _value = null;
45.           setBooleanIgnoreException();
46.   ...
47.       }
48.       private void setBooleanIgnoreException() {
49.   ...
50.       }
51.   }
```

The _List_jsp_*.java file has been generated by WAS' JSP processor, then compiled to generate the .dat data file, then deleted. The amount of imported libraries at the beginning of the generated file is unusual for such a tiny piece of code. JSP programming is generic, and the JSP processor won't spare you from its "generic-ness."

A Second Example: Using the Request Dispatcher

A servlet can update a JSP page because WAS offers interservlet communication through the RequestDispatcher. The RequestDispatcher allows you to forward a request and include a response from another servlet.

Listing 13-4 shows the UpdateJSP servlet. When invoked, this servlet dispatches a message to the Plain.jsp JSP file shown in Listing 13-5.

Listing 13-4   *UpdateJSP servlet*

```
1.    import java.io.*;
2.    import javax.servlet.*;
3.    import javax.servlet.http.*;
4.
5.    public class UpdateJSP extends HttpServlet
6.    {
7.        public void doGet (HttpServletRequest req, HttpServletResponse res)
8.            throws ServletException, IOException
9.        {
10.           String message = "Hello there!";
11.           req.setAttribute("message", message);
12.           RequestDispatcher rd =
      getServletContext().getRequestDispatcher("/Plain.jsp");
13.           rd.forward(req, res);
14.       }
15.   }
```

On line 11, the servlet sets the object message as the attribute named "message" into the context of the web container. Resources that need to be shared in an application are treated as objects that can be added, retrieved, or removed from the servlet context using the ServletContext methods shown in Table 13-1.

On line 13 of Listing 13-4, the servlet uses the javax.servlet.RequestDispatcher interface to forward the request and the response to another resource for further processing. The other resource can be another servlet or another JSP; however, in our example, line 12 shows that the forwarding is directed to Plain.jsp, shown in Listing 13-5.

Listing 13-5   *Plain.jsp*

```
1.    <html>
2.    <head>
3.    </head>
4.    <body>
5.    <h1><servlet code=UpdateJSP></servlet></h1>
6.
7.    <%
8.    String message = (String) request.getAttribute("message");
9.    out.print("message: <b>" + message + "</b>");
10.   %>
11.
12.   </body>
13.   </html>
```

Method	Description
void setAttribute(String name, Object attribute)	Stores an attribute in a context
Object getAttribute(String name)	Gets an attribute from the context
Enumaration getAttributeNames()	Gets the names of all the attributes currently stored in the context
void removeAttribute(String name)	Removes an attribute from the context

Table 13-1 *The ServletContext Methods*

On line 8, getAttribute() is used to get the attribute "message" from the context of the servlet. The following illustration shows the result of requesting the UpsdateJSP servlet.

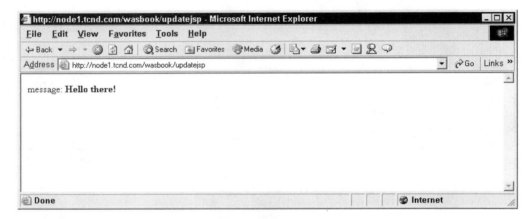

You can modify the TellerLogged servlet discussed in Chapter 12 so that when a user requests the servlet with a GET method, a warning message is returned in the request. Of course, the method to log in is POST so that the userid and password are not being exposed in the query string. Listing 13-6 shows the change in the doGet() method of the TellerLogged servlet.

Listing 13-6 *doGet() method of the TellerLogged servlet*

```
1.   public void doGet(HttpServletRequest request, HttpServletResponse
     response)
2.       throws ServletException, IOException
3.   {
4.       String message =
5.       "<br>" + "Query String: " + request.getQueryString () +
```

```
6.        "<br>" + "Remote User: " + request.getRemoteUser () +
7.        "<br>" + "Remote Address: " + request.getRemoteAddr () +
8.        "<br>" + "Remote Host: " + request.getRemoteHost () +
9.        "<br>" + "Authentication Scheme: " + request.getAuthType () + "<br>"
      + "<hr><p>";
10.       request.setAttribute("message", message);
11.       RequestDispatcher rd =
      getServletContext().getRequestDispatcher("/Warn.jsp");
12.       rd.forward(request, response);
13.   }
```

On line 4, the message is a Java object of type String that is formed of many pieces (lines 5 through 9) appended together to form an HTML-formatted string. Lines 11 and 12 use the RequestDispatcher to forward the request and response of the servlet to Warn.jsp (shown in Listing 13-7), which is running in the same web container and therefore sharing the same context of the servlet.

Listing 13-7   *Warn.jsp*

```
1.    <html>
2.    <head>
3.    </head>
4.    <body>
5.    <h1>Illegal Access<h1>
6.    <h2>
7.    You attempted to login as a teller using
8.    the GET method. Remote logged information follows:
9.    <servlet code=TellerLogged></servlet>
10.   </h2>
11.
12.   <%
13.   String message = (String) request.getAttribute("message");
14.   out.print("TellerLogged returned: <b>" + message + "</b>");
15.   %>
16.
17.   </body>
18.   </html>
```

Line 13 retrieved the information about the remote user by getting the attribute "message" that returns the Java object that has been dispatched from the servlet to the Warn.jsp JSP page. The following illustration shows the result in the browser of teller1 trying to log in explicitly using the GET method. Of course, Warn.jsp is invoked because the TellerLogged servlet does not allow a teller to log in using the GET method.

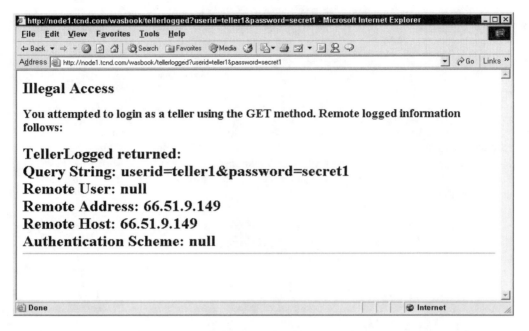

JSP offers you a nongeneric syntax for a contextual inline coding mechanism, making it possible to call Java code from within JSP. At is turns out, Java code can dispatch JSP code from within the servlets by importing the generic javax.servlet classes. The communication between JSP pages and Java servlets is made possible due to the intraservlet communication in a web module.

Servlet Communication

Communication between servlets[3] happens at two levels: *intraservlet* communication occurs inside the web modules and therefore inside the web container; and *interservlet* communication occurs outside the web modules but between the web containers and within the enterprise application.

---

[3] WAS defines an API that allows you to chain a servlet. Chaining a servlet was introduced in Java servlet 1. This technique is not discussed in this book because it is inadequate due to its use of multiple servlets. A cleaner technique will be available to WAS programmers once WAS supports the servlet API 2.3. The servlet API 2.3 introduces the use of filters, with the J2EE web.xml deployment descriptor tag <filter>. The programmer uses filters to do transformation on a request or on a response. Filters are not servlets, but they are objects that act as pre-processors of the request (input to the servlet), or post-processors of the response (output from the servlet)..

Intraservlet Communication

Because JSP pages are turned into Java programs, compiled internally to WAS, and then loaded by the web container, they are treated like servlets in a web application. JSP pages and servlets can collaboratively communicate information within their web context or within the scope of the web container managing them. Servlet to servlet, servlet to JSP page, and JSP page to servlet communication is called intraservlet communication. It is facilitated with the use of the setAttribute() and getAttribute() methods, and the RequestDispatcher's forward and include methods.

The UpdateJSP servlet discussed in a previous section "A Second Example: Using the Request Dispatcher" communicated a message from the servlet to a JSP page using similar methods. You will see more examples about the intracommunication between servlets and JSP pages in the section "Custom Tags: JSP Tag Libraries." You will also learn about their deployment, looking at the J2EE descriptors involved in writing a JSP custom tags library.

Interservlet Communication

In an enterprise application, you can define two or more web applications. For example, in addition to the webapp that was defined in the WASDG application, you can define another webapp2. Within the same enterprise application, servlets in one web application can communicate with servlets in another web application as long as they are both associated with the same virtual host. (Refer to Chapter 4 for a discussion on virtual hosts.) A web application shares data with another web application through its ServletContext object. This object can be accessed by all web applications in the same enterprise application.

Again, the technique here is obviously to use getServletContext(), followed by an access to the request dispatcher. Servlet test1 in webapp can use getServletContext for application webapp2, after which it can access the request dispatcher for servlets in application webapp2 and call the getAttribute() and setAttribute() methods of the servlet context. In the test1 servlet, the sequence of code typically shown is as follows:

```
webapp2context = webappcontext.getContext("/webapp2");
webapp2context.getRequestDispatcher("/test2");
```

Although you can experiment with this technique of sharing data between different web applications on your WAS AEs, in general, you should avoid it because it complicates the programming, understandability, and portability of enterprise web applications in a distributed environment composed of many WAS nodes. Because the ServletContext is constrained to one web application and its Java machine, it can be shared by multiple requests for the target servlet. (Refer to Chapter 8 for the Java machines WAS hierarchy.) It must be clear that a request cannot be shared; therefore, setting attributes on the request will not make the attributes sharable.

Custom Tags: JSP Tag Libraries

JSP pages can call Java-compiled code through customized tags. Custom tags are described in a tag library that is known to the web module through a Tag Library Descriptor (TLD) file.

Such a file has an.tld extension and is deposited in the WEB-INF directory of the web module itself (similar to the web.xml file).

Consider the time.jsp file shown in Listing 13-8 and the corresponding timeTag.java file shown in Listing 13-9. If you request time.jsp from a browser, as shown in the following illustration, the time is printed.

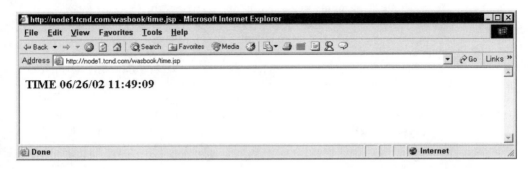

The format of the printed time is formatted according to the format specified on line 5 of Listing 13-8.

Listing 13-8 *time.jsp*

```
1.    <%@ taglib prefix="sample" uri="WEB-INF/sampleTags.tld" %>
2.    <html>
3.      <head></head>
4.      <body>
5.        <h1>TIME  <sample:time format="MM/dd/yy   HH:mm:ss"/></h1>
6.      </body>
7.    </html>
```

The sample:time symbol shown on line 5 is called a *custom tag* and is composed of a prefix and a name known as the *tag name*. To resolve the sample:time symbol, the prefix must be properly mapped to a TLD file, as shown on line 1. On line 1, the taglib directive identifies the prefix sample and maps it to its URI. This way, the file pointed to by the URI is consulted for the custom tag defined subsequently in the rest of the file.

Listing 13-9 *timeTag.java*

```
1.    package com.tcnd.wasdg.tagbin;
2.
3.    import javax.servlet.jsp.tagext.*;
4.    import javax.servlet.jsp.*;
5.    import java.text.SimpleDateFormat;
6.
```

```
7.    public class timeTag extends TagSupport {
8.       String format = "HH:mm:ss";
9.
10.      public void setFormat(String newFormat) {
11.         format = newFormat;
12.      }
13.      public int doEndTag() throws JspException {
14.         SimpleDateFormat sdf;
15.         sdf = new SimpleDateFormat(format);
16.         String time = sdf.format(new java.util.Date());
17.         try {
18.            pageContext.getOut().print(time);
19.         } catch (Exception e) {
20.            throw new JspException(e.toString());
21.         }
22.         return EVAL_PAGE;
23.      }
24.   }
```

The sampleTags.tld file (see Listing 13-10) is called the *tag library descriptor file*. For example, the tag time is described in the descriptor file to identify the classname (tag library) that contains the statement that resolves the tag name time (shown on line 16 of Listing 13-9).

The tag library is actually a class file that must follow a certain convention: it must have a doEndTag()method that returns with EVAL_PAGE, as shown on line 22 of Listing 13-9.

The TLD sampleTags.tld is an XML document that describes the custom tag library.

Listing 13-10   *sampleTags.tld defining the tag named "time"*

```
1.    <?xml version="1.0" encoding="ISO-8859-1" ?>
2.    <!DOCTYPE taglib
3.       PUBLIC "-//Sun Microsystems, Inc.//DTD JSP Tag Library 1.1//EN"
4.       "http://java.sun.com/j2ee/dtds/web-jsptaglibrary_1_1.dtd">
5.
6.    <taglib>
7.       <tlibversion>1.0</tlibversion>
8.       <jspversion>1.1</jspversion>
9.       <shortname>Application Tag Library</shortname>
10.      <uri>http://jakarta.apache.org/taglibs/struts-example-1.0</uri>
11.      <info>
12.         This tag library contains functionality specific to the Struts
13.         Example Application.
14.      </info>
15.      <tag>
16.         <name>time</name>
17.         <tagclass>com.tcnd.wasdg.tagbin.timeTag</tagclass>
18.         <bodycontent>empty</bodycontent>
19.         <info>
```

```
20.            information goes here
21.        and more here
22.        </info>
23.        <attribute>
24.          <name>format</name>
25.          <required>false</required>
26.          <rtexprvalue>false</rtexprvalue>
27.        </attribute>
28.      </tag>
29.    </taglib>
```

Line 1 provides the XML declaration, followed by a definition and validation link (line 2) for the XML document. Lines 15 through 28 are the tag definition: it contains the essential name for the symbol "time" (line 16) and the library where this symbol can be found (line 17); an optional attribute is followed, in which case, it is the "format" attribute. Be aware that the tag handler class implements an attribute using a setter method of the same name in the tag handler's code[4] (the setFormat() method, shown on line 10 of Listing 13-9).

Automating the Process of JSP Tags Library Programming

Let's reconsider the time.jsp and timeTag.java files discussed in the section "Custom Tags: JSP Tag Libraries" to explain a new script that automates the process of generating a tags library. The gentagtld script must be copied to the directory in your search PATH, such as /tools. The gentagtld script, shown in Listing 13-11, reads the tagtld.list file that is usually located in the BASE_DEV directory; the current directory is checked otherwise. Each line in the tagtld.list describes a tag element that is to appear in a TLD file. For instance, to describe the timeTag element, the following line is entered in the tagtld.list file:

```
time   com.tcnd.wasdg.tagbin.timeTag   format&&
```

Listing 13-11   *gentagtld*

```
1.   #!/usr/bin/perl
2.
3.   my $apptld = <<APPTLD;
4.   <?xml version="1.0" encoding="ISO-8859-1" ?>
5.   <!DOCTYPE taglib
6.      PUBLIC "-//Sun Microsystems, Inc.//DTD JSP Tag Library 1.1//EN"
7.      "http://java.sun.com/j2ee/dtds/web-jsptaglibrary_1_1.dtd">
8.
9.   <taglib>
10.
```

---

[4]   Setter methods are similar to those you encounter with a JavaBean.

```
11.    <tlibversion>1.0</tlibversion>
12.    <jspversion>1.1</jspversion>
13.    <shortname>Application Tag Library</shortname>
14.    <uri>http://jakarta.apache.org/taglibs/struts-example-1.0</uri>
15.    <info>
16.      This tag library contains functionality specific to the Struts
17.      Example Application.
18.    </info>
19.
20. TAG_SEGMENT
21.
22. </taglib>
23. APPTLD
24.
25. my $tagsegment = <<TAGSEGMENT;
26.    <tag>
27. TAGCLASS_SEGMENT
28. TAGCLASS_ATTRIBUTES_SEGMENT
29.    </tag>
30. TAGSEGMENT
31.
32. # A tag definition
33. my $tagname = <<TAGNAME_TLD;
34.      <name>TAGNAME</name>
35.      <tagclass>TAGCLASSNAME</tagclass>
36.      <bodycontent>empty</bodycontent>
37.      <info>
38.          information goes here
39.      and more here
40.      </info>
41. TAGNAME_TLD
42.
43. # An attribute definition
44. my $tagattrib = <<TAGATTRIB_TLD;
45.      <attribute>
46.        <name>ATTRIBUTENAME</name>
47.        <required>REQUIRED</required>
48.        <rtexprvalue>RTEXPRVALUE</rtexprvalue>
49.      </attribute>
50. TAGATTRIB_TLD
51.
52. if ( (defined($ENV{BASE_DEV})) && (-d $ENV{BASE_DEV}) ) { $fin =
       "$ENV{BASE_DEV}/tagtld.list"; }
53. else { $fin = "tagtld.list"; }
54. die "It does not seem you have any tagtld.list! Set up the BASE_DEV\n"
       unless (-r $fin);
55. open(FILE,"<$fin");
56. my $i = 0;
57.
58. my $stuffer = "";
59. while (<FILE>) {
```

```
60.        next unless (!( (/^#/) || (/^$/) || (/^\:/) ));
61.
62.        my $s1 = $tagname;
63.        my($name,$class,$attributes) = split(/\s/,$_,3);
64.        $s1 =~ s/TAGNAME/$name/;
65.        $s1 =~ s/TAGCLASSNAME/$class/;
66.
67.        my $stuffer1 = "";
68.        if (defined($attributes) && ($attributes =~ /\&/)) {
69.            chop($attributes);
70.            my @attributes = split(/&/,$attributes);
71.            my $j = 0;
72.            # each attribute must be of the form attrib,flag,flag
73.            while ($j <= $#attributes)
74.            {
75.                my $s = $tagattrib;
76.                $s =~ s/ATTRIBUTENAME/$attributes[$j]/;
77.                if ($attributes[$j+1] =~ /true/i) {
78.                    $s =~ s/REQUIRED/true/;
79.                } else {
80.                    $s =~ s/REQUIRED/false/;
81.                }
82.                if ($attributes[$j+2] =~ /true/i) {
83.                    $s =~ s/RTEXPRVALUE/true/;
84.                } else {
85.                    $s =~ s/RTEXPRVALUE/false/;
86.                }
87.                $stuffer1 .= $s;
88.                $j = $j + 3;
89.            }
90.        }
91.        my $s = $tagsegment;
92.        $s =~ s/TAGCLASS_SEGMENT/$s1/;
93.        $s =~ s/TAGCLASS_ATTRIBUTES_SEGMENT/$stuffer1/;
94.        $stuffer .= $s;
95.    }
96.    $apptld =~ s/TAG_SEGMENT/$stuffer/;
97.    print $apptld;
```

Execute the gentagtld script after setting the BASE_DEV directory. The output is printed on the screen to show the TLD file. When invoked with an argument such as sampleTags, the resettagtld script shown in Listing 13-12 invokes the gentagtld script and generates the sampleTags.tld to be deposited in the directories $BASE_DEV/wasdg.ear/webapp/WEB-INF and $INSTALLEDAPPS/wasdg.ear/webapp/WEB-INF, respectively.

Listing 13-12 *resettagtld*

```
1.   #!/bin/ksh
2.
3.   # genwebxml must be in your search PATH
4.   # BASE_DEV and INSTALLEDAPPS must be set
5.   gentagtld  >  $BASE_DEV/wasdg.ear/webapp/WEB-INF/$1.tld
6.   gentagtld  >  $INSTALLEDAPPS/wasdg.ear/webapp/WEB-INF/$1.tld
```

Registering a Tags Library in the Web Application Descriptor

Using the same deployment strategy discussed in Chapters 11 and 12, you will edit the file servlets.list in your $BASE_DEV directory and add in the following line:

```
:TAGLIB sampleTags
```

Running either svlbuild or resetwebxml will generate a web.xml in which the sampleTags is registered to the web module. In particular, you can locate the segment in the web.xml file shown in Listing 13-13 by running genwebxml in your $BASE_DEV directory.

Listing 13-13 *sampleTags.tld described in the web.xml web application descriptor*

```
1.   <taglib>
2.     <taglib-uri>exampleTags</taglib-uri>
3.     <taglib-location>/META-INF/sampleTags.tld</taglib-location>
4.   </taglib>
```

Line 3 identifies the URI where the sampleTags.tld can be found for our web application.

Summarizing the Steps to Program with a JSP Tags Library

Table 13-2 summarizes the files involved in programming the JSP tags library used with the time.jsp page.

Directory Location	File Type	Processing Agent
wasdg.ear/webapp/	time.jsp	WAS' JSP processor
wasdg.ear/webapp/WEB-INF/classes/com/tcnd/ wasdg/tagbin	timeTag.java	javac
wasdg.ear/webapp/WEB-INF	web.xml	genwebxml
wasdg.ear/webapp/WEB-INF	sampleTags.tld	gentagtld

Table 13-2 *Files involved in programming the JSP tags library used by time.jsp page*

Customizing a Tags Library to Print Typical Messages

You make use of a custom tags library to organize static content used in a web application, for example, e-mail messages that are automatically sent as an autoreply, corporation policy rules that are printed for each category of users, and so on.

Listing 13-14 shows the welcomeTag library that defines the mywelcome attribute.

Listing 13-14 *welcomeTag.java*

```
1.    package com.tcnd.wasdg.tagbin;
2.
3.    import java.util.ArrayList;
4.    import javax.servlet.jsp.tagext.*;
5.
6.    public class welcomeTag extends TagSupport {
7.       private String name = null;
8.       private String welcomeA = "Bank client group A";
9.       private String welcomeB = "Bank client group B";
10.      private String welcomeC = "Bank client group C";
11.
12.      public int doStartTag() {
13.         ArrayList myWelcome = new ArrayList(3);
14.         myWelcome.add(new String(welcomeA));
15.         myWelcome.add(new String(welcomeB));
16.         myWelcome.add(new String(welcomeC));
17.
18.         pageContext.setAttribute("mywelcome", myWelcome);
19.
20.         return SKIP_BODY;
21.      }
22.      public void setName(String newName) {
23.         name = newName;
24.      }
25.   }
```

Listing 13-15 shows the welcome.jsp file that is used to fetch the values passed along with the mywelcome attribute.

Listing 13-15 *welcome.jsp*

```
1.    <%@ taglib prefix="sample" uri="WEB-INF/sampleTags.tld" %>
2.    <html>
3.       <head></head>
```

```
4.      <body>
5.      <sample:clientWelcome/>
6.    <%@ page import="java.util.ArrayList" %>
7.    <%
8.      ArrayList myWelcome =
        (ArrayList)pageContext.getAttribute("mywelcome");
9.    %>
10.   <%
11.     for(int i = 0; i<3; i++) {
12.       out.println("Welcoming client with \"" + i + " -- " +
        myWelcome.get(i) + " <BR>");
13.     }
14.   %>
15.     </body>
16.   </html>
```

To compile and test the welcomeTag custom library, follow these steps:

1. Save welcomeTag.java to the directory $BASE_DEV/wasdg.ear/webapp/ WEB-INF/classes/com/tcnd/wasdg/tagbin, and save welcome.jsp to the directory $BASE_DEV/wasdg.ear/webapp directory.

2. In BASE_DEV, edit the servlets.list and add the following line:

   ```
   :TAGLIB sampleTags
   ```

3. Execute svlbuild:

   ```
   # svlbuild
   ```

4. In BASE_DEV, edit tagtld.list and add the following line:

   ```
   clientWelcome   com.tcnd.wasdg.tagbin.welcomeTag
   ```

   Execute this command:

   ```
   # resettagtld sampleTags
   ```

5. Request welcome.jsp from a browser, as shown in the following illustration.

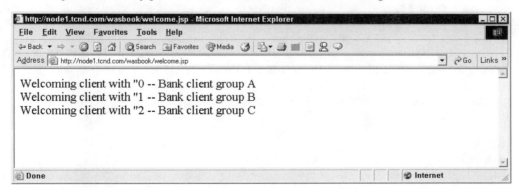

Attribute	Value and Description
autoFlush	True or false. Defaults to true to enable flushing the stream. When set to false, the stream is buffered, and an exception is raised on overflow.
buffer	None or size in K.
contentType	Type or Type; charset=character set. Default is text/html, and the default for the character encoding is ISO-8859-1. (Refer to Appendix C.)
errorPage	A URL. that the JSP will forward processing to whenever an exception is caught.
extends	Java class that implements HttpJspPage. interface.
import	A comma separated list of fully qualified Java packages or type names.
info	A string that is retrieved by the Servlet.getServletInfo() method.
isErrorPage	True or false. If true, the page is used to handle errors, and the implicit script variable `exception` is defined and bound to the offending `Throwable` from the JSP in error.
language	Default to java as the compliant JSP scripting language.
session	True or false. Default to true to indicate that the JSP is session aware.

Table 13-3   *Page Directive Attributes*

On line 6 of the welcome.jsp program shown in Listing 13-15, the page directive syntax is used:

```
<%@ page a_list_of_page_directive_attributes %>
```

Perl programmers would notice that the construct of such syntax using the at symbol (@) to list a set of directives is similar to Perl list syntax. This *may be* partly because the designer of the JSP processor used Perl to write the processor.

The page directive is used to import the java.util.ArrayList. You can use several page directives in your JSP file. Table 13-3 describes the page directive attributes.

For a set of JSP routines that are frequently used, it is possible to write custom tags and archive them into a library. You may find it odd that these routines can include code for some iteration wrappers to cover typical programming functionality such as looping.

Wrapping Up

This chapter focused on how JSP pages are handled within WAS. It provided a technical perspective of JSP page compilation within the web container. We used JSP to perform trivial tasks that are likely to be easily dispatched from our servlets, as in the example with TellerLogged servlet. JSP tags libraries were also discussed, along with automating the generation and deployment of such libraries using the gentagtld script.

The J2EE Web Application in WAS: A Detailed View

IN THIS CHAPTER:

IBM-Specific Deployment Descriptors: A Detailed View

WAS Parsing for the web.xml

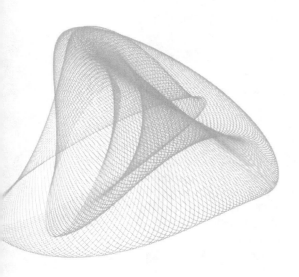

A t this point, you have learned enough about the J2EE web application and its WAS assembly to write interesting programs. There is still much to learn, however. This chapter describes the J2EE web application in detail, along with the deployment descriptor. It also describes the IBM extension and binding files that are specifically generated by the Application Assembly Tool (AAT) and are used by the application server. While the IBM expensions are discussed thoroughly in this chapter, the IBM bindings will be considered in Chapter 18.

These topics, when supplemented with Infocenter pages supplied by IBM, provide enough background to understand how to configure and program web applications under WAS.

IBM-Specific Deployment Descriptors: A Detailed View

It is important to approach the deployment of a web application with some guiding principles in mind. The following sections establish some of these principles; but keep in mind that the prime objective in deploying an application is not to depend on graphical deployment tools, but to gain an understanding of their structure and the descriptors that they generate.

The first step in deploying a web application is to understand the structure established by the deployment tool and to describe it in some concise way. System commands can help you understand how IBM deployment tools work. Consider that the deployment tool: refreshear, we discussed in Chapter 11 archived the web application and invoked the SEAppInstall.sh script to reinstall it. Such a script is of value because it reveals the workings of web application deployment.

IBM Extensions

You may have noticed that when you deployed the web application in Chapter 11, WAS automatically generated some extra files in the deployment directory. To locate the additional files that are terminated with the extension .xmi, use the following command:

```
# find $INSTALLEDAPPS/wasdg.ear | grep  xmi
```

A list of four files will appear:

```
$INSTALLEDAPPS/wasdg.ear/webapp/WEB-INF/ibm-web-bnd.xmi
$INSTALLEDAPPS/wasdg.ear/webapp/WEB-INF/ibm-web-ext.xmi
$INSTALLEDAPPS/wasdg.ear/META-INF/ibm-application-ext.xmi
$INSTALLEDAPPS/wasdg.ear/META-INF/ibm-application-bnd.xmi
```

The first two files are defined inside the web application, whereas the other two are defined to the enterprise application as a whole. All four files define extensions to the J2EE application specification to fulfill the particular schemas as required by IBM WebSphere Application Server. Figure 14-1 shows the tree structure of the wasdg.ear in the $BASE_DEV directory (the top view of the vi window) and in the $INSTALLEDAPPS directory (the bottom view of the vi window) after deploying the WASDG application.

A few other files are also generated by the deployment process of the application, which are discussed later in this chapter.

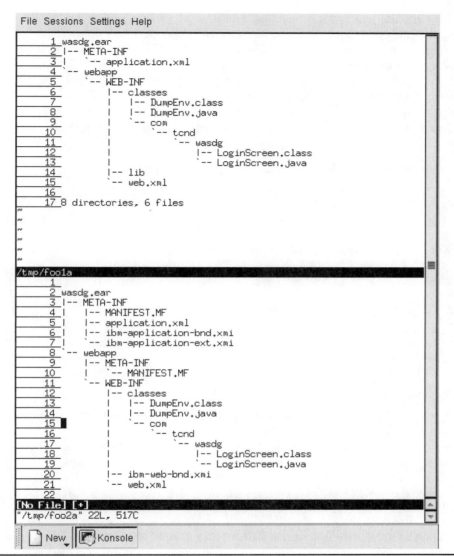

File Sessions Settings Help

```
    1 wasdg.ear
    2 |-- META-INF
    3 |      `-- application.xml
    4 `-- webapp
    5     `-- WEB-INF
    6         |-- classes
    7         |   |-- DumpEnv.class
    8         |   |-- DumpEnv.java
    9         |   `-- com
   10         |       `-- tcnd
   11         |           `-- wasdg
   12         |               |-- LoginScreen.class
   13         |               `-- LoginScreen.java
   14         |-- lib
   15         `-- web.xml
   16
   17 8 directories, 6 files
```

/tmp/foo1a

```
    1
    2 wasdg.ear
    3 |-- META-INF
    4 |   |-- MANIFEST.MF
    5 |   |-- application.xml
    6 |   |-- ibm-application-bnd.xmi
    7 |   `-- ibm-application-ext.xmi
    8 `-- webapp
    9     |-- META-INF
   10     |   `-- MANIFEST.MF
   11     `-- WEB-INF
   12         |-- classes
   13         |   |-- DumpEnv.class
   14         |   |-- DumpEnv.java
   15         |   `-- com
   16         |       `-- tcnd
   17         |           `-- wasdg
   18         |               |-- LoginScreen.class
   19         |               `-- LoginScreen.java
   20         |-- ibm-web-bnd.xmi
   21         `-- web.xml
   22
```

[No File] [+]
"/tmp/foo2a" 22L, 517C

New   Konsole

Figure 14-1 *Tree structure contrasting the tree structure of the deployed application and the files being introduced*

The application.xml file and the web.xml file generated in Chapter 11 with j2tree and genwebxml, respectively, are descriptors that are generically set by the J2EE standard. Yet, descriptors can also be extended by an application server like WAS. If this is the case, they are called IBM extensions to the deployment descriptors, and they are generally specified in .xmi files. If these files do not exist in your web application, WAS automatically generates them whenever you deploy the web application using the SEAppInstall (WAS AEs) or whenever you use the Application Assembly Tool (AAT).

Using the AAT as a first step might be helpful for a beginning student because this will clarify the many descriptor elements from a graphical perspective. Editing the descriptor files later will become more feasible and straightforward. In particular, such editing is possible because the descriptor elements are English words that are easy to understand.

Having extracted the WASDG application and set up the BASE_DEV environment variable properly, you will see the two utility scripts in the next two sections. The first builds the wasdg.ear archive file from the tree of an enterprise web application: we called the script tree2ear. The second script builds the tree of an enterprise application from its wasdg.ear archive file: we called the script ear2tree.

Archiving an Enterprise Application Directory Structure into a File

Before continuing, you need to be familiar with the .ear files that are generated with the `jar` command. You can compact the wasdg.ear directory into an .ear file by the same name and open it with the AAT tool. The reverse is also true; you can go from an .ear file to an EAR tree structure.

The script shown in Listing 14-1 collapses the wasdg.ear tree into the Jar archive wasdg.ear.

Listing 14-1   *tree2ear script*

```
1.    #!/bin/sh
2.
3.    # Create an .ear archive and put it in $BASE_DEV/Dist directory
4.    jar cvf $BASE_DEV/Dist/webapp -C $BASE_DEV/wasdg.ear/webapp .
5.    jar cvf $BASE_DEV/Dist/wasdg.ear -C $BASE_DEV/wasdg.ear META-INF -C
        $BASE_DEV/Dist webapp
6.    rm -f $BASE_DEV/Dist/webapp
```

The -C option in the `jar` command is similar to the one used with the `tar` command, and it means change to a specific directory.

On line 4, the `jar` command archives the web application that is found in the webapp directory. The archive is named webapp and is temporarily deposited in the Dist directory. Line 5 creates the Jar archive wasdg.ear in the Dist directory formed of the META-INF and the webapp (generated previously on line 4), both of which are found in $BASE_DEV/ wasdg.ear and $BASE_DEV/Dist, respectively.

Extracting an Enterprise Application Archive into a Directory Structure

To extract the wasdg.ear file that was generated by the AAT for our application, execute the ear2tree script, shown in Listing 14-2.

Listing 14-2   *ear2tree script*

```
1.    #!/bin/sh
2.
3.    MY_EAR_TREE=wasdg.ear
4.    MY_WAR_TREE=webapp
5.
```

```
6.   (cd $BASE_DEV/$MY_EAR_TREE; jar xvf $BASE_DEV/Dist/$MY_EAR_TREE META-INF)
7.   (cd $BASE_DEV/Dist; jar xvf $BASE_DEV/Dist/$MY_EAR_TREE $MY_WAR_TREE)
8.   (cd $BASE_DEV/$MY_EAR_TREE/$MY_WAR_TREE; jar xvf
     $BASE_DEV/Dist/$MY_WAR_TREE)
9.   (cd $BASE_DEV/Dist; rm -f $BASE_DEV/Dist/$MY_WAR_TREE)
```

The commands on line 6 extract the META-INF file and all its subfolders into the $BASE_DEV/wasdg.ear directory. The commands on line 7 extract the web application webapp into the $BASE_DEV/Dist temporary directory to be further extracted into the $BASE_DEV/wasdg.ear/webapp by the commands on line 8. The commands on line 9 delete the webapp from the temporary directory.

Notice the use of the parentheses in the shell script, which embeds cd as a starting command followed by some other command. By using this technique of changing directory first, before issuing a command, you can manipulate the scope of the command to be within the selected directory.

The next section uses the tree2ear and ear2tree scripts to spot the IBM extensions and binding introduced by the AAT. The method we will use is simple: package the wasdg.ear into an archive, open it with the AAT, save it again from within the AAT tool, extract the wasdg.ear into its tree structure, and finally, spot the differences.

Getting the IBM Extensions

A web application has several attributes that describe how its components are to be dealt with when loaded in the WAS containers. This is basically described at the *inter*module level. For example, if you change the bytecode of a class that has already been loaded in the container of an active WAS, does the new class bytecode get to be loaded again? Although it is possible to go over every single descriptor element or attribute of the deployment descriptors, we choose to use the AAT to look into these attributes. The web application descriptive attributes can be defined by editing the web application using the AAT.

The approach taken here is to load the application into the vendor tool, assemble it with the default setup, save it, and finally, extract it to gather the change.

Consider the webapp discussed in Chapter 11. The webapp is one component of the EAR application: wasdg.ear. From the wasdg.ear directory, we will create a corresponding .ear file by the same name: wasdg.ear. Then we will open this second file with the AAT, possibly make some changes, then save the file, overwriting the previous copy. Finally, we will refresh the wasdg.ear directory with the new .ear file that was generated with the AAT.

Perform the following steps in the BASE_DEV directory:

1. Change the directory to the base development directory, for example /BOOK/14/Code, and make sure the BASE_DEV environment variable is set to it by executing this command:

    ```
    # .  thisbase
    ```

2. Make sure you have the wasdg.ear tree in your base development directory; if not, run j2tree as explained in Chapter 11. List the file in your directory using the `find` and `wc` commands:

```
# find wasdg.ear -type f -exec wc  {} \;  > list1.txt
```

This `find` command iterates over the wasdg.ear directory looking for all files, and printing a line for each of them showing the line counts, words counts, characters counts, and the filename. The output of the command is saved in list1.txt.

3. Archive the wasdg.ear tree into an .ear file that is deposited in the $BASE_DEV/Dist directory. This is done by executing the script tree2ear:

```
# tree2ear
```

4. Start the AAT ($ASSEMBLY) and open the wasdg.ear file: File | Open. Select the wasdg.ear located in the Dist directory as shown in the following illustration.

Browse through the opened file using the AAT. Do not make any changes to the EAR application yet. Make sure you can view the property pane in the AAT console by enabling it: View | Show Property Pane. Figure 14-2 shows the layout of the AAT console, which has three panes.

The left pane is the navigation pane; it represents the topology tree of the enterprise application following the J2EE standard. The navigation pane displays contents and associated assembly properties in an indented tree outlined in Figure 14-3. In this pane, click The WASDG Application.

A tree showing the hierarchy of the assembly properties is shown in the left pane of the AAT. The upper-right pane is the property pane; the lower-right pane is the property dialog box pane. Because you clicked The WASDG Application previously, this pane gives you the option of setting the IBM extensions in it. The property dialog boxes, as shown in the following illustration, typically include five: General, Advanced, Icons, IBM Extensions, and Bindings.

General Advanced Icons IBM Extensions Bindings

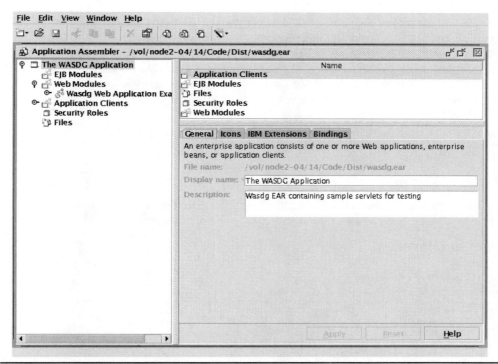

Figure 14-2   *Opening the WASDG application in the AAT*

```
Application display name
├── Application Clients (folder)
│     ├── Application client instances
│     └── Properties for application client instances
├── EJB Modules (folder)
│     └── JAR files
│           ├── Container transactions
│           ├── Entity beans
│           │     ├── Entity bean instances
│           │     └── Properties for entity bean instances
│           ├── Files
│           ├── Method permissions
│           ├── Security roles
│           └── Session beans
│                 ├── Properties for session bean instances
│                 └── Session bean instances
├── Files
├── Security Roles (for the application)
└── Web Modules (folder)
      └── Web applications
            ├── Assembly property extensions
            ├── Files
            ├── Properties for the Web application
            └── Web components
                  ├── Properties for the Web component instance
                  └── Web component instances (servlets or JSP files)
```

Figure 14-3   *Structure of the AAT's navigation pane*

You will use these dialog boxes to add a new module, to modify an already defined module, or to cut and paste archived files and property values between modules. In the left pane, click Web Modules, and you will get webapp. In the right pane, click the IBM Extensions property to view the properties that have been defined by default by the AAT, as shown in Figure 14-4.

Select File | Save As, and then select the wasdg.ear file located in the Dist directory. Accept to overwrite it; this way, the changes made by the AAT are saved into the new generated file.

/vol/node2-04/14/Code/Dist/wasdg.ear already exists.
Do you want to overwrite it?

Yes   No

Extract the newly generated file into the wasdg.ear directory located in your $BASE_DEV directory. Make sure you are in the BASE_DEV directory, and then issue this command:

```
# ear2tree
```

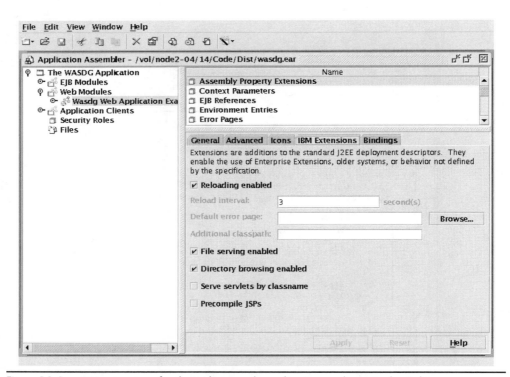

Figure 14-4   *IBM extensions for the webapp web application as shown in the right pane of the AAT*

Inspect the new changes in the wasdg.ear directory. You can quickly spot the changes made by the AAT tool (such as new files created, and any changes made in the descriptor files). Just list the files in the wasdg.ear directory in a list2.txt file (as you did previously in step 2 in the "Getting the IBM Extensions" section), then use the difference to compare list1.txt and list2.txt.

Listing 14-3   *Comparison of list1.txt and list2.txt*

```
[/home/maxou/Code]# diff list1.txt list2.txt
1a2,4
>       3         6        62 wasdg.ear/META-INF/MANIFEST.MF
>       3         9       300 wasdg.ear/META-INF/ibm-application-ext.xmi
>      14        28       789 wasdg.ear/META-INF/ibm-application-bnd.xmi
6c9,12
<      38        69      1552 wasdg.ear/webapp/WEB-INF/web.xml
---
>      39        73      1664 wasdg.ear/webapp/WEB-INF/web.xml
>       5        20       543 wasdg.ear/webapp/WEB-INF/ibm-web-ext.xmi
>       4        12       336 wasdg.ear/webapp/WEB-INF/ibm-web-bnd.xmi
>       3         6        62 wasdg.ear/webapp/META-INF/MANIFEST.MF
```

In Listing 14-3, lines starting with a greater than symbol (>) show the new files that have been introduced or the old files that have been affected in the second instance (list2.txt) of the operation. At the enterprise application level, three new files are listed in the wasdg.ear/META-INF directory, two of which are the ibm-application prefixed .xmi files. At the web application level, three new files are listed as well, in addition to a change in the web.xml file. The meaning of each of the .xmi files can be implied from the filename itself: where *ext* appears in the name, it is an extension file; where *bnd* appears in the name, it is a binding file.

Notice that the usage of the `find`, `wc`, and `diff` commands to compare files in a tree is just a brute approach to detect changes in files between two instances. It is not perfectly accurate because it uses `wc`, and a file that has been changed with the same number of words and lines and characters as the original won't be detected. A more strict way to detect changes in files between two instances is by using the checksum UNIX command: `sum`.

Using the method described in this section, you can practice editing and making changes to the web application using the AAT. You will then be able to edit the affected files and browse through the different elements that are introduced by the AAT in the .xmi files, in the web.xml file, and in the MANIFEST.MF file. For instance, the following illustration shows how to enable serveServletsByClassname in the AAT.

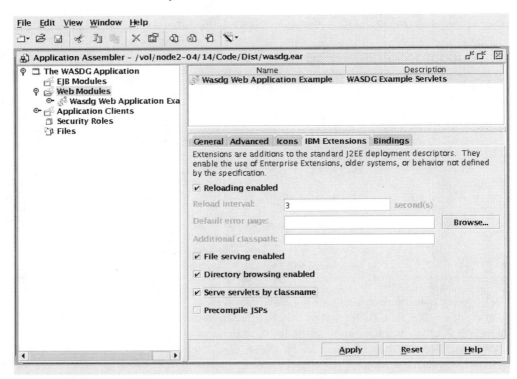

The effect of enabling servlet serving by classname is shown when editing the ibm-web-ext.xmi file, in which the following attribute is enabled:

```
serveServletsByClassnameEnabled="true"
```

Using the AAT requires that you perform some extra steps to manually assemble and deploy the EAR archive of the WASDG application. The alternative is to directly edit the file $BASE_DEV/wasdg.ear/webapp/WEB-INF/ibm-web-ext.xmi and set serveServletsByClassname to true. You then run svlbuild in the BASE_DEV so that the change is also propagated to the deployment directory. You do not need to restart WAS for the change to take effect (as explained in Chapter 15). The following illustration shows the contents of the ibm-web-ext.xmi file in the deployed directory.

You can see the effect of the added extension when you load a servlet using the fully qualified name of the servlet, as shown next. This illustration shows the use of Lynx to request the LoginScreen servlet by class name.

```
File  Sessions  Settings  Help
[root@node2 root]# lynx -dump http://node1.tcnd.com/wasbook/servlet/com.tcnd.wasdg.LoginScreen




    TELLER LOGIN SCREEN
    Teller:    _____
    Password:  _____ Login
[root@node2 root]# █


    New   Konsole
```

In a browser, you also specify the same fully qualified URL name in which the servlet name is specified, as shown here.

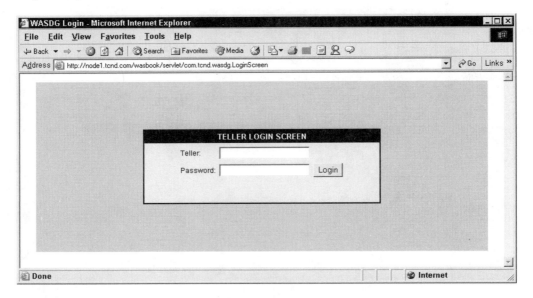

This allows a developer to *directly* test a servlet using the exact name of the servlet. You disable this feature in a production environment.

Using the EARExpander

Collapsing an EAR tree into an .ear file and expanding an .ear file to an EAR tree are possible with the vendor command EARExpander. In WAS AEs, this command is invoked through the shell script EARExpander.sh. The syntax of this command is shown here:

```
EARExpander.sh -ear <ear file or directory> -expandDir <directory
    in which to expand ear> -operation <expand | collapse> [-expansionFlags
    <all | war>]
```

This is a handy command that allows you to view the content of an .ear file; yet, you should be careful about the expanded contents in the tree, because the EARExpander adds the missing extensions and binding files while expanding an .ear file.

Summary of IBM Extensions Attributes

Only one IBM extension applies to an enterprise application as a whole: reloadInterval. You can verify this by using the AAT and browsing through the IBM Extensions property of the WASDG application or any other enterprise application.

The ibm-web-ext.xmi file may contain many other important attributes, some of which are summarized in Table 14-1.

Attribute	Description	Setting
ReloadingEnabled	Improves security and performance in a production environment, where it is set to false. (See Chapter 15 for more information.)	True or false
ReloadInterval	Shows the number of seconds delayed between servlets reloading.	Integer
serveServletsByClassnameEnabled	Invokes servlets by class or code name.	True or false
AdditionalClassPath	Specifies additional directories (and their subdirectories) that contain files such as .jar files that you want to add to the web module classpath without adding it to the .war file. Often used in migrating applications from WAS v3 to WAS v4. This is equivalent to the command-line parameter webModuleAdditionalClassPath, found with the WASPostUpgrade file.	.jar file
FileServingEnabled	Serves servlets, HTML, and other files in the web application without any specific configuration.	True or false
directoryBrowsingEnabled	Makes the content listing for a directory of the web application exposed to the browser.	True or false
PreCompileJSPs	Compiles the .jsp files into their servlets' equivalent bytecode upon starting the web application	True or false

Table 14-1   *Extension Attributes*

In particular, the servlet reloading and servlet serving by classname allow you to practice using your code without restarting WAS, the way svlbuild functions in this book.

WAS v4 supports as IBM extensions the following EJB transaction isolation levels: Serializable, Repeatable read, Read committed, and Read uncommitted. These are supported as IBM extensions because the EJB 1.1 specification does not support transaction isolation anymore.

WAS Parsing for the web.xml

The genwebxml script introduced in Chapter 11 was designed to support the basic elements necessary to describe a web module. Web module description is specific to a particular servlet version specification that is revealed in the first clause of the web.xml file, shown in Listing 14-4. Assuming that BASE_DEV is set properly, you will get the line shown in Listing 14-4, by issuing this command:

```
# genwebxml | grep DOCTYPE
```

Listing 14-4 *Document type as defined in the web.xml*

```
<!DOCTYPE web-app PUBLIC "-//Sun Microsystems, Inc.//DTD Web Application
    2.2//EN" "http://java.sun.com/j2ee/dtds/web-app_2_2.dtd">
```

This clause shows that the DOCTYPE declaration at the head of a web application deployment descriptor file (web.xml) is specific to servlet 2.2. This level is currently supported by WAS v4 and may change with future releases. With a new release of WAS that supports the servlet ARI 2.3, you will be able to edit the genwebxml and make the appropriate change to it (specifically, the line shown in Listing 14-4). This book's approach toward building the J2EE web application is not tied to a specific version or release of WAS.

NOTE

This book does not describe the many elements that can be introduced in the descriptor file. You can visit the site mentioned in Listing 14-4 for details about the web application descriptors.

Following the first clause, shown in Listing 14-5, is an ordered list of elements describing the web application. The approach we will follow to demystify WAS support for the elements used in the web.xml file is the fail-and-discovery method. That is, we will add a malformed element that will cause the failure of WAS while parsing the web.xml; then we will capture the failing statement to list the elements that are supported in the web.xml descriptor file. The failure will be reported in the log file default_server_stdout.log ($WASLOG_STDERR), and the statement shown in Listing 14-5 is consequently printed.

Listing 14-5 *Elements describing the web application*

```
org.xml.sax.SAXParseException: The content of element type "web-app"
must match
"(icon?,display-name?,description?,distributable?,context-param*,serv
let*,servlet-mapping*,session-config?,mime-mapping*,welcome-file-list
?,error-page*,taglib*,resource-ref*,security-constraint*,login-config
?,security-role*,env-entry*,ejb-ref*)"
```

WAS uses an XML parser known as SAX to preprocess the web.xml file. The element type web-app has been described in the Document Type Definition (DTD) for the web application deployment descriptor (web.xml). In WAS AEs, the DTD is the file $WAS_HOME/deploytool/ itp/plugins/com.ibm.etools.j2ee/dtds/*web-app_2_2.dtd*. You can edit and view this file with a simple text editor. The first element described in this file is the web-app element; therefore, the web-app element is the root of the deployment descriptor for a web application.

Each element shown in Listing 14-5 is followed by an operator that describes the element's content, and whose meaning is explained in Table 14-2.

Table 14-3 shows each element that is admissible in the web.xml file, along with its subelements. In the first column, the operator—an asterisk (*) or question mark (?)—that follows each element has been kept for informative reason and is explained in Table 14-2.

WAS v3.5 Components	WAS v4 Components
IBM Developer Kit, Java 2 Tech Ed 1.2.2	IBM Developer Kit, Java 2 Tech Ed 1.3.0
IBM HTTP Server 1.3.12	IBM HTTP Server 1.3.19
InstantDB	InstantDB (sample support only)
UDB v7.1 (with WAS Service Pack 4)	UDB v7.2 (WAS AEs does now ship with UDB, but trail code can be downloaded)
?	Optional

Table 14-2   *Operators That Describe an Element in an .xml Document*

Element and Explanation	Subelements
<icon> (?) References .gif or .jpg icons to be used with the GUI to represent the parent element.	<small-icon> Optionally specifies a 16×16 pixel icon location. <large-icon> Optionally specifies a 32×32 pixel icon location.
<display-name> (?) Contains a short name describing the parent element to be displayed in the GUI.	--
<description> (?) Describes a parent element in the web.xml file.	--
<distributable> (?) Declares that the web application can be deployed in a distributed servlet container.	--
<context-param> (*) Declares a context initialization parameter.	<param-name> Contains the parameter's name. <param-value> Contains the parameter's value. <description> Optional.
<servlet> (*) Declares a servlet.	<icon> Optional. <servlet-name> Contains the servlet name. <display-name> Optional. <description> Optional. <servlet-class> Contains the listener's class name; otherwise, a <jsp-file> specifies the location of a .jsp file relative to the web application. 0 or more <init-param> Contains <param-name> <param-value> and an optional <description>. <load-on-startup> Specifies whether the servlet is to be loaded at startup, and a positive number indicates the order in which to load the servlet. 0 or more <security-role-ref> Maps a role name called from within the servlet along with the name of a security role defined for the web application. Contains an optional <description>, a <role-name>, and a <role-link> pointing to the name of a role defined in the <security-role>.

Table 14-3   *Elements Used in Describing a Web Application*

Element and Explanation	Subelements
<servlet-mapping> (*) Maps a servlet to a URL pattern.	<servlet-name> Contains the name of the servlet declared by <servlet>. <url-pattern> Contains a URL pattern to match.
<session-config> (?) Configures the session tracking for the web application.	<session-timeout> Optional.
<mime-mapping> (*) Maps a filename extension to a MIME type.	<extension> Contains a filename extension. <mime-type> Contains a defined MIME type.
<welcome-file-list> (?) Defines an ordered list of welcome files.	<welcome-file> Contains the filename of a welcome file.
<error-page> (*) Maps an error code or exception type to an error page to be displayed if that error condition arises.	<error-code> Contains an HTTP error code; otherwise, an <exception-type> contains the class name of a Java exception type. <location> Contains the location of the error page resource within the web application.
<taglib> (*) Declares a JSP tag library.	<taglib-uri> Contains the URI to identify the tag library. <taglib-location> Contains the location (relative to the web application) of the .tld file that describes the tag library.
<resource-ref> (*) Declares that the web application references an eternal resource.	<description> Optional. <res-ref-name> Contains the name of the resource factory reference. <res-type> Specifies the type of the data source. <res-auth> Specifies either application or containers. Authorization to the resource is programmatic or to be specified by the application deployer. <res-sharing-scope> Specifies whether the connections can be shared. Is either Shareable or Unshareable.
<security-constraint> (*) Applies security constraints to one or more collections of web resources.	<display-name> <web-resource-collection> 0 or more elements each of which identifies a set of resources within the application, and contains a <web-resource-name>, 0 or more <url-pattern> to match, and 0 or more <http-method> <auth-constraint>. Indicates that the web resources can be accessed by certain user roles, which are then listed with 0 or more <role-name> elements, each of which containing a <security-role-ref> element or the * symbol to indicate all roles in this application. <user-data-constraint> Indicates the level of protection between the client and the application when transmitting data. The element <transport-guarantee> is then set to NONE, INTEGRAL, or CONFIDENTIAL.
<login-config> (?) Configures the authentication mechanism for this application	<auth-method> Optional element to specify the authentication mechanism: BASIC, FORM, DIGEST, CLIENT-CERT. <realm-name> Optional element to specify the real name for the HTTP basic authorization. <from-login-config> Optional element used to specify the <form-login-page> and the <form-error-page> for the FORM-based authentication.

Table 14-3   *Elements Used in Describing a Web Application* (continued)

Element and Explanation	Subelements
\<security-role\> (*)	\<description\> Optional description. \<role-name\> Contains the name of the role.
\<env-entry\> (*) Declares an application's environment entry.	\<description\> Optional description. \<env-entry-name\> Contains the environment entry name. \<env-entry-value\> Contains the environment entry value.\<env-entry-type\> Contains a Java type as the environment entry type: Boolean, String, Integer, Double, Float.
\<ejb-ref\> (*) Declares a reference to an Enterprise JavaBean.	\<description\> \<ejb-ref-name\> Contains the JNDI name of the EJB. \<ejb-ref-type\> Contains the type of the EJB, it is either Entity or Session.\<home\> Contains the type of the EJB's home interface. \<remote\> Contains the type of the EJB's remote interface. \<ejb-link\> Optional element to specify that the EJB reference is linked to the named EJB. \<run-as\> Specifies the application security role that is propagated o the EJB.

Table 14-3   *Elements Used in Describing a Web Application* (continued)

Wrapping Up

This chapter explained how to capture IBM extensions and bindings and how to make use of them by manual editing to their corresponding descriptor files.

Two scripts showed the methodology of compacting the tree of an enterprise application into an .ear file (tree2ear), and vice versa, going from an .ear file to the tree of the enterprise application (ear2tree). The chapter discussed in detail the elements that can be used to describe a J2EE web application. The chapter also demonstrated how to make use of the AAT to extract the implied description of a J2EE web application as it is viewed from WAS.

Classes in WAS: Loading Order versus Visibility Order

IN THIS CHAPTER:

Classpaths and WAS' Classloaders

Initializing and Reloading a Servlet

Module Visibility and Class Reloading

Hot Deployment and Dynamic Reloading

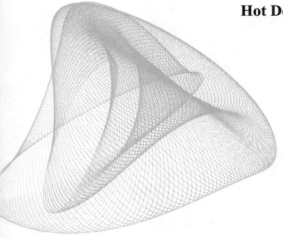

C lasses are loaded within WAS following a predefined hierarchy. The order in which classes are loaded, and the order in which WAS makes them visible, is dictated by the web application classloading specification and by the WAS startup configuration. This is in contrast to what was mentioned in Chapter 11, namely that a web module is usually documented at least at two levels, the *intra-* and the *inter*module levels.

A programmer compiling a program with the Java compiler javac, then executing it by running it within a Java machine started with the `java` command, is in control of the classpath. This situation is different when you program for WAS because, while you will be compiling the code with javac, the interpretation is carried by an already loaded WAS Java machine; therefore, you will not be directly in control of the Java machine and its classloader.

Two aspects characterize class compilation and loading when developing a web application to be run under WAS. Each class undergoes several steps: from editing to compiling to deploying, and then to loading. The first aspect is the resolvability of the symbols used in the class that is accomplished at compilation time. The second aspect is the locality and the visibility of the symbols when running the class. The second aspect requires special consideration because it is run-time dependent and can affect the accessibility of classes (considering Java security), type casting, and the serialization of objects used during the run time of the web module.

The final step in processing a program in a web module is the program's interpretation during run time: the actual carrying out of the meaning of the program statements. This is done by WAS where the servlet container and the Enterprise JavaBeans container are running. The run-time execution of a web module's code can be affected by the locality and by the dynamism of the libraries imported by an application to resolve its symbolic names. *Locality* refers to the placement of the libraries within the WAS tree hierarchy. *Dynamism* refers to the change in code during run time, called *reloading*. However, since everything in Java is based on files, reloading becomes a matter of rewriting or changing the timestamp of a file; for example, rewriting the web.xml file descriptor to $INSTALLEDAPPS/wasdg.ear/webapp/WEB-INF directory.

Classloading can be represented by a top-down tree. While classloading is typically aggregated by WAS through its classloaders, symbolic references are resolved in WAS following a deterministic order: symbols found first take precedence, and class archives are read left to right with the leftmost class taking precedence over the rightmost. This chapter begins by briefly describing the tree hierarchy WAS follows in loading its classes, and then presents a concentric image to help you visualize the loading versus visibility order of classes. You will understand the order of classloading versus its visibility after reading this chapter. It is quite simplistic.

Classpaths and WAS' Classloaders

In this section we will show you how classpaths are defined in WAS configuration. We will use a tree hierarchy to provide a clear understanding of classes visibility order, then you will learn how to add a library or libaries to the WAS startup classpath. Finally, this section conclude with a servlet to print the classpath that is visible to the web application where the servlet itself is defined.

The Classpaths Tree Hierarchy

Classes loaded by a particular classloader can reference other classes that are loaded by the same classloader or by any of its ancestors. The directory tree structure in which WAS is installed maps the hierarchy of classloading. Figure 15-1 depicts the directory structure of WAS and the classloading hierarchy.

A developer can place the class' bytecode of a compiled Java program in several locations. Such freedom can be erratic, however, and should be done taking into account the side effects on the web application. Yet, a developer must know the order of classloading to avoid confusion. A simple explanation of classloading is followed by a simulation to make it clear.

An element of the classpath can be specified in any one of the following directory locations:

- ▶ **Runtime classpath patches (RCP)** $WAS_HOME/classes

- ▶ **Runtime classpath (RC)** $WAS_HOME/lib

- ▶ **Runtime extension (RE)** $WAS_HOME/lib/ext

- ▶ **Application extensions (AE)** $WAS_HOME/lib/app

- ▶ **Application classloaders (AC)**   There are three locations that are searched and looked up in the following order: the root of the WAR file, WEB-INF/classes directory content, .jar files in the WEB-INF/lib directory. In addition to these three locations, a web module can specify more class archives in the MANIFEST following the Class-Path entry.

We need to look more closely at the fifth directory locations of the application classloaders (AC) just mentioned:

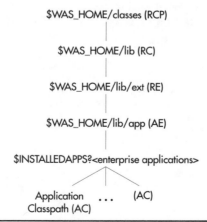

Figure 15-1   *WAS and the classloading hierarchy*

Within an application, there are *two types of modules*: the first is the web module, which pertains to the web container, and the second is the EJB module, which pertains to the EJB container. Web modules can be dynamically loaded, but EJB module must be compiled and loaded first when starting an enterprise web application. For a web module to access an EJB module, the EJB JAR must be specified in the application classloader in the MANIFEST following the Class-Path entry. In the first case, the application classloader is added to the classes found in the web module directories WEB-INF/classes and WEB-INF/lib, and it is made visible to the web module *before* any other classpath just listed (in RCP, RC, RE, AE). This is the default behavior in WAS AEs, and is settable in WAS AE v4 by setting the system property com.ibm.ws.classloader.wasDelegationMode to false:

module classloader, AE, RCP, RC, RE

In the second case, the application classloader is made visible to the EJB module after any other classpath listed (in RCP, RC, RE, AE). This is the default behavior in WAS AEs, and is settable in WAS AE v4 by setting the system property com.ibm.ws.classloader.ejbDelegationMode to true:

AE, RCP, RC, RE, module classloader

The first three instances (TCP, RC, RE) are fixed and defined as the WAS extension directories, using the ws.ext.dirs system property. The classes that are loaded from these directories are referred to as *WAS startup classes,* and the classloader that loads these classes is called the *WAS startup classloader.*[1] Classloading is easy and coherent and requires no technical adroitness: it is just knowing which directory appears first in the classpath of a Java machine that really takes precedence over another.

You can even add more directories to localize the Jar archive, and draw your own hierarchy for classloading by further editing the WAS configuration file. Although such a practice is not recommended, the next section tilts the rule and shows how to extend to the classpath to load the UDB driver. The file setupCmdLine (refer to Chapter 8) is the first script to be executed to set up the WAS_EXT_DIRS and WAS_CLASSPATH environment variables.

---

[1]   Since the premier version of WAS, IBM uses the term *bootstrap classloader* to refer to the WAS *startup classloader*. Although IBM diminished the use of the *bootstrap* term by eliminating the bootstrap.properties file that was part of the premier version of WAS, the term *WAS startup classloader* is more appropriate. Do not confuse the bootstrap classloader with the bootstrap port defined in Chapter 5.

Listing 15-1 shows the WAS_EXT_DIRS and WAS_CLASSPATH defined in the commonly used script setupCmdLine.sh script.

Listing 15-1   *setupCmdLine.sh*

```
1.   #!/bin/sh
2.
3.   COMPUTERNAME=node1

4.   WAS_HOME=/opt/WebSphere/AppServer
5.   JAVA_HOME=$WAS_HOME/java
6.   DBDRIVER_JARS=
7.   DBDRIVER_PATH=
8.   ...
9.

PATH=$JAVA_HOME/ibm_bin:$JAVA_HOME/bin/:$JAVA_HOME/jre/bin:$PATH:$DB2_PATH
10.  DB_TYPE=DB2
11.  DB_INSTANCE_HOME=/home/db2inst1
12. WAS_EXT_DIRS=$JAVA_HOME/lib:$WAS_HOME/classes:$WAS_HOME/lib:$WAS_HOME/lib/
ext:$WAS_HOME/web/help:$DBDRIVER_JARS
13. WAS_CLASSPATH=$WAS_HOME/properties:$WAS_HOME/lib/bootstrap.jar:$WAS_HOME/
lib/j2ee.jar
14.  # Project-12 defined DB2_CLASSPATH
15.  WAS_CLASSPATH=$WAS_CLASSPATH:$DB2_CLASSPATH
16.  ...
```

The three boldface environment variables (lines 12, 13 and 15) are important because they will be further used in the startup script of WAS. For example, the startServer.sh script of WAS AEs for UNIX shows such an entry, as seen in Listing 15-2.

Listing 15-2   *The startup Java machine as defined in the startServer.sh of WAS AEs*

```
$JAVA_HOME/bin/java \
  $WAS_JAVAOPTS \
  $OLT_OPTIONS \
  $DEBUG_OPTIONS \
  -Dcom.ibm.itp.location=$WAS_HOME/bin \
  $SERVERSAS \
```

```
-Dserver.root=$WAS_HOME \
-Dws.ext.dirs=$WAS_EXT_DIRS \
-classpath $WAS_CLASSPATH com.ibm.ws.bootstrap.WSLauncher \
com.ibm.ws.runtime.StandardServer "$@"
```

The fourth case, Application extensions, is fixed by WAS.

After starting WAS, you can view the classpath used by WAS as it is written to the standard output log.

Classes are loaded in the classpath of the WAS startup Java machine following two regimes:

▶ As a regular classpath following the option –classpath. The variable WAS_CLASSPATH is used in this situation, which is the initial classpath; therefore, it must contain the bootstrap.jar[2] to bootstrap the Java machine.

▶ As a property passed to the Java machine so that once the machine that has been bootstrapped is started, it can further start other machines and pass to them the classes that are specified by the property.

The WAS Startup Classpath

When WAS AEs is started, the classpath is printed in the standard output log file. It is customary for a developer to retrieve the WAS startup classpath that is logged to the file $WASLOG_STDOUT. For example, the following command prints the Classpath of WAS startup while WAS is restarting. (To restart WAS, issue the command $STOPWAS; $STARTWAS.)

```
# tail -n 100 $WASLOG_STDOUT | egrep "^ws\.ext\.dirs = |^Classpath = |^Java
Library path = " | splitcp
```

This command assumes that the last 100 lines of the standard output log contain the classpath, which is likely the case after restarting WAS. The egrep is used to look for

---

[2] A bootstrap is the program that starts up a bare machine having an empty memory. Once the bootstrap loader is in memory, it can load the rest of the Java machine(s) classes and WAS in operation. Traditionally, the bootstrap is a short program that acts as a special purpose absolute load module. PC's BIOS uses interrupt 19h as the bootstrap loader service, and PDP-11 uses the LOAD button on the console to invoke the bootstrap.

the starting occurrence of three groups of terms, each of which defines a separate classpath: ws.ext.dirs, Classpath, and Java Library path.

The splitcp is a script (see Listing 15-3) that you can place in your /tools directory.

Listing 15-3 *splitcp*

```
1.    while(<>) {
2.        s/Classpath\s*=\s*//;
3.        s/ws\.ext\.dirs\s*=\s*//;
4.        s/Java Library path\s*=\s*//;
5.        $s .= $_;
6.    }
7.    chop($s);
8.    @l=split(/\n/,$s);
9.    $cp = join(/ /,@l);
10.   print "$_\n" foreach (split(/:/,$cp));
```

The splitcp script reads STDIN to append a full string of information of the classpath; it then splits it into its constituent elements. This is assumed to be a UNIX path specification. For Windows NT, the colon must be turned into a semicolon on line 10.

The following illustration shows the result of running the previous command on a Linux machine.

Our knowledge of classpath loading is still shaky: we need to be definitive about how WAS loads a classpath for an application. Such knowledge of how the WAS startup classpath takes place will become of value as we proceed in this chapter.

Adding Jar Archives to the WAS Startup Classloader

Before adding a Jar archive to the WAS startup classloader, you must fully consider the implications. You must understand the layout of the Java machine processes (the UNIX processes tree as discussed in Chapter 8) and how it maps to the topology tree of WAS. (Refer to Chapters 5 and 8.) The WAS topology tree is typically shown in the left pane of the administrative console.

A resource common to the whole node can be used by *any* application server loaded under the node itself. For example, the JDBC resource shown in the left pane of the tree must be properly set so that it can be used by any of the application servers loaded under WAS; that is, the WASDG application, Petstore, and so on.[3]

Such a resource is said to be global to whole application servers,[4] and may be loaded at once during startup of WAS. To set up the Jar archives for such a global resource, we will edit the setupCmdLine.sh and append the Jar archives to the WAS_CLASSPATH. Recall from Chapter 3, the setj.sh script has an entry that executes our custom db2env.sh script in which the DB2_CLASSPATH is defined. At this time, we append the DB2_CLASSPATH to WAS_CLASSPATH, as shown here:

WAS_CLASSPATH=$WAS_CLASSPATH:**$DB2_CLASSPATH**

Setting the environment variables in setupCmdLine.sh (as shown above) to include specific libraries makes sure that WAS and the application servers are all using the correct UDB Jar archive. Some other UDB run-time libraries must also be added to the path of WAS, as shown on line 9 of Listing 15-1. This is an important point because it shows that WAS run-time libraries are not all Java archives. In particular, persistence to a database may require the loading of run-time libraries not only in the classpath of a Java machine, but within the path of WAS itself. The DB2_PATH shown on line 9 of Listing 15-1 has been set in Chapter 3 through the db2env.sh.

You can restart WAS and monitor the standard output log to retrieve the WAS startup classpath, as discussed in the previous section.

Getting the Application Classpath from within a Servlet

Programmatically, you can get the web application classpath from within a servlet. This is definitely the most obvious way to reveal the classpath visibility to a web application, and in some situations, will help a developer to debug servlets in his or her web modules that might be failing due to missing or colliding libraries. The servlet PrintCp shown in Listing 15-4 is a simple servlet that prints the web application classpath as it is visible from within the context of its web container.

---

[3] In particular, the persistent session manager (which is the subject of Chapter 17) requires a solid definition of the UDB environment variables.

[4] Using WAS is not meant to be specific to one database; you can load different JDBC drivers for other databases when your applications need them. The approach here is to show you a method that developers and administrators can adapt to control classloading in their WAS environment.

Listing 15-4   *PrintCp servlet*

```
1.    import java.io.*;
2.    import java.util.*;
3.    import javax.servlet.*;
4.    import javax.servlet.http.*;
5.
6.    public class PrintCp extends HttpServlet
7.    {
8.        public void service(HttpServletRequest request, HttpServletResponse
      response)
9.        throws ServletException, IOException
10.       {
11.       ServletOutputStream out = response.getOutputStream();
12.       response.setContentType("text/html");
13.
14.       ServletContext context = getServletContext();
15.       String webappclasspath =
String)context.getAttribute("com.ibm.websphere.servlet.application.classpath");
16.
17.       // We don't want to have any descriptive information in this page
18.       //out.println("<html><head><title>Print classpath</title></head>");
19.       out.println("<body bgcolor=\"white\"><h2>" + webappclasspath +
      ")</h2>");
20.
21.       out.println("<hr><p>");
22.       out.close();
23.       }
24.  }
```

Save the servlet to your $BASE_DEV/wasdg.ear/webapp/WEB-INF/classes directory, add an entry in the servlets.list to register this servlet (such as, printcp PrintCp /printcp), and then execute svlbuild to rebuild and update the WASDG application.

A simple request to this servlet using Lynx will return a page full of information about the web application classpath.

Initializing and Reloading a Servlet

It is the responsibility of WAS to load and initialize the servlet the first time it is invoked. The init() method is a one-time-thread initialization of the servlet. When a servlet is invoked the first time, the web container runs the servlet's init() method once.

You can confirm this by following this simple exercise:

1. Restart WAS: $STOPWAS; $STARTWAS.

2. Tail the default_server_stdout.log to your console: tail -f $WASLOG_STDOUT.

3. In another terminal, run the script touchreload, shown in Listing 15-5.

Listing 15-5   *touchreload script to test with servlet reloading*

```
1.  # Login as teller1 then inspect the WASLOG_STDOUT
2.  echo "userid=teller1&password=secret1&---" | lynx -post_data
    http://node1/wasbook/tellerlogged 1>/dev/null
3.  # Login as teller2 then inspect the WASLOG_STDOUT
4.  echo "userid=teller2&password=secret2&---" | lynx -post_data
    http://node1/wasbook/tellerlogged 1>/dev/null
5.  # Change the time stamp of web.xml file then inspect the WASLOG_STDOUT
6.  touch $INSTALLEDAPPS/wasdg.ear/webapp/WEB-INF/web.xml
7.  # Login as teller1 then inspect the WASLOG_STDOUT
8.  echo "userid=teller1&password=secret1&---" | lynx -post_data
    http://node1/wasbook/tellerlogged 1>/dev/null
9.  # Change the time stamp of TellerLogged.class then inspect the
    WASLOG_STDOUT
10. touch $INSTALLEDAPPS/wasdg.ear/webapp/WEB-INF/classes/TellerLogged.class
11. echo "userid=teller1&password=secret1&---" | lynx -post_data
    http://node1/wasbook/tellerlogged 1>/dev/null
```

This script is a mix of `lynx` and `touch` commands. The effect of the script is shown in this illustration.

```
File  Sessions  Settings  Help

[6/17/02 12:27:01:247 EDT]   91d78c8  WebGroup     I SRVE0091I: [Servlet LOG]: tellerlogged: init
[6/17/02 12:27:03:825 EDT]  391438cb  WebGroup     I SRVE0091I: [Servlet LOG]: tellerlogged: destroy
[6/17/02 12:27:04:162 EDT]  391438cb  WebGroup     I SRVE0091I: [Servlet LOG]: JSP 1.1 Processor: init
[6/17/02 12:27:04:170 EDT]  391438cb  WebGroup     I SRVE0091I: [Servlet LOG]: SimpleFileServlet: init
[6/17/02 12:27:04:177 EDT]  391438cb  WebGroup     I SRVE0091I: [Servlet LOG]: InvokerServlet: init
[6/17/02 12:27:04:187 EDT]  391438cb  WebGroup     I SRVE0091I: [Servlet LOG]: DirectoryBrowsingServlet: init
[6/17/02 12:28:14:599 EDT]   91e38c8  WebGroup     I SRVE0091I: [Servlet LOG]: tellerlogged: init

New   Konsole
```

Initially, the script logs in teller1, which makes the web container initialize the TellerLogged servlet, then logs in teller2, which uses the already loaded TellerLogged servlet; therefore, no further initialization occurs. When the `touch` command is used, WAS detects a timestamp change in the web.xml file; therefore, it destroys all initialized servlets (unloading them from the container) and then waits for any request for a servlet to reinitialize the servlet in its web container.

If you touch the timestamp of the TellerLogged servlet, this will not reinitialize the servlet. Yet changing the content of the servlet and then reloading it while WAS is active will reinitialize the servlet.

You need to consider how WAS detects any change in the web module and manages such a change in its web container. Such a change and its associated containment management is referred to as *reloading*.

The default reloadingEnabled is true, in which case, the servlet is reloaded when the servlet .class file has changed. The check occurs at the interval set in the reloadInterval attribute. Recall from Chapter 14 that the reloadingEnabled and reloadInterval are both set in the IBM web module extension file, namely $INSTALLEDAPPS/wasdg.ear/webapp/WEB-INF/ibm-web-ext.xmi.

Module Visibility and Class Reloading

The svlbuild in Chapter 11 sidesteps an important aspect of web application compilation and deployment, that is to say, the problem of module visibility. Our general svlbuild routine has provided a mechanism to build and deploy servlets without having to pay attention to the WAS classloader. This will become much more apparent in Chapter 21, when we have to use JAAS to secure the execution of a privileged class. The svlbuild effectively renders its task because of the work we did in Chapters 3 and 4 in preparing our environment so that the Java compiler javac will use the same libraries that WAS' Java machines use. Having the same classes answers one aspect: the symbol names resolvability. Yet, it does not answer the second aspect, the locality and visibility of the symbol. Additionally, another important configuration factor is set in WAS: module visibility.

Module Visibility

Module visibility refers to how the classes are loaded to a server and to its associated web applications and web modules. Figure 15-2 shows the application server Default Server and the four possibilities to switch its module visibility.

Looking at the topology tree in the left pane of Figure 15-2, recall from Chapter 5 that a node can span one or more application servers. At least one application server is defined, and the default that is preconfigured by WAS AEs installation is the Default Server (see following chart). An application server that is installed under WAS is treated as a server and is managed by its own Java machine.

```
Nodes
|
---node1
     |
     --Application Servers
          |
          -----Default Server
                  (Web applications, Web modules)
```

You can select the module visibility to be one of the following:

► **Global for the whole server (that is, Default Server)**   All web applications classes are loaded in the classpath.

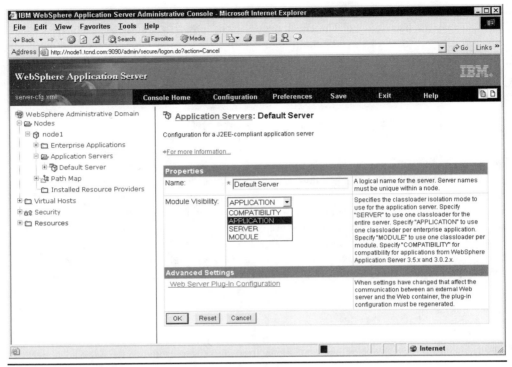

Figure 15-2 *Module visibility*

▶ **Specific to the application server** Web application classes are isolated from each other. For instance, the WASDG application and the Petstore application classes won't be visible to each other.

▶ **Specific to the web module** This choice is available in case more than one module is defined in a web application.

The normal behavior is a visibility at the web application, and is the default setup of WAS AEs. You can practice with the PrintCp servlet shown in Listing 15-5 by putting WAS in a different module visibility setting and then restarting it. The output of PrintCp can be compared for all three module visibilities: application, server, and module. An easy way to do this on WAS AEs is to edit the $WASCFG file and locate the module visibility setting of the application server Default Server:

```
<servers xmi:type="applicationserver:ApplicationServer"
xmi:id="ApplicationServer_1" desiredExecutionState="START"
name="Default Server" id="-1" moduleVisibility="APPLICATION">
```

The specifier moduleVisibility can be set directly with one of the strings that is shown in the drop-down menu of Figure 15-2. For instance, set it to APPLICATION. Restart WAS ($STOPWAS; $STARTWAS), and get the PrintCp servlet using Lynx:

```
# lynx -width=8000 -dump http://was.server.name/wasbook/printcp
```

This command shows you a formatted output for the classpath that is visible to the PrintCp servlet. A line width of 8000 characters might be unrealistic, yet it will direct Lynx to print the maximum line length. Lynx output may be limited to a certain maximum width, in which case, multiple lines will be printed. The Perl script listcp, in Listing 15-6, reads the output of the Lynx command and formats it properly so that we can print the classpath used by the servlet.

Listing 15-6   *listcp Perl script to print the classpath that is visible to the PrintCp servlet*

```
1.    #!/usr/bin/perl
2.    open(F,"lynx -width=8000 -dump http://node1/wasbook/printcp |");
3.    while(<F>) { s/^\s+//; s/\s+$//; $s .= $_ if !(/^_{100,8000}/) }
4.    chop($s);
5.    @l=split(/\n/,$s);
6.    $cp = join(/ /,@l);
7.    print "$cp\n";
8.    # print "$_\n" foreach (split(/:/,$cp));
```

Executing the listcp will print one long line showing the classpath that is visible to the PrintCp servlet. If you uncomment line 8, delete line 7 and run the script, you will get a formatted output showing each element at a time. This assumes that PrintCp is executed on a UNIX system. For Windows NT, you need to split on the semicolon (;) instead of the colon (:).

The following illustration shows the output of the command. Only a few elements of the classpath are shown.

```
File  Sessions  Settings  Help

[root@node1 Order]# ./listcp
/opt/WebSphere/AppServer/installedApps/wasdg.ear/webapp/WEB-INF/classes
/opt/WebSphere/AppServer/installedApps/wasdg.ear/webapp/WEB-INF/lib/glob.jar
/opt/WebSphere/AppServer/installedApps/wasdg.ear/webapp

/opt/WebSphere/AppServer/java/lib
/opt/WebSphere/AppServer/java/lib/dt.jar
/opt/WebSphere/AppServer/java/lib/tools.jar
/opt/WebSphere/AppServer/classes
/opt/WebSphere/AppServer/lib
/opt/WebSphere/AppServer/lib/CMPOpt1026b.zip
/opt/WebSphere/AppServer/lib/EJBCommandTarget.jar
/opt/WebSphere/AppServer/lib/SoapEnabler.jar
/opt/WebSphere/AppServer/lib/WASPostUpgrade.jar
/opt/WebSphere/AppServer/lib/WASPreUpgrade.jar
/opt/WebSphere/AppServer/lib/aat.jar
/opt/WebSphere/AppServer/lib/ace.jar
/opt/WebSphere/AppServer/lib/als.jar
/opt/WebSphere/AppServer/lib/appclient.jar

New    Konsole
```

For readability, you can sort the list by using the keyword (sort split/:/,$cp); however, keep in mind that the initial *order* in which the classes appear is important because the classloader gives priority to the ones encountered first—which makes perfect sense. In APPLICATION mode, the PrintCp servlet will encompass only those classes defined within the web application where the PrintCp is running. Test with the listcp script after switching module visibility settings for the application server and restarting WAS.

The next section shows a classloading simulation in action.

Module Visibility and Reloading Simulation: Hey — Yo

Consider the following program Hey, shown in Listing 15-7. Hey instantiates the class Yo, which is part of the package com.tcnd.wasdg.lorder.

Listing 15-7   *Hey.java*

```
1.    import java.io.*;
2.    import java.util.*;
3.    import javax.servlet.*;
4.    import javax.servlet.http.*;
5.
6.    import com.tcnd.wasdg.lorder.*;
7.
8.    public class Hey extends HttpServlet
9.    {
10.      public void service(HttpServletRequest request, HttpServletResponse
       response)
11.        throws ServletException, IOException
12.        {
13.        Yo o = new Yo();
14.        o.show();
15.
16.        String step = request.getParameter("step");
17.        ServletOutputStream out = response.getOutputStream();
18.        response.setContentType("text/html");
19.
20.        out.println("<html><head><title>Hey -- Yo!</title></head>")
21.        out.println("<body bgcolor=\"white\"><h2> Visibility["+ step + "]  --
       " + o.str + " (" + o.getClass() + ")</h2>");
22.        // out.println("<body bgcolor=\"white\"><h2> Visibility -- " + o.str
       + " (" + o.getClass() + ")</h2>");
23.
24.        out.println("<hr><p>");
25.        out.close();
26.        }
27.  }
```

Listing 15-8 shows the Java class Yo as a simple program that does nothing but print a string showing its fully qualified location.

Listing 15-8 *Yo.java*

```
2.    import java.io.*;
3.
4.    public class Yo implements Serializable {
5.        public String str;
6.
7.        public Yo() {
8.            this.str = "I am in
       $INSTALLEDAPPS/wasdg.ear/webapp/WEB-INF/classes";
9.        }
10.
11.       public void show() {
12.           System.out.println("Yo'str: " + str);
13.       }
14.   }
```

The result of invoking Hey is shown in the following illustration.

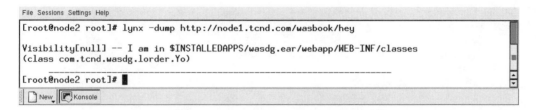

```
File  Sessions  Settings  Help

[root@node2 root]# lynx -dump http://node1.tcnd.com/wasbook/hey

Visibility[null] -- I am in $INSTALLEDAPPS/wasdg.ear/webapp/WEB-INF/classes
(class com.tcnd.wasdg.lorder.Yo)
 _____

[root@node2 root]# █

  New    Konsole
```

An alternative to demystify the visibility order within a web application is through the use of programmatic text processing. This is done with the Perl script subsreload, shown in Listing 15-9. The script writes the servlet Yo to a specific directory and compiles it. The script adds in the appropriate string describing the directory where Yo is being written, along with an identifier that our simulator will make use of.

Listing 15-9 *subsreload*

```
1.    #!/usr/bin/perl
2.
3.    ($step,$loc) = @ARGV;
4.    if (!(defined($loc))) {
5.        print "No directory location defined!\n";
6.    }
7.    elsif (-d ($loc)) {
8.        print "Loading the package Yo in $loc\n";
9.    }
10.   else {
```

```
11.        print "No such location defined on the file system: $loc !\n";
12.  }
13.
14.  # The Yo.java code is assigned to $yo
15.  my $yo = <<YO;
16.  package com.tcnd.wasdg.lorder;
17.  import java.io.*;
18.
19.  public class Yo implements Serializable {
20.      public String str;
21.
22.      public Yo() {
23.          this.str = "[from step STEP] I am in WHERELOCATION ";
24.      }
25.
26.      public void show() {
27.          System.out.println("Yo'str: " + str);
28.      }
29.  }
30.  YO
31.
32.  my $subs = $loc;
33.  if ($subs =~ /\\/) { $subs =~ s/\\/\\\\/g; } # For Windows path name
34.  $yo =~ s/WHERELOCATION/$subs/;
35.  $yo =~ s/STEP/$step/;
36.  open(YO,">com/tcnd/wasdg/lorder/Yo.java");
37.  print YO $yo;
38.  close(YO);
39.
40.  `javac com/tcnd/wasdg/lorder/Yo.java`;
41.  `mkdir -p $loc/com/tcnd/wasdg/lorder`;
42.  `cp com/tcnd/wasdg/lorder/Yo.class $loc/com/tcnd/wasdg/lorder`;
43.
44.  __END__
45.  # See you then
```

The script subsreload takes two arguments: the first is some identifier, and the second is the directory location in which the compiled code of the Yo.java package is to be deposited. As a result, the Yo.class piece of code that is generated by the subsreload script contains some number used as an identifier and a statement to print the location where Yo.class has been deposited. When the Hey servlet calls Yo, the information that has been saved to Yo will be echoed.

The subsreload is invoked from the simreload script at different occasions to load the Yo class in different directory locations before issuing a Lynx request. When simreload invokes the subreload, it will pass the step number to the identifier of subsreload; this way, the step that caused the generation of the Yo class is identified. The simreload script is shown in Listing 15-10.

Listing 15-10   *simreload*

```
1.    #!/bin/ksh
2.
3.    #
4.    # Simulation on module visibility and classes reloading
5.    #
6.    # Make sure that you have created the following directories:
7.    #    mkdir -p $WAS_HOME/classes/com/tcnd/wasdg/lorder
8.    #    mkdir -p
         $INSTALLEDAPPS/wasdg.ear/webapp/WEB-INF/classes/com/tcnd/wasdg/lorder
9.    # Delete any Yo.class file that can be found in any of these directories
         (this may result
10.   #    from an interrupted previous run of this simulator)
11.   # Restart WAS by issuing: $STOPWAS; $STARTWAS
12.   #
13.
14.   echo STEP-1 Loading

\$INSTALLEDAPPS/wasdg.ear/webapp/WEB-INF/classes/com/tcnd/wasdg/lorder/Yo.class
15.   ./subsreload 1 $INSTALLEDAPPS/wasdg.ear/webapp/WEB-INF/classes
16.   echo sleeping 7 seconds, then Lynx gets http://node1/wasbook/hey
17.   lynx -width=160 -dump http://node1/wasbook/hey?step=1
18.
19.   echo STEP-2 Removing

\$INSTALLEDAPPS/wasdg.ear/webapp/WEB-INF/classes/com/tcnd/wasdg/lorder/Yo.class
20.   rm -f

$INSTALLEDAPPS/wasdg.ear/webapp/WEB-INF/classes/com/tcnd/wasdg/lorder/Yo.class
21.   echo sleeping 5 seconds, then Lynx gets http://node1/wasbook/hey
22.   sleep 5
23.   lynx -width=160 -dump http://node1/wasbook/hey?step=2
24.
25.   echo STEP-3 Loading Yo in \$WAS_HOME/classes
26.   ./subsreload 3 $WAS_HOME/classes
27.   echo sleeping 2 seconds, then Lynx gets http://node1/wasbook/hey
28.   sleep 2
29.   lynx -width=160 -dump http://node1/wasbook/hey?step=3
30.
31.
32.   echo STEP-4 Reloading

\$INSTALLEDAPPS/wasdg.ear/webapp/WEB-INF/classes/com/tcnd/wasdg/lorder/Yo.class
33.   ./subsreload 4 $INSTALLEDAPPS/wasdg.ear/webapp/WEB-INF/classes
34.   echo sleeping 2 seconds, then Lynx gets http://node1/wasbook/hey
35.   sleep 2
36.   lynx -width=160 -dump http://node1/wasbook/hey?step=4
37.
38.
```

```
39.  echo STEP-5 Touching
     \$INSTALLEDAPPS/wasdg.ear/webapp/WEB-INF/classes/com/tcnd/wasdg/lorder/Yo.class
40.  echo sleeping 2 seconds, then Lynx gets http://node1/wasbook/hey
41.  sleep 2
42.  lynx -width=160 -dump http://node1/wasbook/hey?step=5
43.
44.  echo STEP-6 Touching
      \$INSTALLEDAPPS/wasdg.ear/webapp/WEB-INF/classes/Hey.class or web.xml
45.  touch $INSTALLEDAPPS/wasdg.ear/webapp/WEB-INF/classes/Hey.class
46.  lynx -width=160 -dump http://node1/wasbook/hey?step=6
47.  echo sleeping 7 seconds, then Lynx gets http://node1/wasbook/hey
48.  sleep 7
49.  lynx -width=160 -dump http://node1/wasbook/hey?step=6
50.
51.  echo STEP-7 Removing

\$INSTALLEDAPPS/wasdg.ear/webapp/WEB-INF/classes/com/tcnd/wasdg/lorder/Yo.class
52.  rm -f

$INSTALLEDAPPS/wasdg.ear/webapp/WEB-INF/classes/com/tcnd/wasdg/lorder/Yo.class
53.  lynx -width=160 -dump http://node1/wasbook/hey?step=7
54.  echo sleeping 7 seconds, then Lynx gets http://node1/wasbook/hey
55.  sleep 7
56.  lynx -width=160 -dump http://node1/wasbook/hey?step=7
57.
58.  echo STEP-8 Removing \$WAS_HOME/classes/com/tcnd/wasdg/lorder/Yo.class
59.  rm -f $WAS_HOME/classes/com/tcnd/wasdg/lorder/Yo.class
60.  lynx -width=160 -dump http://node1/wasbook/hey?step=8
61.  echo sleeping 7 seconds, then Lynx gets http://node1/wasbook/hey
62.  sleep 7
63.  lynx -width=160 -dump http://node1/wasbook/hey?step=8
64.  echo sleep all you want... et c\'est tout!
```

```
File Sessions Settings Help
[6/17/02 19:13:02:133 EDT]  ec356c4 SystemOut   U Yo'str: [from step 3] I am in /opt/WebSphere/AppServer/classes
[6/17/02 19:13:06:201 EDT]  ec616c4 SystemOut   U Yo'str: [from step 3] I am in /opt/WebSphere/AppServer/classes
[6/17/02 19:13:08:260 EDT]  ec356c4 SystemOut   U Yo'str: [from step 3] I am in /opt/WebSphere/AppServer/classes
[6/17/02 19:13:08:312 EDT]  ec096c4 SystemOut   U Yo'str: [from step 3] I am in /opt/WebSphere/AppServer/classes
[6/17/02 19:13:10:284 EDT]  527596c7 WebGroup   I SRVE0091I: [Servlet LOG]: hey: destroy
[6/17/02 19:13:10:516 EDT]  527596c7 WebGroup   I SRVE0091I: [Servlet LOG]: JSP 1.1 Processor: init
[6/17/02 19:13:10:547 EDT]  527596c7 WebGroup   I SRVE0091I: [Servlet LOG]: SimpleFileServlet: init
[6/17/02 19:13:10:690 EDT]  527596c7 WebGroup   I SRVE0091I: [Servlet LOG]: InvokerServlet: init
[6/17/02 19:13:10:701 EDT]  527596c7 WebGroup   I SRVE0091I: [Servlet LOG]: DirectoryBrowsingServlet: init
[6/17/02 19:13:15:477 EDT]  ec096c4 WebGroup    I SRVE0091I: [Servlet LOG]: hey: init
[6/17/02 19:13:15:479 EDT]  ec356c4 SystemOut   U Yo'str: [from step 4] I am in /opt/WebSphere/AppServer/installedApps/wasdg.ear/webapp/WEB
-INF/classes
[6/17/02 19:13:15:539 EDT]  ec356c4 SystemOut   U Yo'str: [from step 4] I am in /opt/WebSphere/AppServer/installedApps/wasdg.ear/webapp/WEB
-INF/classes
[6/17/02 19:13:16:726 EDT]  497896d9 WebGroup   I SRVE0091I: [Servlet LOG]: hey: destroy
[6/17/02 19:13:16:965 EDT]  497896d9 WebGroup   I SRVE0091I: [Servlet LOG]: JSP 1.1 Processor: init
[6/17/02 19:13:16:973 EDT]  497896d9 WebGroup   I SRVE0091I: [Servlet LOG]: SimpleFileServlet: init
[6/17/02 19:13:16:980 EDT]  497896d9 WebGroup   I SRVE0091I: [Servlet LOG]: InvokerServlet: init
[6/17/02 19:13:16:991 EDT]  497896d9 WebGroup   I SRVE0091I: [Servlet LOG]: DirectoryBrowsingServlet: init
[6/17/02 19:13:22:619 EDT]  ec356c4 SystemOut   I SRVE0091I: [Servlet LOG]: hey: init
[6/17/02 19:13:22:621 EDT]  ec356c4 SystemOut   U Yo'str: [from step 3] I am in /opt/WebSphere/AppServer/classes
[6/17/02 19:13:22:673 EDT]  ec096c4 SystemOut   U Yo'str: [from step 3] I am in /opt/WebSphere/AppServer/classes
[6/17/02 19:13:29:728 EDT]  ec096c4 SystemOut   U Yo'str: [from step 3] I am in /opt/WebSphere/AppServer/classes

  New   Konsole
```

Restart WAS ($STOPWAS; $STARTWAS). Make sure you have loaded the initial Hey servlet. Run simreload. Assuming that the module visibility of WAS is set to APPLICATION, executing the simreload script results in the output shown in Listing 15-11.

Listing 15-11   *Result of running simreload*

```
1.    STEP-1 Loading
         $INSTALLEDAPPS/wasdg.ear/webapp/WEB-INF/classes/com/tcnd/wasdg/lorder/Yo.class
2.    Loading the package Yo in
         /opt/WebSphere/AppServer/installedApps/wasdg.ear/webapp/WEB-INF/classes
3.    sleeping 7 seconds, then Lynx gets http://node1/wasbook/hey
4.
5.    Visibility[1] -- [from step 1] I am in
         /opt/WebSphere/AppServer/installedApps/wasdg.ear/webapp/WEB-INF/classes
         (class com.tcnd.wasdg.lorder.Yo)
6.
```

```
7.    STEP-2 Removing
         $INSTALLEDAPPS/wasdg.ear/webapp/WEB-INF/classes/com/tcnd/wasdg/lorder/Yo.class
8.    sleeping 5 seconds, then Lynx gets http://node1/wasbook/hey
9.
10.      Error 500: com/tcnd/wasdg/lorder/Yo
11.
12.   STEP-3 Loading Yo in $WAS_HOME/classes
13.   Loading the package Yo in /opt/WebSphere/AppServer/classes
14.   sleeping 2 seconds, then Lynx gets http://node1/wasbook/hey
15.
16.   Visibility[3] -- [from step 3] I am in /opt/WebSphere/AppServer/classes
         (class com.tcnd.wasdg.lorder.Yo)
17.
```

```
18.   STEP-4 Reloading
         $INSTALLEDAPPS/wasdg.ear/webapp/WEB-INF/classes/com/tcnd/wasdg/lorder/Yo.class
19.   Loading the package Yo in
         /opt/WebSphere/AppServer/installedApps/wasdg.ear/webapp/WEB-INF/classes
20.   sleeping 2 seconds, then Lynx gets http://node1/wasbook/hey
21.
22.   Visibility[4] -- [from step 3] I am in /opt/WebSphere/AppServer/classes
         (class com.tcnd.wasdg.lorder.Yo)
23.
```

```
24.  STEP-5 Touching
       $INSTALLEDAPPS/wasdg.ear/webapp/WEB-INF/classes/com/tcnd/wasdg/lorder/Yo.class
25.  sleeping 2 seconds, then Lynx gets http://node1/wasbook/hey
26.
27.  Visibility[5] -- [from step 3] I am in /opt/WebSphere/AppServer/classes
       (class com.tcnd.wasdg.lorder.Yo)
28.
```

```
29.  STEP-6 Touching $INSTALLEDAPPS/wasdg.ear/webapp/WEB-INF/classes/Hey.class
       or web.xml
30.
31.  Visibility[6] -- [from step 3] I am in /opt/WebSphere/AppServer/classes
       (class com.tcnd.wasdg.lorder.Yo)
32.
```

```
33.  sleeping 7 seconds, then Lynx gets http://node1/wasbook/hey
34.
35.  Visibility[6] -- [from step 4] I am in
       /opt/WebSphere/AppServer/installedApps/wasdg.ear/webapp/WEB-INF/classes
       (class com.tcnd.wasdg.lorder.Yo)
36.
```

```
37.  STEP-7 Removing

$INSTALLEDAPPS/wasdg.ear/webapp/WEB-INF/classes/com/tcnd/wasdg/lorder/Yo.class
38.
39.  Visibility[7] -- [from step 4] I am in
       /opt/WebSphere/AppServer/installedApps/wasdg.ear/webapp/WEB-INF/classes
       (class com.tcnd.wasdg.lorder.Yo)
40.
```

```
41.  sleeping 7 seconds, then Lynx gets http://node1/wasbook/hey
42.
43.  Visibility[7] -- [from step 3] I am in /opt/WebSphere/AppServer/classes
       (class com.tcnd.wasdg.lorder.Yo)
44.
```

```
45.  STEP-8 Removing $WAS_HOME/classes/com/tcnd/wasdg/lorder/Yo.class
46.
```

```
47.  Visibility[8] -- [from step 3] I am in /opt/WebSphere/AppServer/classes
     (class com.tcnd.wasdg.lorder.Yo)
48.
```

```
49.  sleeping 7 seconds, then Lynx gets http://node1/wasbook/hey
50.
51.  Visibility[8] -- [from step 3] I am in /opt/WebSphere/AppServer/classes
     (class com.tcnd.wasdg.lorder.Yo)
52.
```

```
53.  sleep all you want... et c'est tout!
```

After simreload finishes execution, the standard output of WAS shows the activities that have been carried out during reloading.

The output of the script shows the loading activity of WAS. You may need to compare each step shown in the output to the one shown in the script (see Listing 15-10).

In step 1, Yo is loaded in the webapp classes directory, and a soft reload will take place during the 7 seconds sleep time after which the lynx command is issued to request the Hey servlet. Line 5 shows that the visibility of Yo in step 1 is for a Yo that has been set in step 1.

In step 2 (line 7), the Yo is removed from the classes directory of the webapp, and after a sleep of 5 seconds, a request to the Hey servlet will fail (line 10).

Step 3 loads Yo in the run-time classpath of WAS. The visibility in step 3 for the Yo is as set in step 3 to be located in the WAS classpath (line 16).

Step 4 loads the Yo in the webapp classes directory, but this will not have any effect. The visibility in step 4 for the Yo is for a Yo that has been loaded in step 3, namely in the WAS run-time classpath.

Step 5 tries to change the timestamp of the Yo.class in the webapp classes directory; however, this will do nothing because the Yo is still the same as the one set in step 3 (line 27).

Step 6 touches the Hey servlet loaded in the webapp so that WAS reloads the servlet in the web container. (See the previous illustration.) However, the visibility in this step is still for a Yo loaded in step 3 (line 31). This is true because we need a few seconds for the change to take effect.

Still in the same step: after waiting seven seconds (line 33), the visibility of Yo has changed. Line 35 shows that the visibility changed to a Yo loaded in the webapp (as it has been set in step 4).

In step 7, the Yo is removed from the webapp classes directory. For a few seconds, the Yo is still loaded as shown on line 39. Yet this will change to the Yo that has been loaded in step 3 after 7 seconds, as shown on line 43.

Step 8 shows that the removal of Yo from the WAS run-time classpath has no effect as long as WAS is still active. Only restarting the WAS after deleting the Yo from the run-time classpath will make the reference to this Yo disappear.

Hot Deployment and Dynamic Reloading

By writing a new servlet or a new .jsp file in our webapp web module, then running the svlbuild script to compile and update the files in the $INSTALLEDAPPS/wasdg.ear directory, we have done a *hot deployment*.

By touching the class file of a servlet that is already loaded in the WAS web container, we provoke WAS to dynamically reload the servlet. *Touching a file* means to change its timestamp, and, in a WAS perspective, it is equivalent to making a change to a file.

We will refer to hot deployment as HD, to dynamic reloading as DR, and to reloading as RLD. Changes in WAS are divided into four categories:

▶ **Changes at the web module level**   These changes include preexisting components, or adding new components, such as servlets, JSP files, or enterprise beans to an already loaded web module. These changes can also be reflected in the deployment descriptor (web.xml) of the web application. An example is the webapp that we deployed in Chapter 11. Such changes can take effect without stopping and starting the application server (WAS) if dynamic reloading (DR) is enabled.

▶ **Changes at the application level**   We will undertake these changes on a running enterprise application, i.e., wasdg.ear. These changes can affect all web modules configured within it. Other changes are in the attributes of the .xmi configuration files of the application discussed in Chapter 14.

▶ **Changes at the application server level**   These changes are reflected in the server-cfg.xml.

▶ **Changes at the plug-in level**   These changes are necessary where configuration data of the plug-in needs to be changed for the following reasons: changing the servlet mapping of a web application in the web.xml file; changing the HTTP transport port or the virtual host in the server-cfg.xml file.

Because WAS is constituted from one or more Java machines that are running an enterprise web application and its constituent components, the concentric rings can be used to show the effect of WAS and its deployment. The concentric ring image shown in Figure 15-3 is well integrated into the understanding of classloading that WAS undertakes while containing and managing its web applications.

The WAS administration server running in the innermost rings can access data objects in the outer rings. The WebSphere Application Server is running in the inner ring.

The following four tables summarize the effects of making changes in any WAS components. The tables start from the outer ring and move to the inner ring. An RLD* (reloading) appears in a cell to imply that reloading is possible if it has been enabled in the web .xmi file of the application. A *Y* appears in a row for a Yes for that particular action. A *(Y)* appears in the Srv

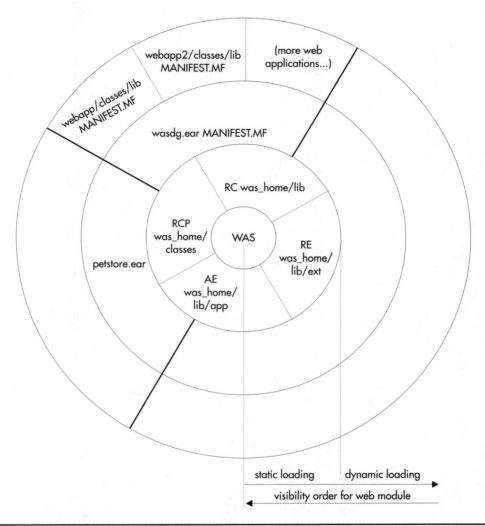

Figure 15-3   *Concentric rings showing the loading order versus visibility order in WAS*

(server restart) column to indicate that it may be necessary to restart WAS depending on other conditions. In the Location column, the asterisk (*) is used to denote anything present in that directory.

Table 15-1 shows the effects of changes made at the web module level.

Table 15-2 shows the effects of changes made at the Enterprise JavaBeans .jar files level.

Table 15-3 shows the effects of changes made at the enterprise application level.

Changes	Location	HD	DR	Module	Appl	Srv	Other
Change an existing JSP file.	webapp/*	-	Y				.
Add a JSP file.	webapp/*	Y	Y				.
Change an existing servlet class.	webapp/ WEB-INF/ classes webapp/ WEB-INF/ [lib or classes]	-	Y			(Y)	RLD*
Change a dependent class of an existing servlet class.	ibid	-	Y			(Y)	RLD*
Add a new servlet using the Invoker facility (serve servlets by class name) or add a dependent class to an existing application.	ibid	Y	-			(Y)	RLD*
Add a new servlet, including a new definition of the servlet in the web.xml deployment descriptor for the application.	ibid WEB-INF/ web.xml	Y	-			(Y)	RLD*
Modify the web.xml file of an application, except security roles and login-config.	web.xml	Y	Y			(Y)	RLD*
Modify the web.xml file of an application's properties: security roles and login-config.	web.xml	Y	Y	DrAdmin		(Y)	RLD*
Modify the ibm-web-ext.xmi of an application without disabling RLD by setting the reloadInterval property to zero (0) or by setting the reloadEnabled property to false.		-	Y			(Y)	RLD*
Modify the ibm-web-ext.xmi of an application to enable reloading RLD.		-	-	DrAdmin			
Modify the ibm-web-bnd.xmi of an application.	-	-	-	Y	Restart		

Table 15-1 *When a Change Is Made at the Web Module Level*

Changes	HD	DR	Module	Appl	Srv	Other
Modify ejb-jar.xml of an application.	-	Y	Restart			
Modify ibm-ejb-jar-ext.xmi.	-	Y	Restart (DrAdmin)			
Modify ibm-ejb-jar-bnd.xmi.	-	Y	Restart (DrAdmin)			
Modify Table.ddl for an EJB Jar (location of the database table schema).	-	-				Rerun the DDL file on user database server.

Table 15-2 *When a Change Is Made at the EJB .Jar Files Level*

Changes	HD	DR	Module	Appl	Srv	Other
Modify the Map.mapxmi or Schema.dbxmi files for an EJB Jar (.jar location).	-	Y	DrAdmin			Redeploy the EJB and restart the module.
Update the implementation class for an EJB or a dependent class of the implementation class for an EJB ($INSTALLEDAPPS/ \<ear-application\>/*).	-	Y			(Y) Recommended	Restart all dependent applications/ modules.
Update Home/Remote interface classes for an EJB.	-	Y		Y		Regenerate code artifact. Redeploy EJB.Md/App Visibility for classloading.*
Add a new EJB to a running server. The addition is to an existing EJB Jar file.	Y	Y		DrAdmin		Apply the new Jar to the installedApps folder and restart the application.

Table 15-2 _When a Change Is Made at the EJB .Jar Files Level_ (continued)

Table 15-4 shows the effect of changes made at the server configuration and HTTP plug-in level.

Changes	HD	DR	Appl	Srv	Other
Modify the application.xml for an application.	-	Y	Y		Restart the application.
Modify the ibm-app-ext.xmi file for an application.	-	Y	Y		Restart the application.
Modify the ibm-app-bnd.xmi file for an application.	-	Y	Y		Restart the application.
Modify a nonmodule Jar contained in the EAR.	Y	Y	DrAdmin		Restart the application containing the modified .jar file.
Add a new EJB module to an existing, running application (server-cfg.xml).	N	N		Y	Restart the server.
Add a new web module to an existing, running application (change to server-cfg.xml).	N	N		Y	Restart the server.
Add a new application to server-cfg.xml of running server.	N	N		Y	Restart the server.

Table 15-3 _When a Change Is Made at the Enterprise Application Level_

Changes	Location	HD	DR	Other
Modify a server-cfg.xml file of running server.	server-cfg.xml	N	N	Restart WAS.
Modify application.xml to change the context root of a war file.	web application application.xml file	Y	Y	Generate the plug-in config file through the administrative console or through the GenPluginCfg.bat/sh script.
Modify web.xml to add, remove, or modify a servlet mapping.	web module web.xml file	Y	Y	Possibly, regenerate the http plug-in configuration file (GenPluginCfg.bat/sh), e.g., adding or changing the URI context mapping of a servlet.
Modify server-cfg.xml to add, remove, or modify a HTTP transport, to add or remove a virtual host, or to add, remove, or modify a virtual host alias.	plugin-cfg.xml	Y	Y	Generate the plug-in config file through the web browser admin or through the GenPluginCfg.bat/sh file.

Table 15-4 *When a Change Is Made at the Server Configuration or HTTP Plug-In Level*

When you restart WAS, whatever changes you have made, at any level, will be in effect. If after making a change to the web module, you are in doubt about the behavior of WAS, the enterprise application, or any of the configuration files, restart WAS and test again. You can assess the situation and determine whether the changes were picked up properly by the WAS Java machine(s).

Wrapping Up

Classloading is arcane and organized. It is predefined in the WAS startup configuration, and can be modified by directly editing these configuration files, or through the administrative console. Direct modification of the configuration file is necessary when adding classes globally that are to be shared by all application servers, in particular, for those resources that are not application-specific but that pertain globally to the whole node. For example, we have discussed how to add the UDB Jar library files to the WAS startup classloader. In addition to the Jar archive files, WAS may also need other libraries to be dynamically loaded; this is also the situation with the UDB to implement session persistence. (Refer to the "Adding Jar Archives to the WAS Startup Classloader" section.)

When WAS is started, the *WAS startup classloader* (misleadingly and inconsistently called *bootstrap classloader* in IBM documentation since the premier version of WAS) is started with a classpath defined in the ws.ext.dirs, as discussed in the section "Classpaths and WAS' Classloaders." Module visibility and class reloading refer to the symbolic name resolution of a class(es) from within a web module while WAS is in an active state and reloading of classes is enabled.

# CHAPTER 6

Session Identification and the HTTP Protocol

IN THIS CHAPTER:

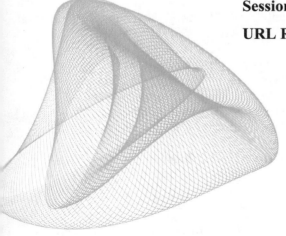

W hen transitioning information between an Internet browser and a server, data flows in dribs and drabs. If the browser were totally connected to the server, the browser and the HTTP server could communicate information through shared memory. However, all browsers are merely agents that run on devices that are totally disconnected from the web server. Because browsers can adequately handle communication protocols, and at least the HTTP protocol, you can simulate memory sharing by marking a browser identity to a dashboard where objects are held.

Three functional aspects simulate such memory sharing between the browser and the application server.[1] First, the browser identity is saved as an identifier known to the browser as a cookie. Second, the dashboard is handled within the application server through a mechanism known as session management. Third, session management adheres to timing functions whose parameters can be programmatically set so that continuity and interruption of sessions is controllable.

These three functional aspects work collectively to handle user sessions, and programmers are offered a set of routines to manage user sessions. The first aspect is totally protocol-dependent; therefore, it is handled by the web server. The second aspect is handled by the application server, and the third aspect is handled by both the web server and the application server.

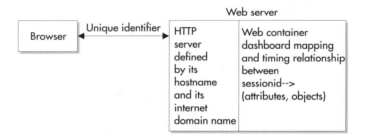

Whether you decide to use Java servlets or CGI scripts, state information between a browser and an HTTP server is handled with the CGI environment variables—not because CGI originated before Java, but because CGI is compatible with all network router and firewall brands. Information is communicated in a very simple way, in particular, with the Set-Cookie header.

You can easily master the programming technique to manage sessions; however, the difficulty is not in using Java methods or CGI Perl modules to carry out such a task. Rather, it is in defining a deterministic approach that can help you progressively write, modify, and test your code. The approach discussed in this chapter defines the commands that can assist you in finding the most optimal way to program effectively and disclose the transitional information between your program and an agent browser.

The chapter also discusses the coexistence of CGI programs within an application server in maintaining a user session.

---

[1]   Notice that the communication is between the browser and the application server, not the web server. The application server has the functional algorithms and mnemonic capacity to handle session management.

Identifying User Logins

You have seen how a teller logs in and becomes authorized to gain access to the CreditDebit servlet so that he or she can operate on a client account. However, the CreditDebit servlet is reentrant through its doGet() method, which does not adequately protect a banker account. A barrier is needed to prevent nonprivileged users from modifying banker accounts. In fact, it is always possible to put a request to any servlet; however, the servlet should implement such a barrier and filter the request by identifying its issuer. The most common way to perform this task is to implement a filtering routine that will detect the submitter of the request before allowing him or her further action. This is accomplished by determining whether the user who put in the request is in session. Session management is part of the WAS web container (see the illustration).

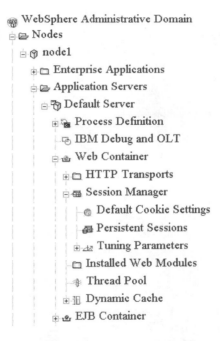

However, before discussing session scope and its containment (the topic of Chapter 17), a discussion about cookies is required to clarify how a session is identified.

Getting the mime_header

One of the most direct ways to reveal Internet transition states between client and server is through an application that can demystify the communication carried through the HTTP or HTTPS protocols, such as Lynx. Table 16-1 summarizes some options you need to be familiar with while testing with Lynx.

Option	Description
accept_all_cookies	Makes Lynx accept all cookies sent by the server.
cookies	Toggles the Set-Cookies headers' handler.
cookie_file	Used as -cookie_file=FILENAME, from which Lynx reads the cookies. When not specified, Lynx reads the cookies from ~/.lynx_cookies.
cookie_save_file	Used as -cookie_save_file=FILENAME, to which Lynx writes the cookies. When not specified, Lynx writes the cookies as specified by -cookie_file (the previous option).
dump	Directs Lynx to write the output to the standard output. This option is often used to help developers quickly test their code, such as servlets.
from	Uses -from to toggle transmission of From headers.
head	Used with the -mime_header option to send a HEAD request for the MIME headers.
post_data	Used when posting data to a form that handles the POST method. Data is read from standard input (STDIN) using the conventional HTTP posting stream. (The ampersand (&) and equal sign (=) are used to separate and set equality to each field, respectively. The input is terminated with three hyphens (---) beginning on a new line.)
mime_header	Prints the MIME header of a fetched document when used with the -head option.
trace	Turns on the Lynx trace mode.

Table 16-1   *Essential Lynx Options for Developers*

Cookies

Cookies are part of the HTTP headers; hence, they are handled by the HTTP protocol and not by the application server. It is important to notice such a disassociation (between the HTTP server and the application server) for three reasons. First, it allows you to incorporate an application server in a web site where session management still depends on CGI scripts. Second, you can gain a clear understanding of the session management mechanism and debug your code by tracking down the session identifier that is passed in the MIME header. Third, one of the variables that a cookie may depend on is the domain name of the issuer server; therefore, a cookie[2] sent through internal HTTP transport (default port 9080) of the application server is not the same as the one sent through the HTTP server. To compound the complexity, virtual hosting where domain name mapping plays a role can also impact the mechanism of reading back a cookie from the client browser.

Programming cookies is simple. The difficulty is defining a concise way that developers can test the flow between the web server and the client browser when cookies are involved.

---

[2]   This is also true for a session, because the session identifier is being sent as a cookie known as JSESSIONID.

Cookies with CGI

Cookies originated as CGI variables that were set in the browser header. Even if you will be programming in Java, knowing how to manipulate cookies using CGI scripts is essential for any good web programming. Such understanding makes you realize how to solve issues with session management.

Setting Cookies with CGI Script

The setcookies.cgi script, shown in Listing 16-1, sets two cookies: the LAPERLA cookie and the SESSIONID cookie. Lines 13 through 17 define five of the parameters of SESSIONID: the cookie name itself, the domain and pathname that can have access to this cookie, the security, and the expiration time set to 65 seconds.

Listing 16-1   *setcookies.cgi sets two cookies in the client browser*

```
1.   #!/usr/bin/perl
2.
3.   use CGI qw/:standard/;
4.
5.   my($cooknameN)="LAPERLA";
6.   my($cooknameN_Domain)='.tcnd.com';
7.   my($cooknameN_Path)='/';
8.   my($cooknameN_Secure)=0;
9.   #my($cooknameN_Expire)="27-Apr-2008 10:10:10 GMT";
10.  #my($cooknameN_Expire)="01-Jan-1970 00:00:10 GMT";
11.  my($cooknameN_Expire)="+5s";
12.
13.  my($cooknameI)="SESSIONID";
14.  my($cooknameI_Domain)='.tcnd.com';
15.  my($cooknameI_Path)='/';
16.  my($cooknameI_Secure)=0;
17.  my($cooknameI_Expire)="+65s";
18.
19.
20.  my(%h1) = ('a'=>1,'b'=>2,'c'=>3,'d'=>4,8=>'Z','username'=>'dave');
21.  my $loc = 'http://node1.tcnd.com/wasbook/dumpcook';
22.
23.  my $sessionid = unpack('H*',pack('Ncs', time, $$ & 0xff, rand(0xffff)));
24.
25.  &sign_cookies();
26.  print "OK.";
27.
28.  sub sign_cookies {
29.      my $name1 = $cooknameN;
30.      my $name2 = $cooknameI;
31.
32.      my $c1 = cookie(
33.          '-name'      => $name1,      # name of the cookie
```

```
34.              '-value'    => \%h1,    # value of the cookie
35.              '-expires'  => $cooknameN_Expire,    # expires after 1 hour
36.              '-domain'   => $cooknameN_Domain,    # valid for our domain
37.              '-path'     => $cooknameN_Path,      # only for CGI scripts
38.              '-secure'   => $cooknameN_Secure     # 0 normal, 1 for HTTPS
39.         );
40.      my $c2 = cookie(
41.              '-name'     => $name2,        # name of the cookie
42.              '-value'    => $sessionid,    # value of the cookie
43.              '-expires'  => $cooknameI_Expire, # expires after 1 hour
44.              '-domain'   => $cooknameI_Domain, # valid for our domain
45.              '-path'     => $cooknameI_Path,   # only for CGI scripts
46.              '-secure'   => $cooknameI_Secure  # 0 normal, 1 for HTTPS
47.         );
48.
49.      if ( (defined($loc)) && ($loc ne '') ) {
50.           print header('-cookie' => [$c1,$c2],-header=>
       redirect(-uri=>$loc));
51.      }
52.      else {
53.           print header('-cookie' => [$c1,$c2]);
54.      }
55.  }
```

Figure 16-1 shows the result of requesting setcookies.cgi. The script sets the cookies first, then sends the redirection to the URI /wasbook/dumpcook in the header, as shown on line 50. The DumpCook servlet is explained in the section "Using Cookies Through HTTP Java Servlets" later in this chapter.

One important aspect of the Perl program shown in Listing 16-1 is the way information is organized before being sent to the browser. In particular, it is clear enough that the header is printed first (line 50 or line 53) before shipping out any other content to the browser. Before committing the response, programmers need to add any cookie to be sent in it first; this ensures that the cookie is sent properly in the HTTP header. Each cookie is described with six parameters. For example, the first cookie is described in its six attributes shown on lines 33 through 38; they are name, value, expires, domain, path, and secure. Invoking Lynx to print the MIME header, you will get all six parameters on one line, one for each cookie.

In the following illustration, Set-Cookie: appears on two lines: the first is for the LAPERLA cookie, in which security is enabled (set it to 1) only for illustrative purposes, and the second is for the SESSIONID cookie. For each cookie, the name, value, domain, path, expires, and secure attributes are listed on one line. The location is also set to be redirected to http://node1.tcnd.com/wasbook/dumpcook.

```
[root@node1 root]# lynx  -head  -mime_header  http://node1.tcnd.com/cgi-bin/setcookies.cgi
HTTP/1.1 302 Found
Date: Fri, 03 May 2002 02:37:34 GMT
Server: IBM_HTTP_SERVER/1.3.19.1  Apache/1.3.20 (Unix)
HEADER="Status: 302 Moved
Set-Cookie: LAPERLA=8&2&username&dave&a&1&b&2&c&3&d&4; domain=.tcnd.com; path=/; expires=Fri, 03-May-2002 02:37:39 GMT; secure
Set-Cookie: SESSIONID=3cd1f7ee210e1b; domain=.tcnd.com; path=/; expires=Fri, 03-May-2002 02:38:39 GMT
Location: http://node1.tcnd.com/wasbook/dumpcook
Connection: close
Content-Type: text/html; charset=iso-8859-1

[root@node1 root]#
```

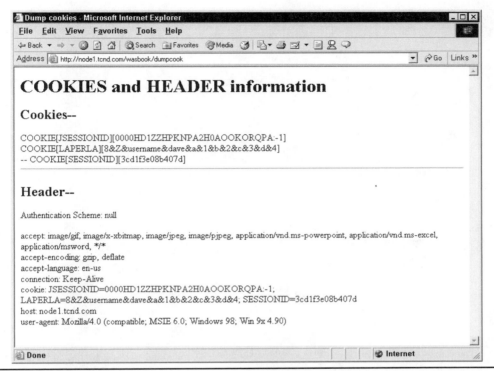

Figure 16-1   *DumpCook servlet resulting from the redirected request of setcookies.cgi*

Reading a Cookie in CGI Script

Reading back the value of the cookie is quite simple. You request the cookie by name and then iterate over its (key-value) pairs, as shown in getlaperla.cgi, Listing 16-2. The following script retrieves the value of the cookie previously set. When you request this CGI script within less than 6 seconds from requesting the setcookies.cgi, you will be able to fetch back the values of the LAPERLA cookie, as seen in the following illustration.

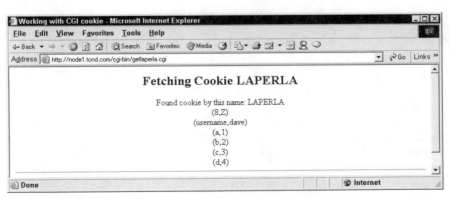

Listing 16-2   *getlaperla.cgi reads the cookie named LAPERLA*

```
1.    #!/usr/bin/perl
2.
3.    use CGI qw/:standard/;
4.
5.    my($cooknameN)="LAPERLA";
6.
7.    my $out = &htmlheader();
8.    print $out;
9.    print "<html><head><title>Working with CGI cookie</title></head> <body
          bgcolor=\"white\"><P><center> <h2>Fetching Cookie LAPERLA</h2>";
10.   &query_laperla();
11.   print "<hr><p></html>";
12.
13.
14.   sub query_laperla {
15.       my $name = $cooknameN;
16.       my $key;
17.       my %cookie;
18.       if (cookie(-name => $name)) {
19.           print "Found cookie by this name:\n $name<br>\n\n";
20.           %cookie = cookie(-name => $name);
21.           foreach $key (keys %cookie) {
22.               print "($key,$cookie{$key})<br>";
23.           }
24.           return 1;
25.       }
26.       else {
27.           print "No cookie by this name:\n cookie Name:$name!\n\n";
28.           return 0;
29.       }
30.   }
31.
32.   sub htmlheader () {
33.           return qq~Content-type: text/html
34.           Pragma: no-cache\n\n~;
35.   }
```

Understanding the Reasoning Behind the Hash as the Value of a Cookie

The setcookies.cgi script shows how a hash can be passed as the value of a cookie, and the getlaperla.cgi script shows how the hash can be fetched back from the cookie. Therefore, it is possible to hold the information of a browser within the MIME header by assigning it to a cookie. This is adequate if the size of the hash is optimal, certainly less than 4096 bytes. This size fits the requirement of a web-based real-time system; for example, a couple of coordinates are required to be communicated between CGI scripts, or maybe the user registration data of a client on a web site.

In addition, this technique is semipersistent because the cookie is always held on the client browser and is written to his hard disk when the browser is closed. It is considered to be *semipersistent* because the data is not saved in the event of a power loss or system freeze on the user workstation where the browser is running. In most cases, this is sufficient for commercial web sites, and the cost of network traffic in transmitting cookies' information back and forth is justifiable compared to the cost of application server licensing and administration.

Perl CGI programming can take advantage of cookie programming in particular because it is possible to pass a hash as the value in a cookie. The hash is then iterated through using `foreach` to initialize a set of data access methods (similar to the getter/setter methods described in Chapter 10). An object-oriented Perl class can be implemented as an iterator class that consists of two methods: a constructor method that takes the content of the hash (the cookie value) to be blessed in the iterator class, and an iteration method that can get each pair of elements (key and value) extracted from the flattened hash (a list of elements in the cookie value). Although the implementation of the Perl iterator class can be accomplished in 14 lines of code, it is beyond the scope of this book.

Using Cookies Through HTTP Java Servlets

In the past, using CGI programming was essential to understanding programming with cookies. However, now it is possible to use HTTP Java servlets to set and retrieve information from a cookie.

Setting Cookies from Within a Servlet: SetCookie

Like a CGI script, a Java servlet needs to address the setting of a cookie using the CGI variable: cookie. A simple servlet to set cookie in the browser its requester is shown in Listing 16-3. The SetCookie servlet uses the class javax.servlet.http.Cookie class provided by the Servlet API. On line 20, the Cookie() constructor creates a cookie object that can be prepared to be sent to the client by passing this object to the addCookie() method of the HttpServletResponse (line 29.)

Listing 16-3   *SetCookie servlet*

```
1.    import java.io.*;
2.    import java.util.*;
3.    import javax.servlet.*;
4.    import javax.servlet.http.*;
5.
6.    public class SetCookie extends HttpServlet
7.    {
8.
9.        public void doGet (HttpServletRequest request, HttpServletResponse
      response)
10.        throws ServletException, IOException
11.        {
12.            PrintWriter out;
```

```
13.            // set mime type
14.            response.setContentType("text/html");
15.            out = response.getWriter();
16.
17.            String someName = "SESSIONID";
18.            String someValue = "12345";
19.
20.            Cookie c = new Cookie(someName, someValue);
21.            c.setValue("123456");
22.            c.setVersion(0); // Netscape's most popular, 1 experimental
23.            c.setDomain(".tcnd.com");
24.            c.setPath("/wasbook/");
25.            c.setMaxAge(15); // expire in 15 seconds
26.            c.setSecure(false); // not secure
27.            // VERSION 1 only   c.setComment("a comment goes here");
28.
29.            response.addCookie(c);
30.
31.            String content = "<HTML><HEAD><TITLE> Testing SetCookie
       </TITLE></HEAD>" +
32.                "<BODY><P><CENTER><H1>Test SetCookie</H1><HR><P></HTML>";
33.            out.println(content);
34.      }
35.  }
36.
```

The HTTP header for the cookie contains many details about the cookie that are handled by the servlet API. Like the CGI script, the servlet may set the value (line 21,) the consequent domain (line 23,) the consequent path (line 24,) the expiration (line 25,) and the security flag (line 26.)

On line 29, the cookie is added to the response, because cookie is sent via the HTTP header.

Setting Cookies Through the POST Method: PostCookie

Passing the session value and the expiration time of a cookie is possible through the PostCookie servlet shown in Listing 16-4.

Listing 16-4   *The PostCookie servlet posts a cookie with a selected value and name*

```
1.    import java.io.*;
2.    import java.util.*;
3.    import javax.servlet.*;
4.    import javax.servlet.http.*;
5.
6.    public class PostCookie extends HttpServlet {
7.        public void doGet (HttpServletRequest request, HttpServletResponse
       response)
8.        throws ServletException, IOException
```

```
9.        {
10.           PrintWriter out;
11.           response.setContentType("text/html");
12.           out = response.getWriter();
13.
14.           String sessvalue = request.getParameter("sessvalue");
15.           String sesstime = request.getParameter("sesstime");
16.
17.           Cookie c = new Cookie("SESSIONID", sessvalue);
18.           c.setMaxAge(Integer.parseInt(sesstime)); // Netscape's most
       popular, 1 for RFC 2109 experimental
19.           c.setDomain("node1.tcnd.com");
20.           c.setPath("/"); //c.setPath("/wasbook/");
21.           c.setVersion(0);
22.           c.setSecure(false);
23.
24.           response.addCookie(c);
25.
26.           String content = "<HTML><HEAD><TITLE> Testing PostCookie
       </TITLE></HEAD>" +
27.                  "<BODY><P><CENTER><H1>This cookie will expire in: " +
       sesstime + " seconds</H1><HR><P></HTML>";
28.           out.println(content);
29.        }
30.     public void doPost(HttpServletRequest request, HttpServletResponse
       response)
31.             throws ServletException, IOException
32.        {
33.              doGet(request,response);
34.        }
35.  }
```

You can test the PostSession servlet by placing a request to its URL in the browser, as in the following example:

http://node1.tcnd.com/wasbook/postcookie?sesstime=5&sessvalue=abc

After placing such a request, within less than 6 seconds, you can place another request to the DumpCook servlet to echo the cookie (SESSIONID) back in your browser:

http://node1.tcnd.com/wasbook/dumpcook

The PostSession servlet uses the doGet() method to retrieve the data passed in the URL. Usually, the time and value of the cookie are defined by the server; they are not posted selectively by the client unless there is an obvious reason to implement a trivial security problem using the callback mechanism. However, a security implementation with callback is not discussed in this chapter.

Let's take a look at a more interesting example to test the servlet, this time using Lynx. First, we will issue a POST method and read the MIME header of the reply back, looking for the Set-Cookie header, as in the following command:

```
# echo "sesstime=5&sessvalue=abc&---" | lynx  -accept_all_cookies
     -mime_header -post_data -post_data
        http://node1.tcnd.com/wasbook/postcookie
  | grep Set-Cookie; date
```

Next, we will parallel this command consecutively with another Lynx command:

```
# for i in 1 2 3; do echo "sesstime=1$i&sessvalue=abc&---" | lynx
     -accept_all_cookies  -post_data
        http://node1.tcnd.com/wasbook/postcookie; cat /root/.lynx*;
done
```

Figure 16-2 shows the result of both commands just issued.

The first command requested from the PostCookie servlet sets the session ID value to abc and times it out in 5 seconds. The command is followed by the date command to print the current date and time. Looking at Figure 16-2, the Set-Cookie header has been filtered from the MIME header, and it shows an expiration time that is 5 seconds from the printed date.

The second command is an iteration of that result in requesting to post a cookie three times. Each time the command is executed, the content of the .lynx_cookies file is printed, which is where Lynx saves the cookies after exiting. However, no cookie information is kept from one command to another because Lynx deletes these cookies from its saved file (for example, from ~/.lynx_cookies) as the setup of the application server dictates (for example, -1 to delete the cookie after the browsing agent exited.) In fact the application server does

```
[root@node1 root]#
[root@node1 root]# echo "sesstime=5&sessvalue=abc&---" | lynx  -accept_all_cookies -mime_header
-post_data -post_data http://node1.tcnd.com/wasbook/postcookie  | grep Set-Cookie; date
Set-Cookie: SESSIONID=abc;Domain=node1.tcnd.com;Expires=Thu, 02-May-2002 21:24:41 GMT;Path=/
Thu May  2 17:24:36 EDT 2002
[root@node1 root]#
[root@node1 root]#
[root@node1 root]# for i in 1 2 3; do echo "sesstime=1$i&sessvalue=abc&---" | lynx  -accept_all_
cookies  -post_data http://node1.tcnd.com/wasbook/postcookie; cat /root/.lynx*; done

               This cookie will expire in: 11 seconds
        _____
node1.tcnd.com  FALSE   /       FALSE   1020374691      SESSIONID     abc

               This cookie will expire in: 12 seconds
        _____
node1.tcnd.com  FALSE   /       FALSE   1020374692      SESSIONID     abc

               This cookie will expire in: 13 seconds
        _____
node1.tcnd.com  FALSE   /       FALSE   1020374693      SESSIONID     abc
[root@node1 root]#
```

Figure 16-2 *Getting the MIME header of PostCookie requests*

nothing beside setting the maximum age of the cookie to −1. The deletion of the cookies from the browser is usually handled in the following fashion:

1. The cookie is held in memory during browsing and while the browser process is effectively running on the client system.

2. When the browser exits, the cookie is written and saved to a file with some its associated timing information.

3. When the browser is started again, the file in which the cookies are stored is being parsed by the browser, and all cookies that needed to be deleted after closing the browser are deleted at this time.

Quite awkward, but this is how it is!

While the HTTP protocol passes information in the MIME header file (shown in the first command of Figure 16-2), the browser agent fetches this information and saves it within its environment to further maintain its states (shown in the second command).

Now it should be clear that the statewise communication between the browser and the web server occurs purely through the HTTP protocol at one end and an agent saving data to either memory or to a file at the other end.

Fetching Cookies: DumpCook

A common utility servlet is the DumpCook shown in Listing 16-5. This servlet prints all cookies found in the header of a browser. Of course only these cookies that can be echoed back to the consequent domain and program are printed.

Listing 16-5   *The DumpCook servlet to iterate through the cookies and print them out*

```
1.    import java.io.*;
2.    import java.util.*;
3.    import javax.servlet.*;
4.    import javax.servlet.http.*;
5.
6.    public class DumpCook extends HttpServlet
7.    {
8.
9.        public void service(HttpServletRequest request, HttpServletResponse
      response)
10.       throws ServletException, IOException
11.       {
12.       ServletOutputStream out = response.getOutputStream();
13.       response.setContentType("text/html");
14.       out.println("<html><head><title>Dump cookies</title></head><body
      bgcolor=\"white\">");
15.       out.println("<h1>COOKIES and HEADER information</h1>");
16.       out.println("<h2>Cookies--</h2>");
17.       int j;
18.       Cookie[] cookies = request.getCookies();
```

```
19.      for (j=0; j< cookies.length; j++) {
20.          // Fetch a cookie
21.          Cookie aCookie = cookies[j];
22.          String n = aCookie.getName();
23.              String v = aCookie.getValue();
24.          // Looking for the cookie with SESSIONID
25.          if (n.equals("SESSIONID")) {
26.          out.println("-- COOKIE[" + n + "][" + v + "] <br>");
27.          }
28.          else {
29.          out.println("COOKIE[" + n + "][" + v + "] <br>");
30.          }
31.      }
32.      out.println("<hr><p>");
33.      out.println("<h2>Header--</h2>");
34.      out.println("Authentication Scheme: "+request.getAuthType()+"<br>");
35.      out.println("<p>");
36.      Enumeration names = request.getHeaderNames();
37.      while (names.hasMoreElements())
38.          {
39.          String header = (String) names.nextElement();
40.          out.println(header + ": " + request.getHeader(header) + "<br>");
41.          }
42.      out.close();
43.      }
44.  }
45.
```

On line 18, the cookies are read from the request because cookies are stored in the HTTP header. The cookies are saved into an array of cookies. Line 19 iterates over the array, getting each element at a time (line 21) and printing the getting the cookie name and its value (line 22, 23). All parameters found in the HTTP header are also printed (line 36 to 41).

Logging Cookie Information by Redirecting System.out: DumpCookLog

It is possible to redirect System.out.println() to print to a local file, to log in information from within the servlet to a local file. Such an implementation of System.out redirection is important particularly because an HTTP servlet is mostly used to read and write data while running within its container. The DumpCookLog servlet shown in Listing 16-6 shows such an example. This servlet is basically the same as the DumpCook servlet seen in the previous section except that it has an init() and destroy() method where the initialization and the closing of a print streamer have been dictated.

Listing 16-6   *The DumpCookLog servlet redirecting System.out to a file*

```
1.   import java.io.*;
2.   import java.util.*;
3.   import javax.servlet.*;
```

```
4.    import javax.servlet.http.*;
5.    import java.sql.Timestamp;
6.
7.    public class DumpCookLog extends HttpServlet
8.    {
9.        public static final String FILE = "/tmp/cooklog.txt";
10.       FileOutputStream outStr;
11.       PrintStream printStream;
12.
13.       public void init() throws ServletException
14.       {
15.           try
16.           {
17.               outStr = new FileOutputStream(FILE,true);
18.               printStream = new PrintStream(outStr);
19.               System.setOut(printStream);
20.               Timestamp now = new Timestamp( System.currentTimeMillis() );
21.               System.out.println(now.toString() + ": Shipping out
      characters");
22.           }
23.           catch (IOException e)
24.           {
25.               e.printStackTrace();
26.               // ...
27.           }
28.
29.       }
30.
31.       public void service(HttpServletRequest request, HttpServletResponse
      response)
32.       throws ServletException, IOException
33.       {
34.   ...
35.       }
36.
37.       public void destroy()
38.       {
39.           // super.destroy();
40.           try
41.           {
42.               outStr.close();
43.               printStream.close();
44.           }
45.           catch (IOException e)
46.           {
47.               e.printStackTrace();
48.               // ...
49.           }
50.       }
51.   }
```

The System.out stream is wrapped by a new stream so that it is redirected to another source.[3] On line 17, the file /tmp/cooklog.txt is created, and the append flag is set to true. To connect to the System.out stream, on line 18, a print stream is created. On line 19, System.out is redirected to printStream.

The DumpCookLog servlet shows you two important aspects when programming an HTTP servlet: the initialization of the redirection taking place in the init() method and the termination of the redirection taking place in the destroy() method. These methods are important; otherwise, if the creation and the closing of the print stream took place within the service() method, the logging of information in the /tmp/cooklog.txt file might be erratic because each thread (one per service() call) would be creating (in append mode) a connection and closing it. However, threads are concurrent, and they might be opening the print stream concurrently. There is no need to run a servlet as a single thread to cure this problem.

The System.out stream of the DumpCookLog servlet will print to the /tmp/cooklog.txt, as well as all the servlets in which System.out occurs and that have been defined within the same web container. For example, use the `tail` command with the -f option to print the tail of the /tmp/cooklog.txt file and invoke the DumpCookLog servlet to make sure that the init() method did all the creation (and open in append mode if the file previously exists).[4] Next, try to log in as teller1 while observing the content of the /tmp/cooklog.txt file.

As you can see in the following illustration, the record of teller1 has also been logged to the same file that is opened by the DumpCookLog servlet. This results from the statement aEmp.show(), which prints information about the aEmp object. (Refer to Chapter 10 for more details.) In the TellerLogged servlet, the first statement shown next instantiates and initializes the aEmp object; the second statement invokes the show() method, using System.out.println() to print the object content.

```
[root@node1 root]# tail -f /tmp/cooklog.txt
2002-05-02 09:58:15.726: Shipping out characters
COOKIE[JSESSIONID][0000OMAZ5L4TH4WEAQGKVN4WAOY:-1]
userID: teller1
password: null
frstName: Jane1
lastName: Doe1
image: ../images/teller1
ssn: 000000000
empno: 1
email: teller1@wasette.com
contact: somecontact
counter: 0
If session persistence is enabled then the following will write to the datastore
```

---

[3]   Perl supports tying a filehandle to a package to override I/O behavior of the filehandle; therefore, Perl users have a different approach to redirect the print stream output to an open file handle.

[4]   Remarkably, you should learn about file I/O flags in C, where you can demystify the meaning of these flags.

```
EmpAccnt aEmp = iDAO.getEmpAccnt();
aEmp.show();
```

Limitations and Naming Conventions of Cookies

Although generating cookies is not an issue, a browser can accept only a certain number of cookies from your HTTP server: 20 cookies per site, up to 300 in total. Each cookie can hold up to 4KB, or 4096 bytes. Cookie names cannot contain any of the following characters:

[ ] ( ) = , \ / " @ ? : ; SPACE

Session Management

A web server identifies a client browser by setting a session ID as a cookie in the MIME header when sending information to the browser. The application server dictates that the session ID to be passed is named JSESSIONID, according to the J2EE spec. To enable session management in WAS, you start the administrative console and make sure that Enable Cookies is checked (WebSphere Domain | Nodes | <node name> | Application Servers | Default Server | Web Container | Session Manager,) as shown in Figure 16-3.

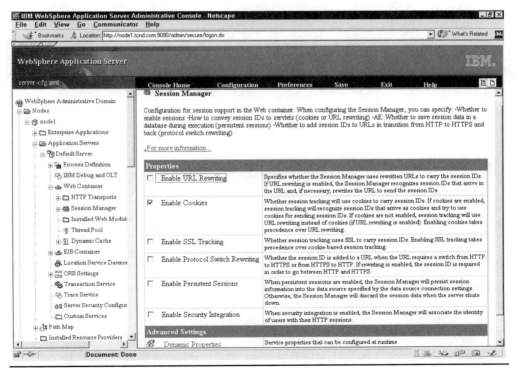

Figure 16-3   *Enabling cookie in the WAS AEs administrative console*

In addition, for the JSESSIONID cookie identifier, you need to set Maximum Age to −1 and Path to /, (WebSphere Domain | Nodes | *<node name>* | Application Servers | Default Server | Web Container | Session Manager | Default Cookie Settings,) as shown in Figure 16-4. Setting Maximum Age to −1 means that the session identified by the JSESSIONID cookie will be deleted when the client browser is exited.

The way a client browser operates on cookies is simple: first, during browsing, all cookies are cached in memory; when the client exits the browser, the cookies are written to a file; when the client starts the browser again, the cookies are checked for expiration, and if a −1 has been set, the cookies are deleted. If you use the `lynx` command with the options -dump or -post_data, Lynx is instantaneously started and then exited, which leads to the same effect as starting and exiting the browser.

This section discusses session management specific to WAS. It also explains how to use a WAS session from within CGI programs.

Identifying a Session with the JSESSIONID Cookie

The session identifier is preset to the JSESSIONID cookie. When a cookie is enabled, you will not need to refer to it using any of the cookie methods. WAS provides you with a set of methods that you can use to manage a user session without referring to JSESSIONID. On the

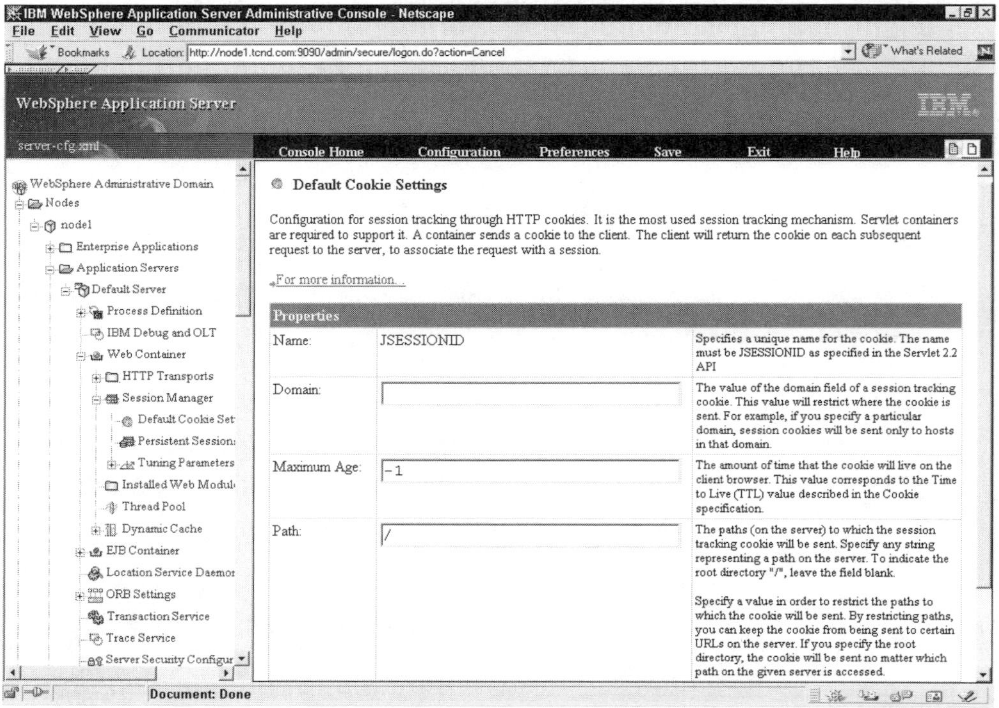

Figure 16-4   *Setting the JSESSIONID identifier parameters*

other hand, if you need to track a user session while using CGI script along with the application server, then you need to track the JSESSIONID cookie. The following section provides a simple example.

A Simple Session Servlet: Session

The Session servlet, shown in Listing 16-7, determines whether the user is in session or not. The user session is read from the request on line 21, then checked if it is true on line 22. The statements on both lines will create a session if the user is not in session. Otherwise, the servlet prints that the user is already in session.

Listing 16-7   *The Session servlet*

```
1.    import java.io.*;
2.    import java.util.*;
3.    import javax.servlet.*;
4.    import javax.servlet.http.*;
5.
6.    public class Session extends HttpServlet
7.    {
8.        public void doGet (HttpServletRequest req, HttpServletResponse res)
9.        throws ServletException, IOException
10.       {
11.
12.        String content1 = "<HTML><HEAD><TITLE> Testing Session
      </TITLE></HEAD>" +
13.            "<BODY><P><CENTER><H1> You were not in session
      </H1><HR><P></HTML>";
14.        String content2 = "<HTML><HEAD><TITLE> Testing Session
      </TITLE></HEAD>" +
15.            "<BODY><P><CENTER><H1> You are already in session
      </H1><HR><P></HTML>";
16.        PrintWriter out;
17.        res.setContentType("text/html");
18.        out = res.getWriter();
19.
20.        // create a new session
21.        HttpSession session = req.getSession(true);
22.        if (session.isNew())
23.            out.println(content1);
24.        }
25.        else
26.        {
27.            out.println(content2);
28.        }
29.    }
30. }
```

FlipSession

Invalidating a session means deleting the session identifier and freeing all associated objects bound to it. The FlipSession servlet shown in Listing 16-8 keeps on flipping the sessions by invalidating the previous session (if any) and then creating a new session each time the servlet is requested.

Listing 16-8 *The FlipSession servlet*

```
1.    import java.io.*;
2.    import java.util.*;
3.    import javax.servlet.*;
4.    import javax.servlet.http.*;
5.
6.    public class FlipSession extends HttpServlet
7.    {
8.
9.        public void doGet (HttpServletRequest req, HttpServletResponse res)
10.       throws ServletException, IOException
11.       {
12.           PrintWriter out;
13.           res.setContentType("text/html");
14.           out = res.getWriter();
15.
16.           // get current session object (creating one if not found)
17.           HttpSession session = req.getSession();
18.           if (session.isNew()) {
19.               out.println("You are not in session but I have just created
      one: " + session.getId() + "!");
20.           }
21.           else
22.           {
23.               out.println("You were in session (" + session.getId() + ")
      but I have just invalidated it!");
24.               session.invalidate();
25.           }
26.       }
27.   }
28.
```

Every time you request the FlipSession servlet, if a session is not found, then it is created (line 18) and a message is printed acknowledging the requester of it (line 19). Otherwise, the requester was in session, and his or her session is invalidated (line 24).

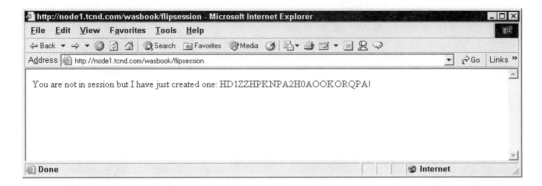

A typical output of four consecutive requests can be shown in the browser at four instances, as summarized next:

```
You are not in session but I have just created one: 5NT05N5LV4G45ZOHC5GTT3A!
You were in session (5NT05N5LV4G45ZOHC5GTT3A) but I have just invalidated it!
You are not in session but I have just created one: PCB5DDTBUI0BW5BAFHLYKUA!
You were in session (PCB5DDTBUI0BW5BAFHLYKUA) but I have just invalidated it!
and so on
```

As you can see, the first request created the session 5NT05N5LV4G45ZOHC5GTT3A, and the second request invalidated it, and so on.

Invalidating a Session

The ResetSession servlet shown in Listing 16-9 shows how a session can hold three objects, of which two are identical (the same memory reference).

Listing 16-9   *The ResetSession servlet*

```
1.    import java.io.*;
2.    import java.util.*;
3.    import javax.servlet.*;
4.    import javax.servlet.http.*;
5.
6.    public class ResetSession extends HttpServlet {
7.
8.        public void doGet (HttpServletRequest request, HttpServletResponse
      response)
9.            throws ServletException, IOException {
10.
11.        String content1 = "<HTML><HEAD><TITLE> Testing Session
      </TITLE></HEAD>" +
12.            "<BODY><P><CENTER><H1> First time in session
      </H1><HR><P></HTML>";
13.
14.        String content2 = "<HTML><HEAD><TITLE> Testing Session
      </TITLE></HEAD>" +
```

```
15.            "<BODY><P><CENTER><H1> I invalidated your session and created a
      new one.</H1><HR><P></HTML>";
16.
17.
18.        PrintWriter out;
19.        response.setContentType("text/html");
20.        out = response.getWriter();
21.
22.        // create a new session
23.        HttpSession session = request.getSession(true);
24.        // if session is new (user not in session) then create one
25.        if (session.isNew() == true) {
26.            out.println(content1);
27.        }
28.        else
29.        {
30.            // invalidate and create a new session with three (attr,obj)
      pairs
31.            session.invalidate();
32.            session = request.getSession();
33.            // session.setMaxInactiveInterval(5); // 5 seconds ! zapp it
34.            String s1 = "Bonjour monsieur!"; // a first string as an
      object
35.            String s2 = "Bonjour madame!"; // a second string as an
      object
36.            session.setAttribute("a1",s1); // a1-to-object s1
37.            session.setAttribute("a2",s2); // a2-to-object s2
38.            session.setAttribute("a3",s2); // a3-to-object s2
39.            out.println(content2);
40.        }
41.    }
42. }
43.
```

If the user is not in session, ResetSession creates a new session for the user without any attributes associated with it. Within the session time constraint, the second time the user requests ResetSession, servlet invalidates the session and creates a new one with three associated attributes a1, a2, and a3, shown on lines 36, 37, and 38 consecutively. The attributes a2 and a3 point to the same object s2.

To test with this servlet, request the URI /wasbook/resetsession relative to your web server; then follow it by a request to the URI /wasbook/dumpsession. Repeat the operation to see the difference in your browser. If you are using the browser Back button, remember to reload to see the most current session state.

Timing Out the Web Application Sessions

Sessions that have been defined in a web module can collectively be set to time out after a certain period of inactivity. The time out is a configurable value that is set in the deployment descriptor of the web application: web.xml. You set the time out in this file as follows:

```
<session-config id="SessionConfig_1">
        <session-timeout>1</session-timeout>
</session-config>
```

You do not need to edit the web.xml file to add these tagged descriptors, because web.xml is always generated when you run svlbuild. To add the time out of one minute, you edit the servlets.list (discussed in Chapter 11) and add the following line in it:

```
:SESSIONTIME 1
```

You run svlbuild again, and the change will take effect. In fact, svlbuild calls the genwebxml script to generate the web.xml file, adding the appropriate session-config descriptive segment in the file. This is much easier and quicker than editing manually or using the Application Assembly Tool. You may test with different time values, but we set it to one minute because it is quicker to test code within this time range. When :SESSIONTIME is not specified in servlets.list, the session-config descriptor is ignored.

Remember that at any time, you can look at the output generated by genwebxml by executing the script on the command line. Normally, you execute the script in the BASE_DEV directory where the servlets.list file is present; however, the script will attempt to locate a file by also looking for one in $BASE_DEV.

Printing Out the Session Data: DumpSession

A handy servlet to print the session identifier, the session objects, and other session statistics is essential to helping you understand session management and that dashboard mechanism mentioned in the introduction. The DumpSession servlet, shown in Listing 16-10, prints session information.

Listing 16-10   *The DumpSession servlet*

```
1.    import java.io.*;
2.    import java.util.*;
3.    import javax.servlet.*;
4.    import javax.servlet.http.*;
5.    import java.sql.Timestamp;
6.
7.    import com.tcnd.wasdg.common.*;
8.
9.    public class DumpSession extends HttpServlet
10.   {
11.       public void service(HttpServletRequest request, HttpServletResponse
      response)
12.       throws ServletException, IOException
13.       {
14.       HttpSession session = request.getSession();
15.       EmpAccnt aEmp = (EmpAccnt)session.getAttribute("teller");
16.
17.       ServletOutputStream out = response.getOutputStream();
```

```
18.        response.setContentType("text/html");
19.        out.println("<html><head><title>Dumping session
     object</title></head>");
20.        out.println("<body bgcolor=\"white\"><h1>Session object
     content</h1>");
21.        out.println("<h2>JSESSIONID = " +  session.getId() + "</h2>");
22.
23.        // Dump the EMPACCNT object if it is not null
24.        if (aEmp != null)
25.            {
26.            out.println("FRSTNAME: " + aEmp.getFrstName() + " <br>");
27.            out.println("LASTNAME: " + aEmp.getLastName() + " <br>");
28.            out.println("IMAGE: " + aEmp.getImage() + " <br>");
29.            out.println("SSN: " + aEmp.getSsn() + " <br>");
30.            out.println("EMPNO: " + aEmp.getEmpno() + " <br>");
31.            out.println("EMAIL: " + aEmp.getEmail() + " <br>");
32.            out.println("CONTACT: " + aEmp.getContact() + " <br>");
33.            out.println("COUNTER: " + aEmp.getCounter() + " <br><br>");
34.            aEmp.show(); // print it to STDOUT
35.            }
36.        else
37.            out.println("Object is null!<br>");
38.
39.        out.println("<hr><p>");
40.
41.        Enumeration list = session.getAttributeNames();
42.        while (list.hasMoreElements()) {
43.            String n = (String) list.nextElement();
44.            String v = session.getAttribute(n).toString();
45.            out.println(n + ": " + v + "<br>");
46.        }
47.        out.println("<hr><p>");
48.
49.        String sessinfo =
50.            "Created on: " + session.getCreationTime() + " or " + new
     Date(session.getCreationTime()) + "<br>" +
51.            "Last accessed on: " + session.getLastAccessedTime() + " or " +
     new Date(session.getLastAccessedTime()) + "<br>" +
52.            "Expire after: " + session.getMaxInactiveInterval() + " seconds "
     + "<br>" +
53.            "Session ID from cookie: " +
     request.isRequestedSessionIdFromCookie() + "<br>" +
54.            "Session ID from URL: " + request.isRequestedSessionIdFromURL() +
     "<br>" +
55.            "OK to request session ID: " +
     request.isRequestedSessionIdValid() + "<br>";
56.        out.println(sessinfo);
57.        out.println("<hr><p>");
58.
59.        int j;
```

```
60.        Cookie[] cookies = request.getCookies();
61.        for (j=0; j< cookies.length; j++) {
62.            // Fetch a cookie
63.            Cookie aCookie = cookies[j];
64.            String n = aCookie.getName();
65.                String v = aCookie.getValue();
66.            out.println("COOKIE[" + n + "][" + v + "] <br>");
67.        }
68.
69.        out.close();
70.        }
71.   }
```

To test the DumpSession servlet, log in as teller1 and click on dumpsession. Figure 16-5 shows the result of such a dump, in particular, the EmpAccnt object that the attribute teller pointed to (line 15). Wait a minute and click Reload, and you won't see the object anymore: when the object times out, you won't be able to refer to that object anymore. It is null (line 24).

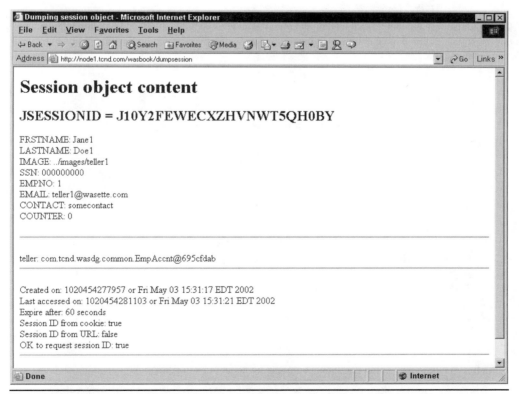

Figure 16-5   *DumpSession servlet showing the EmpAccnt object for a teller in session*

WAS Session Identifier Visibility to CGI Programs

Assuming that session management uses the JSESSIONID as a session identifier, you can design a general-purpose CGI script that can flow in the session, as shown in Listing 16-11:

Listing 16-11   *getjsessionid.cgi reads the JSESSIONID set by the application server*

```perl
1.    #!/usr/bin/perl
2.
3.    use CGI qw/:standard/;
4.
5.    my($cooknameI)="JSESSIONID";
6.
7.    my $out = &htmlheader()
8.    print $out;
9.    print "<html><head><title>Working with CGI cookie</title></head> <body
         bgcolor=\"white\"><P><center> <h2>Fetching cookie JSESSIONID</h2>";
10.   &query_jsessionid();
11.   print "<hr><p></html>";
12.
13.
14.   sub query_jsessionid {
15.       my $name = $cooknameI;
16.       my $key;
17.       my %cookie;
18.       if (cookie(-name => $name)) {
19.           print "Found cookie by this name:\n $name<br>\n\n";
20.           %cookie = cookie(-name => $name);
21.           foreach $key (keys %cookie) {
22.               print "$key";
23.           }
24.           return 1;
25.       }
26.       else {
27.           print "No cookie by this name:\n cookie Name:$name!<br>\n\n";
28.           return 0;
29.       }
30.   }
31.
32.   sub htmlheader () {
33.           return qq~Content-type: text/html
34.           Pragma: no-cache\n\n~;
35.   }
36.
```

The getjsessionid.cgi looks for the cookie named JSESSIONID and prints it value.

The CGI script cannot do that much to retrieve and manipulate session objects from the web container;[5] however, it is possible to keep on identifying the user session from within CGI programs. It might not be obvious why CGI programs should coexist in a WebSphere region (discussed in Chapter 5) unless you consider old legacy systems or special systems that are built based on CGI programs. The use of Simple Object Access Protocol (SOAP) may fill the gap of interchanging information with other CGI-based servers. However, there are obvious reasons to use Perl and Perl/CGI in a web site, especially when you consider programming tools that are heavily dependent on parsing regular expressions, such as search tools, data mining tools, or document transformation tools (from XML to HTML). The main corporate page for the vendor of WebSphere Application Server uses Perl CGI as a search tool as shown in Chapter 1.

SessionFairy

JSP was already discussed in Chapter 13. As you will recall, JSP fills in one of the gaps of Java-compiled language: online coding and text preprocessing for views and presentations. To contrast the need to have different means to perform preprocessing while coding web applications, this section walks you through the SessionFairy servlet.

The SessionFairy servlet does some preprocessing on its own using the Perl interpreter. Here is its functionality:

▶   Gathers information about the session identifier known to the browser.

▶   Gets the attribute name and classname to which it maps.

▶   Tries to locate the classname referred to previously and introspect it. Writes the information to a temporary file.

▶   Invokes the Perl i2jsp script to process the introspected information written to the temporary file and dynamically generates the SessionFairy.jsp file. Finally, you can request this .jsp file to gather information about the current session.

It is possible to perform all preprocessing internally inside the servlet itself instead of representing it to the Perl interpreter in this fashion. However, Java does not promote powerful

---

[5]   This is not necessarily true. A programmer can write routines that can extrapolate information from the web container; this is something we will explore in the next section.

string processing when carrying out such a task; although its library is rich, it is still too bulky as an object-oriented language to help with such a task.

Gathering Information from the Session Identifier

The SessionFairy servlet shown in Listing 16-12 proceeds by opening the file /tmp/ SessionFairy.tmp (line 11, 16 and 17) to write the information about the objects found in the browser session (line 21) and are pointed to by the session attributes (line 30.)

Listing 16-12   *The SessionFairy servlet*

```
1.    import java.io.*;
2.    import java.util.*;
3.    import javax.servlet.*;
4.    import javax.servlet.http.*;
5.    import java.lang.reflect.*;
6.
7.    import com.tcnd.wasdg.common.*;
8.
9.    public class SessionFairy extends HttpServlet
10.   {
11.       public static final String FILE = "/tmp/SessionFairy.tmp";
12.
13.       public void service(HttpServletRequest request, HttpServletResponse
      response)
14.       throws ServletException, IOException
15.       {
16.           FileOutputStream outStr = new FileOutputStream(FILE,false);
17.           PrintStream printStream = new PrintStream(outStr);
18.           System.setOut(printStream);
19.           System.out.println("# SessionFairy.tmp");
20.
21.           HttpSession session = request.getSession();
22.           EmpAccnt aEmp = (EmpAccnt)session.getAttribute("teller");
23.
24.           ServletOutputStream out = response.getOutputStream();
25.           response.setContentType("text/html");
26.           out.println("<html><head><title>Session Fairy --
      Introspect</title></head>");
27.           out.println("<body><h1>Session object content</h1>");
28.           out.println("<body><h2>SESSIONID = " + session.getId() +
      "</h2>");
29.
30.           Enumeration list = session.getAttributeNames();
31.           while (list.hasMoreElements())
32.           {
33.               // get the name of this listed element
34.               String n = (String) list.nextElement();
35.               // get the value of the attribute and convert it to a string
36.               String v = session.getAttribute(n).toString();
```

```
37.                 // trim the value to get only the class name
38.                 String c = StrTool.trimSessionString(v);
39.                 System.out.println("ATTRIBUTE: " + n );
40.                 System.out.println("CLASSNAME: " + c );
41.                 out.println(n + ": " + v + "    (" + c + ")" + "<br>");
42.                 try
43.                 {
44.                     Class sessProv = Class.forName(c);
45.                     Field field[] = sessProv.getDeclaredFields();
46.                     for (int i=0; i<field.length; i++)
47.                     {
48.                         out.println("Field " + i + " = " + field[i] +
        "<br>");
49.                         System.out.println("#Field: " + field[i]);
50.                     }
51.                     Constructor con[] = sessProv.getDeclaredConstructors();
52.                     for (int i=0; i<con.length; i++)
53.                     {
54.                         out.println("Constructor " + i + " = " + con[i]+
        "<br>");
55.                         System.out.println("#Constructor: " + field[i]);
56.                     }
57.                     Method m[] = sessProv.getDeclaredMethods();
58.                     for (int i=0; i<m.length; i++) {
59.                         out.println("Method " + i + " = " + m[i] + "<br>");
60.                         System.out.println("Method: " + m[i]);
61.                     }
62.                 }
63.                 catch (ClassNotFoundException e)
64.                 {
65.                     out.println("No magic today.. Cannot!");
66.                 }
67.             }
68.         out.println("<hr><p>");
69.
70.         String sessinfo =
71.             "Created on : " + session.getCreationTime() + "(" + new
        Date(session.getCreationTime()) + ")" + "<br>" +
72.             "Last access on: " + session.getLastAccessedTime() + "(" +
        new Date(session.getLastAccessedTime()) + ")" + "<br>" +
73.             "Expiration on: " + session.getMaxInactiveInterval() +
        "seconds" + "<br>" +
74.             "Session ID from cookie: " +
        request.isRequestedSessionIdFromCookie() + "<br>" +
75.             "Session ID from URL: " +
        request.isRequestedSessionIdFromURL() + "<br>" +
76.             "OK to request session ID: " +
        request.isRequestedSessionIdValid() + "<br>";
77.         out.println(sessinfo);
78.         out.println("<hr><p>");
79.         out.close();
80.
```

```
81.          Process p = Runtime.getRuntime().exec("/usr/local/bin/perl
      /BOOK/16/Code/Dist/i2jsp");
82.
83.     }
84. }
```

The SessionFairy gets the name of each object (line 34), converts it to a string (line 36), trims it to get the classname (line 38), then prepares it to introspect the classname (line 44). Because the introspection for the fields and constructors is not important, line 46 and 54 print a # at the beginning of each line for these introspected values. The introspected methods (line 57) are of importance, because they might have the getter and setter methods.

Figure 16-6 shows the result of invoking the SessionFairy servlet.

Generating the SessionFairy.jsp

The Perl script i2jsp, shown in Listing 16-13, reads in the introspected data written to the /tmp/SessionFairy.tmp file and generates the SessionFairy.jsp file to be deposited in the current web application. Most Perl regular expressions are similar to those found in the metacharacters used in UNIX programs (sed, awk, grep, egrep, vi, ed, and so on), and computer science readers should be familiar with them.

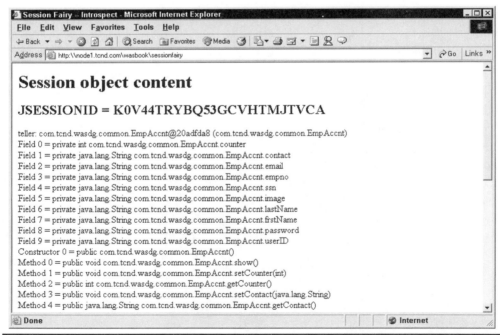

Figure 16-6   *The SessionFairy servlet request returns the result of introspection on the class pointed to by the session.*

On lines 8 and 9 in Listing 16-13, @page has been escaped so that Perl does not interpret it as being a list. Notice the similarity between JSP and Perl. The JSP page is defined as an encore string from lines 5 to 34, which is preprocessed by substituting all these strings that are identified anywhere a ziff_ appears.

Listing 16-13   *The i2jsp Perl script generates the SessionFairy.jsp file*

```
1.    #!/usr/bin/perl
2.
3.    use strict;
4.
5.    my $jsp = <<JSPTEMPLATE;
6.    <!--SessionFairy.jsp-->
7.    <!--You have to escape these @'s in Perl. -->
8.    <%\@page import = "java.util.*"%>
9.    <%\@page import = "<!--ziff_CLASSNAME-->"%>
10.   <html> <head><title>JSP generated by the SessionFairy</title></head>
11.      <body bgcolor="white">
12.      <%
13.         String objname = "<!--ziff_CLASSNAME-->";
14.         String attribute = "<!--ziff_ATTRIBUTE-->";
15.       <!--ziff_CLASSNAME-->  <!--ziff_DUMMYOBJECT--> =
      (<!--ziff_CLASSNAME-->)session.getAttribute(attribute);
16.         String heading = null;
17.         if (anObject == null) {
18.            heading = "Strange, I thought I can do magic!";
19.         } else {
20.            heading = "... et voila!";
21.         out.println("This attribute name: " + attribute + " <br>");
22.         out.println("This object name: " + objname + " <br><br>");
23.         <!--ziff_GETTERMETHODS-->
24.         }
25.      %>
26.
27.      <h1> <%=heading%> </h1>
28.      <p>
29.      <hr>
30.      Session ID: <%=session.getId()%><br>
31.      Time created: <%=new Date(session.getCreationTime())%><br>
32.      Last time accessed: <%=new Date(session.getLastAccessedTime())%><br>
33.      </body> </html>
34.   JSPTEMPLATE
35.
36.   my($a,$c,@m); #attribute, classname, methods
37.   my($i)=0;
38.
39.   open(FILE,"</tmp/SessionFairy.tmp");
40.   while(<FILE>) {
41.       # print ">> $p\n";
```

```
42.       if (/^ATTRIBUTE:/i) {
43.           s/^ATTRIBUTE:\s+//; s/\s+$//;
44.           $a = $_;
45.       }
46.       if (/^CLASSNAME:/i) {
47.           s/^CLASSNAME:\s+//; s/\s+$//;
48.           $c = $_;
49.       }
50.       if (/^METHOD:/i) {
51.           s/^METHOD:\s+//i; s/\s+$//;
52.           s/(.)*$c\.//;
53.           if (/^get/) {
54.               $m[$i]=$_;
55.               $i++;
56.           }
57.       }
58.   }
59.   close(FILE);
60.
61.   $jsp =~ s/<!--ziff_ATTRIBUTE-->/$a/g;
62.   $jsp =~ s/<!--ziff_CLASSNAME-->/$c/g;
63.
64.   my($getters)="";
65.   my($o)="anObject";
66.   $jsp =~ s/<!--ziff_DUMMYOBJECT-->/$o/g;
67.
68.   foreach(@m) {
69.       my $n = $_;
70.       $n =~ s/^get//; $n =~ s/\(\)(.)*$//;
71.       $getters .= "out.println(\"$n: \" + $o.$_ + \" <br>\");";
72.   }
73.   $jsp =~ s/<!--ziff_GETTERMETHODS-->/$getters/g;
74.
75.   open(OUT,">$ENV{INSTALLEDAPPS}/wasdg.ear/webapp/SessionFairy.jsp");
76.   print OUT $jsp;
77.   close(OUT);
```

Line 52 filters out the method name by deleting anything preceding it up to the class name. Obviously, the class name is the object itself. Line 53 determines if the method is a data access method that starts with a get, and then it adds it to its list of accessors. The list is then used on line 68 to form a string of getters that will print the object attribute (line 71).

i2jsp generated the SessionFairy.jsp file shown in Listing 16-14. This file is generated every time you put a request to the SessionFairy servlet. You can locate it in the directory $INSTALLEDAPPS/ wasdg.ear/webapp. You will normally place a request to this .jsp file, as in the following:

```
http://node1.tcnd.com/wasbook/SessionFairy.jsp
```

Figure 16-7 shows how the SessionFairy.jsp file prints the object attributes pointed to by the session identifier. The object scope is retrieved from the same web container as the one in

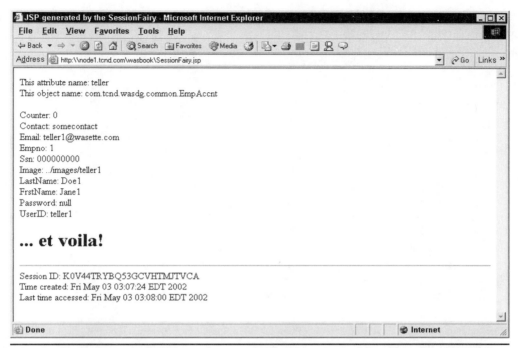

Figure 16-7   *Requesting that the SessionFairy.jsp print the content of the object pointed to by the session identifier*

which the SessionFairy servlet is running. One more point to note: you need to be quick and issue both requests to the SessionFairy servlet and the SessionFairy.jsp file within one minute—the time constraint to expire an inactive session as set in the earlier section, "Timing Out the Web Application Sessions."

The generating of the SessionFairy.jsp, Listing 16-14, is a consequence of requesting and hence executing the SessionFairy servlet. The JSP file can then be requested to get each attribute from the object being introspected.

Listing 16-14   *The generated file SessionFairy.jsp*

```
<!--SessionFairy.jsp-->
<%@page import = "java.util.*"%>
<%@page import = "com.tcnd.wasdg.common.EmpAccnt"%>
<html> <head><title>JSP generated by the SessionFairy</title></head>
  <body bgcolor="white">
  <%
    String objname = "com.tcnd.wasdg.common.EmpAccnt";
    String attribute = "teller";
```

```
    com.tcnd.wasdg.common.EmpAccnt  anObject =
       (com.tcnd.wasdg.common.EmpAccnt)session.getAttribute(attribute);
   String heading = null;
   if (anObject == null) {
     heading = "Strange, I thought I can do magic!";
   } else {
     heading = "... et voila!";
   out.println("This attribute name: " + attribute + " <br>");
   out.println("This object name: " + objname + " <br><br>");
   out.println("Counter: " + anObject.getCounter() + " <br>");
   out.println("Contact: " + anObject.getContact() + " <br>");
   out.println("Email: " + anObject.getEmail() + " <br>");
   out.println("Empno: " + anObject.getEmpno() + " <br>");
   out.println("Ssn: " + anObject.getSsn() + " <br>");
   out.println("Image: " + anObject.getImage() + " <br>");
   out.println("LastName: " + anObject.getLastName() + " <br>");
   out.println("FrstName: " + anObject.getFrstName() + " <br>");
   out.println("Password: " + anObject.getPassword() + " <br>");
   out.println("UserID: " + anObject.getUserID() + " <br>");
   }
%>

<h1> <%=heading%> </h1>
<p>
<hr>
Session ID: <%=session.getId()%><br>
Time created: <%=new Date(session.getCreationTime())%><br>
Last time accessed: <%=new Date(session.getLastAccessedTime())%><br>
</body> </html>
```

This SessionFairy is an example that shows you how preprocessing on strings can be carried in programming. In this specific example, we started with a servlet then generated a JSP file, which is going to be turned into a servlet once the JSP file is requested.

URL Rewriting and Hidden Parameters

For the session manager to operate properly, the JSESSIONID must be held consistently in the browser when a user is navigating from one page to another. So far, to hold the session ID, we have been relying on the cookie. However, recall from Figure 16-3 that the session manager also supports URL rewriting for those users who disabled the cookie in their browser. This section discusses two techniques to show you how JSESSIONID can be held in the browsers of cookie-cautious individuals.

URL Rewriting

You disable cookies and enable URL rewriting by editing the server-cfg.xml configuration file of WAS AEs. Do not use the administrative console, because it is web-based and will not function property when carrying out this step; this is partly because the administrative application shares the same cookie setting as the rest of the applications. To disable the cookie, in the server-cfg.xml file, locate the line where the sessionManager word is specified, reverse the flag of enableCookies from true to false, and reverse the flag of enableUrlRewriting from false to true.

```
<sessionManager xmi:id="SessionManager_1" enable="false"
    enableUrlRewriting="true" enableCookies="false"
    enableSSLTracking="false" enableProtocolSwitchRewriting="false"
    enablePersistentSessions="false"
enableSecurityIntegration="false">
```

Similarly, you can use the subs script to make this change easily:

```
# subs $WASCFG enableUrlRewriting=\"true\" enableUrlRewriting=\"false\"

# subs $WASCFG enableCookies=\"false\" enableCookies=\"true\"
```

The subs script, shown in Listing 16-15, is a simple script that substitutes a source string by replacing it by a target string. The script takes three arguments and uses the /tmp directory for temporary storage:

```
subs  filename  source-string  replace-with-string
```

You will place the subs script in the /tools directory so that it can be made available in the environment path.

Listing 16-15   *The subs script to replace the source string with a target string*

```
#!/usr/bin/ksh
sed -e "s/$2/$3/g" $1  > /tmp/subs.t.$$
mv $1 /tmp/subs.$$
mv /tmp/subs.t.$$  $1
```

Restart WAS:

```
# $STOPWAS; $STARTWAS
```

Now you should be able to test with URL rewriting. First, you need to compile the code for this chapter using svlbuild. From a browser, log in as teller1 with password secret1. Then in the next page presented to you in the browser, click the selection to test URL rewrite.

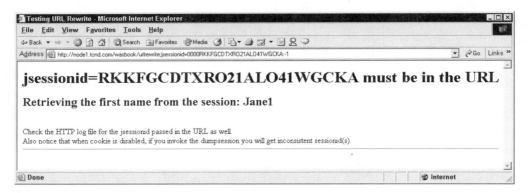

Notice that the jsessionid is passed in the URL itself. To confirm this, in the HTTP log file, an entry showing the jsessionid is also written:

```
66.51.9.149 - - [01/May/2002:01:45:48 -0400] "GET
      /wasbook/urlrewrite;jsessionid=0000RKKFGCDTXRO21ALO41WGCKA:-1
HTTP/1.1"
      200 418 "http://node1.tcnd.com/wasbook/tellerlogged"
"Mozilla/4.0
      (compatible; MSIE 6.0; Windows 98; Win 9x 4.90)"
```

Now log in again, but this time, rather than clicking on URL rewrite, click Dumpsession. You will realize that the data of the teller cannot be retrieved from the object held in the web container because the servlet does not have a valid reference saved in the JSESSIONID. Unlike the UrlRewrite servlet, the DumpSession servlet is cookie-based.

Before looking at the code, consider the following illustration summarizing the flow of the request:

The LoginScreen servlet posts the userid and password of the teller to the TellerLogged servlet. The latter creates a session and prepares a reference to point to it. However, cookies are not enabled, and UrlRewrite is the only servlet that will be able to gather the JSESSIONID. When URL Rewrite is enabled, the encodeURL() method must be used and referred to with an HREF. The TellerLogged servlet does this by using string substitution, as shown in the following code fragments:

```
"<font face=\"arial,helvetica,geneva,sans-serif\" size=\"+2\" >Click here to
      test <a href=\"ziff_URLREWRITE\">URL rewrite." +
```

```
content = StrTool.replaceUnsensitive( content, "ziff_URLREWRITE",
    response.encodeURL("/wasbook/urlrewrite") );
```

By following the HREF from the page just mentioned, the UrlRewrite servlet is invoked. This servlet has nothing special (refer to the code distribution for this chapter). The URL rewriting code is simply done by the TellerLogged servlet.

You may still be able to get the JSESSIONID from the cookie or by invoking the HttpSession getId() method, but such methods must not be used as the result is totally inconsistent, as shown in Figure 16-8.

Form Hidden Fields

Like any other field, the JSESSIONID can also be held as an input element in an HTML form. Hidden fields fall between <form> ... </form> of an HTML page, and are tagged, as in <input type=hidden name=*some-name* value=*some-value*>. For example, in the EditTeller servlet, the following statement makes a replacement in the form editteller to hide the JSESSIONID in the form:

```
content = StrTool.replaceUnsensitive(content,
"<!--HIDDEN_INPUT_IN_HERE-->",
"<input type=\"hidden\" name=\"JSESSIONID\" value=\""
    + session.getId() +"\">");
```

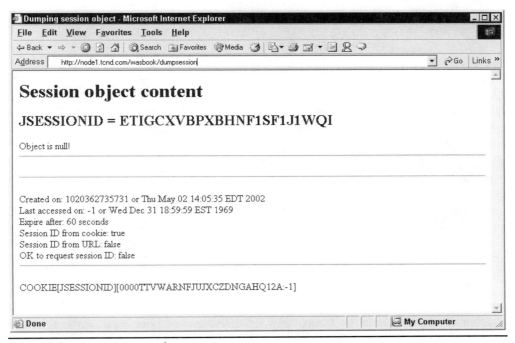

Figure 16-8   *Inconsistent result*

To view the net effect of such a substitution, log in as teller1 and then select the editteller profile. This will put you in the Teller Profile screen shown in Figure 16-9.

View the source of the page and locate the <form> tag. You should see the hidden field with the value of the session ID.

```
<content><form action="/wasbook/updateprofile">
<input type="hidden" name="JSESSIONID"
value="USPFIXCORJ2UCG0B01G2RDQ">
```

The hidden field will be reflected in the CGI parameters when /wasbook/updateprofile is invoked, and it can be retrieved from this request: request.getParameter("JSESSIONID").

In this chapter, the application does not support hidden fields for session IDs. The example shown here is used to illustrate how to hide the session ID as a form field parameter. Hidden fields cannot be passed in static pages where no <form></form> tags are defined. In this situation, the programmer has to pass the session ID as a parameter in the URL.

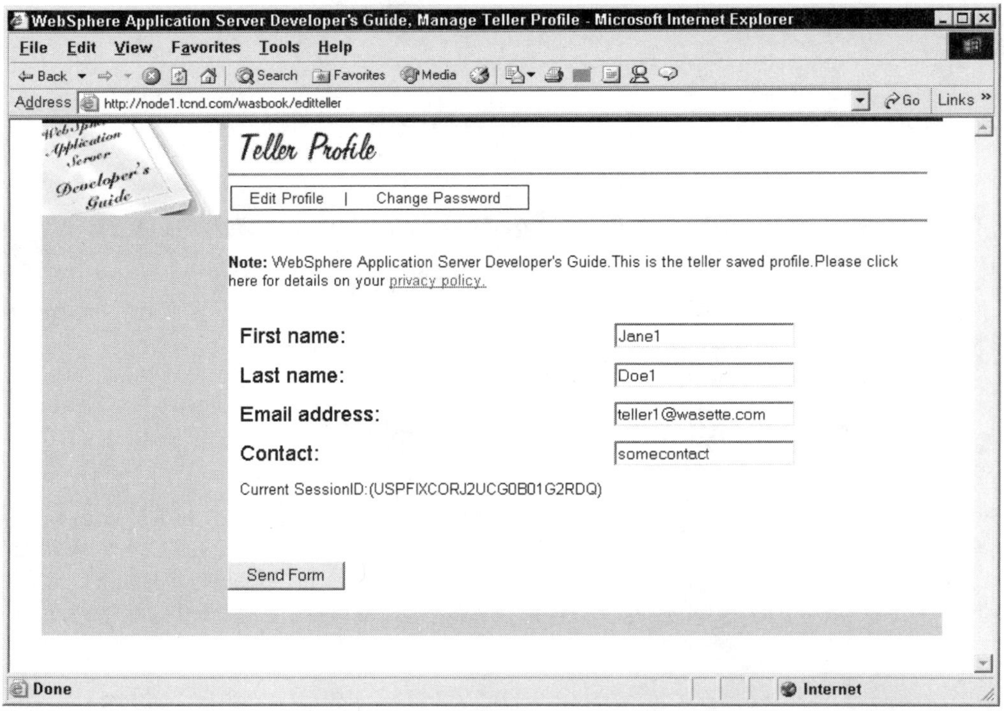

Figure 16-9   *Teller Profile screen*

Wrapping Up

This chapter discussed the important aspects of the HTTP protocol when communicating state information between the web server and the browser. It also clarified the difference between cookie functionality and session management. The former is just a CGI variable that can hold a value that can be used as an identifier, and it is set in the MIME header as dictated by the HTTP protocol. The latter is a set of routines that are managed by the application server web container to hold particular objects for a certain time.

The combination of the session ID, the time variables held in the web container, and some time-sensitive processing routines give the feeling of session continuity.

While a browser can set more than one cookie at a time, and therefore more than one session ID at a time (coming from different web containers), there is a one-to-one relationship between the browser and the session ID set by a web container. In other words, the scope of the session is held solely within one web container. Chapter 17 discusses in more detail the scope of a session.

This chapter also discussed how CGI scripts can coexist with an application server while maintaining the session flow.

Introspection has been used in the SessionFairy servlet, and Perl is invoked to generate the SessionFairy.jsp file to disclose and read from the session object the data held within the session scope.

The chapter concluded with an alternative to maintain the JSESSIONID when cookies are disabled: URL rewriting and HTML form hidden fields.

Session Scope and IBM Session Persistence

IN THIS CHAPTER:

Think of a session as a reference to an object address (in memory) with two properties. First, while an object address names an object location in the local Java machine[1], a session is an application server domainwide address that uniquely names an object. Thus, any object can be named by a session through its attributes. Second, the session reference falls within the scope of a single Java machine and cannot be referenced from another Java machine.

Session management in WAS is quite simple: a session reference is synonymous with a Java object. WAS session management, therefore, can address as many sessions as objects can fit into memory. However, a client browser can have only one session defined from a web container.

IBM WebSphere Application Server defines two types of sessions which, in WAS terminology, are known as an in-memory session and a persistent session. This chapter discusses session scope and IBM session persistence in detail.

Examining Session Scope and Affinity

As it is referred to in this chapter, session may have two different meanings. In fact, there are two different views you can take while reading about a session and session management. A *session* is just an identifier that is held as a cookie in the client browser. *Session management* refers to the (application server) management of the Java objects that are pointed to by the identifier. To refer to a cookie identifying a session, the term *session identifier* is used; otherwise, session refers to the containment of the session and the objects to which it refers.

The following sections clarify two important topics in IBM session management that you need to be aware of: scope of a session and session affinity.

Understanding Session Scope

Session management takes place within the web container of an application server. This can be seen in the hierarchy tree of the administrative server of WAS AEs: WAS Domain | Nodes | *node name* | Application Servers | Default Server | Web Container | Session Manager.

---

[1] Because the local Java machine is running the web container, this is equivalent to saying that an object address names an object located in the web container.

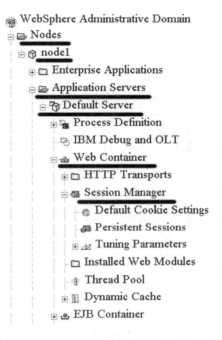

As a result, the scope of a session is defined within the same web container of the web application (that is, the Java machine that is running the wasdg.ear/webapp) where the session has been initialized. This means that the objects that have been added to a session by a servlet or JSP code can be visible only to programs that are running in the same web container of the web application. In other words, the HttpSession objects are scoped within the same web application containment (and fall within this web application context), and they cannot be shared between web application contexts. This is enforced in WAS v4 due to its support of the Servlet 2.2 spec.

To clarify this point, consider the TellerLogged servlet from Chapter 16. Locate the statement that set the first name of the teller to XYZ and uncomment it; then run svlbuild for the change to take effect.

```
session.setAttribute("teller",aEmp);
aEmp.setFrstName("XYZ");
```

Notice that the second statement comes after the session statement that maps the attribute to the object aEmp, and commit the change in memory or persistently. Actually, whether the aEmp.setFrstName() statement falls before or after the setAttribute() statement, the change to the first name will still take effect in the object itself. Any servlet that is running in the same web container of WAS must be able to see the change. For example, within the time constraint of the session (the default is 30 minutes), click Edit Profile to request the EditTeller servlet. Figure 17-1 shows that the first name of employee XYZ has been retained in the object and is visible to a different servlet that is contained in the same web application.

You can go back and reload the TellerLogged servlet from the previous posted value, or you can request the DumpSession servlet, and you can still see that XYZ has been retained in the object and is visible from within all these servlets managed within the same web container.

Understanding Session Affinity

Using WAS Advanced Edition, a WebSphere domain can span several application servers in the same bailiwick A web application is contained only in one of these application servers; therefore, a session is managed solely in one of these application servers. In other words, once a client browser logs in, the session must be managed by the same server and by the

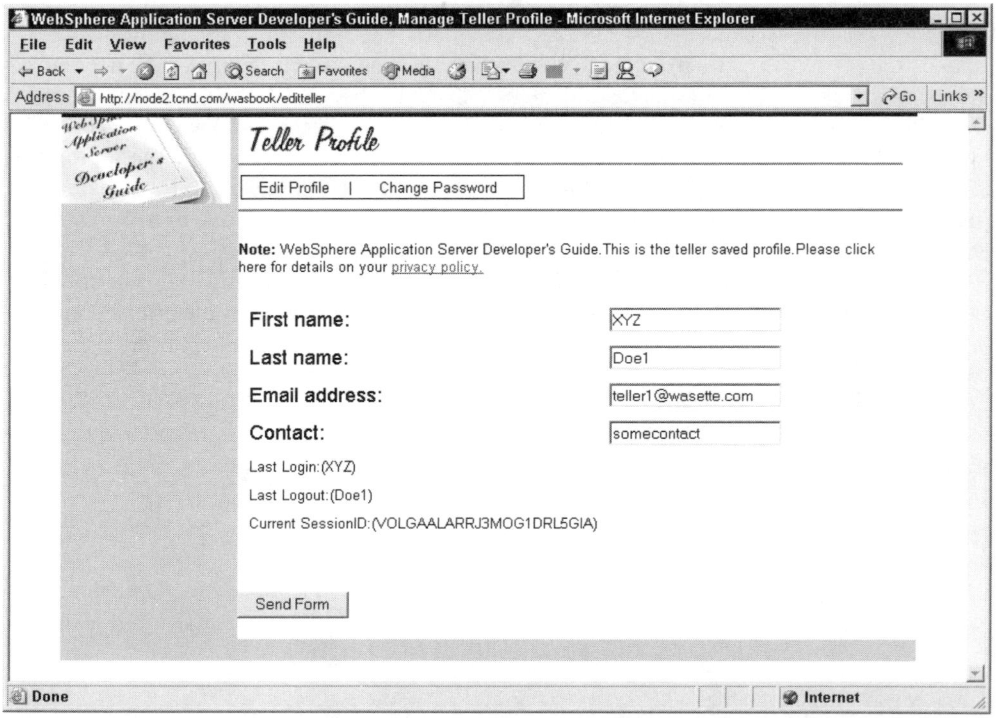

Figure 17-1   *Setting the first name of the teller to XYZ falls within the scope of the session object*

same web container (Java machine) that first assigned that client to the session ID. This is called *session affinity*.

The session affinity mechanism is purely another mapping that is maintained within a cluster of application servers. The common SESSIONS table allows a new server to pick up the objects from the database and assign the client browser to a new server. If you are using WAS AE, you can request the MIME header to look up the value of the JSESSIONID. The following example posts a request to the TellerLogged servlet:

```
echo "userid=teller1&password=secret1&---" | lynx -accept_all_cookies
    -post_data -mime_header
    http://node2.tcnd.com/wasbook/tellerlogged |
    grep Set-Cookie
Set-Cookie: JSESSIONID=00015GC20EX0GCBSCDIKK5ZV4QQ:t(&tre;Path=/
```

The value shown reflects a cache ID (the first four digits), and the server ID reads from the plugin-cfg.xml[2] (whatever follows the colon and precedes the semicolon). By maintaining such information in the MIME header, WAS session affinity can be effectively managed through its server group and workload management. This is to ensure a failover solution and smooth continuity of operation on business machines.

Session affinity dictates that when a client is in a session, all his or her session requests will be sent to the same Java machine, and therefore, to the same web application. This is required by the Servlet 2.2 spec. In a clustered environment, WAS v4, through its web server plug-in, provides session affinity in a server group.

Examining Session Persistence: Setup, Configuration, and Testing

This section shows you how to set up session persistence in WAS AEs. First, a program that looks up JNDI (Jana Naming and Directory Interface) names is introduced so that you can ensure that a defined DataSource has been properly configured in WAS. You will also learn how to test the session persistence configuration after a first run of WAS (where session persistence has been enabled).

Setting Up and Configuring a Session

The setup requires you to create a database so that it can be accessed by WAS. Then configure JNDI naming in the administrative console and make sure that WAS can properly resolve it.

Session persistence is enabled manually because the WAS AEs administrative console cannot ensure a proper administrative operation through its web console while session persistence is enabled.

---

[2] WAS AEs is a stand-alone server; therefore, there is no session affinity with such a product. The server ID shows as –1 for this product.

Exploring a Roadmap of Setup and Configuration

The following steps walk you through the details of setup and configuration:

1. Locate your JDBC driver to be used by WAS' session persistence components. These drivers must be loaded in the WAS startup environment. When using UDB, all drivers and libraries located in /usr/IBMdb2/V7.1/java12 and /usr/IBMdb2/V7.1/lib must be loaded.

2. If you want the SESSION database to be defined on a remote server, install the UDB client components on each machine where an application server is running. WAS v4 requires this because the connection manager uses the type 2 database driver. You also need to catalog the database on the node on which the application server is running. Chapter 2 discusses the type 2 database driver; Chapter 4 discusses cataloging a database.

3. Log into the administrative console and create the JDBC provider, as seen in Figure 17-2: WebSphere Domain | Resources | JDBC Drivers | Db2JdbcDriver. If you are using UDB, use the db2java.zip located in the /usr/IBMdb2/V7.1/java12 directory. Save the changes just made by selecting File | Save.

4. Also in the administrative console, create the data source pointing to the SESSION database created in step 2. Usually, WAS AEs comes preconfigured with this setting, but you need to set up the username and password that is authorized to create and

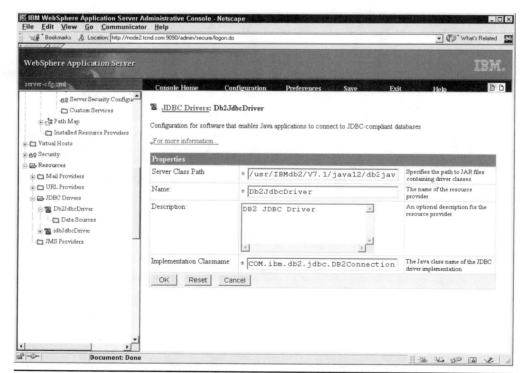

Figure 17-2 *Configuring the JDBC provider*

access the SESSION database. Select the Session Persistence Datasource from the administrative console, as shown in Figure 17-3: WebSphere Domain | Resources | JDBC Drivers | Db2JdbcDriver | Data Sources . On the same menu the section headed Connection Pool Settings does not need to be modified, and is not important for our example. Save the changes by selecting File | Save. Restart WAS: # `$STOPWAS;` `$STARTWAS`

	Name	JNDI Name	Description	Category
□	Session Persistence datasource	jdbc/Session	Data source for session persistence	Samples

5. Make sure you can look up the JNDI name of the data source. Use the WasJndi program (see Listing 17-1) to verify whether you can look up the data source name. This step is summarized in the section "Looking Up JNDI Names" later.

6. In the administrative console, configure the session manager database authorization as shown in Figure 17-4. Do not check the persistence yet because this must be done manually and not through the administrative console. Save your configuration and exit the console.

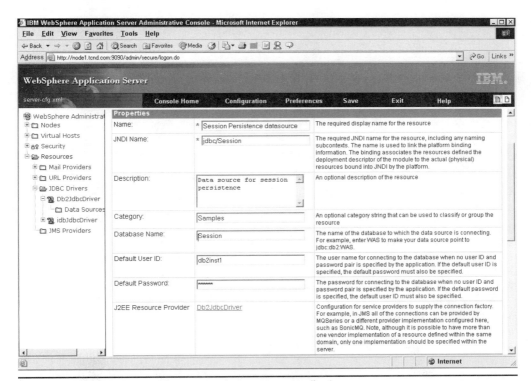

Figure 17-3   *Configuring the setting to the DataSource jdbc/Session*

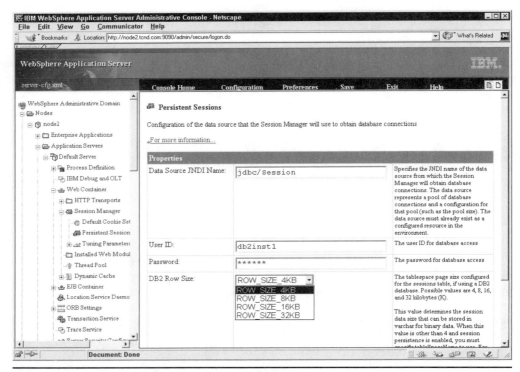

Figure 17-4   *Session manager DataSource configuration*

7. Stop WAS ($STOPWAS) and edit the server-cfg.xml file to enable session persistence. You do this by locating the enablePersistentSessions identifier and setting its flag to true:

```
<sessionManager xmi:id="SessionManager_1"
enableUrlRewriting="false" enableCookies="true"
enableSSLTracking="false" enableProtocolSwitchRewriting="false"
enablePersistentSessions="false"
enableSecurityIntegration="false">
```

8. Start the application server: $STARTWAS. Request the login servlet, and before logging in with a teller account, query the SESSIONS table in the SESSION database and inspect the first record created. The section "Testing Session Persistence" (later in this chapter) discusses how to query the SESSIONS table.

Looking Up JNDI Names

After configuring a resource and binding a name to it in the administrative console, you need to verify whether the resource can be looked at programmatically. This step will save you a lot of time, because it ensures that no configuration issues exist with your JNDI naming. To perform this task, you will edit and save the program shown in Listing 17-1. The JNDI API is an implementation-independent library for directory and naming systems. WAS includes a JNDI service provider so that different service providers can connect to different directory services.

Listing 17-1   *WasJndi to look up WAS' JNDI names*

```
import javax.naming.Context;
import javax.naming.InitialContext;
import javax.naming.Binding;
import javax.naming.NamingEnumeration;
import javax.naming.NamingException;
import java.util.Hashtable;

public
class WasJndi
{
    public static void main(String [] args)
    {
        try
        {
            // Read the first argument if specified, otherwise
            // set the URL to our localhost:900 as a default
            String providerURL;
            if (args.length == 0)
            {
                providerURL = "iiop://localhost:900";
            }
            else
            {
                providerURL = args[0];
            }

            // Create the initial context.
            Hashtable hs = new Hashtable();
            hs.put( Context.INITIAL_CONTEXT_FACTORY,
"com.ibm.websphere.naming.WsnInitialContextFactory");
            hs.put( Context.PROVIDER_URL, providerURL);
            Context context = new InitialContext(hs);
            // If no name is specified on the command line starting
            // as a second parameter than list, then list all
            // of the names in the specified context and the object
            // they are bound to.
            if (args.length <= 1)
            {
                NamingEnumeration listNames = context.listBindings("");
                while (listNames.hasMore())
                {
                    Binding binding = (Binding)listNames.next();
                    System.out.println( binding.getName() + " " +
binding.getObject());
```

```
                   }
              }
              // One or more names have been specified after the
              // URL on the command prompt. List each name and its binding
              else
              {
                   for (int i = 1; i < args.length; i++)
                   {
                        Object object = context.lookup(args[i]);
                        System.out.println( args[i] + " " + object);
                   }
              }
              context.close();
         } catch (NamingException namingexception)
         {
              namingexception.printStackTrace();
         }
    }
}
```

To obtain the JNDI context, you need to specify the WAS initial context factory:
`com.ibm.websphere.naming.WsnInitialContextFactory`. When WasJndi
is invoked without any argument, it looks up the localhost iiop://localhost:900 for all names.
When it is invoked with one argument, this will be read as the host from which to read the
name. You can specify the name(s) to look up by typing them after the hostname. For instance,
to look up the jdbc/Session name and find out whether it has been properly configured in the
administrative console, you run this command:

`# java WasJndi iiop://was.host.name:900   jdbc/Session`

This command returns to the standard output:

```
1.    jdbc/Session WebSphere DataSource:CMProperties for DataSource "Session
      Persistence datasource"
2.     DataSource Properties [COM.ibm.db2.jdbc.DB2ConnectionPoolDataSource]:
      {user=db2inst1;password=XXXXXXX;description=Data source for session
      persistence;databaseName=Session;}
3.     Connection Pool Properties:
4.        minConnectionPoolSize        = 1
5.        maxConnectionPoolSize        = 30
6.        connTimeout                  = 180
7.        idleTimeout                  = 1800
8.        orphanTimeout                = 1800
9.        maxStatementCacheSize        = 3
10.       autoConnectionCleanupDisabled= false
11.       errorMap                     = null
12.       informixLockModeWait         = 0
13.       oracleStmtCacheSize          = 0
```

Such an output guarantees that your JNDI lookup name is working fine. Notice also the output of the jdbc/Session—it reflects the configuration data that you entered in the administrative console in the previous setup. The Connection Pool Properties is also printed showing the default settings.

On WAS AEs, the output conforms to the description of the data source session persistence defined in the server configuration file grep jndiName ($WASCFG) shown here:

```
<factories xmi:type="resources:DataSource" xmi:id="DataSource_1"
name="Session Persistence datasource" jndiName="jdbc/Session"
description="Data source for session persistence"
defaultUser="db2inst1" defaultPassword="{xor}Lyg7b29o"
...>
```

Using WAS Components in Persisting a Session

WAS persists a session by storing it to a database. Within WAS, several components[3] work together to carry out the task of such storage. The following components operate when session persistence is enabled:

- ▶ WebSphere Server Runtime (WSRV)
- ▶ Servlet Engine (SRVE)
- ▶ Connection Manager (CONM)
- ▶ Cache Management (DYNA)
- ▶ Session and User Profiles (SESN)
- ▶ WebSphere Transactions (WTRN)

You will better understand WAS components and how to monitor them after reading Chapter 24.

Testing Session Persistence

Sessions are held persistently in the SESSION database. The table SESSIONS is created the first time you run WAS in which session persistence has been enabled. We will examine the SESSIONS table that is created, after enabling session persistence, and during the first run of WAS. The program qry_session is also presented as a handy program to query the SESSIONS table.

Performing the First Run of Session Persistence

Once you stop and restart WAS AEs, the application server will effectively go through its first run to create the database table (and only one table) for session persistence: the SESSIONS

---

[3]   WAS has as many as 40 components. For their classification, refer to Chapter 24.

table. Usually, this is done after you put in a first request to a servlet, for example, requesting the LoginScreen servlet: http://was.server.name/wasbook/login. To see the table created, just log in as the UDB instance user who has been granted access to the database, connect, and list the tables:

```
# db2 connect to SESSION
# db2 describe table SESSIONS show detail
```

Table 17-1 summarizes each field in the database. The last three fields, SMALL, MEDIUM, and LARGE, reveal how a session object is persisted. The data types of these fields suggest the following: any HttpSession object must be serialized to be persisted, and it must be converted to a stream of bytes so that it can be persisted. The ID holds the value of the JSESSIONID of the client browser. These fields will become clearer after you read the section "Using a Teller Login Scenario to Test Session Persistence" later in this chapter.

Querying the SESSIONS Table

For a new programmer, development might be hard without knowing what is happening in the background while the WAS web container is managing the persistent session. You can query the database using the db2 command, but with such lengthy output, this method of debugging might not be preferable.

The program qry_session, shown in Listing 17-2, can assist you to dump the SESSIONS table in a formatted way while debugging your code.

Column Name	Typename	Length	Scale	Nulls
ID	VARCHAR	128	0	No
PROPID	VARCHAR	128	0	No
APPNAME	VARCHAR	128	0	Yes
LISTENERCNT	SMALLINT	2	0	Yes
LASTACCESS	BIGINT	8	0	Yes
CREATIONTIME	BIGINT	8	0	Yes
MAXINACTIVETIME	INTEGER	4	0	Yes
USERNAME	VARCHAR	256	0	Yes
SMALL	VARCHAR	3122	0	Yes
MEDIUM	LONG VARCHAR	32700	0	Yes
LARGE	BLOB	2097152	0	Yes

Table 17-1   *The SESSIONS Table and Its Fields as Defined in the SESSION Database*

Listing 17-2   *Perl DBI program qry session to query the SESSION table*

```perl
#!/usr/bin/perl

use strict;
use DBI;
require "session.pl";

my @ord=('ID','PROPID','APPNAME','LISTENERCNT','LASTACCESS','CREATIONTIME',
'MAXINACTIVETIME','USERNAME','SMALL','MEDIUM','LARGE');

$SIG{`INT`} = sub { die };  # Enable Control-C to terminate the program

my($dbuname)=$dbguide::dbuname;
my($dbpw)=$dbguide::dbpw;
my($dbname)=$dbguide::dbname;
my($dbinstance)=$dbguide::dbinstance;

my($session)=$dbguide::session;

my ($conn,$cursor,@values);

$conn = DBI->connect("DBI:DB2:$dbname",$dbuname,$dbpw);
die "Cannot connect to conn: $DBI::errstr\n" unless ($conn);

print "Connected.\n";

# Prepare an SQL query.
$cursor = $conn->prepare("SELECT * FROM $dbinstance.$session");

# Execute the query.
$cursor->execute();

if ($cursor->err()) {
    die "Cannot query conn: $DBI::errstr\n";
}

# Extract the data.
my $i = 0;
while (@values = $cursor->fetchrow() ) {
    print "\nRow $i ------\n";
    my $j = 0;
    foreach (@values) { print "$j $ord[$j] -- $_\n"; $j++; }
    $i++;
}
# we are done with the cursor.
$cursor->finish();
# disconnect
$conn->disconnect or warn "Disconnection failed: $DBI::errstr\n";
```

You have already seen a few other DBI programs in Chapter 9 to populate and query the DBGUIDE database. Similarly, the qry_session program is based on Perl DBI, and it can assist you to quickly read the content of the SESSIONS table. The following shows the output of the program after the first run of WAS-enabled session persistence:

```
# qry_session
Connected.
Row 0 ------
0 ID -- default_host/wasbook
1 PROPID -- default_host/wasbook
2 APPNAME --
3 LISTENERCNT --
4 LASTACCESS -- 1019462431985
5 CREATIONTIME --
6 MAXINACTIVETIME -- -1
7 USERNAME --
8 SMALL --
9 MEDIUM --
10 LARGE --
```

This record is an initial record in the SESSIONS table. Each row is numbered and printed to the user screen, one column on a line. The column number is followed by the column name, followed by two hyphens (--), and finally, followed by the data saved in the column itself. Do not pay too much attention to this first record, but getting it initially ensures that your web application session persistence table (SESSIONS) has been properly created and WAS can write to it. On the other hand, if the table has not been created, then the program returns an SQL0204N telling that the SESSIONS table is an undefined name.

Instead of using the db2 command to query the database, the qry_session will be employed next.

Programming Considerations

The wasdg.ear application, which you already deployed in chapters 11 and 12 and used in Chapter 16, is also used in this chapter to test session persistence. There are almost no changes in the programming code to fulfill this requirement; in fact, most changes are administrative[4] and need to be carried out at the application server level.

However, you must be aware of a couple of points while you are writing your programs, in particular, when implementing the serializable interface for these objects to be stored in the persistent HTTP session. Also, you must be aware of which HttpSession methods will commit the objects to the data store and which methods will delete the objects from the data store.

---

[4]   In reality you should pay attention on where to put your classes that are involved with session persistence. Consistency of the classes might be violated whenever you dynamically load and unload classes from the reloadable web application classpath.

Serializing Persistent HTTP Session Objects

Objects to be persisted must be serialized; otherwise, your application will run erratically, and the objects may not be persisted properly and will throw errors.

Looking at the TellerLogged servlet from Chapter 16, recall these statements:

```
EmpAccnt aEmp = iDAO.getAccnt();

session.setAttribute("teller",aEmp);
```

The second statement just shown maps the attribute name `teller` to the object aEmp within the scope of the client session. The object aEmp has been defined in the class EmpAccnt; therefore, you need to make a change to the declaration of the class itself:

```
public class EmpAccnt implements java.io.Serializable
{

}
```

After making this change, recompile and update the deployed web application by running svlbuild again.

The classes used by Java objects that must be serialized and deserialized can be placed in the web application classpath as long as you do not alter the web application during run time by unloading these classes. The class loader scope will suffer otherwise. It is also recommended in a production environment that you move these classes to the WAS system classpath instead of loading them from the web application classpath (see Chapter 15).

Invalidating the Session on Logoff

When closing a session, you need to release the HttpSession objects by using the javax.servlet.htt.HttpSession.invalidate() method. This ensures that the user session record has been deleted from the data store. Usually, when you shut down WAS AEs, the application server will attempt to invalidate all *staled sessions*: those that have timed out but whose records are still dangling in the database.

The Logoff servlet shown in Listing 17-3 shows how to invalidate a session. In the section "Using a Teller Login Scenario to Test Session Persistence," you will see the effect of Logoff on the database.

Listing 17-3   *Logoff servlet invalidates the HttpSession and releases its associated objects*

```
1.    import java.io.*;
2.    import javax.servlet.*;
3.    import javax.servlet.http.*;
4.    import java.util.Hashtable;
5.
6.    import com.tcnd.wasdg.dataaccess.*;
```

```
7.   import com.tcnd.wasdg.common.*;
8.
9.   public class Logoff extends javax.servlet.http.HttpServlet {
10.
11.  public void init() throws ServletException {
12.  }
13.
14.  public void doGet(HttpServletRequest request, HttpServletResponse
     response)
15.          throws IOException{
16.      String content = "Bye.";
17.
18.      HttpSession session = request.getSession(true);
19.      // make sure to get rid of a staled session
20.      if (session.isNew() == false) {
21.          System.out.println("LOG OUT. No staled session, invalidation in
     progress...");
22.          session.invalidate();
23.          // do not uncomment below, as this will create session record in
     the database. Careful!
24.          // session = request.getSession(true);
25.      }
26.
27.      response.setContentType("text/html");
28.      response.setHeader("Pragma", "no-cache");
29.      response.setHeader("Cache-Control", "no-cache");
30.      response.setDateHeader("Expires", 0);
31.
32.      ServletOutputStream out = response.getOutputStream();
33.      out.println(content);
34.      out.close();
35.  }
36.  }
```

On line 24, the commented line shows a statement with the getSession() method. If you enable this statement, every time the Logoff servlet is called, it creates a record in the data store. This statement has been left here on purpose for educational purposes. Just imagine if a developer threw such a statement in a production code; the result would be disastrous!

Committing Changes in a Persistent Session

It is important that you use setAttribute() every time you make a change in a session. Although it will appear to your program as though the change has taken effect, such a change will not be recorded to the database unless you call setAttribute() in your servlet. As for the JSP code, you may either write a scriptlet to explicitly call setAttribute(), or you can use the session manager to change the Write contents (see Table 17-2) from the default *Write changed* to *Write all* so that any change in the session is written to the database. It is advisable to use

Session Settings	In Memory	In DB	Description
Base in-memory session pool size	Y	Y	Fully use system capacity.
Session affinity	Y	Y	Session context is in the same JVM. This is enforced by Servlet 2.2 spec.
Tablespace and row size	N	Y	Optimize the writing to the database.
Multirow schema	N	Y	Use all database capacity.
Write contents	N	Y	Determine what session data to write.
Schedule invalidation	N	Y	Update database to last access time only, and schedule the invalidation of requested sessions.

Table 17-2   *Changing the Write Contents*

setAttribute() instead of this drastic solution, which can result in performance degradation because more data needs to be written unnecessarily to the database.

Although it is advisable to refrain from using JSP for anything other than dynamic HTML, WAS v4 offers the dosetattribute flag in its JSP InitParameter. When this flag is set to true, JSP session-scoped beans always call setAttribute().

Understanding Session Impact When Reloading a Servlet or a .jsp

Whether persistence is enabled, reloading a servlet or a .jsp file will not impact the sessions managed by web applications. You have already seen how the SessionFairy servlet builds and reloads the SessionFairy.jsp file to gather session information from webapp without restarting WAS.

Writing to the Persistent Database: sync()

The changes in the object session can be written to the database by calling the method sync(). This method is defined in the interface com.ibm.websphere.servlet.session.IBMSession. Usually, you call sync() after your servlet is done with the session object. For sync() to write the data to the database, either the manual update or the time-based update must be enabled.

Using a Teller Login Scenario to Test Session Persistence

In this section, you will practice with session persistence using the teller web application: wasdg.ear/webapp. In the first approach, the browser is used to explain how a session is seen from the client browser perspective; in the second approach, Lynx is used to tap into the protocol data sent in the header of the page. An example showing how to overflow the session table is also provided. The discussion concludes with a brief overview of session id mapping.

Examining a Teller Login Scenario Using the Browser

The following exercise consists of eight steps you can use to practice with session persistence.

1. Request the LoginScreen servlet and log in as teller1. After you log in, your browser will show you that you are in-session, as seen in Figure 17-5. The last line in the figure shows the session identifier value to be the following:

   5V4ZT2SJJIMHORCSJ2V0LII

   This value will also match the value in the SESSIONS table.

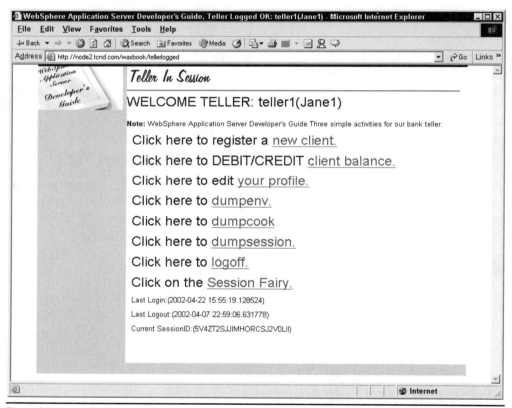

Figure 17-5 *Teller in session after login*

2. Run qry_session, and you will get the record where the session identifier has been set, as shown next:

```
Row 1 ------
0 ID -- 5V4ZT2SJJIMHORCSJ2V0LII
1 PROPID -- 5V4ZT2SJJIMHORCSJ2V0LII
2 APPNAME -- default_host/wasbook
3 LISTENERCNT -- 0
4 LASTACCESS -- 1019508676164
5 CREATIONTIME -- 1019508676164
6 MAXINACTIVETIME -- 1800
7 USERNAME -- anonymous
8 SMALL -- (object as stream of bytes)
9 MEDIUM --
10 LARGE --
```

3. Dump the session by clicking on dumpsession. This will show the value of the session, as seen in Figure 17-6.

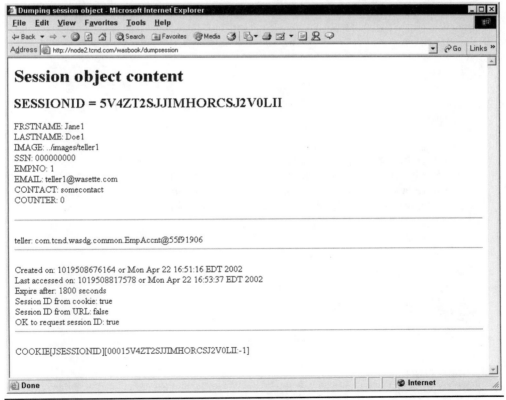

Figure 17-6   *dumpsession reveals the contents of the user session object*

4. Click on the Back button of the navigator, and you will get a message saying that the data has expired.

5. Click Reload to post the form again from the previous data. However, calling the TellerLogged servlet again will invalidate the previous session identifier (line 5) and will re-create another session identifier:

```
1.              // create a new session
2.              HttpSession session = request.getSession(true);
3.              // make sure to get rid of a staled session
4.              if (session.isNew() == false) {
5.                  session.invalidate();
6.                  session = request.getSession(true);
7.              }
8.              System.out.println("If session persistence is
enabled then the following will write to the datastore");
9.              session.setAttribute("teller",aEmp);
```

Although the session is not really a staled session, the code on line 5 will delete the previously set session ID from the SESSIONS table. This servlet did not recognize that you were in session, and you are using the Back button of the browser. For this reason, the Back button is usually implemented within the context of the page being viewed.

Now, let's take a look at the SESSIONS table:

```
Connected.

Row 0 ------
0 ID -- default_host/wasbook
1 PROPID -- default_host/wasbook
2 APPNAME --
3 LISTENERCNT --
4 LASTACCESS -- 1019508990402
5 CREATIONTIME --
6 MAXINACTIVETIME -- -1
7 USERNAME --
8 SMALL --
9 MEDIUM --
```

```
10 LARGE --

Row 1 ------
0  ID -- 3YZ1E3L1U1XZE5BUEBSYTHI
1  PROPID -- 3YZ1E3L1U1XZE5BUEBSYTHI
2  APPNAME -- default_host/wasbook
3  LISTENERCNT -- 0
4  LASTACCESS -- 1019508973247
5  CREATIONTIME -- 1019508973247
6  MAXINACTIVETIME -- 1800
7  USERNAME -- anonymous
8  SMALL -- (object as stream of bytes)
9  MEDIUM --
10 LARGE --
```

Notice that the previous record has been deleted, and a new one is created with a different session ID. This one is 3YZ1E3L1U1XZE5BUEBSYTHI.

6. Test session introspection. Click Session Fairy to introspect the object that is tied to the session attribute. You should see a screen full of information about the aEmp class being introspected, as shown in Figure 17-7.

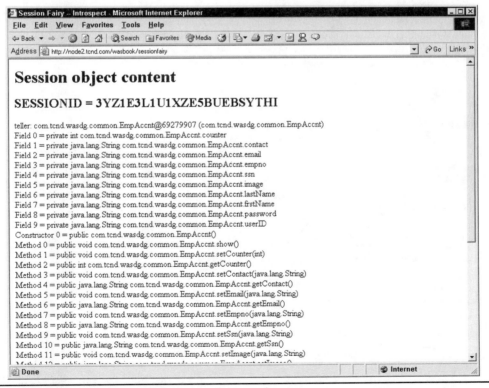

Figure 17-7   *Introspection with the SessionFairy servlet*

7. Now request the SessionFairy.jsp by typing the URL explicitly in the browser. The result of this request is shown in Figure 17-8.

8. Reinspect the SESSIONS table verifying that the session ID previously shown has been stored in a record. Invoke the Logoff servlet: http://was.server.name/wasbook/logoff. This will print *Bye*. Inspect the SESSIONS table again: the record should be cleared by now.

Examining a Teller Login Scenario Using Lynx

Using a graphical-based browser as we did previously is artistically sound and obviously prettier than a textual-based browser. Note also that it may require enough typing and clicking to flow from one request to another. Lynx is not only an alternative for textual browsing, but it is also an indispensable agent that developers need to be acquainted with. It will save you and your organization a lot of time when debugging your application.

We will use Lynx here to request the MIME header and show how the records are being stacked up in the data store after each request.

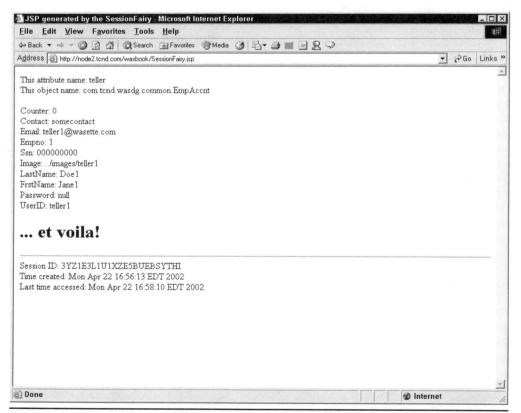

Figure 17-8 *SessionFairy.jsp reveals the content of the session object*

Three Repetitive Lynx Requests

In this example, you will invoke Lynx with the command as shown in line 2 in Listing 17-4. This command puts a POST request to the TellerLogged servlet and passes in the userid and password of the employee teller1. It then gets the MIME header along with the page, and filters any line containing the Set-Cookie term.

Listing 17-4   *Issuing three consecutive Lynx commands to log in teller1*

```
1.   #
2.   #  echo "userid=teller1&password=secret1&---" |
         lynx -accept_all_cookies -post_data -mime_header
            http://node2.tcnd.com/wasbook/tellerlogged |
               grep Set-Cookie
3.   Set-Cookie: JSESSIONID=0001BL13IMQRF5R2LBOOPTJ1M1Q:-1;Path=/
4.   # !!
5.   Set-Cookie: JSESSIONID=0001T24R31YXSIDQQAAXVZHQ2FQ:-1;Path=/
6.   # !!
7.   Set-Cookie: JSESSIONID=0001EST2GQYFFLT1R3KDQ1W4R0Y:-1;Path=/
8.   #
9.
```

Lines 4 and 6 repeat the command from the history. So far, there are three commands executed (lines 2, 4, and 6) that are all similar. After the execution of each command, a different session ID is printed. This occurs because Lynx POSTs the data, and then it exits after each command without holding in the session ID.

Now let's look at the SESSIONS table to see what is happening in the background. The qry_session is employed here. After running the qry_session, the output shows that all three session IDs are stacked in the SESSIONS table, as shown in Listing 17-5.

Listing 17-5   *Output result when issuing qry_session to query the SESSIONS table*

```
Connected.

Row 0 ------
0 ID -- default_host/wasbook
1 PROPID -- default_host/wasbook
2 APPNAME --
3 LISTENERCNT --
4 LASTACCESS -- 1019550767082
5 CREATIONTIME --
6 MAXINACTIVETIME -- -1
7 USERNAME --
8 SMALL --
```

```
9 MEDIUM --
10 LARGE --

Row 1 ------
0 ID -- BL13IMQRF5R2LBOOPTJ1M1Q
1 PROPID -- BL13IMQRF5R2LBOOPTJ1M1Q
2 APPNAME -- default_host/wasbook
3 LISTENERCNT -- 0
4 LASTACCESS -- 1019550936764
5 CREATIONTIME -- 1019550936764
6 MAXINACTIVETIME -- 1800
7 USERNAME -- anonymous
8 SMALL -- (object as stream of bytes)
9 MEDIUM --
10 LARGE --

Row 2 ------
0 ID -- T24R31YXSIDQQAAXVZHQ2FQ
1 PROPID -- T24R31YXSIDQQAAXVZHQ2FQ
2 APPNAME -- default_host/wasbook
3 LISTENERCNT -- 0
4 LASTACCESS -- 1019550938441
5 CREATIONTIME -- 1019550938441
6 MAXINACTIVETIME -- 1800
7 USERNAME -- anonymous
8 SMALL -- (object as stream of bytes)
9 MEDIUM --
10 LARGE --

Row 3
0 ID -- EST2GQYFFLT1R3KDQ1W4R0Y
1 PROPID -- EST2GQYFFLT1R3KDQ1W4R0Y
2 APPNAME -- default_host/wasbook
3 LISTENERCNT -- 0
4 LASTACCESS -- 1019550941108
5 CREATIONTIME -- 1019550941108
6 MAXINACTIVETIME -- 1800
7 USERNAME -- anonymous
8 SMALL -- (object as stream of bytes)
9 MEDIUM --
10 LARGE --
```

Be cautious when designing code that handles a session, whether the session is held only in memory and/or persistently in a data store.

The next section emphasizes the consequences of such common coding.

Session Harassment with Lynx

When you design your web application, be sure you know when and where to use session persistence. In a trusted environment, such as the intranet of a governmental agency, information might flow as expected because the people accessing the web server are not expected to do anything malicious. However, this is not true on the Internet, and a user who is using a quick Internet commander such as Lynx may be able to overflow a web site. The following is an example.

Recall from the scenario discussed previously, a teller logged in through the LoginScreen servlet and then logged off via the Logoff servlet. This is the normal cycle of most clients accessing a web site where login is involved. Say that teller1 logs in using Lynx; each time she logs in, she exits without holding the JSESSIONID of the web container in her browsing agent. For each login (without a logoff), an entry is created in the data store. The entry will be marked stale (remember to enable this cleanup in your configuration) and will be deleted in 30 minutes. Now, the user runs the command in the nebbish.sh shell script shown in Listing 17-6.

Listing 17-6   *nebbish.sh script*

```
1.    #!/bin/ksh
2.
3.    # --- Integer variables
4.    typeset -i counter=0
5.
6.    while [[ $counter -lt 15 ]] ; do
7.      echo $counter
8.        echo "userid=teller1&password=secret1&---" | lynx -accept_all_cookies
        -post_data -mime_header http://node2.tcnd.com/wasbook/tellerlogged
        1>/dev/null
9.        (( counter = $counter + 1 ))
10.   done
11.
```

On line 6, the loop has been set to 15 times, but imagine if the script loop was set to thousands of times. Obviously, thousands of records would be written. Also, even if the session persistence were turned off, thousands of objects would be held in memory. The solution to this problem is a careful implementation of the login procedure: the entry that has the first method to the isNew() method. Your servlet has to gather the time of the user's last login and last logout (as depicted in the EMPPWD table) and employ a heuristic to find out whether the user account should be disabled because it might exhaust the system resources.

Using Multiple Sessions to One Web Container

A teller can have only one session coming from the same web container. However, if you are thinking about allowing two tellers to operate from the same browser, then you can arrange your code to handle multiple objects (one for each teller) to be mapped by the attribute of the session id. For example, a switch statement can branch to fetch the appropriate object in question. But who would like to implement such a ragged program?

Recall from Chapter 16, a session is scoped within a web container; therefore, there is a one-to-one correspondence between a session id saved in the client browser and the web container. Because a session can map one or more objects to different named attributes, there is a one-to-N correspondence between a session id saved in the client browser and the mapped attribute object pairs (A1,O1), ... (An,On), where O1, ...On are all contained in the web container as shown in the illustration. The web container keeps track of the time of the jsession id, so it can clean the objects at expiration time.

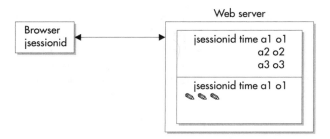

A problem occurs when multiple objects are referenced by a session. For example, if one object references another object in the same session, and the multirow configuration has been put in place to support session data that is larger than 2MB, this will result in a circular reference unless you pay close attention to keep on *sync()*ing the objects. You should avoid such a style of programming because your application will suffer from portability and will be costly and complex to maintain and debug.

Tuning the Session Manager

Persistent sessions are stored to a database. This adds another factor that can sabotage the smoothness of performance. Two approaches are considered to help you gain more performance: systemic tuning of the database, and WAS containment cache settings. The former, because of its database administrative aspect, is discussed in Chapter 25. The latter is discussed in this section.

In the administrative console, walk down the tree to locate the session tuning parameters: Nodes | *node name* | Application Servers | Default Server | Web Container | Session Manager | Tuning Parameters. The session manager properties can be selectively set in this menu (see Figure 17-9).

You can also select the invalidation schedule menu, as shown in Figure 17-10, for the persistent session. These settings are briefly described in the WAS AEs server configuration file, as shown in Listing 17-7.

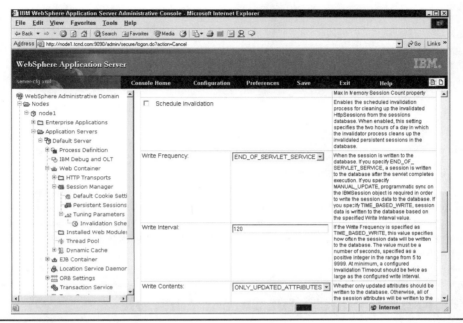

Figure 17-9   *Session manager properties*

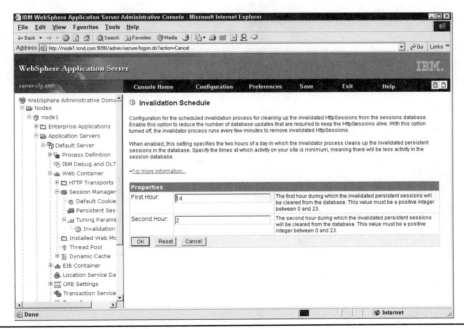

Figure 17-10   *Invalidation schedule menu*

Listing 17-17   *WAS containment cache setting for the session manager*

```
<tuningParams xmi:id="TuningParams_1"
usingMultiRowSchema="false" allowOverflow="true"
scheduleInvalidation="false"
writeFrequency="END_OF_SERVLET_SERVICE"
writeInterval="120"
writeContents="ONLY_UPDATED_ATTRIBUTES"
invalidationTimeout="30">
<invalidationSchedule xmi:id="InvalidationSchedule_1"
firstHour="14" secondHour="2"/>
```

The invalidationTimeout for 30 minutes that we mentioned earlier in the section "Session Harassment with Lynx" resulted from this setup. At this time, the reader should have enough understanding (along the programs and tools) and feel comfortable in testing with different setup for these parameters.

Considering Page Sizes Larger Than 4K

You can selectively set the page size of a session to 8K, 16K, or 32K.

The db2 procedure shown in Listing 17-8 tells you how to create a UDB buffer pool SESSIONBP of size 8K. Line 8 shows how to create a table space SESSTS of size 8K and assign it to the buffer pool SESSBUFF.

Listing 17-18   *Setting a buffer pool for an 8K session size*

```
1.   connect to session
2.   drop table SESSIONS
3.   connect reset
4.   connect to session
5.   create bufferpool SESSIONBP size 1000 pagesize 8K
6.   connect reset
7.   connect to session
8.   create tablespace SESSTS pagesize 8K managed by system using
        ('/home/db2inst1/db2inst1/NODE0000/SQL00004/SESSTS.0') bufferpool
        SESSIONBP
9.   connect reset
10.  disconnect session
```

The procedure to follow on the WAS side in order to change the table space size is summarized here:

1. Stop WAS AEs: $STOPWAS.

2. Edit the server-cfg.xml file. Locate the line that contains the identifier db2RowSize, set its value to ROW_SIZE_8KB, and add in the tableSpaceName="SESSTS" to this tagged line:

```
<persistentSessions xmi:id="SessionPersistence_1"
datasourceJNDIName="jdbc/Session" userId="db2inst1"
password="{xor}Lyg7b29o" db2RowSize="ROW_SIZE_8KB"
tableSpaceName="SESSTS"/>.
```

In the server-cfg.xml file, locate the following tag and delete it:

```
<tableSpaceName xsi:nil="true"/>.
```

3. Start WAS AEs: $STARTWAS.

Based on the page size specified, the session manager will create the SESSIONS table in the specified tablespace.

Recall that you should not use the administrative console (or web console) of WAS AEs v4.0.2 when session persistence is enabled. For this reason, manual editing for the server-cfg.xml file is necessary, as explained previously in the section "Setting Up and Configuring a Session."

Understanding the Reasoning Behind Persistence

The reasoning behind session persistence is to write and organize the client state data on a nonvolatile medium, so that if the client gets disconnected from the web server, he or she will be able to resume the session from the point of interruption. (The word *disconnected* is used solely for explanation.)

In fact, whether the client is in or out of session, he or she is always disconnected from the server, which explains why session persistence is in fact based only on timeout of the session identifier. This is seen clearly in the record of the session itself (refer to Table 17-1).

Another reason to support session persistence is plainly commercial. Because persistence requires a lot of disk space and a couple of database engines that are good enough to manage the writing of persistent data, enterprises need to make the data store highly available, and make the database servers run without interruption. Such data store is quite expensive both in hardware and management. IBM has been known to deliver high-performance disk arrays of serial drives known as SSAs[5] (Serial Storage Architecture) that can be arranged into loops spanning multiple SSA adapters on AIX systems.

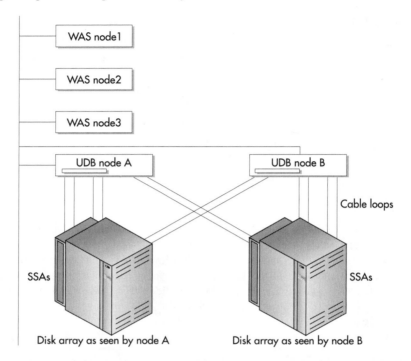

Disk array as seen by node A   Disk array as seen by node B

On the other hand, the availability of the database server must be ensured with the use of High Availability Cluster Multi-Processing (HACMP,) which adds to the administrative cost of the whole shebang.

Persistence is important to secure the availability of critical data that needs to be communicated to different clients throughout an application, such as real-time data collected and used in aviation, in hospitals, and so on. Whether a company decides to implement session persistence to secure the content of a shopping cart might be unwise or might just be a matter of taste.

Wrapping Up

This chapter explored IBM Session Persistence that are specific to WebSphere Application Server. Although the session persistence is handled by WAS, developers should be aware

---

[5]   SSAs are used in enterprise environment. An SSA throughput is estimated to 160MB/second, and an array of 128 devices at a time is possible; however you need an iceberg to cool these drives.

of how to write proper code that will not undermine the system performance. In other words, both administration and coding must be managed carefully to achieve an optimal performing application.

While Chapter 16 introduced the in-memory session management and defined the session scope, this chapter complemented the previous one with the in-database session management. The reader can use the many servlets and tools offered in these chapters as a fundamental basis to understand and test with WAS session manager.

The chapter also showed the limitation and the negative impact on the system resources, as well as the cost in both administration and hardware when using the persistent session management.

Enterprise JavaBeans Programming

Apart from the web container used to load the servlets of the WASDG application, WAS has a container called the Enterprise JavaBeans container (EJB container) that can hold and execute a set of Java programs known as Enterprise JavaBeans (EJBs). This chapter focuses on removing the data access component (DAC) programming from the servlets and separating it as a business logic. The logic or programming of all database access is delegated to the EJB container. Therefore, the prime function of the EJB container is to separate the business logic from the servlets. The benefits of such a separation are scalability,[1] security, data verification, ease of modification of the web pages, and separation of the roles in an enterprise; in addition, EJB's can be developed centrally and accessed by many applications, giving all the usual benefits of reuse, etc.

Servlets are loaded once in the web container; similarly, Enterprise JavaBeans are also loaded once in the EJB container. As a result, moving the DAC to the EJB container makes it possible to spare the system resources because a connection to the database can be shared by multiple servlets. Recall in Chapter 12 that a DAC was used carefully in servlets to make the DAC a shareable object—but shareable and local only to the servlet itself. The DAC was loaded only once at servlet initialization (through the init() method), yet the scope of such a DAC is local to the servlet.

The objective in this chapter is to gain more performance and granularity in moving the DAC functionality to the EJB container. This is one important characteristic of web application programming that you will understand after reading this chapter. Figure 18-1 contrasts the use of the DataAccessComponent object within the servlet to the use of a DataAccessComponent object that is managed by an EJB.

By moving the connectivity operations of the DAC to delegate it to the EJB container, the servlet programs neither need to connect to the database directly nor need to use any of the DAC methods.

EJB programming is a stub programming style; therefore, it requires close attention to the nomination of classes. In particular, the use of a regulated nomination for the classes and the tree hierarchy makes the programming and deployment procedure easy; otherwise, it is expensive and time consuming to understand and realize.

Like the web container, the EJB container runs on the server; objects that are loaded in the web container fall in the web container context. Objects that are loaded in the EJB container fall in the EJB container context. The programs that are loaded in the web container are called servlets, and the programs that are loaded in the EJB container are called Enterprise JavaBeans. All servlets are loaded once in the web container, and all EJBs are loaded once in the EJB container.

Because WAS can start several web and EJB containers, the *WAS containment* is used generically to refer to the WAS containers and their contexts as a whole. The words "bean"

---

[1] This point is debatable when it comes to a WAS single server versus a WAS domain spanning multiple nodes. Chapter 25 provides a note about EJB performance. Also, Chapter 22 discusses how to stress-test the web application; a quick stress test reveals that the WASDG application outperforms its equivalent that uses EJBs.

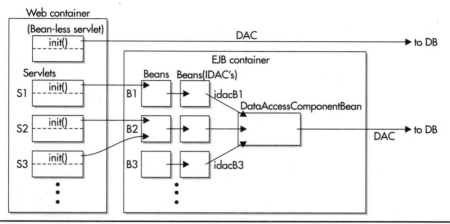

Figure 18-1   *DataAccessComponent in the servlet versus EJB*

or "beans" are used to refer to an Enterprise JavaBean or a set of Enterprise JavaBeans.[2] Therefore, in this chapter the words "bean," "EJB," and "Enterprise JavaBean" are used interchangeably.

You should also refer to the code distribution for this chapter and read the README.TXT file to install and practice with the code. Extract the code archive in the /BOOK/18 directory. This chapter uses the code from Chapter 16, so you should extract the Chapter 16 code in the /BOOK/16 directory. Knowing the basics of Enterprise JavaBeans and the mechanism of using home and remote interfaces will help you fully comprehend this chapter.

Enterprise JavaBeans for the WASDG Application

In Chapters 12 and 16, the servlets defined a DAC object in their init() methods for the readiness of accessing the database in their service(), doGet(), or doPost() methods. For instance, the code segment in Listing 18-1 shows how the QueryTable servlet makes such an initialization.

Listing 18-1   *QueryTable servlet defines a DAC object in the init() method*

```
1.    import java.io.*;
2.    import javax.servlet.*;
3.    import javax.servlet.http.*;
4.    import javax.servlet.http.HttpServlet;
```

---

[2]   A JavaBean and an Enterprise JavaBean are not the same. In this book, we are not interested in JavaBeans at all. The focus is only on the *beans* that can be contained in WAS' EJB container, which are called Enterprise JavaBeans.

```
5.
6.    import com.tcnd.wasdg.dataaccess.*;
7.    import com.tcnd.wasdg.common.*;
8.
9.    public class QueryTable extends javax.servlet.http.HttpServlet
10.   {
11.       DataAccessComponent DAC;
12.
13.   public void init() throws ServletException {
14.       DAC = new DataAccessComponent();
15.   }
16.
17.   public void doGet(HttpServletRequest request, HttpServletResponse
      response)
18.       throws ServletException, IOException
19.   {
20.       String dbTable = request.getParameter("table");
21.
22.       IDataAccessObject iDAO = DAC.createDAObject();
23.
24.       iDAO.setCommandString("SELECT * FROM DB2INST1." + dbTable);
25.       iDAO = DAC.executeQuery(iDAO);
26.       DataSet dataSet = iDAO.getDataSet();
27.
28.       response.setContentType("text/html");
29.       response.setHeader("Pragma", "no-cache");
30.       response.setHeader("Cache-Control", "no-cache");
31.       response.setDateHeader("Expires", 0);
32.
33.       // Iterate through the dataSet and print content
34.       PrintWriter out = response.getWriter();
35.

61.   }
62.
63.    public void doPost(HttpServletRequest request, HttpServletResponse
      response)
64.        throws ServletException, IOException
65.   {
66.       doGet( request, response);
67.   }
68.   }
```

As discussed in Chapter 12, the DAC is defined and loaded only once: the first time the servlet is requested (lines 13 through 15). The servlet shown in Listing 18-1 also exposes the business logic of how to access the database on lines 22 through 26.

Consider the QueryTable9 servlet shown in Listing 18-2. This is a simpler servlet, which is easier to program for two reasons. First, the DAC is not being used; therefore, the servlet programmer does not need to know how to make use of the DAC. Yet, the programmer needs to follow a standard way to take advantage of the business logic: in general, this is a cut-and-paste operation of a block of code shown on lines 22 through 40. Second, all the programmer has to do is pass a set of parameters to a specific method that will return to the caller the specific data.

Listing 18-2   *The QueryTable9 servlet using the FetchTableBean*

```
1.    import java.io.*;
2.    import javax.servlet.*;
3.    import javax.servlet.http.*;
4.    import javax.servlet.http.HttpServlet;
5.    import javax.rmi.*;
6.    import javax.naming.*;
7.    import javax.ejb.*;
8.    import java.util.*;
9.    import com.tcnd.wasdg.ejb.MapRequest;
10.   import com.tcnd.wasdg.ejb.fetchtable.*;
11.
12.   import com.tcnd.wasdg.common.DataSet;
13.
14.   public class QueryTable9 extends javax.servlet.http.HttpServlet
15.   {
16.       InitialContext jndiCtx;
17.       FetchTableHomeRemote fHome = null;
18.       FetchTableRemote fRemote = null;
19.
20.
21.   public void init() throws ServletException {
22.       try
23.       {
24.           // Get System properties for JNDI initialization
25.           java.util.Properties properties = new java.util.Properties();
26.           properties.put(javax.naming.Context.PROVIDER_URL, "iiop:///");
27.           properties.put(javax.naming.Context.INITIAL_CONTEXT_FACTORY,
"com.ibm.websphere.naming.WsnInitialContextFactory");
28.           // Form an initial context
```

```
29.             jndiCtx = new InitialContext(properties);
30.             System.out.println("Good QueryTable9 -- init() got initial
        context");
31.             java.lang.Object o = jndiCtx.lookup("FetchTable");
32.             fHome =
        (FetchTableHomeRemote)javax.rmi.PortableRemoteObject.narrow(o,
        FetchTableHomeRemote.class);
33.             System.out.println("Good QueryTable9 -- init() got home
        interface");
34.             fRemote = fHome.create();
35.             System.out.println("Good QueryTable9 -- init() create");
36.         }
37.         catch (Exception e)
38.         {
39.             System.out.println( "QueryTable9 servlet error when retrieving
        the home interface: " + e.getMessage());
40.         }
41.     }
42.
43.     public void doGet(HttpServletRequest request, HttpServletResponse
        response)
44.         throws ServletException, IOException {
45.
46.         MapRequest mReq = new MapRequest();
47.         DataSet dataSet = null;
48.
49.         String dbTable = request.getParameter("table");
50.         mReq.setParam("tablename",dbTable);
51.         try
52.         {
53.             dataSet = fRemote.fetch(mReq);
54.         }
55.         catch (Exception e)
56.         {
57.             System.out.println( "QueryTable9 servlet error:" +
        e.getMessage());
58.         }
59.         response.setContentType("text/html");
60.         response.setHeader("Pragma", "no-cache");
61.         response.setHeader("Cache-Control", "no-cache");
62.         response.setDateHeader("Expires", 0);
63.
64.         // Iterate through the dataSet and print content
65.         // The code is not shown here, but it is similar to the code in
        Listing 18-1
```

```
66.  ...
67.  }
68.  ...
69.  }
```

On line 49 the table is read from the servlet request, and then it is set to tablename on line 50. On line 53, the table is fetched and the result returned in the dataSet.

QueryTable9 can be requested to query a table such as the EMPACCNT table, as shown in Figure 18-2. The table's contents are returned by FetchTableBean as a data set (line 53). Notice the ease of programming in QueryTable9: set the parameters (line 50), and then call the fetch method (line 53) to execute and return the result on the specified operation.

Typically, the data that is passed through the request of a servlet, like the table name on line 49, should be validated before it is passed to the bean. (This chapter does not discuss data validation.)

QueryTable9 is a servlet program that is loaded in the web container, and the FetchTableBean is a bean that is loaded in the EJB container. Both programs are subject to WAS containment, and consequently, run on the application server.

This chapter introduces seven Enterprise JavaBeans:

▶   An essential bean that accesses the database: DataAccessComponentBean.

▶   Three beans to query a database table, to credit or debit a banker account, and to perform an operation on an employee (or teller) account: FetchTableBean, CreditDebitBean, and OperationEmpBean, respectively.

▶   Three beans that allow the previously listed beans to interact with the DataAccessComponentBean. More specifically, the three beans mentioned previously, FetchTableBean, CreditDebitBean, and OperationEmpBean, interface with the DataAccessComponentBean by using IDACFecthTableBean, IDACCreditDebitBean, and IDACOperationEmpBean, respectively.

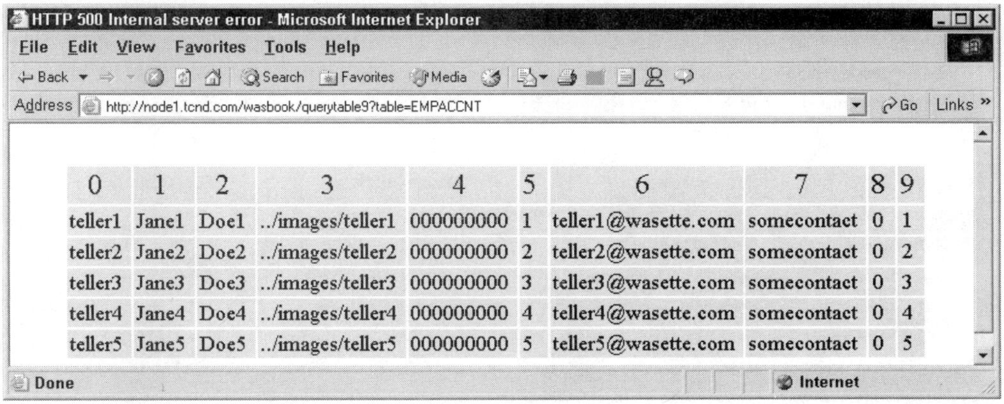

Figure 18-2   *The QueryTable9 servlet executing the EJB class FetchTableBean to query a database table*

Table 18-1 summarizes the seven beans introduced in this chapter.

We did not get into programming specifics, but we are carefully selecting and regulating the nomination of the beans by following these guidelines:

▶ An operation to be carried by some program *AbcXyz* can be represented by a bean with an EJB class named *AbcXyz*Bean, whose home interface is *AbcXyz*HomeRemote and whose remote interface is *AbcXyz*Remote.

▶ In addition, the EJB class *AbcXyz*Bean accesses the database using the EJB class name IDAC*AbcXyz*Bean, whose home interface is IDAC*AbcXyz*HomeRemote and whose remote interface is IDAC*AbcXyz*Remote.

Such a nomination is important when you realize that programming beans follows a repetitive pattern that can be automatically generated with a scripting language such as Perl. How to turn a program such as AbcXyz into an EJB session bean is explained in the section "Turning the Programs into Session Beans."

The following illustration shows the tree structure in which the development of the beans takes place. The ejb directory holds the business logic and each subdirectory. Additionally, the dataaccess directory contains the idac subdirectory that holds the IDAC's beans that correspond and map to each of the operational beans found in the parent directory ejb (with the exception to the dataaccess directory). To clarify this last point, the reader should refer to Figure 18-3, which details the content of the directories.

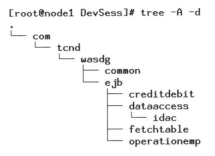

To separate the business logic from the servlets, you first classify into objects the business operations to be carried by a servlet, each of which is then implemented as a bean, and add

Bean Name	Home Interface	Remote Interface	Makes Use Of
DataAccessComponentBean	DataAccessComponentHomeRemote	DataAccessComponentRemote	-
FetchTableBean	FetchTableHomeRemote	FetchTableRemote	IDACFetchTableBean
CreditDebitBean	CreditDebitHomeRemote	CreditDebitRemote	IDACCreditDebitBean
OperationEmpBean	OperationEmpHomeRemote	OperationEmpRemote	IDACOperationEmpBean
IDACFetchTableBean	IDACFetchTableHomeRemote	IDACFetchTableRemote	DataAccessComponentBean
IDACCreditDebitBean	IDACCreditDebitHomeRemote	IDACCreditDebitRemote	DataAccessComponentBean
IDACOperationEmpBean	IDACOperationEmpHomeRemote	IDACOperationEmpRemote	DataAccessComponentBean

Table 18-1 *EJB Session Beans Introduced in this Chapter*

it to the ejb directory. For example, the FetchTableBean is a bean defined in the directory com/tcnd/wasdg/ejb/fetchtable.

On the other hand, the FetchTableBean interfaces with the DataAccessComponentBean via IDACFetchTableBean. Therefore, the IDACFetchTableBean is defined in the directory com/tcnd/wasdg/ejb/dataaccess/idac, which was chosen for clarity.

Figure 18-3 shows the programs and the development tree structure discussed in this chapter. The directories are highlighted in gray.

Notice that the ejb directory contains the beans that are to be contained in WAS' EJB container. Table 18-2 summarizes the Enterprise JavaBeans, their relative directories, and their mapping names. Mapping the names helps you locate an Enterprise JavaBean in the container.

There are two characteristics about the name mapping. The first is programmatic and is achieved with a Java program such as HmLookup, shown in Listing 18-3. The second characteristic is configuration-specific and is achieved at two points: during the archiving of the EJB module and during the deployment of the whole Enterprise JavaBeans shebang. Both points are explained in the section "Deploying the EJB Module WasdgBeans.jar."

```
[root@node1 DevSess]# tree -A -f
.
├── ./Properties
│   └── ./Properties/dbguide.properties
├── ./com
│   └── ./com/tcnd
│       └── ./com/tcnd/wasdg
│           ├── ./com/tcnd/wasdg/common
│           │   ├── ./com/tcnd/wasdg/common/DataSet.java
│           │   └── ./com/tcnd/wasdg/common/StrTool.java
│           └── ./com/tcnd/wasdg/ejb
│               ├── ./com/tcnd/wasdg/ejb/BeanBase.java
│               ├── ./com/tcnd/wasdg/ejb/HmLookup.java
│               ├── ./com/tcnd/wasdg/ejb/MapRequest.java
│               ├── ./com/tcnd/wasdg/ejb/creditdebit ──────────1 bean (creditdebit)
│               │   ├── ./com/tcnd/wasdg/ejb/creditdebit/CreditDebitBean.java
│               │   ├── ./com/tcnd/wasdg/ejb/creditdebit/CreditDebitHomeRemote.java
│               │   └── ./com/tcnd/wasdg/ejb/creditdebit/CreditDebitRemote.java
│               ├── ./com/tcnd/wasdg/ejb/dataaccess ──────────1 bean (data access)
│               │   ├── ./com/tcnd/wasdg/ejb/dataaccess/CliAccnt.java
│               │   ├── ./com/tcnd/wasdg/ejb/dataaccess/DataAccessComponentBean.java
│               │   ├── ./com/tcnd/wasdg/ejb/dataaccess/DataAccessComponentHomeRemote.java
│               │   ├── ./com/tcnd/wasdg/ejb/dataaccess/DataAccessComponentRemote.java
│               │   ├── ./com/tcnd/wasdg/ejb/dataaccess/EmpAccnt.java
│               │   ├── ./com/tcnd/wasdg/ejb/dataaccess/IDataAccessObject.java
│               │   ├── ./com/tcnd/wasdg/ejb/dataaccess/idac ───3 beans
│               │   │   ├── ./com/tcnd/wasdg/ejb/dataaccess/idac/IDACCreditDebitBean.java
│               │   │   ├── ./com/tcnd/wasdg/ejb/dataaccess/idac/IDACCreditDebitHomeRemote.java
│               │   │   ├── ./com/tcnd/wasdg/ejb/dataaccess/idac/IDACCreditDebitRemote.java
│               │   │   ├── ./com/tcnd/wasdg/ejb/dataaccess/idac/IDACFetchTableBean.java
│               │   │   ├── ./com/tcnd/wasdg/ejb/dataaccess/idac/IDACFetchTableHomeRemote.java
│               │   │   ├── ./com/tcnd/wasdg/ejb/dataaccess/idac/IDACFetchTableRemote.java
│               │   │   ├── ./com/tcnd/wasdg/ejb/dataaccess/idac/IDACOperationEmpBean.java
│               │   │   ├── ./com/tcnd/wasdg/ejb/dataaccess/idac/IDACOperationEmpHomeRemote.java
│               │   │   └── ./com/tcnd/wasdg/ejb/dataaccess/idac/IDACOperationEmpRemote.java
│               ├── ./com/tcnd/wasdg/ejb/fetchtable ──────────1 bean (fetchtable)
│               │   ├── ./com/tcnd/wasdg/ejb/fetchtable/FetchTableBean.java
│               │   ├── ./com/tcnd/wasdg/ejb/fetchtable/FetchTableHomeRemote.java
│               │   └── ./com/tcnd/wasdg/ejb/fetchtable/FetchTableRemote.java
│               └── ./com/tcnd/wasdg/ejb/operationemp ──────────1 bean (operationemp)
│                   ├── ./com/tcnd/wasdg/ejb/operationemp/OperationEmpBean.java
│                   ├── ./com/tcnd/wasdg/ejb/operationemp/OperationEmpHomeRemote.java
│                   └── ./com/tcnd/wasdg/ejb/operationemp/OperationEmpRemote.java
```

Figure 18-3   *Programs and development tree structure for the EJB session beans*

Enterprise JavaBean Home Interface	Directory (Relative to com/tcnd/wasdg)	Alias Mapping Name
DataAccessComponentHomeRemote	ejb/dataaccess	DataAccessComponent
FetchTableHomeRemote	ejb/fetchtable	FetchTable
IDACFetchTableHomeRemote	ejb/dataacess/idac	IDACFetchTable
CreditDebitHomeRemote	ejb/creditdebit	CreditDebit
IDACCreditDebitHomeRemote	ejb/dataaccess/idac	IDACCreditDebit
OperationEmpHomeRemote	ejb/operationemp	OperationEmp
IDACOperationEmpHomeRemote	ejb/dataaccess/idac	IDACOperationEmp

Table 18-2 *Enterprise JavaBeans Introduced in this Chapter*

The Java class HmLookup, shown in Listing 18-3, acts as a switchboard: given an Enterprise JavaBean alias name, HmLookup looks (in the EJB container) for the home interface of the corresponding Enterprise JavaBean and then returns it to the caller.

Listing 18-3 *HmLookup*

```
1.    package com.tcnd.wasdg.ejb;
2.
3.    import javax.naming.*;
4.    import javax.rmi.*;
5.    import com.tcnd.wasdg.ejb.dataaccess.*;
6.    import com.tcnd.wasdg.ejb.dataaccess.idac.*;
7.    import com.tcnd.wasdg.ejb.fetchtable.*;
8.    import com.tcnd.wasdg.ejb.creditdebit.*;
9.    import com.tcnd.wasdg.ejb.operationemp.*;
10.
11.   public class HmLookup
12.   {
13.       static private DataAccessComponentHomeRemote dacHomeRemote = null;
14.
15.       static private FetchTableHomeRemote fetchtableHomeRemote = null;
16.       static private IDACFetchTableHomeRemote idac_fetchtableHomeRemote =
      null;
17.
18.       static private CreditDebitHomeRemote creditdebitHomeRemote = null;
19.       static private IDACCreditDebitHomeRemote idac_creditdebitHomeRemote =
      null;
20.
21.       static private OperationEmpHomeRemote operationempHomeRemote = null;
22.       static private IDACOperationEmpHomeRemote idac_operationempHomeRemote
      = null;
23.
```

```
24.  public static Object getHome(String beanAlias) // throws WasdgException
25.  {
26.      try
27.      {
28.          if (beanAlias.equals("DataAccessComponent"))
29.          {
30.              if (dacHomeRemote == null)
31.                  dacHomeRemote =
        (DataAccessComponentHomeRemote)getNarrowedClass( "DataAccessComponent",
        DataAccessComponentHomeRemote.class);
32.              return dacHomeRemote;
33.          }
34.
35.          if (beanAlias.equals("FetchTable"))
36.          {
37.              if (fetchtableHomeRemote == null)
38.                  fetchtableHomeRemote =
        (FetchTableHomeRemote)getNarrowedClass( "FetchTable",
        FetchTableHomeRemote.class);
39.              return fetchtableHomeRemote;
40.          }
41.          if (beanAlias.equals("IDACFetchTable"))
42.          {
43.              if (idac_fetchtableHomeRemote == null)
44.                  idac_fetchtableHomeRemote =
        (IDACFetchTableHomeRemote)getNarrowedClass( "IDACFetchTable",
        IDACFetchTableHomeRemote.class);
45.              return idac_fetchtableHomeRemote;
46.          }
47.  ...
48.      }
49.      catch (Exception e)
50.      {
51.      }
52.      return null;
53.  }
54.
55.  private static Object getNarrowedClass(String jndiName, Class className)
        // throws WasdgException
56.  {
57.      Object ro = null;
58.      try
59.      {
60.          Context jndiCtx = new InitialContext();
61.          Object o = jndiCtx.lookup(jndiName);
62.          ro = PortableRemoteObject.narrow(o, className);
63.      }
64.      catch (Exception e)
65.      {
```

```
66.     }
67.     return ro;
68. }
69. }
```

Programming the HmLookup is simple because a clear correspondence exists between the Enterprise JavaBeans and their associated names. Lines 13 through 22 define all the EJB home interfaces (as static and private). On line 24, the method getHome(String beanAlias) takes an alias name as an argument; it then returns the home interface that corresponds to the specified alias.[3]

The home interface of a specific EJB is located only once, and only if the variable that is pointing to the specified interface is null. (See lines 30, 37, and 43.)

Like the web container, the EJB container has a context that the programmer can access. Because the EJBs are located in the EJB container, the EJB classes can be looked up within the EJB container context, as shown on lines 60 through 62. The PortableRemoteObject narrows a reference to a specific type; it converts a remote reference from a general type to a specific type as required by Java RMI-IIOP.

If you want to add another EJB, first you need to edit the HmLookup and add the additional mapping alias; second, you need to edit the ejb-jar.xml file and add the corresponding mapping alias. The EJB deployment descriptor ejb-jar.xml is discussed in the section "Deploying the EJB Module WasdgBeans.jar." The ejb-jar.xml will be automatically generated with a Perl script.

Turning the Programs into Session Beans

Disregarding the syllogistics behind the Java classes that are involved in programming a session bean, each EJB class needs to include a series of imports and a series of methods. For example, the EJB class FetchTableBean shown in Listing 18-4 imports these Java classes and defines a series of EJB methods that are highlighted with bold in the listing. The boldface sections are repetitive and true for every bean.

Listing 18-4 *FetchTableBean*

```
1.   package com.tcnd.wasdg.ejb.fetchtable;
2.
3.   import com.tcnd.wasdg.common.DataSet;
4.   import com.tcnd.wasdg.ejb.dataaccess.*;
5.   import com.tcnd.wasdg.ejb.dataaccess.idac.*;
6.   import com.tcnd.wasdg.ejb.BeanBase;
7.   import com.tcnd.wasdg.ejb.HmLookup;
8.   import com.tcnd.wasdg.ejb.MapRequest;
9.   import javax.ejb.*;
```

---

[3] We derived the alias name of a bean from the bean name so that the mapping in the program HmLookup coincides with the mapping in the descriptor ejb-jar.xml.

```
10.
11.    public class FetchTableBean extends BeanBase implements SessionBean
12.    {
13.        private javax.ejb.SessionContext ctx = null;
14.        public void setSessionContext(javax.ejb.SessionContext ctx) {
       this.ctx = ctx; }
15.        public void ejbActivate() {}
16.        public void ejbPassivate() {}
17.        public void ejbCreate() {}
18.        public void ejbRemove() {}
19.        public javax.ejb.SessionContext getSessionContext() { return ctx; }
20.
21.        public DataSet fetch(MapRequest mReq) throws
       javax.ejb.CreateException, java.rmi.RemoteException
22.        {
23.            IDACFetchTableRemote idac =
       ((IDACFetchTableHomeRemote)HmLookup.getHome("IDACFetchTable")).create();
24.            baseDataset = idac.fetch(mReq);
25.            return baseDataset;
26.        }
27.    }
```

To expose the fetch() method (line 21) of the FetchTableBean, two other Java classes are needed: the home interface FetchTableHomeRemote and the remote interface FetchTableRemote, shown in Listings 18-5 and 18-6, respectively.

Listing 18-5   *FetchTableHomeRemote*

```
1.    package com.tcnd.wasdg.ejb.fetchtable;
2.
3.    import java.rmi.RemoteException;
4.    import javax.ejb.CreateException;
5.    import com.tcnd.wasdg.ejb.fetchtable.FetchTableRemote;
6.
7.    public interface FetchTableHomeRemote extends javax.ejb.EJBHome
8.    {
9.        FetchTableRemote create() throws CreateException, RemoteException;
10.   }
```

Listing 18-6   *FetchTableRemote*

```
1.    package com.tcnd.wasdg.ejb.fetchtable;
2.
3.    import java.rmi.RemoteException;
```

```
4.    import com.tcnd.wasdg.common.DataSet;
5.    import com.tcnd.wasdg.ejb.MapRequest;
6.
7.    public interface FetchTableRemote extends javax.ejb.EJBObject
8.    {
9.        DataSet fetch(MapRequest arg1) throws java.rmi.RemoteException,
      javax.ejb.CreateException; 10.  }
```

The FetchTableBean does not access the database directly; rather, it uses the bean IDACFetchTableBean to interact with the bean DataAccessComponentBean. The session bean DataAccessComponentBean is the medium (hub) through which all accesses to the database are performed. Listings 18-7, 18-8, and 18-9 show the bean IDACFetchTableBean, its home, and its remote interface, respectively.

Listing 18-7   *IDACFetchTableBean*

```
1.    package com.tcnd.wasdg.ejb.dataaccess.idac;
2.
3.    import com.tcnd.wasdg.common.DataSet;
4.    import com.tcnd.wasdg.ejb.dataaccess.IDataAccessObject;
5.    import com.tcnd.wasdg.ejb.dataaccess.*;
6.    import com.tcnd.wasdg.ejb.HmLookup;
7.    import com.tcnd.wasdg.ejb.MapRequest;
8.    import java.rmi.RemoteException;
9.    import javax.ejb.*;
10.
11.   public class IDACFetchTableBean implements SessionBean
12.   {
13.       private javax.ejb.SessionContext ctx = null;
14.       final static String jndiName = "DataAccessComponent";
15.       protected IDataAccessObject iDAO = null;
16.       protected DataAccessComponentRemote dacRemote = null;
17.
18.       public void setSessionContext(javax.ejb.SessionContext ctx) {
      this.ctx = ctx; }
19.       public void ejbActivate() {}
20.       public void ejbPassivate() {}
21.       public void ejbCreate() {}
22.       public void ejbRemove() {}
23.       public javax.ejb.SessionContext getSessionContext() { return ctx; }
24.
25.       public DataSet fetch(MapRequest mReq) throws
      javax.ejb.CreateException, java.rmi.RemoteException
```

```
26.     {
27.          DataSet ds = null;
28.          dacRemote =
       ((DataAccessComponentHomeRemote)HmLookup.getHome(jndiName)).create();
29.          iDAO = dacRemote.createDAObject();
30.          String dbTable = mReq.getParam("tablename");
31.          iDAO.setCommandString("SELECT * FROM DB2INST1." + dbTable);
32.          iDAO = dacRemote.executeQuery(iDAO);
33.          ds = iDAO.getDataSet();
34.          return ds;
35.     }
36.  }
```

Listing 18-8   *IDACFetchTableHomeRemote*

```
1.    package com.tcnd.wasdg.ejb.dataaccess.idac;
2.
3.    import java.rmi.RemoteException;
4.    import javax.ejb.CreateException;
5.    import com.tcnd.wasdg.ejb.dataaccess.idac.IDACFetchTableRemote;
6.
7.    public interface IDACFetchTableHomeRemote extends javax.ejb.EJBHome
8.    {
9.        IDACFetchTableRemote create() throws CreateException,
      RemoteException;
10.   }
```

Listing 18-9   *IDACFetchTableRemote*

```
1.    package com.tcnd.wasdg.ejb.dataaccess.idac;
2.
3.    import com.tcnd.wasdg.common.DataSet;
4.    import com.tcnd.wasdg.ejb.MapRequest;
5.    import javax.ejb.CreateException;
6.    import java.rmi.RemoteException;
7.
8.    public interface IDACFetchTableRemote extends javax.ejb.EJBObject
9.    {
10.       DataSet fetch(MapRequest mReq) throws CreateException,
      RemoteException;
11.   }
```

The Data Access Component as a Session Bean: DataAccessComponentBean

The DataAccessComponentBean, shown in Listing 18-10, is the essential program that provides methods to select, insert, and update a database. Chapter 10 discussed the data access component and its interface objects: DataAccessComponent and IDataAccessObject. Listing 18-10 shows only the changes made to the original program DataAccessComponent to turn it into a bean. The reader should compare the DataAccessComponentBean source code to the DataAccessComponent source code.

Listing 18-10   *DataAccessComponentBean*

```
1.    package com.tcnd.wasdg.ejb.dataaccess;
2.
3.    import javax.ejb.*;
4.    import java.rmi.RemoteException;
5.    import java.util.*;
6.    import java.sql.*;
7.    import java.io.*;
8.    import com.tcnd.wasdg.ejb.dataaccess.IDataAccessObject;
9.    import com.tcnd.wasdg.common.DataSet;
10.   import com.tcnd.wasdg.ejb.dataaccess.EmpAccnt;
11.   import com.tcnd.wasdg.ejb.dataaccess.CliAccnt;
12.   import com.tcnd.wasdg.common.StrTool;
13.
14.   public class DataAccessComponentBean implements SessionBean
15.   {
16.       private javax.ejb.SessionContext ctx = null;
17.       private java.sql.Connection conn;
18.   ...
19.       private static final String
dbguidePropertiesFileName="/BOOK/18/DevSess/Properties/dbguide.properties";
20.       private String dbDriver;
21.       private String dbUrl;
22.       private String dbUser;
23.       private String dbPassword;
24.
25.       public void setSessionContext(javax.ejb.SessionContext ctx) {
      this.ctx = ctx; }
26.       public void ejbActivate() {}
27.       public void ejbPassivate() {}
28.       public void ejbCreate() {}
```

```
29.        public void ejbRemove() {}
30.        public javax.ejb.SessionContext getSessionContext() { return ctx; }
31.
32.        public DataAccessComponentBean()
33.        {
34.            super();
35.            loadDefaultConnectionSettings();
36.        }
37.        private void loadDefaultConnectionSettings()
38.        { ... }
39.    ...
40.        private void connect(IDataAccessObject iDAO) // throws WasdgException
41.        { ... }
42.        private void disconnect() // throws WasdgException
43.        { ... }
44.        public IDataAccessObject executeQuery(IDataAccessObject iDAO) throws
       java.rmi.RemoteException
45.        { ... }
46.        public IDataAccessObject executeUpdate(IDataAccessObject iDAO) throws
       java.rmi.RemoteException
47.        { ... }
48.    ...
49.        public IDataAccessObject createDAObject() throws
       java.rmi.RemoteException
50.        {
51.            IDataAccessObject iDAO = new IDataAccessObject();
52.            return iDAO;
53.        }
54.        public IDataAccessObject fetchEmpAccount(IDataAccessObject iDAO)
       throws java.rmi.RemoteException
55.        { ... }
56.        public IDataAccessObject fetchCliAccount(IDataAccessObject iDAO)
       throws java.rmi.RemoteException
57.        { ... }
58.    }
```

Using the DataAccessComponentBean is simple. Every bean located in the ejb/dataaccess/idac directory is suffixed with IDAC and is called an IDAC bean. Such an IDAC bean locates the DataAccessComponentBean class and creates a *data access object* using the createDAObject() method. The createDAObject() method is made available to other IDAC's EJBs via the remote interface DataAccessComponentRemote shown in Listing 18-11. As in chapters 10, 12, and 16, you can use the returned object to select, insert, or update the database.

Listing 18-11   *DataAccessComponentRemote*

```
1.   package com.tcnd.wasdg.ejb.dataaccess;
2.
3.   import com.tcnd.wasdg.ejb.dataaccess.IDataAccessObject;
4.   import java.rmi.RemoteException;
5.
6.   public interface DataAccessComponentRemote extends javax.ejb.EJBObject
7.   {
8.       IDataAccessObject createDAObject() throws RemoteException;
9.       IDataAccessObject executeQuery(IDataAccessObject arg0) throws
     RemoteException;
10.      IDataAccessObject executeUpdate(IDataAccessObject arg0) throws
     RemoteException;
11.      IDataAccessObject fetchCliAccount(IDataAccessObject arg0) throws
     RemoteException;
12.      IDataAccessObject fetchEmpAccount(IDataAccessObject arg0) throws
     RemoteException;
13.  }
```

Programmatically, turning the DataAccessComponent into a bean requires little change (adding the imports and declaring the SessionBean methods, generating stubs/interfaces, and the deployment descriptors); however, a programmer must pay special attention to object serialization of the returned type of some of the methods that are available in the EJB remote interface. In particular, the following classes must be serialized: IDataAccessObject, CliAccnt, and EmpAccnt. Such serialization in bean coding requires that we put the three classes mentioned earlier in the *same directory* as the DataAccessComponentBean.

Figure 18-4 shows the development tree of the data access component as discussed in Chapter 10, and the current development tree as we made this component an Enterprise JavaBeans.

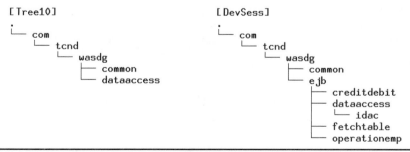

Figure 18-4   *Data access component development tree from Chapter 10 (left) versus Chapter 18 (right)*

Extending the BeanBase to Communicate the Returned Objects

Each of the three beans—FetchTableBean, CreditDebitBean, and OperationEmpBean—extends the BeanBase class to be able to communicate the returned values from the IDAC beans. The BeanBase is shown in Listing 18-12.

Listing 18-12   *BeanBase*

```
1.    package com.tcnd.wasdg.ejb;
2.    import javax.naming.*;
3.    import javax.rmi.*;
4.    import com.tcnd.wasdg.common.DataSet;
5.    import com.tcnd.wasdg.ejb.dataaccess.CliAccnt;
6.    import com.tcnd.wasdg.ejb.dataaccess.EmpAccnt;
7.
8.    public class BeanBase {
9.        protected DataSet baseDataset = new DataSet();
10.       protected CliAccnt baseCli = new CliAccnt();
11.       protected EmpAccnt baseEmp = new EmpAccnt();
12.   }
```

All three returned object types—DataSet, CliAccnt, and EmpAccnt—have been serialized. Such a serialization (implements java.io.Serializable) is necessary because these object types are returned by the methods in the remote interface of the EJBs.

Optimizing the EJB Container with a Larger Bean: MapRequest.setOperation()

For each of the beans FetchTableBean and CreditDebitBean, a specific functionality has been implemented. The first fetches a table from a database, and the second credits or debits a banker account. The bean OperationEmpBean is different in that the programmer needs to specify the kind of operations, for example, mReq.setOperation(*someoperation*), before calling the method OperationEmpBean.execute(MapRequest mReq).

For example, the segment of the UpdateTeller9 servlet in Listing 18-13 shows how the programmer needs to specify the kind of operation before calling execute() through the remote interface of OperationEmpBean.

Listing 18-13 *UpdateTeller9*

```
1.    import java.io.*;
2.    import javax.servlet.*;
3.    import javax.servlet.http.*;
4.    import javax.rmi.*;
5.    import javax.naming.*;
6.    import javax.ejb.*;
7.    import java.util.*;
8.    import com.tcnd.wasdg.ejb.MapRequest;
9.    import com.tcnd.wasdg.ejb.operationemp.*;
10.   import com.tcnd.wasdg.ejb.dataaccess.EmpAccnt;
11.   import com.tcnd.wasdg.common.StrTool;
12.
13.   public class UpdateProfile9 extends javax.servlet.http.HttpServlet
14.   {
15.       InitialContext jndiCtx;
16.       OperationEmpHomeRemote fHome = null;
17.       OperationEmpRemote fRemote = null;
18.
19.   public void init() throws ServletException
20.   {
21.       try
22.       {
23.           // Get System properties for JNDI initialization
24.           java.util.Properties properties = new java.util.Properties();
25.           properties.put(javax.naming.Context.PROVIDER_URL, "iiop:///");
26.
      properties.put(javax.naming.Context.INITIAL_CONTEXT_FACTORY,"com.ibm
.websphere.naming.WsnInitialContextFactory");
27.           // Form an initial context
28.           jndiCtx = new InitialContext(properties);
29.           java.lang.Object o = jndiCtx.lookup("OperationEmp");
30.           fHome =
      (OperationEmpHomeRemote)javax.rmi.PortableRemoteObject.narrow(o,
      OperationEmpHomeRemote.class);
31.           fRemote = fHome.create();
32.           System.out.println("Good UpdateProfile9 -- init() after
      create");
33.       }
34.       catch (Exception e)
35.       {
36.           System.out.println("UpdateProfile servlet error when retrieving
      the home interface: " + e.getMessage());
37.       }
38.   }
39.
40.   public void doGet(HttpServletRequest request, HttpServletResponse
      response
41.             throws ServletException, IOException
```

```
42.   {
43.   ...
44.   }
45.
46.   public void doPost(HttpServletRequest request, HttpServletResponse
        response)
47.       throws IOException
48.   {
49.       // Get the session object EmpAccnt in aEmp
50.       HttpSession session = request.getSession();
51.       EmpAccnt aEmp = (EmpAccnt)session.getAttribute("teller");
52.
53.       MapRequest mReq = new MapRequest();
54.
55.       // Get the userid from the session set by TellerLogged9
56.       String userid = aEmp.getUserID();
57.       // the following parameters need to be read from the request because
        they may have been changed
58.       String frstname = request.getParameter("firstname");
59.       String lastname = request.getParameter("lastname");
60.       String email = request.getParameter("email");
61.       String contact = request.getParameter("contact");
62.
63.       mReq.setOperation("__OPERATIONEMP_UPDATEINFO__");
64.       mReq.setParam("userid",userid);
65.       mReq.setParam("frstname",frstname);
66.       mReq.setParam("lastname",lastname);
67.       mReq.setParam("email",email);
68.       mReq.setParam("contact",contact);
69.       try
70.       {
71.           EmpAccnt aEmp2 = new EmpAccnt();
72.           aEmp2 = fRemote.execute(mReq);
73.           if (aEmp2 != null)
74.           {
75.               // update the Session object EmpAccnt if the UPDATE was
        successful
76.               aEmp.setFrstName(frstname);
77.               aEmp.setLastName(lastname);
78.               aEmp.setEmail(email);
79.               aEmp.setContact(contact);
80.           }
81.       }
82.       catch (Exception e)
83.       {
84.           System.out.println("UpdateProfile servlet error: " +
        e.getMessage());
85.       }
86.       ServletOutputStream out = response.getOutputStream();
87.       out.print("Teller userid: " + aEmp.getUserID());
```

```
88.        out.print("<br>Firstname: " + aEmp.getFrstName());
89.        out.print("<br>Lastname: " + aEmp.getLastName());
90.        out.print("<br>Email: " + aEmp.getEmail());
91.        out.print("<br>Contact: " + aEmp.getContact());
92.        out.close();
93.    }
94.    }
```

On line 63, the __OPERATIONEMP_UPDATEINFO__ is set in the request. Lines 64 through 68 define the parameters to be passed with the request. Line 72 executes the request through the remote interface of the OperationEmpBean. The flow diagram shown in Figure 18-5 depicts how a program calls the execute() method.

Usually, this set of operations must be bundled;[4] however, for clarity, we have explicitly coded and defined four of these operations:

▶ **__OPERATIONEMP_FETCH__**   This operation requests a fetch of the employee or teller account. An employee account is of type com.tcnd.wasdg.ejb.dataaccess.EmpAccnt.

▶ **__OPERATIONEMP_UPDATEINFO__**   This operation requests to update an employee or teller account.

▶ **__OPERATIONEMP_LOGIN__**   This operation is to verify the credentials of a teller and authorize the login of the subject. The operation replaces the one found in the original servlet TellerLogged in Chapter 16. In this chapter, we had to add to the EmpAccnt a getter and setter for the timestamps of the teller login and logout time. Initially, the EmpAccnt maps the fields in the EMPACCNT table, yet the timestamps for the login and logout are set in the EMPPWD table. The IDACOperationEmpBean will make the necessary changes to the EmpAccnt object before returning; this is to avoid the use of a join.[5]

▶ **__OPERATIONEMP_LOGOUT__**   This operation invalidates the user session and updates the logout's timestamp of the teller. This operation replaces the one found in the original servlet Logout in Chapter 16. The explanation on updating the teller's login- and logout- time, shown in the preceding bullet, apply here.

Therefore, the IDACOperationEmpBean, shown in Listing 18-14, first creates the home interface and then uses the if-statement to transfer control to the appropriate block of statements to perform the requested operation. The creation of the home interface is done once for any of the four operations.

---

[4]   The bundle manager class BundleManager is discussed in Chapter 23. For clarity, we will not use any additional class at this point in the programming discussion.

[5]   When programming entity beans, you will not have this flexibility. The matter becomes much more complicated when joining data between two tables, and the number of database accesses becomes much more significant—a concern in scalability.

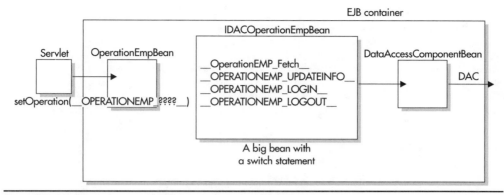

Figure 18-5   *Flow diagram for the IDACOperationEmpBean*

Listing 18-14   *IDACOperationEmpBean*

```
1.    package com.tcnd.wasdg.ejb.dataaccess.idac;
2.
3.    import com.tcnd.wasdg.ejb.dataaccess.*;
4.    import com.tcnd.wasdg.ejb.HmLookup;
5.    import com.tcnd.wasdg.ejb.MapRequest;
6.    import com.tcnd.wasdg.common.DataSet;
7.
8.    import java.rmi.RemoteException;
9.    import javax.ejb.*;
10.
11.   public class IDACOperationEmpBean implements SessionBean
12.   {
13.       private javax.ejb.SessionContext ctx = null;
14.       final static String jndiName = "DataAccessComponent";
15.       protected IDataAccessObject iDAO = null;
16.       protected DataAccessComponentRemote dacRemote = null;
17.
18.       public void setSessionContext(javax.ejb.SessionContext ctx) {
      this.ctx = ctx; }
19.       public void ejbActivate() {}
20.       public void ejbPassivate() {}
21.       public void ejbCreate() {}
22.       public void ejbRemove() {}
23.       public javax.ejb.SessionContext getSessionContext() { return ctx; }
24.
25.   public EmpAccnt execute(MapRequest mReq) throws
          javax.ejb.CreateException, java.rmi.RemoteException
26.   {
27.       EmpAccnt aEmp = null;
28.
```

```
29.      dacRemote =
       ((DataAccessComponentHomeRemote)HmLookup.getHome(jndiName)).create();
30.      iDAO = dacRemote.createDAObject();
31.
32.      if (mReq.getOperation().equals("__OPERATIONEMP_FETCH__"))
33.      {
34.          iDAO.setParameters(mReq.getParamTable());
35.          iDAO.setCommandString("SELECT * FROM DB2INST1.EMPACCNT WHERE
       USERID = ':userid'");
36.          iDAO = dacRemote.fetchEmpAccount(iDAO);
37.          if (iDAO.getCommandResult())
38.              aEmp = iDAO.getEmpAccnt();
39.          else {} // throw WasdgException: Teller not found!
40.      }
41.      if (mReq.getOperation().equals("__OPERATIONEMP_UPDATEINFO__"))
42.      {
43.          iDAO.setParameters(mReq.getParamTable());
44.          iDAO.setCommandString("UPDATE DB2INST1.EMPACCNT SET FRSTNAME =
       ':frstname' , LASTNAME = ':lastname' , EMAIL = ':email' , CONTACT =
       ':contact' WHERE USERID = ':userid'");
45.          iDAO = dacRemote.executeUpdate(iDAO);
46.          // If update is committed to database, then read record from
       database and return aEmp
47.          if (iDAO.getCommandResult())
48.          {
49.              iDAO.setCommandString("SELECT * FROM DB2INST1.EMPACCNT WHERE
       USERID = ':userid'");
50.              iDAO = dacRemote.fetchEmpAccount(iDAO);
51.              aEmp = iDAO.getEmpAccnt();
52.          }
53.          else {} // throw WasdgException: Teller account not updated !
54.      }
55.      if (mReq.getOperation().equals("__OPERATIONEMP_LOGIN__"))
56.      {
57.          iDAO.setParameters(mReq.getParamTable());
58.          iDAO.setCommandString("SELECT * FROM DB2INST1.EMPPWD WHERE
       (USERID = ':userid' AND PASSWORD = ':password')");
59.          iDAO = dacRemote.executeQuery(iDAO);
60.          if (iDAO.getCommandResult())
61.          {
62.              // Get the timestamps for login and logout from the EMPPWD
       table
63.              DataSet dataSet = iDAO.getDataSet();
64.              dataSet.seekFirstRow();
65.              String tmlogin = dataSet.getValue("tmlogin");
66.              String tmlogout = dataSet.getValue("tmlogout");
67.
68.              // Fetch the employee account first, then update the aEmp
       object with the timestamps
69.              iDAO.setCommandString("SELECT * FROM DB2INST1.EMPACCNT WHERE
```

```
      USERID = ':userid'");
70.              iDAO = dacRemote.fetchEmpAccount(iDAO);
71.              aEmp = iDAO.getEmpAccnt();
72.              aEmp.setTmLogin(tmlogin);
73.              aEmp.setTmLogout(tmlogout);
74.              // Update the timestamps in the table EMPPWD
75.              iDAO.setCommandString("UPDATE DB2INST1.EMPPWD SET TMLOGIN =
      (CURRENT TIMESTAMP) WHERE USERID = ':userid'");
76.              iDAO = dacRemote.executeUpdate(iDAO);
77.          }
78.          else {} // throw WasdgException: Teller not found!
79.      }
80.      if (mReq.getOperation().equals("__OPERATIONEMP_LOGOUT__"))
81.      {
82.          iDAO.setParameters(mReq.getParamTable());
83.          iDAO.setCommandString("UPDATE DB2INST1.EMPPWD SET TMLOGOUT =
      (CURRENT TIMESTAMP) WHERE USERID = ':userid'");
84.          iDAO = dacRemote.executeUpdate(iDAO);
85.      }
86.      return aEmp;
87. }
88. }
```

The reason for setting and getting the operations as implemented by the IDACOperationEmpBean is to have *a bigger bean* that can perform many of the tasks at once. The impact of having a big bean like this one, or to split its functionality into several smaller beans, can affect the performance of your application server. EJB caching plays a major role in performance tuning of the EJB container. Chapter 25 addresses this issue.

Regulating the Beans Nomination

Regulating the nomination of the programs involved in developing the EJB module seriously impacts the effectiveness of the programming and deployment of the module. This will become more evident to you when we discuss the deployment process in the next section. For now, just consider the Perl script listbeans shown in Listing 18-15.

Listing 18-15 *listbeans*

```
1.  #!/usr/bin/perl
2.
3.  @BeansDir=
4.  (
5.  'com/tcnd/wasdg/ejb/dataaccess',
6.  'com/tcnd/wasdg/ejb/dataaccess/idac',
7.  'com/tcnd/wasdg/ejb/creditdebit',
8.  'com/tcnd/wasdg/ejb/operationemp',
```

```
9.      'com/tcnd/wasdg/ejb/fetchtable'
10.     );
11.     foreach (@BeansDir) {
12.         @B = glob($_ . '/' . '*Bean.java');
13.         foreach (@B) {
14.             s/Bean\.java$//; s/\//./g;
15.             push(@L,$_);
16.         }
17.     }
18.     $i=0;
19.     foreach (@L) {
20.         @p=split(/\./);
21.         ($n,$h,$r,$c)=($p[$#p],$_ . "HomeRemote",$_ . "Remote",$_ . "Bean");
22.         $i++;
23.     print
24.     "<session id=\"Session_$i\">
25.         <ejb-name>$n</ejb-name>
26.         <home>$h</home>
27.         <remote>$r</remote>
28.         <ejb-class>$c</ejb-class>
29.         <session-type>Stateless</session-type>
30.         <transaction-type>Bean</transaction-type>
31.     </session>
32.     \n";
33.     }
```

When you run listbeans in the $BASE_DEVBEAN, a mapping of the beans is generated, as shown in Listing 18-16.

Listing 18-16   *Output generated by the listbeans script*

```
1. <session id="Session_1">
2.   <ejb-name>DataAccessComponent</ejb-name>
3.   <home>com.tcnd.wasdg.ejb.dataaccess.DataAccessComponentHomeRemote</home>
4.   <remote>com.tcnd.wasdg.ejb.dataaccess.DataAccessComponentRemote</remote>
5.   <ejb-class>com.tcnd.wasdg.ejb.dataaccess.DataAccessComponentBean</ejb-class>
6.   <session-type>Stateless</session-type>
7.   <transaction-type>Bean</transaction-type>
8. </session>
9. ...
10.<session id="Session_7">
11.   <ejb-name>FetchTable</ejb-name>
12.   <home>com.tcnd.wasdg.ejb.fetchtable.FetchTableHomeRemote</home>
13.   <remote>com.tcnd.wasdg.ejb.fetchtable.FetchTableRemote</remote>
14.   <ejb-class>com.tcnd.wasdg.ejb.fetchtable.FetchTableBean</ejb-class>
15.   <session-type>Stateless</session-type>
16.   <transaction-type>Bean</transaction-type>
17.</session>
```

For illustrative purposes, the output in Listing 18-16 has been truncated to show the mapping of only two beans: DataAccessComponentBean and FetchTableBean.

Based on the listbeans script, the following section shows the use of the Perl script j2ejb that generates the deployment descriptor of the beans in the $BASE_DEVBEAN/META-INF directory. In Listing 18-15, lines 5 through 9 list the directories of the beans to be contained in the EJB container. You can program additional beans by adding more branches to the ejb directories. You also need to add these directories to the list variable @BeansDir of the Perl script j2ejb (used in the following section) to get the mapping of these beans in the deployment descriptor.

This regulated nomination helps you realize a well-structured development tree showing the beans that will be contained in WAS' EJB container, as discussed in the next few sections.

Deploying the EJB Module WasdgBeans.jar

From the $BASE_DEVBEAN directory, we will generate the EJB module WasdgBeans.jar. This module will then be subject to the verification procedure to ensure that it is compatible with the current release of the WAS EJB container specification. Once the EJB module WasdgBeans.jar passes the verification procedure, we will use the administrative console to generate the enterprise application WasdgBeans.ear and register it in WAS configuration data.

Generating the EJB Module: WasdgBeans.jar

All the beans that implement the programming logic to be used within the WASDG application are coded in a separate directory. In our discussion, we have considered /BOOK/18/DevSess to be such a directory, and we will set the environment variable $BASE_DEVBEAN to point to this directory. Having a separate directory such as $BASE_DEVBEAN for programming the beans means that these beans can be developed independently from the web application. The compilation of the programs, the generation of the deployment descriptors, and the archiving (or assembly) of the resulting EJB component is realized in the $BASE_DEVBEAN directory. These three activities just mentioned are realized in three subsequent commands.

Change directory to $BASE_DEVBEAN and issue the following commands:

1. Compile the beans:

   ```
   "# "./jall
   ```

2. Generate the metafiles and the deployment descriptors in the directory META-INF: ejb-jar.xml, ibm-ejb-jar-bnd.xmi, ibm-ejb-jar-ext.xmi, and MANIFEST.MF:

   ```
   "# "./j2ejb
   ```

3. Make the .jar archive WasdgBeans.jar:

   ```
   "# "jar "-Mcvf "../WasdgBeans.jar  "-C "./  "META-INF "-C "./ "com
   ```

The WasdgBeans.jar consists of all subdirectories and files under the directories META-INF and com. The WasdgBeans.jar is called the EJB module. Such an EJB module is ready to be used in the web application. For example, a servlet of the WASDG application uses a bean from the EJB module to request business data; therefore, the beans in the EJB container are often called programs that implement the business logic. Whatever it is being called, it is important for you to know how to make use of these beans, and therefore of the EJB module.

For the servlets to make use of the beans, the EJB module must be explicitly known to WAS' containment. In other words, it must be known first to the run time of the EJB container and next to the web container where servlets (using the beans) are loaded.

First, it is evident that the beans must be loaded and started in the EJB container. The section "Generating and Registering the Enterprise Application: WasdgBeans.ear" shows how to add the beans to the run time of the EJB container.

Second, the servlets that use the beans and that are loaded in the web container need to resolve the symbolic names for references known in the EJB module. Having the class files is enough unless you want to compile .java servlets that use the beans. For example, the QueryTable9.java servlet needs to resolve symbolic names and requires the .java programs that form the EJB module (specifically, those .java programs in $BASE_DEVBEAN). The section "Testing the EJB Module WasdgBeans.jar's Beans'" explains this second point in more detail.

Every time you make a change to the beans in the $BASE_DEVBEAN directory, you can clean up all classes using this command:

```
"# "find ". "-name ""*.class" "-exec "rm "-f "{} "\;
```

Then you issue the previous three commands to rebuild the WasdgBeans.jar file. That is all you need to do to generate the WasdgBeans.jar EJB module. Eventually, it is quicker than the AAT wizard! Once you have the WasdgBeans.jar, you may need to verify it to see if it is compliant with WAS EJB container specifications. The next section discusses how to verify the EJB module.

Verifying the EJB Module

This is an easy step that you perform by using the AAT.

1. Start the AAT:

   ```
   # $ASSEMBLY &
   ```

2. Select File | Open and select the WasdgBeans.jar.

3. Select File | Verify and read the output that resulted from the verification. The following illustration shows such results.

```
Validating EJB module deployment descriptor
Validating com.tcnd.wasdg.ejb.dataaccess.idac.IDACCreditDebitRemote.
Validating com.tcnd.wasdg.ejb.operationemp.OperationEmpRemote.
Validating com.tcnd.wasdg.ejb.dataaccess.idac.IDACOperationEmpHomeRemote.
Validating com.tcnd.wasdg.ejb.dataaccess.idac.IDACOperationEmpRemote.
Validating com.tcnd.wasdg.ejb.creditdebit.CreditDebitHomeRemote.
Validating com.tcnd.wasdg.ejb.fetchtable.FetchTableBean.
CHKJ2400W: Public com.tcnd.wasdg.common.DataSet com.tcnd.wasdg.ejb.fetchtable.FetchTableBean.fetch(com.tcnd.wasdg.ejb.MapRequest) throws
Validating com.tcnd.wasdg.ejb.dataaccess.DataAccessComponentRemote.
Validating com.tcnd.wasdg.ejb.fetchtable.FetchTableHomeRemote.
Validating com.tcnd.wasdg.ejb.operationemp.OperationEmpHomeRemote.
```

[Verify] [Stop] [Help]

You can ignore the warning messages. For a list of warning and error messages in WAS AEs v4, the properties file ejbvalidator.properties is usually in the directory $WAS_HOME/ deploytool/itp/plugins/com.ibm.etools.j2ee. This file contains the descriptive messages used by the validation component.[6]

Generating and Registering the Enterprise Application: WasdgBeans.ear

In the left pane of the WAS AEs administrative console, walk down the WAS topology tree: WebSphere Administrative Domain | Nodes | *nodeName* | Enterprise Applications. Select Install to install the J2EE application (EAR) file WasdgBeans.ear. Notice you do not have the .ear file at this point, but through the administrative console, the install process will build it from the WasdgBeans.jar file. Figure 18-6 shows the console in which you will specify the location of WasdgBeans.jar . Assuming you started the administrative console on a server where the directory containing the EJB module WasdgBeans.jar is mounted, browse through the directory and select the WasdgBeans.jar file in the Path box. In the Application Name box, enter **WasdgBeans**, as shown in Figure 18-6.

Click Next, and select Everyone for the security-roles-to-users mapping. As shown in Figure 18-7, you need to select the Everyone check box before going to the next step.

Each bean in the EJB module must be bound to a JNDI (Java Naming and Directory Interface) name. This is the configuration specification mentioned earlier in the section "Enterprise JavaBeans for the WASDG Application." Refer to Table 18-2 and Listing 18-3 to see the mapping that we followed from the beginning of this chapter. Figure 18-8 shows the mapping that corresponds with Table 18-2. A bean mapped to a JNDI name is also said to be a bean *bound* to a JNDI name. *Object binding* is the association of a distributed object with an identifier, and it is usually provided by a naming service. Such a naming service uses its lookup API, then uses the identifier to locate the object. On Java clients, the JNDI used by Enterprise JavaBeans is a lookup API.

---

[6]   The properties file ejbvalidator.properties may not be consistent with the generated messages because the validator may be using a different file. Because it is not documented by IBM, the property file just mentioned may not be available with newer releases of WAS.

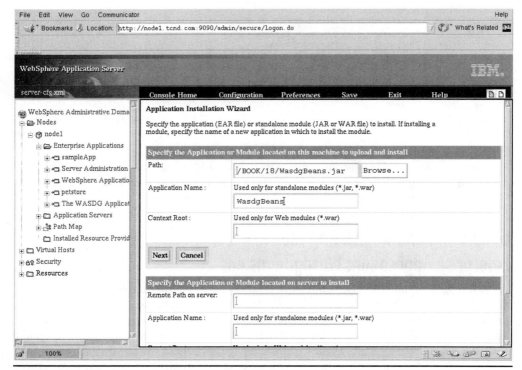

Figure 18-6   WasdgBeans

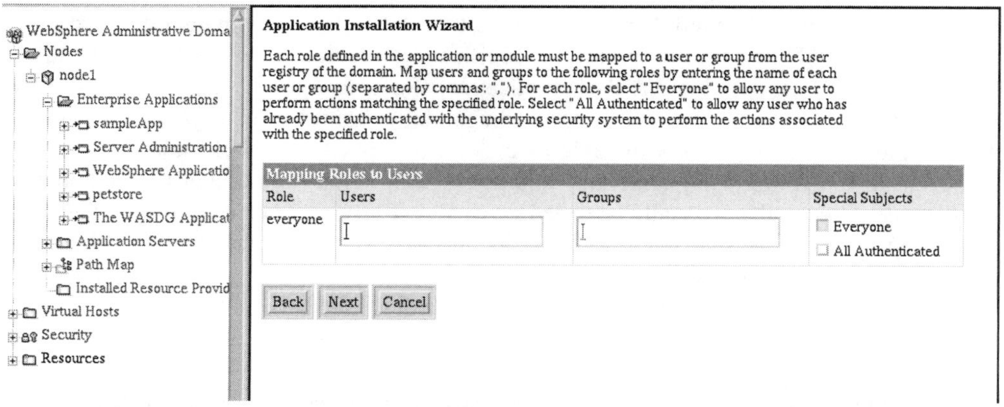

Figure 18-7   Map the special user subject Everyone for the role defined in the module

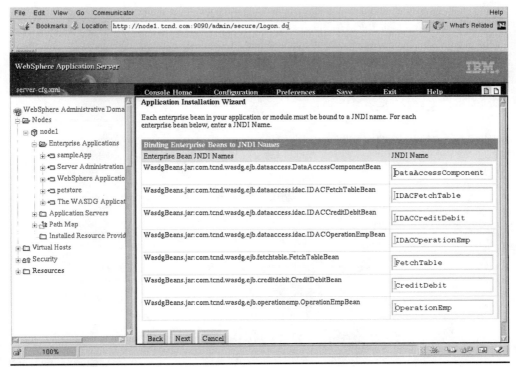

Figure 18-8   *Beans to JNDI name mapping*

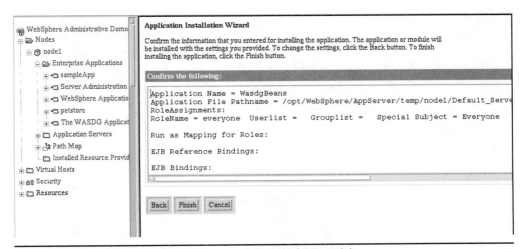

Figure 18-9   *The final step to confirm the installation of the module*

The next step is the final step in which the code is generated, and the WAS configuration is updated with the new J2EE application to be started. As shown in Figure 18-9, click Finish in the administrative console to confirm the build of WasdgBeans.ear.

During the compilation, tail the $WASLOG_STDOUT to see the build process. You will read messages similar to the ones shown in Listing 18-17.

Listing 18-17   *WAS' workbench generating logs while making the enterprise application WasdgBeans.ear*

```
1.   [8/9/02 7:04:11:259 EDT] 5d124dd5 SystemOut       U >>> EJB jar ...
2.   [8/9/02 7:05:37:372 EDT] 4bf48dc0 SystemOut       U Starting workbench.
3.   [8/9/02 7:05:43:028 EDT] 4bf48dc0 SystemOut       U Creating the project.
4.   [8/9/02 7:05:43:196 EDT] 4bf48dc0 SystemOut       U   Creating EJB
     Project...
5.
6.   ...
7.
8.   [8/9/02 7:05:51:261 EDT] 4bf48dc0 SystemOut       U Generating deployment
     code
9.
10.  ...
11.
12.  [8/9/02 7:06:02:251 EDT] 4bf48dc0 SystemOut       U Building:
     /Deployed_WasdgBeans.jar.
13.  [8/9/02 7:06:02:273 EDT] 4bf48dc0 SystemOut       U   Invoking Java Builder
     on /Deployed_WasdgBeans.jar.
14.
15.  ...
16.
17.  [8/9/02 7:06:07:586 EDT] 4bf48dc0 SystemOut       U Invoking RMIC.
18.
19.  ...
20.
21.  [8/9/02 7:06:27:474 EDT] 4bf48dc0 SystemOut       U EJBDeploy complete.
22.  [8/9/02 7:06:27:475 EDT] 4bf48dc0 SystemOut       U 0 Errors, 0 Warnings, 0
     Informational Messages
```

Listing 18-17 has been truncated. You do not need to know about the many programs involved in this stub programming, except the last line (line 22), which shows the bottom line result as 0 Errors.

Once the J2EE application WasdgBeans.ear has been built successfully, the administrative console returns with a list of the J2EE applications that are registered in its configuration data (for example, server-cfg.xml). As shown in Figure 18-10, you should see the WasdgBeans listed with a small icon showing that it has not been started.

Before exiting the administrative console, save the configuration data to update the server-cfg.xml file. Usually, two entries will be created, as shown in Listing 18-18. A new reference is created to the EJB module, EJBModuleRef_13, and a tag is created for the

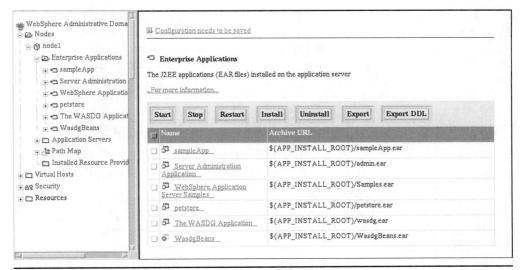

Figure 18-10   *WasdgBeans listed as an installed application*

installedApps WasdgBeans.ear. Note that the incremental reference number depends on the sequence of EJB modules installed in WAS configuration data.

Listing 18-18   *WasdgBeans.ear as registered in WAS AEs server-cfg.xml*

```
1.    <ejbContainer xmi:id="EJBContainer_1"
      passivationDirectory="${WAS_ROOT}/temp"
      inactivePoolCleanupInterval="30000" installedEJBModules="EJBModuleRef_2
      EJBModuleRef_1 EJBModuleRef_3 ...  EJBModuleRef_13"
      defaultDatasource="DataSource_1">
2.    ...
3.    <installedApps xmi:id="ApplicationRef_6" name="WasdgBeans"
      archiveURL="${APP_INSTALL_ROOT}/WasdgBeans.ear">
4.     <modules xmi:type="applicationserver:EJBModuleRef"
      xmi:id="EJBModuleRef_13" uri="WasdgBeans.jar"/>
5.    </installedApps>
```

Restart WAS so the WasdgBeans.ear starts:

```
# STOPWAS; $STARTWAS
```

While WAS is restarting, a message appears in the standard output file showing the success of starting WasdgBeans.ear, as shown in Listing 18-19.

Listing 18-19   *WAS EJB Engine starting WasdgBeans*

```
[8/9/02 7:17:49:750 EDT] 616af3a1 EJBEngine      I WSVR0037I: Starting EJB jar:
   WasdgBeans
```

Also notice that at the end of the build process just discussed, the directory $INSTALLEDAPPS/ WasdgBeans.ear is created, which contains the J2EE enterprise application WasdgBeans.ear. During the build process, the administrative console uses a scratch directory to generate and compile the code of the WasdgBeans.jar. This book does not discuss the programming behind the architecture of the EJB container; however, you can obtain the generated source code of the J2EE application WasdgBeans.ear by using the ejbdeploy, as shown in the next section.

Using ejbdeploy.sh to Generate the Code for Deployment

We used the AAT to generate the EJB module WasdgBeans.jar, then to verify it. The deployment of the EJB module is then carried through the use of the administrative console, as discussed in the preceding section.

At this time, you can inspect the files that have been generated during the deployment. The directory $INSTALLEDAPPS/WasdgBeans.ear contains the enterprise application: WasdgBeans.ear. The files in this directory are shown in the tree structure of the following illustration.

```
WasdgBeans.ear
├── META-INF
│   ├── MANIFEST.MF
│   ├── application.xml
│   ├── ibm-application-bnd.xmi
│   └── ibm-application-ext.xmi
└── WasdgBeans.jar
```

The WasdgBeans.jar is called the *deployed-ejb* for the EJB module WasdgBeans.jar. The deployed-ejb file WasdgBeans.jar is different than the EJB module WasdgBeans.jar that we generated with the AAT: a deployed-ejb file contains the additional generated and compiled classes that are required for deployment.

WAS distribution provides the shell script ejbdeploy.sh (or ejbdeploy.bat on NT) to generate a deployed-ejb. Run the script ejbdeploy.sh without any argument to get a list of the supported options. The syntax of ejbdeploy.sh is shown here:

```
ejbdeploy input_JAR_name working_directory output_JAR_name [-codegen]
    [-cp classpath] [-dbname name] [-dbschema name]
    [-dbvendor name] [-ignoreErrors] [-keep] [-noinform] [-novalidate]
    [-nowarn] [-quiet] [-rmic options] [-trace] [-35]
```

You can use ejbdeploy.sh to generate the deployed-ejb WasdgBeans.jar:

```
# ejbdeploy.sh /BOOK/18/WasdgBeans.jar /tmp/source /tmp/WasdgBeans.jar -nowarn
```

In this command, /BOOK/18/WasdgBeans.jar is the EJB module inputted file, and /tmp/ WasdgBeans.jar is the outputted deployed-ejb file. The directory /tmp/source is used as a scratch directory during the generation process of the deployed-ejb file.

When using ejbdeploy.sh, the bean binding to the JNDI name cannot be customized and is taken as the default as generated by the ejbdeploy.sh script. Recall that in Figure 18-8 we were able to specify our own aliases for the beans binding to JNDI name. In which case, the binding is found in the META-INF/ibm-ejb-jar-bnd.xmi of the archived file $INSTALLEDAPPS/ WasdgBeans.ear/WasdgBeans.jar.

Extract the /tmp/WasdgBeans.jar and compare the file ibm-ejb-jar-bnd.xmi to its counterpart described in the preceding sentence. For example, the binding for the DataAccessComponent to JNDI name, as set in Figure 18-8, is customized thus:

```
<ejbBindings xmi:id="EnterpriseBeanBinding_1" jndiName="DataAccessComponent">
  <enterpriseBean xmi:type="ejb:Session"
      href="META-INF/ejb-jar.xml#Session_1"/>
</ejbBindings>
```

The binding for the DataAccessComponent to JNDI name as set by the ejbdeploy.sh is set to the default as shown here:

```
<ejbBindings xmi:id="EnterpriseBeanBinding_1"
jndiName="com/tcnd/wasdg/ejb/dataaccess/DataAccessComponentHomeRemote">
  <enterpriseBean xmi:type="ejb:Session"
      href="META-INF/ejb-jar.xml#Session_1"/>
</ejbBindings>
```

You can always wrap the ejbdeploy.sh in a Perl script to do the appropriate preprocessing of the bean binding to JNDI name; this will save you the extra steps of using the administrative console.

If you omit the option -nowarn then warning messages are printed during the generation of the deployed-ejb. These messages are equivalent to the one shown in the section "Verifying the EJB Module."

The interested reader can generate the source code of the deployed-ejb WasdgBeans.jar by using the option -keep:

```
# ejbdeploy.sh /BOOK/18/WasdgBeans.jar /tmp/source /tmp/WasdgBeans.jar -keep -nowarn
```

The /tmp/source will then contain the source code of the deployed-ejb.

An EJB module can be debugged during run time. In this case, you need to specify the option -debug when generating the deployed-ejb archive of the module. The option -debug is available with the ejbdeploy of WAS v5.

Testing the EJB Module WasdgBeans.jar's Beans

Using the same code as the WASDG application in Chapters 16 and 17, we will expand the web application to test a set of servlets that use the EJBs developed in this chapter. These servlets are compiled in $BASE_DEVBEAN, and are called servlets-9. Each servlet-9 has a counterpart servlet (in Chapter 16) with equivalent functionality, except a servlet-9 uses primarily the objects in the $BASE_DEVBEAN (EJBs) instead of those defined in the web application development directory $BASE_DEV.

For example, the servlet TellerLogged9 calls the method in the bean OperationEmpBean to authenticate the user, and gets an object for the employee or teller account in com.tcnd. wasdg.ejb.dataaccess.EmpAccnt. TellerLogged9 then uses the object to set an HTTP session: session.setAttribute("teller",aEmp). In this section, we will install a fresh copy of the WASDG application from chapters 16 and 17.

After installing the web application, we will discuss two methods to make the beans of the EJB module WasdgBeans available to the WASDG application: the first method uses an explicit copy of the named files in the directory $BASE_DEVBEAN, and the second method uses a symbolic link from the directory $BASE_DEV to the directory $BASE_DEVBEAN.

Installing the WASDG Application

Install the WASDG application as we did in Chapter 16 by following these six steps:

```
# rm -rf $INSTALLEDAPPS/wasdg.ear
# cd /BOOK/18/Code
# . thisbase
# ./j2tree wasdg.ear webapp wasbook
# refreshear
# ./svlbuild
```

The code in /BOOK/18/Code is similar to /BOOK/16/Code except for the servlets.list, which contains the mapping of the servlets-9. The series of commands just shown install a fresh copy of the WASDG application from Chapters 16 and 17.

Using Explicit Copy to Merge the EJBs to the WASDG Development Tree

To provide a dynamic development environment for EJB programming, we will merge the code in the directory $BASE_DEVBEAN (/BOOK/18/DevSess) to the directory $BASE_DEV/wasdg.ear/webapp/WEB-INF/classes (/BOOK/18/Code/wasdg.ear/webapp/WEB-INF/classes).

We will use the cpfl tool to copy named files relative to their subdirectory. (The cpfl tool is distributed with the Gramercy Toolkit. Appendix A explains how to download the toolkit.)

```
# cpfl -name "*.class" -from /BOOK/18/DevSess -to
$BASE_DEV/wasdg.ear/webapp/WEB-INF/classes -v
# cpfl -name "*.class" -from /BOOK/18/DevSess -to
$INSTALLEDAPPS/wasdg.ear/webapp/WEB-INF/classes -v
```

Now you can test simply by requesting the QueryTable9 servlet. In a browser, request was.server.name:9080/wasbook/querytable9?table=EMPACCNT.

If successful, this request prints the debugging messages in WAS standard output (tail -f $WASLOG_STDOUT), as shown in Listing 18-20.

Listing 18-20   *QueryTable9 printing messages to WAS standard output*

```
1.    [8/9/02 7:18:13:274 EDT] 4bd0f3ad WebGroup        I SRVE0091I: [Servlet
      LOG]: querytable9: init
2.    [8/9/02 7:18:13:300 EDT] 4bd0f3ad SystemOut       U Good -- init() got
      initial context
```

```
3.   [8/9/02 7:18:13:305 EDT] 4bd0f3ad SystemOut      U Good -- init() got home
     interface
4.   [8/9/02 7:18:13:548 EDT] 4bd0f3ad SystemOut      U Good QueryTable9 --
     init() after create
5.   [8/9/02 7:18:13:608 EDT] 4bd0f3ad SystemOut      U >>>>> Querying the
     table: EMPACCNT
6.   [8/9/02 7:18:14:234 EDT] 4bd0f3ad SystemOut      U Good -- After fetch
```

The messages on lines 1 through 4 are printed only once during the lifetime of the servlet because the init() method of a servlet is invoked only once as the servlet is requested the first time. This means that for the lifetime of the QueryTable9 servlet, it uses the init() method to get at an initial context and create a remote reference to FetchTableBean.

The previous two commands using cpfl are necessary because cpfl creates the missing directories to which .class files are to be copied. Therefore, these two commands use the cpfl tool to perform two tasks at once:

▶ Creates the directories following the tree hierarchy found in /BOOK/18/DevSess relative to $BASE_DEV/wasdg.ear/webapp/WEB-INF/classes and to $INSTALLEDAPPS/ wasdg.ear/webapp/WEB-INF/classes

▶ Copies the .class files to their relative created directories

Figure 8-11 shows the structure of the web application development directory $BASE_DEV after copying the files from $BASE_DEVBEAN to $BASE_DEV.

The gray area shows the directories that have been copied from $BASE_DEVBEAN to $BASE_DEV.

At this point, you can test with the beans in WasdgBeans by simply starting with a request to LoginScreen9: was.server.name/wasbook/login9. As you noticed, it is not necessary to run svlbuild because you have been copying the .class files.

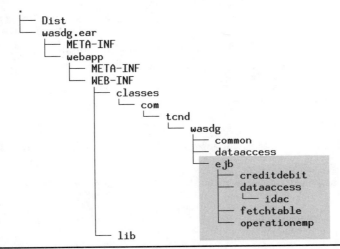

Figure 18-11   *The base development directory (BASE_DEV) after copying the beans*

However, if you copy the servlets' source code from $BASE_DEVBEAN to $BASE_DEV/wasdg.ear/webapp/WEB-INF/classes, then you also need to copy all .java programs from $BASE_DEVBEAN because the svlbuild needs to build the classes. The following command copies the named file "*.java":

```
# cpfl -name "*.java" -from /BOOK/18/DevSess -to
$BASE_DEV/wasdg.ear/webapp/WEB-INF/classes -v
```

Now you can practice by writing new servlets that use the beans in WasdgBeans. Just change directory to $BASE_DEV and issue the command `svlbuild` every time you change any of the servlets.

The method in the next section shows an alternative way to make the code in the directory $BASE_DEVBEAN visible to the web application in $BASE_DEV tree.

Using a Symbolic Link to Link the EJBs to the WASDG Development Tree

Merging the $BASE_DEVBEAN with the $BASE_DEV requires you to move the files explicitly. Yet there is a simpler way to establish a web application build tree in which the classes in the $BASE_DEVBEAN are made visible. You can accomplish this task by using the UNIX command `ln` to establish a symbolic link to the ejb directory in $BASE_DEVBEAN. It is simpler than the method discussed in the previous section because it guarantees the homogeneity of the EJB directory.

Say a programmer named Dave is programming the beans in the directory $BASE_DEVBEAN, and Sue is programming the servlets in the directory $BASE_DEV. Sue will be able to compile servlets that use the current version of Dave's beans without explicitly replicating the contents of Dave's $BASE_DEVBEAN directory every time Dave makes a change to it.

First, expand the WASDG application development directory and install the web application using the same six-step procedure described earlier in the section "Installing the WASDG Application."

Second, in the $INSTALLEDAPPS directory, establish the missing tree structure found relative to $BASE_DEVBEAN. The `cpfl` command can do that:

```
# cpfl -name "*.class" -from /BOOK/18/DevSess -to
$INSTALLEDAPPS/wasdg.ear/webapp/WEB-INF/classes -v
```

Third, in the $BASE_DEV directory, establish the missing tree structure found relative to $BASE_DEVBEAN, but use the symbolic link[7] instead of an explicit copy with the cpfl script:

```
# ln -s $BASE_DEVBEAN/com/tcnd./wasdg/ejb
$BASE_DEV/wasdg.ear/webapp/WEB-INF/classes/com/tcnd/wasdg/ejb
```

Figure 18-12 shows the resulting web application tree.

---

[7] When using the symbolic link, make sure the -follow option is used with the `find` command in the jall and svlbuild scripts. The -follow option is used to dereference symbolic links.

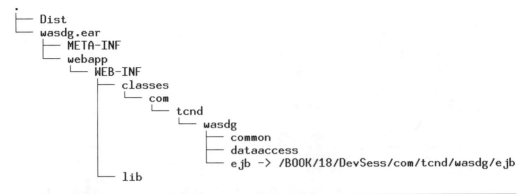

```
 
├── Dist
└── wasdg.ear
     ├── META-INF
     └── webapp
          └── WEB-INF
               ├── classes
               │    └── com
               │         └── tcnd
               │              └── wasdg
               │                   ├── common
               │                   ├── dataaccess
               │                   └── ejb -> /BOOK/18/DevSess/com/tcnd/wasdg/ejb
               └── lib
```

Figure 18-12   *The base development directory (BASE_DEV) using a symbolic link to the ejb directory*

From now on, you can test writing new servlets that use the EJBs. As in Chapter 16, you will write servlets and deploy them with the svlbuild command. Make sure you are in $BASE_DEV, and you can issue the command ./svlbuild every time you write a new servlet or make a change to an existing servlet.

Modifying and Verifying the EJB Module Code

By now you should have realized that you have organized your code in two directories: the beans development directory $BASE_DEVBEAN and the web application development directory $BASE_DEV. The beans programming is carried in the directory $BASE_DEVBEAN (such as /BOOK/18/DevSess). You will develop, compile, and generate the EJB module WasdgBeans.jar from this directory. Of course, after getting the EJB module, you will deploy it using the administrative console of WAS AEs: an essential step to generate the EJB enterprise application WasdgBeans.ear and to register it in the server-cfg.xml file.

If you modify the code in the $BASE_DEVBEAN directory, you need to carry out two important actions.

▶   After generating the WasdgBeans.jar and before deploying it using the administrative console, verify the WasdgBeans.jar. This is important to resolve major issues that might result from the EJB level specification that is supported by WAS.[8]

▶   If you are not using a symbolic link to link the EJBs to the WASDG development tree (see the section "Using a Symbolic Link to Link the EJBs to the WASDG Development Tree"), you need to make a proper replication for the named file from $BASE_DEVBEAN to $BASE_DEV. Clean all .class files that resulted from a previous replication of the $BASE_DEVBEAN.

---

[8]   Notice that the approach taken here is not to discuss a particular EJB container version and its specification. Rather, you use the AAT shipped with the WAS version to verify whether your EJB module is compatible with the WAS' EJB container. You also use the AAT to generate the initial metafiles and deployment descriptors that you will use as a skeleton in your Perl script.

▶ Even a minor modification to any of the class files in $BASE_DEVBEAN needs to be propagated to the $BASE_DEV directory. For example, consider adding a new method to the EmpAccnt. You must remember to propagate the change to the $BASE_DEV directory; otherwise, you might encounter run-time errors, such as a loader constraints violation (shown in Listing 18-21).

Listing 18-21   *A loader constraints violation*

```
1.   [1/1/02 8:25:35:413 EST] 321c3868 WebGroup      X Servlet Error: Class
     com/tcnd/wasdg/ejb/dataaccess/EmpAccnt violates loader constraints:
     java.lang.LinkageError: Class com/tcnd/wasdg/ejb/dataaccess/EmpAccnt
     violates loader constraints
2.           at UpdateProfile9.doPost(UpdateProfile9.java:85)
3.           at javax.servlet.http.HttpServlet.service(HttpServlet.java:760)
```

For the simplicity of coding within a WAS containment context, a servlet that sets an HTTP session within the web container context must use objects that are equivalent to the ones used by the EJB container.[9] These objects are serialized (implements java.io.serializable) and can easily be made available to the beans and the servlets if you have considered organizational tree programming. This is an easy step when you consider the build tree shown in Figure 18-12.

Test Scenario

In a browser, you can request the LoginScreen9 servlet to start testing with the servlets-9 series. Figure 18-13 shows the login screen.

Log in as a teller, for example, teller1 with password secret1, and click Login to see the welcome screen shown in Figure 18-14.

You should be familiar with the screen in Figure 18-14. It is derived from the TellerLogged servlet from chapters 12 and 16. You can still request the LoginScreen servlet (/wasbook/login) to get the TellerLogged servlet welcome screen. There is a major difference between the login process started by LoginScreen versus LoginScreen9. The difference is in the object com.tcnd.wasdg.ejb.dataaccess.EmpAccnt that is used through the login9 (LoginScreen9) to maintain an HTTP session. It is this object that is used by the beans. For ease of programming, it is recommended that you use the same object for both the web container and the EJB container.

Having the same object to satisfy the WAS containment context is important. For example, Emp and Emp are not equivalent, and casting is not allowed. (Refer to DumpSession in the bulleted list that follows.) It becomes necessary to copy the object from EmpAccnt to EmpAccnt.[10]

---

[9]   In web application programming, using the same objects within the context of the web container and the EJB container is typical, considering that beans return data from the database and servlets use the web container context to cache such data. For example, when a teller logs in, the employee record is fetched from the database table EMPACCNT, and its attributes are set in the object ejb/dataaccess/EmpAccnt. This object must be used if it is to be saved in the HTTP session so that the other servlets that use the EJBs in the WASDG application can use the object to the left of an assignment of an EJB method call.

[10] For educational purposes, we left both com.tcnd.wasdg.common.EmpAccnt and com.tcnd.wasdg.ejb.dataaccess.EmpAccnt in the WASDG application of this chapter.

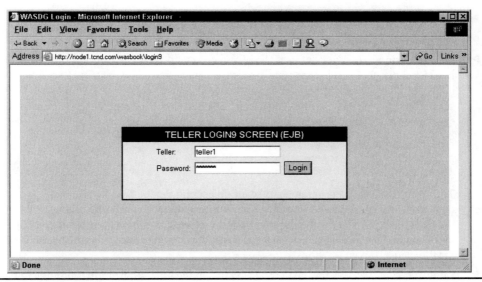

Figure 18-13   *LoginScreen9*

The following summarizes the link references available in the welcome screen shown in Figure 18-14.

▶ **CreditDebit9**   This servlet uses the CreditDebitBean.

▶ **EditTeller9**   This servlet uses the OperationEmpBean.

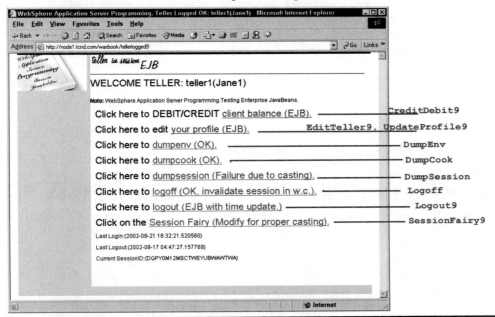

Figure 18-14   *TellerLogged9 servlet generating the welcome screen*

▶ **DumpEnv**   There is no change to this generic servlet.

▶ **DumpCook**   There is no change to this generic servlet.

▶ **DumpSession**   This servlet uses the object com.tcnd.wasdg.common.EmpAccnt, and it will fail due to a servlet run-time error throwing a java.lang.ClassCastException. This is because the object of type com.tcnd.wasdg.ejb.dataaccess.EmpAccnt that has been set in the HTTP session by the TellerLogged9, and that is returned in DumpSession by session.getAttribute("teller"), cannot be cast to be of this type:

```
com.tcnd.wasdg.common.EmpAccnt.
com.tcnd.wasdg.common.EmpAccnt aEmp =
(com.tcnd.wasdg.common.EmpAccnt) session.getAttribute("teller");
```

The com.tcnd.wasdb.common.EmpAccnt object and the com.tcnd.wasdg.ejb.dataaccess.EmpAccnt object are not equivalent, although the EmpAccnt.java file is the same in both directories: com/tcnd/wasdg/common and com/tcnd/wasdg/ejb/dataaccess. Furthermore, casting is not permitted specifically for the clause shown previously.

▶ **Logout9**   This servlet has been modified to use the OperationEmpBean to invalidate the teller HTTP session after updating the EMPPWD table with the time the teller logged off the system.

▶ **SessionFairy9**   The only change you need to make to SessionFairy to turn it into SessionFairy9 is to import the correct EmpAccnt that has been set in the session: import com.tcnd.wasdg.ejb.dataaccess.EmpAccnt.

Although you have added the methods EmpAccnt.setTmLogin() and EmpAccnt.setTmLogout(), the SessionFairy9 results with a SessionFairy.jsp that exposes both methods. Because the SessionFairy9 servlet introspects the com.tcnd.wasdg.ejb.dataaccess.EmpAccnt object, it will be able to discover these two new setter methods and make them available in the SessionFairy.jsp. Recall from Chapter 16 that the servlet SessionFairy calls the Perl interpreter on i2jsp to generate the JSP previously mentioned. The i2jsp is expected to be in the directory /BOOK/16/Code/Dist:

```
Process p = Runtime.getRuntime().exec("/usr/local/bin/perl
/BOOK/16/Code/Dist/i2jsp");
```

Refer to the source code of the SessionFairy9 servlet.

Assembling the EJB Module WasdgBeans.jar: Using the AAT

The use of the AAT becomes essential whenever the programmer needs to get the original set of *metafiles*: J2EE deployment descriptors that can be parsed properly by WAS. This is important especially when you realize that WAS, in addition to the J2EE standard, might be adding extensions and binding to describe an EJB module. Also, generating the original set of metafiles and deployment descriptors guarantees that the current version of WAS will parse these files, properly disregarding issues with J2EE compliance. In other words, instead of following the J2EE specification and determining if WAS can parse the syntax properly, you will use the AAT to generate the metafiles and the deployment descriptors.

Once you get these files, programming becomes easier because subsequent use of AAT is not necessary. The following section discusses how to change the code and reassemble the EJB module without the extensive use of the AAT.

Generating the WasdgBeans.jar Using the AAT

In the section "Generating the EJB Module: WasdgBeans.jar" we have efficiently generated the WasdgBeans.jar (in the DevSess build tree) by using the j2ejb script and the `jar` command.

Using the AAT to generate the WasdgBeans.jar is a simple but a lengthy process. This section is presented to show the reader the steps to follow in using the AAT when generating the WasdhBeans.jar. The reader can obtain the steps to follow in using the AAT by downloading the file ch18_aat.pdf from Osborne web site.

Modifying the Code of an Assembled EJB Module

Assembling an EJB module using the AAT is tedious and time consuming. You do not need to reassemble an EJB module using the AAT every time you make a change to the internal flow of its programs. You can use the `jar` command instead.

NOTE

The AAT herein is essentially used to generate the metafiles and deployment descriptors of the EJB module. As long as the EJB's mapping is unaffected in the deployment descriptor, you can use the same set of files generated by the AAT in the META-INF directory. This saves you a lot of time.

1. After assembling your application using the AAT for the first time and saving the EJB module to a file, such as WasdgBeans.jar, extract the file to the META-INF subdirectory and its contents to the $BASE_DEVBEAN directory. Change directory to $BASE_DEVBEAN (such as /BOOK/18/DevSess), and then from the generated WasgBeans.jar, extract the META-INF directory and its contents. Assuming the WasdgBeans.jar is in the directory /BOOK/18, issue the following command:

   ```
   # jar -xf ../WasdgBeans.jar  META-INF
   ```

2. At this point, you can make changes to the code in $BASE_DEVBEAN, provided you do not move the programs around in the tree hierarchy and you keep working with the same set of imports (imported libraries). In other words, it is admissible to make a change in the logic and the work flow of your beans, for example, adding an if clause for another operation in the IDACOperationEmpBean, or changing the SQL statement in a bean clause. After making such a change in $BASE_DEVBEAN, recompile with jall:

   ```
   # ./jall
   ```

3. Use the "jar command to generate the EJB module WasdgBeans.jar, overwriting the previous one:

   ```
   # jar -Mcvf ../WasdgBeans.jar -C ./ com -C ./ META-INF
   ```

4. Verify the EJB module WasdgBeans.jar with the $ASSEMBLY. Refer to the section "Verifying the EJB Module."

5. Use the administrative console to uninstall the enterprise application WasdgBeans if it has been previously installed: WebSphere Administrative Domain | Nodes |

nodeName | Enterprise Applications. Select WasdgBeans to uninstall. Restart WAS and then deploy WasdgBeans.ear again, as explained in the section "Deploying the EJB Module: WasdgBeans.jar."

6. Remember to update the $BASE_DEV (such as /BOOK/18/Code) web application development directory with the new source code in case you want to test with servlets that use the EJBs. Refer to the section "Modifying and Verifying the EJB Module Code."

You do not need to repeat the first step unless you reassemble the WasdgBeans.jar using the AAT for a major change in the build tree that can affect the mapping. Also notice that the EJB module WasdgBeans.jar created in the third step contains a .java source file. This should not cause a problem; however, if you want to include only .class files, then you need to resort to a different build procedure, that is, extract the original EJB module to a desired directory, move all "*.class" named files from the $BASE_DEVBEAN using the cpfl, and so on.

Wrapping Up

In this chapter, the word "bean" refers to an Enterprise JavaBean (EJB), and the term "WAS containment" refers to the WAS' web and 'EJB container as a whole. WAS can start zero or more of the specified containers, yet the role of the programmer is to make use of WAS containment. More specifically, a programmer can organize two development trees: the first tree is to develop the beans to be registered and loaded in WAS' EJB container, and the second tree is to develop the servlets to be contained in the web container. Because the servlets fall into the web container context and these servlets can use the beans that fall in the EJB container context, you should carefully select the branch (Java package) in the development tree where serialized objects exist.

You also saw that because a branch of the development tree is mapped to a Java package, it is easy to move these serialized objects used by the beans and make them visible to the web container. You learned two methods to realize this point: the first method uses the cpfl script to copy named files from the $BASE_DEVBEAN directory relative to their subdirectories' location in the directories $BASE_DEV and $INSTALLEDAPPS/wasdg.ear; and the second method uses the UNIX command ln to establish a simple symbolic link to make available (dereference) the package in the $BASE_DEVBEAN directory and make it available to the web application defined in the $BASE_DEV directory.

Programs that are to be turned into beans should have been tested and debugged first. Once the logic of these programs is error free, they can be easily turned into beans. To turn a program into a bean, you use stub programming where mostly a cut-and-paste operation is performed. (Use the emacs buffer, or vi yank, which takes a few seconds to carry out such text processing with either one of these editors.) For example, the DataAccessComponentBean resulted from a stepwise build starting with a first design and programming of the component in Chapter 10 (DataAccessComponent), and then turning the component into a bean.

The $BASE_DEVBEAN directory holds a well-structured build tree, where a selected and regulated nomination of the programs involved in building the beans live. This directory has made it possible to generate the EJB module WasdgBeans.jar with simple commands in a matter of seconds.

The chapter also showed you how to deploy the enterprise application WasdgBeans.ear and how to test it using the WASDG application.

Apache SOAP Programming in WAS

It is possible to make the Enterprise JavaBeans (EJBs) developed in Chapter 18 open to the public. By exposing the EJBs through the use of Apache-SOAP, these EJBs will be simple open routines that are available on the Internet. In this case, they are termed *web services*.

SOAP uses the HTTP protocol[1] to provide communication to an EJB, a standard Java program, a script of a certain type, database stored procedures, or programs that communicate using the MIME header such as a Perl/CGI program. Because SOAP uses the HTTP protocol, the web services that SOAP provides are based on *interweb* communication. To secure these open web services, HTTP-based security needs to be established. This chapter focuses on SOAP programming specific to WAS v4 and v5. We will use WAS AEs to quickly deploy the SOAP enterprise application. (This chapter does not discuss security.)

Figure 19-1 shows the three elements involved to allow a company connected to the Internet to perform specific business action on the WASDG application: for example, to fetch a database table such as the employee table or to credit or debit a banker account.

The beans that we programmed in Chapter 18 are ready to provide web services. This chapter explains how to use Apache SOAP to provide such web services. The chapter considers both programming and deployment of the Apache SOAP application under WAS. It also addresses basic debugging approaches for SOAP programming. It is assumed that you have read Chapters 11 and 18, so you know the basis of J2EE deployment and the programming of EJBs. If you are a beginner, you should supplement the information in this chapter with Apache SOAP information available on http://xml.apache.org/soap/docs/guide/.

Deploying the SOAP Application: wasdgsoap.ear

This section explains how to turn programmatically the business logic developed in Chapter 18 into web services. We will focus first on deploying the SOAP-based enterprise application; then we will focus on the SOAP programming of two beans—CreditDebitBean and FetchTableBean—and how to open their business as a service accessible on the Web.

Figure 19-2 shows the basic tree structure for our EAR application: wasdgsoap.ear.

This tree is similar to the first J2EE development tree discussed in Chapter 11. In addition, the script refreshsoapear, shown in the illustrated tree, is a variation on the refreshear script discussed in Chapter 11.

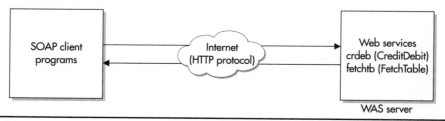

Figure 19-1 *Web services to the WASDG application provided through Apache SOAP*

---

[1] The HTTP protocol is not used exclusively. However, it is the protocol used most often and the one discussed in this chapter.

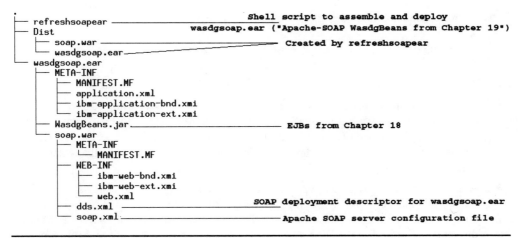

```
.
├── refreshsoapear ──────────────────────  Shell script to assemble and deploy
├── Dist                                    wasdgsoap.ear ("Apache-SOAP WasdgBeans from Chapter 19")
│   ├── soap.war ──────────────────────────── Created by refreshsoapear
│   └── wasdgsoap.ear──
└── wasdgsoap.ear
    ├── META-INF
    │   ├── MANIFEST.MF
    │   ├── application.xml
    │   ├── ibm-application-bnd.xmi
    │   └── ibm-application-ext.xmi
    ├── WasdgBeans.jar──────────────────────── EJBs from Chapter 18
    ├── soap.war
    │   ├── META-INF
    │   │   └── MANIFEST.MF
    │   ├── WEB-INF
    │   │   ├── ibm-web-bnd.xmi
    │   │   ├── ibm-web-ext.xmi
    │   │   └── web.xml
    │   ├── dds.xml ──────────────────── SOAP deployment descriptor for wasdgsoap.ear
    │   └── soap.xml ────────────────── Apache SOAP server configuration file
```

Figure 19-2 *The wasdgsoap.ear development tree*

The script refreshsoapear, shown in Listing 19-1, builds the wasdgsoap.ear from the development tree and deposits it in the Dist directory. In addition, the script reinstalls the wasdgsoap.ear application.

Listing 19-1 *refreshsoapear*

```
1.   #!/bin/sh
2.
3.   # Uninstall the SOAP application and delete it from any previous install
4.   $SEAPPINSTALL -uninstall "Apache-SOAP WasdgBeans from Chapter 19" -delete
     true
5.
6.   # First archive the web application, then the enterprise application
7.   jar cvf $BASE_DEV/Dist/soap.war -C $BASE_DEV/wasdgsoap.ear/soap.war .
8.   jar cvf $BASE_DEV/Dist/wasdgsoap.ear -C $BASE_DEV/wasdgsoap.ear META-INF
      -C $BASE_DEV/Dist soap.war -C $BASE_DEV/wasdgsoap.ear WasdgBeans.jar
9.
10.  # Install the application
11.  $SEAPPINSTALL -install $BASE_DEV/Dist/wasdgsoap.ear
         -precompileJsp false -interactive false
12.
13.  # Restart WAS
14.  $STOPWAS
15.  $STARTWAS
```

Before running refreshsoapear, make sure you have set the BASE_DEV environment variable to your development directory. Change the directory to your development directory, and issue this command:

```
# . thisbase
```

When refreshsoapear runs, the following actions are performed:

▶ A cleanup of the "Apache-SOAP WasdgBeans from Chapter 19" application from a previous deployment, if any (line 4).

▶ An assembly of the soap.war (line 7) to be deposited in the Dist directory.

▶ An assembly of the application wasdgsoap.ear (line 8) after assembling soap.war (line 7). Notice also that the WasdgBeans.jar[2] is the same as the web module that we developed in Chapter 18. Yet, there is one exception in the programming of this module: the MapRequest has been replaced with java.util.Hashtable. The reason for making this change is clarified in the section "Passing Parameters."

▶ A deployment of the assembled application wasdgsoap.ear (line 11) to be registered under the name "Apache-SOAP WasdgBean in Chapter 19." Such deployment verifies and compiles the EJB module; then it deploys the wasdgsoap.ear in the $INSTALLEDAPPS directory and modifies the WAS AEs configuration data in server-cfg.xml (or using the environment variable from Chapter 4, $WASCFG). For example, after deployment of the wasdgsoap.ear, the following new entries are introduced in the $WASCFG:

```
1.   <installedApps xmi:id="ApplicationRef_9"
              name="Apache-SOAP WasdgBeans from Chapter 19"
              archiveURL="${APP_INSTALL_ROOT}/wasdgsoap.ear">
2.    <modules xmi:type="applicationserver:WebModuleRef"
         xmi:id="WebModuleRef_12" uri="soap.war"/>
3.    <modules xmi:type="applicationserver:EJBModuleRef"
         xmi:id="EJBModuleRef_15" uri="WasdgBeans.jar"/>
4.   </installedApps>
```

▶ A restart for WAS as it is reflected on lines 14 and 15. After refreshsoapear finishes running, WAS is restarted (lines 14 and 15). Make sure WAS has properly started the web module. If so, an entry in WAS' standard output file is logged, as shown here:

```
[9/3/02 12:03:40:863 EDT] 68856f6d ServletEngine A SRVE0169I:
Loading Web Module: Apache-SOAP Wrapper.
```

The "Apache-SOAP Wrapper" string reflects the name of the soap.war application that is registered as the display name of the web application. The next section looks closely at the content of the deployment descriptor that describes the web module: soap.war.

The soap.war Web Application

The layout of the web module soap.war is typical for any Apache SOAP application. Its deployment descriptor web.xml, shown in Listing 19-2, does not vary unless security is put in place. The deployment descriptor contains two servlets that put together the SOAP

---

[2]   The reader may refer to the README file found in the code distribution of this chapter for further explanation on how to generate WasdgBeans.jar.

mechanism to communicate procedural information over the wire: using XML over the HTTP protocol. This is an extension to the HTTP headers associated with an encapsulation of the requests in an HTTP M-POST method, in which the body contains XML structure. We are not interested in the implementation of Apache-SOAP but, rather, with those elements needed to program a SOAP application.

Two essential servlets make accessibility to the web services possible: the first routes RPC requests, and the second routes messages.

The org.apache.soap.server.http package contains three classes: two servlets and one utility class, listed here:

▶ **org.apache.soap.server.http.RPCRouterServlet**   This servlet routes RPC requests to the intended method of the intended object.

▶ **org.apache.soap.server.http.MessageRouterServlet**   This servlet routes messages to the appropriate listener method.

▶ **org.apache.soap.server.http.ServerHTTPUtils**   This utility class provides extra utilities for HTTP SOAP programming.

We are interested in only the first two classes because they are the ones that need to be mapped in the web application deployment descriptor web.xml of a SOAP-enabled web application. Listing 19-2 shows the web.xml of our web application soap.war.

The RPCRouterServlet and MessageRouterServlet servlets have public constructors RPCRouterServlet() and MessageRouterServlet(), respectively, with the typical methods: init(), doGet(), and doPost(). The init() method overrides the GenericServlet, and doGet() and doPost() override their counterpart in the javax.servlet.http.HttpServlet.

Listing 19-2   *The web.xml deployment descriptor for the soap.war web module*

```
1.    <?xml version="1.0" encoding="UTF-8"?>
2.    <!DOCTYPE web-app PUBLIC "-//Sun Microsystems, Inc.//DTD Web Application
      2.2//EN" "http://java.sun.com/j2ee/dtds/web-app_2_2.dtd">
3.      <web-app id="WebApp_1">
4.        <icon>
5.          <small-icon></small-icon>
6.          <large-icon></large-icon>
7.        </icon>
8.        <display-name>Apache-SOAP Wrapper< Wrapper/display-name>
9.        <description>
            Provide the SOAP router URL and the SOAP message router
          </description>
10.       <servlet id="Servlet_1">
11.         <servlet-name>rpcrouter</servlet-name>
12.         <display-name>Apache-SOAP RPC router servlet</display-name>
13.         <description>no description</description>
14.<servlet-class>org.apache.soap.server.http.RPCRouterServlet</servlet-class>
```

```
15.             <init-param id="InitParam_1">
16.                <param-name>faultListener</param-name>
17.
       <param-value>org.apache.soap.server.DOMFaultListener</param-value>
18.             </init-param>
19.          </servlet>
20.          <servlet id="Servlet_2">
21.             <servlet-name>messagerouter</servlet-name>
22.             <display-name>Apache-SOAP message router servlet</display-name>
23.       <servlet-class>
             org.apache.soap.server.http.MessageRouterServlet
</servlet-class>
24.             <init-param id="InitParam_2">
25.                <param-name>faultListener</param-name>
26.
       <param-value>org.apache.soap.server.DOMFaultListener</param-value>
27.             </init-param>
28.          </servlet>
29.          <servlet-mapping id="ServletMapping_1">
30.             <servlet-name>rpcrouter</servlet-name>
31.             <url-pattern>/servlet/rpcrouter</url-pattern>
32.          </servlet-mapping>
33.          <servlet-mapping id="ServletMapping_2">
34.             <servlet-name>messagerouter</servlet-name>
35.             <url-pattern>/servlet/messagerouter</url-pattern>
36.          </servlet-mapping>
37.       </web-app>
```

Be aware that the soap.xml file is not a SOAP deployment descriptor; it is a file that is essentially copied to the root directory of a SOAP web module. The soap.xml file is called the Apache SOAP configuration file. Its contents are shown here:

```
<!-- Apache SOAP Server Configuration File -->
<soapServer>
  <configManager value="com.ibm.soap.server.XMLDrivenConfigManager"/>
  <serviceManager>
    <option name="SOAPInterfaceEnabled" value="false"/>
  </serviceManager>
</soapServer>
```

Testing the wasdgsoap.ear and Demystifying the SOAP Message

As a first step to test your deployment, determine whether the web application servlet RPCRouterServlet is reachable by using Lynx to dump the MIME header. Make a request to the rpcrouter, as shown in Figure 19-3. If the supplied URL provides an RPC route, you will get a dump of the MIME header similar to the one shown in Figure 19-3; otherwise, HTTP error 404 is printed for "document cannot be found," which implies that the wasdgsoap.ear did not deploy properly.

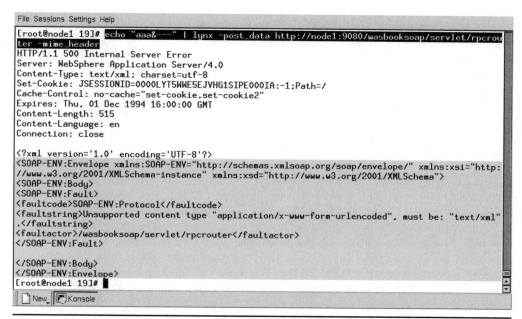

Figure 19-3   *Using Lynx to ensure that the RPC router is reachable*

The gray area in Figure 19-3 reveals the HTTP headers added in the response by SOAP. A SOAP message in an HTTP request or HTTP response always uses the text text/xml content type. The Content-Type is text/xml, as shown in Figure 19-3. A SOAP message typically has three elements:

▶ An envelope as the root element of the XML document

▶ A body as a child of the envelope and the body of the message

▶ A header as an optional element to add attributes and properties to the message

Uninstalling and Installing the wasdgsoap.ear

You can uninstall the application at any time by issuing this command:

```
# $SEAPPINSTALL -uninstall "Apache-SOAP WasdgBeans from Chapter 19" -delete true
```

To install the application, issue this command:

```
# $SEAPPINSTALL -install $BASE_DEV/Dist/wasdgsoap.ear -ejbdeploy true
-interactive false
```

You do not need to reinstall the wasdgsoap.ear if you make a change to the SOAP deployment descriptor dds.xml. However, you must restart WAS for the change to take effect.

Apache SOAP Deployment Descriptors Used by WAS

The SOAP descriptor for a SOAP service contains binding information for a service definition needed by SOAP run time to invoke the service. Such a SOAP descriptor resides on the server, and it is called the SOAP *deployment descriptor.*

Four types of Apache deployment descriptors are known to WAS' SOAP programming. The first deployment descriptor is known for a standard Java class whose methods are to be advertised within the distributed system environment. The second deployment descriptor is for a service that exposes one or many Enterprise JavaBeans. The third deployment descriptor is for a service that exposes methods implemented using the Bean Scripting Framework (BSF) script. The fourth deployment descriptor is for services rendered by database stored procedures.

Because SOAP exposes programs that can be any Java class, Java method, script, or other procedure, we will use the word "open" to refer to any of the previously listed programs. Using the word "open" makes the programmer more cautious about the security breach that can occur by using SOAP programming. Of course, because a SOAP application is used in the context of J2EE web application, the logical security implemented by J2EE also applies to a web application that uses SOAP and can be programmed in the web.xml deployment descriptor. In addition, because SOAP is based on the HTTP protocol, the secure HTTPS protocol can be used as an essential administrative security. This chapter does not address how to apply security in SOAP programming.

Listing 19-3 shows the Apache SOAP deployment descriptor artifact for an open standard Java class.

Listing 19-3   *Artifact for an open standard Java class*

```
<isd:service xmlns:isd="http://xml.apache.org/xml-soap/deployment"
             id="urn:unique-urn-service" [type="message"]>
  <isd:provider type="java"
             scope="Request | Session | Application"
             methods="list-of-advertised-methods">
    <isd:java class="specified-classname" [static="true|false"]/>
  </isd:provider>
<isd:faultListener>org.apache.soap.server.DOMFaultListener</isd:faultListener>
</isd:service>
```

Listing 19-4 shows the Apache SOAP deployment descriptor artifact for an open EJB class.

Listing 19-4   *Artifact for an open EJB class*

```
<isd:service xmlns:isd="http://xml.apache.org/xml-soap/deployment"
             id="urn:unique-urn-service">
<isd:provider type="provider-class-type"
             scope="Application"
             methods="list-of-advertised-methods">
  <isd:option key="FullHomeInterfaceName" value="home-name" />
```

```
  <isd:option key="JNDIName" value="jndi-name"/>
  <isd:option key="ContextProviderURL" value="URL-to-JNDI-provider"/>
  <isd:option key="FullContextFactoryName"
            value="classname-of-context-factory" />
</isd:provider>
<isd:faultListener>org.apache.soap.server.DOMFaultListener</isd:faultListener>
</isd:service>
```

The provider class type is specified as follows:

▶ For a stateless session bean, use com.ibm.soap.providers.WASStatelessEJBProvider.

▶ For a stateful session bean, use com.ibm.soap.providers.WASStatefulEJBProvider.

▶ For an entity bean, use com.ibm.soap.providers.WASEntityEJBProvider.

In our example, we will use the default name for the iiop URL key and its value:

```
<isd:option key="ContextProviderURL" value="iiop://localhost:900" />
```

We will also use the default name for the context provider key and its value:

```
<isd:option key="FullContextFactoryName"
value="com.ibm.websphere.naming.WsnInitialContextFactory" />
```

Listing 19-5 shows the Apache SOAP deployment descriptor artifact for the BFS script.

Listing 19-5   *Artifact for the BFS script*

```
<isd:service xmlns:isd="http://xml.apache.org/xml-soap/deployment"
              id="urn:unique-urn-service">
  <isd:provider type="script"
              scope="Request | Session | Application"
              methods="list-of-advertised-methods">
      <isd:script language="language-name" [source="source-filename"]>
      [script-body-code]
      </isd:script>
</isd:provider>
<isd:faultListener>org.apache.soap.server.DOMFaultListener</isd:faultListener>
</isd:service>
```

Listing 19-6 shows the Apache SOAP deployment descriptor artifact for the database stored procedure.

Listing 19-6   *Artifact for universal database (UDB) stored procedures*

```
<isd:service xmlns:isd="http://xml.apache.org/xml-soap/deployment"
              id="urn:unique-urn-ervice">
  <isd:provider type="com.ibm.soap.providers.WASDB2SPProvider"
```

```
                scope="Application"
                methods="* | EXPOSED_METHODS">
    [<isd:option key="fullContextFactoryName"
          value="com.ibm.websphere.naming.WsnInitialContextFactory |
                context-factory"/>
     <isd:option key="datasourceJNDI" value="jndi-name"/>
    ]
     [<isd:option key="dbDriver" value="COM.ibm.db2.jdbc.app.DB2Driver | db-driver"/>
      <isd:option key="dbURL" value="jdbc:db2:somedb | db-url"/>
     ]
      <isd:option key="userID" value="db-userid"/>
      <isd:option key="password" value="db-password"/>
</isd:provider>
<isd:faultListener>org.apache.soap.server.DOMFaultListener</isd:faultListener>
</isd:service>
```

Generating an Apache SOAP Deployment Descriptor Using gensoap-ejb

The utility script gensoap-ejb provided with this book's distribution code is a SOAP deployment descriptor generator. Use the script to generate SOAP deployment descriptors for EJBs: dds.xml.

Although you can certainly manually edit the dds.xml file, the gensoap-ejb script allows you to parse the information as it is listed in canonical form in the file soap-ejbfactory.list. Listing data canonically has three advantages. First, it automates the building process of SOAP applications similar to the way the j2ejb script was automated in Chapter 18. Second, it minimizes the chances of entering an ambiguous data string in a dds.xml file. Third, the configuration data defined in the dds.xml is maintained and reposed in the main file soap-ejbfactory.list. For example, Listing 19-7 shows the soap-ejbfactory.list file that is processed by gensoap-ejb. Each line that contains data and does not start with a hash (#) forms a record. Such records start with the unique URN name and are shown in the following listing:

Listing 19-7   *soap-ejbfactory.list*

```
1.   # ejbfactory.list file contains canonical data of SOAP D.D. for EJB
2.   # (1)ServiceURN, (2)EJBType, (3)ContextProviderURL,
       (4)FullHomeInterfaceName, (5)JNDIName, (6)FullContextFactoryName,
       (7)Methods-list
3.   # 1st, 2nd, 4nd, 5th, and 7th fields must be specified. Always use a
       comma as a separator
4.   # MAPPINGS are identified by #MAPPINGS_<unique-urn-service> followed by:
5.   #            encoding-uri, qname-namespace, qname-element, java-type,
       serializer, deserializer
6.
7.   crdeb, Stateless, iiop://localhost:900,
       com.tcnd.wasdg.ejb.creditdebit.CreditDebitHomeRemote, CreditDebit,
```

```
        com.ibm.websphere.naming.WsnInitialContextFactory, creditdebit,
        dummymethod1, dummymethod2
8.    #MAPPINGS_crdeb: http://schemas.xmlsoap.org/soap/encoding/,
        xml-soap-cliaccnt-demo, cliaccnt,
        com.tcnd.wasdg.ejb.dataaccess.CliAccnt,
        org.apache.soap.encoding.soapenc.BeanSerializer,
        org.apache.soap.encoding.soapenc.BeanSerializer
9.
10.   fetchtb, Stateless, iiop://localhost:900,
        com.tcnd.wasdg.ejb.fetchtable.FetchTableHomeRemote, FetchTable,
        com.ibm.websphere.naming.WsnInitialContextFactory, fetch
11.   #MAPPINGS_fetchtb: http://schemas.xmlsoap.org/soap/encoding/,
        xml-soap-dataset-demo, dataset, com.tcnd.wasdg.common.DataSet,
        com.tcnd.wasdg.common.DataSetSerializer,
        com.tcnd.wasdg.common.DataSetSerializer
```

Mappings are described as records that start on a line with #MAPPINGS_<unique-urn-service>. Type mappings are discussed in the section "Specifying Type Mappings in a SOAP Deployment Descriptor," later in this chapter. When gensoap-ejb is executed, it looks for the soap-ejbfactory.list file in the current directory; then it generates the SOAP deployment descriptor to be used with the EJBs and prints it to standard output.

There are two options for gensoap-ejb:

▶ **-qname** To tabulate and print the qualified names (QName) listed in the soap-ejbfactory.list file. These are the entries that start with #MAPPINGS_<unique-urn-service>. Use q-name to see the qualified names clearly and to resolve ambiguity when mapping Java types.

▶ **-jndi** To print the JNDI name information.

Figure 19-4 (on page 13) shows the result when executing gensoap-ejb with the options -qname and –jndi, consecutively.

When using the option q-name, the last column of the printed table will show the Java type. If an (SD) is printed, then the specific Java type has been set with a custiom (de)serializer.

To generate the dds.xml file, execute gensoap-ejb without any option and pipe the output to dds.xml as follows:

```
# gensoap-ejb  >  dds.xml
```

Listing 19-8 shows the dds.xml file generated for our example.

Listing 19-8 *SOAP deployment descriptor: dds.xml generated by gensoap-ejb*

```
1.    <root>
2.    <isd:service xmlns:isd="http://xml.apache.org/xml-soap/deployment"
3.                 id="urn:crdeb">
4.      <isd:provider type="com.ibm.soap.providers.WASStatelessEJBProvider"
5.                 scope="Application"
```

```
6.                    methods="creditdebit dummymethod1 dummymethod2">
7.       <isd:option key="FullHomeInterfaceName"
      value="com.tcnd.wasdg.ejb.creditdebit.CreditDebitHomeRemote" />
8.       <isd:option key="JNDIName" value="CreditDebit" />
9.       <isd:option key="ContextProviderURL" value="iiop://localhost:900" />
10.      <isd:option key="FullContextFactoryName"
      value="com.ibm.websphere.naming.WsnInitialContextFactory" />
11.    </isd:provider>
12.<isd:faultListener>org.apache.soap.server.DOMFaultListener</isd:faultListener>
13.    <isd:mappings>
14.      <isd:map encodingStyle="http://schemas.xmlsoap.org/soap/encoding/"
15.             xmlns:x="urn:xml-soap-cliaccnt-demo" qname="x:cliaccnt"
16.             javaType="com.tcnd.wasdg.ejb.dataaccess.CliAccnt"
17. java2XMLClassName="org.apache.soap.encoding.soapenc.BeanSerializer"
18. xml2JavaClassName="org.apache.soap.encoding.soapenc.BeanSerializer"/>
19.    </isd:mappings>
20.  </isd:service>
21.
22.  <isd:service xmlns:isd="http://xml.apache.org/xml-soap/deployment"
23.             id="urn:fetchtb">
24.    <isd:provider type="com.ibm.soap.providers.WASStatelessEJBProvider"
25.               scope="Application"
26.               methods="fetch">
27.      <isd:option key="FullHomeInterfaceName"
      value="com.tcnd.wasdg.ejb.fetchtable.FetchTableHomeRemote" />
28.      <isd:option key="JNDIName" value="FetchTable" />
29.      <isd:option key="ContextProviderURL" value="iiop://localhost:900" />
30.      <isd:option key="FullContextFactoryName"
      value="com.ibm.websphere.naming.WsnInitialContextFactory" />
31.    </isd:provider>
32.

<isd:faultListener>org.apache.soap.server.DOMFaultListener</isd:faultListener>
33.    <isd:mappings>
34.      <isd:map encodingStyle="http://schemas.xmlsoap.org/soap/encoding/"
35.             xmlns:x="urn:xml-soap-dataset-demo" qname="x:dataset"
36.             javaType="com.tcnd.wasdg.common.DataSet"
37.             java2XMLClassName="com.tcnd.wasdg.common.DataSetSerializer"
38.             xml2JavaClassName="com.tcnd.wasdg.common.DataSetSerializer"/>
39.    </isd:mappings>
40.  </isd:service>
41.  </root>
```

After deploying the wasdgsoap.ear, you can modify the content of the dds.xml simply by rewriting the dds.xml file and then restarting WAS. For instance, to add a new mapping for a qualified name, you will edit the soap-ejbfactory.list and then add the mapping to it. Save

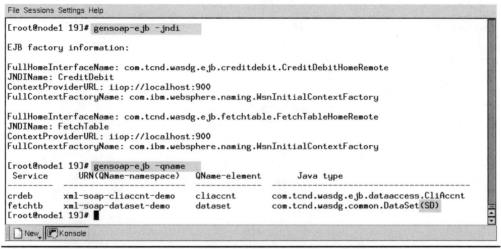

Figure 19-4 *gensoap-ejb printing a SOAP deployment descriptor*

your changes made to the soap-ejbfactory.list, and run these two commands to test with the new dds.xml:

```
# gensoap-ejb > $INSTALLEDAPPS/wasdgsoap.ear/soap.war/dds.xml
# $STOPWAS; $STARTWAS
```

The dds.xml reflects the definition of an open EJB class that has been detailed in the previous section. The <mappings> segment is specifically used to map Java objects that needs to be passed back and forth between the client and the server. These objects need to be byte-wise flattened and then reconstructed, or using Java terms, such objects need to be serialized and deserialized. The <mappings> segment of code is explained in the next section.

Passing Parameters

When passing parameters (of a service or a Java class) between a client and a server over the wire, data needs to be serialized. Parameters are characterized by data type, and their transmission over the wire is traditionally known as marshalling and unmarshalling of their data type.

Apache SOAP provides a mechanism to recognize serialization by providing a default registry for known and commonly used data types, as well as a default class that can serialize beans. In the web module WasdgBeans.jar, we replaced com.tcnd.wasdg.ejb.MapRequest with a simple java.util.Hashtable. This is a simple solution[3] that allows us to communicate

---

[3]   This is not the best solution because typically a web module should not be altered to fit into Apache SOAP programming. Also, the MapRequest played a major role in which this type of class can have additional code that validates the data handed by the servlets and passed on to the beans. Replacing MapRequest with java.util.Hashtable is a simple solution and is shown here for educational reasons.

between the SOAP client programs and the EJBs. The java.util.Hashtable is a predefined Java type already supported by SOAP encoding.

The SOAPMappingRegistry for the SOAP encoding style includes mappings for the predefined Java types listed here:

▶   The Java primitive types and their corresponding wrapper classes

▶   Java arrays

▶   java.lang.String

▶   java.util.Date

▶   java.util.GregorianCalendar

▶   java.util.Vector

▶   java.util.Hashtable

▶   java.util.Map (whenever it is supported by the Java editions)

▶   java.math.BigDecimal

▶   javax.mail.internet.MimeBodyPart

▶   java.io.InputStream

▶   javax.activation.DataSource

▶   javax.activation.DataHandler

▶   org.apache.soap.util.xml.QName

▶   org.apache.soap.rpc.Parameter

▶   java.lang.Object (a deserializer for null objects only)

To register type-mapping information into an Apache SOAP server, you must do this programmatically on the SOAP server and the SOAP client. On the server, you register the type mappings information within each service in the deployment descriptor dds.xml. On the client, you create an instance of the SOAPMappingRegistry and use the mapTypes() method to add new mappings.

The following sections discuss how to qualify names in a SOAP client program, how to specify corresponding mappings information on the SOAP server, and how to program a customized serializer that conforms to Apache SOAP specification. Finally, the last section discusses the correspondence between qualified names (on the client) and their mappings (on the server).

Qualifying Names on the SOAP Client: QName

We will refer to the class org.apache.soap.util.xml.QName as QName for short. QName is used to represent the fully qualified name of a variable. The constructor of this class allows you to specify QName with or without arguments, as follows:

▶   QName()

▶ QName(org.w3c.dom.Node *node*)

▶ QName(java.lang.String *namespaceURI*, java.lang.String *localPart*)

We are interested in the third form of the constructor. QName() is used in a SOAP client program, and its arguments must be defined on the server. The *namespaceURI* corresponds to the name space for an XML element, and *localPart* corresponds to the name of the XML element. The two arguments of QName *must* also be defined in the SOAP deployment descriptor dds.xml that is on the server. Such a definition is accomplished by specifying type mappings within each service definition in the dds.xml.

Specifying Type Mappings in a SOAP Deployment Descriptor

Type-mapping information for RPC services is specified in the deployment descriptors through the use of a <mappings> element, which may be optionally specified as a child of the <service> element. Listing 19-9 shows the <mappings> artifact specified within a service definition in the dds.xml.

Listing 19-9   *<mappings> artifact*

```
<isd:mappings [defaultRegistryClass="registry-subclass"]>
  <isd:map encodingStyle="encoding-uri"
           xmlns:x="qname-namespace" qname="x:qname-element"
           javaType="java-type"
           java2XMLClassName="serializer"
           xml2JavaClassName="deserializer"/>
</isd:mappings>
```

The boldface elements shown in Listing 19-9 are explained as follows:

▶ **registry-subclass**   An optional attribute to specify the default type-mapping registry. It is a fully qualified Java subclass of org.apache.soap.encoding.SOAPMappingRegistry.

▶ **encoding-uri**   The URI for the encoding method; typically, this is set for standard SOAP encoding as http://schemas.xmlsoap.org/soap/.

▶ **qname-namespace**   The name space for the XML element.

▶ **qname-element**   The name of the XML element.

▶ **java-type**   The fully qualified Java class for which you are providing the mapping.

▶ **serializer**   The fully qualified Java class that implements org.apache.soap.util.xml .Serializer.

▶ **deserializer**   The fully qualified Java class that implements org.apache.soap.util.xml .Deserializer.

Type Mappings for the CliAccnt Object

The CreditDebitBean returns null on failure, otherwise, it credits or debits the client account and returns a CliAccnt object on success. CreditDebitBean is a bean that is defined in WAS' EJB container, therefore the object returned by the bean is returned by the server. Because, the CliAccnt is a typical JavaBean with a series of setter and getter methods (refer to Chapter 10), then it is possible to serialize it and deserialize it using the SOAP encoding style by simply passing "org.apache.soap.encoding.soapenc.BeanSerializer" as the last two parameters when you register the type mapping for the CliAccnt object. The public properties of the bean will become named accessors (elements) in the XML form.

Listing 19-10 shows the type mappings for the CliAccnt object to be returned by the URN service crdeb (CreditDebitBean).

Listing 19-10   *The <mappings> child of the URN service crdeb*

```
<isd:mappings>
   <isd:map encodingStyle="http://schemas.xmlsoap.org/soap/encoding/"
            xmlns:x="urn:xml-soap-cliaccnt-demo" qname="x:cliaccnt"
            javaType="com.tcnd.wasdg.ejb.dataaccess.CliAccnt"
 java2XMLClassName="org.apache.soap.encoding.soapenc.BeanSerializer"
 xml2JavaClassName="org.apache.soap.encoding.soapenc.BeanSerializer"/>
   </isd:mappings>
```

Type Mappings for the DataSet Object

The FetchTableBean is also defined in WAS container, and it is run on the server. However, the object returned by the bean is an object that is neither a JavaBean nor a standard Java type that is a part of the registered SOAP encoding style.

The DataSet object that is returned by the bean (on the server) needs to be serialized. This is done with a customized class com.tcnd.wasdg.common.DataSetSerializer. The programming of this class is explained in the next section, "Programming the DataSetSerializer."

Listing 19-11 shows the type mappings for the DataSet object to be returned by the URN service fetchtb (FetchTableBean).

Listing 19-11   *The <mappings> child of the URN service fetchtb*

```
<isd:mappings>
    <isd:map encodingStyle="http://schemas.xmlsoap.org/soap/encoding/"
            xmlns:x="urn:xml-soap-dataset-demo" qname="x:dataset"
            javaType="com.tcnd.wasdg.common.DataSet"
    java2XMLClassName="com.tcnd.wasdg.common.DataSetSerializer"
    xml2JavaClassName="com.tcnd.wasdg.common.DataSetSerializer"/>
  </isd:mappings>
```

Programming the DataSetSerializer

According to the Apache SOAP implementation, any Serializer must implement the org.apache.soap.util.xml.Serializer interface. Similarly, any Deserializer must implement the org.apache.soap.util.xml.Deserializer interface. These interfaces declare the methods marshall() and unmarshall() that handle the serialization and deserialization of the Java data type in the context to and from XML document instance.

We will write the class com.tcnd.wasdg.common.DataSetSerializer to handle the transmission of the com.tcnd.wasdg.common.DataSet object properly. Looking at the com.tcnd.wasdg.common.DataSet , shown in Listing 19-12, you can see that this class defines two objects: ht of type java.util.Hashtable (line 16), and rows of type java.util.Vector (line 17). The DataSetSerializer needs to marshall and unmarshall both of these objects.

Listing 19-12   *Data types used in the class com.tcnd.wasdg.common.DataSet*

```
1.    package com.tcnd.wasdg.common;
2.    import java.io.*;
3.    import java.util.*;
4.    public class DataSet implements java.io.Serializable
5.    {
6.    ...
7.
8.      // DataSet store the result of a SQL statement
9.      // The ht Hashtable stores
10.     //    the column name as a key and the column index as a value.
11.     // The rows vector contains all the row objects.
12.     // The row vector contains all the values of one row, as string
13.
14.     public DataSet()
15.     {
16.       ht = new Hashtable();
17.       rows = new Vector();
18.       row = new Vector();
19.       currentRow = new Vector();
20.     }
21.     ...
22.    }
```

The DataSetSerializer is typically a variation on the code that is implemented in the org.apache.soap.encoding.soapenc.BeanSerializer. Listing 19-13 shows code for the com.tend.wasdg.common.DataSetSerializer. The source code of the DataSetSerializer can be found within the distribution code.

Listing 19-13   *DataSetSerializer's basic statements*

```
1.    package com.tcnd.wasdg.common;
2.
3.    import java.io.*;
4.    import org.w3c.dom.*;
5.    import org.apache.soap.*;
6.    import org.apache.soap.encoding.soapenc.*;
7.    import org.apache.soap.rpc.*;
8.    import org.apache.soap.util.*;
9.    import org.apache.soap.util.xml.*;
10.   import java.util.Hashtable;
11.   import java.util.Vector;
12.   import com.tcnd.wasdg.common.DataSet;
13.
14.   public class DataSetSerializer implements Serializer, Deserializer
15.   {
16.     public void marshall(String inScopeEncStyle, Class javaType,
17.     Object src, Object context, Writer sink,
18.     NSStack nsStack, XMLJavaMappingRegistry xjmr, SOAPContext ctx)
19.     throws IllegalArgumentException, IOException
20.     {
21.       nsStack.pushScope();
22.       SoapEncUtils.generateStructureHeader(inScopeEncStyle, javaType,
      context, sink, nsStack, xjmr);
23.       sink.write(StringUtils.lineSeparator);
24.       DataSet src2 = (DataSet)src;
25.       Parameter param;
26.       param = new Parameter("ht", Hashtable.class, new Hashtable(src2.ht),
      null);
27.       xjmr.marshall(inScopeEncStyle, Parameter.class, param, null, sink,
      nsStack, ctx);
28.       sink.write(StringUtils.lineSeparator);
29.       param = new Parameter("rows", Vector.class, new Vector(src2.rows),
      null);
30.       xjmr.marshall(inScopeEncStyle, Parameter.class, param, null, sink,
      nsStack, ctx);
31.       sink.write(StringUtils.lineSeparator);
32.       sink.write("</" + context + '>');
33.       nsStack.popScope();
34.     }
35.     public Bean unmarshall(String inScopeEncStyle, QName elementType, Node
      src, XMLJavaMappingRegistry xjmr, SOAPContext ctx)
36.     throws IllegalArgumentException
37.     {
38.       Element root = (Element)src;
39.       Element tempEl = DOMUtils.getFirstChildElement(root);
40.       DataSet target;
41.       try
```

```
42.      {
43.        target =
44.          (DataSet)DataSet.class.newInstance();
45.      }
46.      catch (Exception e)
47.      {
48.        throw new IllegalArgumentException("Problem instantiating bean: " +
      e.getMessage());
49.      }
50.      while (tempEl != null)
51.      {
52.        Bean paramBean = xjmr.unmarshall(inScopeEncStyle,
      RPCConstants.Q_ELEM_PARAMETER, tempEl, ctx);
53.        Parameter param = (Parameter)paramBean.value;
54.        String tagName = tempEl.getTagName();
55.        if (tagName.equals("ht"))
56.        {
57.          target.ht = (Hashtable)param.getValue();
58.        }
59.        if (tagName.equals("rows"))
60.        {
61.          target.rows = (Vector)param.getValue();
62.        }
63.        tempEl = DOMUtils.getNextSiblingElement(tempEl);
64.      }
65.      return new Bean(DataSet.class, target);
66.  }
67. }
```

Marshalling

You do not need to know the specifics on how the marshall() and unmarshall() methods work, but the following sections give a brief explanation of the process.

Marshalling or serialization is the process of mapping Java objects to the XML instance.

In Listing 19-3, Line 21 creates a new namespace scope in the nsStack object. All namespaces used within the application call are pushed on the NSStack. This stack can therefore be used to query a namespace within a given URI.

Line 22 generates the opening element for the structure header, which is then followed by a newline character (line 23).

Lines 26 to 28 marshall the ht parameter of the DataSet.

Line 26 creates a Parameter object with the java.util.Hashtable object that will be passed to the marshall() method on line 27.

Line 27 calls the XMLJavaMappingRegistry.marshall() method and passes the corresponding type of the parameter. By passing the Java data type for the parameter to be serialized, the marshall method of the SOAPMappingRegistry will call the corresponding Serializer for the passed Java data type. To finish with the ht parameter, line 28 writes a newline character.

Lines 29 to 31 follow the same explanation as previously (for the ht parameter) but this time for the rows parameter.

Finally, line 32 closes the element, and the NSStack is popped on line 33.

Unmarshalling

Unmarshalling or deserialization is the construction of Java objects out of the XML instance. This is done by traversing the DOM Node of the XML instance of the specific Java object, locating the tags that correspond to the attributes (and their values) of the customized Java type.

In Listing 19-3, lines 50 to 66 define a loop that traverse the Node object to obtain the elements and inspect their tag names. In the loop process, every child element is unmarshalled to a Bean object that holds the type of the returned object (line 52).

The Bean object holds a value as a reference to a java.lang.Object that is casted to a Parameter object (line 53).

A comparison between the tag names and the QNames of the attributes of the Java object is performed (lines 55 and 59). Whenever there is a match, the appropriate value is returned from the Parameter object after casting it to the corresponding data type (lines 57 and 61).

Finally, on line 65, the unmarshall() returns the type org.apache.soap.util.Bean that holds a reference to the destination Java type.

The class com.tcnd.wasdg.common.DataSetSerializer follows the Apache SOAP implementation in these ways:

▶ The DataSetSerializer is a serializer that implements the org.apache.soap.util.xml .Serializer interface

▶ The DataSetSerializer is a deserializer that implements the org.apache.soap .util.xml.Deserializer interface

Edit and save the DataSetSerializer.java to the directory com/tcnd/wasdg/common of the EJB module WasdgBeans.jar. For example, change to a development directory, such as /BOOK/19/DevSess18Hashed; then compile the DataSetSerializer.java with the following command:

```
# javac  com/tcnd/wasdg/common/DataSetSerializer.java
```

If the compilation is successful, you can add the DataSetSerializer.class to the WasdgBeans.jar of the deployment application using the `addjar` command:

```
# modjar -arc WasdgBeans.jar -name DataSetSerializer.class -from /BOOK/19/DevSess18Hashed
```

The `modjar` command is a utility script that takes a .jar file; add to it named file(s) while keeping the same tree structure. Refer to Appendix D for the syntax of modjar.

Matching a Client's QName() to Its Server Mappings

Table 19-1 shows the correspondence between the qualified name used in a SOAP client and its mapping in the <mappings> child of a URN service.

	Name Space for XML Element	Name of the XML Element
QName() CLIENT	namespaceURI	localPart
dds.xml SERVER	qname-namespace	qname-element

Table 19-1 *Matching Client Qualified Name to Its Corresponding URN Service <mappings>*

Consider the fragment of code shown in Listing 19-14. This code corresponds to the SOAP client program testsoap2, which maps the Java DataSet. The program testsoap2 is provided with the distribution code of this chapter.

Listing 19-14 *A code fragment of a SOAP client program*

```
1.      SOAPMappingRegistry smr = new SOAPMappingRegistry();
2.      // Create an instance of the Serializer class
3.      DataSetSerializer dsSer = new DataSetSerializer();
4.
5.      // Map the type
6.      smr.mapTypes(Constants.NS_URI_SOAP_ENC,
7.          new QName("urn:xml-soap-dataset-demo", "dataset"),
8.                  DataSet.class, dsSer, dsSer);
9.
10.     // Build the call
11.     Call call = new Call();
12.     call.setSOAPMappingRegistry(smr);
13.     call.setTargetObjectURI("urn:fetchtb");
14.     call.setMethodName("fetch");
15.     call.setEncodingStyleURI(Constants.NS_URI_SOAP_ENC);
16.     Vector params = new Vector();
17.     params.addElement(new Parameter("mReq", Hashtable.class, mReq,
    null));
18.     call.setParams(params);
19.     System.out.println("\n**** Calling EJB FetchTableBean Web service\n");
20.     Response resp;
21.     try
22.     {
23.         resp = call.invoke(url, ""); // router_URL, actionURI
24.     }
```

On line 7, the qualified name should match its corresponding <mappings> for the specific service defined in dds.xml. Listing 19-11 shows the <mappings> child of the corresponding URN service.

On line 17 the mReq is of type java.util.Hashtable, therefore there is no need to specify any type mappings for this parameter. mReq will be automatically handled by SOAP default encoding.

Accessing Beans Using a SOAP Client

When calling a bean using a SOAP client, the SOAP run time handles the calling of that bean's create method. The SOAP run time calls the create method only if this method has not been called previously.

The CreditDebitBean bean that we deployed in the SOAP application previously is called a *web service*. When the stateless session bean CreditDebitBean is running in the context of the SOAP run-time's bean base, such a bean is therefore said to act as a web service to perform a database action: crediting or debiting a banker account record. When the SOAP client makes a call to the method of this service and an instance of the bean is not available, the SOAP run time will make a first call to the EJB create method to obtain a stateless session, and then it will call the requested method.

The next section discusses the SOAP client and setting the environment to run such a client.

Setting the SOAP Client Environment

To successfully compile and run a SOAP client program, you need to add several .jar files to the CLASSPATH environment variable.[4] The soapcp script shown in Listing 19-15 appends the necessary libraries to the CLASSPATH, and it further defines the environment variable SOAPCP to contain the additional .jar archives needed by a SOAP client program.

Listing 19-15   *soapcp*

```
#/bin/sh

wh=$WAS_HOME
CP=$wh/lib/soap.jar
CP=$CP:$wh/lib/xerces.jar
CP=$CP:$wh/lib/certpath.jar
CP=$CP:$wh/lib/xss4j-dsig.jar
CP=$CP:$wh/lib/xalan.jar
CP=$CP:$wh/lib/soap-sec.jar
CP=$CP:$wh/lib/tools.jar
export SOAPCP=$CP
export CLASSPATH=$CLASSPATH:$CP
```

To set up the environment where you will start testing with a SOAP client program, at the command prompt, execute soapcp in its current environment:

```
# .  soapcp
```

---

[4]   The setj.sh (introduced in Chapter 3) includes the necessary libraries to develop with Apache SOAP under WAS. This is to facilitate the programming of the (de)serializer such as the com.tcnd.wasdg.common.DataSetSerializer.

This assumes that the soapcp is in the search PATH; otherwise, you need to explicitly specify its location. If soapcp is in the current directory, then execute this command:

```
# .  ./soapcp
```

Testing with SOAP Clients

In the code distribution, find the source code of two test programs: testsoap1.java and testsoap2.java. Compile the program and test your SOAP application. The program testsoap1 is a SOAP client program that credits or debits a client account. Invoke the program as show here:

```
#java testsoap1 http://your.server:9080/wasbooksoap/servlet/rpcrouter
       client1 5
```

This command will credit client1 with $5.

The program testsoap2 accesses the fetchtb service to return a database table. For example, to fetch the CLIACCNT table from the DBGUIDE database, issue the following command:

```
#java testsoap2 http://your.server:9080/wasbooksoap/servlet/rpcrouter
       CLIACCNT
```

This command will print the CLIACCNT table.

Debugging SOAP Client in a Nutshell

Debugging the SOAP application is fairly simple. The following is a guideline for programmers to follow:

▶ **Ensure there is a functional URL that provides a SOAP router**   Use Lynx to get a quick dump on the MIME header as you did in the section "Deploying the SOAP Application: wasdgsoap.ear." This will return a fault, but it ensures that the URL to the rpcrouter servlet is reachable. In case there is no reachable SOAP route in the web application, the Lynx command will return a 404 error code. This means the org.apache.soap.server.http.RPCRouterServlet servlet is unreachable.

▶ **Ensure that the SOAP deployment descriptor is parsed properly by the application server (WAS)**   If the SOAP deployment descriptor dds.xml cannot be parsed properly by the server, the WAS reports an error in the standard output and/or standard error file.

▶ **Make use of the Fault class to print any Fault code and Fault message returned in the SOAP response**   After invoking a SOAP call, you can check on the success of the response by getting the boolean value returned by response.generatedFault(). If a fault is generated, then you can get the fault by instantiating response.getFault().The getFaultCode() returns the code that shows whether the error is due to the client or the server. The getFaultString() gives a more descriptive message of the error. It is also recommended to read any message printed to the WAS standard output and standard error files.

Wrapping Up

Apache SOAP programming allows you to expose your application on the Internet and make it available to other applications, making application-to-application communication possible.

This chapter explained how to program and debug a SOAP application in WAS. The chapter used the WasdgBeans example developed in Chapter 18 to turn these beans into web services. The SOAP deployment descriptors, the SOAP client programs, and the SOAP server configuration file were discussed throughout this chapter. In addition, you learned how to write a custom (de)serializer to (un)marshall specific Java data types.

Fundamental Security Programming: Applying JAAS

IN THIS CHAPTER:

Installing the Java Authentication and Authorization Service (JAAS)

Programming JAAS

A JAAS Example: FetchFile and PrivilegedFetchFile

Securing the Teller Login/Logout

The Future of JAAS

Cipher

Almost every computer science book contains a chapter on security; but because security is precious, a single chapter on it must be just as precious. Therefore, this chapter addresses security using the latest goodies of Java delivery: the Java Authentication and Authorization Service (JAAS), Cipher, and a combination of both with UNIX[1] system authorization.

Security falls into four separate categories: client browser security, users and groups role security at the application level, application-level security, and system-level security. At the client browser level, the HTTPS has been adopted to protect a user's browser data from another user's browser. Using users and groups role security is a logical approach (adopted in J2EE) to map security roles to promote the portability of the web application.

Nonetheless, protecting the web application from the rest of the world requires the implementation of security at the application level. System-level security protects saved user data from being tempered with by means of development tools or administrative tools, programs or programmers, or system commands. This chapter addresses how to combine both application-level security and system-level security to protect user data from developers. The discussion is based on the teller application, which uses JAAS, UNIX authentication, and database authorization together to demonstrate how efficiently Java coding handles security in a web application. You should also study HTTPS and J2EE security, which are beyond the scope of this book.

This chapter addresses JAAS rather than J2EE application security because J2EE application security is still exposed in plain text to developers, and it is not yet reliable for enterprises. J2EE and its successors will eventually provide a more adequate way to configure security rather than in the XML descriptor files.

This chapter takes into consideration the release of the Java 2 SDK, Standard Edition v1.4 (hopefully, it will be supported in the future version of WAS) so that the example will run on the current WAS v4 and can be easily migrated to the later version.

Using JAAS at one end and Cipher at the other forms a good programming basis. Therefore, the chapter concludes with an example in which Cipher is used to sign HTML pages treated as Java objects. JAAS is used here with the assumption that you have thoroughly read the JAAS documentation available at the Sun Microsystems site: http://java.sun.com. Within the examples, the discussion of the differences between IBM Java 2 v1.3 and Sun v1.3 (using JNDI 1.2 security) is minimal. Such differences will eventually be eradicated with the new release of WAS supporting Java 2 v1.4.

---

[1] The aim is to use the security that is implemented on each platform, whether it is UNIX, NT, Linux, Solaris, or any other platform. This chapter uses common ground between all platforms to explain JAAS security, which is becoming a standard under the Java 2 SDK v1.4. The code will work on any platform with any version of WAS.

Installing the Java Authentication and Authorization Service (JAAS)

The setj.sh script, discussed in Chapter 3, sets the JAAS library in the classpath. At this point, you can set your environment with this command:

```
# .  /tools/env/setj.sh  w130
```

Check whether your environment has been properly set to point to the JAAS library:

```
# set | grep -i jaas
```

Although your environment is pointing to the JAAS libraries, you must download JAAS from the Sun Microsystems web site. Extract the archive and move the jaas.jar file to the appropriate directory shown in your environment, for example, the $JAVA_HOME/jre/lib/ext directory.

You will also need to add the jaas.jar file to the WAS startup classpath. Edit the setupCmdLine.sh file and add the fully qualified name of the jaas.jar file to WAS_CLASSPATH; for example, you may have copied the jaas.jar file to $JAVA_HOME/jre/lib/ext/jaas.jar as shown on line 21 in Figure 20-1. The rest of the highlighted segment in Figure 20-1 is explained in the section "Securing the Teller Login/Logout" later in this chapter.

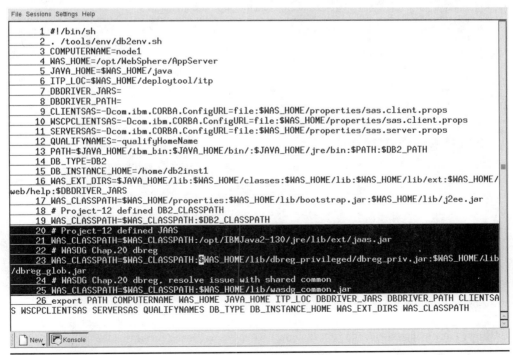

Figure 20-1   *setupCmdLine.sh of WAS AEs v4 showing how to enable JAAS in WAS*

Instead of the colon (:), you will use a semicolon (;) on Windows NT to separate the elements of the classpath. You should also read the documentation associated with the JAAS package and run the sample example to make sure your environment is properly set. The JAAS binary is usually packaged with a sample application that you can locate in the directory doc/samples where you extracted the package. The sample example is a good tool to experiment with to learn about the doAs() and callback methods of JAAS. Although this chapter does not discuss JAAS in detail, it is applied to show you how to make use of it in a web application that is loaded and run under WAS, such as the WASDG application.

To test whether JAAS has been added properly to the WAS classpath, restart WAS and either look into the standard output for the startup classpath of WAS (refer to Chapter 15,) or run the `ps` command and grep for the word "jaas.jar." The `ladder` command result can be seen in this illustration.

```
File  Sessions  Settings  Help
root      15272 15960   0 13:01 pts/21    00:00:00 /opt/WebSphere/AppServer/java/jre/bin/exe/java -
classpath /opt/WebSphere/AppServer/properties:/opt/WebSphere/AppServer/lib/bootstrap.jar:/opt/We
bSphere/AppServer/lib/j2ee.jar:/home/db2inst1/sqllib/java/sqlj.zip:/home/db2inst1/sqllib/functio
n:/home/db2inst1/sqllib/java12/db2java.zip:/opt/IBMJava2-130/jre/lib/ext/jaas.jar:/opt/WebSphere
/AppServer/lib:/opt/WebSphere/AppServer/lib/dbreg_privileged/dbreg_priv.jar:/opt/WebSphere/AppSe
rver/lib/dbreg_glob.jar:/opt/WebSphere/AppServer/lib/wasdg_common.jar -Xmx256m -Djava.security.p
olicy=/BOOK/20/dbreg_sysprotected/java.policy -Djava.security.auth.policy=/BOOK/20/dbreg_sysprot
ected/jaas.policy -Djava.security.auth.login.config=/BOOK/20/dbreg_sysprotected/login.conf -Dcom
.ibm.CORBA.ConfigURL=file:/opt/WebSphere/AppServer/properties/sas.server.props -Dws.ext.dirs=/op
t/WebSphere/AppServer/java/lib:/opt/WebSphere/AppServer/classes:/opt/WebSphere/AppServer/lib:/op
t/WebSphere/AppServer/lib/ext:/opt/WebSphere/AppServer/web/help: -Dws.server.config=/opt/WebSphe
re/AppServer/config/server-cfg.xml -Dserver.root=/opt/WebSphere/AppServer -Dcom.ibm.itp.location
=/opt/WebSphere/AppServer/bin -Dcom.ibm.ws.launcher.port=34312 com.ibm.ws.bootstrap.WSLauncher c
om.ibm.ws.runtime.StandardServer -configFile /opt/WebSphere/AppServer/config/server-cfg.xml -nod
eName node1 -serverName Default Server
root      15276 30285   0 13:01 pts/23    00:00:00 grep jaas
You have new mail in /var/spool/mail/root
[root@node1 doas]#
  New    Konsole
```

Programming JAAS

JAAS is used to explicitly enforce permission on users and/or developers when reading/ writing files or executing a program or a piece of code. A JAAS-enabled program can be set to prompt the user to log in (instantiating a LoginContext object). If successful, it is followed by a single method invocation using one of two methods: doAs() or doAsPrivileged(), where the user's login-object is passed along with the code to be executed. Within the context just created, policy files and login configuration files play a role in specifying permission on the code to be executed, and whether any file is to be accessed. You will gain a clear understanding through examples. The code in the section "A JAAS Example: FetchFile and PriviligedFetchFile" is in the doas directory of the extracted code archive of this chapter. The code in the section "Another JAAS Example" is in the doas-zen directory.

The first example is based on a program that runs from the command prompt. The second example makes changes to the first to show JAAS-based servlet programs that run in a WAS web container.

A JAAS Example: FetchFile and PrivilegedFetchFile

The package discussed here is for a program that can fetch the contents of the file /tmp/foo.txt. The foo.txt file has only one line: "Hello jaas!" The program FetchFile is authorized to run the PrivilegedFetchFile program after a successful login. The FetchFile login is carried with a custom login module DbregLoginModule. The login module verifies whether the credentials of the FetchFile (usually read from a callback prompt) match the ones saved internally. The loginname and the loginpassword are not read from a callback method but from a property file; this way, we can use this example as a building block to modify the WASDG application. Note that a servlet running in the web container cannot have a callback method implemented because it is not possible to prompt the user to log in from within a terminal.[2] For this reason, the credentials for all examples throughout this chapter will be read from property files.

The following illustration shows the tree structure of the JAAS-enabled package.

```
File Sessions Settings Help

[root@node2 doas]# numln /tmp/jj123 68
1.   .
2.   ├── README
3.   ├── com
4.   │   └── tcnd
5.   │       └── wasdg
6.   │           ├── common
7.   │           │   ├── StrTool.class
8.   │           │   └── StrTool.java
9.   │           └── dbreg
10.  │               ├── DbregLoginModule.class
11.  │               ├── DbregLoginModule.java
12.  │               ├── DbregPrincipal.class
13.  │               ├── DbregPrincipal.java
14.  │               ├── FetchFile$NullCallbackHandler.class
15.  │               ├── FetchFile.class
16.  │               └── FetchFile.java
17.  ├── dbreg_privileged
18.  │   └── com
19.  │       └── tcnd
20.  │           └── wasdg
21.  │               └── dbreg
22.  │                   ├── PrivilegedFetchFile.class
23.  │                   └── PrivilegedFetchFile.java
24.  ├── jaas.policy
25.  ├── jall
26.  ├── java.policy
27.  └── login.conf
28.
29.  10 directories. 16 files
[root@node2 doas]#
```

Be sure to compile and execute this example successfully. Although you will be executing one Java program to fetch the /tmp/foo.txt file, namely the FetchFile class, a few programs

---

2   It may be possible to implement the callback to be a servlet. For example, if you start a session with a servlet like PostCookie in Chapter 16, the password does not need to be cached by the login module because it can be saved in the session. Such implementation is not covered in this chapter.

are involved in the authorization that you need to code. We will use our own custom authentication scheme and write the DbregLoginModule, shown in Listing 20-2, that implements the LoginModule interface javax.security.auth.spi.LoginModule.

You need to write a login configuration file, for example, login.conf, and pass it in the system settings when starting the Java machine, for example, -Djava.security.auth.login.config= login.conf. Listing 20-1 shows such a login.conf file in which the DbregLoginModule has been selected as the custom login module.

Listing 20-1 *login.conf*

```
FetchFile {
     com.tcnd.wasdg.dbreg.DbregLoginModule required debug=true;
};
```

The FetchFile is the name of the class that we will execute. Of course, the FetchFile is also part of the package that is reflected in the fully qualified name of the class DbregLoginModule. Listing 20-2 shows the DbregLoginModule of our first example.

Listing 20-2 *DbregLoginModule (first example)*

```
1.    package com.tcnd.wasdg.dbreg;
2.
3.    import java.util.*;
4.    import java.io.*;.
6.    import javax.security.auth.*;
7.    import javax.security.auth.callback.*;
8.    import javax.security.auth.login.*;
9.    import javax.security.auth.spi.*;
10.
11.   public class DbregLoginModule implements LoginModule
12.   {
13.       private Subject subject;
14.       private CallbackHandler callbackHandler;
15.       private DbregPrincipal principal;
16.       private Map cacheMap;
17.       private Map options;
18.       private boolean debug;
19.
20.       // State information for the currently authenticated user
21.       private String loginname = "dbreg";
22.       private String dbregloginname = null;
23.       private char[] password = {'p','w','d','0','0','7'};
24.       private char[] dbregpassword = new char[80];
25.       private int length_dbregpassword;
26.
27.       private boolean succeeded = false;
```

```
28.      private boolean commitSucceeded = false;
29.
30.      private static final String
dbguidePropertiesFileName="/BOOK/20/dbreg_sysprotected/dbreg_login.properties"
31.
32.      private void loadDefaultConnectionSettings()
33.      {
34.          java.util.Properties prop;
35.          prop = new Properties();
36.          try
37.          {
38.              prop.load(new FileInputStream(dbguidePropertiesFileName));
39.          }
40.          catch (Exception e)
41.          {
42.              e.printStackTrace();
43.          }
44.          dbregloginname = prop.getProperty("dbregloginname");
45.          String s = prop.getProperty("dbregpassword");
46.          s.getChars(0,s.length(),dbregpassword,0);
47.          length_dbregpassword = s.length();
48.
49.          // Print these to make sure we have the correct data
50.          System.err.println(" -- dbreg_login.properties: " +
     dbregloginname);
51.          System.err.println(" -- dbreg_login.properties: " + s);
52.
53.      }
54.
55.  public void initialize(Subject s, CallbackHandler cb, Map cacheMap,
     Map options)
56.      {
57.          subject = s;
58.          callbackHandler = cb;
59.          cacheMap = cacheMap;
60.          options = options;
61.
62.
63.          loadDefaultConnectionSettings();
64.          // initialize any configured options
65.          debug = "true".equalsIgnoreCase((String)options.get("debug"));
66.          // If any shared map, then put it in here
67.      }
68.
69.  public boolean login() throws LoginException
70.      {
71.          if (debug)
72.              System.err.println("DbregLoginModule login() " +
     dbregloginname);
```

```
73.
74.             // Normally, we'd set this from the getName() method of
75.             // the name callback, or from the user environment.
76.
77.             // Check password and return true if correct
78.             if (loginname.equals(dbregloginname) && (password.length ==
      length_dbregpassword))
79.                {
80.                int i = 0;
81.                while ( i < length_dbregpassword )
82.                   {
83.                   if ( password[i] != dbregpassword[i] ) break;
84.                   i++;
85.                   }
86.                if (i == password.length)
87.                   succeeded = true;
88.                else
89.                   succeeded = false;
90.                }
91.          else
92.             succeeded = false;
93.
94.          if (succeeded)
95.             return true;
96.          else
97.             {
98.                loginname = null;
99.                for (int i = 0; i < password.length; i++) password[i] = ' ';
100.               password = null;
101.               throw new FailedLoginException("Hmm!");
102.            }
103.       }
104.
105.    public boolean commit() throws LoginException
106.       {
107.       if (debug)
108.          System.err.println("DbregLoginModule commit()");
109.
110.       if (!succeeded)
111.          {
112.             // Someone authenticated the user. Clean up...
113.             // Don't add principal to the subject
114.             // the subject
115.             loginname = null;
116.             return false;
117.          }
118.
119.       principal = new DbregPrincipal(loginname);
120.       // dbreg might already be in the subject if another module
121.       // authenticated him.
```

```
122.            if (!subject.getPrincipals().contains(principal))
123.            {
124.                subject.getPrincipals().add(principal);
125.            }
126.
127.            // Clean up our internal state
128.            loginname = null;
129.            commitSucceeded = true;
130.            return true;
131.        }
132.
133.    public boolean abort() throws LoginException
134.        {
135.            if (debug)
136.                System.err.println("DbregLoginModule abort()");
137.
138.            if (succeeded == false)
139.                // We failed, and so did someone else, so just clean up
140.                return false;
141.            else if (succeeded == true && commitSucceeded == true)
142.            {
143.                // login succeeded, but another required module failed
144.                // We must remove our principal and clean up
145.                logout();
146.            }
147.        else
148.            {
149.                // commit failed, even though login succeeded
150.                succeeded = false;
151.            }
152.            return true;
153.        }
154.
155.    public boolean logout() throws LoginException
156.        {
157.            if (debug)
158.                System.err.println("DbregLoginModule logout()");
159.
160.            subject.getPrincipals().remove(principal);
161.            principal = null;
162.            loginname = null;
163.            succeeded = commitSucceeded = false;
164.            return true;
165.        }
166. }
```

Writing a login module that implements the DbregLoginModule interface requires writing a class with the following five methods:

▶ `public void initialize(Subject, CallbackHandler, Map, Map)`, shown on line 55, initializes the login module. One part of the initialization adopted in this chapter is shown in `loadDefaultConnectionSettings()` being called on line 63, and defined on lines 32 to 53. The dbregloginname is read from the property file as a string, and the dbregpassword is set as an array of characters (line 46). The length of the dbregpassword is held in length_dbregpassword, on line 47, so that we can compare it to the original password. On line 65, the debug is initialized to true, since this value has been set in the login.conf file that has been specified in the system settings, for example, using the `Djava.security.auth.login.config=login.conf`. Any option can be passed to the DbregLoginModule by listing it in the login.conf file. Recall, our login.conf file is the following:
```
FetchFile {
com.tcnd.wasdg.dbreg.DbregLoginModule required debug=true;
};
```

▶ public boolean `login()`, on line 69, authenticates the user and returns true for a successful authentication and returns false otherwise. Line 78 compares whether the loginname matches the string dbregloginname and whether the length of the passwords are the same. The passwords are compared character by character, as shown on line 83.

▶ `public boolean commit()`, on line 105, is called if the user is authenticated by the DbregLoginModule as it has been set (as required) in the login.conf file. Once authenticated, the login module must add the appropriate principal objects to the stored object (lines 119 to 125).

▶ `public boolean abort()`, shown on line 133, aborts from the login upon user authentication failure.

▶ `public boolean logout()`, shown on line 155, logs the user out by removing any principal from the saved subject and setting the loginname to null. All the login module states are reset (line 163).

Authorizing the Execution of the FetchFile

The FetchFile program, shown in Listing 20-3, calls the doAs() method to execute the PrivilegedFetchFile. The code is straightforward because it hides all the complexity behind JAAS methods.

Listing 20-3   *FetchFile*

```
1.    package com.tcnd.wasdg.dbreg;
2.
3.    import javax.security.auth.*;
```

```
4.   import javax.security.auth.callback.*;
5.   import javax.security.auth.login.*;
6.
7.   public class FetchFile
8.   {
9.       static class NullCallbackHandler implements CallbackHandler
10.      {
11.          public void handle(Callback[] cb)
12.          {
13.              throw new IllegalArgumentException("Not implemented.");
14.          }
15.      }
16.
17.      static LoginContext lc = null;
18.      public static void main(String[] args)
19.      {
20.          // use the configured LoginModules for the FetchFile entry
21.          try
22.          {
23.              lc = new LoginContext("FetchFile", new
     NullCallbackHandler());
24.          }
25.          catch (LoginException le)
26.          {
27.              le.printStackTrace();
28.              System.exit(-1);
29.          }
30.          try
31.          {
32.              lc.login();
33.          }
34.          catch (Exception e)
35.          {
36.              System.out.println("Login failed: " + e);
37.              System.exit(-1);
38.          }
39.
40.          // At this point the authenticated user can execute the code
41.          String c = (String)Subject.doAs(lc.getSubject(), new
     PrivilegedFetchFile());
42.          System.out.println("FETCHED FILE CONTENT: " + c);
43.          System.exit(0);
44.      }
45.  }
```

On line 32, the DbregLoginModule is consulted to verify whether the login is successful before executing the doAs() method on line 41. The FetchFile itself is also secured and will not be executed unless it falls into the context of the Java policy file, for example, java.policy shown in Listing 20-4.

Listing 20-4   *java.policy*

```
1.    grant codebase "file:/BOOK/20/doas/" {
2.        permission java.security.AllPermission;
3.    };
4.    /***
5.    grant codebase "file:[path]sample.jar" {
6.        permission javax.security.auth.AuthPermission
"createLoginContext";
7.        permission javax.security.auth.AuthPermission "doAs";
8.        permission java.io.FilePermission "foo.txt", "read";
9.    };
10.   */
```

Only the first three lines are active in the java.policy file; the rest of the lines summarize another security setting that is possible even at the code level (the sample.jar archive on line 5). This file grants all code in the /BOOK/20/doas all permissions. When loading the code in WAS, this file will not have any effect. You see why in the section "Another JAAS Example: ZenFile Servlet and PrivilegedFetchFile," when we experiment with the JAAS-enabled servlet. In fact, the java.security is managed by WAS' Java machine, and your code will not override or have any effect on the Java security handled by WAS' Java machine.

Securing the PrivilegedFetchFile Program

The PrivilegedFetchFile program, shown in Listing 20-5, implements PrivilegedAction so that the run() methods execute the code of its body. This is like a run-time evaluation of a program that is protected and is executed only by selected authorized callers. In our case, the caller is FetchFile (see Listing 20-3,) and the authorization is done in the DbregLoginModule (see Listing 20-2).

Listing 20-5   *PrivilegedFetchFile*

```
1.    package com.tcnd.wasdg.dbreg;
2.
3.    import com.tcnd.wasdg.common.StrTool;
4.
5.    import java.io.*;
6.    import java.security.*;
7.
8.    class PrivilegedFetchFile implements PrivilegedAction
9.    {
10.       public Object run()
11.       {
12.           String content = StrTool.getFile("/tmp/foo.txt");
13.           return new String(content);
```

```
14.        }
15.    }
```

On line 12 in Listing 20-5, the permission of the /tmp/foo.txt file is granted to be read.

On line 15 of Listing 20-2, the DbregPrincipal is a Java class that you need to implement. Listing 20-6 shows such a simple class with a getter method for the name of the authenticator, and a comparison method for objects' equality since the name of a Java string object of type String.

Listing 20-6   *DbregPrincipal*

```
1.     package com.tcnd.wasdg.';
2.
3.     import java.security.*;
4.     import java.io.*;
5.
6.     public class DbregPrincipal implements Principal, Serializable {
7.         private String name;
8.
9.         public DbregPrincipal(String s) {
10.            name = s;
11.        }
12.
13.        public String getName() {
14.            return name;
15.        }
16.
17.        public boolean equals(Object o) {
18.            if (!(o instanceof DbregPrincipal))
19.                return false;
20.            return ((DbregPrincipal) o).name.equals(name);
21.        }
22.    }
```

Login Configuration and Policy Files

Along with the application, three files determine the behavior of the JAAS application, namely the execution of the FetchFile program. One of them, the login.conf (see Listing 20-1), was already discussed. The other two are the Java policy configuration file (java.policy, shown in Listing 20-4) and the JAAS policy configuration file (jaas.policy, shown in Listing 20-7).

Listing 20-7   *jaas.policy file*

```
1.     grant codebase "file:/BOOK/20/doas/dbreg_privileged/"
2.         Principal com.tcnd.wasdg.dbreg.DbregPrincipal "dbreg" {
```

```
3.      permission java.io.FilePermission "${/}tmp${/}foo.txt",
"read";
4.  };
```

While these policy files can be easily changed to test with a different setting, this will become much harder to do when you use JAAS in WAS. These policy files are loaded as system properties when you start WAS, and for any change to take effect, you need to restart WAS. This is normal because WAS is started as a Java machine similarly to when you execute the java bare command. The changes in the login.conf file are dynamic because the content of the file is read by the login module during run time.

Executing the FetchFile program

The command to execute the FetchFile program is lengthy. It must list four of the system properties to be passed to the Java machine. Make sure you are in the directory where you compiled your code, for example, /BOOK/20/doas, and issue the command shown in the following illustration. The result is obvious: Hello jaas!

NOTE

The distribution code provided for this chapter also shows the reader how to test with the many programs discussed in this chapter.

```
File  Sessions  Settings  Help
[root@node1 doas]# java -classpath .:./dbreg_privileged  -Djava.security.manager -Djava.security
olicy=java.policy -Djava.security.auth.policy=jaas.policy -Djava.security.auth.login.config=logi
conf  com.tcnd.wasdg.dbreg.FetchFile
 -- dbreg_login.properties: dbreg
 -- dbreg_login.properties: pwd007
DbregLoginModule login() dbreg
DbregLoginModule commit()
FETCHED FILE CONTENT: Hello jaas!
[root@node1 doas]#
New  Konsole
```

Another JAAS Example: ZenFile Servlet and PrivilegedFetchFile

Applying JAAS to secure the access to a file system or to execute the bytecode of a file requires a particular discipline in programming. There is no deployment methodology in applying JAAS; however, this section provides guidelines that you can follow to ease the operation in applying JAAS security to your web application.

The principal name, selected directories on the file system, policy files, login configuration file, and Java programs all are involved in JAAS programming. The method discussed here derives the program names, the directory names, the directory-holding property files, the login configuration file and policy files, and the Java package name from the name of the principal. Although this is not dictated in JAAS programming guidelines, it is recommended to enforce such a methodology in your programming, first to minimize confusion in your programs, and second, to have the possibility to expand your code for as many principals as you need. Usually, an application needs a few principals to be assigned privileged authority on classes and signed files.

The principal in question is the user dbreg. This user will be the only one to have the privilege of fetching a file by executing the PrivilegedFetchFile program. Select a base directory where you will prepare the programs for this section, for example, /BOOK/20/ doas-zen. For the principal dbreg, we will create three directories, as shown in Table 20-1:

For each of the directories shown in Table 20-1, the following files are used in this example:

- ▶ **com/tcnd/wasdg/dbreg/** DbregPrincipal.java, DbregLoginModule.java, and ZenFile.java

- ▶ **dbreg_privileged/com/tcnd/wasdg/dbreg/** PrivilegedFetchFile.java

- ▶ **dbreg_sysprotected/** login.conf, java.policy, and jaas.policy

In addition to these files, you will use the jall script to compile the package, and the dbreg2was script to deploy the package. The dbreg2was is a custom script that is run from within the directory holding the package com.tcnd.wasdg.dbreg, for example, /BOOK/20/ doas-zen, and will be explained later in the section "Deploying the Code in WAS."

The tree structure for the com.tcnd.wadg.dbreg package is shown in Figure 20-2.

Compile the package by executing jall. This will generate a class file for each program. The ZenFile.java servlet will have two class files: ZenFile.class (line 16) and ZenFile$NullCallbackHandler.class (line 15). On line 14, the class file FetchFile. class~ illegalaccessor has been added on purpose and is explained later in this section.

Directory	Description
com/tcnd/wasdg/dbreg	This directory will contain the package com.tcnd.wasdg.dbreg. All Java classes using JAAS should be privatized and contained in the same package.
dbreg_privileged	The user dbreg is the only user who has the privilege to execute classes from within this directory. However, as mentioned previously, because all Java classes using JAAS must be contained in the same package, you must create the directory to hold the package com.tcnd.wasdg.dbreg in this directory: dbreg_privileged/com/tcnd/wasdg/dbreg.
dbreg_sysprotected	This directory can be accessed only by root. It contains property, policy, and configuration files. All files are set as read only for user root. Therefore, developers need to have root access to access any of these files.

Table 20-1 *Directories Created for the First JAAS Example*

```
File Sessions Settings Help
1.  .
2.  ├── ./Dist
3.  ├── ./com
4.  │       └── ./com/tcnd
5.  │               └── ./com/tcnd/wasdg
6.  │                       ├── ./com/tcnd/wasdg/common
7.  │                       │       ├── ./com/tcnd/wasdg/common/StrTool.class
8.  │                       │       └── ./com/tcnd/wasdg/common/StrTool.java
9.  │                       └── ./com/tcnd/wasdg/dbreg
10. │                               ├── ./com/tcnd/wasdg/dbreg/DbregLoginModule.class
11. │                               ├── ./com/tcnd/wasdg/dbreg/DbregLoginModule.java
12. │                               ├── ./com/tcnd/wasdg/dbreg/DbregPrincipal.class
13. │                               ├── ./com/tcnd/wasdg/dbreg/DbregPrincipal.java
14. │                               ├── ./com/tcnd/wasdg/dbreg/FetchFile.class~illegalaccessor
15. │                               ├── ./com/tcnd/wasdg/dbreg/ZenFile$NullCallbackHandler.class
16. │                               ├── ./com/tcnd/wasdg/dbreg/ZenFile.class
17. │                               └── ./com/tcnd/wasdg/dbreg/ZenFile.java
18. ├── ./dbreg2was
19. ├── ./dbreg_privileged
20. │       └── ./dbreg_privileged/com
21. │               └── ./dbreg_privileged/com/tcnd
22. │                       └── ./dbreg_privileged/com/tcnd/wasdg
23. │                               └── ./dbreg_privileged/com/tcnd/wasdg/dbreg
24. │                                       ├── ./dbreg_privileged/com/tcnd/wasdg/dbreg/PrivilegedFetchFile.class
25. │                                       └── ./dbreg_privileged/com/tcnd/wasdg/dbreg/PrivilegedFetchFile.java
26. ├── ./jall
27. └── ./javafiles.list
28.
29. 11 directories, 15 files
```

New   Konsole

Figure 20-2   *Directory tree structure where the com.tcnd.wasdg.dbreg package is compiled*

NOTE

Line 6 shows that com.tcnd.wasdg.common defines the StrTool class: although you might have this class available in the web application (as set in Chapters 16 and 17) for example, $INSTALLEDAPPS/wasdg.ear/ webapp/WEB-INF/classes/com/tcnd/wasdg/common directory, you still need to move such a package out of the web application deployment directory and make it available in the WAS classpath (as shown in Figure 20-1, line 25). This is important because JAAS-enabled applications will not use the symbols from web application libraries. In addition, your JAAS-enabled application might suffer from class casting issues at the session level (explained in the section "Class Casting and Symbolic Name Resolution" later in this chapter).

Deploying the Code in WAS

In most of the previous chapters, the code developed was easily tested with the use of the svlbuild script. Recall that svlbuild recompiles servlets and copies them to the web application tree in the $INSTALLEDAPPS directory. Using svlbuild is not possible in this example for two reasons. First, JAAS programs need to be loaded in the WAS startup because system properties need to be set. Second, the libraries referred to by a JAAS-enabled servlet cannot use the classes that are defined in the web application tree (for example, $INSTALLEDAPPS/ wasdg.ear/webapp/WEB-INF/classes), even though their visibility comes in the first order (discussed in Chapter 15).

Deploying the Code in WAS Startup   To deploy the code in WAS, the dbreg2was script shown in Listing 20-8 is a sufficient script to package and deploy the sample application for this second example.

Listing 20-8   *dbreg2was*

```
1.   #!/bin/sh
2.
3.   # This script is invoked from within the doas-zen directory
4.   #
5.   # Archive the dbreg global login (dbreg_glob.jar) and the privileged
6.   # programs to access (dbreg_priv.jar) then move them to $WAS_HOME/lib
7.   # and $WAS_HOME/lib/dbreg_privileged respectively.
8.
9.   # Start clean
10.  (cd Dist; rm -rf com)
11.  # The program and its associated JAAS
12.  (cd Dist; tar cvf - -C ../ com/tcnd/wasdg/dbreg | tar xvf - )
13.  (cd Dist; jar cvf dbreg_glob.jar com/tcnd/wasdg/dbreg)
14.  # Move it to WAS_HOME/lib
15.  (cd Dist; rm -rf com; mv -f dbreg_glob.jar $WAS_HOME/lib )
16.  # Clean again
17.  (cd Dist; rm -rf com)
18.  # The privileged program(s)
19.  (cd Dist; tar cvf - -C ../dbreg_privileged com/tcnd/wasdg/dbreg -C ../
         com/tcnd/wasdg/common | tar xvf - )
20.  (cd Dist; jar cvf dbreg_priv.jar com/tcnd/wasdg)
21.
22.  # Make sure we have a dbreg_privileged directory in WAS_HOME/lib
23.  (cd $WAS_HOME/lib; mkdir dbreg_privileged)
24.  # Move it to WAS_HOME/lib/dbreg_privileged
25.  (cd Dist; rm -rf com; mv -f dbreg_priv.jar
         $WAS_HOME/lib/dbreg_privileged)
26.  # Clean before you leave
27.  (cd Dist; rm -rf com)
28.  echo DONE
```

You are left with such a specific script on purpose: to obtain a clearer understanding of how to load a JAAS-enabled servlet. The script is commented to avoid detailed explanation.

Adding the ZenFile Servlet to the Web Application   You need to register the ZenFile servlet in the web.xml descriptor. Change the directory to BASE_DEV (for example, /BOOK/20/Code) and edit the servlets.list file, adding this line:

```
zenfile   com.tcnd.wasdg.dbreg.ZenFile   zen
```

Save the servlets.list file and run the resetwebxml script to update the web.xml file in the BASE_DEV directory and in the deployment directory.

Adding the System Properties   Start the administrative console to add three system properties to the startup of the Java machine. In the left pane, select WebSphere Domain | Nodes | <nodename> | Application Servers | Process Definition | JVM Settings. Then scroll down the right pane and click System Properties. Click New to add each of the three system properties listed in Table 20-2.

Figure 20-3 shows how to add a system property.

Figure 20-4 shows all three properties after being added. Remember to save your settings before exiting the administrative console.

> **CAUTION**
>
> *Do not add the java.security.manager as a system property. This will cause WAS to hang.*

Edit and make the appropriate changes in the policy files and the login configuration file.

We have already seen these files in the section "Programming JAAS:" login.conf (see Listing 20-1), java.policy (see Listing 20-4), and jaas.policy (see Listing 20-7). Refer to the code distribution of the current example for the content of these files.

Restart WAS.

```
# $STOPWAS; $STARTWAS
```

Test your servlet by requesting the URI /wasbook/zen, as illustrated here.

System Property Name	Value
java.security.policy	/BOOK/20/dbreg_sysprotected/java.policy
java.security.auth.policy	/BOOK/20/dbreg_sysprotected/jaas.policy
java.security.auth.login.config	/BOOK/20/dbreg_sysprotected/login.conf

Table 20-2   *System Properties and Their Values*

NOTE

Both the jaas.policy and the java.policy are not enforced when JAAS is used in WAS; however, the login process and the privileged action of JAAS are perfectly operational. The section "Securing the Teller Login/Logout" shows how to apply such a login and apply authorization to the Logout servlet solely to update a teller's logout time.

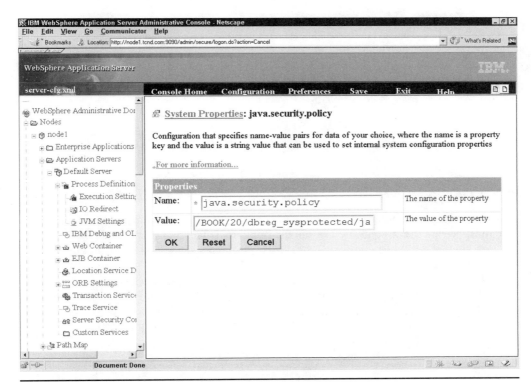

Figure 20-3   *Adding java.security.policy as a WAS system property*

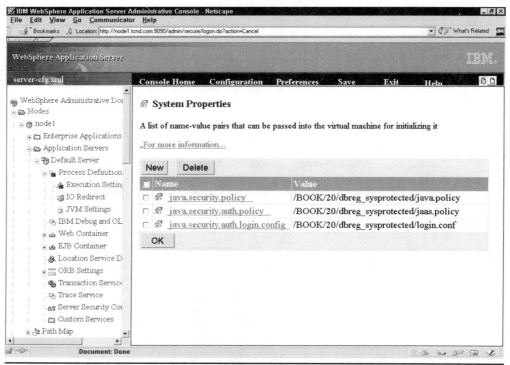

Figure 20-4   *java.policy, jaas.policy, and login.conf added as system properties in WAS*

Illegal Accessor

Until now everything has gone well, and the ZenFile servlet fetched the foo.txt file; however, you must be sure that no one else can run the PriviligedFetchFile piece of code. In any event, such an attempt to run the code using the doAs() (without a successful login authorization) from a servlet other than ZenFile is called an illegal access.

In Figure 20-2 on line 14, the bytecode of a FetchFile servlet has been saved in the file FetchFile.class~illegalaccessor. Rename this class to FetchFile.class and repeat the deployment as explained previously in the section "Deploying the Code in WAS." Then register this servlet in the web.xml file: change the directory to /BOOK/20/Code and edit the servlets.list to add the following line:

```
illegalfetch    com.tcnd.wasdg.dbreg.FetchFile    fetch
```

Update the web.xml by running resetwebxml, and request the FetchFile servlet by typing in the browser **http://your.web.server/wasbook/fetch**. Inspect the standard output file to locate the error:

```
1.   [5/15/02 23:31:37:645 EDT] 102573d6 WebGroup      X Servlet Error: try to
     access class com/tcnd/wasdg/dbreg/PrivilegedFetchFile from class
     com/tcnd/wasdg/dbreg/FetchFile: java.lang.IllegalAccessError: try to
     access class com/tcnd/wasdg/dbreg/PrivilegedFetchFile from class
     com/tcnd/wasdg/dbreg/FetchFile
2.      at com.tcnd.wasdg.dbreg.FetchFile.doGet(FetchFile.java:57)
3.      at javax.servlet.http.HttpServlet.service(HttpServlet.java:740)
4.      at javax.servlet.http.HttpServlet.service(HttpServlet.java:853)
```

IllegalAccessorError is a run-time error that occurs when a program attempts to access or modify a field or call a method to which it does not have access.

Alternative Login Modules

At the beginning of this chapter, you practiced with a JAAS application run on the command prompt, and next, you practiced with a simple JAAS servlet application deployed in WAS. As you can see, the user (or developer) with the login name dbreg does not need to be authenticated on the system to be able to use JAAS. This is called *custom login,* because we customized the login module with DbregLoginModule that implements the LoginModule.

The next version of WAS is expected to support Java 2 v1.4, in which more system authentication is available, such as NIS+. (This is currently available only with JNDI v1.2 from Sun Microsystems.) Therefore, you can authenticate the dbreg user using the operating system or NIS+. For such a change to take effect, all you need to do is have dbreg as a valid account on your UNIX system, and his or her password is mapped with the NIS+/YP map. Then edit the login.conf file and change the authentication method to refer to the JNDI login module as shown in the following example:

```
1.   ZenFile {
2.      com.sun.security.auth.module.JndiLoginModule required
3.         user.provider.url="nis://node1.tcnd.com/arayech/user"
4.         group.provider.url="nis://node1.tcnd.com/arayech/system/group";
5.   };
```

This assumes that NIS+/YP is installed on the network of tcnd.com, and that the system on which the authentication will occur is bound. To check whether or not the system is bound, use the command ypwhich, or look into the directory /var/yp for the binding. In the preceding example, node1.tcnd.com is the hostname and arayech is the YP domain name.

You can also use other authentication methods such as those provided by the Windows NT and UNIX operating systems.

Securing the Teller Login/Logout

When a teller logs in, the first screen shows the last time he or she logged in and logged out. Printing such information the first time a teller enters the web application is a good, informative approach to protect the teller. This is similar to the classical login approach that is followed on a UNIX or mainframe green screen. The following illustration shows the time-sensitive information for a teller logging in to the WASDG application.

However, developers have access to the database and can alter the timestamp of the teller's last login/logout. This is possible because programmers of the WASDG application can write Java programs that instantiate the DataAccessComponent (see Chapter 9), and they can also look at the dbguide.properties file in which the authentication of the dbuser is stored. Such a security issue might be more contrasted in financial, governmental, and military agencies where security must be distributed between the responsible individuals or the programmers. In fact, security is realized by segregating the application and distributing it to unrelated individuals (even programmers), each of whom will be set with a different authorization schema.

To better understand this concept, we will redesign the WASDG application to take care of such a security hole. Changes will apply only to the Logout servlet; the TellerLogged servlet is kept as it is for comparison. In the next section, JAAS is briefly discussed before making the application JAAS-enabled. You will also learn more about the classes' loading order (discussed in Chapter 15) and how it can affect session management (discussed in Chapters 16 and 17), in particular, how the symbolic resolution of a name can affect the class casting.

JAAS-Enabling the Logout of the WASDG Application

In the earlier section "Securing the PrivilegedFetchFile Program" we used dbreg in the package name com.tcnd.wasdg.dbreg. Any other name can be used for a package, but we chose dbreg to keep consistency in our nomination throughout the chapter. We will enforce such consistency so that our code can be easily understood and used as a building block when JAAS-enabling a web application.

The previous section discussed how the dbreg principal gains access to and executes the PrivelegedFetchFile program. The dbreg is not really a UNIX user, and his or her authentication has been set using our custom DbregLoginModule. In this section, we will create the dbreg account as a UNIX user account that is granted access to update the EMPPWD table. The dbuser previously set in Chapter 9 will be denied from updating records in the EMPPWD table.

Segregation of the Developer's Roles

Users, developers, and administrators use the web application all at once. To separate and protect the application from developers, you need to put a hierarchy in place, in which your

	System Auth	JAAS Auth to Execute Privileged Code (login.conf)	Control UDB Instance	UPDATE Table EMPPWD (grant command)	Authorized Property Directory (UNIX chmod 700)	Authorized Property Directory (JAAS jaas.policy)
root	Y	-	Y (use *su*)	Y (use *su*)	Y	-
db2inst1	Y	-	Y	Y	-	-
dbreg	Y	Y	-	Y	-	Y
dbuser	Y	-	-	-	-	-

Table 20-3   *Authority of the Four Main Users*

application is protected by hiding authorization data, such as login configuration data. To better understand this, consider all four users who might be involved in the web application, from starting the application server to writing a servlet. Table 20-3 summarizes the authority of users: root, db2inst1, dbreg, and dbuser.

Table 20-4 shows the authority of dbreg and dbuser to access system-protected files, and to execute privileged (JAAS-protected) code during WAS run time. The (Y) appears when WAS does not appear to promote the JAAS policy as dictated in our jaas.policy file. The Y appears when the user authority is in effect for the entity shown in the column. Such an entity can be a servlet, a Java class, a property file, or a directory.

When designing your application with JAAS authorization, it is customary to list the essential data that is needed per each principal. For example, here is a list for the dbreg user:

► Principal dbregloginname to be checked against JAAS loginname: dbreg

► Principal dbregloginpassword: pwd12345

► Principal can execute privileged class file: need to read the login.conf file

► Principal system account: dbreg

► Principal system password: pwd007

	Logout	PrivilegedDbregAuth	dbreg_sysprotected	secure_emppwd_dbguide.properties	DataAccessComponent
dbreg	Y	Y	(Y)	Y	Y
dbuser	Y	-	-	-	Y

Table 20-4   *User Authority on doAs() of JAAS-Enabled Servlets and Miscellaneous Property Files*

All property files, policy files, and login configuration files are contained and secured in the dbreg_sysprotected directory. The UNIX security is applied in here, masking all bits except for the root to be able to read these files as shown in the illustration.

```
File Sessions Settings Help
[root@node1 20]# ls -ld dbreg_sysprotected
drwx------   2 root     root         4096 May 15 22:26 dbreg_sysprotected
[root@node1 20]# ls -l dbreg_sysprotected
total 20
-r--------   1 root     root           43 May 15 18:01 dbreg_login.properties
-r--------   1 root     root          491 May 15 18:17 jaas.policy
-r--------   1 root     root          734 May 15 18:22 java.policy
-r--------   1 root     root          363 May 15 22:26 login.conf
-r--------   1 root     root          115 May 15 22:16 update_emppwd_dbguide.properties
[root@node1 20]# █
```

The Privileged Tree Structure for the Logout Servlet

The following illustration shows the build tree we will compile the JAAS-enabled Logout servlet used in the WASDG application.

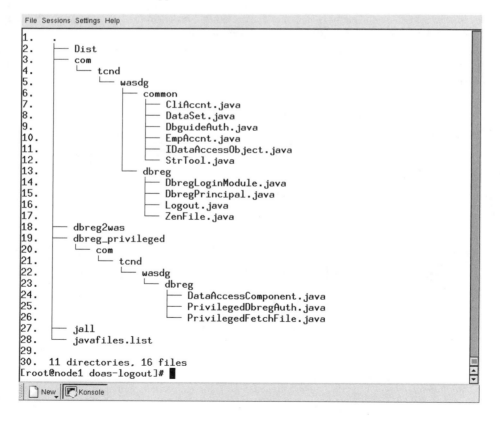

```
File Sessions Settings Help
1.  .
2.  ├── Dist
3.  ├── com
4.  │   └── tcnd
5.  │       └── wasdg
6.  │           ├── common
7.  │           │   ├── CliAccnt.java
8.  │           │   ├── DataSet.java
9.  │           │   ├── DbguideAuth.java
10. │           │   ├── EmpAccnt.java
11. │           │   ├── IDataAccessObject.java
12. │           │   └── StrTool.java
13. │           └── dbreg
14. │               ├── DbregLoginModule.java
15. │               ├── DbregPrincipal.java
16. │               ├── Logout.java
17. │               └── ZenFile.java
18. ├── dbreg2was
19. ├── dbreg_privileged
20. │   └── com
21. │       └── tcnd
22. │           └── wasdg
23. │               └── dbreg
24. │                   ├── DataAccessComponent.java
25. │                   ├── PrivilegedDbregAuth.java
26. │                   └── PrivilegedFetchFile.java
27. ├── jall
28. └── javafiles.list
29.
30.  11 directories, 16 files
[root@node1 doas-logout]# █
```

Changes in the Database

Once again, consider the dbguide.sql script in Chapter 9. The dbuser has been granted access to delete, insert, and update the EMPPWD table.

```
GRANT CONNECT ON DATABASE TO USER DBUSER
GRANT SELECT, INSERT, UPDATE ON TABLE EMPPWD TO USER DBUSER
```

Granting the update on the EMPPWD table to the dbuser was necessary so that the TellerLogged servlet and the previously discussed Logout servlet can update the teller record upon login and logout. The dbuser has been granted all access rights on the DBGUIDE table for simplicity; therefore, all servlets that access the DBGUIDE database instantiate the DataAccessComponent in their init() method. Such instantiation leads to a default loading of the dbguide.properties file.

However, the dbuser must be restricted from updating the table EMPPWD, and dbreg is the only one authorized to update such a table. The dbguide-20.sql reflects such a change in the DBGUIDE database.

```
GRANT CONNECT ON DATABASE TO USER DBREG
GRANT CONNECT ON DATABASE TO USER DBUSER
GRANT SELECT, INSERT, UPDATE ON TABLE EMPPWD TO USER DBREG
GRANT SELECT, INSERT ON TABLE EMPPWD TO USER DBUSER
```

First, you need to create the dbreg account that is granted access to update the EMPPWD and CLIPWD tables. Second, you need to rebuild the database by running db2 -f /BOOK/20/DB/dbguide-20.sql, and repopulate the database by executing the ins_dbguide as we already did in Chapter 9.

Edit the property file update_emppwd_dbguide.properties and save it in the dbreg_sysprotected directory. Set its UNIX access bits to 700 (for example, chmod update_emppwd_dbguide.properties 700). The update_emppwd_dbguide.properties is shown in Listing 20-9.

Listing 20-9   *update_emppwd_dbguide.properties*

```
1.   dbdriver=COM.ibm.db2.jdbc.app.DB2Driver2.   dburl=jdbc:db2:DBGUIDE
3.   dbuser=dbreg
4.   dbpassword=pwd007
5.   dbinstance=DB2INST1
```

Changes in the Logout Servlet

The Logout servlet, shown in Listing 20-10, is a JAAS-enabled servlet. It has the privilege to run the PrivilegedDbregAuth (line 48) after a successful login (line 44). The PrivilegedDbregAuth() returns the object that holds the authorization to access and update the database table EMPPWD. The returned object is then passed to the DataAccessComponent to allow such an authorized update on the EMPPWD table, in particular, on the timestamp for the TMLOGOUT field (line 74). Also, line 11 shows that the com.tcnd.wasdg.dataaccess has been commented out, because the DataAccessComponent is now part of the com.tcnd.wasdg.dbreg package.

The changes in the Logout servlet are depicted from lines 1 to 58. The callback is handled in the init() part of the servlet; therefore, the login.conf file is being read only once: every time the servlet is reinitialized. Because the servlet is part of a JAR archive loaded at WAS startup time (for example, $WAS_HOME/lib/dbreg_glob.jar), to reload it so any changes in the login.conf take effect, you need to restart WAS.

Listing 20-10   *Logout*

```
1.   package com.tcnd.wasdg.dbreg;
2.
3.   import javax.security.auth.*;
4.   import javax.security.auth.callback.*;
5.   import javax.security.auth.login.*;
6.
7.   import java.io.*;
8.   import javax.servlet.*;
9.   import javax.servlet.http.*;
10.  import java.util.Hashtable;
11.  // Changed -- import com.tcnd.wasdg.dataaccess.*;
12.  import com.tcnd.wasdg.common.*;
13.
14.  public class Logout extends javax.servlet.http.HttpServlet
15.  {
16.      static class NullCallbackHandler implements CallbackHandler
17.      {
18.          public void handle(Callback[] cb)
19.          {
20.          // we won't implement this one
21.              throw new IllegalArgumentException("Not implemented.");
22.          }
23.      }
24.
25.      static LoginContext lc = null;
26.
27.      DataAccessComponent DAC;
28.
29.      public void init() throws ServletException
30.      {
31.          System.out.println(" > INIT Logout!");
32.          // use the configured LoginModules for the Logout
33.          try
34.          {
35.              lc = new LoginContext("Logout", new NullCallbackHandler());
36.          }
37.          catch (LoginException le)
38.          {
39.              // throw exception -1
40.              le.printStackTrace();
41.          }
```

```
42.          try
43.          {
44.              lc.login();
45.              // At this point the authenticated user can execute the code
46.              // Get the privileged object holding the authorization to the
     DBGUIDE
47.              // specifically for the principal dbreg, and instantiate a
     DAC
48.              DbguideAuth dbregObj =
     (DbguideAuth)Subject.doAs(lc.getSubject(), new PrivilegedDbregAuth());
49.              // Show to standard output only for learning reason, must be
     deleted otherwise.
50.              dbregObj.show();
51.              DAC = new DataAccessComponent(dbregObj);
52.          }
53.          catch (Exception e)
54.          {
55.              // throw exception -1
56.              System.out.println("Login failed: " + e);
57.          }
58.      }
59.
60.
61.
62.      public void doGet(HttpServletRequest request, HttpServletResponse
     response)
63.              throws IOException
64.      {
65.          String content = null;
66.
67.          HttpSession session = request.getSession(true);
68.          // make sure to get rid of the session
69.          if (session.isNew() == false) {
70.              content = "LOGOUT: TMLOGOUT updated and session invalidated.
     Bye!";
71.              // Update the login time in two statements
72.              EmpAccnt aEmp = (EmpAccnt)session.getAttribute("teller");
73.              IDataAccessObject iDAO = DAC.createDAObject();
74.              iDAO.setCommandString("UPDATE DB2INST1.EMPPWD SET TMLOGOUT =
     (CURRENT TIMESTAMP) WHERE USERID = '" + aEmp.getUserID() + "'");
75.              iDAO = DAC.executeUpdate(iDAO);
76.              session.invalidate();
77.          }
78.          else
79.          {
80.              content = "Not in session... Bye anyway!";
81.          }
82.
83.          response.setContentType("text/html");
84.          response.setHeader("Pragma", "no-cache");
85.          response.setHeader("Cache-Control", "no-cache");
```

```
86.            response.setDateHeader("Expires", 0);
87.
88.            ServletOutputStream out = response.getOutputStream();
89.            out.println(content);
90.            out.close();
91.        }
92.    }
```

Line 48 shows that the PrivilegedDbregAuth() is called to return the object DbguideAuth. The DbguideAuth is shown in Listing 20-11. This is just a simple class that contains a list of accessor methods.

Listing 20-11   *DbguideAuth*

```
1.    package com.tcnd.wasdg.common;
2.
3.    // public class DbguideAuth
4.    public class DbguideAuth implements java.io.Serializable
5.    {
6.        private String dbDriver;
7.        private String dbUrl;
8.        private String dbUser;
9.        private String dbPassword;
10.
11.       public DbguideAuth()
12.       {
13.       }
14.
15.       public String getDbDriver() {return dbDriver;}
16.       public void setDbDriver(String s) {dbDriver = s;}
17.
18.       public String getDbUrl() {return dbUrl;}
19.       public void setDbUrl(String s) {dbUrl = s;}
20.
21.       public String getDbUser() {return dbUser;}
22.       public void setDbUser(String s) {dbUser = s;}
23.
24.       public String getDbPassword() {return dbPassword;}
25.       public void setDbPassword(String s) {dbPassword = s;}
26.
27.       public void show()
28.       {
29.           System.out.println("dbDriver: " + dbDriver);
30.           System.out.println("dbUrl: " + dbUrl);
31.           System.out.println("dbUser: " + dbUser);
32.           System.out.println("dbPassword: " + dbPassword);
33.       }
34.    }
```

In the Logout, the JAAS login authentication is set to DbregLoginModule as required. This is shown in the login.conf in Listing 20-12.

Listing 20-12   *login.conf*

```
Logout {
    com.tcnd.wasdg.dbreg.DbregLoginModule required debug=true;
};

ZenFile {
    com.tcnd.wasdg.dbreg.DbregLoginModule required debug=true;
};
```

Changes in the DataAccessComponent

In terms of coding, the change in the DataAccessComponent is minimal. Copy the program from Chapter 12 to the tree structure of our JAAS-enabled application, making it part of the com.tcnd.wasdg.dbreg package. Then add two methods to the program: DataAccessComponent(DbguideAuth o) and loadDefaultConnectionSettings(DbguieAuth o).

Listing 20-13 shows part of the DataAccessComponent where the authorization on the DBGUIDE database has been enforced.

Listing 20-13   *Changes in the DataAccessComponent*

```
1.    package com.tcnd.wasdg.dbreg;
2.
3.    import java.util.*;
4.    import java.sql.*;
5.    import java.io.*;
6.
7.    import com.tcnd.wasdg.common.*;
8.
9.    public class DataAccessComponent
10.   {
11.       private java.sql.Connection conn;
12.       private static final boolean SUCCESS = true;
13.       private static final boolean FAILURE = false;
14.       private boolean someData;
15.       private static final String dbguidePropertiesFileName=
"/BOOK/20/dbreg_sysprotected/update_emppwd_dbguide.properties";
16.       private String dbDriver;
17.       private String dbUrl;
18.       private String dbUser;
19.       private String dbPassword;
```

```
20.
21.     public DataAccessComponent()
22.     {
23.         super();
24.         loadDefaultConnectionSettings();
25.     }
26.
27.     public DataAccessComponent(DbguideAuth o)
28.     {
29.         super();
30.         loadDefaultConnectionSettings(o);
31.     }
32.
33.     private void loadDefaultConnectionSettings()
34.     {
35.         // ...
36.     }
37.     private void loadDefaultConnectionSettings(DbguideAuth o)
38.     {
39.         dbDriver = o.getDbDriver();
40.         dbUrl = o.getDbUrl();
41.         dbUser = o.getDbUser();
42.         dbPassword = o.getDbPassword();
43.     }
44.
```

Class Casting and Symbolic Name Resolution

Be extremely careful when deploying a web application under WAS. The symbolic names of your programs being resolved by WAS can affect type casting. The way and the order in which WAS loads it classes and then makes them visible to your program can affect the type casting in your program. WAS class casting is totally bound to the location[3] of the library from which the symbolic names are being resolved. This is an important statement that every WAS programmer must remember. You will understand this point more clearly after reading the following example.

Say that the com.tcnd.wasdg.common package is defined in two places: in $WAS_HOME/lib/wasdg_common.jar and in the web application directory $INSTALLEDAPPS/wasdg.ear/webapp/WEB-INF/classes/com/tcnd/wasdg/common. Because the visibility order[4] for the TellerLogged servlet takes precedence over the web application directory, the session for the EmpAccnt has been initialized from the common web application package. On the other hand, the Logout servlet is JAAS-enabled and will be looking for the common package from

---

[3]   The location is really in the URI, which is the relative location of the directory from which WAS will look up the symbolic names your program uses.

[4]   Refer to Chapter 15 for a thorough discussion on WAS classloader.

the $WAS_HOME/lib/wasdg_common.jar. Now when the Logout servlet is invoked, a ClassCastException occurs, as shown next.

```
1.   [5/16/02 2:41:51:490 EDT]  5d3a5e2 SystemOut     U If session persistence
        is enabled then the following will write to the datastore
2.   [5/16/02 2:41:57:272 EDT]  5d3a5e2 WebGroup      X Servlet Error:
        com.tcnd.wasdg.common.EmpAccnt: java.lang.ClassCastException:
com.tcnd.wasdg.common.EmpAccnt
3.       at com.tcnd.wasdg.dbreg.Logout.doGet(Logout.java:72)
4.       at javax.servlet.http.HttpServlet.service(HttpServlet.java:740)
```

Move the common package out from the web application and restart WAS to cure this problem. This way, both the TellerLogged servlet and the Logout servlet can resolve symbols from the same package. Even though two packages are identical, the URI of the package is important during run time, when programs have to resolve symbolic names.

The Future of JAAS

The new release of the Java 2 SDK v1.4, standard edition, is expected to support Simple Authentication and Security Layer (SASL) authentication using Digest-MD5 and GSS-API/ Kerberos. Hopefully, IBM will port the APIs to support the many missing authentications in their new version of WAS.

Table 20-5 summarizes some of the user authentication APIs supported with the release of Java 2 SDK v1.4.

The approach followed in this chapter minimizes such differences between Java 2 SDK v1.3 and v1.4 and adequately implements security that can be ported to the new version.

The example discussed in this chapter to JAAS-enable the Logout servlet can be applied to the other servlets: adding a new teller, logging a teller, adding a new banker, and so on.

APIs in Java 2 SDV v1.4	Description
JndiLoginModule	Prompts for a username and password and then verifies the password against the password stored in a directory service configured under JNDI
KeyStoreLoginModule	Provides a JAAS login module that prompts for a key store alias and populates the subject with the alias' principal and credentials
Krb5LoginModule	Authenticates users using Kerberos protocols
NTLoginModule	Renders a user's NT security information as some number of `Principals` and associates them with a `Subject`
UnixLoginModule	Imports a user's UNIX `Principal` information (`UnixPrincipal`, `UnixNumericUserPrincipal`, and `UnixNumericGroupPrincipal`) and associates them with the current `Subject`
UnixSystem	Retrieves and makes available UNIX UID/GID/groups information for the current user

Table 20-5   *User Authentication APIs Supported in Java 2 SDK v1.4*

Cipher

This final section provides an example of Cipher encryption. The example consists of two Java programs and one servlet. The programs Cfile and then Dfile are run from the command prompt to cipher a file using a password, and then to decrypt the file using the same password. The FetchSignedFile servlet can decrypt a file and present it to the browser.

The Cfile, shown in Listing 20-14, takes three arguments:

```
java Cfile original-filename ciphered-filename password
```

For example:

```
# java Cfile loginscreen.html loginscreen.signed pwd123
```

This command writes loginscreen.signed as a file that can be fetched and decrypted with either Dfile or FetchSignedFile. To view the file, invoke the Dfile with this command:

```
# java Dfile loginscreen.signed pwd123
```

Listing 20-14   *Cfile*

```
1.   import java.io.*;
2.   import java.util.*;
3.   import java.lang.*;
4.
5.   import javax.crypto.*;
6.   import javax.crypto.spec.*;
7.
8.   /**
9.    * Read a file content, sign the content as object, then write it
10.   * java Cfile filename signedfile password
11.   **/
12.
13.  class Cfile {
14.
15.  public static void main(String argv[]) {
16.
17.      String fn = argv[0];
18.      String signedfn = argv[1];
19.      String content = getFile(fn);
20.      writeSignedFile(argv[2], content, signedfn);
21.  }
22.
23
24.  public static void writeSignedFile(String password, String stream, String
     fn) {
25.      try {
```

```
26.            byte[] salt = {
27.                (byte) 0x35, (byte)0x46,
28.                (byte) 0x25, (byte)0xc6,
29.                (byte) 0x85, (byte)0xa6,
30.                (byte) 0xe5, (byte)0x16
31.            };
32.            PBEParameterSpec pbeParamSpec = new PBEParameterSpec(salt, 20);
33.            char[] secret = (password).toCharArray();
34.            PBEKeySpec keySpec = new PBEKeySpec(secret);
35.            SecretKeyFactory keyFac =
        SecretKeyFactory.getInstance("PBEWithMD5AndDES");
36.            SecretKey sKey = keyFac.generateSecret(keySpec);
37.
38.            Cipher cipher = Cipher.getInstance("PBEWithMD5AndDES");
39.            cipher.init(Cipher.ENCRYPT_MODE,sKey,pbeParamSpec);
40.            FileOutputStream fout = new FileOutputStream(fn);
41.            ObjectOutputStream oout = new ObjectOutputStream(fout);
42.            SealedObject sealed = new SealedObject(stream, cipher);
43.            oout.writeObject(sealed);
44.            oout.flush();
45.        } catch (Exception e) {
46.            System.out.println("Encryption error:"+e);
47.        }
48.    }
49.
50.
51. public static String getFile(String fn) {
52.        String content = "";
53.        try {
54.            RandomAccessFile file = new RandomAccessFile(fn,"r");
55.            long seek = 0;
56.            long length = file.length();
57.            while(seek < length) {
58.                String s = file.readLine();
59.                content = content + s;
60.                seek = file.getFilePointer();
61.            }
62.        } catch (IOException e)
63.        {
64.            e.printStackTrace();
65.        }
66.        return content;
67.    }
68.
69.  }
```

The Dfile decrypts what the program Cfile has encrypted. The Dfile is shown in Listing 20-15.

Listing 20-15   *Dfile*

```
1.    import java.io.*;
2.    import java.util.*;
3.    import java.lang.*;
4.
5.    import javax.crypto.*;
6.    import javax.crypto.spec.*;
7.
8.
9.    /**
10.   * fetch the signed file: java Dfile filename password
11.   **/
12.
13.   class Dfile {
14.
15.   public static void main(String argv[]) {
16.
17.       String signedfn = argv[0];
18.       String content = getSignedFile(argv[1],signedfn);
19.       System.out.println(content);
20.   }
21.
22.
23.   public static String getSignedFile(String password, String fn) {
24.       String stream = "";
25.       try {
26.           byte[] salt = {
27.               (byte) 0x35,  (byte)0x46,
28.               (byte) 0x25,  (byte)0xc6,
29.               (byte) 0x85,  (byte)0xa6,
30.               (byte) 0xe5,  (byte)0x16
31.           };
32.           PBEParameterSpec pbeParamSpec = new PBEParameterSpec(salt, 20);
33.           char[] secret = (password).toCharArray();
34.           PBEKeySpec keySpec = new PBEKeySpec(secret);
35.           SecretKeyFactory keyFac =
      SecretKeyFactory.getInstance("PBEWithMD5AndDES");
36.           SecretKey sKey = keyFac.generateSecret(keySpec);
37.
38.           Cipher cipher = Cipher.getInstance("PBEWithMD5AndDES");
39.           cipher.init(Cipher.DECRYPT_MODE,sKey,pbeParamSpec);
40.           FileInputStream fin = new FileInputStream(fn);
```

```
41.              ObjectInputStream oin = new ObjectInputStream(fin);
42.              SealedObject sealed = (SealedObject) oin.readObject();
43.              stream = (String) sealed.getObject(cipher);
44.          } catch (Exception e) {
45.              System.out.println("Encryption error:"+e);
46.          }
47.          return stream;
48.      }
49
50.  }
51.
```

Use the FetchSignedFile to decrypt a ciphered file. You enter the filename and password in the form before submitting it. You can use the FetchSignedFile, shown in Listing 20-16, to request an authorized login screen or an authorized registration screen or to view a ciphered document.

Listing 20-16   *FetchSignedFile*

```
1.   import java.util.*;
2.   import java.lang.*;
3.   import javax.crypto.*;
4.   import javax.crypto.spec.*;
5.
6.   import java.io.*;
7.   import javax.servlet.*;
8.   import javax.servlet.http.*;
9.
10.  import com.tcnd.wasdg.common.*;
11.
12.  public class FetchSignedFile extends javax.servlet.http.HttpServlet {
13.      String step1content =
14.
15.  "<HTML>" +
16.  "<HEAD>" +
17.  "<TITLE>WASDG - Fetch a signed file and print its content to the
     browser</TITLE>" +
18.  "</HEAD>" +
19.  "<BODY>" +
20.  "<H1>FETCH A CIPHERED FILE AND PRINT IT AS HTML CONTENT</H1>" +
21.  "<FORM METHOD=\"POST\" ACTION=\"/wasbook/fetchsigned\">" +
22.  "" +
23.  "<HR>" +
24.  "<H2>Enter the file name to read as an HTML content:</H2>" +
25.  "<font size=-1>(this is relative to the base directory specified in the
     context-param)</font>" +
26.  "<P>File name:<INPUT TYPE=\"text\" NAME=\"fname\" SIZE=\"20\">" +
27.  "<P>Signature:<INPUT PASSWORD=\"text\" NAME=\"password\" SIZE=\"20\">" +
```

```
28.    "<HR>" +
29.    "<INPUT TYPE=\"submit\" VALUE=\"Fetch\"><INPUT TYPE=\"reset\">" +
30.    "</FORM>" +
31.    "</BODY>" +
32.    "</HTML>" +
33.    "";
34.
35.
36.    public void doGet(HttpServletRequest request, HttpServletResponse
         response)
37.            throws IOException{
38.
39.        ServletOutputStream out = response.getOutputStream();
40.
41.        response.setContentType("text/html");
42.        response.setHeader("Pragma", "no-cache");
43.        response.setHeader("Cache-Control", "no-cache");
44.        response.setDateHeader("Expires", 0);
45.
46.        out.println(step1content);
47.    }
48.
49.    public void doPost(HttpServletRequest request, HttpServletResponse
         response)
50.            throws IOException{
51.
52.        String fname = request.getParameter("fname");
53.        String password = request.getParameter("password");
54.        ServletContext context = getServletContext();
55.        String fromdir = context.getInitParameter("fromdir");
56.
57.        // Change:  String content = StrTool.getFile(fromdir + fname);
58.        String content = getSignedFile(password,fromdir + fname);
59.
60.        ServletOutputStream out = response.getOutputStream();
61.        response.setContentType("text/html");
62.        response.setHeader("Pragma", "no-cache");
63.        response.setHeader("Cache-Control", "no-cache");
64.        response.setDateHeader("Expires", 0);
65.
66.        out.println(content);
67.    }
68.
69.    public static String getSignedFile(String password, String fn) {
70.        String stream = null;
71.        try {
72.            byte[] salt = {
73.                    (byte) 0x35, (byte)0x46,
74.                    (byte) 0x25, (byte)0xc6,
75.                    (byte) 0x85, (byte)0xa6,
```

```
76.                  (byte) 0xe5, (byte)0x16
77.              };
78.              PBEParameterSpec pbeParamSpec = new PBEParameterSpec(salt, 20);
79.              char[] secret = (password).toCharArray();
80.              PBEKeySpec keySpec = new PBEKeySpec(secret);
81.              SecretKeyFactory keyFac =
       SecretKeyFactory.getInstance("PBEWithMD5AndDES");
82.              SecretKey sKey = keyFac.generateSecret(keySpec);
83.
84.              Cipher cipher = Cipher.getInstance("PBEWithMD5AndDES");
85.
86.              cipher.init(Cipher.DECRYPT_MODE,sKey,pbeParamSpec);
87.              FileInputStream fin = new FileInputStream(fn);
88.              ObjectInputStream oin = new ObjectInputStream(fin);
89.              SealedObject sealed = (SealedObject) oin.readObject();
90.              stream = (String) sealed.getObject(cipher);
91.          } catch (Exception e) {
92.              System.out.println("Encryption error:"+e);
93.          }
94.      return stream;
95.  }
96.
97.  }
```

The following two illustrations show how to request the ciphered document signed by invoking the FetchSignedServlet. The first illustration shows how to request a signed file along with its password. The second shows the content of the decrypted file.

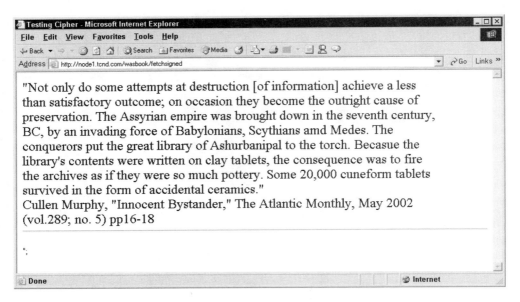

"Not only do some attempts at destruction [of information] achieve a less than satisfactory outcome; on occasion they become the outright cause of preservation. The Assyrian empire was brought down in the seventh century, BC, by an invading force of Babylonians, Scythians amd Medes. The conquerors put the great library of Ashurbanipal to the torch. Becasue the library's contents were written on clay tablets, the consequence was to fire the archives as if they were so much pottery. Some 20,000 cuneform tablets survived in the form of accidental ceramics."
Cullen Murphy, "Innocent Bystander," The Atlantic Monthly, May 2002 (vol.289; no. 5) pp16-18

You can also secure the registration of a new user by signing the static HTML form so that only privileged personal can request the signed form and deciph it using the FetchSignedServlet. For instance, sign the form reg_client.html into reg_client.signed with a password. Requesting the signed form is shown in the following illustration.

Wrapping Up

At the code level, Java security cannot be bypassed in a distributed system. This chapter showed you how to JAAS-enable servlets under WAS. JAAS is really a lightweight, highly secure library, and is not expected to slow a web application as much as J2EE security enablement will. The JAAS LoginModule should work with WAS. This chapter also discussed an important point about WAS type casting that can be affected by the visibility order of the library (see Chapter 15). In addition, the Cipher engine was used to provide a brief example of how to secure documents and important registration forms.

Enterprise Application Development

IN THIS CHAPTER:

Reconsidering the Build Process Using the make Utility

Concurrent Development: Source Code Control, Compiling, and Testing

Considering the Environment for Concurrent Programmers

Documentation

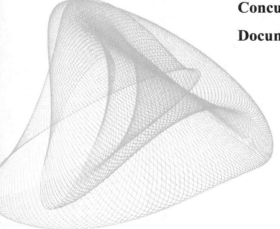

Much of the complexity in web application programming is due to the intricacies of compiling, assembling[1], and deploying code in the application server. The code itself may depend on other pieces of code to be imported from another library or another package, which complicated matters. Furthermore, assembling the application is tedious and time-consuming for a programmer in a dynamic development environment.

You must closely observe the dependency on other pieces of code because module visibility is hierarchical[2] and is managed by the application server's Java machines. As a result, you should carefully consider casting, serialization, and signed archives while deploying the dependent libraries.

When you assemble the application using a graphical tool such as the Application Assembly Tool (AAT), many important parts of the code may be hidden that the programmer needs to know about. This problem affects debugging and makes it harder to determine why a program is performing inadequately.

So far, our approach to using scripts (such as svlbuild and refreshear) has been straightforward, quick, and clear. In particular, if you practice programming under WAS based on the WASDG application, the svlbuild script can compile and deploy tons of servlets in a web application in a matter of a few seconds, even on a mediocre processor such as the Pentium II 333 MHz.

But now, we need to slightly modify the build procedure so that code compilation[3] is not enforced unless there is a change in a program or in any of the libraries upon which it depends (a different .class or .jar file). We will use the make utility, which is regulated and concise; no doubt, it is the foundation of any application builder that you would find described in the literature.

It is regulated because it is based on rules that can save you a tremendous amount of time when building a project formed of many pieces of code. It is concise because the make utility's rules are based on time, in particular, the timestamp of each program file. Once you put the build procedure in place, and this happens only once for the lifetime of a project, you and other developers can easily use make to compile and test the application.

The Java compiler (javac) and the make utility work perfectly together. Whereas the former has the ability to resolve symbol dependencies that need to be imported or looked at from the current directory or the supplied classpath, the latter can detect the time change of all the files on which the target program depends.

Because Java packages map into the directory, the make utility is a perfect fit as it works on the timestamp of files and directories, and it processes inference rules based on file extensions.

This chapter explores how two or more developers can work concurrently on creating a web application. To achieve this goal, we will use the make utility and the Revision Control System (RCS). A few utility scripts are introduced to facilitate quick application-building and documentation.

---

[1] Although compilation is performed independently from the application server and its assembly tool, assembling may involve the AAT. The application server administrative console may also be involved in the deployment, which is the case with Enterprise JavaBeans deployment.

[2] Refer to Chapter 15 for explanation on classes loading order versus visibility order.

[3] We are also considering moving such a compiled piece of code to the deployment tree. Such a piece of code must be moved comprehensively to the deployed tree when not moving the whole tree structure, or taking the time-consuming approach in reassembling the web application and re-expanding it.

The method discussed here is adequate for a group of users (college students, or many developers in an organization). RCS is used for pedagogical reasons, so that you will understand the functionality of a source control.

This chapter concludes with an explanation about how to generate online documentation using the javadoc utility.

Reconsidering the Build Process Using the make Utility

Figure 21-1 shows the J2EE tree structure of the WASDG application. Based on this tree structure, we have already been developing the web application in Chapters 11, 12, 13, 16, 17, and 20.

The svlbuild script introduced in Chapter 11 looked for all the Java files in the base development tree and collectively compiled them before moving them to the deployment tree. If the development of the WASDG application takes place in the wasdg.ear directory, the build process of this application relies on two specified locations:

▶ **The base development tree**   Pointed to with the environment variable $BASE_DEV, and which we will call the *source tree.* The WASDG application is then developed in the $BASE_DEV/wasdg.ear directory.

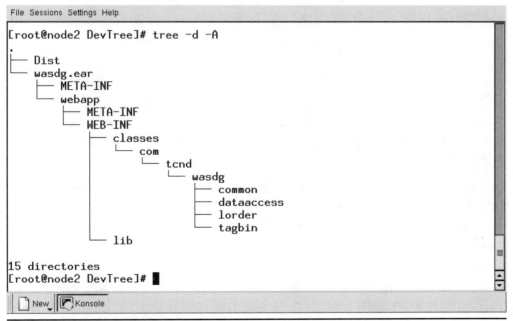

Figure 21-1   *Tree structure of the J2EE application, WASDG*

▶ **The deployment tree** Pointed to with the environment variable $INSTALLEDAPPS, and which we will call the *factual tree*. The WASDG application is then deployed to the $INSTALLEDAPPS/wasdg.ear directory; such a directory is also known as the deployment directory of the WASDG application.

The parallelism between the source tree and the factual tree makes the writing of a deployment tool or script fairly easy. Figure 21-2 shows the correspondence between the source tree and the factual tree.

The code is compiled in the source tree and then moved to the factual tree. The following section focuses on the compilation process.

Compiling Code Using the make Utility

As a rule of thumb, wherever a .java file is found in any subtree of the source tree, the javac is invoked to compile a file. Starting with a simple example, consider compiling the .java files in the $BASE_DEV/wasdg.ear/webapp/WEB-INF/classes directory using the make utility. In this directory, we will save the hidden file .jlist (see Listing 21-1) and the Makefile (see Listing 21-2). The .jlist file contains a list of all the .java files that are found in the same directory where .jlist is saved.

Listing 21-1 *.jlist*

```
JSRCS= BruteConn.java CreditDebit.java DumpCook.java DumpCookLog.java
       DumpEnv.java DumpSession.java EditTeller.java FetchFile.java
       FlipSession.java Hey.java Logoff.java Logout.java PostCookie.java
       PrintCp.java QueryEmpAccnt.java QueryTable.java ResetSession.java
       SelectTable.java Session.java SessionFairy.java SetCookie.java
       TellerLogged.java UrlRewrite.java
```

Listing 21-2 shows the Makefile saved in each directory of the web application where a .java file happens to be saved.

Listing 21-2 *Makefile*

```
1.   OBJDIR=/BOOK/21/DevTree/wasdg.ear/webapp/WEB-INF/classes
2.   # Uncomment below to enable silent
3.   #.SILENT:
4.
5.   JAVAC=$(JAVA_HOME)/bin/javac
6.   # Enable deprecation if you are porting an old application
7.   #JAVACOPT= -deprecation  -classpath ${OBJDIR}:${CLASSPATH}
8.   JAVACOPT= -classpath ${OBJDIR}:${CLASSPATH}
9.
10.  include .jlist
```

```
11.    JCLASSES=${JSRCS:.java=.class}
12.
13.    all:: ${JCLASSES}
14.
15.    #force explicitly a rebuild
16.    rebuild: ${JCLASSES}
17.        $(JAVAC) $(JAVACOPT) $(JSRCS)
18.
19.    ${JCLASSES}: ${JSRCS}
20.
21.    #
22.    # suffix rule
23.    #
24.    .SUFFIXES :
25.    .SUFFIXES : .java .class
26.
27.    .java.class:
28.        $(JAVAC) $(JAVACOPT) $<
```

Three user-defined macros exist in this Makefile:

▶ **OBJDIR**   Specifies the base or root directory of this Java application (line 1).

▶ **JAVAC**   Specifies the host Java compiler (line 5).

▶ **JAVACOPT**   Specifies the options to be passed to the Java compiler (line 8). The root directory of this Java application (OBJDIR) and the classpath defined by the environment variable CLASSPATH form the classpath of this compilation.

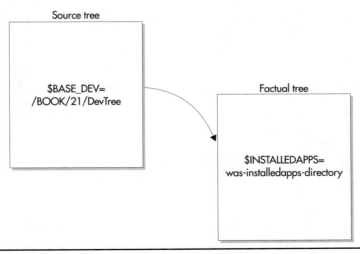

Figure 21-2   *Source tree and factual tree*

Line 10 uses the preprocessing directive include to insert the.jlist file as part of this Makefile. The .jlist file is expected to be in the current directory.

Specifying .SUFFIXES: without any file extensions on line 24 requires make to ignore its built-in list; then line 25 uses another .SUFFIXES: with extensions, setting make extensions only to those listed here: .java and .class.

Lines 27 and 28 form what is called an *inference rule,* and consists of an implicit target, an implicit dependency, and one or more implicit commands. The rule starts with .java.class, indicating that we can have a .java file as our source and can generate a .class file from it. The .java part of .java.class is called *implicit dependency,* and the .class part of .java.class is called *implicit target.* The command following the inference rule tells the make utility how to turn a .java file into a .class file:

▶ Use the value of JAVAC to invoke the Java compiler with the flags option specified in JAVACOPTS.

▶ Use the current dependent file ($<) that is out of date with respect to the target.

The dollar sign and less-than symbol ($<) shown on line 28 is a make predefined macro, which stands for the synonym for the dependent file with a timestamp older than the target.

Automating the Process

The AppMaker1 script shown in Listing 21-3 visits each subdirectory of the BASE_DEV directory looking for .java files; if one is encountered, it deposits two files, .jlist and Makefile, in the subdirectory where at least one .java file is found. In addition, two files are created in the BASE_DEV directory: the makeit shell script, which can invoke each of the Makefiles that have been generated in a subdirectory, and the makejar file, which can package in a library all the .java files or all the .class files.

Listing 21-3   *AppMaker1*

```
1.    #!/usr/bin/perl
2.
3.    if ( (defined($ENV{BASE_DEV})) && (-d $ENV{BASE_DEV}) ) { $base =
      $ENV{BASE_DEV}; }
4.    else { die "BASE_DEV!\n"; }
5.
6.    $m = <<MAKE;
7.    OBJDIR=$base/wasdg.ear/webapp/WEB-INF/classes
8.    # Uncomment below to enable silent
9.    #.SILENT:
10.
11.   JAVAC=\$(JAVA_HOME)/bin/javac
12.   # Enable deprecation if you are porting an old application
13.   #JAVACOPT= -deprecation  -classpath \${OBJDIR}:\${CLASSPATH}
14.   JAVACOPT= -classpath \${OBJDIR}:\${CLASSPATH}
```

```
15.
16.   include .jlist
17.   JCLASSES=\${JSRCS:.java=.class}
18.
19.   all:: \${JCLASSES}
20.
21.   #rebuild: \$(JCL)
22.   rebuild: \${JCLASSES}
23.       \$(JAVAC) \$(JAVACOPT) \$(JSRCS)
24.
25.   \${JCLASSES}: \${JSRCS}
26.
27.   #
28.   # suffix rule
29.   #
30.   .SUFFIXES :
31.   .SUFFIXES : .java .class
32.
33.   .java.class:
34.       \$(JAVAC) \$(JAVACOPT) \$<
35.
36.   MAKE
37.
38.   $mj = <<MAKEJAR;
39.
40.   OBJDIR=$base/wasdg.ear/webapp/WEB-INF/classes
41.
42.   #.SILENT:
43.   BASE_DEV=$base
44.   CLASSLIB=wasdg.jar
45.   JAVALIB=wasdg_src.jar
46.   CLASS_FILES='(cd \$(OBJDIR); find . -name "*.class")'
47.   JAVA_FILES='(cd \$(OBJDIR); find . -name "*.java")'
48.
49.   jar_class::
50.       (cd \$(OBJDIR); jar cvf \$(BASE_DEV)/Dist/\$(CLASSLIB)
       \$(CLASS_FILES))
51.
52.   jar_java::
53.       (cd \$(OBJDIR); jar cvf \$(BASE_DEV)/Dist/\$(JAVALIB) \$(JAVA_FILES))
54.
55.   #sign_jar_class::
56.
57.   MAKEJAR
58.
59.   open(D,"find $base -type d |");
60.   $dir.=$_ while(<D>);
61.   #print "$dir\n";
62.   @dir=split(/\n/,$dir);
63.   #print "@dir\n";
```

```
64.   open(OUT,">fileslist.txt"); print OUT "FILESLIST.TXT\n\n"; close(OUT);
65.   foreach (@dir) {
66.       #print "\t$_\n";
67.       undef(@jlist); undef(@f);
68.       @jlist=glob("$_/*.java");
69.       if (defined @jlist) {
70.           foreach $f (@jlist) { $f =~ s/$_\///; $f =~ s/\.java$//;
      push(@f,"$f.java"); }
71.           open(OUT,">>fileslist.txt");
72.           print OUT "$_\n";
73.           foreach $f (sort @f) { print OUT "\t$f\n"; }
74.           close(OUT);
75.           open(OUT,">$_/.jlist");
76.           print OUT "JSRCS= @f\n";
77.           close(OUT);
78.           open(OUT, ">$_/Makefile");
79.           print OUT "$m\n";
80.           close(OUT);
81.           print "\t$_\n";
82.           push(@D,"(cd $_ ; time make \$1)\n");
83.       }
84.   }
85.   open(OUT,">makeit");
86.   print OUT @D;
87.   close(OUT);
88.   'chmod 750 makeit';
89.
90.   open(OUT,">makejar");
91.   print OUT $mj;
92.   close(OUT);
```

The AppMaker1 script finds all the directories that are located under the BASE_DEV
directory and pushes them on a list (line 59), visiting each of the directories (line 65) looking
for .java files (line 70). After at least one .java file is located, jmake deposits a .jlist and
Makefile (lines 75 and 78) in the subdirectory and remembers the visited directory by
pushing the command shown on line 82 (cd $_; time make \$1), which is interpreted
as follows: change directory to the directory where one or more .java files are found and then
time the make command with one argument passed to the Makefile through the shell script.
The $1 has been escaped so that Perl does not interpret the symbol as a variable.

In the BASE_DEV directory, the makeit file is then created (line 85), followed by the makejar
file (line 90).

Listing 21-4 shows the makeit file generated by AppMaker1. To build the web application,
all you have to do is to run makeit with one of these options:

▶   **all**   Make compiles these .java files that have been changed, or with a source file with
a timestamp that is more recent than their target.

▶   **rebuild**   Make compiles all .java files explicitly, whether they have changed or not.

For example, after making a change to the Session.java source file, you can recompile it by running this command:

```
# makeit  all
```

Listing 21-4   *makeit*

```
(cd /BOOK/21/DevTree/wasdg.ear/webapp/WEB-INF/classes ; time make $1)
(cd /BOOK/21/DevTree/wasdg.ear/webapp/WEB-INF/classes/com/tcnd/wasdg ; time
    make $1)
(cd /BOOK/21/DevTree/wasdg.ear/webapp/WEB-INF/classes/com/tcnd/wasdg/common ;
    time make $1)
(cd
    /BOOK/21/DevTree/wasdg.ear/webapp/WEB-INF/classes/com/tcnd/wasdg/dataaccess
    ; time make $1)
(cd /BOOK/21/DevTree/wasdg.ear/webapp/WEB-INF/classes/com/tcnd/wasdg/lorder ;
    time make $1)
(cd /BOOK/21/DevTree/wasdg.ear/webapp/WEB-INF/classes/com/tcnd/wasdg/tagbin ;
    time make $1)
```

So far, we have been compiling the source code in the source tree without moving any of the compiled files to the factual tree. Yet, moving the corresponding code is quite simple. Consider the following change in the rule of how to generate a .class file from a .java file:

```
1.    .java.class:
2.        $(JAVAC) $(JAVACOPT) $<
3.        cp $(OBJDIR)/$*.class $(FACTUAL)/$*.class
```

These three lines are read as follows: when a source .java file has been changed or does not have a corresponding target .class file (line 1), compile it using the source program (line 2) to generate the target .class file, and then copy the corresponding generated target to the factual tree (line 3). The dollar sign and asterisk ($*) refer to the current target without an extension. The extension (suffix) class is added to the $* to build the filename that needs to be copied from the source tree to the factual tree.

The makejar file that is also generated by the AppMaker1 script is invoked as follows:

```
make -f makejar jar_class
make -f makejar jar_java
```

These two options are explained in the next section, where the AppMaker1 script is slightly modified to write a more interesting script.

An Initial Makefile for the BASE_DEV

Having a shell script such as makeit is obviously a simple way to generate a utility shell script. A better solution to compile code of an enterprise web application is to write a common

Makefile that resides in the root directory of the source tree: $BASE_DEV. To generate such a common Makefile, we employ the scipt AppMaker shown in Listing 21-5. The complete code for the AppMaker script is part of the distribution code for this book.

Listing 21-5 *AppMaker*

```perl
1.    #!/usr/bin/perl
2.
3.    if ( (defined($ENV{BASE_DEV})) && (-d $ENV{BASE_DEV}) ) { $base =
      $ENV{BASE_DEV};
4.    else { die "BASE_DEV!\n"; }
5.    if ( (defined($ENV{INSTALLEDAPPS})) && (-d $ENV{INSTALLEDAPPS}) ) {
      $factual = $ENV{INSTALLEDAPPS}; }
6.    else { die "factual tree INSTALLEDAPPS!\n"; }
7.
8.    $m = <<MAKE;
9.    OBJDIR=$base/wasdg.ear/webapp/WEB-INF/classes
10.   FACTUAL=$factual/wasdg.ear/webapp/WEB-INF/classes
11.   # Uncomment below to enable silent
12.   #.SILENT:
13.
14.   JAVAC=\$(JAVA_HOME)/bin/javac
15.   # Enable deprecation if you are porting an old application
16.   #JAVACOPT= -deprecation  -classpath \${OBJDIR}:\${CLASSPATH}
17.   JAVACOPT= -classpath \${OBJDIR}:\${CLASSPATH}
18.
19.   include .jlist
20.   JCLASSES=\${JSRCS:.java=.class}
21.
22.   all:: \${JCLASSES}
23.
24.   #force explicitly a rebuild
25.   rebuild: \${JCLASSES}
26.       \$(JAVAC) \$(JAVACOPT) \$(JSRCS)
27.
28.   \${JCLASSES}: \${JSRCS}
29.
30.
31.   # suffix rule
32.   .SUFFIXES :
33.   .SUFFIXES : .java .class
34.
35.   .java.class:
36.       \$(JAVAC) \$(JAVACOPT) \$<
37.       cp \$(OBJDIR)\/\$*.class \$(FACTUAL)\/\$*.class
38.   MAKE
39.
40.   $mj = <<MAKEJAR;
```

```
41.   OBJDIR=$base/wasdg.ear/webapp/WEB-INF/classes
42.
43.   BASE_DEV=$base
44.   CLASSLIB=wasdg.jar
45.   JAVALIB=wasdg_src.jar
46.   CLASS_FILES='(cd \$(OBJDIR); find . -name "*.class")'
47.   JAVA_FILES='(cd \$(OBJDIR); find . -name "*.java")'
48.
49.   include .jdir
50.
51.   jar_class::
52.       (cd \$(OBJDIR); jar cvf \$(BASE_DEV)/Dist/\$(CLASSLIB)
        \$(CLASS_FILES))
53.
54.   jar_java::
55.       (cd \$(OBJDIR); jar cvf \$(BASE_DEV)/Dist/\$(JAVALIB) \$(JAVA_FILES))
56.
57.   #sign_jar_class::
58.
59.   make_all :
60.       for subdir in \${DIRS} ; \\
61.       do \\
62.           cd \$\${subdir} ; make all ; \\
63.       done
64.
65.   make_rebuild :
66.       for subdir in \${DIRS} ; \\
67.       do \\
68.           cd \$\${subdir} ; make rebuild ; \\
69.       done
70.
71.   make_rcs :
72.       for subdir in \${DIRS} ; \\
73.       do \\
74.           cd \$\${subdir} ; mkdir RCS; chmod 755 RCS; ci -u1 *.java ; \\
75.       done
76.   MAKEJAR
77.
78.   open(D,"find $base -type d |");
79.   $dir.=$_ while(<D>);
80.   @dir=split(/\n/,$dir);
81.   open(OUT,">fileslist.txt"); print OUT "FILESLIST.TXT\n\n"; close(OUT);
82.   foreach (@dir) {
83.       #print "\t$_\n";
84.       undef(@jlist); undef(@f);
85.       @jlist=glob("$_/*.java");
86.       if (defined @jlist) {
87.           foreach $f (@jlist) { $f =~ s/$_\///; $f =~ s/\.java$//;
        push(@f,"$f.java"); }
88.           open(OUT,">>fileslist.txt");
```

```
89.          print OUT "$_\n";
90.          foreach $f (sort @f) { print OUT "\t$f\n"; }
91.          close(OUT);
92.          open(OUT,">$_/.jlist");
93.          print OUT "JSRCS= @f\n";
94.          close(OUT);
95.          open(OUT, ">$_/Makefile");
96.          print OUT "$m\n";
97.          close(OUT);
98.          print "\t$_\n";
99.          push(@L,"(cd $_ ; time make \$1)\n");
100.         push(@D,"$_ ");
101.         # The following is used only to link RCS in a user holding tree
102.         my $subtree = $_; $subtree =~ s/^$base//;
103.         push(@LINK,"ln -s $_/RCS  \$BASE_DEV$subtree/RCS\n");
104.         push(@LINK,"(cd \$BASE_DEV$subtree; co -rl RCS/*,v)\n");
105.    }
106. }
107. open(OUT,">makeit"); print OUT @L; close(OUT); 'chmod 750 makeit';
108. open(OUT,">Makefile"); print OUT $mj; close(OUT);
109. open(OUT,">.jdir"); print OUT "DIRS= @D\n"; close(OUT);
110. open(OUT,">linkrcs"); print OUT "@LINK\n"; close(OUT);
```

The generated common Makefile is shown in Listing 21-6.

The Makefile in the root of the holding tree is called the *initial* Makefile and can be invoked with the following options:

▶ **make_all**   Visit every directory where a .java file is located in the $BASE_DEV/ wasdg.ear directory and compile the code of a source file that has changed.

▶ **make_rebuild**   Visit every directory where a .java file has been located and explicitly compile it.

▶ **jar_class**   Package all .class files in a .jar file for a binary distribution.

▶ **jar_java**   Package all .java files in a .jar file for a source code distribution.

▶ **make_rcs**   Add in the RCS directories and check in the .java files.

Listing 21-6   *Makefile generated in the base directory of the source tree*

```
1.
2.    OBJDIR=/BOOK/21/DevTree/wasdg.ear/webapp/WEB-INF/classes
3.
4.    #.SILENT:
5.    BASE_DEV=/BOOK/21/DevTree
6.    CLASSLIB=wasdg.jar
7.    JAVALIB=wasdg_src.jar
8.    CLASS_FILES='(cd $(OBJDIR); find . -name "*.class")'
```

```
9.    JAVA_FILES='(cd $(OBJDIR); find . -name "*.java")'
10.
11.   include .jdir
12.
13.   jar_class::
14.       (cd $(OBJDIR); jar cvf $(BASE_DEV)/Dist/$(CLASSLIB) $(CLASS_FILES))
15.
16.   jar_java::
17.       (cd $(OBJDIR); jar cvf $(BASE_DEV)/Dist/$(JAVALIB) $(JAVA_FILES))
18.
19.   #sign_jar_class::
20.
21.   make_all :
22.       for subdir in ${DIRS} ; \
23.       do \
24.           cd $${subdir} ; make all ; \
25.       done
26.
27.   make_rebuild :
28.       for subdir in ${DIRS} ; \
29.       do \
30.           cd $${subdir} ; make rebuild ; \
31.       done
32.
33.   make_rcs :
34.       for subdir in ${DIRS} ; \
35.       do \
36.           cd $${subdir} ; mkdir RCS; chmod 755 RCS; ci -u1 *.java ; \
37.       done
```

The make of jar_class (line 13) and of jar_java (line 16) are functionally similar, so only one is explained here. To build the .jar file of all classes, the CLASS_FILES macro on line 8 is assigned the set of all .class files relative to the OBJDIR. Line 14 defines the rule of how to make the .jar; again, this is done relative to the OBJDIR. All the .class files that have been defined in the set are added to the same archive and deposited in the $BASE_DEV/Dist directory.

CAUTION

Be careful when coding a Makefile. The syntax is extremely important. Sometimes the syntax of Shell programming that is properly parsed by the Shell interpreter will become faulty and cause error when included in a Makefile.

On lines 24 and 30, it is necessary to end the command with a semicolon and backslash (;\); otherwise, a syntax error is produced such as this:

```
/bin/sh: -c: line 2: syntax error: unexpected end of file
```

Lines 33 through 37 define the checking of the .java files in an RCS directory. The make_rcs option directs the Makefile to create an RCS directory in each subdirectory where a .java file is encountered (Figure 21-3). Then all the .java files are being checked in (ci -u1 *.java) in the created directory with version number 1. The ci -u1 command causes the .java files to not only be checked in, but also to be checked out by unlocking the retrieved revision. For more information, read the man pages of the RCS commands: rcs, ci, co, ident, rcsdiff, rcsmerge, and rlog.

The make_rcs option is available to prepare a source tree with the RCS subdirectories. The source tree will be further exploited by a programmer who will copy it into his or her home directory. The AppMaker program also deposits the linkrcs script into the base directory of the source tree. (To avoid confusion, at this point we will not discuss the linkrcs script besides stating its importance in preparing a programmer's development tree.)

Building and Deploying a Two-in-One Script: AppBuild

You've learned how to compile code and distribute it using the make utility. Now it's time to learn how to create the factual tree and generate the necessary files that describe the J2EE application, such as application.xml and web.xml.

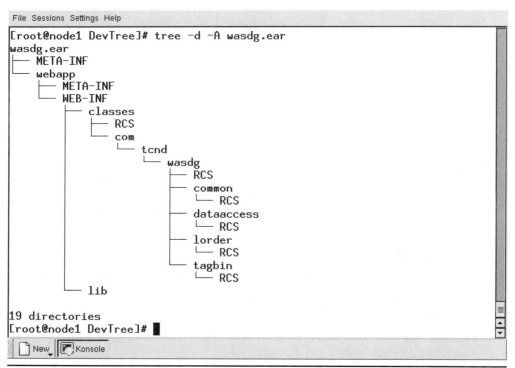

Figure 21-3   *RCS subdirectories created by the* `make make_rcs` *command*

The factual tree is a J2EE tree. You can create it the first time you start building the project by using the same method discussed in Chapter 11. Namely, only the first time, you use the j2tree script followed by refreshear: the first command builds the J2EE-compliant source tree, and the second command builds the factual tree from the source tree.

After that, you use the `AppBuild` command to generate the necessary Makefile to compile your project. Listing 21-7 shows the AppBuild script that combines the `AppMaker` command, followed by the code to move .jsp, .xmi, and .tld files to the factual tree and generate the web.xml descriptor file.

Listing 21-7   *AppBuild*

```ksh
1.   #!/bin/ksh
2.
3.   deployDir=$INSTALLEDAPPS
4.
5.   ./AppMaker
6.   make make_all
7.
8.   for dir in 'find . -type d -print'
9.   do
10.      ls -l $dir/*.jsp > /dev/null 2>&1
11.      if [ $? = 0 ] ; then
12.      (
13.        print "copying from $dir to $deployDir/$dir"
14.        cp $dir/*.jsp $deployDir/$dir
15.      )
16.      fi
17.  done
18.
19.  for dir in 'find . -type d -print'
20.  do
21.      ls -l $dir/*.xmi > /dev/null 2>&1
22.      if [ $? = 0 ] ; then
23.      (
24.        print "copying from $dir to $deployDir/$dir"
25.        cp $dir/*.xmi $deployDir/$dir
26.      )
27.      fi
28.  done
29.
30.  for dir in 'find . -type d -print'
31.  do
32.      ls -l $dir/*.tld > /dev/null 2>&1
33.      if [ $? = 0 ] ; then
```

```
34.        (
35.           print "copying from $dir to $deployDir/$dir"
36.           cp $dir/*.tld $deployDir/$dir
37.        )
38.        fi
39.  done
40.
41.  resetwebxml
```

Some of the code in AppBuild is similar to the svlbuild script (refer to Chapter 11). It does not explicitly compile the .java files, and it does not move all the .class files found in the source tree to the factual tree. On line 5, the AppMaker script is called to generate all necessary Makefiles to be subsequently invoked with make make_all (line 6), which causes the compilation of the Java code and deployment of the .class bytecode. The last line of the script rebuilds the web.xml file and deposits it in the appropriate directories of the source tree and the factual tree. Recall that resetwebxml parses the servlets.list file in the current directory to build the web.xml file.

Concurrent Development: Source Code Control, Compiling, and Testing

The previous section discussed how to compile, deploy, and package code. Most of the actions taken were between the source tree and the factual tree. Now, you'll learn how two or more developers can share the same set of source code files while they each compile and test the enterprise application in their own environment and in their own WAS instance. To be able to achieve such a task, three points need to be realized, programmatically and administratively:

▶ Create user accounts along with their home directories.

▶ Control the source tree and allow a replication of the source tree into a user home directory. The user replicates the source tree into a holding tree. For example, the user dave's holding tree is /home/dave/DevTree.

▶ Install WAS to be run by a particular user. Such a WAS installation is referred to as a *WAS instance.*

To create user accounts on the UNIX system, use the adduser command. Consult the man pages about this command. The following sections discuss the second two points just mentioned. Assume that the users dave, jane, and rosa have valid accounts on the UNIX server node1, and their home directories are /home/dave, /home/jane, and /home/rosa, respectively. Dave and Jane are two programmers who are being supervised by senior programmer Rosa.

A User-Specific Development Tree: Holding Tree

The section "Reconsidering the Build Process Using the make Utility"mentioned that the source tree contains code that is deployed to the factual tree. All three users, dave, jane, and rosa, can replicate the source tree into their home directories.

For example, assuming the source tree is /BOOK/21/DevTree, and the user dave wants to replicate it into his holding tree /home/dave/DevTree, dave will change the directory to /home/dave/DevTree and then issue the following command:

```
# tar cf -  --exclude RCS  -C  /BOOK/21/DevTree . | tar xf -
```

Also, dave needs to clean the .java files and .class files that may have been deposited into his holding tree:

```
# find . -name ".class" -exec rm -f {} \;
# find . -name ".java" -exec rm -f {} \;
```

Now dave is ready to run the script linkrcs, shown in Listing 21-8, to link his holding tree to the source tree, then check out the code of a specific release from it. First of all, the user dave sets his BASE_DEV to /home/dave/DevTree, and then he executes the script linkrcs:
/export BASE_DEV=/home/dave/DevTree # linkrcs.

Listing 21-8 *linkrcs*

```
1.   ln -s /BOOK/21/DevTree/wasdg.ear/webapp/WEB-INF/classes/RCS
     $BASE_DEV/wasdg.ear/webapp/WEB-INF/classes/RCS
2.   (cd $BASE_DEV/wasdg.ear/webapp/WEB-INF/classes; co -r1 RCS/*,v)
3.   ln -s
     /BOOK/21/DevTree/wasdg.ear/webapp/WEB-INF/classes/com/tcnd/wasdg/RCS
     $BASE_DEV/wasdg.ear/webapp/WEB-INF/classes/com/tcnd/wasdg/RCS
4.   (cd $BASE_DEV/wasdg.ear/webapp/WEB-INF/classes/com/tcnd/wasdg; co -r1
     RCS/*,v)
5.   ln -s
     /BOOK/21/DevTree/wasdg.ear/webapp/WEB-INF/classes/com/tcnd/wasdg/common/RCS
     $BASE_DEV/wasdg.ear/webapp/WEB-INF/classes/com/tcnd/wasdg/common/RCS
6.   (cd $BASE_DEV/wasdg.ear/webapp/WEB-INF/classes/com/tcnd/wasdg/common; co
     -r1 RCS/*,v)
7.   ln -s
     /BOOK/21/DevTree/wasdg.ear/webapp/WEB-INF/classes/com/tcnd/wasdg/dataaccess/RCS

     $BASE_DEV/wasdg.ear/webapp/WEB-INF/classes/com/tcnd/wasdg/dataaccess/RCS
8.   (cd
     $BASE_DEV/wasdg.ear/webapp/WEB-INF/classes/com/tcnd/wasdg/dataaccess; co
     -r1 RCS/*,v)
9.   ln -s
     /BOOK/21/DevTree/wasdg.ear/webapp/WEB-INF/classes/com/tcnd/wasdg/lorder/RCS
     $BASE_DEV/wasdg.ear/webapp/WEB-INF/classes/com/tcnd/wasdg/lorder/RCS
```

```
10.   (cd $BASE_DEV/wasdg.ear/webapp/WEB-INF/classes/com/tcnd/wasdg/lorder; co
      -rl RCS/*,v)
11.   ln -s
      /BOOK/21/DevTree/wasdg.ear/webapp/WEB-INF/classes/com/tcnd/wasdg/tagbin/RCS
      $BASE_DEV/wasdg.ear/webapp/WEB-INF/classes/com/tcnd/wasdg/tagbin/RCS
12.   (cd $BASE_DEV/wasdg.ear/webapp/WEB-INF/classes/com/tcnd/wasdg/tagbin; co
      -rl RCS/*,v)
```

Say, for example, that user dave sets up his BASE_DEV environment variable to /home/
dave/DevTree by invoking this command:

```
# linkrcs
```

This command creates in the RCS a symbolic link in each directory of the user dave's
holding tree, where the source code of a Java program is found (for example, line 1). The
RCS link is to the original source tree directory. The code in the RCS is also checked out
for release number 1 of the web application (for example, line 2).

The user dave will then use this holding tree as if it is his own source tree to check in a new
.java file (using ci -u1 filename.java) and editing the older file (by checking it out first
with locking co -l filename.java). When co is used with the option -l, the file is
being checked out and locked.

Similarly, when user jane tries to check out the locked file with the co -l filename, she
will be warned that this file is in use. Editing the same file concurrently is always possible
because user jane can check out the file in read-only mode and modify it, but then she
needs to use the rcsdiff command to merge her changes with dave's changes. We are
not going to digress into RCS commands and their options; however, you can consult a UNIX
manual or the man pages for further exploration with RCS.[4]

The linkrcs script makes symbolic links for the RCS directories that contain code to be
commonly shared by dave, jane, and rosa. The only difference is that rosa is the authority
to issue the RCS administrative command rcs to control the source code.

For simplicity, the discussion herein assumes that all three developers are trusted; otherwise,
the user rosa must use the administrative command rcs to control the accessibility of the
checked in files (using the option -a: rcs -ausers).

Figure 21-4 shows the correspondence between the source tree, the holding tree, and the
factual tree.

The source tree contains one copy of the initial code checked in the RCS directories. The
holding tree contains a copy of the source tree with code checked out from the RCS directories.
The code is compiled in the holding tree of a user and then replicated to the factual tree. The
factual tree is in the $INSTALLEDAPPS directory.

Once a user creates a holding tree, he or she will use it exactly as if it is the source tree.
Therefore, user dave will have his environment variable BASE_DEV pointing to the holding

---

[4]   RCS is used here due to its availability on the UNIX system. You can also use SCCS, CVS, or any other
       source control. More sophisticated source control applications are available, like IBM CMVC, or whatever
       IBM has decided to call it lately. Usually, using such an application turns the web application project into
       a source control project!

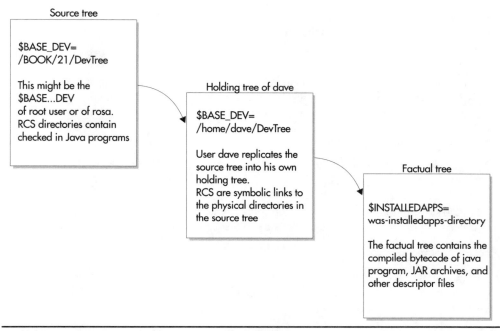

Figure 21-4   *Source tree, holding tree, and factual tree*

tree /home/dave/DevTree, and he will subsequently compile and deploy his code by using the AppBuild script, as described in the previous section. Yet, dave needs to have his own WAS instance because it is not possible to share the same WAS application between all three users.

NOTE

It is possible for the holding tree and the factual tree to be the same tree. In other words, a user can compile his or her code directly in the factual tree. In this situation, the user must own the WAS instance.

Installing Multiple Instances of WebSphere Domains on the Same Server

WAS is started by a Java machine. Because multiple Java machines can be running on the same server, you can have two or more WebSphere domains defined and running on the same server. This allows multiple users to share the same physical machine while each of them is running WAS in its own memory space. The direct way to show you how this is possible is by going straight into the procedure. We will use WAS AEs because it is the most realistic WAS product for a programmer to develop and test code with.

After installing WAS AEs, say in the /opt/WebSphere/AppServer directory, you will make an image of the installation product (similar to the method described in Chapter 8). The image to be created is of the AppServer directory. The following command shows you how to create such an image and deposit it into the /tmp directory:

```
# tar cf /tmp/wasaes4.tar -C /opt/WebSphere AppServer
```

After creating the image, a user can extract it in his or her own working space (for example, in his or her home directory) and must preprocess the files that are in the bin, config, and properties directories to substitute the following:

▶ The predefined ports with another set of ports

▶ The directory location of the initially installed product with the new location where the image has been extracted

For the substitutions mentioned here, the subs script (see Chapter 17) is sufficient to perform the processing on these files. Recall that subs takes three arguments:

```
subs filename originalstring newstring
```

Let's say the user dave has an account on the node1 machine, and his home directory is /home/dave. The user dave logs in and extracts the WAS product image into his home directory by issuing the following command:

```
# cd /home/dave; tar xf /tmp/wasaes4.tar
```

This command creates the /home/dave/AppServer directory containing the binary distribution of the WAS product. Before dave starts the product, he needs to make the one-time change in the configuration files of WAS: mapping the ports to another set of ports and correcting the directory location.

Mapping the Ports to Another Set of Ports

To identify the ports used by WAS, consider the wasports script shown in Listing 21-9. This script iterates over all the files in the current directory and guesses which ports are in use. Put the script in your search PATH, for example, in the /tools directory, change the directory to $WAS_HOME/config, and invoke it.

Listing 21-9 *wasports*

```perl
1.    #!/usr/bin/perl
2.
3. my @likely=('objectleveltracesettings','locationservicedaemon',
                'orbsettings','transports');
4.
5.    my(@files)=glob("./*");
6.    foreach my $f (@files) {
7.        print ">> DOING FILE $f\n";
8.        open(F,"<$f");
```

```
9.        while(<F>) {
10.          foreach $s (@likely) {
11.              if ( (/$s/i) && (/[Pp]ort=\"\d{2,5}\"/) ) {
12.                  s/^(.)*[Pp]ort=\"//;
13.                  s/\"(.)*//;
14.                  print "$s ++ $_\n";
15.              }
16.          }
17.      }
18.  }
```

The wasports script reveals the preconfigured ports to be used by a WAS installation, as shown in this illustration.

The wasports script looks for a likely occurrence of particular strings that might be followed by port numbers (line 11), and then it isolates the port numbers (lines 12 and 13) to print them (line 14).

Assigning the Ports for a WAS Instance and Modifying the Directory of a WAS Instance

Each instance of a running WAS exclusively consumes a set of ports; therefore, you need to change the ports to make sure no two instances of WAS conflict in using the same ports. Listing 21-10 shows the script that the user dave will run in his /home/dave/AppServer/config directory to substitute all the ports with his own set of ports.

Listing 21-10   *subswasports*

```
1.    subs admin-server-cfg.xml   2102 12102
2.    subs admin-server-cfg.xml   9001 19001
3.    subs admin-server-cfg.xml   901 10901
4.    subs admin-server-cfg.xml   9091 19091
5.
6.    subs server-cfg.xml   2102 12102
7.    subs server-cfg.xml   9000 19000
8.    subs server-cfg.xml   900 10900
9.    subs server-cfg.xml   9080 19080
10.   subs server-cfg.xml   9443 19443
11.   subs server-cfg.xml   9090 19090
12.   subs server-cfg.xml   7000 17000
13.
14.   subs template-server-cfg.xml   2102 12102
15.   subs template-server-cfg.xml   9000 19000
16.   subs template-server-cfg.xml   900 10900
17.   subs template-server-cfg.xml   9080 19080
18.   subs template-server-cfg.xml   9443 19443
19.   subs template-server-cfg.xml   9090 19090
20.   subs template-server-cfg.xml   7000 17000
```

The user `dave` also needs to rectify the directory location from which WAS is started. The subswasdir, shown in Listing 21-11, takes one argument as the name of the user who owns the WAS instance and makes the appropriate substitution to point to the directory of the user owning the instance. The script assumes that the product extracted in the /home/someuser/AppServer directory originated from an image of the initial product that has been installed in /opt/WebSphere/AppServer. The user `dave` issues the following command:

```
# subswasdir  dave
```

This command makes all the appropriate changes in the configuration files of WAS to point to the new location of the installed product.

Listing 21-11   *subswasdir*

```
1.    #!/bin/ksh
2.
3.    # example: subswasdir dave
4.
5.    (cd /home/$1/AppServer/bin; subs setupCmdLine.sh
        "\/opt\/WebSphere\/AppServer" "\/home\/$1\/AppServer")
6.    (cd /home/$1/AppServer/config; subs admin-server-cfg.xml
        "\/opt\/WebSphere\/AppServer" "\/home\/$1\/AppServer")
7.    (cd /home/$1/AppServer/config; subs server-cfg.xml
```

```
        "\/opt\/WebSphere\/AppServer" "\/home\/$1\/AppServer")
8.   (cd /home/$1/AppServer/config; subs template-server-cfg.xml
        "\/opt\/WebSphere\/AppServer" "\/home\/$1\/AppServer")
9.   (cd /home/$1/AppServer/config; subs plugin-cfg.xml
        "\/opt\/WebSphere\/AppServer" "\/home\/$1\/AppServer")
10.  (cd /home/$1/AppServer/properties; subs sas.client.props
        "\/opt\/WebSphere\/AppServer" "\/home\/$1\/AppServer")
```

Now that the user `dave` has made the changes to his WAS image, he can start a WAS instance on his own by running /home/dave/AppServer/bin/startServer.sh.

Similarly, the user `jane` can set her WAS instance with a different set of ports and different directory location for the installed product. On the same directory shared by `dave` and `jane`, one person can run the `ps` command to realize that two instances of WAS are running in different memory space.

Setting the Environment

The setj.sh script introduced in Chapter 3 takes one argument to prepare the development environment of a user according to the WASDG environment. If you invoke it with a w130 argument, it will set the environment according to your platform for WAS v4. If you are on a Linux platform, then setj.sh executes the shell script setw4lin.sh to set up the part of the environment that pertains to WAS v4 for Linux. In particular, the WAS_HOME directory is generically set to /opt/WebSphere/AppServer.

Let's modify setw4lin.sh to make WAS_HOME point to $HOME/AppServer unless the user is root. The modification is simple as we will add a conditional statement that checks the login id, then accordingly the global variable WAS_HOME is set to point to the appropriate directory. Listing 21-12 shows the code that needs to be added to the setw4lin.sh script.

Listing 21-12   *Code added to modify setw4lin.sh*

```
#Only root own the original install of WAS
USER='whoami'
if [ $USER = "root" ]
then
  WAS_HOME=/opt/WebSphere/AppServer
else
  WAS_HOME=$HOME/AppServer
fi
```

This modification enforces the setting of the environment variables that relates to WAS to be relative to the home directory of a user. For instance, when the user `dave` logs in, the WAS_HOME directory is set to /home/dave/AppServer, and every subsequent environment variable that points to the WAS installation directory will point to the directory just mentioned.

Naming the WebSphere Domain

The method of configuring and running multiple instances of WAS on the same server proved that the name of the WebSphere domain is totally immaterial. In other words, in the previous example, both `dave` and `jane` were running WAS with a WebSphere domain by the same default name: WebSphere Administrative Domain. Naming a WebSphere domain has no technical value; it is just a label.[5] Therefore, our approach in defining a WebSphere domain in Chapter 5 was coherent as we took the systemic approach to discuss it.

Considering the Environment for Concurrent Programmers

Timestamping transactions is very important in a networked environment. Any literature about an application that is distributed on several machines must have a section that discusses—at least briefly—the importance of synchronizing the clocks of the machines located on the same subnet.

Having the clocks in sync between all machines is important for shared file systems (NFS or AFS), for the make utility, for security transactions across platform, for Kerberos authentication, and so on.

When building a project using the make utility, it is important for the time between all networked machines to be in sync. The obvious and accurate way to synchronize the clock between all TCP/IP-networked machines is by using the Network Time Protocol (NTP). NTP is a protocol built on top of TCP/IP that assures local timekeeping with reference to precise clocks, such as atomic clocks that are available on the Internet. The protocol synchronizes distributed clocks within milliseconds over long time periods.[6]

In a networked environment, you can have a machine that acts as the time server. An Intel 386 with 32MB running Linux suffices to be such a server because NTP imposes minimal load on a server. You will install the basic Linux operating system on such a machine, enable only the essential services on this machine (for example, inetd), and configure the ntpd (NTP daemon) on it. Consider the arayech.tcnd.com machine in a networked environment in the following illustration. The arayech machine peers with the timeservers and broadcasts time for all machines on the local network of tcnd.com.

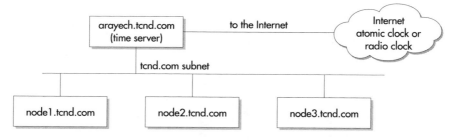

---

5   WAS v5 does not use the term "WebSphere domain" but *WebSphere cluster*. The notion of WebSphere domain (known in WAS v3.5 and v4) that spans many nodes has been replaced with the WebSphere cluster that spans many cells.

6   Refer to RFC 1119 for the Network Time Protocol Specification and Implementation.

The arayech machine must start the ntpd after synchronizing its clock with a precise clock on the Internet. For this reason, the /etc/rc.d/init.d/ntpd file that starts the ntpd on a Linux machine should have a start entry, as shown in Listing 21-13.

Listing 21-13   *start of ntpd*

```
1.   start() {
2.       /usr/sbin/ntpdate -o 1 tock.usno.navy.mil clock.llnl.gov
3.       # Start daemons.
4.       echo -n "Starting ntpd: "
5.       daemon ntpd -A
6.       RETVAL=$?
7.       echo
8.       [ $RETVAL -eq 0 ] && touch /var/lock/subsys/ntpd
9.       return $RETVAL
10.  }
```

On line 2, the `ntpdate` command updates the time with two time servers before starting its daemon (line 5).

Also on arayech, the /etc/ntpd.conf file contains a configuration file, shown in Listing 21-14.

Listing 21-14   *ntpd.conf on time server arayech.tcnd.com*

```
1.   server time.ien.it
2.   server canon.inria.fr
3.   peer arayech.tcnd.com
4.   driftfile /var/adm/ntp.drift
5.   restrict 66.51.9.0 mask 255.255.255.192 nomodify
6.   restrict 127.0.0.1
7.   restrict default notrust nomodify
```

NOTE

The configuration file may contain many entries to enable tracing and to collect statistics, which are beyond the scope of this book.

Now arayech is a time server, and all machines in the tcnd.com domain can synchronize their clocks with it. For instance, because the arayech clock is now in sync with the time servers time.ien.it and canon.inria.fr, the node1.tcnd.com machine can also be running the ntpd and try to synchronize its clock directly with arayech.tcnd.com. The node1 machine will have an /etc/htp.conf file, as shown in Listing 21-15.

Listing 21-15   */etc/ntp.conf on node1.tcnd.com*

```
1.  server arayech.tcnd.com
2.  driftfile /var/adm/ntp.drift
3.  restrict 206.148.52.0 mask 255.255.255.192 nomodify
4.  restrict 127.0.0.1
5.  restrict arayech.tcnd.com nomodify
6.  restrict default notrust nomodify
```

Line 1 shows that node1.tcnd.com is looking for arayech.tcnd.com as the time server. Line 3 again restricts the broadcast of time to outside machines that are not part of the tcnd.com network.

The `ntpdc` command can be used on node1.tcnd.com to confirm the synchronization of the clock with arayech, as shown next.

```
# ntpdc
ntpdc> peers
remote          local      st poll reach delay    offset    disp
=================================================================
=arayech.tcnd.co 66.51.9.155   16   64    0 0.00000  0.000000 0.00000
```

After running `ntpdc`, invoke the `peers` command to locate the remote time server with which a machine is synchronizing its clock.

A Windows NT machine can also synchronize with the arayech time server, provided it has an NTP client application installed on it. The following illustration shows the use of Hummingbird's network time application when synchronizing the clock with arayech.

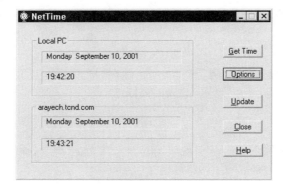

Another issue that confronts a skilled programmer is how to copy or move files or directories around in a distributed environment. Moving a file or a set of files between machines or file systems is necessary to replicate an installation, to distribute mirrored files in a clustered environment, to restore a backup copy of a set of files, to archive a web application for testing or distribution, and so on. There are many ways to perform this task by using a combination of basic commands such as `tar, jar, dump, cpio, backup,` and `restore` (AIX only), or by employing all these commands across machines and distributed file systems by using the piping capability of UNIX commands and the `rsh` command.

The following command replicates /tmp/sometree1 from the local AIX machine to the directory /export/public of the remote AIX populi machine:

```
backup -i -f - < /tmp/sometree1 | rsh populi ' cd /export/public ; restore -f - '
```

Yet, we can use a generic UNIX command such as tar and wrap it in an rsh to replicate directories across any UNIX system. The following command shows you how to do so, provided you have rexec configured on your system:

```
# rsh node1 tar cvf - -C /opt/WebSphere/AppServer/InstalledApps wasdg.ear | tar xvf -
```

This command replicates to the wasdg.ear application directory from the host node1 and extract it in the current directory of the machine where the command is issued.

Documentation

You can easily document the packages of a web application by using javadoc. The javadoc utility is used to parse Java source files looking for text and tags embedded between slashes and asterisks (/** and */) to generate HTML files describing these source files. Because the Java compiler (javac) treats the text that falls in between /** and */ as a comment, such online tagged documentation doesn't affect your compiled code.

The format of the javadoc command follows:

```
javadoc [options] [packagenames] [sourcefiles] [classnames] [@files]
```

Let's use javadoc with the find and sed commands to quickly generate the appropriate documentation for the packages used in our web application developed in Part III of this book.

1. Create a directory to deposit the documentation for the packages. Usually, the directory is the document root of the HTTP server. However, for testing purpose, create one in the /tmp directory:

   ```
   mkdir /tmp/test
   ```

2. Locate the webapp directory that contains the package and run the find command to walk through each directory. Then use the sed command to substitute each directory separator (/) with a dot (.) so that it can be presented as a package name to the javadoc command.

   ```
   cd $BASE_DEV/wasdg.ear/webapp/WEB-INF/classes
   find com/tcnd/wasdg -type d -print | sed 's/\///./g' | xargs javadoc -d /tmp/test
   ```

This command creates the documentation that corresponds to the packages located in com/tcnd/wasdg. This works fine because Java packages map exactly to the directory hierarchy on the file system.

The javadoc command creates an index.html and a packages.html file and deposits them into the /tmp/test directory.

Wrapping Up

In this chapter, you learned that when a web application is written by two or more developers, the source code must be made available on a sharable directory. Using a source control application resolves the issue of concurrently editing source files. Each developer can copy the shared web application from the source tree to his own holding tree. The developer can edit files in the holding tree, then test the web application by deploying it to the factual tree. Testing occurs on a WAS domain that is assigned specifically to the developer.

As a result, two or more developers can deploy and test the application, as long as their deployment occurs on a disjoint WebSphere Application Server. You can run several WAS domain instances on the same server as long as they have been installed in separate directories, and each instance uses a disjoint set of ports.

This chapter concluded by explaining how to generate Java documentation with `javadoc`.

Stress-Testing, Tracing, and Debugging

OBJECTIVES

► Programming a Stress Tester

► Writing a Logger

► Writing an Exception Handler

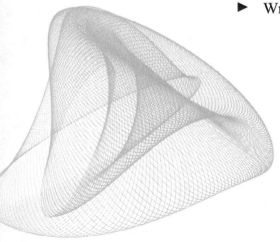

Stress-Testing

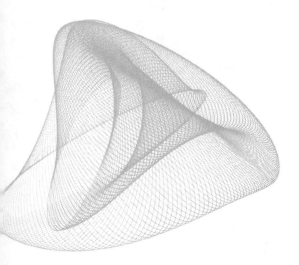

S tress-testing an application server and collecting statistical data is the last step in a web development project. Yet, this is true only if the web application is performing adequately and properly when a fair number of users are realizing their tasks on the web application. In this book, we have considered several scripts to facilitate programming and simulation for a developer.

Chapters 3 and 4 presented the scripts to automatically set up the user development environment (the WASDG environment), Chapter 7 presented scripts to extrapolate WAS configuration and generate reports, Chapter 9 presented scripts to quickly rebuild the DBGUIDE database, Chapter 11 presented scripts to automate the build and deployment process of a J2EE application under WAS (such as the WASDG application), Chapter 15 presented a simulator script to prove the loading order versus visibility order of classes, and Chapter 17 showed the commands that may cause session harassment under WAS.

This chapter presents the simulator to stress-test a web application such as the WASDG application. In particular, to simulate a set of users or tellers working concurrently on crediting and debiting bankers accounts, we need to write a script at the level of system programming: a teller's browser is a forked process, and his or her repetitive requests[1] to URIs (also called hits) are an iteration within the process.

The scripts considered in this chapter to stress-test the web server are based on Perl and form the foundation of methods to stress-test web application servers on an intranet. (I called it *intranet* instead of *Internet* because the servers will be isolated in a lab so it is possible to collect accurate data while stress-testing a web application.) The discussion in this chapter does not consider tangential situations such as proxy server, firewall crossing, router-based load distribution, etc. None of these are considered to be part of WebSphere Application Server, and the delay they may provoke must be addressed separately and independently from WAS. Yet, the approach used in this chapter could apply to Lynx for any of the aforementioned situations, because Lynx is based on Perl libwww-perl (LWP) and support proxies, secure HTTP protocol, etc.

Although WAS offers many Java APIs that can be used to programmatically monitor the application server, they do not form an adequate basis to collect statistical data; therefore, they must be disabled or commented out from the web application code. Calling an API's methods from within an application will eventually make the system too busy to execute such methods. Only proper simulation for a number of active users or clients on their web browsers must be considered when stress-testing a web application.

---

[1] A more rigorous technical description of a web hit is provided in the Web Statistical Analysis and Probability (WSAP) application, written by the author and which you can download from www.tcnd.com.

Basic Timing for HTTP Requests

One view of stress-testing is to look at the elapsed time it takes to complete a successful user request. The elapsed time means from the time the request is issued to the time it is satisfied and returned with some data to the user. A failing request is a request that returns no data to the client. This means if we consider the data returned to be a stream of bytes assigned to a variable $buf (using Perl notation), then a failing request accounts for such a returned stream whose length equals zero (length($buffer)). This means if a client tries to log in and fails due to bad authentication, his or her request is considered successful as long as some data is returned to the client browser.

One simple way to time a teller login to the WASDG Login application is by using the command shown in Listing 22-1.

Listing 22-1   *Timing a teller login*

```
# time echo "userid=teller1&password=secret1&---" | lynx -post_data
    http://node1/wasbook/tellerlogged | grep WELCOME
                    WELCOME TELLER: teller1(Jane1)

real    0m0.698s
user    0m0.050s
sys     0m0.020s
```

Because it is possible to place the `time` command before anything you normally put on the command line, we can have a sequence of URL requests in a shell script where tellers may issue several requests after logging in to the application. The someurls script shown in Listing 22-2 is such a script.

Listing 22-2   *someurls*

```
1.    echo "userid=teller1&password=secret1&---" | lynx -post_data
        http://node1/wasbook/tellerlogged | grep WELCOME
2.    echo "clientid=client12&amount=5&---" | lynx -post_data
        http://node1/wasbook/creditdebit | grep Juggle
3.    echo "clientid=client12&amount=15&---" | lynx -post_data
        http://node1/wasbook/creditdebit | grep Juggle
4.    echo "userid=teller2&password=secret2&---" | lynx -post_data
        http://node1/wasbook/tellerlogged | grep WELCOME
5.    echo "clientid=client12&amount=10&---" | lynx -post_data
        http://node1/wasbook/creditdebit | grep Juggle
6.    echo "clientid=client14&amount=1&---" | lynx -post_data
        http://node1/wasbook/creditdebit | grep Juggle
```

It's easy to time the URLs by running the `time` command against the script. The following illustration shows that it took approximately 3 seconds to execute all the URLs.

```
File Sessions Settings Help
[root@node2 misc]# time ./someurls
                         WELCOME TELLER: teller1(Jane1)
   Juggle:c client12:b 35:d# 0:c# 4:
   Juggle:c client12:b 50:d# 0:c# 5:
                         WELCOME TELLER: teller2(Jane2)
   Juggle:c client12:b 60:d# 0:c# 6:
   Juggle:c client14:b 2:d# 0:c# 2:

real    0m3.210s
user    0m0.130s
sys     0m0.190s
[root@node2 misc]#

 New   Konsole
```

At the end of each run, the `time` command returns elapsed real time, user time, and system time. The user time and system time result from the fact that as the commands in the someurls scripts are executed, they switch back between user mode and kernel mode. Mainly, it is in user mode that any program starts its execution, but the intervention of the operating system is necessary whenever the program needs I/O services, network services, and other services.

No doubt, placing an HTTP request requires network services and therefore, the attention of the operating system (the kernel itself under UNIX). Switching between user mode and system or kernel mode is typical. Adding the user time to the system time produces the CPU time (CPU time = user time + system time). Chapter 25 shows more thorough commands to count CPU time.

In designing a subroutine to be processed by a known algorithm to stress-test a web server, you must first examine the HTTP methods to be performed on the web server. There are basically two commonly known and widely used HTTP methods: GET and POST. The reader should be cautious about the nomination used in here when referring to GET and POST as methods. The word method is used here as per the HTTP nomenclature, abd it has nothing to do with Java class programming.

A workstation on which Lynx is installed will eventually have the LWP, URI, and HTTP Perl modules installed. GET and POST are two Perl scripts that are used as commands and that are installed with such a library. To log in as a teller, you can post the URL with the POST command, as shown in Listing 23-3.

Listing 23-3   *Posting an HTTP request using the Perl POST script*

```
# POST http://node1.tcnd.com/wasbook/tellerlogged [ENTER]
Please enter content (application/x-www-form-urlencoded) to be POSTed:
userid=teller1&password=secret1&
[CONTROL-D]
```

After issuing the POST command and pressing ENTER, you will be asked to enter the data to be posted. Each entered line must end with a carriage return (by pressing ENTER), and you will end the input of data by pressing CTRL-D.

You can also get a URL with the GET command:

```
# GET http://node1.tcnd.com/wasbook/dumpenv
```

This command returns the data returned by the DumpEnv servlet. The data returned is printed to your console without any formatting; it also shows the header content of the page returned with such a request.

Programming a Stress-Tester

The method shown previously is simple, but it lacks important simulation aspects. First, the script starts a process that requests URLs serially, whereas multiple clients' or tellers' requests need to be executed concurrently. Second, when repetitive requests are made, the browser's delay to set up its variables is not accounted for. Third, it lacks automation because it requires an explicit set of URLs to be typed in. Fourth, the method lacks the randomness in the process of selecting a client and placing his or her requests.

The ZappUrl script discussed in this section addresses two of these points: concurrency, and accuracy in accounting for the time. As for automation and random selection of the URLs, these are discussed in the section "Stress-Testing the WASDG Application with SharkUrl."

Special Considerations for the HTTP Methods

In the rest of the chapter, only the GET method is considered while designing the program to stress-test the web server.[2] The POST method requires some extra specific programming using the LWP, URI, and HTTP Perl modules, which is beyond the scope of this book. Also, depending on whether we use the POST or the GET method to stress-test the server, there might be a minimal difference in the result because the procedure of handling either method relates to the HTTP server rather than WebSphere Application Server.

Let's open a socket and write a stream of bytes to it that we consider to be a hit. For instance, if $s is the variable representing the stream of bytes, then such a variable is set to a value, as shown in Listing 22-4.

Listing 22-4   *Preparing the stream of bytes to be shipped to the HTTP socket*

```
$s =  <<EOF;
GET $uri HTTP/1.0
Content-type: text/html
User-Agent: WASDG-ZappUrl
```

---

[2]   The reader should consider re-deploying the WASDG application in the code distribution for this chapter. A few servlets, such as the TellerLogged servlet, have been mondified to make use of the service() and doGet methods instead of the doPost(). This is a minor change in the code of the servlets that we consider exclusively in this chapter.

```
Cookie: $cookie

EOF
} else {
$s =  <<EOF;
GET $uri HTTP/1.0
Content-type: text/html
User-Agent: WASDG-ZappUrl

EOF
}
```

Forking Concurrent Processes for Concurrent Users

For multiple tellers or users accessing the web application, consider forking a process for each user. Listing 22-5 shows the forking of processes for a number of clients.

Listing 22-5   *Code to iterate and fork processes for a number of clients*

```
1.    # Fork one process for each client, and fetch the url $nhits
time in each
       forked process
2.    for(my $i=0;$i<$clients;$i++) {
3.        $stress{$i}{success} = $stress{$i}{fail} = 0;
4.        if (($pid = fork) == 0) {
5.            # child process
6.            print STDERR "[ > COMMENCING CHILD PROCESS $i / $$]\n"
if
       $verbose;
7.            my $start = time;
8.            while ($nhits > 0) {
9.                &hitit($i, $destination, $port, $uri);
10.               $nhits--;
11.               # set the name of this running process
12.               $0 = "ZappUrl $i:$nhits"
13.            }
14.            my $end = time;
15.            my $delay = $end - $start;
16.            print STDERR "\n[ < ENDING CHILD PROCESS $i /$$
       $stress{$i}{success}/$stress{$i}{fail}  ($delay secs)]\n" if
$verbose;
17.            exit 0; # terminate process
18.        }
```

```
19.   }
20.
21.   for(my $i=0;$i<$clients;$i++) {
22.       wait; # wait for the child process to terminate
23.   }
```

Iterating to Place Multiple Requests Within Each Process

Although forked processes run concurrently, which is the normal behavior when several clients or tellers are accessing a web application, each of these forked processes needs to serially issue a number of hits. Therefore, once a process is forked, an iteration is started within the process to serially execute a number of hits. Listing 22-6 shows such iteration.

Listing 22-6   *Iteration started within each forked process*

```
1.    while ($nhits > 0) {
2.        &hitit($i, $destination, $port, $uri);
3.        $nhits--;
4.        # set the name of this running process
5.        $0 = "ZappUrl $i:$nhits"
6.    }
7.    ...
8.    sub hitit {
9.    ...
10.   }
```

The ZappUrl Script

You're still left with a few tasks. The code to process the command prompt and set up the final script variables is required. The code to open a socket where the HTTP protocol is listening is also needed. All the code is shown in the final ZappUrl script, shown in Listing 22-7.

Table 22-1 shows the options of the ZappUrl script.

It is required to specify only the number of clients, the number of hits, the target HTTP server, and the URI. The verbosity is set with the option -v or -vv. While -v prints information about when a process is started and when it is exited, -vv prints additional information such as the content of the page returned by the HTTP server.

Option	Required	Description
-v	N	Verbose
-vv	N	Verbose prints everything
-vj	N	Views JSESSIONID
-c \<n\>	Y	Number of clients
-h \<n\>	Y	Number of hits per client
-f \<n\>	N	Number of frequency to report the hits. Must be multiple of the number of hits. Do not specify for the default of 1.
-t \<server\>	Y	Target server
-u \<uri\>	Y	URI
-C \<cookie\>	N	Cookie
-R \<filename\>	N	Prints comma-delimited format report to filename. If filename is STDOUT, then print.

Table 22-1   *Options of the ZappUrl Stress-Tester*

The -vj option is important in particular to clearly print the JSESSIONID, in case you do not specify the more raw-printing -vv option. Once you locate the JSESSIONID, you can use it in a successive request with the -C option.

The following example clarifies how to use the ZappUrl script. Figure 22-1 shows the ZappUrl requesting one client with one hit to login teller1. Because the -vv option prints the header and the content of the HTML page returned, we use the `grep` command with the -v option to delete the line returned where \<html\> occurs (which is the content of the page). The -R option followed by stderr requested to print the output to the STDERR, which is the console or window where the command is issued.

Figure 22-1   *ZappUrl requesting one client with one hit to login teller1*

The following illustration shows a similar login for teller1; however, we requested to print only the important information (options -v -vj): the start and end of the process, the elapsed time, and the JSESSIONID if any returned in the header of the page.

```
File  Sessions  Settings  Help
[root@node2 Stress]# perl zappurl -c 1 -h 1 -t node1.tcnd.com  -u /wasbook/tellerlogged?userid=teller1
\&password=secret1 -R stderr -v -vj
[ > COMMENCING CHILD PROCESS 0 / 2523]
[JSESSIONID 0000214BAKJWZ2X03TVO41STH1Y:-1]
        client,hit,flag,hits,bytes,success,failure [0, 1,  1, 4129, 1, 0]

[ < ENDING CHILD PROCESS 0 /2523 1/0  (0 secs)]
Elapsed:    0
[root@node2 Stress]# 

 New   Konsole
```

The JESSIONID shows the session id saved in the WAS web container for the previous request (Chapter 16). Consequently, we use it with another request to dump the session by invoking the DumpSession servlet, as shown in the following illustration.

```
File  Sessions  Settings  Help
[root@node2 Stress]# perl zappurl -c 1 -h 1 -t node1.tcnd.com  -u /wasbook/dumpsession -R stderr -C
JSESSIONID=0000214BAKJWZ2X03TVO41STH1Y:-1 -vv
[ > COMMENCING CHILD PROCESS 0 / 2548]
HTTP/1.1 200 OK
Date: Fri, 05 Jul 2002 15:06:38 GMT
Server: IBM_HTTP_SERVER/1.3.19.1  Apache/1.3.20 (Unix)
Connection: close
Content-Type: text/html
Content-Language: en

<html><head><title>Dumping session object</title></head>
<body bgcolor="white"><h1>Session object content</h1>
<h2>JSESSIONID = 214BAKJWZ2X03TVO41STH1Y</h2>
FRSTNAME: Jane1 <br>
LASTNAME: Doe1 <br>
IMAGE: ../images/teller1 <br>
SSN: 000000000 <br>
EMPNO: 1      <br>
EMAIL: teller1@wasette.com <br>
CONTACT: somecontact <br>
COUNTER: 0 <br><br>
<hr><p>
teller: com.tcnd.wasdg.common.EmpAccnt@723cfd02<br>
<hr><p>
Created on: 1025881546203 or Fri Jul 05 11:05:46 EDT 2002<br>Last accessed on: 1025881598851 or Fri
Jul 05 11:06:38 EDT 2002<br>Expire after: 60 seconds <br>Session ID from cookie: true<br>Session ID
from URL: false<br>OK to request session ID: true<br>
<hr><p>
COOKIE[JSESSIONID][0000214BAKJWZ2X03TVO41STH1Y:-1] <br>
        client,hit,flag,hits,bytes,success,failure [0, 1,  1, 927, 1, 0]

[ < ENDING CHILD PROCESS 0 /2548 1/0  (0 secs)]
Elapsed:    0
[root@node2 Stress]# 

 New   Konsole
```

Listing 22-7   *ZappUrl script to stress-test a web server with a single URI*

```
1.    #!/usr/bin/perl
2.
3.    # ZappUrl    --- bulk request urls to stress-test a web server
4.
5.    use strict;
6.
7.    my %stress; # holds a stresser object of success and failure
8.    my $freq = 1;
9.    # Initialize
10.   my $version = "HTTP 1.0"; # default
11.   my $clients = 1;
12.   my $nhits = 1;
13.
14.   my $verbose = 0; # verbose flag disabled
15.   my $vsess = 0; # view jsession
16.   my $report; # flag set to print report
17.   my $fh;
18.   my $output;
19.
20.   my
($target,$cookie,$uri,$hostname,$destination,$port,$pid,$elapsed,$nbytes,$nhits);
21.   while(@ARGV) {
22.   if ($ARGV[0] eq "-v") {
23.      $verbose = 1;
24.      shift @ARGV;
25.   }
26.   if ($ARGV[0] eq "-vv") {
27.      $verbose = 2;
28.      shift @ARGV;
29.   }
30.   if ($ARGV[0] eq "-vj") {
31.      shift @ARGV;
32.      $vsess = 1;
33.   }
34.   elsif ($ARGV[0] eq "-R") {
35.       $report = 1;
36.       shift @ARGV;
37.       $output = shift @ARGV;
38.       if ( ($output =~ /stderr/i) || ($output =~ /stdout/i) )
39.       {
40.           $fh = 'STDERR';
41.       }
42.       else {
43.           $fh = 'REPORT';
44.           open(REPORT,">$output");
45.       }
46.   }
47.   elsif ($ARGV[0] eq "-C") {
```

```perl
48.       shift @ARGV;
49.       $cookie = shift @ARGV;
50.   }
51.
52.   elsif($ARGV[0] eq "-f") {
53.       shift @ARGV;
54.       $freq = shift @ARGV;
55.   }
56.   elsif($ARGV[0] eq "-c") {
57.       shift @ARGV;
58.       $clients = shift @ARGV;
59.   }
60.   elsif($ARGV[0] eq "-h") {
61.       shift @ARGV;
62.       $nhits = shift @ARGV;
63.   }
64.   elsif($ARGV[0] eq "-t") {
65.       shift @ARGV;
66.       $target = shift @ARGV;
67.   }
68.   elsif($ARGV[0] eq "-u") {
69.       shift @ARGV;
70.       $uri = shift @ARGV;
71.   }
72.   else { last; }
73.
74.   }
75.
76.   die "Usage: zappkurl [-v] [-vv] [-vj] [-R filereport] [-c clients] [-h
      hits] -t server -u uri\n" unless
77.       ( defined($clients) && defined($nhits) && defined($target) &&
      defined($uri) );
78.
79.   chop($hostname = `hostname`);
80.
81.
82.   if ($target =~ ':') {
83.       ($destination, $port) = split(/\:/,$target);
84.   }
85.   else {
86.       $port = 80;
87.       $destination = $target;
88.       # ($destination, $uri) = split(/\//,$target,2);
89.   }
90.
91.   my $start = time;
92.
93.   # Fork one process for each client, and fetch the url $nhits time in each
      forked process
94.   for(my $i=0;$i<$clients;$i++) {
```

```
95.        $stress{$i}{success} = $stress{$i}{fail} = 0;
96.    if (($pid = fork) == 0) {
97.            # child process
98.            print STDERR "[ > COMMENCING CHILD PROCESS $i / $$]\n" if
       $verbose;
99.            my $start = time;
100.           while ($nhits > 0) {
101.                &hitit($i, $destination, $port, $uri);
102.                $nhits--;
103.                # set the name of this running process
104.                $0 = "ZappUrl $i:$nhits"
105.            }
106.            my $end = time;
107.            my $delay = $end - $start;
108.            print STDERR "\n[ < ENDING CHILD PROCESS $i /$$
       $stress{$i}{success}/$stress{$i}{fail}  ($delay secs)]\n" if $verbose;
109.            exit 0; # terminate process
110.    }
111. }
112.
113. for(my $i=0;$i<$clients;$i++) {
114.    # wait for the child process to terminate, and return process pid
115.    wait;
116. }
117.
118. $elapsed = time - $start;
119. print STDOUT "Elapsed:    $elapsed\n";
120.
121. #for(my $i=0;$i<$clients;$i++) {
122. #    print "STRESS Client $i $stress{$i}{success} / $stress{$i}{fail}\n";
123. #}
124.
125. ###################################
126.
127. sub hitit {
128.    my($i, $destination, $port, $uri) = @_;
129.
130.    if ($nbytes = &requrl($destination, $port, $uri)) {
131.        if (($nhits % $freq) == 0) {
132.            $stress{$i}{success}++;
133.            my $s = "\tclient,hit,flag,hits,bytes,success,failure [$i,
       $nhits,  1, $nbytes, $stress{$i}{success}, $stress{$i}{fail}]\n";
134.            syswrite($fh,$s,length($s)) unless !$report;
135.        }
136.    } else {
137.        $stress{$i}{fail}++;
138.        my $s = "\tclient,hit,flag,bytes,success,failure [$i, $nhits,  0,
       $nbytes, $stress{$i}{success}, $stress{$i}{fail}]\n";
139.        syswrite($fh,$s,length($s)) unless !$report;
140.    }
```

```
141.  }
142.
143.  sub requrl {
144.      my ($destination, $remoteport, $uri) = @_;
145.      my $AF_INET = 2;
146.      my $SOCK_STREAM = 1;
147.      my $targ;
148.      if (!(defined $targ)) {
149.          $targ = pack('S n a4 x8', $AF_INET, $remoteport,
      (gethostbyname($destination))[4]);
150.      }
151.      socket(SOCKET, $AF_INET, $SOCK_STREAM, (getprotobyname('tcp'))[2]) ||
      die $!;
152.
153.      if (!connect(SOCKET, $targ)) {
154.          close(SOCKET);
155.          return(-1);
156.      }
157.
158.      select(SOCKET);
159.      $| = 1;
160.      select(STDOUT);
161.
162.      my $s;
163.      if ($cookie) {
164.          $s =  <<EOF;
165. GET $uri HTTP/1.0
166. Content-type: text/html
167. User-Agent: WASDG-ZappUrl
168. Cookie: $cookie
169.
170. EOF
171.  } else {
172.          $s =  <<EOF;
173. GET $uri HTTP/1.0
174. Content-type: text/html
175. User-Agent: WASDG-ZappUrl
176.
177. EOF
178.  }
179.      print SOCKET $s;
180.
181.      my $len = 0;
182.      my $buf;
183.      my ($junk,$sid);
184.      while (sysread(SOCKET,$buf,4096)) {
185.          $len += length($buf);
186.          print $buf if ($verbose>1);
187.          if ($buf =~ /Set-Cookie:\s+/) {
188.              ($junk,$sid) = split(/JSESSIONID=/,$buf);
```

```
189.              ($sid,$junk) = split(/;/,$sid);
190.          }
191.          $buf = undef;
192.      }
193.      print "[JSESSIONID $sid]\n" if ($vsess);
194.      close(SOCKET);
195.      return($len);
196. }
```

ZappUrl script is copyrighted © 2002 by Total Computing & Network Design, Inc. All rights reserved.

Stress-Testing the WASDG Application with SharkUrl

The SharkUrl[3] script is a stress-tester for web applications in which randomness of user login and URI selections has been accounted for. You can download SharkUrl from the publisher's web site. SharkUrl takes many options, as summarized in Table 22-2.

Files Preprocessed by the SharkUrl Script

When SharkUrl is invoked with the -i option, the list of files that follow this option are being preprocessed in the internal queue of SharkUrl. For example, in the previous example, simulate1.inc and simulate2.inc are two Perl files. Listing 22-8 shows the content of simulate1.inc.

Listing 22-8   *Include file simulate1.inc to be processed by SharkUrl*

```
1.   #[!1]
2.   {
3.       use randuser;
4.       $userid = undef;
5.       $password = undef;
6.
7.   sub  {
8.       my $id = shift;
9.
10.      # randomly select a userid and password when it is not defined
11.      if (!defined $userid)  {
12.          ($userid,$password) = randuser::userpwd($nusers);
13.      }
14.
15.      print STDERR "\t$id (userid=$userid password=$password)\n" if
     ($verbose>1);
16.
```

```
17.      my @bunch =
18.      (
19.  "/wasbook/tellerlogged?userid=$userid&password=$password&",
20.  "/wasbook/creditdebit?clientid=client1&amount=5",
21.  "/wasbook/dumpsession",
22.  "/wasbook/creditdebit?clientid=client1&amount=15",
23.  "/wasbook/creditdebit?clientid=client1&amount=-5",
24.  "/wasbook/creditdebit?clientid=client1&amount=10",
25.  "/wasbook/creditdebit?clientid=client1&amount=-15",
26.  "/wasbook/logout"
27.      );
28.
29.      return @bunch;
30.  } # end sub
31.
32.  }
```

The simulate1.inc file starts with a first line with a special coding syntax #[!1] to identify itself as being a file to be preprocessed once by SharkUrl. The number following the exclamation mark specifies the number of times you want SharkUrl to preprocess the file.

The include file simulate1.inc also contains an anonymous subroutine. We use anonymous subroutine (a subroutine without a name) because we are concerned with only the reference to the created subroutine. Line 3 defines the usage of a package named randuser to be invoked

Option	Required	Description
-v	N	Verbose
-vv	N	Verbose prints everything.
-vj	N	Views JSESSIONID
-c \<n\>	Y	Number of clients. Defaults to 1.
-h \<n\>	Y	Number of hits per client. Defaults to 1.
-f \<n\>	N	Number of frequency to report the hits. Must be a multiple of the number of hits. Do not specify for the default of 1. Use this option to limit the output on a large number of hits.
-t \<server\>	Y	Target server where the web application is served
-i \<f1,f2,...\>	Y	A series of filenames to include in SharkUrl preprocessor. Use comma to separate the filenames; do not use spaces. You need to include at least one file.
-R \<filename\>	N	Prints a comma-delimited format report to filename. If filename is STDOUT, then print to standard output. If *default* is specified as a filename, then output is written to shark.*timestamp* file.

Table 22-2   *Options of the SharkUrl Stress-Tester*

in a statement on line 12, where a userid, password-value pair is randomly selected for the preprocessed script.

In this listing, the bunch of URIs listed and then returned by the anonymous subroutine are important.

The URI on line 19 starts the user's login process. The URI on line 20 requests to credit the client1 account by $5. The URI on line 21 invokes the DumpSession servlet and has been placed intentionally to prove that JSESSIONID has been carried over from the first URI (line 19) all the way down. DumpSession reveals the content of the session (Chapters 16 and 17). The rest of the URIs are self-explanatory: they credit or debit the banker account with id client1.

Eventually, the URIs where a login, a logout, and a credit or debit are requested will cause network activity between WAS and the UDB where the data is stored. This makes our example an adequate one to test the performance of WebSphere Application Server and the UDB in real time. The section "Sniffing the Network to Measure WAS Performance" later in this chapter addresses such network-based performance-monitoring issues.

Running SharkUrl

To illustrate how to run SharkUrl to stress-test a web application, we will write two include files: simulate1.inc shown previously in Listing 22-8, and simulate2.inc, shown in Listing 22-9. An excellent example to run SharkUrl and test the performance of WAS is the WASDG application because it is simple and clear enough to collect normal data that describes the performance of WAS. The operations of a teller describe typical and standard activities carried against a web application: login, authentication, followed by a series of credits and debits to banker accounts, and finally, logout[4] of the account (as shown on line 22 of Listing 22-9).

Listing 22-9   *Include file simulate2.inc to be processed by SharkUrl*

```
1.    #[!1]
2.    {
3.        use randuser;
4.        $userid = undef;
5.        $password = undef;
6.
7.    sub {
8.        my $id = shift;
9.
10.       # randomly select a userid and password when it is not defined
11.       if (!defined $userid)  {
```

---

[4]   The Logout servlet is different than the Logoff servlet. Logout updates the database with the time the teller logged off the system, whereas the Logoff servlet does not. Refer to Chapter 20 for more details.

```
12.            ($userid,$password) = randuser::userpwd($nusers)
13.        }
14.        print STDERR "\t$id (userid=$userid password=$password)\n" if
       ($verbose>1);
15.
16.        my @bunch =
17.        (
18.     "/wasbook/tellerlogged?userid=$userid&password=$password&",
19.     "/wasbook/creditdebit?clientid=client3&amount=15",
20.     "/wasbook/creditdebit?clientid=client2&amount=15",
21.     "/wasbook/creditdebit?clientid=client4&amount=-15",
22.     "/wasbook/creditdebit?clientid=client1&amount=-10",
23.     "/wasbook/logout"
24.        );
25.
26.        return @bunch;
27.  } # end sub
28.
29.  }
```

You start running the SharkUrl with a single client, but with a number of hits that are more than the number of the bunch of URIs listed in any of the include files.

Assuming we have the include files simulate1.inc and simulate2.inc, we will run the SharkUrl as shown next:

```
# ./SharkUrl -c 1 -h 10 -t node1 -i simulate1.inc,simulate2.inc -R stderr
```

The result of the command is shown in the following illustration.

You can also print the comma-delimited record that resulted from such a run by specifying the option -R stdout, in which case, the output is similar to that shown in the next illustration.

```
File Sessions Settings Help
[root@node1 Stress]# ./SharkUrl -c 1 -h 10 -t node1 -i simulate1.inc,simulate2.inc -R stdout
simulate1.inc simulate2.inc
0, 0, 0, 1, 266, 1, 0, [!simulate1.inc   1], /wasbook/tellerlogged?userid=teller2&password=secret2&
0, 1, 0, 1, 800, 2, 0, [!simulate1.inc   1], /wasbook/creditdebit?clientid=client1&amount=5
0, 2, 0, 1, 784, 3, 0, [!simulate1.inc   1], /wasbook/dumpsession
0, 3, 0, 1, 800, 4, 0, [!simulate1.inc   1], /wasbook/creditdebit?clientid=client1&amount=15
0, 4, 0, 1, 800, 5, 0, [!simulate1.inc   1], /wasbook/creditdebit?clientid=client1&amount=-5
0, 5, 0, 1, 800, 6, 0, [!simulate1.inc   1], /wasbook/creditdebit?clientid=client1&amount=10
0, 6, 0, 1, 800, 7, 0, [!simulate1.inc   1], /wasbook/creditdebit?clientid=client1&amount=-15
0, 7, 0, 1, 228, 8, 0, [!simulate1.inc   1], /wasbook/logout
0, 8, 0, 1, 266, 9, 0, [!simulate2.inc   1], /wasbook/tellerlogged?userid=teller2&password=secret2&
0, 9, 0, 1, 800, 10, 0, [!simulate2.inc   1], /wasbook/creditdebit?clientid=client3&amount=15
Elapsed:    0
[root@node1 Stress]#
    New    Konsole
```

A total of nine fields exist, numbered 0 through 8. The order of the fields in a comma-delimited record is described as follows:

▶ **Field 0**   Client number

▶ **Field 1**   Hit number

▶ **Field 2**   An indicative number for the delay in seconds for the hit to complete

▶ **Field 3**   Success (1) or failure (0) flag

▶ **Field 4**   Number of bytes received

▶ **Field 5**   Total number of successes

▶ **Field 6**   Total number of failures

▶ **Field 7**   Include file being preprocessed

▶ **Field 8**   URI being requested

You can test with different include files and different setups of the WASDG application. For instance, stress-test the web application after enabling security with JAAS (as explained in Chapter 20) to see the effect of the doas() method. Also, you can stress-test the application when session persistence (Chapter 17) is enabled, or when using EJB (Chapter 18).

Generating and Interpreting a Report

You will specify the -R option of SharkUrl script to generate and write a report to a file. The report to be generated is typically formed of comma-delimited records, each written on a single line. Therefore, the interpretation of the report can be done with an application that can read comma-delimited reports and map them to tables. Here we use the BwjSort[5] utility to sort and interpret such tables.

---

[5]   BwjSort is supplied with Gramercy Toolkit. Refer to Appendixes D for syntax on using the BwjSort command.

Generating the Report

Generating a comma-delimited file describing the run of SharkUrl is realized with the -R option. For example, to generate the report myrun.txt, you follow the -R option with the filename, as in -R foo.txt. The only exception is the word "default," which is specifically interpreted differently. When -R default is specified, SharkUrl creates the file shark_<timestamp>. You can still use the verbose options -v, -vv, and -vj; this should not affect the reported data because these options print their output to console (STDERR). The following illustration shows the effect of the -vj option while the data is being written to the foo.txt file.

```
File Sessions Settings Help
[root@node2 Stress]# ./sharkurl -c 1 -h 10 -t node1 -i simulate1.inc,simulate2.inc -R foo.txt -vj
simulate1.inc simulate2.inc
[JSESSIONID 0000LQ23HOQZRZ34W54Z0ZV1HFQ:-1]
[CARRY OVER JSESSIONID=0000LQ23HOQZRZ34W54Z0ZV1HFQ:-1]
[CARRY OVER JSESSIONID=0000LQ23HOQZRZ34W54Z0ZV1HFQ:-1]
[CARRY OVER JSESSIONID=0000LQ23HOQZRZ34W54Z0ZV1HFQ:-1]
[CARRY OVER JSESSIONID=0000LQ23HOQZRZ34W54Z0ZV1HFQ:-1]
[CARRY OVER JSESSIONID=0000LQ23HOQZRZ34W54Z0ZV1HFQ:-1]
[JSESSIONID 0000GRIWKWMGUCPRP4GRK113A3Y:-1]
[CARRY OVER JSESSIONID=0000GRIWKWMGUCPRP4GRK113A3Y:-1]
[CARRY OVER JSESSIONID=0000GRIWKWMGUCPRP4GRK113A3Y:-1]
[CARRY OVER JSESSIONID=0000GRIWKWMGUCPRP4GRK113A3Y:-1]
[CARRY OVER JSESSIONID=0000GRIWKWMGUCPRP4GRK113A3Y:-1]
Elapsed:    4
[root@node2 Stress]# █


  New   Konsole
```

The -vj option reveals that the JSESSIONID that is initially set with the first hit of the include file has been carried over to every subsequent hit within the same include file. Because seven hits have occurred with the same JSESSIONID, simulate2.inc has been chosen randomly from the SharkUrl preprocessor, and is totally consumed for the first seven hits. As the client continues hitting, another JSESSIONID is being generated because once a preprocessed include file is totally consumed, the session id is undefined so that it won't be carried over to the next preprocessed include.

The following example shows the run of SharkUrl for 32 clients or tellers, each doing 12 hits. The command issued is highlighted.

```
File Sessions Settings Help
[root@fs Stress]# ./sharkurl -c 32 -h 12 -t node1 -i simulate1.inc,simulate2.inc -R foo.txt
simulate1.inc simulate2.inc
Elapsed:    58
[root@fs Stress]# █


  New   Konsole
```

Although we have defined only four tellers, the WASDG application does not restrict two or more tellers by the same teller id to log in concurrently. You can also redefine the database to have as many tellers and bankers as you want. (Refer to Chapter 9.)

The run took a total elapsed time of 58 seconds, and there has been no failure. SharkUrl has been started on fs.tcnd.com (a dual Pentium Pro 200 MHz with 512MB of RAM), the WASDG application is running on node1.tcnd.com (a Pentium II 333 MHz with 1GB of RAM), and the UDB is running on a similar but really busy server whose hostname is node2.tcnd.com. Session persistence is disabled, and JAAS security is not configured.

Listing 22-10 shows a snapshot of the default report generated by SharkUrl. This report, specifically, is based on a secondary run that took 77 seconds to complete. In the rest of chapter we will consider the stress-testing run discussed previously, and which took 58 seconds to complete.

Listing 22-10   *Snapshot of the report foo.txt generated by SharkUrl*

```
1.    0, 0, 3,   1, 4129, 1, 0, [!simulate1.inc  1],
         /wasbook/tellerlogged?userid=teller2&password=secret2&
2.    1, 0, 3,   1, 4129, 1, 0, [!simulate2.inc  1],
         /wasbook/tellerlogged?userid=teller3&password=secret3&
3.    9, 0, 3,   1, 4129, 1, 0, [!simulate1.inc  1],
         /wasbook/tellerlogged?userid=teller2&password=secret2&
4.    8, 0, 4,   1, 4129, 1, 0, [!simulate2.inc  1],
         /wasbook/tellerlogged?userid=teller2&password=secret2&
5.    7, 0, 4,   1, 4129, 1, 0, [!simulate2.inc  1],
         /wasbook/tellerlogged?userid=teller4&password=secret4&
6.    ...
7.    15, 2, 16,  1, 927, 3, 0, [!simulate1.inc  1], /wasbook/dumpsession

8.    13, 1, 16,  1, 1031, 2, 0, [!simulate2.inc  1],
         /wasbook/creditdebit?clientid=client3&amount=15
9.    16, 1, 17,  1, 1031, 2, 0, [!simulate2.inc  1],
         /wasbook/creditdebit?clientid=client3&amount=15
10.   0, 3, 17,  1, 1035, 4, 0, [!simulate1.inc  1],
         /wasbook/creditdebit?clientid=client1&amount=15
11.   1, 2, 18,  1, 1031, 3, 0, [!simulate2.inc  1],
         /wasbook/creditdebit?clientid=client2&amount=15
12.   ...
13.   26, 3, 28,  1, 1033, 4, 0, [!simulate2.inc  1],
         /wasbook/creditdebit?clientid=client4&amount=-15
14.   28, 3, 29,  1, 1033, 4, 0, [!simulate2.inc  1],
         /wasbook/creditdebit?clientid=client4&amount=-15
15.   30, 3, 29,  1, 1033, 4, 0, [!simulate2.inc  1],
         /wasbook/creditdebit?clientid=client4&amount=-15
16.   29, 4, 29,  1, 1035, 5, 0, [!simulate1.inc  1],
         /wasbook/creditdebit?clientid=client1&amount=-5
17.   ...
18.   17, 9, 70,  1, 1033, 10, 0, [!simulate2.inc  1],
         /wasbook/creditdebit?clientid=client4&amount=-15
19.   1, 11, 70,  1, 1035, 12, 0, [!simulate1.inc  1],
         /wasbook/creditdebit?clientid=client1&amount=10
```

```
20.   0, 11, 70,  1, 1033, 12, 0, [!simulate2.inc  1],
      /wasbook/creditdebit?clientid=client4&amount=-15
21.  15, 11, 70,  1, 1035, 12, 0, [!simulate1.inc  1],
      /wasbook/creditdebit?clientid=client1&amount=15
22.  ...
```

The report shown in Listing 22-10 reveals that client 0 had to wait 70 seconds for the eleventh hit to complete (line 20), similar to how long it took client 15 (line 21). This proves the randomness of the SharkUrl hitting strategy. Line 1 shows that client 0's login took 3 seconds, and the third hit (line 10) took 17 seconds to complete crediting a banker account—as time goes on, WAS is being stressed to satisfy other clients requests, and the time to wait for client 0 to satisfy a request is escalating. On line 20, it took 70 seconds to satisfy client 0 debiting the banker account.

Interpreting the Report

Among the tools supplied with this book is the BwjSort utility. This tool is a generic command that makes it easy to sort comma-delimited record files. BwjSort takes a series of arguments to properly map the fields used in each record of a file before initiating its sorting procedure. The following command shows how you can sort the foo.txt file by ascending client order (field 0), followed by descending elapsed time order (field 2) per hit:

```
# BwjSort -in foo.txt -n 7 -f 0,2 -o a,d -d i,i,i,i,i,i,i,s,s  -2 tab | more
```

The result of the command is shown in the next illustration.

```
 File Sessions Settings Help
[root@fs Stress]# ./bwjsort -in foo.txt -n 7 -f 0,2 -o a,d -d i,i,i,i,i,i,i,s,s  -2 tab | more
0      11    55    1    1035    12   0
0      10    48    1    1035    11   0
0       9    41    1    1035    10   0
0       7    39    1    1033     8   0
0       8    39    1     927     9   0
0       6    34    1    4129     7   0
0       5    28    1     317     6   0
0       4    27    1    1033     5   0
0       3    21    1    1031     4   0
0       2    17    1    1031     3   0
0       1     8    1    1029     2   0
0       0     1    1    4129     1   0

1      11    56    1    1035    12   0
1      10    52    1    1035    11   0
1       9    42    1    1035    10   0
1       7    39    1    1033     8   0
1       8    39    1     927     9   0
1       6    35    1    4129     7   0
1       5    31    1     317     6   0
1       4    28    1    1035     5   0
1       3    24    1    1031     4   0
1       2    18    1    1031     3   0
1       1    12    1    1029     2   0
1       0     1    1    4129     1   0
--More--
 New  Konsole
```

Knowing that clients have been frustrated waiting forever for their request to be fulfilled but also pointing to the hit number when such delays occurred, we will sort the report by descending elapsed time order (field 2), followed by ascending hit count order (field 1).

```
File Sessions Settings Help
[root@fs Stress]# ./bwjsort -in foo.txt -n 7 -f 2,1 -o d,a -d i,i,i,i,i,i,i,s,s  -2 tab | more
30      11      58      1       1031    12      0
23      11      58      1       317     12      0
22      11      58      1       317     12      0
27      10      57      1       1035    11      0
30      10      57      1       1031    11      0
19      10      57      1       1035    11      0
20      10      57      1       1035    11      0
23      10      57      1       1035    11      0
22      10      57      1       1035    11      0
2       11      57      1       317     12      0
3       11      57      1       317     12      0
31      11      57      1       1035    12      0
6       11      57      1       317     12      0
15      11      57      1       317     12      0
12      11      57      1       317     12      0
16      11      57      1       317     12      0
19      11      57      1       317     12      0
29      11      57      1       1031    12      0
20      11      57      1       317     12      0
26      11      57      1       1031    12      0
28      11      57      1       1035    12      0
27      11      57      1       1035    12      0
23      9       56      1       1031    10      0
22      9       56      1       1031    10      0
2       10      56      1       1035    11      0
--More--
 New  Konsole
```

You can also print the URI by specifying a column count equal to 9:

```
# BwjSort -in foo.txt -n 9 -f 2,1 -o d,a -d i,i,i,i,i,i,i,s,s  -2 tab | more
```

You now have sufficient tools to evaluate WAS performance. Realistically, the performance analysis shown in our example is fine because the WASDG application coding is simple and does not use unnecessary Java coding.

Sniffing the Network to Measure WAS Performance

When SharkUrl ran in the previous example, three essential elements communicated together to send and receive data over TCP/IP: WAS, the UDB, and the client browsers (SharkUrl's forked processes). We are concerned with the communication between WAS and the UDB. For this reason, we will use a network analyzer such as the IBM DataGlance Network Analyzer or a similar analyzer such as Sniffer, to monitor the network while running the previous example.

Figure 22-2 shows the results of our analysis in the IBM Network Analyzer during the 58-second run.

We made sure that the network activity is minimal before starting the test. It is minimal because network-dependent applications such as NFS and NTP will periodically broadcast minimal data on the network. We started the Network Analyzer first, and then issued the SharkUrl command. (See the section "Running SharkUrl" earlier.) The analysis shows that the network is busy and most of the frames are being sent during the first 30 seconds, and

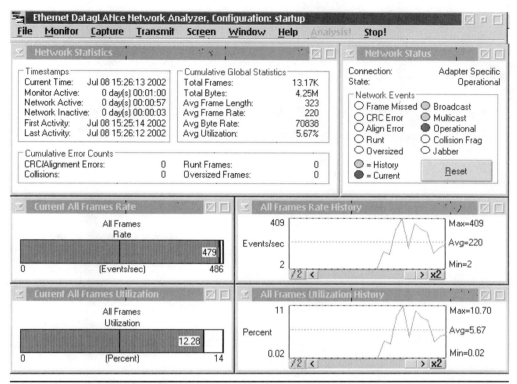

Figure 22-2 *The IBM Network Analyzer*

then the frames being sent scaled down during the next 30 seconds: obviously, this is the effect of caching.

Because we are interested in the communication between the WAS server and the UDB server, let's peek at the frames being sent between 66.51.9.175 or 66.51.9.151 (WAS) and 66.51.9.152 (UDB). WAS is installed on a server with two network adapters, each of which has an IP that is known in the routing table of the server machine. Figure 22-3 shows the content of the frame being sent by the WAS server to the UDB server where the DBGUIDE is defined; the user and password can also be seen.

Figure 22-4 shows the reply back from the UDB server to the WAS server. A tremendous amount of frames are being sent back and forth between WAS and UDB, although persistence is disabled. In our situation, we can attribute the delay to this extensive network dependency on the database, yet we should not conclude that most of the delay is caused solely by the database access. Sometimes, a programmer might be porting an application that can impact the performance due to unnecessary multithreading or poor coding that is not appropriate to be deployed under WAS. Chapter 25 considers how to monitor memory, CPU, and threads consumption.

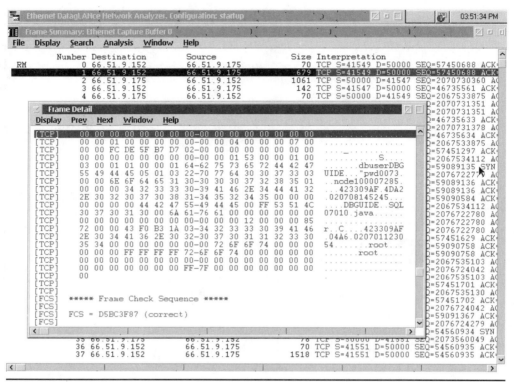

Figure 22-3 *Content of the frame sent by the WAS station requesting a query to DBGUIDE*

If you do not have a network analyzer at your disposal, you can still measure the network performance by collecting data with the `netstat` command. (See Chapter 25.)

The usage of the network analyzer or the sniffer can show the immense difference in network traffic between using stateless session beans and persistent entity beans as explained in Chapter 18. We will not present an analysis on the performance of Enterprise JavaBeans realize that an EJB-enabled application (for example, the WASDG application of Chapter 18), does not perform as well as the beans-less application of Chapter 16. A quick analysis using the SharkUrl for 10 clients and 12 hits per client showed that the beans-less application outperformed the EJB-enabled appliction by a ratio of 3:4 (30 seconds compared to 40 seconds). Refer to the README.TXT file in the distribution code of this chapter.

A Final Note about the Preprocessed Includes

Because the include files that are passed to and preprocessed by SharkUrl are Perl code, you can specify your own package and subroutine within these files. Do not alter the content of SharkUrl because it is a copyrighted product.

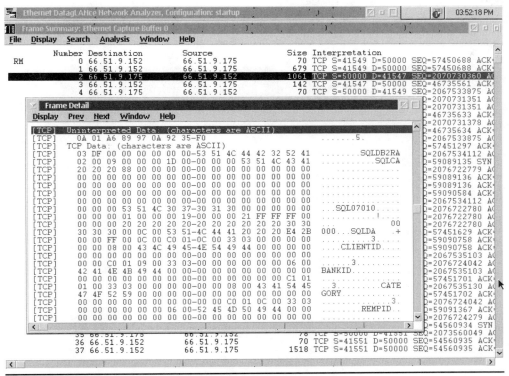

Figure 22-4 *Content of the frame sent by the UDB station in reply to the query*

Wrapping Up

This chapter demonstrated how to stress-test WebSphere Application Server. The approach followed here was to look at WAS from the outside in, and then address timing URLs to the WASDG application. The zappurl was introduced to show the essential elements in coding a simulator to stress-test a web application. A professional stress tester, SharkUrl, was then presented.

In the example discussed in this chapter, we could suggest counting the transactions taking place during the 11 hits of each client (2 logins, 2 logouts, and 7 credits or debits); yet such a counting method is theoretical (or academic), and the result might fall beyond expectation. For a web application, like any distributed application, the proper technical approach in measuring performance is to stress-test and have a network analyzer pinpoint the reasons in case the application does not perform adequately.

A developer's programming style can definitely impact the performance of a web application. Also, it's not advisable to throw exceptions for the sake of generality and garnish the code with a surplus of debugging APIs. We kept the exception handling in the WASDG application to a minimum in this chapter because Chapter 23 covers this subject in detail.

We also need to consider other factors when doing performance analysis: it is basically the systematic consumption of threads, memory, CPU, and network data structures (sockets and their state). For completeness, many of these points are addressed in Chapter 25.

Writing an Exception Handler, Logging, and Debugging

IN THIS CHAPTER:

S hipping characters out to standard output is a simple technique used in tracing programs. Because the nature of web application programming basically approximates an I/O in perpetuity between a client browser and the web application, or between the web application and a remote database, this technique is simple, and it is the most adequate one to trace and debug web applications.

To trace servlets and EJB components code, you use the System.out.println() or System .err.println() methods in your code. The output from these println statements appears in the application server stdout and stderr logs, respectively. Chapter 16 discussed how to redirect I/O from a specific servlet to WAS' standard output file. This chapter presents a set of programs that provides the function of I/O control and error handling to form a unified exception-handling API.

Typically, I/O routines are presented with a user-defined package, such as com.tcnd .wasdg.log package. A user's program to carry out I/O invokes the Log.log() method, which performs the necessary printing actions on his or her behalf. This I/O as seen by the programmer is simple. This simplification of I/O makes it possible to control the writing and formatting of the data by hiding the complex methods from the programmer's code.

This chapter also shows you how to programmatically put in place an error-handling mechanism by using a routine (or class) that implements Java's Throwable interface. Such error handling is called exception handling[1] and is characterized by a stack trace that allows you to view the stacked messages when an error is caught. Because messages are stacked, the printing of the stack shows a trace back. Here, you implement the com.tcnd.wasdg .wasdgexceptions package that prints the predefined state of your custom exceptions.

Implementing this package depends on two other packages or libraries: the com .tcnd .wasdg.log mentioned previously, and the BundleManager class discussed in its own section. The first is used to direct I/O to a log file, and the second is used to identify informative or error messages that have been bundled into properties files.

As a prerequisite for the programs considered in this chapter, consult a Java programming manual for the following Java classes: java.io.PrintWriter, java.io.BufferedWriter, java.io .FileWriter, java.util.PropertyResourceBundle, and java.lang.Exception.

For completeness, the chapter concludes with a section that shows how to use alternative debugging techniques using extra applications or tools.

Logging, Tracing, and Debugging with Exception Handling

Three packages provide logging messages and exception handling of the WASDG application to a log file. Figure 23-1 shows the development tree and the programs that are presented in this chapter.

---

[1] Perl programmers should realize that the try, catch, throw used in Java corresponds to eval, $@, die in Perl. If die is called, then Perl die's error string is passed to $@, and the program proceeds to the statement following the evaluated block. Java and Perl are both interpreted languages.

```
.
|-- Properties
|   |-- base.properties
|   |-- components.properties
|   |-- log.properties
|   |-- messages.properties
|   |-- severity.properties
|   |-- test1.properties
|   `-- test2.properties
|-- com
|   `-- tcnd
|       `-- wasdg
|           |-- common
|           |   `-- BundleManager.java
|           |-- log
|           |   |-- Log.java
|           |   |-- LogWriter.java
|           |   |-- LogWriterFile.java
|           |   `-- LogWriterStdout.java
|           `-- wasdgexceptions
|               |-- WasdgException.java
|               `-- WasdgMessages.java
`-- jall
```

Figure 23-1   *Development tree hierarchy for logging and exception-handling packages*

The following describes each directory in the tree hierarchy shown in Figure 23-1:

▶ **Properties directory**   Contains all .properties files used for the application programs

▶ **com/tcnd/wasdg/common directory**   Contains the BundleManager that will cache all key-value pairs found in the .properties files or bundles just mentioned

▶ **com/tcnd/wasdg/log directory**   Contains the programs that initialize a LogWriter and allow logging of messages with the Log.log() method

▶ **com/tcnd/wasdg/wasdgexceptions**   Contains the WasdgException class that extends Exception and allows throwing of customized Throwable exceptions for our application

Each of the last three directories just described represents a package discussed in this chapter. The Properties directory is discussed along with the BundleManager.

The net outcome of all the programming in this chapter is to come up with three procedures or Java methods: the first is used to effectively and transparently log messages, the second is used to simply fetch a value of a specific property, and the third is used to throw exceptions that are specific to the WASDG application. These three methods are listed next:

▶ **Log.log(String message)**   Writes a message to the log file

► **BundleManager.getString(String bundleFilename, String propertyName)**   Reads
  a cached property

► **WasdgException(String mnemonic, Throwable eThrowable)**   Used to throw an
  exception as in throw new WasdgException(mnemonic)

The first time the Log.log() method is invoked, a LogWriter is created. The LogWriter can
directly println to standard output or to a log file. To print to a log file, the LogWriter creates a
PrintWriter object that is attached to a buffered FileWriter object. In turn, the FileWriter object
is attached to an open file on the file system. Any further call to Log.log() will subsequently
write to the log file on the already created LogWriter.

For example, the following statement writes the message "Hello there!" to the log file:

```
Log.log("Hello there!");
```

When a property file is deposited in the Properties directory, for example, /BOOK/23/
Properties, it will be automatically cached by the BundleManager the first time the
BundleManager.init() runs. All key-value pairs of the .properties files can then be retrieved
with the BundleManager .getString() method. For example, if the test1.properties file contains
an entry for the property TEST1=abc, then a programmer can retrieve the property of TEST1
as follows:

```
String value = BundleManager.getString("test1.properties","TEST1");
```

The string assigned to the value is then abc.

The WasdgException() functions like this. We will signal our own exceptions with the throw
statement. The throw keyword is followed by an object of type Throwable or a subclass that
extends the Exception class. When an exception is thrown as in the following clause:

```
throw new WasdgException("DATA0001E");
```

the program execution stops at that point, and the interpreter looks for a corresponding catch
clause to handle the exception.

Assuming that logging is directed to the /tmp/wasdg.log file, the previous statement will
throw an exception that can be caught and written to the log file, as shown in the following
illustration.

```
File Sessions Settings Help
[root@node1 Tree]# cat /tmp/wasdg.log
LogWriterFile.startWriter: Start the /tmp/wasdg.log
21/08/02 21:15:49:449   Test0.main: Simple test for exceptions handling with WasdgException
21/08/02 21:15:49:458   -------- dataaccess X DATA0001E: Database error: There is no connection
 to the remote database. Make sure that you can access the remote database from the current serv
er
com.tcnd.wasdg.wasdgexceptions.WasdgException: DATA0001E
        at Test0.m(Test0.java:23)
        at Test0.main(Test0.java:13)


[root@node1 Tree]#
 New   Konsole
```

The WasdgException presented in this chapter can handle regular exceptions, multiple exceptions, and nested exceptions. This is obviously possible because exceptions are saved on a stack that can be retrieved and appended to a string as further Throwable exceptions propagate.

Logging Information: Log.log()

The Log class provides logging services for application debugging. To write to the log file, the programmer needs to simply call the log() method with a java.lang.String stream of information passed as a parameter:

```
Log.log("Test.main: This is a stream");
```

When logging the information, the Log class will first timestamp the message with the current time before writing the information. For example, the previous statement would have resulted with a logged message of this form:

```
21/08/02 23:16:37:739    Test.main: This is a stream
```

The Log uses two writers: LogWriterStdout and LogWriterFile. Both of the writers extend the default log writer class LogWriter, shown in Listing 23-1. The first writer class directs the printing to the standard output, and the second writer class directs the printing to a specified file on the file system. Either writer can be selected through the log.properties file entry shown here:

```
LogTo=FILE
```

Processing the content of the log.properties file is explained in the section "Bundling Information with the BundleManager."

Listing 23-1 *LogWriter*

```
1.    package com.tcnd.wasdg.log;
2.
3.    // Default log writer class.  Extend this class to create new log
      writers
4.    public class LogWriter
5.    {
6.    // Default constructor.
7.    public LogWriter() {
8.        super();
9.    }
10.
11.   public void finalize()
12.   {
13.       stopWriter();
```

```
14.     }
15.     public void init() {} // rotate previous log files, and open new file
16.     public void flushWriter() {} // flush buffered stream
17.     public void startWriter() {} // open the file
18.     public void stopWriter() {} // close the file
19.     public void writeMessage(String aMessage) {}
20.     }
```

The LogWriterFile class opens a file and uses the PrintWriter object to attach to the open file.[2] Subsequently, all messages to the former file are printed through the println() method. Listing 23-2 shows how the LogWriterFile extends LogWriter.

Listing 23-2   *LogWriter File*

```
1.     package com.tcnd.wasdg.log;
2.     ...
3.     // Extends LogWriter to write log messages to a file
4.     public class LogWriterFile extends LogWriter
5.     {
6.         private String currentFileName;
7.         private PrintWriter fStream;
8.         private int numToBack;
9.     ...
10.    // Constructor with a filename and number of backups
11.    public LogWriterFile(String fileName, int logBackup)
12.    {
13.        super();
14.        currentFileName = fileName;
15.        numToBack   = logBackup;
16.        init(); // open a new log and backup previous logs
17.    }
18.
19.    // Start a new log.  Rotate old logs by appending a number to an
20.    // old log file. More recent logs have lower numbers.
21.    public synchronized void init()
22.    {
23.        // Rotate files (optional)
24.    ...
25.        startWriter();
26.    }
27.
28.    // Initialize the writer and start it up by opening the file specified in
           the constructor
29.    public void startWriter()
```

---

[2]   Chapter 16 used a different approach to redirect I/O using the PrintStream object.

```
30.  {
31.      try
32.      {
33.          fStream = new PrintWriter(
34.              new BufferedWriter(new FileWriter(currentFileName)));
35.          writeMessage("LogWriterFile.startWriter: Start the " +
     currentFileName);
36.      }
37.      catch (Exception e)
38.      {
39.          e.printStackTrace();
40.      }
41.  }
42.  ...
43.  // Write one message to the destination.
44.  public void writeMessage(String aMessage)
45.  {
46.      fStream.println(aMessage);
47.      fStream.flush();
48.  }
49.  }
```

Line 7 shows that the fStream is a static variable of type PrintWriter. On line 33, a new PrintWriter is initialized and is assigned to the static variable fStream. Lines 44 through 48 show how the writeMessage() method uses the fStream to println and flush a string to the open file.

The complete source code for the LogWriterFile and LogWriterStdout are in the distribution code of this chapter.

The Log class is shown in Listing 23-3. This class is simple.

Listing 23-3   *Log*

```
1.   package com.tcnd.wasdg.log;
2.
3.   import com.tcnd.wasdg.common.BundleManager;
4.   import java.text.*;
5.   import java.util.*;
6.
7.   /**
8.    * This class provides logging services for applications tracing.
9.    * The logging API is:
10.   * <p><code>
11.   * Log.log( "message" );
12.   * <p>
13.   * Two writers are provided: LogWriterStdout and LogWriterFile.
14.   * The file "log.properties" contains the location where the log file
```

```
15.      * is created, and whether to write data to stdout or to a file.
16.      * <p><code>
17.      * LogTo=FILE              - write to a file
18.      * LogFile=/tmp/wasdg.log    - logfile name
19.      * LogBackup=3              - Number of logs to rotate
20.      * </code>
21.      */
22.    public class Log
23.    {
24.        private static LogWriter          lWriter;
25.        // timestamp format
26.        private static SimpleDateFormat dateFormat = new
         SimpleDateFormat("dd/MM/yy HH:mm:ss:SSS");
27.
28.    // Default constructor is private. Do not instantiate.
29.    private Log()
30.    {
31.        super();
32.    }
33.
34.    // Write messages to output
35.    public static void flush()
36.    {
37.        lWriter.flushWriter();
38.    }
39.
40.    public static void init()
41.    {
42.        // Log to FILE
43.        if (BundleManager.getString("log","LogTo").compareTo("FILE") == 0)
44.        {
45.            String LogName = BundleManager.getString("log","LogFile");
46.            String LogBackup = BundleManager.getString("log","LogBackup");
47.            if (LogName.equals("")) LogName = "foo.log";
48.            if ( LogBackup.equals("") )
49.                lWriter = new LogWriterFile(LogName);
50.            else
51.                lWriter = new
         LogWriterFile(LogName,Integer.parseInt(LogBackup));
52.            lWriter.startWriter();
53.        }
54.        else // to STDOUT
55.        {
56.            lWriter = new LogWriterStdout();
57.            lWriter.startWriter();
58.        }
59.    }
60.
```

```
61.    // Write a message to the log.
62.    // The formatted message is shipped out: timestamp \t message
63.    public static void log(String message )
64.    {
65.        Calendar    longDate;
66.        String      datedMessage;
67.
68.        if (null == lWriter) init();
69.
70.        // Add current date & time to message
71.        longDate = GregorianCalendar.getInstance(TimeZone.getDefault());
72.        datedMessage = dateFormat.format(longDate.getTime())+ "\t" +
       message;
73.        lWriter.writeMessage(datedMessage);
74.    }
75.
76.    public static void stopLog()
77.    {
78.        if (null == lWriter) return;
79.        lWriter.stopWriter();
80.    }
81.    }
```

Mentioning how to retrieve a property from a cached bundle prematurely, on line 43, if the LogTo property is set to FILE, then LogWriterFile() is instantiated (line 49 or line 51); otherwise, the LogWriterStdout() is instantiated to direct printing to standard output.

Such an instantiation occurs only once, if and only if the first time the Log.log(String message) is called (on line 63) and the lWriter variable has not been initialized (line 68).

Lines 71 through 73 show how a timestamped message is written by the Log.log() method.

Bundling Information with the BundleManager

The configuration data specific to the programs of a web application must not be hard-coded in the source code of the application.[3] Such configuration data is saved in property files and bundled together in a specific base directory. There is one initial file base.properties, for example, /BOOK/23/Code/Properties/base.properties shown in Listing 23-4, that points to the location of the directory where all properties files are saved.

Listing 23-4   *base.properties*

```
properties.dir=/BOOK/23/Code/Properties
```

---

[3]   Configuration data of an application needs to be tabulated using specification sheets. Tabulation is traditionally done in assembly language programming or when writing an interpreter.

Once the BundleManager reads this file, it locates the directory where all property files are located, and then it reads them all to save and cache the properties. For simplicity, it is appropriate to deposit all properties files for an application in a single directory relative to the application source directory. Therefore, we will place all the properties files for this chapter's application in the same directory as the file base.properties: /BOOK/23/Code/Properties.

The BundleManager is shown in Listing 23-5. On line 8, the location of the base.properties file is set explicitly in the class code, and on line 9, the base filename is specified without the extension. The first time the BundleManager.getString() is called, the BundleManager will initialize by calling its init() method. Upon initialization, the BundleManager will locate the directory in which the properties files are located (line 45). The elements of the base.properties file is then cached (line 46), and every property file that is located in the specified directory (for example, /BOOK/23/Code/Properties) is then cached, as shown on line 55.

Listing 23-5   *BundleManager*

```
1.    package com.tcnd.wasdg.common;
2.
3.    import java.util.*;
4.    import java.io.*;
5.
6.    public class BundleManager
7.    {
8.        private static final String
      wasdgPropertiesFileName="/BOOK/23/Code/Properties/base.properties";
9.        private static String baseFile = "base";
10.       private static Hashtable mBundles;
11.
12.   private BundleManager() {super();}
13.
14.   private static PropertyResourceBundle createBundle(String file)
15.   {
16.       PropertyResourceBundle baseBundle = null;
17.       try
18.       {
19.           baseBundle =  new PropertyResourceBundle(
20.               new BufferedInputStream(new FileInputStream(file +
      ".properties")));
21.       }
22.       catch (Exception IOException)
23.       {
24.           System.out.println("BundleManager.createBundle: File " + file +
      ".properties not found!");
25.       }
26.       return baseBundle;
27.   }
28.
```

```
29.   public static void init() throws Exception
30.   {
31.       String baseDir;
32.       String fileName;
33.       Vector baseList;
34.       PropertyResourceBundle baseBundle;
35.
36.       java.util.Properties prop;
37.       prop = new Properties();
38.       try
39.       {
40.           prop.load(new FileInputStream(wasdgPropertiesFileName));
41.       } catch (Exception e)
42.       {
43.           e.printStackTrace();
44.       }
45.       baseDir = prop.getProperty("properties.dir");
46.       baseBundle = createBundle(baseDir + "/" + baseFile);
47.
48.       mBundles = new Hashtable();
49.       mBundles.put("base",baseBundle);
50.
51.       baseList = listFiles(baseDir);
52.       for (int i = 0; i < baseList.size(); i++ )
53.       {
54.           fileName = (String) baseList.elementAt(i);
55.           baseBundle = createBundle(baseDir + "/" + fileName);
56.           mBundles.put(fileName, baseBundle);
57.       }
58.   }
59.
60.   public static PropertyResourceBundle getBundle(String bundleName)
61.   {
62.       try
63.       {
64.           if (mBundles == null) BundleManager.init();
65.           return (PropertyResourceBundle) mBundles.get( bundleName );
66.       }
67.       catch (Exception e)
68.       {
69.           return null;
70.       }
71.   }
72.
73.   // Get a property from a cached bundle
74.   public static String getString(String bundleName, String propertyName)
75.   {
76.       try
77.       {
```

```
78.              if (mBundles == null) BundleManager.init();
79.              PropertyResourceBundle bundle = getBundle(bundleName);
80.              if (bundle == null) return "";
81.              return bundle.getString(propertyName);
82.          }
83.      catch (Exception e)
84.      {
85.          return "";
86.      }
87.  }
88.
89.  // Given the base directory (baseDir), return a list of all properties
90.  // files in specified directory, otherwise return an empty Vector.
91.  private static Vector listFiles(String baseDir)
92.  {
93.      Vector filesList = new Vector();
94.      int    k;
95.      try
96.      {
97.          File dir = new File(baseDir);
98.          String[] files = dir.list();
99.
100.         for (int i=0; i<files.length; i++)
101.         {
102.             String fileName = files[i];
103.             k = fileName.lastIndexOf(".");
104.             if (k > 0)
105.                 fileName = fileName.substring(0, k);
106.             filesList.addElement(fileName);
107.         }
108.     }
109.     catch (Exception e)
110.     {
111.     }
112.     return filesList;
113. }
114. }
```

On line 74, the getString(String bundleName, String propertyName) method is often used in the application programs to get the value of a specific propertyName listed in a bundleName.

One advantage of having the BundleManager to preprocess all properties files from a localized base directory is transparency of controlling the properties of the application. The BundleManager makes it possible to deposit a new .properties file in the specified property directory so that the application developer can automatically fetch a defined property value during run time. The following two sections consider the log.properties file that specifies properties for the Log class, and three other properties files used while handling exceptions for the WASDG application.

Considering the log.properties File

The Log class discussed in the section "Logging Information: Log.log()" reads its configuration properties from the log.properties file shown in Listing 23-6.

Listing 23-6 *log.properties*

```
1.   # Properties for the Log class
2.   LogTo=FILE
3.   LogFile=/tmp/wasdg.log
4.   LogBackup=3
```

On line 2, the LogTo specifies that the log is written to a file. On line 3, the LogFile specifies the location and the name of the log file where messages are printed. On line 4, the LogBackup is optional, and it specifies the number of logs to rotate before writing logging information to the wasdg.log file specified previously.

Considering the Exception-Handling Properties Files

A good approach to organizing the error codes of an application is to categorize and tabulate them according to certain criteria, such as the component that generated such an error, the severity level of the error, and a description of the error. In this chapter, an error code is referred to as a *mnemonic* because it is a well-defined symbol (or a symbolic representation) formed of nine characters that a programmer can memorize. A mnemonic does not necessarily refer only to an error code; it may refer to any useful information that can be thrown and logged to trace an application.

The informative mnemonic codes, their components grouping, and their severity codes are saved as pairs of values in the properties files: messages.properties, components.properties, and severity.properties, respectively.

Listings 23-7, 23-8, and 23-9 show all three properties files, respectively, for a mnemonic's descriptive information, the component name it pertains to, and the severity code it is associated with. These properties files are limited in entry for illustrative reasons.

Listing 23-7 *messages.properties*

```
1.   DATA0001E=Database error: There is no connection to the remote database. Make
sure that you can access the remote database from the current server
2.   DATA0002I=Using default settings for DBGUIDE database in dbguide.properties
3.   DATA0003W=Cannot update database
4.   UREG0001I=Updating database with new user registration
5.   UREG0002I=Validating user registration
6.   UREG0003W=Last name is required for user registration
7.   UREG0004E=User has been denied access. User cannot login!
8.   UREG0005W=User already registered
9.   SESS0001I=Invalidating user session
10.  SESS0002E=User logins or sessions are in excess than permitted!
```

Consider the mnemonic DATA0001E: its descriptive message shows that this is a "Database error: There is no connection to..." and the component group that this exception belongs to is dataaccess, as shown in Listing 23-8. This means that programs in the dataaccess component will throw such an exception mnemonic.

Listing 23-8 *components.properties*

```
1.   DATA0001E=dataaccess
2.   DATA0002I=dataaccess
3.   DATA0003W=dataaccess
4.   UREG0001I=registration
5.   UREG0002I=registration
6.   UREG0003W=registration
7.   UREG0004E=registration
8.   UREG0005W=registration
9.   SESS0001I=login
10.  SESS0002E=login
```

DATA0001E has a severity level of X, as shown in Listing 23-9.

Listing 23-9 *severity.properties*

```
1.   # The severity level is one of these: I informative, W warning, X fatal
error, A audit
       A audit
2.   DATA0001E=X
3.   DATA0001I=I
4.   DATA0001W=W
5.   UREG0001I=I
6.   UREG0002I=I
7.   UREG0003W=W
8.   UREG0004E=X
9.   UREG0005W=W
10.  SESS0001I=A
11.  SESS0002E=A
```

Of course, an exception mnemonic is unique, and it pertains to a specific component with which it has an associated severity code. Maintaining the uniqueness of a mnemonic is usually achieved by maintaining a common database table with the mnemonic attribute as the key of a record; alternatively, this can also be more adequately realized with a simple Perl script that can process a common repository[4] and generate all three properties files. This chapter does not discuss either method to maintain the uniqueness of the mnemonic.

---

[4]   For example, a common repository consists of the application components, the corresponding four-character code of each component, a sequence of four-digit numbers as message codes, the severity of the message code per component, an explanatory message, and maybe a macro that can be processed by Tcl.

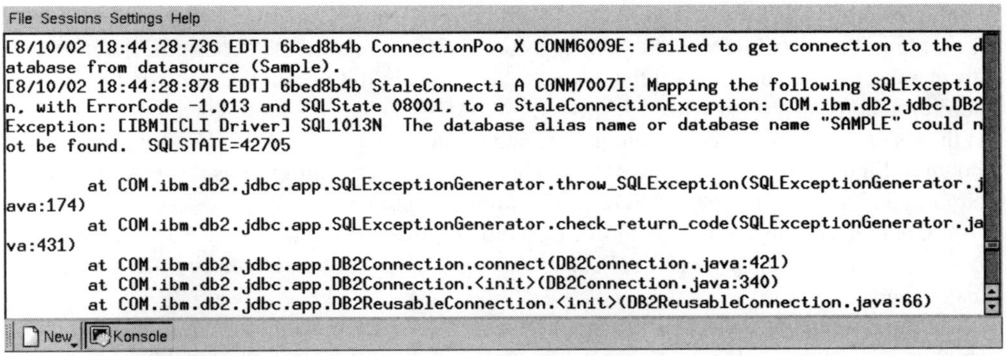

```
File  Sessions  Settings  Help
[8/10/02 18:44:28:736 EDT] 6bed8b4b ConnectionPoo X CONM6009E: Failed to get connection to the d
atabase from datasource (Sample).
[8/10/02 18:44:28:878 EDT] 6bed8b4b StaleConnecti A CONM7007I: Mapping the following SQLExceptio
n, with ErrorCode -1,013 and SQLState 08001, to a StaleConnectionException: COM.ibm.db2.jdbc.DB2
Exception: [IBM][CLI Driver] SQL1013N  The database alias name or database name "SAMPLE" could n
ot be found.  SQLSTATE=42705

        at COM.ibm.db2.jdbc.app.SQLExceptionGenerator.throw_SQLException(SQLExceptionGenerator.j
ava:174)
        at COM.ibm.db2.jdbc.app.SQLExceptionGenerator.check_return_code(SQLExceptionGenerator.ja
va:431)
        at COM.ibm.db2.jdbc.app.DB2Connection.connect(DB2Connection.java:421)
        at COM.ibm.db2.jdbc.app.DB2Connection.<init>(DB2Connection.java:340)
        at COM.ibm.db2.jdbc.app.DB2ReusableConnection.<init>(DB2ReusableConnection.java:66)
  New, Konsole
```

Figure 23-2   *WAS' exception format*

The following section on exception handling shows you how to make use of the properties files discussed in this section to throw customized exceptions.

Exception Handling

When throwing an exception from within the WASDG application, you want to write it to the log file. The thrown exception will be formatted somehow similarly to the way WAS writes its exceptions to the standard output file. For example, compare the WAS exception shown in Figure 23-2 to the WasdgException shown in Figure 23-3.

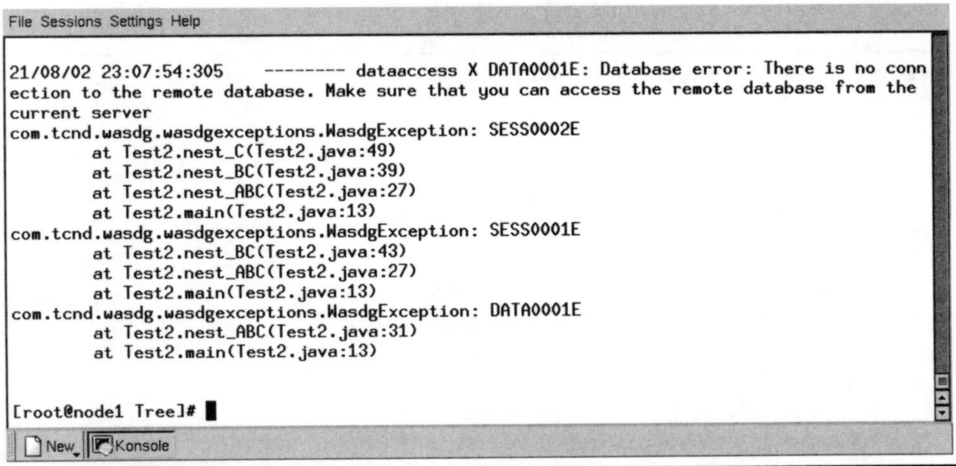

```
File  Sessions  Settings  Help
21/08/02 23:07:54:305      -------- dataaccess X DATA0001E: Database error: There is no conn
ection to the remote database. Make sure that you can access the remote database from the
current server
com.tcnd.wasdg.wasdgexceptions.WasdgException: SESS0002E
        at Test2.nest_C(Test2.java:49)
        at Test2.nest_BC(Test2.java:39)
        at Test2.nest_ABC(Test2.java:27)
        at Test2.main(Test2.java:13)
com.tcnd.wasdg.wasdgexceptions.WasdgException: SESS0001E
        at Test2.nest_BC(Test2.java:43)
        at Test2.nest_ABC(Test2.java:27)
        at Test2.main(Test2.java:13)
com.tcnd.wasdg.wasdgexceptions.WasdgException: DATA0001E
        at Test2.nest_ABC(Test2.java:31)
        at Test2.main(Test2.java:13)


[root@node1 Tree]# █
  New, Konsole
```

Figure 23-3   *WasdgException format*

The exception thrown in Figure 23-3 resulted from running a Test2 program that is available in the distribution code. (Refer to the section "Testing the Programs" later in this chapter.) A web application that throws exceptions in the format just specified can be monitored and supervised with WASMON. WASMON is the subject of Chapters 24 and 26. At the risk of misleading you, without getting into the specifics of WASMON, its console is shown in Figure 23-4 just for illustration. This figure demonstrates the use of WASMON in trapping and monitoring the WASDG application exceptions.

In Chapter 26, the section "Monitoring Web Applications with WASLED/WASMON" shows how to monitor any web application that uses the exception handler implemented in this chapter.

Listing 23-10 shows the WasdgException class that extends the java.lang.Exception class, which is a subclass of java.lang.Throwable. Because an exception is an object, it can contain data and define methods.

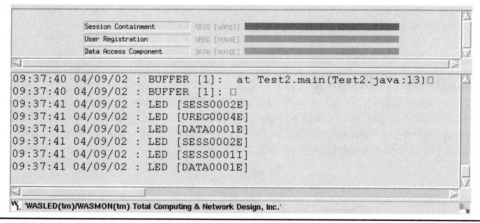

Figure 23-4   *WASMON trapping and monitoring the WASDG application exceptions*

Listing 23-10   *WasdgException*

```
1.    package com.tcnd.wasdg.wasdgexceptions;
2.
3.    import com.tcnd.wasdg.log.Log;
4.    import java.io.StringWriter;
5.    import java.io.PrintWriter;
6.    import java.util.*;
7.    import java.lang.*;
8.
9.    // WasdgException class extends Exception to support multiple messages in
      a single exception.
10.   // In debug mode new exceptions can hold references to old exceptions.
11.   // getStackTraceString() get information from the entire chain
12.
13.   public class WasdgException extends Exception
14.   {
15.       // Control nesting for debugging
16.       public static boolean debugMode = true;
17.       // Chain of exceptions
18.       private Throwable nestedChainException = null;
19.       // Stack trace from nested exceptions
20.       private String nestedStackTrace = null;
21.       // Support for multiple messages
22.       private Vector arrayMessages = new Vector(10);
23.
24.   // Default constructor, no message or nested exception
25.   public WasdgException()
26.   {
27.       super();
28.       init( null, null );
29.   }
30.
31.   // Constructor with mnemonic
32.   public WasdgException(String mnemonic)
33.   {
34.       super(mnemonic);
35.       init(mnemonic,null);
36.   }
37.
38.   // Constructor with nested exception
39.   public WasdgException(Throwable eThrowable)
40.   {
41.       super();
42.       init( null, eThrowable );
43.   }
44.
45.   // Constructor with mnemonic and nested exception
```

```
46.    public WasdgException(String mnemonic, Throwable eThrowable)
47.    {
48.        super(mnemonic);
49.        init( mnemonic, eThrowable );
50.    }
51.
52.    // Converts the stack trace information of the provided exception to a
       string
53.    static public String generateStackTraceString(Throwable eThrowable)
54.    {
55.        StringWriter lWriter = new StringWriter();
56.        eThrowable.printStackTrace(new PrintWriter(lWriter));
57.        return lWriter.toString();
58.    }
59.
60.    // Returns nested exception, null otherwise
61.    public Throwable getNestedException()
62.    {
63.        return nestedChainException;
64.    }
65.
66.    // Returns the stack trace string information about this exception and
       all nested ones
67.    public String getStackTraceString()
68.    {
69.        return nestedStackTrace;
70.    }
71.
72.    // On creation of a new exception, store the mnemonic and stack trace
       from this exception
73.    // In debug mode: log the new exception, get stacktrace information from
       any nested
74.    // exception and chain to the nested exception.
75.
76.    private void init(String mnemonic, Throwable eThrowable)
77.    {
78.        // Save mnemonic
79.        if (mnemonic != null)
80.            setMessage(mnemonic);
81.
82.        // If debugMode and nested exception then get nested exception stack
       trace
83.        if ((debugMode) && (eThrowable != null))
84.        {
85.            nestedChainException = eThrowable;
```

```
86.              if (nestedChainException instanceof WasdgException)
87.              {
88.                  WasdgException e = (WasdgException) eThrowable;
89.                  nestedStackTrace = e.getStackTraceString();
90.              }
91.              else
92.              {
93.                  nestedStackTrace =
        generateStackTraceString(nestedChainException);
94.              }
95.          }
96.
97.      // Update the stack trace string
98.      if ( null == nestedStackTrace )
99.          nestedStackTrace = generateStackTraceString(this);
100.     else
101.         nestedStackTrace = nestedStackTrace +
        generateStackTraceString(this);
102.
103.     if (debugMode)
104.         Log.log( " -------- "
105.         + WasdgMessages.getComponentCode(mnemonic) + " " +
     WasdgMessages.getSeverityCode(mnemonic) + " " + mnemonic + ": " +
     WasdgMessages.getDescriptiveMessage(mnemonic)
106.             + "\n" + nestedStackTrace
107.             + "\n");
108. }
109.
110. // Add a mnemonic to the list of messages for this exception
111. private void setMessage(String mnemonic)
112. {
113.     arrayMessages.addElement(mnemonic);
114. }
115. }
```

On line 39, the WasdgException takes a Throwable object as an argument. The Throwable object is at the top of the Exception class hierarchy, and it defines a human-readable error message of type String that can be inherited by all exception classes.

On line 105, the writing of the exception is similar to the way WAS writes its exception, as shown in Figure 23-2. To realize this, WasdgException calls WasdgMessages to retrieve an exception code or mnemonic from the bundled properties file discussed in the section "Considering the Exception-Handling Properties Files" earlier in this chapter.

The WasdgMessages, shown in Listing 23-11, offers three methods to fetch information about a specific exception mnemonic, as summarized in Table 23-1.

Method	Properties File	Description
getDescriptiveMessages	messages.properties	Gets an elaborated explanation about the mnemonic
getComponentCode	components.properties	Gets the symbolic name of the component to which the mnemonic pertains
getSeverityCode	severity.properties	Gets a one-character severity code level under which the mnemonic is categorized

Table 23-1 *Methods Used to Fetch Information About a Specific Exception or Message Mnemonic*

On Lines 12, 13, and 14 of WasdgMessages, shown in Listing 23-11, the three variables of type PropertyResourceBundle—componentCodes, descriptiveMessages, and serverityCodes—are used to cache the property bundles.

Listing 23-11 *WasdgMessages*

```
1.    package com.tcnd.wasdg.wasdgexceptions;
2.
3.    // This class contains the methods to return a descriptive message,
4.    // the severity code, and the component name of an exception mnemonic
5.
6.    import java.io.*;
7.    import java.util.*;
8.    import com.tcnd.wasdg.common.BundleManager;
9.    import com.tcnd.wasdg.log.Log;
10.
11.   public class WasdgMessages {
12.       private static PropertyResourceBundle componentCodes;
13.       private static PropertyResourceBundle descriptiveMessages;
14.       private static PropertyResourceBundle severityCodes;
15.       static
16.       {
17.           componentCodes = BundleManager.getBundle("components");
18.           descriptiveMessages = BundleManager.getBundle("messages");
19.           severityCodes = BundleManager.getBundle("severity");
20.       }
21.
22.   // constructor
23.   public WasdgMessages() { super(); }
24.
25.   //  This method returns the description of a message mnemonic
26.   public static String getDescriptiveMessage(String mnemonic) throws
      MissingResourceException
27.   {
28.       try
29.       {
```

```
30.            return descriptiveMessages.getString(mnemonic);
31.        }
32.        catch (MissingResourceException e)
33.        {
34.            Log.log("WasdgMessages.getDescriptiveMessage: Not found for " +
      mnemonic);
35.            return "?";
36.        }
37.    }
38.
39.    // This method returns the severity code of a message mnemonic
40.    public static String getSeverityCode(String mnemonic) throws
      MissingResourceException
41.    {
42.    ...
43.    }
44.
45.    // This method returns the severity code of a message mnemonic
46.    public static String getComponentCode(String mnemonic) throws
      MissingResourceException
47.    {
48.    ...
49.    }
50.    }
```

On line 26, the getDescriptiveMessage() method returns the information of a specific exception mnemonic; otherwise, upon failure, an exception is thrown and the value is returned as a question mark (?). This allows the programmer to point to an undefined exception mnemonic when reading the log file. Listing 23-11 does not show the code for getSeverityCode() and getComponentCode() because they are programmatically similar to getDescriptiveMessage() just discussed.

Testing the Programs

The distribution code comes with several programs to test the packages discussed in this chapter. Table 23-2 summarizes each of the testing programs.

Program Name	Description
TestLog	Tests the Log.log() method
TestBundleManager	Tests the BundleManager
Test0	Tests the WasdgException: throwing simple exception
Test1	Tests the WasdgException: throwing multiple exceptions
Test2	Tests the WasdgException: nested exception

Table 23-2   *Simple Testing Programs for Chapter 23*

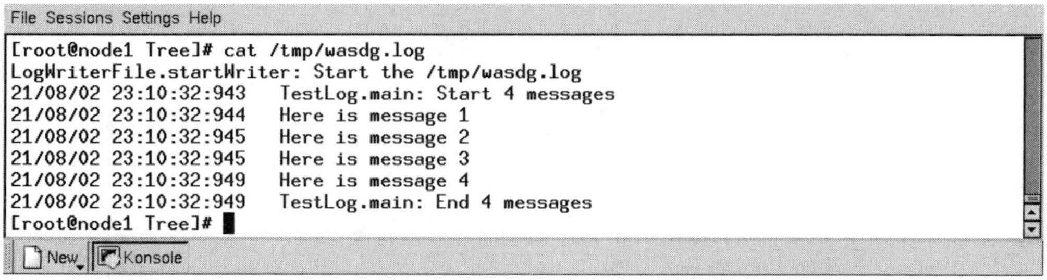

```
File Sessions Settings Help
[root@node1 Tree]# cat /tmp/wasdg.log
LogWriterFile.startWriter: Start the /tmp/wasdg.log
21/08/02 23:10:32:943    TestLog.main: Start 4 messages
21/08/02 23:10:32:944    Here is message 1
21/08/02 23:10:32:945    Here is message 2
21/08/02 23:10:32:945    Here is message 3
21/08/02 23:10:32:949    Here is message 4
21/08/02 23:10:32:949    TestLog.main: End 4 messages
[root@node1 Tree]#
  New   Konsole
```

Figure 23-5   *Messages written to the log file by TestLog*

When executing the TestLog program, messages are written to the wasdg.log file as specified in the log.properties file. Such messages are shown in Figure 23-5.

Test0, Test1, and Test2 programs, show the usage of the WasdgException in handling exceptions. Figure 23-6 shows the exceptions caught and thrown when executing the program Test1.

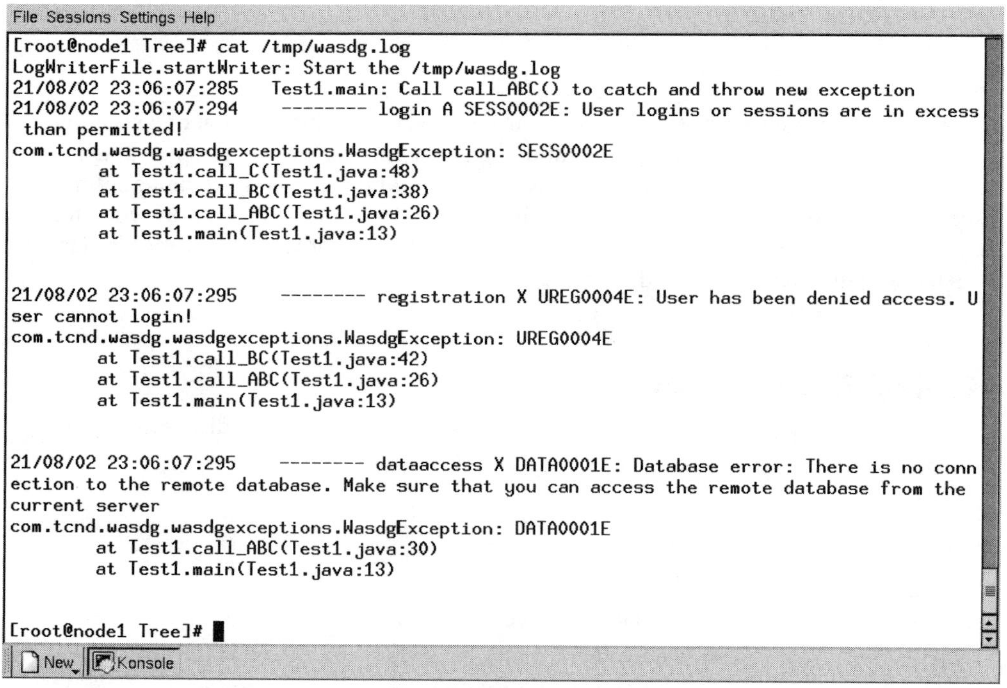

```
File Sessions Settings Help
[root@node1 Tree]# cat /tmp/wasdg.log
LogWriterFile.startWriter: Start the /tmp/wasdg.log
21/08/02 23:06:07:285    Test1.main: Call call_ABC() to catch and throw new exception
21/08/02 23:06:07:294    -------- login A SESS0002E: User logins or sessions are in excess
 than permitted!
com.tcnd.wasdg.wasdgexceptions.WasdgException: SESS0002E
        at Test1.call_C(Test1.java:48)
        at Test1.call_BC(Test1.java:38)
        at Test1.call_ABC(Test1.java:26)
        at Test1.main(Test1.java:13)


21/08/02 23:06:07:295    -------- registration X UREG0004E: User has been denied access. U
ser cannot login!
com.tcnd.wasdg.wasdgexceptions.WasdgException: UREG0004E
        at Test1.call_BC(Test1.java:42)
        at Test1.call_ABC(Test1.java:26)
        at Test1.main(Test1.java:13)


21/08/02 23:06:07:295    -------- dataaccess X DATA0001E: Database error: There is no conn
ection to the remote database. Make sure that you can access the remote database from the
current server
com.tcnd.wasdg.wasdgexceptions.WasdgException: DATA0001E
        at Test1.call_ABC(Test1.java:30)
        at Test1.main(Test1.java:13)


[root@node1 Tree]#
  New   Konsole
```

Figure 23-6   *WasdgException catching and throwing new exceptions when running Test1*

IBM Object Level Trace (OLT) and Object Level Debugger (OLD)

Because we mostly use an HTTP servlet to send requests or receive responses, tracing web application servlets with breakpoints is time consuming and useless. Tracing with breakpoints is usually helpful in debugging programs with complex numerical routines. There is no usability to implement and test such mathematical programs in a distributed environment; therefore, we will skim over the usage of IBM's offering for its trace debuggers: OLT/OLD. The OLT/OLD debuggers are represented here only for completeness.[5]

On the other hand, when facing performance issues in a distributed web application, you must resort to the use of a sniffer or a network analyzer as an accurate real-time debugging technique, as shown in Chapter 22.

OLT allows you to trace and step through debugging the code running in your application server runtime. You need to have a workstation on which you can run the OLT trace viewer. This workstation will be used to debug user code that runs in a distributed environment. Let's say the machine jade.tcnd.com is such a Windows NT workstation, and the application is being run on the default server of WAS on the server node1.tcnd.com.

In the admin console, you need to enable IBM debugging and OLT and to specify the directory where the source code reside: select Nodes | node1 | Application Servers | Default Server | IBM Debug and OLT. Then restart WAS AEs with the debugging flags, as follows:

```
startServer.sh -oltEnable -debugEnable -host jade -jdwPort 8001 -port 2102
```

You can now start tracing a program's source code using the OLT viewer. You start the OLT on Windows NT workstation (whose hostname is jade) using the batch file olt.bat. You need to specify the server and port where the OLT-enabled application is running, for example, node1.tcnd.com on port 2102.

You start the IBM debugger by issuing the `ibmdebug` command; you specify the server name and the port number where the OLD-enabled application is running, for example, node1.tcnd .com on port 8001.

Wrapping Up

A good programmer always knows when an exception is expected and the reason it is being thrown; if not, then the use of exception handling is justified, as you learned in this chapter. Therefore, the excessive use of the Throwable objects to complement source code in a generalized way is not advised because it will slow down the web application.

---

[5]   OLT/OLD are mostly used by the vendor of WAS in debugging the application server code itself, which
      is outside the scope of this book.

You also learned that exception handling is useful in methods that need to connect to other distributed resources, in which case, if the resource is not available, a person can be notified. An application can throw its own exceptions by extending the Exception class: the WasdgException is such a class. Exceptions can be symbolized using mnemonics that are separated into groups. We used the BundleManager in this chapter to classify and cache the values of our exception mnemonics.

You also learned that the printing of messages and exceptions is handled using the Log.log() method that initialized a PrintWriter object.

Monitoring, Tuning, and Risk Management

OBJECTIVES

► Monitoring WAS and Web Applications

► Monitoring System Resources and Threads

► WAS Tuning and Performance

► Risk Managing a WebSphere Region

WAS Monitoring with WASLED™ and WASMON™

Monitoring WAS activity is crucial in a WebSphere region. A monitor program is a basic application that can trap[1] events and combine logical conditions; if satisfied, the program may send appropriate alerts to developers and administrators, and may trigger some routines to heuristically resolve the problem.

Unfortunately, WAS, like many other application servers, does not provide you with a monitoring tool to assess its running state. This chapter address the topic of monitoring WAS with the WASLED/WASMON application.

WASLED is an application that assists you in graphically monitoring the activities of WAS components. WASMON has the same features as WASLED, in addition to some extra monitoring features that allow you to specify triggers and filters on specific WAS events. Triggers are any program that you can execute at the command prompt; these are usually shell scripts, Perl scripts, compiled Java programs, or just a simple command. Filters are patterns that can detect the occurrence of WAS events. Such patterns are usually regular expressions.

WASMON runs as a server, listening to incoming data from a client. The data is the WAS log data that is written to WAS' standard output. For instance, for WAS AEs it is written to the file default_server_stdout.log. This chapter discusses how to monitor WAS using WASMON.

Monitoring Objective

Let's pause a moment and look at the WAS big picture: The WAS program consists of four major parts: a listener routine; resource grouping routines; containment routines; and an output routine. The main purpose of the resource grouping routines is to deliver the client's URI input through the listener to the appropriate container after parsing the URI, validate it, and then bind to it the appropriate resource names. When a user requests a servlet, to satisfy his or her request, all parts of WAS must execute satisfactorily. During execution, if any error occurs, an administrator must be notified. Errors may be caught, scripts automatically triggered, and an alert made to specific users.

Component Message Numbers as LED

WAS has as many as 40 components (see Table 24-1). Each component is identified with an ID number. The ID follows the form *CCCC* and is used as a suffix to identify the source of a message number. The message number is of the form *NNNN* and is appended to the suffix to form a unique identifier for such a named message, which WASLED™ refers to as a LED. A final optional character may also terminate or suffix each LED to highlight the severity of the message. Therefore, a LED is of the form *CCCCNNNN*[*s*], where [*s*] is one of the following:

- ▶ **E**   An error severity is 1 (red)
- ▶ **W**   A warning severity is 2 (orange)
- ▶ **I**   An informational message with the lowest severity 3 (green)
- ▶ **A**   Not documented by IBM, however, assuming it is an audit, WASLED shows this message severity in black
- ▶ **Not specified**   (blue)

In the previous list, the color shown corresponds to the LED light that shows off in WASMON console. For example, consider the following illustration showing the tail of WAS standard output log file after starting the application server. The command `tail $WASLOG_STDOUT` printed the messages as they are, while the command `tail $WASLOG_STDOUT | awk '{ print $7 }` printed the 7th field of each message. This field describes the component, the LED number, and its severity level.

```
[root@node1 /]# tail $WASLOG_STDOUT
[6/5/02 10:54:18:297 EDT] 61e03385 WebGroup        I SRVE0091I: [Servlet LOG]: DirectoryBrowsingServlet: init
[6/5/02 10:54:18:389 EDT] 61e03385 ServletEngine   A SRVE0169I: Loading Web Module: Wasdg Web Application Exa
mple.
[6/5/02 10:54:18:630 EDT] 61e03385 WebGroup        I SRVE0091I: [Servlet LOG]: JSP 1.1 Processor: init
[6/5/02 10:54:18:638 EDT] 61e03385 WebGroup        I SRVE0091I: [Servlet LOG]: SimpleFileServlet: init
[6/5/02 10:54:18:828 EDT] 61e03385 WebGroup        I SRVE0091I: [Servlet LOG]: InvokerServlet: init
[6/5/02 10:54:18:839 EDT] 61e03385 WebGroup        I SRVE0091I: [Servlet LOG]: DirectoryBrowsingServlet: init
[6/5/02 10:54:18:901 EDT] 61e03385 HttpTransport   A SRVE0171I: Transport http is listening on port 9,080.
[6/5/02 10:54:20:740 EDT] 61e03385 HttpTransport   A SRVE0171I: Transport https is listening on port 9,443.
[6/5/02 10:54:20:742 EDT] 61e03385 HttpTransport   A SRVE0171I: Transport http is listening on port 9,090.
[6/5/02 10:54:20:781 EDT] 61e03385 Server          A WSVR0023I: Server Default Server open for e-business
[root@node1 /]# tail $WASLOG_STDOUT | awk '{ print $7 }'
SRVE0091I:
SRVE0169I:
SRVE0091I:
SRVE0091I:
SRVE0091I:
SRVE0091I:
SRVE0171I:
SRVE0171I:
SRVE0171I:
WSVR0023I:
[root@node1 /]#
```

Note that this previous example is shown as a simple educative illustration, and does not form the basis on which WASMON/WASLED internal processing is based on. Table 24-1 describes the WAS components.

Component ID	Component Description
AATL	Application Assembly Tool
ADGU	Administrative GUI
ADMR	Administrative repository
ADMT	Administrative tasks

Table 24-1   *WAS Components' Identifications and Their Descriptions*

Component ID	Component Description
ADMS	Administrative server
ALRM	Alarm
CHKJ	IBM validation tool
CHKW	WebSphere Server validation
CNTR	EJB container
CONM	Connection manager
DBMN	Database manager
DRSW	Data replication service
DYNA	Cache management
INST	Install
J2CA	Connector architecture (J2C)
JORB	IBM Java ORB
JSAS	Security Association Service
JSPG	JavaServer Pages
LTXT	Localizable text
MSGS	Messaging
MIGR	WebSphere migration tools
NMSV	JNDI name services
PLGN	Web Server plug-ins and native code
PMON	Performance Monitor
SECJ	WebSphere Security
SESN	Session and User Profiles
SMTL	WebSphere Systems Management Utilities
SRVE	Servlet Engine
TRAS	Tracing Component
WCMD	WebSphere Systems Management Commands
WINT	Request Interceptors
WOBA	WebSphere Object Adapter
WPRS	WebSphere Persistence
WSCL	Client
WSCP	WSCP Command Line
WSVR	WebSphere Server Runtime
WTRN	WebSphere Transactions
WTSK	WebSphere Systems Management Tasks
WWLM	EJB Work Load Management
XMLC	XML Configuration

Table 24-1   *WAS Components' Identifications and Their Descriptions* (continued)

Installing and Starting Up WASMON™

Installing and starting WASMON™ is fairly simple. The product consists basically of the following parts:

▶ **The wasmon program**[1]   Requires Perl Tk as a prerequisite to run

▶ **The wasmon.conf configuration script**   Defines the filters and their associated triggers to be executed and recipients to be notified

▶ **Miscellaneous files**   Include the LED database flat file *wasleddb* (or alternately wasleddb_s_r402), a couple of bitmap images in the lib directory, and the *wasmontkt* that processes the wasmon.conf file

▶ **The TriggersPool directory**   Allows you to deposit your own script

▶ **The wasmoncl program**   Is copied to and run on a client machine to which to forward WAS log activity to it

▶ **The wasmonhelper program and its associated files**   wasmonhelper.conf and wasmonvar, which the reader should ignore for now, as they will be discussed in Chapter 26

You can download the product as TAR or ZIP archive from the Osborne web site or from www.tcnd.com. Extract the archive to a directory of your choice. The directory where you extracted the archive will look like this:

```
|-- README
|-- helper (this directory is not needed in this chapter)
|-- lib-emu (contains the bitmaps)
|-- TriggersPool
|   |-- chekjndi.pl
|   |-- wm_0001.sh
|   |-- wm_0002.sh
|   |-- wm_0003.sh
|   |-- wm_0004.sh
|   |-- wm_0005_kill-all-WAS4-processes-on-NodeX.sh
|   |-- wm_0006.sh
|   |-- wm_0008.sh
|   `-- wm_0010.sh
|-- wasleddb (might also be named wasleddb_<s|l>_r<version>)
|-- wasmon
|-- wasmon.conf
|-- wasmoncl
|-- wasmonhelper (not needed in this chapter)
`-- wasmontkt
```

---

[1]   Not all the features of WASLED/WASMON are available when you run the product on Windows NT.

After extracting the contents of the application archive, locate the README file and read the license agreement before running the WASMON™/WASLED™ program.

To start WASMON, simply issue this command:

```
# wasmon
```

Alternatively, start the program explicitly by running it through the Perl interpreter with this command:

```
# perl wasmon
```

The WASMON console will appear, as shown in Figure 24-1.

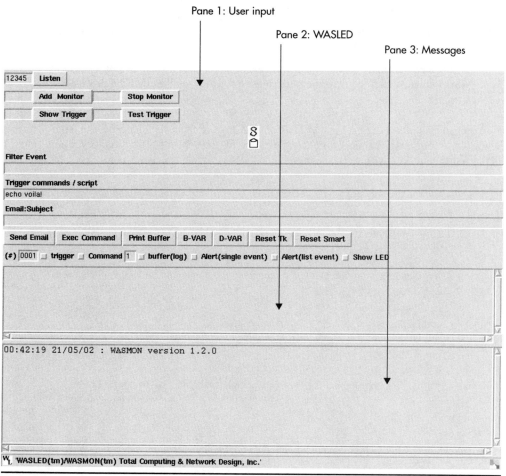

Figure 24-1   *The WASMON console*

The console consists of three panes:

▶ The first pane is where you make entries using the keyboard or the mouse to interact with the wasmon program. In addition, this pane shows two blinking throbs, discussed in the section "Monitoring WAS Containment" later in this chapter.

▶ The second pane is where WASLED activities are monitored. Colors represent the severity of each component.

▶ The third pane is where the wasmon program's activities are logged.

The First Pane: The User Input Pane

You interact with WASMON through this pane and enters data here for one of three reasons: to view and to test configuration data from within WASMON; to request from WASMON to process specific data;or to alter or to reset the queues and buffers of WASMON.

12345	Stop Listening			
	Add Monitor		Stop Monitor	
0001	Show Trigger		Test Trigger	

Filter Event
CNTR[0-9][0-9][0-9][0-9]E

Trigger commands / script
echo voila!

Email:Subject

Send Email	Exec Command	Print Buffer

(#) 0001 ⬛ trigger ⬛ Command 1 ⬛ buffer(log) ⬛ Alert(single event) ⬛ Alert(list event) ⬛ Show LED

For instance, to view trigger content and to test its functionality, you enter its four digits and click on Show Trigger or Test Trigger, respectively.

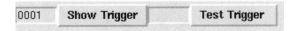

To filter an event while WASMON is running, you can just enter the string to be matched in the Filter Event text box; once the event is detected, it is printed in the third pane, and it is also possible to execute an associated trigger on such a detection.

The Second Pane: The WASLED Activities Pane

This pane refers to the WASLED activities; it shows the graphical representation of the activities of WAS components.

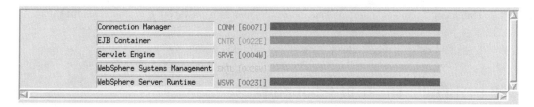

When one of the more than 40 WAS components is detected by WASMON, it is dynamically allocated a graphical object to show its current state. Therefore, each component is represented on one line, as shown in this illustration:

```
Servlet Engine                SRVE [0004W]
```

The line is formed of three parts: the component's descriptive name; the last LED component processed by WASMON, however its color reflects the state of the LED previously processed; and a colored bar that shows the severity of the current processed component. For example the previous line shows that the Servlet Engine component's current LED is SRVE0004W (W=warning=orange), which is graphically shown in orange. The Servlet Engine's previous state was normal, as reflected by the green color of SRVE0004W (the second part).

All 40 WAS components are initially monitored by WASMON. However, a component will show up only if it is detected by WASMON. You can also exclude a component from the list by entering its four-character ID number (*CCCC*) in the first pane and by clicking Stop Monitor. Add Monitor does the opposite.

The Third Pane: The WASMON Activities Pane

Many WASMON activities can be shown in this scrollable pane. It is useful to know what is happening in the background while WASMON is processing the WAS activities log.

```
00:45:22 21/05/02 : FILTER [CNTR[0-9][0-9][0-9][0-9]E].
00:45:23 21/05/02 : FILTER [CNTR[0-9][0-9][0-9][0-9]E].
00:45:27 21/05/02 : stop listening on 12345
00:45:27 21/05/02 : OK, slam the socket closed!
00:45:30 21/05/02 : B-VAR: BOOL_ACTIVEPORT_node2:50000 1
00:45:30 21/05/02 : B-VAR: BOOL_ACTIVEPORT_node2:50009 0
00:45:30 21/05/02 : B-VAR: BOOL_JNDILOOKUP_node1:900/WSsamples/AccountHome 1
00:45:30 21/05/02 : B-VAR: BOOL_JNDISERVER_node1:900 1
00:45:30 21/05/02 : B-VAR: BOOL_LOOKFILE_15951_ 0
```

'WASLED(tm)/WASMON(tm) Total Computing & Network Design, Inc.'

For example, if you select the Show LED check box in the first pane while WASMON is running, the WAS' LEDs will be printed in this window.

Activating and Connecting to the WASMON Server

By now, you should have the WASMON console on your workstation. The program is initially in a waiting state. You need to enter a socket number in the upper-left corner of the console and click the Listen button. At this time, WASMON is ready to accept connection from the client that will forward WAS' activity log to it. To put the program back into its inactive state, just Click on Stop Listening again.

WASMON is successfully active when you see the message NowAccepting on *socket-number* in the third pane. Make sure that the WASMON is started and is listening before you start the client discussed next.

Now, you can run wasmoncl on any workstation that has access to the WAS server log where STDOUT is written. You do not need to start the client wasmoncl on the same server on which WAS is installed and running; what is important is to have access to the file system to which WAS is logging its STDOUT data. For instance, to check for the default log you can issue this command:

```
# tail $WAS_HOME/logs/default_server_stdout.log
```

This command should print a couple of lines on your screen. If the test was successful, you can start wasmoncl The following example assumes that the workstation on which the wasmoncl is started has access to WAS' default_server_stdout.log file:

```
# tail -f $WAS_HOME/logs/default_server_stdout.log | wasmoncl 12345
pleiade
```

The previous command also assumes that WASMON has been started on the workstation whose hostname is pleiade, and is listening and accepting connection on socket 12345.

As more data is written to the default_server_stdout.log file by WAS, the previous command will send the data to the server pleiade on socket 12345, provided that wasmoncl has successfully connected to the WASMON server running on the machine pleiade. A successful connection to the server is shown in the third pane of WASMON as a message "Good, Here We Connect!"

```
00:42:19 21/05/02 : WASMON version 1.2.0
00:43:09 21/05/02 : Trying to listen on 12345
00:43:09 21/05/02 : Now, accepting clients on 12345
00:43:51 21/05/02 : Great! -- Someone is trying to connect!
00:43:51 21/05/02 : Good, here we connect!
```

'WASLED(tm)/WASMON(tm) Total Computing & Network Design, Inc.'

Monitoring WAS Containment

Once the connection has been established, the center of the first WASMON pane will show two activities of WAS containers: the web container (servlet engine) and the EJB container.

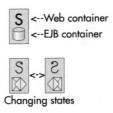

The throb on the top will change state when the WAS web container is active, for example, when a servlet is loaded. The throb in the bottom will change state when the WAS EJB container is active. Both throbs will be blinking whether WASMON detects any activities or not.

To test the web container throb, keep on looking at the throb while putting a request to a servlet.

Filtering WAS Events and Firing Action with WASMON

While colors are more intuitive to work with log records and script commands are more direct and intelligent to work with (or to realize a goal), the combination of both makes us better comprehend the behavior of a software application to successfully achieve the task of application monitoring. WASMON is an extension of WASLED with additional features that allow the administrator to monitor WAS components and trigger specific scripts according to certain condition. The following summarizes the essential capabilities of WASMON:

▶   Filters messages

▶   E-mails or pages a set of users when a condition or a set of conditions is met

▶   Triggers scripts when a condition or a set of conditions is met

▶   Includes miscellaneous features such as buffering messages, on-line filtering, and on-line trigger activation capabilities.

The wasmon.conf file takes several directives of which only six are of interest to you at this time. These directives are referred to as Direct Alert directives to contrast them from another set of directives known as Logical Alert directives. The Logical Alert directives are discussed in the section Conditional Monitoring later in this chapter. Table 24-2 summarizes the Direct Alert directives.

Directive	Description
ALERT ON COMPONENT FAULT	Alert when a component error (E) is detected
ALERT ON COMPONENT WARN	Alter when a component warning (W) is detected
ALERT ON COMPONENT LIST FAULTS	Alert when one or many component errors (E) are detected
ALERT ON COMPONENT LIST WARNS	Alert when one or many component warnings (W) are detected
ALERT ON FILTER	Alert when a user-defined filter is detected
ALERT ON LIST FILTERS	Alert when a list of user-defined filters are all detected

Table 24-2   *Direct Alert Directives Used in the wasmon.conf File*

Each directive is specified on a single line, followed by comma-separated entries. The comma-separated entries form a record in which the position of each field is important. If we look at field1 occupying a slot1 in the record, and field2 occupying slot2 in the record, and so on; therefore we look at a record as being formed of nine slots followed by at least one slot to depict a filter:

slot1, slot1,slot2,...,slot9,filterslot1[,filterslot2[...][,filterslot*N*]]

The content of the record can be summarized as follows:

```
n1,n2,DDDD, trig-options, e-mail-address, cc-e-mail-address,
e-mail-subject,e-mail-body, logical-expression,
filter1[,filter2[...][,filterN]]
```

The *DDDD* stands for the four digits of the trigger number, and *e-mail-address* is the address to which to send the e-mail, with the subject *e-mail-subject* and the body *e-mail-body* when the condition is met. You must specify either a *DDDD*, an e-mail-address, or both. The filter1 through *filterN* represent the expressions that you are trying to detect while processing the WAS STDOUT logging. The *DDDD* trigger number is explained in the section "Triggering Scripts" later in this chapter. The *trig-options* is a list of options that you want to pass to the script being triggered; this is optional and can be kept empty if you do not need to specify any option. The *logical-expression* is not used with the Direct Alert directives but you must keep the comma as a placeholder for it.

The *n1* and *n2* are two positive integers that tell how many times to send an e-mail notification, and how many times to execute the *DDDD* trigger respectively every time the condition on the filter or filters is met. Every time a list of filters is met, WASMON sends the e-mail and executes the trigger; then it resets to FALSE its condition on the filter listing. For a list of *N* filters, a condition is met when "*filter*1 AND *filter*2 --- AND *filter*N" are all truly detected. For a list of component faults or warns, the filters correspond to a comma delimited component acronyms, for example "SRVE,DYNA,CONM." When selecting a list of component faults, WASMON will detect each of the components listed that generate an error (E). When selecting a list of components warns, WASMON will detect each of the components listed that generate a warning (W).

Because the comma is used to separate the entries on each line, do not use the comma in any of the fields.

Let's take a look at an example::

```
ALERT ON COMPONENT
FAULT:3,1,0002,Hmm,maxou@ibmsos.com,admin@ibmsos.com,ALERT: SRVE
ERROR,,,SRVE
```

When WASMON reads this line from its configuration file, it parses it; then it directs its internal monitoring engine to do the following:

- ▶ **ALERT ON COMPONENT FAULT**   Alerts when an error (E) occurred in a component. The component here is SRVE, which identifies the web container.

- ▶ **3**   Sends an e-mail notification to the recipient three times every time the condition is met. The first time the condition is met, a first e-mail is sent out and the filtering pool is reset. The second e-mail will be sent if the condition is met again, and so is the third e-mail. That is because WASMON monitor WAS in real time, and an error can be filtered at different instances as time go on. WASMON stops sending e-mail after the third one is being sent. In the first pane, you can press on Reset Tk button to reset the queue of all Direct Alert directives so that WASMON will continue sending another three e-mails whenever the condition is met.

- ▶ **1**   Executes the trigger only once when condition is met.

- ▶ **0002**   Trigger number that corresponds to a script whose name starts with wm_0002* and is located in the TriggersPool directory. The triggers naming convention is explained later on in the section "Triggering Scripts."

- ▶ **Hmm**   To be passed as an option to the triggered script. This is a simple example, but in reality you may need to trigger a script with more rigorous options, such as restart, halt, or retry. The options passed to a trigger are sent as one single argument to the triggered script, and must all be alphanumeric in addition to the following characters: / _ - :

- ▶ **maxou@ibmsos.com**   Recipient to which to send the e-mail

- ▶ **admin@ibmsos.com**   Will also receive a carbon copy (cc)

- ▶ **ALERT SRVE ERROR**   The subject sent in the e-mail

- ▶ **Insert comma as a placeholder to skip this field**   Usually this is the entry of the body of the e-mail message.

- ▶ **Insert comma as a placeholder**   This entry must be skipped and will be used when we discuss the Logical Alert directives.

- ▶ **SRVE**   Filter to detect any error caused in the web container

The program wasmontkt reads the wasmon.conf file and generates a report that can be easily understood. You will use this report to locate a ticket sent to a user along with the conditions processed that generated such a ticket. The report can also be used to check if the wasmon.conf file has been properly configured. As an example, consider the configuration file shown in Listing 24-1. This is a simple example that summarizes each of the directives shown in Table 24-2.

Listing 24-1   *wasmon.conf sample configuration file*

```
1.    #
2.    # WASLED(tm)/WASMON(tm)
3.    # (C) COPYRIGHT TOTAL COMPUTING & NETWORK DESIGN Corp. 2002
4.    #
5.    # wasmon.conf contains the additional configuration for the wasmon
      program.
6.    # Blank lines or lines starting with a hash (#) are not processed
7.    #
8.
9.    ALERT ON COMPONENT FAULT: 1,1,0002,
      Hello,root@node1,admin@node2,ALERT:EJB CONTAINER ERROR,,,CNTR
10.   ALERT ON COMPONENT FAULT: 1,1,0002,,root@node1,admin@node2,ALERT:EJB
      CONTAINER ERROR,,,CNTR
11.   ALERT ON COMPONENT FAULT:
      1,1,0002,dummy-options,root@node1,admin@node2,ALERT:EJB CONTAINER
      ERROR,,dummy,CNTR
12.   ALERT ON COMPONENT WARN:
      2,2,0002,dummy-options,maxou@node2.tcnd.com,admin@node2.tcnd.com,ALERT:SRVE
      WARNING,,,SRVE
13.
14.   ALERT ON FILTER: 2,2,0002,dummy-options, admin@ibmsos.com,, ALERT:SRVE
      ERROR,,,SRVE[0-9][0-9][0-9][0-9]E
15.   ALERT ON FILTER: 0,1,0002,dummy-options, maxou@ibmsos.com,, ALERT:SRVE
      WARN,,,SRVE[0-9][0-9][0-9][0-9]W
16.   ALERT ON FILTER: 2,2,0002,, maxou@ibmsos.com,, ALERT:FILTER,,,connection
      pool(.)*destroyed
17.
18.   ALERT ON COMPONENT LIST WARNS: 1,1,0005,,maxou@ibmsos.com,,WASMON:
      WARNING ON SRVE and SMTL,,,SRVE,SMTL
19.   ALERT ON COMPONENT LIST FAULTS: 0,,,,maxou@ibmsos.com,,ALERT:SOMETHING
      ERROR,,,SRVE,CNTR
20.
21.   ALERT ON LIST FILTERS: 0,1,0002,,root@node1,,ALERT:SOMETHING
      FILTERED,,,SRVE[0-9][0-9][0-9][0-9]W,SRVE[0-9][0-9][0-9][0-9],connection
      pool(.)*source,CONM6007I,CNTR[0-9][0-9][0-9][0-9]
```

When you run wasmontkt,[2] a report is printed on your console that is similar to that seen in Figure 24-2.

If the user root@node2 receives an e-mail message with a ticket TK41, this is due to the filters that are listed in the report. A typical e-mail message received by root@node1 is shown in Listing 24-2.

Listing 24-2 *E-mail received by recipient reflects ticket number TK41 in body of the message*

```
From root   Tue Apr 16 23:54:03 2002
Return-Path: <root@node1.tcnd.com>
Received: (from root@localhost)
        by node1.tcnd.com (8.11.6/8.11.6) id g3H3s3617860;
        Tue, 16 Apr 2002 23:54:03 -0400
Date: Tue, 16 Apr 2002 23:54:03 -0400
Message-Id: <200204170354.g3H3s3617860@node1.tcnd.com>
To: root@node1.tcnd.com
From: wasmon@node1.tcnd.com
Subject: ALERT:SOMETHING FILTERED
cc:
WASMON [TK41] 23:54:03 16/04/02
```

Looking again at the report generated by wasmontkt, the first digit shown in the TRIGGER and the E-MAIL columns reflects the number of times the trigger and the e-mail will be executed and sent respectively.

Note also that when WASMON parses the fields of each line in the configuration file, it deletes all spaces found at the beginning and end of a field, except the for filter fields (which happen to be listed and comma separated at the end of each configuration line.)

Even though you might have a valid wasmon.conf file and WASMON server is running, the monitoring activities will not take place unless you select the Alert(Single Event) and Alert(List Event) check boxes.

The Alert(Single Event) check box is used to process only those directives whose condition does not include a list of assertions: ALERT ON COMPONENT FAULT, ALERT ON COMPONENT WARN, and ALERT ON FILTER.

The Alert(List Event) check box enables these directives that contain a list of assertions: ALERT ON COMPONENT LIST FAULTS, ALERT ON COMPONENT LIST WARNS, and ALERT ON LIST FILTERS.

---

[2]   The TK301, TK401, and TK402 shown in the illustration result from other directives that are not shown in Listing 24-1. These directives will be explained later in this chapter.

```
File  Sessions  Settings  Help

[root@node1 DB]# ./wasmontkt
TICKET   TRIGGER   TRIGGER SUB     EMAIL             CC           SUBJECT           FILTER
------   -------   -----------     -----             --           -------           ------
TK11     1/0002    wm_0002.sh      1/root@node1      admin@node   ALERT:EJB CONTA   CNTR[0-9][0-9][0-9][0-9]E
TK12     1/0002    wm_0002.sh      1/root@node1      admin@node   ALERT:EJB CONTA   CNTR[0-9][0-9][0-9][0-9]E
TK13     1/0002    wm_0002.sh      1/root@node1      admin@node   ALERT:EJB CONTA   CNTR[0-9][0-9][0-9][0-9]E
TK14     2/0002    wm_0002.sh      2/maxou@node2.    admin@node   ALERT:SRVE WARN   SRVE[0-9][0-9][0-9][0-9]W
TK21     2/0002    wm_0002.sh      2/admin@ibmsos                 ALERT:SRVE ERRO   SRVE[0-9][0-9][0-9][0-9]E
TK22     0/0002    wm_0002.sh      1/maxou@ibmsos                 ALERT:SRVE WARN   SRVE[0-9][0-9][0-9][0-9]W
TK23     2/0002    wm_0002.sh      2/maxou@ibmsos                 ALERT:FILTER      connection pool(.)*destroye
TK31     1/0005    wm_0005_kill-a  1/maxou@ibmsos                 WASMON: WARNING   SMTL[0-9][0-9][0-9][0-9]W
                                                                                   SRVE[0-9][0-9][0-9][0-9]W
TK32     0/                        /maxou@ibmsos.                 ALERT:SOMETHING   SRVE[0-9][0-9][0-9][0-9]E
                                                                                   CNTR[0-9][0-9][0-9][0-9]E
TK41     0/0002    wm_0002.sh      1/root@node1                   ALERT:SOMETHING   SRVE[0-9][0-9][0-9][0-9]W
                                                                                   SRVE[0-9][0-9][0-9][0-9]
                                                                                   connection pool(.)*source
                                                                                   CONM6007I
                                                                                   CNTR[0-9][0-9][0-9][0-9]
TK301    1/0002    wm_0002.sh      1/maxou@ibmsos                 ALERT:SOMETHING   SRVE[0-9][0-9][0-9][0-9]E
                                                                                   CNTR[0-9][0-9][0-9][0-9]W
                                                                                   exp: (c1 || c2)
TK401    0/0002    wm_0002.sh      1/root@node1                   ALERT:SOMETHING   SRVE[0-9][0-9][0-9][0-9]W
                                                                                   SRVE[0-9][0-9][0-9][0-9]
                                                                                   connection pool(.)*source
                                                                                   CONM6007I
                                                                                   CNTR[0-9][0-9][0-9][0-9]
                                                                                   exp: (c1 && c2) && ((c3 ||
TK402    0/0002    wm_0002.sh      1/root@node1                   ALERT:SOMETHING   SRVE[0-9][0-9][0-9][0-9]W
                                                                                   SRVE[0-9][0-9][0-9][0-9]
                                                                                   connection pool(.)*source
                                                                                   CONM6007I
                                                                                   CNTR[0-9][0-9][0-9][0-9]
                                                                                   exp: (c1 && @BOOL_URL_node1

[root@node1 DB]# ▮
```

New Konsole

Figure 24-2   *wasmontkt report*

E-Mailing an Alert

You can send e-mails or pages to a set of users while monitoring specific events. This capability is configurable in the wasmon.conf file. However, it is also possible to directly send a notification via e-mail to a single user through the first pane of the WASMON™ console.

E-Mail: The Subject Dialog Box and Send E-mailButton

In the first pane of WASMON, you can enter an e-mail to directly send a notification to a user. This is mainly used for testing purposes and is not associated with the online filtering available in the first pane.

For example, to test whether the recipient admin@ibmsos.com can successfully receive e-mail from WASMON, you type in the E-mail:Subject text box **admin@ibmsos.com^ALERT:TESTING WASMON** as shown in the following illustration.

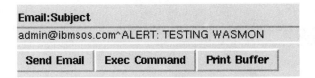

The e-mail will be sent when we press on Send E-mail and a message will be written in the activity pane.

```
14:34:55 17/04/02 : Alerting "root@node1.tcnd.com^ALERT: TESTING WASMON".
```

The caret (^) is used to separate the e-mail address from the subject. Also, there is a reason to use the Send E-mail button: dynamically updating e-mail will send a bunch of messages to the wrong addresses by the time you are typing an e-mail.

Filtering Events and E-Mailing Users

Because WASMON can filter regular expression while processing the WAS log, you can filter specific strings and notify a developer via e-mail when such a condition is met. For example, a developer can write specific data to the WAS' standard output using the System.out.println() method, and WASMON can filter such data while processing the log.

Triggering Scripts

Shell and Perl scripts are the most efficient way to achieve quick[3] results in administering computer systems. WASMON reads the scripts from the TriggersPool directory. This is where you will deposit the scripts that you need WASMON to execute when a condition is detected.

There are three possible ways to take functional action with WASMON:

▶ Through online filters and online commands

▶ Through online filters and online triggers

▶ Automatically through the wasmon.conf file and by selecting the appropriate checkboxes in the first pane of WASMON

The first and the second methods are based on operator interaction, since the data needs to be input in the first pane of WASMON.

The Online Filter Command and the Online Command

The online command is input in the first pane of the console.Here you type in a command that can refer to a shell script, or just a simple command that can be interpreted in your environment. For example, enter **echo voila!** and test it by clicking Exec Command. Usually, you need to associate such an action with a condition, for this reason, the online command is usually used in conjunction with the online filter command. The filtering command is enabled by checking the Command check button, and by typing in the text entry dialog labeled Filter Event a regular expression, a direct string, or a combination of both that you want to filter from the activity of WAS.

---

[3]   Also the cheapest, unlike using third-party application such as Tivoli and its nonportable macro language.

For instance, Figure 24-3 shows the filtering of the CNTR component followed by four digits and ending with an E (for error.) When the condition is met, the command that is entered in the text box labeled "Trigger commands / script" is executed. Notice that when you enter a command you must delimit it with the ^ character. For example, ^echo voila!^ is a valid command. The caret (^) is reserved to delimit inputted commands. You need to type in the ending caret (^) after you finish typing the command, so that the proper command will be executed. Do not attempt to insert or delete characters between the beginning and ending carets while WASMON is running and Command filter box is checked. WASMON keeps on dynamically updating the command, and by the time you finish your insertion between two carrets wrong commands will be executed.

Online Filter and Online Trigger

You can place all the scripts that you intend to invoke from within the wasmon program in the TriggersPool directory. Each filename must start with wm_*DDDD* as a prefix, where *DDDD* stands for a four-digit number. As an example, wm_0005_this_one_will_haltWAS.sh is a valid script name. From inside WASMON, the script number 0005 is used to refer to such a script. Only alphanumeric characters and the underscore character (_) are allowed in the script name. It is possible to specify an online trigger in the first pane of the WASMON console.

NOTE

0000 and 9001 to 9999 are reserved for internal WASMON use.

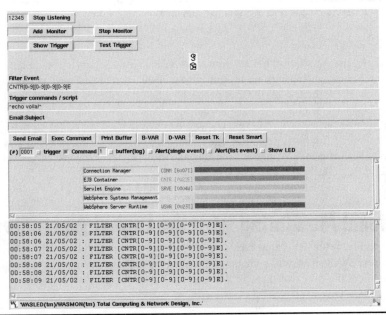

Figure 24-3   *Online filtering for the CNTR[0-9][0-9][0-9][0-9]E LED*

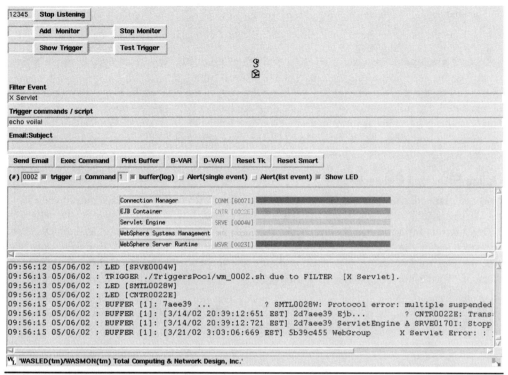

Figure 24-4   *Entering a filter and trigger manually in WASMON console*

For example, the illustration below shows the online filter X Servlet being entered in the Filter Event text box, and the online trigger number 0002 entered as well as the "trigger" checkbox is checked; the trigger 0002 is executed when the filter is detected by WASMON (see Figure 24-4).

We enabled the buffer with one line (as you can see in the first pane) so that we can print the content of the buffer to show the occurrence of the string being filtered "X Servlet" in the third pane. You need to click on Print Buffer after the trigger is executed to print the buffer content.

Conditional Monitoring with the Logical Alert Directives

WASMON can be set to send alert based on a combination of conditions. To build an assertion where WASMON will send an alert based on such a combination on conditions, WASMON offers the user two directives known as Logical Alert directives. Table 24-3 summarizes these two directives.

Directive	Filter Description
LOGICAL ALERT ON COMPONENT LIST	Filter components of WAS based on their severity criteria.
LOGICAL ALERT ON LIST FILTERS	Filters are regular expression

Table 24-3   *Logical Alert directives used in WASMON configuration file*

The Logical Alert directives are distinguished from the Direct Alert directives that we discussed previously for the following main reason: these directives allow you to enter a logical expression to be evaluated at run time; such that the conditional variables of the regular expression are mapped to the filters. An example will clarify this. Consider the following entries of the Logical Alert directives in wasmon.conf, as shown in Listing 24-3.

Listing 24-3   *Logical Alert directives defined in wasmon.conf*

```
1.    # Logical Alert directive for (any SRVE in error OR any CNTR in Warning)
2.    LOGICAL ALERT ON COMPONENT LIST:
        1,1,0002,dummy,maxou@ibmsos.com,,ALERT:SOMETHING ERROR,,(c1 ||
        c2),SRVE-E,CNTR-W
3.
4.    # Logical Alert directive using a condition on filters
5.    LOGICAL ALERT ON LIST FILTERS: 0,1,0002,,root@node1,,ALERT:SOMETHING
        FILTERED,,(c1 && c2) && ((c3 || c4) &&
        c5),SRVE[0-9][0-9][0-9][0-9]W,SRVE[0-9][0-9][0-9][0-9],connection
        pool(.)*source,CONM6007I,CNTR[0-9][0-9][0-9][0-9]
6.
7.    # Logical Alert directive using a B-VAR in the conditional expression
8.    LOGICAL ALERT ON LIST FILTERS: 0,1,0002,,root@node1,,ALERT:SOMETHING
        FILTERED,,(c1 && @BOOL_URL_node1.tcnd.com/wasbook/dumpenv) && (( c2 ||
        c3 || c4) &&
        c5),SRVE[0-9][0-9][0-9][0-9]W,SRVE[0-9][0-9][0-9][0-9],connection
        pool(.)*source,CONM6007I,CNTR[0-9][0-9][0-9][0-9]
```

For the entry on line 5, WASMON will evaluate the expression (c1 && c2) && ((c3 || c4) && c5) after mapping each of the numbered c's to each corresponding filter. The filters are numbered from left to right. There are as many numbered c's as the number of filters. In our example, we have five filters and five numbered c's. The c1,c2,c3,c4,c5 do not need to appear in order in the expression, however you should not specify a numbered condition (c's) more than once. If you do, you must specify the filter repetitively so that it match a numbered condition. Otherwise, WASMON will map the first numbered c's that it occurs to the filter in order going left to right.

NOTE

WASMON does not do validation, either on your logical construct, or on any entry in the wasmon.conf file. However, a lightweight validation is possible through the wasmontkt program. You need to input your configuration data in the wasmon.conf file, save it, and then run wasmontkt to see if your configuration file will be properly parsed by WASMON.

On line 8, the string @*BOOL_URL_node1.tcnd.com/wasbook/dumpenv* is called a b-var, it is a boolean variable that will evaluate to 1 (true) if the url *node1.tcnd.com/wasbook/dumpenv* is reachable from WASMON, and 0 (false) otherwise. b-var's are part of WASMON internal variables which we will not discuss in this chapter, but will be considered in Chapter 26 "Risk Management with WASMON™."

Wrapping Up

WASMON/WASLED is a simple monitoring application that can monitor WAS and its many runtime components. It is based solely on Perl Tk; therefore, it is easy and cost-effective to use. While it is a fine utility for monitoring WAS, it is also certainly a great tool to assist developers in understanding WAS activities.

WASMON console consists of three panes; the first pane allows you to interact with WASMON; the second pane is the WASLED part associated to the WASMON program, it shows WAS components activities; the third pane is where WASMON prints its messages.

In addition, two throbs in the first pane reveal the containment activities of WAS: the web container and the EJB container.

When transitioning from one severity level to another within the same component, WASLED (in the second pane) shows the color of the previous instance in its LED name and the color of the current instance in its LED light.

While the first pane of WASMON allows a limited filtering on the WAS activities, you can configure WASMON to process a filter, a list of filters, and logical expressions by editing the wasmon.conf file. Entries in this file are divided into two groups of directives: Direct Alert directives, and Logical Alert directives.

The wasmontkt program can parse the wasmon.conf file to generate a report about your configuration file. The report can be used for two reasons: first it shows if the wasmon.conf file is a properly formatted file, and second, you can use the report to get the mapping of a ticket toward the condition that caused the generation of such a ticket.

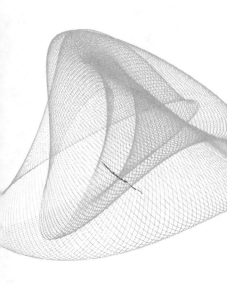

Monitoring and Tuning the System Resources

U NIX offers a set of standard commands to monitor system resources; in addition to these commands, AIX offers specific ones to accurately collect statistics on systemic resources. Because many WAS components run as Java processes that snowball a series of threads on a computer system, monitoring the system threads is of major importance in a WebSphere region.

Monitoring the system is an important activity that teaches us about the behavior of an application running on the system; WebSphere Application Server is such an application. In this chapter, you will learn about how the thread table and the activity of threads on the system helps us to understand the performance of Java-based application servers. AIX is the best system for organizing and scheduling threads.

This chapter also presents two tools: MrThread and MrTop. MrThread allows you to capture the following during run time: new threads being created, old threads being deleted, the distribution of the threads on an SMP system, and any change of a thread running on the system. On a Linux system, MrTop is the counterpart of MrThread. (For a clear understanding of Linux threads with WAS v4, refer to Chapter 8.)

This chapter uses many commands to monitor the system resources of any of these three platforms: AIX, Linux, and Windows NT. Some scripts are also presented to assist you in assessing WAS consumption of system resources. Finally, the chapter addresses caching EJB and tuning the UDB database parameters setting, such as the persistent session database.

Preparing Your Systems for the Performance Commands

This section briefly discusses the availability of the system commands to collect statistics or to measure performance on AIX, Linux, and Windows NT. You will also find out which software you must install to use extra commands and run some of the scripts presented in this chapter.

Performance Commands on AIX and Linux

AIX comes with a set of UNIX standard commands that are also known to Linux RedHat v7.2 or later. Table 25-1 shows the various UNIX standard commands that are available to both AIX and Linux.

In addition to these standard commands, we use the AIX performance pack that is installed from the perfagent.tools fileset. Table 25-2 shows some of the AIX proprietary commands that can assist you with measuring and tuning performance of applications running on AIX systems.

Command	Description
ps	Processes table statistics
sar	Provides a snapshot of the system activity
iostat	Provides usage statistics for CPU/IO subsystem
netstat	Displays contents of various system tables
nfsstat	Provides statistics on NFS/RPC interfaces
vmstat	Processes queue, memory, paging, CPU statistics, and so on
pstat	Prints content of kernel tables. This command is currently not available with the default installation of Linux Red Hat 7.2
top	Is available on Linux systems. Do not port this utility to AIX

Table 25-1   *Standard UNIX Tuning Commands*

Installing the System Agent on AIX

The System Agent for AIX is part of the filesets distributed on the CD-ROM of the AIX operating system. To install the System Agent on an earlier version of AIX than v4.3.3, follow these steps:

1. Install the perfagent.tools fileset and the perfagent.server fileset from your existing AIX 4.3 media before updating an existing AIX 4.3 system from the AIX 4.3.3.0 maintenance level.

2. Install the perl.rte fileset that is shipped with the AIX 4.3.3.0 maintenance level prior to updating an existing AIX 4.3 system.

Command	Description
svmon	Provides a snapshot of virtual memory
rmss	Simulates real memory configuration
vmtune	Sets virtual memory parameters
netpmon	Monitors network activity
no	Sets network variables
filemon	Provides statistics on file system performance
lockstat	Reports kernel lock statistics

Table 25-2   *AIX-Specific Tuning Commands*

This update causes the sysmgt.websm.apps 4.3.3.0 to be updated first to satisfy any prerequisites that the AIX 4.3.3.0 maintenance level install needs— which might fail otherwise.

Requirement for Windows NT

Windows NT also has some of the basic sets of commands to measure performance. To make sure of their availability, install the Windows NT performance pack. Additionally, in this chapter, we assume that you have installed the MKS Toolkit and Perl version 5 or later for Windows NT.

Essential Monitoring Commands: `ps`, `sar`, and `vmstat`

The `ps` command is an essential command to monitor the processes on a UNIX system. No other tool can give you a more accurate result in monitoring UNIX processes. Therefore, we will explore a few of the options of the `ps` command. Because the options differ between different UNIX platforms, you should read the manual pages of the `ps` command on your own system. Two other commands, `sar` and `vmstat`, are also discussed in this section. The following discussion applies to AIX and Linux.

Monitoring Processes with the `ps` Command

To get a snapshot of all the percentages of memory usage, on Linux, issue the `ps -e vg` command and on AIX, issue the `ps vgc` command. To monitor WAS process 1234, issue the `ps v 1234` command.

On Linux, the `ps` command is not fully compatible with the `ps` command of AIX systems, but at least it supports the AIX format descriptors and their codes, shown in Table 25-3.

Such support for the AIX format descriptors in the `ps` command is good because you will be able to select specific columns from the process table to monitor and wrap such a command in a script.

We will use the -o option to format the displayed information. The format variable can take multiple fields, as in the following command:

```
# ps -e -o comm=CMD -o pri,nice,vsz=SZ,stime
```

To print a specific header for a column, you assign the header title to the field name, as in comm=CMD. The previous command will print the processes with the following column header:

```
CMD PRI NI SZ ST
```

To monitor the memory usage of a process, use the v option followed by the process number, as in the following command:

```
# ps v 10842
```

Code	Normal	Header
%C	pcpu	%CPU
%G	group	GROUP
%P	ppid	PPID
%U	user	USER
%a	args	COMMAND
%c	comm	COMMAND
%g	rgroup	RGROUP
%n	nice	NI
%p	pid	PID
%r	pgid	PGID
%t	etime	ELAPSED
%u	ruser	RUSER
%x	time	TIME
%y	tty	TTY
%z	vsz	VSZ

Table 25-3   *Format Descriptors Used After the -o Option of the* ps *Command*

On AIX, this command returns the following information: PID, TTY, STAT, TIME, PGIN, SIZE, RSS, LIM, TSIZ, TRS, %CPU, %MEM, COMMAND.

The data collected is more meaningful when you wrap the previous command in a loop. The psv script, shown in Listing 25-1, is invoked as a command. The syntax of psv is shown next:

```
psv -p processNumber -s sleepTime
```

The *processNumber* is the numerical number of the process running on the system, and the *sleepTime* is the number of seconds to wait between each invocation of the ps command.

Listing 25-1   psv

```
1.   #!/usr/bin/perl
2.
3.   while(@ARGV) {
4.   if ($ARGV[0] eq "-p") {
5.       shift @ARGV;
6.       $process = shift @ARGV;
7.   }
8.   if ($ARGV[0] eq "-s") {
9.       shift @ARGV;
10.      $sleep = shift @ARGV;
```

```
11.  }
12.  else {
13.      last;
14.  }
15.  }
16.
17.  $i = 1;
18.  while (1) {
19.      $psv = 'ps v $process';
20.      ($headln,$dataln) = split(/\n/,$psv);
21.      # replace one or more spaces with semicolon
22.      $dataln =~ s/\s+/;/g;
23.      # get rid of any starting semicolon
24.      $dataln =~ s/^;//;
25.      ($pid,$tty,$stat,$time,$pgin, $size,$rss,$lim,$tsiz,
      $trs,$cpu,$mem,$command) = split(/;/,$dataln);
26.      print "$pid,$tty,$stat,$time,$pgin, $size,$rss,$lim,$tsiz,
      $trs,$cpu,$mem,$command\n";
27.      sleep $sleep;
28.      $i += 1;
29.  }
```

As shown in the following illustration, the psv script reports the data in a comma-delimited format about the process specified. Assume you want to monitor the processes started by WAS on AIX. Because each application server contains one Java machine, you will monitor the Java machine process started for a specific application server. As for monitoring the web application, you need to further monitor the thread started by the main process. Monitoring the thread is considered in the section "Threads and Processes" later in this chapter.

The report can be further used to correlate the extracted data to another set of data collected from other commands, or you can direct the output to a file and sort it with the BwjSort utility that we used in Chapter 22. The advantage of using the ps command is the possibility to isolate and monitor a specific process.

Next, we will discuss two commands, sar and vmstat, that report statistics about memory and CPU usage for the whole system.

Monitoring Memory and CPU with `sar` and `vmstat`

You can also monitor the memory and CPU usage for the system as a whole by using the `sar` and `vmstat` commands. These commands are useful to pinpoint a performance problem that is caused by an application such as WAS. For example, the Java machine appears to be idle, but it is really trying to search for free memory on the system.

The `sar` command results in a timestamped report about the system activities. The options of the `sar` command are different for AIX and Linux.

To report the memory paging activity on Linux, use the -B option, and on AIX, use the -r option. For example, on a Linux system, consider stress-testing the WASDG application using the SharkUrl utility discussed in Chapter 22, and then run the following command:

```
# sar -B 1 100
```

Listing 25-2 shows the results of this command.

Listing 25-2   *Output of* `sar -B 1 100`

```
1.   [root@node1 root]# sar -B 1 100
2.   Linux 2.4.9-13custom (node1)     08/30/2002
3.
4.   02:12:34 PM   pgpgin/s pgpgout/s  activepg  inadtypg  inaclnpg  inatarpg
5.   02:12:35 PM       0.00      0.00     53069     79468      6926     65535
6.   02:12:36 PM       0.00    416.00     53071     79493      6926     65535
7.   02:12:37 PM       0.00      0.00     53071     79516      6926     65535
8.   02:12:38 PM       0.00      0.00     53071     79538      6926     65535
9.   02:12:39 PM       0.00      0.00     53071     79558      6926     65535
10.  02:12:40 PM       0.00      0.00     53071     79580      6926     65535
11.  02:12:41 PM       0.00    700.00     53072     79607      6926     65535
12.  02:12:42 PM       0.00      0.00     53072     79631      6926     65535
13.  02:12:43 PM       0.00      0.00     53072     79653      6926     65535
14.  02:12:44 PM       0.00      0.00     53072     79654      6926     65535
15.  02:12:45 PM       0.00      0.00     53072     79654      6926     65535
16.  02:12:46 PM       0.00    408.00     53074     79654      6926     65535
17.  02:12:47 PM       0.00      0.00     53074     79654      6926     65535
18.  02:12:48 PM       0.00      0.00     53074     79654      6926     65535
19.  02:12:49 PM       0.00      0.00     53074     79654      6926     65535
20.  02:12:50 PM       0.00      0.00     53074     79654      6926     65535
21.  02:12:51 PM       0.00     24.00     53074     79654      6926     65535
```

During this stress test, the web application has adequately performed, even though the system has been paging at three peeks (lines 6, 11, and 16) and the number of inactive pages has been kept the same (inaclnpg). This reveals that the Java machine maintained enough free memory throughout the stress-test. Later, in the section "Monitoring Linux Processes with

MrTop (Mister Top)," you will learn how MrTop confirms that the heap of the Java machine is totally maintained in physical memory.

You can repeat the stress-test to realize that the context-switching of the system was highly active by issuing the `sar -w 1 100` command.

You can use the `sar` command on SMP systems. AIX offers the -P option, which allows you to report per-processor statistics for a specific processor. On Linux, the -U option is the counterpart of the -P option just mentioned.

Next, we will discuss the use the `vmstat` command. It provides statistics about CPU and memory usage. To iterate 100 times and collect data every three seconds, you issue this command: `vmstat 3 100`. Figure 25-1 shows the result if the `vmstat` command on Linux versus AIX.

Although the reported data is formatted differently on Linux than on AIX, the report commonly organizes the data into sections to reveal the following:

- **Statistics about the state of the runnable processes** This is reported under the header procs, and it shows the number of runnable processes in the column r, and the number of blocked processes waiting for I/O in the column b. On Linux, a third column labeled w for the number of swapped-out runnable processes is not important and must always be 0.
- **Memory usage and availability** This is reported under the header memory.

```
File Sessions Settings Help
[root@node2 /]# vmstat 3 100
   procs                      memory    swap          io     system         cpu
 r  b  w   swpd   free   buff  cache  si  so    bi    bo   in    cs  us  sy  id
 0  0  0      0   8580 241196 349732   0   0     0     2    8    13   0   0   7
 1  0  0      0   8580 241196 349732   0   0     0     0  273   919   6   1  93
 1  0  0      0   8580 241204 349732   0   0     0   395  207   475   2   1  98
 1  0  0      0   8580 241204 349732   0   0     0     0  307  1097   6   1  93
 0  0  0      0   8580 241204 349732   0   0     0     0  154   272   1   0  99
 0  0  0      0   8580 241204 349732   0   0     0     1  145   174   1   0  99
 0  0  0      0   8580 241204 349732   0   0     0     0  144   172   1   0  99
New Konsole
```

```
File Sessions Settings Help
# vmstat 3 100
kthr     memory             page              faults        cpu
----- ----------- ------------------------ ------------ -----------
 r  b   avm   fre  re  pi  po  fr   sr  cy  in   sy  cs us sy id wa
 0  0 10796 74251   0   0   0   0    0   0 171  231  48  1  3 93  3
 0  0 10796 74250   0   0   0   0    0   0 168   66  30  0  0 99  0
 0  0 10796 74250   0   0   0   0    0   0 167   46  30  0  0 99  0
 0  0 10796 74250   0   0   0   0    0   0 168   46  29  0  1 99  0
 0  0 10796 74250   0   0   0   0    0   0 168   67  30  0  0 99  0
 0  0 10796 74250   0   0   0   0    0   0 167   46  30  0  1 99  0
New Konsole
```

Figure 25-1 *`vmstat` report on Linux and on AIX*

► **Paging activity on AIX or swapping activity on Linux**   This is reported under the header page on AIX and the header swap on Linux. On AIX, several subcolumns are shown under the Page column, but you will be interested in the following: the pi column for the number of pages that have been paged, the po column for the number of pages that have been paged out, the fr column for the steal rate, and the sr column for the page scan rate. When the ratio of sr to fr is high, an application process, such as the Java machine of a web application that has been started under WAS, will seem to be idle as it is searching for available memory.

► **I/O operations, context-switching rates, and overall interrupt**   This is reported under the header Faults on AIX, and the headers io and system on Linux.

► **Percentage of CPU time**   This is reported under the header cpu, and it reflects the percentage of CPU time devoted for user average time (us column), system average time (sy column), idle average time (id column), and disk I/O wait average time (wa column, on AIX only).

Considering Windows NT Memory Usage

We will use the `sysinf` command to print the memory information from the GlobalMemoryStatus system call. The `sysinf` command is available only on Windows NT systems where the MKS Toolkit has been installed. For example, the command:

```
# sysinf memory -v
```

returns the following information about the memory: memory load, total physical memory, available physical memory, total page file bytes, available page file bytes, total virtual bytes, and available virtual bytes.

The w_mm script, shown in Listing 25-3, uses the `sysinf memory` command to print to standard output the difference in memory every 2 seconds on Windows NT. To run this script, you need to have Perl installed on your Windows NT system. This script will help you detect the difference in memory usage over time while running an application such as WAS.

Listing 25-3   *The w_mm script to monitor Windows NT memory*

```
1.   format top =
2.   LOAD       TPHY       APHY       TPAG       APAG       TVIR       AVIR
      DIFF-APHY DIFF-APAG DIFF-AVIR
3.      .
4.   format STDOUT =
5.   @<<<<<<<< @<<<<<<<< @<<<<<<<<< @<<<<<<<< @<<<<<<<< @<<<<<<<< @<<<<<<<<
      @<<<<<<<< @<<<<<<<< @<<<<<<<<
6.   $mem_load $mem_tphy $mem_aphy $mem_tpag $mem_apag $mem_tvir $mem_avir
      $diff_mem_aphy $diff_mem_apag $diff_mem_avir
7.      .
8.   .
```

```
9.    $==5;
10.
11.   $memstate = 'sysinf memory';
12.   @memlist = split('\\s+',$memstate);
13.   $mem_load = $memlist[0];
14.   $mem_tphy = $memlist[1]; $mem_aphy = $memlist[2];
15.   $mem_tpag = $memlist[3]; $mem_apag = $memlist[4];
16.   $mem_tvir = $memlist[5]; $mem_avir = $memlist[6];
17.
18.   until ( 1 == 2 ) {
19.   sleep(2);
20.   $mem_load_0 = $mem_load;
21.   $mem_tphy_0 = $mem_tphy; $mem_aphy_0 = $mem_aphy;
22.   $mem_tpag_0 = $mem_tpag; $mem_apag_0 = $mem_apag;
23.   $mem_tvir_0 = $mem_tvir; $mem_avir_0 = $mem_avir;
24.
25.   $memstate = `sysinf memory`;
26.   @memlist = split('\\s+',$memstate);
27.   $mem_load = $memlist[0];
28.   $mem_tphy = $memlist[1]; $mem_aphy = $memlist[2];
29.   $mem_tpag = $memlist[3]; $mem_apag = $memlist[4];
30.   $mem_tvir = $memlist[5]; $mem_avir = $memlist[6];
31.
32.   $mem_load_1 = $mem_load;
33.   $mem_tphy_1 = $mem_tphy; $mem_aphy_1 = $mem_aphy;
34.   $mem_tpag_1 = $mem_tpag; $mem_apag_1 = $mem_apag;
35.   $mem_tvir_1 = $mem_tvir; $mem_avir_1 = $mem_avir;
36.
37.   $diff_mem_load = $mem_load_0 - $mem_load_1;
38.   $diff_mem_tphy = $mem_tphy_0 - $mem_tphy_1; $diff_mem_aphy = $mem_aphy_0
          - $mem_aphy_1;
39.   $diff_mem_tpag = $mem_tpag_0 - $mem_tpag_1; $diff_mem_apag = $mem_apag_0
          - $mem_apag_1;
40.   $diff_mem_tvir = $mem_tvir_0 - $mem_tvir_1; $diff_mem_avir = $mem_avir_0
          - $mem_avir_1;
41.
42.   write;
43.   }
```

Figure 25-2 shows the output of w_mm.

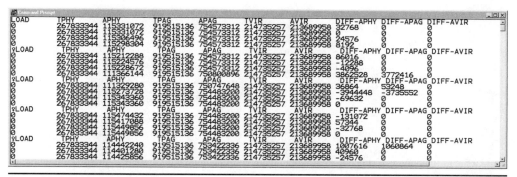

Figure 25-2   *The output of the w_mm script*

Considering Windows NT Network Usage

The `netstat` command is also available on Windows NT. When this command is used with the -s option, statistics about the many network protocols available on the system are printed. To print the network usage on Windows NT in real time, we will write a script to wrap the `netstat -s` command in a loop. The w_ipstat script, shown in Listing 25-4, prints the network usage on the system every two seconds.

Listing 25-4   *The w_ipstat script to monitor network usage on Windows NT*

```
1.   #!/usr/bin/perl
2.
3.   format top =
4.   RX-IP      TX-IP      REQ-IP     RXD-IP     TXD-IP     ERR-IP     DIS-IP
      REA-REQ    REA-OK     REA-BAD
5.   .
6.   format STDOUT =
7.   @<<<<<<<< @<<<<<<<< @<<<<<<<< @<<<<<<<< @<<<<<<<< @<<<<<<<< @<<<<<<<<
      @<<<<<<<< @<<<<<<<< @<<<<<<<<
8.   $ip_packets_rec $ip_packets_del $ip_out_req $diff_ip_packets_rec
      $diff_ip_packets_del $err_diff_ip_packets $ip_route_discard
      $diff_ip_reassembly_required $diff_ip_reassembly_successful
      $diff_ip_reassembly_failures
9.   .
10.
11.
12.  $ip_packets_rec = 0;
13.  $ip_packets_del = 0;
```

```
14.   $ip_reassembly_required = 0;
15.   $ip_reassembly_successful = 0;
16.   $ip_reassembly_failures = 0;
17.
18.
19.
20.   while (1) {
21.   sleep(2);
22.   $instant = time;
23.   $ip_packets_rec_0 = $ip_packets_rec;
24.   $ip_packets_del_0 = $ip_packets_del;
25.   $ip_reassembly_required_0 = $ip_reassembly_required;
26.   $ip_reassembly_successful_0 = $ip_reassembly_successful;
27.   $ip_reassembly_failures_0 = $ip_reassembly_failures;
28.   $netstat = 'netstat -s ';
29.   chop($netstat);
30.
31.   @lines = split('\n',$netstat);
32.   $i = 0;
33.   while ($i <= $#lines) {
34.       $line = $lines[$i];
35.       if ($line =~ /Segments Received/){
36.           @parts=split("=", $line);
37.           $parts[1] =~ s/\s//;$tcp_seg_rec=$parts[1];
38.       }
39.       if ($line =~ /Segments Sent/) {
40.           @parts = split("=", $line);
41.           $parts[1] =~ s/\s//;
42.           $tcp_seg_sent = $parts[1];
43.       }
44.       if ($line =~ /Packets Received/) {
45.           @parts = split("=", $line);
46.           $parts[1] =~ s/\s//;
47.           $ip_packets_rec = $parts[1];
48.       }
49.       if ($line =~ /Packets Delivered/) {
50.           @parts = split("=", $line);
51.           $parts[1] =~ s/\s//;
52.           $ip_packets_del = $parts[1];
53.       }
54.       if ($line =~ /Routing Discards/) {
55.           @parts = split("=", $line);
56.           $parts[1] =~ s/\s//;
57.           $ip_route_discard = $parts[1];
58.       }
59.       if ($line =~ /Output Requests/) {
60.           @parts = split("=", $line);
61.           $parts[1] =~ s/\s//;
62.           $ip_out_req = $parts[1];
```

```
63.       }
64.       if ($line =~ /Reassembly Required/) {
65.           @parts = split("=", $line);
66.           $parts[1] =~ s/\s//;
67.           $ip_reassembly_required = $parts[1];
68.       }
69.       if ($line =~ /Reassembly Successful/) {
70.           @parts = split("=", $line);
71.           $parts[1] =~ s/\s//;
72.           $ip_reassembly_successful = $parts[1];
73.       }
74.       if ($line =~ /Reassembly Failure/) {
75.           @parts = split("=", $line);
76.           $parts[1] =~ s/\s//;
77.           $ip_reassembly_failure = $parts[1];
78.       }
79.       if ($line =~ /Datagrams Received/) {
80.           @parts = split("=", $line);
81.           $parts[1] =~ s/\s//;
82.           $udp_datagram_rec = $parts[1];
83.       }
84.       if ($line =~ /Datagrams Sent/) {
85.           @parts = split("=", $line);
86.           $parts[1] =~ s/\s//;
87.           $udp_datagram_sent = $parts[1];
88.       }
89.       $i++;
90.  } # end while
91.  $ip_packets_rec_1 = $ip_packets_rec;
92.  $ip_packets_del_1 = $ip_packets_del;
93.  $diff_ip_packets_rec = $ip_packets_rec_1 - $ip_packets_rec_0;
94.  $diff_ip_packets_del = $ip_packets_del_1 - $ip_packets_del_0;
95.  $err_diff_ip_packets = $diff_ip_packets_rec - $diff_ip_packets_del;
96.
97.  $ip_reassembly_required_1 = $ip_reassembly_required;
98.  $ip_reassembly_successful_1 = $ip_reassembly_successful;
99.  $ip_reassembly_failures_1 = $ip_reassembly_failures;
100. $diff_ip_reassembly_required = $ip_reassembly_required_1 -
         $ip_reassembly_required_0;
101. $diff_ip_reassembly_successful = $ip_reassembly_successful_1 -
         $ip_reassembly_successful_0;
102. $diff_ip_reassembly_failures = $ip_reassembly_failures_1 -
         $ip_reassembly_failures_0;
103.
104. write; # end while (1)
105. }
```

You use the w_ipstat script to collect network data as the application server is running on the system. The result of running w_ipstat is shown in Figure 25-3.

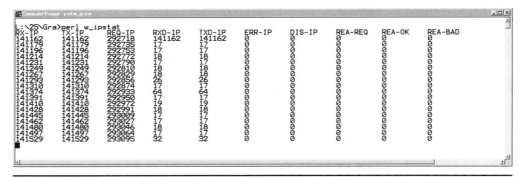

Figure 25-3 *The output of w_ipstat*

Threads and Processes

Thread support was added to AIX version 4 to add scalability to the execution of applications on AIX systems, in particular, to implement and exploit thread-intensive applications on SMP systems. In AIX version 4, the CPU scheduler dispatches threads that require less processing and less memory usage than the dispatching of processes known in previous versions of AIX. AIX version 4 is a good operating system to manage WAS processes considering the high use of threads.

A *process* is a collection of physical resources (memory and files access) required to run a program. A *thread* is the execution state of an instance of the program holding its own contents of the instruction-address register and the general-purpose register but sharing the process resources. Multiple threads can be started within a single process sharing the process resources.

Three major characteristics distinguish AIX v4.3.3 threads from all other operating systems: they can be prioritized, they can be scheduled, and they can be further scheduled according to a selective scheduling policy. The details of thread scheduling are beyond the scope of this book.

This section discusses how to monitor the threads on both AIX and Linux systems. On AIX, we will use the pstat command and MrThread command. On Linux, we will use the top command and MrTop command. Both MrThread and MrTop are part of the Gramercy Toolkit. Refer to Appendix A for instructions on downloading and using the Gramercy Toolkit.

Threads Statistics on AIX

On AIX, the contents of the various system tables can be interpreted and shipped out to standard output with the pstat command. The tables represent the mapping of the structures found in the /usr/include/sys/*.h header files.

In particular, when the -A option is used with pstat, the entries in the kernel thread table are displayed, as shown here:

```
# pstat -A
```

This command prints the thread table information, as shown in this illustration.

```
File Sessions Settings Help
# pstat -A
THREAD TABLE:

SLT ST    TID     PID    CPUID   POLICY PRI CPU    EVENT  PROCNAME    FLAGS
  0 s      3       0       0      FIFO   10  78            swapper
         t_flags: wakeonsig kthread
  1 s     105      1       0      other  3c   0            init
         t_flags: local wakeonsig cdefer
  2 r     205     204      0      FIFO   7f  78            wait
         t_flags: sig_avail kthread
  3 s     307     306      0       RR    24   0            netm
         t_flags: sig_avail kthread
  4 s     409     408      0       RR    25   0            gil
         t_flags: sig_avail kthread
  5 s     50b     408      0       RR    25   0 0020446c   gil
         t_flags: sig_avail kthread
  6 s     60d     408      0       RR    25   0 0020446c   gil
         t_flags: sig_avail kthread
  7 s     70f     408      0       RR    25   0 0020446c   gil
         t_flags: sig_avail kthread
  8 s     811     408      0       RR    25   0 0020446c   gil
         t_flags: sig_avail kthread
  9 s     91d    105a      0      other  3c   0            srcmstr
         t_flags: wakeonsig
                  sel
 10 s     aad     978      0      other  3c   0            dtlogin
         t_flags: wakeonsig cdefer
                  sel
 11 s     b27     71e      0      other  3c   0            lvmbb
         t_flags: sig_avail kthread
 New  Konsole
```

For each thread, there are 11 fields listed in the order shown in Table 25-4.

Attribute	Description
SLT	The slot number the thread occupies in the thread table.
ST	A status code
TID	The thread ID of the kernel thread
PID	The parent process ID of the thread
CPUID	The CPU number on which the thread is running. Threads in the same process can run on different CPUs at the same time.
POLICY	FIFO, RR, or other
PRI	The priority of the process or kernel thread. The higher the number, the lower the priority.
CPU	The percentage of time the process has used the CPU since the process started. This value is equal to the total time the process used the CPU divided by the elapsed time of the process, divided by the number of available CPUs in the system.
EVENT	-
PROCNAME	The process name that started the thread
FLAGS	The flags specific to each thread that describe the thread state

Table 25-4   *Attributes of Each Thread*

To get the default number of threads started by WAS on an AIX system, you run the `pstat` command, filtering the java threads, and counting these threads occurrences:

```
# pstat -A | grep java | wc
```

This command should be executed at two instances: before starting WAS and after starting WAS. Then you compute the difference to get the number of java threads started initially by WAS. Looking at the number of threads as the user load increases will give you an idea of whether the max threads number is being reached, which is also useful.

The following illustration shows the `pstat` command run at the two instances mentioned previously.

```
File Sessions Settings Help
# pstat -A | grep java | wc
        0        0        0
# pstat -A | grep java | wc
      110     1092     7370
# █

 New    Konsole
```

The result of the first command is 0 because no java threads are started at all. The result of the second command reveals that there are 109 java threads after starting WAS.

If you need to monitor the WAS threads, you need to poll the thread table at different instances as WAS is being used. You then compare the results between different instances to analyze how the system resources are being used in conjunction with the java threads started by WAS. This task is not that simple because the `pstat` command returns the information about all threads in an unformatted table that is not that simple to filter specific entries from it by using the commonly known UNIX commands.

Monitoring specific threads can be done programmatically with the command `MrThread` discussed in the following section.

Monitoring the Threads with *MrThread* (Mister Thread)

To use `MrThread` (Mister Thread), you should have installed the Gramercy Toolkit.

`MrThread` is a utility that runs on AIX to monitor any change in the threads on the computer system. The only requirement for `MrThread` to run is the `pstat` command and the Perl interpreter. The former is part of the standard UNIX tools, and the latter is installed by default on any AIX system.

The basic command to invoke `MrThread` is shown next and explained in detail in the bulleted list that follows:

```
MrThread -p processName [-d delay] [-n instances] [-f fieldsList] [-o
sortOrder] [-v] [-tt] [--Version]
```

▶ **processName**   The name of the process associated with the thread. For example, on an AIX system where WAS has been started, we will be looking for java as a process name.

▶ **delay**   The number of seconds to wait between each invocation of MrThread to poll the thread table. The default is 4 seconds. You need to specify a number that is likely to fit the responsiveness of your system when you issue the pstat command consecutively.

▶ **instances**   The number of instances desired to poll in the thread table. The default is 5. If you specify 3 for the number of instances, then MrThread will generate two outputs:
Output 1: compare instance 1 to instance 2
Output 2: compare instance 2 to instance 3
By looking at the changes in the threads, you can realize how the system is being used to run the application. For instance, on a multiprocessor system, a change in the CPUID can be detected to find out if the system processing resources are in use.

▶ **fieldsList**   A comma-delimited ordered list of the fields by which the reported data is sorted. The fields are within the following list: SLT, TID, PID, CPUID, PRI, and CPU. The following is an example of such a list:

▶ **sortOrder**   A comma-delimited ordered list showing the criteria of the sort of the fieldsList. Values in this list are either *a* for ascending or *d* for descending.

▶ **-v**   The printing of verbose information about the processes being considered by MrThread.

▶ **-tt**   The printing of thread tables processed by MrThread is enabled. The default mode of MrThread is silent.

▶ **--Version**   The printing of the version number of MrThread and the supported platforms.

MrThread compares the result of the thread table, waiting four seconds between two instances, and then it reports the threads in four groups, as shown is Table 25-5.

The following command prints a formatted thread table for all java threads started on the system:

```
# MrThread -p java -n 1 -tt
```

Threads Status	Description
All processName Threads	Enabled with the -more option. All processname threads are printed in case there is a difference in the threads between two subsequent instances.
Active Changing processName Threads	Prints any of the processname threads in which a change has been detected between two subsequent instances.
Vanished processName Threads	Prints the threads that existed in a previous instance but have been deleted in a subsequent instance.
Newly Created processName Threads	Prints any newly created thread that has been created in a subsequent instance.

Table 25-5   *Four Groups of Threads Reported by* MrThread

The result of the command is shown in Figure 25-4. Notice that only one instance is selected with the option -n 1.

The first command of Figure 25-4 shows that we have 109 java threads, and the second command uses `MrThread` to print these java threads.

You can also print it in ascending order of the priority (PRI) and descending order of the CPUID of the thread:

```
# MrThread -p java -n 1 -tt -f PRI,CPUID -o a,d
```

Say that the WAS startup on an AIX system takes approximately 90 seconds. To see how WAS initializes the java threads, follow these two steps:

1. Stop WAS on the system with the `kill` command. You can get the WAS processes that need to be killed simply with the `ps -f -o comm,pid` command. You then select these PIDs associated with the `java` command.
2. Run the command: `# MrThread -p java -d 25 -n 3 -more -v`.

Then start up the WAS server, and you will be able to see how the java threads are being started. Figure 25-5 shows the output of `MrThread` as WAS is starting.

To see how WAS creates a new thread, here is a simple example. Run `MrThread` with the following command:

```
# MrThread -p java -d 4 -n 5
```

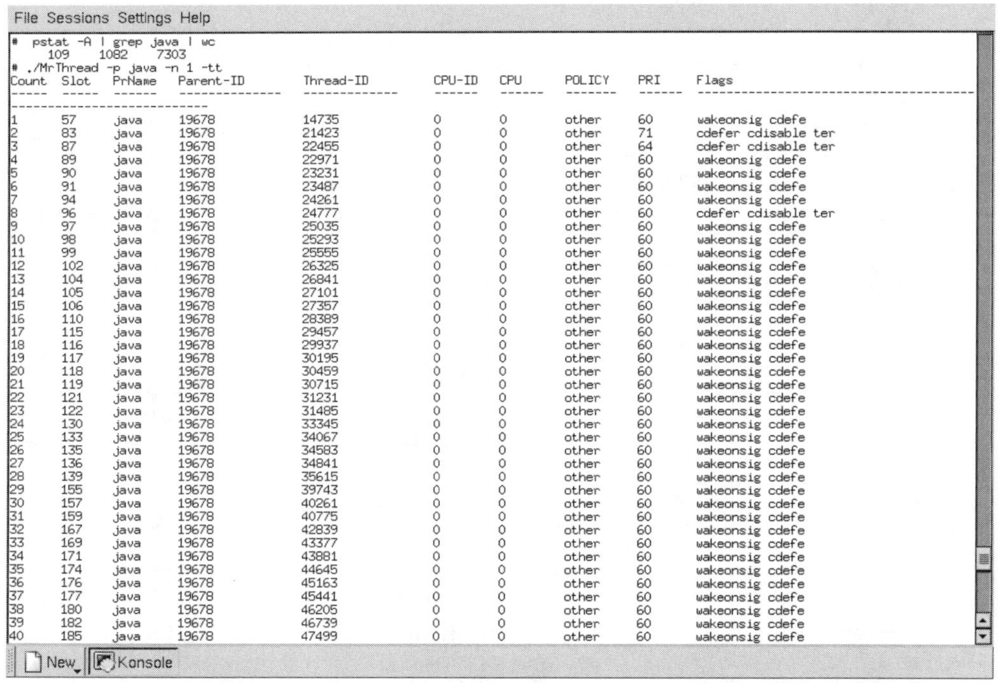

```
File Sessions Settings Help
#  pstat -A | grep java | wc
    109    1082    7303
# ./MrThread -p java -n 1 -tt
Count Slot  PrName Parent-ID      Thread-ID      CPU-ID CPU    POLICY  PRI    Flags
----- ----- ------ -------------- -------------- ------ ------ ------- ------ ----------------------------------------
--------------------------
1     57    java   19678          14735          0      0      other   60     wakeonsig cdefe
2     83    java   19678          21423          0      0      other   71     cdefer cdisable ter
3     87    java   19678          22455          0      0      other   64     cdefer cdisable ter
4     89    java   19678          22971          0      0      other   60     wakeonsig cdefe
5     90    java   19678          23231          0      0      other   60     wakeonsig cdefe
6     91    java   19678          23487          0      0      other   60     wakeonsig cdefe
7     94    java   19678          24261          0      0      other   60     wakeonsig cdefe
8     96    java   19678          24777          0      0      other   60     cdefer cdisable ter
9     97    java   19678          25035          0      0      other   60     wakeonsig cdefe
10    98    java   19678          25293          0      0      other   60     wakeonsig cdefe
11    99    java   19678          25555          0      0      other   60     wakeonsig cdefe
12    102   java   19678          26325          0      0      other   60     wakeonsig cdefe
13    104   java   19678          26841          0      0      other   60     wakeonsig cdefe
14    105   java   19678          27101          0      0      other   60     wakeonsig cdefe
15    106   java   19678          27357          0      0      other   60     wakeonsig cdefe
16    110   java   19678          28389          0      0      other   60     wakeonsig cdefe
17    115   java   19678          29457          0      0      other   60     wakeonsig cdefe
18    116   java   19678          29937          0      0      other   60     wakeonsig cdefe
19    117   java   19678          30195          0      0      other   60     wakeonsig cdefe
20    118   java   19678          30459          0      0      other   60     wakeonsig cdefe
21    119   java   19678          30715          0      0      other   60     wakeonsig cdefe
22    121   java   19678          31231          0      0      other   60     wakeonsig cdefe
23    122   java   19678          31485          0      0      other   60     wakeonsig cdefe
24    130   java   19678          33345          0      0      other   60     wakeonsig cdefe
25    133   java   19678          34067          0      0      other   60     wakeonsig cdefe
26    135   java   19678          34583          0      0      other   60     wakeonsig cdefe
27    136   java   19678          34841          0      0      other   60     wakeonsig cdefe
28    139   java   19678          35615          0      0      other   60     wakeonsig cdefe
29    155   java   19678          39743          0      0      other   60     wakeonsig cdefe
30    157   java   19678          40261          0      0      other   60     wakeonsig cdefe
31    159   java   19678          40775          0      0      other   60     wakeonsig cdefe
32    167   java   19678          42839          0      0      other   60     wakeonsig cdefe
33    169   java   19678          43377          0      0      other   60     wakeonsig cdefe
34    171   java   19678          43881          0      0      other   60     wakeonsig cdefe
35    174   java   19678          44645          0      0      other   60     wakeonsig cdefe
36    176   java   19678          45163          0      0      other   60     wakeonsig cdefe
37    177   java   19678          45441          0      0      other   60     wakeonsig cdefe
38    180   java   19678          46205          0      0      other   60     wakeonsig cdefe
39    182   java   19678          46739          0      0      other   60     wakeonsig cdefe
40    185   java   19678          47499          0      0      other   60     wakeonsig cdefe
New Konsole
```

Figure 25-4 *The thread table printed by `MrThread` and showing the java threads started by WAS*

```
File Sessions Settings Help
# ./MrThread -p java -d 25 -n 3 -more -v
starting polling instance 1
ending instance 1 [196 lines processed]
========================================================================
starting polling instance 2
ending instance 2 [245 lines processed]
========================================================================

21 57 74 97 102 103 105 112 122 124 141 157 185 189 197 201 203 204
=============== All java Threads
=============== Active Changing java Threads
=============== Vanishes java Threads
=============== Newly Created java Threads
Count  Slot  PrName  Parent-ID      Thread-ID     CPU-ID  CPU   POLICY   PRI    Flags
-----  ----  ------  ---------      ---------     ------  ----  ------   ---    -----
1      21    java    20490          5537          0       0     other    68     wakeonsig cdefe
2      57    java    16676          14739         0       b     other    71     cdefer cdisable ter
3      74    java    20490          19153         0       0     other    68     wakeonsig cdefe
4      97    java    16676          25041         0       0     other    60     wakeonsig cdefe
5      102   java    16676          26329         0       0     other    60     wakeonsig cdefe
6      103   java    16676          26589         0       1     other    60     wakeonsig cdefe
7      105   java    16676          27105         0       0     other    60     wakeonsig cdefe
8      112   java    16676          28909         0       0     other    60     wakeonsig cdefe
9      122   java    16676          31233         0       0     other    60     wakeonsig cdefe
10     124   java    16676          31757         0       0     other    60     wakeonsig cdefe
11     141   java    16676          36153         0       2     other    61     wakeonsig cdefe
12     157   java    16676          40265         0       0     other    60     wakeonsig cdefe
13     185   java    16676          47503         0       1     other    64     cdefer cdisable ter
14     189   java    20490          48535         0       0     other    68     wakeonsig cdefe
15     197   java    16676          50645         0       0     other    60     wakeonsig cdefe
16     201   java    16676          51697         0       0     other    60     wakeonsig cdefe
17     203   java    20490          52077         0       0     other    68     wakeonsig cdefe
18     204   java    16676          52357         0       43    other    93     cdefe
starting polling instance 3
ending instance 3 [267 lines processed]
========================================================================
21 57 74 97 102 103 105 112 122 124 141 157 185 189 197 201 203 204
21 57 74 76 97 102 103 105 112 116 121 122 124 141 156 157 158 161 162 171 185 189 190 197 201 203 204
=============== All java Threads
1      57    java    16676          14739         0       b/0/0/ other    71     cdefer cdisable ter
2      97    java    16676          25041         0       0     other    60     wakeonsig cdefe
3      102   java    16676          26329         0       0     other    60     wakeonsig cdefe
4      103   java    16676          26589         0       1     other    60     wakeonsig cdefe
5      105   java    16676          27105         0       0     other    60     wakeonsig cdefe
6      112   java    16676          28909         0       0     other    60     wakeonsig cdefe
  New   Konsole
```

Figure 25-5   `MrThread` *showing the new threads created by WAS while the application server is starting*

As the command is executing, request the BeenThere test servlet (refer to Chapter 6) using the ZappUrl stress-tester that was discussed in Chapter 22:

```
# ZappUrl -c 12 -h 32 -t was.server.name -u
/webapp/examples/BeenThere -R stderr -vv
```

The `MrThread` output will show the newly created java threads, as shown in this illustration.

```
File Sessions Settings Help
=============== Active Changing java Threads
=============== Vanishes java Threads
=============== Newly Created java Threads
1      67    java    16694          17307         0       0     other    60     wakeonsig cdefe
2      74    java    16694          19161         0       0     other    60     wakeonsig cdefe
3      104   java    16694          26849         0       0     other    60     wakeonsig cdefe
4      108   java    16694          27881         0       0     other    60     wakeonsig cdefe
5      120   java    16694          30725         0       0     other    60     wakeonsig cdefe
6      125   java    16694          32019         0       0     other    60     wakeonsig cdefe
7      127   java    16694          32527         0       0     other    60     wakeonsig cdefe
8      145   java    16694          37173         0       0     other    60     wakeonsig cdefe
9      164   java    16694          42075         0       0     other    60     wakeonsig cdefe
10     165   java    16694          42333         0       0     other    60     wakeonsig cdefe
=============== Active Changing java Threads
=============== Vanishes java Threads
=============== Newly Created java Threads
1      67    java    16694          17307         0       0     other    60     wakeonsig cdefe
2      74    java    16694          19161         0       0     other    60     wakeonsig cdefe
3      104   java    16694          26849         0       0     other    60     wakeonsig cdefe
4      108   java    16694          27881         0       0     other    60     wakeonsig cdefe
5      120   java    16694          30725         0       0     other    60     wakeonsig cdefe
6      125   java    16694          32527         0       0     other    60     wakeonsig cdefe
7      127   java    16694          32527         0       0     other    60     wakeonsig cdefe
8      145   java    16694          37173         0       0     other    60     wakeonsig cdefe
9      164   java    16694          42075         0       0     other    60     wakeonsig cdefe
10     165   java    16694          42333         0       0     other    60     wakeonsig cdefe
#
  New   Konsole
```

Monitoring Linux Processes with MrTop (Mister Top)

MrTop (Mister Top) is a utility that is available with the distribution of the Gramercy Toolkit. MrTop can be used to print statistics on Linux processes and forked threads.[1] The syntax for the MrTop command is shown next, which is explained in detail in the bulleted list that follows:

```
# MrTop -t topOutput [-p processName] [-f fieldsList] [-o sortOrder]
[-v] [--Version]
```

► **topOutput**   A filename that contains the output from the top command on a Linux system. The current top version used is 2.0.7, and it can be reported on your system with this command: top -Version.

► **processName**   The name of the process MrTop will select from the output reported by the top command. For example, on a Linux system where WAS has been started, we will be looking for java as a process name. If not specified, the default is java.

► **fieldsList**   A comma-delimited ordered list of the fields by which the reported data is sorted. The fields are within the following list: PRI, NI, PID, CPU, MEM, RSS, SHARE, and SIZE. If this option is not specified, then the MrThread sort criteria is by PID followed by MEM in ascending order.

► **sortOrder**   A comma-delimited ordered list showing the criteria of the sort of the fieldsList. Values in this list are either *a* for ascending or *d* for descending.

► **-v**   The enabling of verbosity with -v so that MrTop prints the tables being processed. The default mode of MrTop is silent.

► **--Version**   The printing of the version of MrTop and the supported platforms; same as invoking MrTop without any option.

MrTop is still in beta; the final version of this utility will support instance comparisons of processes or threads similar to MrThread. You can obtain the final version of MrTop from www.tcnd.com.

Unlike MrThread, which works in real time on the AIX system, MrTop needs to read the data collected with the top command from a file. The next example shows how to use MrTop on a Linux system. It requires the stress-tester SharkUrl (refer to Chapter 22), the top command, and the MrTop utility. You will run the top command.

---

[1]   Refer to Chapter 5 for handling processes and threads on Linux.

Let's say the total elapsed time for the stress-test of a scenario as discussed in Chapter 22 is approximately 20 seconds. After restarting WAS, and before repeating the scenario, you execute the `top` command to collect data for approximately 28 seconds:

```
# top -n 14 -d 2 > top.data
```

This command iterates 14 times with a delay of 2 seconds, writing the output of the `top` command to the top.data file.[2] Then, as you start executing the previous command, you repeat the stress-test scenario. Finally, the top.data file is processed by `MrTop` with this command:

```
# MrTop -f top.data -p java
```

Figure 25-6 shows the output of `MrTop` for five iterations with a delay of 4 seconds in stress-testing the TellerLogged servlet.

`MrTop` revealed that during the stress-testing, there was no need to swap memory pages in and out. This is good because the Java machine heap is totally allocated to real memory.

To print more verbose information about the forked processes and the CPU usage time, use the -v option:

```
# MrTop -f top.data -p java -f CPU -o a -v
```

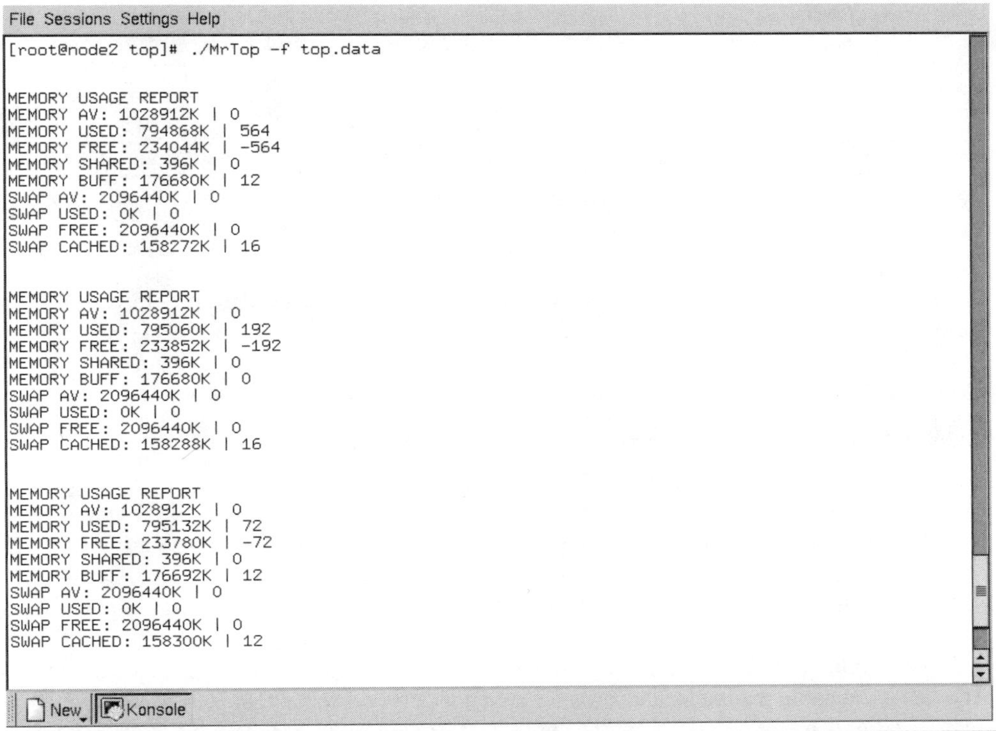

```
File Sessions Settings Help

[root@node2 top]# ./MrTop -f top.data

MEMORY USAGE REPORT
MEMORY AV: 1028912K | 0
MEMORY USED: 794868K | 564
MEMORY FREE: 234044K | -564
MEMORY SHARED: 396K | 0
MEMORY BUFF: 176680K | 12
SWAP AV: 2096440K | 0
SWAP USED: 0K | 0
SWAP FREE: 2096440K | 0
SWAP CACHED: 158272K | 16

MEMORY USAGE REPORT
MEMORY AV: 1028912K | 0
MEMORY USED: 795060K | 192
MEMORY FREE: 233852K | -192
MEMORY SHARED: 396K | 0
MEMORY BUFF: 176680K | 0
SWAP AV: 2096440K | 0
SWAP USED: 0K | 0
SWAP FREE: 2096440K | 0
SWAP CACHED: 158288K | 16

MEMORY USAGE REPORT
MEMORY AV: 1028912K | 0
MEMORY USED: 795132K | 72
MEMORY FREE: 233780K | -72
MEMORY SHARED: 396K | 0
MEMORY BUFF: 176692K | 12
SWAP AV: 2096440K | 0
SWAP USED: 0K | 0
SWAP FREE: 2096440K | 0
SWAP CACHED: 158300K | 12

New   Konsole
```

Figure 25-6   *MrTop* output showing the memory usage

---

[2]   For a large workload, you can enlarge the delay time and reduce the iteration time.

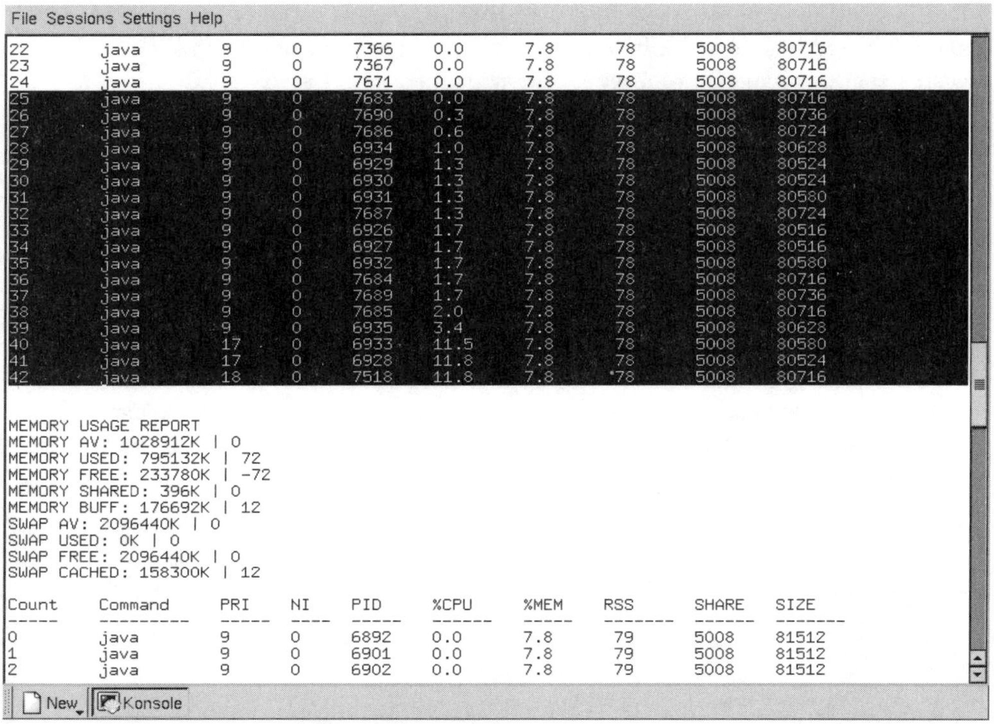

File Sessions Settings Help

```
22      java    9    0    7366    0.0    7.8    78    5008    80716
23      java    9    0    7367    0.0    7.8    78    5008    80716
24      java    9    0    7671    0.0    7.8    78    5008    80716
25      java    9    0    7683    0.0    7.8    78    5008    80716
26      java    9    0    7690    0.3    7.8    78    5008    80736
27      java    9    0    7686    0.6    7.8    78    5008    80724
28      java    9    0    6934    1.0    7.8    78    5008    80628
29      java    9    0    6929    1.3    7.8    78    5008    80524
30      java    9    0    6930    1.3    7.8    78    5008    80524
31      java    9    0    6931    1.3    7.8    78    5008    80580
32      java    9    0    7687    1.3    7.8    78    5008    80724
33      java    9    0    6926    1.7    7.8    78    5008    80516
34      java    9    0    6927    1.7    7.8    78    5008    80516
35      java    9    0    6932    1.7    7.8    78    5008    80580
36      java    9    0    7684    1.7    7.8    78    5008    80716
37      java    9    0    7689    1.7    7.8    78    5008    80736
38      java    9    0    7685    2.0    7.8    78    5008    80716
39      java    9    0    6935    3.4    7.8    78    5008    80628
40      java   17    0    6933   11.5    7.8    78    5008    80580
41      java   17    0    6928   11.8    7.8    78    5008    80524
42      java   18    0    7518   11.8    7.8    78    5008    80716


MEMORY USAGE REPORT
MEMORY AV: 1028912K  |  0
MEMORY USED: 795132K  |  72
MEMORY FREE: 233780K  |  -72
MEMORY SHARED: 396K  |  0
MEMORY BUFF: 176692K  |  12
SWAP AV: 2096440K  |  0
SWAP USED: 0K  |  0
SWAP FREE: 2096440K  |  0
SWAP CACHED: 158300K  |  12

Count   Command   PRI    NI    PID    %CPU    %MEM    RSS    SHARE   SIZE
-----   -------   ---    --    ---    ----    ----    ---    -----   ----
0       java      9      0     6892   0.0     7.8     79     5008    81512
1       java      9      0     6901   0.0     7.8     79     5008    81512
2       java      9      0     6902   0.0     7.8     79     5008    81512
```

New Konsole

Figure 25-7 *MrTop showing the java threads CPU usage on Linux*

This command prints the CPU usage in ascending order for the forked java threads during the five iterations, as shown in Figure 25-7.

Considering the Swap Paging Space

No matter how much memory is available on a computer system, you should give special consideration to the swap space. It is arguable whether huge (infinite) memory would be faster to access than swapping pages to spinning devices (such as hard disks). These hot static arrays of RAM can represent a buffer frame that can melt an iceberg and still reach a breakeven point after which they will become slower than swapped memory pages.

It is desirable to help the operating system kernel to swap pages in and out quickly. On AIX, the swappable paging space is implemented as a round-robin four-way algorithm. For this reason, it is better to have a paging space swapped on four separate hard disk drives that adhere to the swap page algorithm being in use.

Usually a swap space accounts for 1.8 times the real memory available in the system.

Considering EJB Caching

The performance penalty of a web application in a distributed system is due to the complexity of transferring object data into and out of a container. This is first because the protocols involved in these transfers have to operate heavily on large objects. The amount of information that we should account for in distributed objects must account for the extra network data that is saved in the object and is not visible to the programmer. In addition, some extra milestones of delay might be added if data security and encryption are put in place on these objects.

On the other hand, protocols using name resolution for the generality—to promote distributed processing—of enterprise programming are normally much slower than the processor. Also, what is more significant than the operational characteristics of the protocol, is the fact that the object transfer runs independently of the processing agent container. That is, usually the timing to transfer an object must be controlled internally to the container: this is called *synchronization*. WAS uses cache to gain some performance for the containment of the EJB. Yet, for a multithreaded application such as WAS, the solution is harsh: pausing the containment processing every time the cash needs to be cleaned.

WAS maintains a cache for the containment of the EJB. On WAS AE, the cache property is configurable through a set of five parameters: Cache size, Cache preferred limit, Cache absolute limit (or hard limit), Cache cleanup interval (or Cleanup interval), and Passivation directory. For simplicity, we will consider only WAS AEs EJB caching, as shown in Figure 25-8, where only two parameters need to be set: Cache size and the Cleanup interval. The cache size is the number of buckets in the cache's hash table.

For the WAS' EJB container caching, a thread is running in the background along with the thread(s) that are normally running under the EJB container. The latter is then termed a foreground thread. The problem is obviously lateral regarding how the foreground and background threads are going to cooperate to carry out a task on a shared chunk of memory. All threads run at the same level. However, there is more to consider in terms of which one would be using the processor time: if the background thread attempts to free entries while the application server threads are running, then there is performance cost due to the cache manager run time. In a production environment, the application server threads are unlikely to be idle.

The cache property in WAS does not provide us with a scheduling priority for such a thread.

Because WAS AEs runs on a single client, the update to the data source is exclusively done by the EJB container of the application server, in which case, there is a potential performance benefit from using a larger cache size.[3] To minimize the cost of Java machine heap size, and to allow the EJB container to optimize caching, it is recommended that you deploy your EJBs in a single container per application server.

If you increase the number of beans in cache, you also need to increase the Java machine heap size (as long as it fits in real memory).

---

[3]   In WAS AE, the database access is shared by multiple nodes and is titled *sharable,* in which case, the beans are cached for the duration of the transaction they are involved in: caching in a multinode WAS AE has little effect.

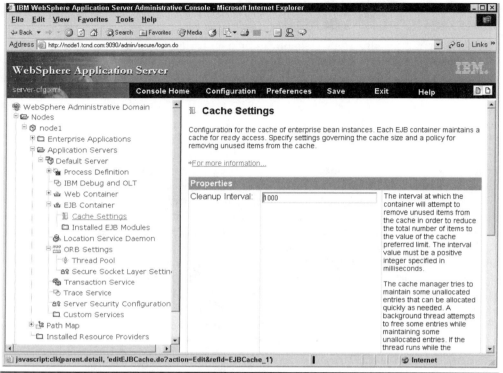

Figure 25-8   *EJB container cache setting in WAS AEs*

Considering Performance for the SESSION Database

Persistent sessions are stored to a database. Two approaches are available to help you gain more performance: WAS containment cache settings and systematic tuning of the database. The former is discussed in Chapter 17; in this section, we consider the latter, and we assume that our database name is SESSION.

Every database in the UDB has a set of parameters that can affect the performance of the application trying to pull or to push information to the database. Table 25-6 summarizes these parameters.

The database parameter settings can be updated simply with the db2 update command. For example, to update the applheapsz to 512 blocks, issue this command:

```
db2 update db cfg for <database> using applheapsz 512
```

Parameter	Default Value
BUFFPAGE	1000 with each page size equal to 4KB
APPLHEAPSZ	128 with each page size equal to 4KB
MAXAPPLS	40
PCKCACHESZ	max(8*MAXAPPLS,32)
DFT_DEGREE	1
MAXAGENTS	200
LOCKLIST	100 with each page size equal to 4KB
LOCKTIMEOUT	−1 (second)
MAXLOCKS	10 percent

Table 25-6   *UDB Database Parameter Settings*

The following summarizes each of the UDB database parameters and their estimated value.

▶   **applheapsz**   This parameter defines the memory blocks allocated to the application heap by the UDB. Test the performance by setting this value to 256 and 512. Usually a value of 512 is adequate.

▶   **maxappls parameter**   This parameter reflects the maximum number of applications that can connect to the database. You can estimate the value of this parameter by using the following formula: max application = maximum number of connections from an application server to the data source × number of cloned servers + any other connection from miscellaneous applications. Cloned servers are replicated WAS servers considered with WAS AE solely (refer to Chapter 5). Miscellaneous applications include the DBI-based scripts discussed in Chapter 9. To update the value of maxappls:

```
# db2 update db cfg for SESSION using maxappls <number>
```

Keep the value of maxappls lower than maxlocks; otherwise, increase the locklist. For the definition of maxlocks and locklist, refer to the parameters in this section.

▶   **maxagents parameter**   This parameter must be as large as the total number of maxapplszs for all databases allowed to be accessed concurrently. Take into account all EJB entity accesses, the administrative repository accesses, and all data source accesses from the administrative servers and their clones. To change this value, use the following command:

```
# db2 update dbm cfg using maxagents <number>
```

Enlarging the buffer pools reduces the disk access activity as the data is kept in memory. Before increasing the buffer pools, it is common to check the current usage of buffer pages by analyzing the data collected by the UDB system monitor. The UDB's system monitor collects statistical data as determined by the setting of its monitor switches. Enable the buffer-related information switch by using the following command:

```
# db2 update monitor switches using bufferpool on
```

This command affects only the current application, and the value is reset to off when the application terminates. An alternate command that enables the switch temporarily for all applications that are not currently connected to the database is shown here:

```
# db2 update dbm cfg using dft_mon_bufpool on
```

You can check on the settings of the monitor switches any time by issuing db2 get monitor switches. To reset the statistics, issue the command db2 reset monitor all.
At this point, you can view the buffer pool statistics:

```
# db2 get snapshot for bufferpools on SESSION
```

In the snapshot, locate the two lines that show the total buffer pool read time and total buffer pool write time. Both of these reflect the physical activity to the disk when reading and writing data. Progressively try to enlarge the buffer pools to reduce these times close to zero. First, get to know about the current number of pages by connecting to the target database, and then issue this command:

```
# db2 connect to SESSION; db2 "select * from syscat.bufferpools"
```

Usually, the default value is 1000 or 4MB, as reflected in the value of NPAGES, shown in Listing 25-5.

Listing 25-5   *Getting the number of pages used in the buffer pools*

```
# db2 connect to SESSION; db2 "select * from syscat.bufferpools"

   Database Connection Information

 Database server      = DB2/LINUX 7.1.0
 SQL authorization ID = DB2INST1
 Local database alias = SESSION

BPNAME        BUFFERPOOLID NGNAME       NPAGES   PAGESIZE  ESTORE
------------- ------------ ------------ -------- --------- ------
IBMDEFAULTBP           1 -                 1000      4096 N

  1 record(s) selected.
```

If your session data is estimated to be 16MB, you need to set NPAGES to –1 and then update the buffer page BUFFPAGE to 4000 or 16MB by issuing the following two commands consecutively:

```
# db2 alter bufferpool ibmdefaultbp size -1
# db2 update db cfg for SESSION using buffpage 4000
```

Restart your testing and get a snapshot of the UDB monitor as discussed previously. Your application should gain some performance as disk access is reduced.

▶ **locklist, maxlocks parameters**   These parameters can be used to lock tables and rows in a database so that the database manager can control the access of concurrent applications to the database. Each database uses one locklist, settable with the locklist parameter, to indicate the amount of storage held by these connected applications:

```
db2 update db cfg for SESSION using locklist <number>
```

Each application uses a percentage of the locklist that is held in maxlocks, which can be adjusted. Use UDB-monitoring to justify your setting for the locklist and maxlocks values. Set the lock switch to on, reset the snapshot, connect to the database, and then get a snapshot about the locks:

```
db2 update monitor switches using lock on
db2 reset monitor all
db2 connect to SESSION
db2 get snapshot for locks on SESSION
```

▶ **dft_degree parameter**   This parameter specifies whether to use SMP parallel procedures. To use SMP, set it to –1 by issuing the command db2 update db cfg <database> using dft_degree -1. SMP parallel procedure is not enabled by default as this value is set to 1. Do not use SMP parallel procedures unless your application retrieves information from the database using only the select statement.

▶ **applheapsz parameter**   This parameter is the number of memory blocks used by UDB to process application requests. Each memory block is 4KB, and the default number of blocks being set is typically 128KB. You need to change this value to 256 or higher by issuing the following command:

```
# db2 update db cfg for SESSION using applheapsz 512
```

Wrapping Up

WAS is a thread-intensive application. This chapter discussed how to gather information about processes, memory, and threads using the `ps`, `pstat`, `sar`, `vmstat` and `top` commands. You learned about two commands: `MrThread` and `MrTop`. `MrThread` can print the thread table along with information of the threads as being allocated in an SMP system. `MrTop` is an alternative to monitor forked processes (threads) on a Linux platform.

This chapter also introduced two scripts to measure memory and network usage on Windows NT. It concluded with a discussion on WAS EJB container caching and setting the UDB database parameters for the SESSION database.

Risk Management with WASMON

I f you are ambitious, you can configure WASMON to replace a failing WebSphere Application Server. You can start WASMON in supervisor mode so that the systemic and network resources of one or many servers can be *periodically* probed. Upon failure of any specific resource or service, a script can be triggered to take administrative action; for example, restart an application, reboot a server, or initiate a server takeover. You can also be notified of any failure, then enter in parole with WASMON to remotely order a specified action. The word "parole" is used because WASMON adopts a fiduciary relationship with the operator, allowing him or her freedom to roam while the systems in a WebSphere region are always under surrogate surveillance. Figure 26-1 shows WASMON monitoring the HTTP server, the WAS node, and the UDB server in a WebSphere region. WASMON communicates with a roaming operator via e-mail.

When you use WASMON, you can avoid having to manually assess the systemic data of its surrounding environment by assigning it to its *delegator,* also known as the WASMON helper program (wasmonhelper). The wasmonhelper periodically scrutinizes the surrounding systems by assigning tasks to gather systemic data to its delegatees: Java programs, system commands, shell and Perl scripts, and so on. In the rest of this chapter, the wasmonhelper program is referred to as the WASMON delegator or the delegator program.

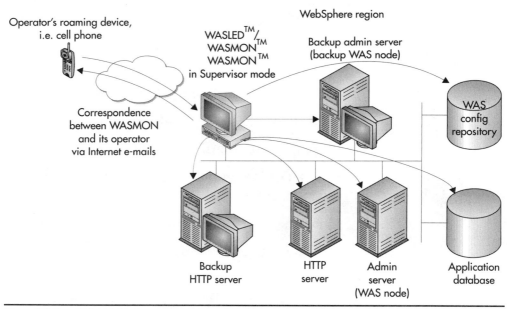

Figure 26-1 *WASMON in supervisor mode monitoring a WebSphere region*

The delegator prepares a set of variables that are used internally by WASMON and are part of the WASMON *internal variables*. Using these variables, you can program WASMON to take part in risk-managing applications and application servers in a WebSphere region.

There are four types of WASMON internal variables: s-var, b-var, d-var, and g-var. These variables play a major role in automating WASMON to excavate a failing server or its processes.

This chapter follows a top-down approach. It starts with a generic example using WASMON in supervisor mode and then proceeds with an explanation about configuration, using the delegator program. The WASMON internal variables are also explained, and examples are provided.

Chapter 24 did not use the full processing capabilities of WASMON, in which case, using a Linux server running on an Intel 486 processor with 64MB of RAM was sufficient[1]. Working with WASMON as explained in this chapter requires a Pentium II processor 333MHz (or better) with 256MB of RAM. For some of the WASMON variables to evaluate properly, you also need to have Lynx, remote shell (rsh), and a Java machine set on the system where the "wasmon" program is executed.

This chapter concludes with a discussion on how to use WASMON to generically monitor other log files, such as WAS' standard error file to which WAS writes errors when it is low on memory. Web applications that use the exception handler (discussed in Chapter 23) can also be monitored using WASMON.

Risk Management with WASMON: A Simple View

The WASMON supervisor mode is configurable through the SUPERVISOR directive that is specified in wasmon.conf. The supervisor mode evolved to provide two fundamental characteristics for WASMON monitoring. First, reliability is increased because the supervisor keeps on inspecting whether the other resources related to WAS are functional whenever no more WAS data flows to WASMON. Second, the supervisor can enter in parole with an operator, allowing such an operator to remotely request an administrative action via WASMON.

Putting WASMON in Supervisor Mode

You can start WASMON in supervisor mode by entering the following line in the wasmon.conf file:

```
SUPERVISOR:ON,15,1,1,0003,maxou@node4,SUPERVISOR ALERT,,(0)
```

After saving the wasmon.conf file to the directory where WASMON is installed, simply start "wasmon" by issuing the following command:

```
# perl wasmon
```

The third pane of Figure 26-2 shows that WASMON started in supervisor mode. The delta time is set at 15 seconds, as shown in the message.

---

[1]   WASLED/WASMON has been tested on a Linux 2.4.9 server installed on an Intel 486 with 64MB. It has also been tested on Windows NT server v4 running on Intel 200 MHz with 256MB. Not all functionality is available on Windows NT.

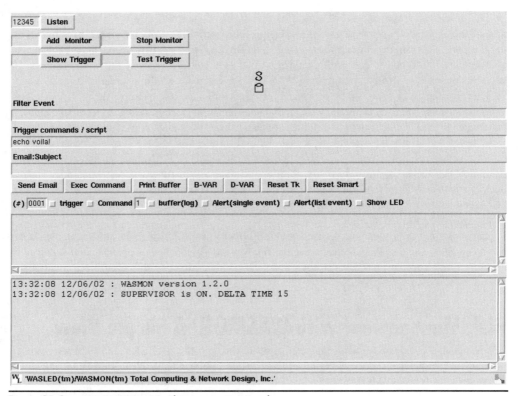

Figure 26-2 *WASMON started in supervisor mode*

In wasmon.conf, the SUPERVISOR directive is used to put the WASMON program in supervisor mode. This directive is followed by nine descriptive fields listed in order as follow:

1. **ON**   Field 1 is to switch on the supervisor. Can be ON or OFF.

2. **15**   Field 2 is the number of seconds set to the periodicity of the supervisor. This time is referred to as the *delta time* of the supervisor, for example, every delta time = 15 seconds the supervisor performs its checkup. Usually this number should be bigger, for example, 600 for checking every 10 minutes.

3. **1**   Field 3 is the number of times to send an e-mail as an alert. Can be 0 for none or 1 to send one e-mail.

4. **1**   Field 4 is the number of times to execute the trigger. It can be 0 for none or 1 to execute the trigger only once.

5. **0003**   Field 5 is the trigger number. You can use any triggers from 0001 to 9000 for the triggers saved in the TriggersPool directory. (Refer to Chapter 24.) 0000 and 9001 to 9999 are reserved for internal WASMON use.

6. **maxou@node1**   Field 6 is the e-mail address to which WASMON sends the alert.

7. **SUPERVISOR ALERT**   Field 7 is the subject.

8. **e-mail body**   Field 8 is the e-mail body is skipped, but a comma reserves its place.

9. **(0)**   Field 9 is a logical expression. By specifying (0), it always evaluates to false; therefore, the supervisor will not execute the alert. The logical expression is a Boolean expression that evaluates to true or false. It can be formed of one or more Boolean variables or sub-Boolean expressions. The following are three examples of Boolean expressions:

▶ (!(b1) && !(b2) && !(b3))

▶ (d1 || (d2 && !(b1)))

▶ (!(b1) && !(b2)) || (d1 && !(b3))

The *b*'s and *d*'s are all Boolean variables. In these examples, we assume that the *b*'s and *d*'s stands for b-var and d-var, respectively. The section "WASMON's Four Types of Internal Variables" later in this chapter explains the meaning of b-var and d-var. A Boolean expression's syntax is the same as the one evaluated in Perl. The exclamation point (!) is for negation.

Click on Listen, and WASMON will enter into a periodic cycle with delta time = 15 seconds. Assuming you do not have any data being sent to WASMON, the third pane of the console shows such a cycle.

```
13:32:08 12/06/02 : WASMON version 1.2.0
13:32:08 12/06/02 : SUPERVISOR is ON. DELTA TIME 15
13:32:25 12/06/02 : Trying to listen on 12345
13:32:25 12/06/02 : Now, accepting clients on 12345
13:32:25 12/06/02 : IDLE -- NOW: 2452440133225 NEXT SANE AT: 2452440133240  NO WAS ACTIVITY
13:32:41 12/06/02 : IDLE -- NOW: 2452440133241 NEXT SANE AT: 2452440133256  NO WAS ACTIVITY
```
`WL  'WASLED(tm)/WASMON(tm) Total Computing & Network Design, Inc.'`

Start the wasmoncl to send WAS data to WASMON, as explained in Chapter 24. For example, log in to a workstation that has access to a WAS standard output log file, and issue this command:

```
# tail -f $WAS_HOME/logs/default_server_stdout.log | wasmoncl 12345 pleiade
```

The supervisor is interrupted and does not enter its routine check as long as WAS data flows to WASMON within a time interval that is less than the delta time of the supervisor. The following illustration shows how the supervisor enters its routine check at time 13:22:25, 13:32:41, and 13:22:57. At time 13:33:04, a connection is established, and WASMON's supervisor will not be active unless there is no data flowing from WAS between 13:32:57 and 13:33:13.

```
13:32:08 12/06/02 : WASMON version 1.2.0
13:32:08 12/06/02 : SUPERVISOR is ON. DELTA TIME 15
13:32:25 12/06/02 : Trying to listen on 12345
13:32:25 12/06/02 : Now, accepting clients on 12345
13:32:25 12/06/02 : IDLE -- NOW: 2452440133225 NEXT SANE AT: 2452440133240  NO WAS ACTIVITY
13:32:41 12/06/02 : IDLE -- NOW: 2452440133241 NEXT SANE AT: 2452440133256  NO WAS ACTIVITY
13:32:57 12/06/02 : IDLE -- NOW: 2452440133257 NEXT SANE AT: 2452440133312  NO WAS ACTIVITY
13:33:04 12/06/02 : Great! -- Someone is trying to connect!
13:33:04 12/06/02 : Good, here we connect!
```
`WL  'WASLED(tm)/WASMON(tm) Total Computing & Network Design, Inc.'`

Either stop WAS or stop the wasmoncl so that no more data flows from WAS to WASMON, and the supervisor will be reactivated again, as shown in this illustration.

```
13:34:46 12/06/02 : Great! -- Someone is trying to connect!
13:34:46 12/06/02 : Good, here we connect!
13:34:51 12/06/02 : Hmm, zero length data from recv = graceful socket closure!
13:34:51 12/06/02 : kick client.
13:35:00 12/06/02 : IDLE -- NOW: 2452440133500 NEXT SANE AT: 2452440133515 LAST WAS AT: 2452440133451
13:35:16 12/06/02 : IDLE -- NOW: 2452440133516 NEXT SANE AT: 2452440133531 LAST WAS AT: 2452440133451
13:35:32 12/06/02 : IDLE -- NOW: 2452440133532 NEXT SANE AT: 2452440133547 LAST WAS AT: 2452440133451
13:35:48 12/06/02 : IDLE -- NOW: 2452440133548 NEXT SANE AT: 2452440133603 LAST WAS AT: 2452440133451
```

'WASLED(tm)/WASMON(tm) Total Computing & Network Design, Inc.'

The supervisor acts independently of WAS and is started periodically to evaluate its logical expression during the time when WAS is inactive.

In the supervisor's field 9, having a logical expression of (0) or (1) is not efficient, but it can prove to be a good way for testing. The following section shows how to put the WASMON supervisor in an active state by setting the logical expression to (1).

Putting the Supervisor in an Active State

The logical expression shown in the previous example is neutral, and it always evaluates to false. Consider having (1) as a logical expression so that it always evaluates to true. This will put the supervisor in an active state. Edit the wasmon.conf file and modify the SUPERVISOR logical expression:

```
SUPERVISOR: ON,15, 1,1,0003,maxou@node.tcnd.com,SUPERVISOR ALERT,,(1)
```

Save the change to the wasmon.conf file and restart WASMON. Click Listen and inspect the messages in the third pane. The supervisor is entered after 15 seconds, and an e-mail alert (Listing 26-1) is sent, along with the execution of the trigger 0003. This is done only once as specified in the properties of the SUPERVISOR.

```
13:43:45 12/06/02 : WASMON version 1.2.0
13:43:45 12/06/02 : SUPERVISOR is ON. DELTA TIME 15
13:43:58 12/06/02 : Trying to listen on 12345
13:43:58 12/06/02 : Now, accepting clients on 12345
13:44:01 12/06/02 : IDLE -- NOW: 2452440134401 NEXT SANE AT: 2452440134416  NO WAS ACTIVITY
13:44:01 12/06/02 : TICKET SENT: TK00 SUPERVISOR  Recipient[ maxou@node1 ]
13:44:01 12/06/02 : TICKET TRIGGER: TK00 SUPERVISOR  Trigger [ 0003 ]
13:44:17 12/06/02 : IDLE -- NOW: 2452440134417 NEXT SANE AT: 2452440134432  NO WAS ACTIVITY
```

'WASLED(tm)/WASMON(tm) Total Computing & Network Design, Inc.'

The e-mail alert is shown in Listing 26-1. The body of the e-mail shows a ticket of TK00, identifying the supervisor ticket number.

Listing 26-1   *Alert sent as e-mail to user maxou@node.tcnd.com*

```
1.    Date: Wed, 12 Jun 2002 13:44:01 -0400
2.    Message-Id: <200206121744.g5CHi1G04064@node1.tcnd.com>
```

```
3.    To: maxou@node1.tcnd.com
4.    From: wasmon@monitor.tcnd.com
5.    Subject: SUPERVISOR ALERT
6.    cc:
7.
8.    WASMON [TK00 SUPERVISOR] 13:44:01 12/06/02
```

Although the e-mail is sent to maxou@node1.tcnd.com, it is not required to have the e-mail of the recipient defined on the monitored node. The example used here is only for illustration. In addition, the e-mail functionality of WASMON requires that the workstation on which WASMON is running has the sendmail properly configured on it. Chapter 24 explained how to test whether or not WASMON can properly send e-mail through its console.

Entering in Parole with the Supervisor

You can enter in parole with WASMON via e-mail because WASMON can initiate such an e-mail-conversation. Entering in parole means that WASMON sends you an e-mail with a unique identifier. You reply using the identifier in the subject, asking WASMON to take a specific action by triggering a script. This simple task allows you to act remotely on a faulty application, a faulty server, or its services.

You enable parole in a logical expression that is to be negotiated and asserted by WASMON. The keyword PAROLE, when entered as the first word preceding the logical expression, will put WASMON *in parole state*. For example, the entry *PAROLE(1)* for the SUPERVISOR logical expression (field 9) will put WASMON in parole state because the logical expression is true by default.

Whenever the logical expression evaluates to true, WASMON will send you an e-mail with an identifier and then it will look for your reply. For this reason, a *wasmon* user account must be created on the same machine on which WASMON is running. The wasmon e-mail account must be used only by WASMON. The directive WASMON MAIL FILE is used to define the fully qualified name of the file where the e-mails of wasmon's user are written: for example, if WASMON is running on the server node1.tcnd.com on which the wasmon account has been created, then sending an e-mail to wasmon@node1.tcnd.com will end up being written to the file /var/spool/mail/wasmon (see Listing 26-2).

Listing 26-2   *Defining the WASMON e-mail file and the SUPERVISOR configuration property in wasmon.conf*

```
WASMON MAIL FILE: /var/spool/mail/wasmon
SUPERVISOR:ON,15, 1,1, 0003,
     maxou@node1.tcnd.com, SUPERVISOR ALERT,,PAROLE(1)
```

The SUPERVISOR definition shown on the second line must be entered on one line. Make sure that when the PAROLE keyword is used, the WASMON MAIL FILE is also set to point to the wasmon mail file. Also, make sure that the UNIX file permission for the e-mail file is set to allow WASMON to read this file.

Stop and restart WASMON. Because the logical expression (1) has been preceded by the keyword PAROLE, the supervisor will enter in parole by sending the user maxou@node1.tcnd.com (see Listing 26-3) an e-mail with a unique identifier. The following illustration shows the messages printed in the third pane of WASMON when it enters in parole.

```
14:56:56 12/06/02 : WASMON version 1.2.0
14:56:56 12/06/02 : SUPERVISOR is ON. DELTA TIME 15
14:57:48 12/06/02 : Trying to listen on 12345
14:57:48 12/06/02 : Now, accepting clients on 12345
14:57:49 12/06/02 : IDLE -- NOW: 2452440145749 NEXT SANE AT: 2452440145804  NO WAS ACTIVITY
14:57:49 12/06/02 : TICKET SENT: TK00 SUPERVISOR  Recipient[ maxou@node1 ]
14:57:49 12/06/02 : SUPERVISOR ENTERING PAROLE: IDENTIFIER 3d0799ad9dc291 RECIPIENT[ maxou@node1 ]
14:57:50 12/06/02 : TICKET TRIGGER: TK00 SUPERVISOR  Trigger [ 0003 ]
14:58:05 12/06/02 : IDLE -- NOW: 2452440145805 NEXT SANE AT: 2452440145820  NO WAS ACTIVITY
```
`W  'WASLED(tm)/WASMON(tm) Total Computing & Network Design, Inc.'`

The body of the e-mail contains the ticket number TK00 as the reason for sending this e-mail, followed by the unique identifier. Refer to Chapter 24 for directions on how to interpret the ticket numbers.

Listing 26-3   *E-mail sent to maxou@node1 by the WASMON supervisor via the PAROLE keyword*

```
1.   Date: Wed, 12 Jun 2002 14:57:49 -0400
2.   Message-Id: <200206121857.g5CIvnM06843@node1.tcnd.com>
3.   To: maxou@node1.tcnd.com
4.   From: wasmon@monitor.tcnd.com
5.   Subject: SUPERVISOR ALERT
6.   cc:
7.
8.   WASMON [TK00 SUPERVISOR] 14:57:49 12/06/02
9.   Reply back with subject: 3d0799ad9dc291_DDDD_R:sec:bf
```

The operator maxou replies with a plain body e-mail, but he will enter the unique identifier in the subject line and append to it his request: **3d0799ad9dc291**_0004_R:65:3.

Listing 26-4 shows the e-mail delivered to the wasmon user account and written to the file specified after the directive WASMON MAIL FILE shown in Listing 26-2.

Listing 26-4   *E-mail delivered to the wasmon account*

```
Date: Wed, 12 Jun 2002 14:58:57 -0400
From: root <maxou@node1.tcnd.com>
Message-Id: <200206121858.g5CIwv906918@node1.tcnd.com>
To: wasmon@monitor.tcnd.com
Subject: 3d0799ad9dc291_0004_R:65:3
```

The WASMON supervisor in parole detects the e-mail, and then it exits from its awaiting-for-reply state and enters in standby mode. The standby mode duration is 65 seconds in this particular example. The following illustration shows the activities taking place within WASMON.

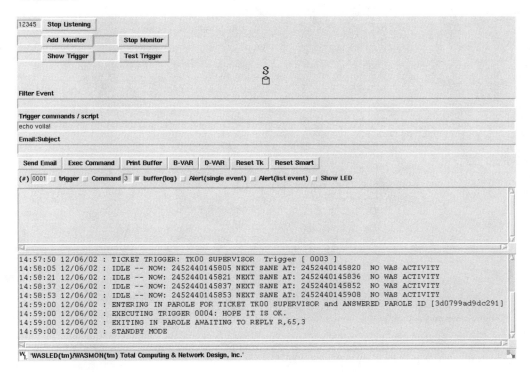

The WASMON supervisor processes maxou's request "0004_R:65:3" to trigger script number 0004, to switch the buffer line's size to 3, to enable buffering (shown in the next illustration), and to wait 65 seconds in standby mode before replying (R) with a report. Notice that the WASMON console is remotely controlled, the buffer line is set to 3, and the Buffer check box is highlighted.

After 65 seconds, an e-mail is sent to maxou@node1.tcnd.com, and WASMON closes its standby mode, as shown here.

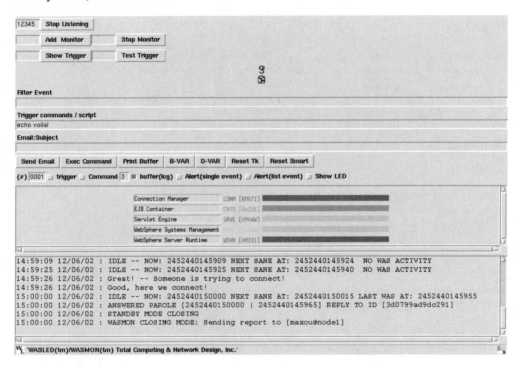

Listing 26-5 shows the e-mail whose body contains a generic report composed of @BVAR, @DVAR, and @BUFF.

Listing 26-5   *E-mail sent by WASMON to maxou@node1.tcnd.com as a final report*

```
1.    Date: Wed, 12 Jun 2002 15:00:00 -0400
2.    Message-Id: <200206121900.g5CJ00Q06960@node1.tcnd.com>
3.    To: maxou@node1.tcnd.com
4.    From: wasmon@monitor.tcnd.com
5.    Subject: WASMON CLOSING REPLY ID [3d0799ad9dc291]
6.    BOOL_ACTIVEPORT_node2_50000: 1
7.    BOOL_JNDILOOKUP_node1_900_WSsamples/AccountHome: 1
8.    BOOL_JNDISERVER_node1_900: 1
9.
10.

      BOOL_LOOKFILE_/opt/WebSphere/AppServer/installedApps/wasdg.ear/
      webapp/WEB-INF/ibm-web-ext.xmi_reloadingEnabled=\"true\"
```

```
11.   BOOL_LOOKPROCESS_18056:1
12.   BOOL_PING_node2:1
13.   BOOL_RSHLOOKFILE_node2_/etc/hosts_wasdb.tcnd.com:1
14.
```

```
BOOL_RSHLOOKFILE_node2_/opt/WebSphere/AppServer/installedApps/wasdg.
ear/webapp/WEB-INF/ibm-web-ext.xmi_reloadingEnabled=\"true\":1
15.
```

```
BOOL_RSHURI_node2_/opt/WebSphere/AppServer/installedApps/wasdg.ear/
webapp/WEB-INF/web.xml:1
16.
       BOOL_URI_/opt/WebSphere/AppServer/installedApps/wasdg.ear/webapp/WEB-
INF/web.xml:1
17.   BOOL_URL_node1.tcnd.com:9080_/wasbook/dumpenv:1
18.   BOOL_URL_node1.tcnd.com:9090_/admin:1
19.   BOOL_URL_node1.tcnd.com_/wasbook/dumpenv:0
20.
       DVAL1_CHECKSUM_/opt/WebSphere/AppServer/installedApps/wasdg.ear/webap
p/WEB-INF/web.xml:42848
       11
21.   DVAL1_LOOKPROCESS_18056:18056
22.
```

```
DVAL1_RSHCHECKSUM_node2_/opt/WebSphere/AppServer/installedApps/wasdg.
ear/webapp/WEB-INF/web.xml:42848
         11
23.   DVAL1_RSHLOOKPROCESS_node2_17061:17061
24.
       DVAL2_CHECKSUM_/opt/WebSphere/AppServer/installedApps/wasdg.ear/webap
p/WEB-INF/web.xml:42848
       11
25.   DVAL2_LOOKPROCESS_18056:18056
26.
```

```
DVAL2_RSHCHECKSUM_node2_/opt/WebSphere/AppServer/installedApps/wasdg.
```

```
ear/webapp/WEB-INF/web.xml:42848
        11
27.  DVAL2_RSHLOOKPROCESS_node2_17061:17061
28.
      DVAR_CHECKSUM_/opt/WebSphere/AppServer/installedApps/wasdg.ear/webapp
/WEB-INF/web.xml:0
29.  DVAR_LOOKPROCESS_18056:0
30.

DVAR_RSHCHECKSUM_node2_/opt/WebSphere/AppServer/installedApps/wasdg.
ear/webapp/WEB-INF/web.xml:0
31.  DVAR_RSHLOOKPROCESS_node2_17061:0
32.
33.
34.  ...
35.  SMTL0028W: Protocol error: multiple suspended transaction
36.  [3/14/02 20:39:12:651 EST] 2d7aee39 Ejb...        ? CNTR0022E:
      Transaction coord
37.  [3/14/02 20:39:12:721 EST] 2d7aee39 ServletEngine A SRVE0170I: Stopping
      Web Modu
38.  [3/21/02 3:03:06:669 EST] 5b39c455 WebGroup      X Servlet
Error: :
      java.lang.Nu
39.  llPointerException
```

The variables @BVAR, @DVAR, and @BUFF are discussed in the section "WASMON's Four Types of Internal Variables" later in this chapter. Mentioning @BUFF prematurely, this variable returns the content of the buffer that can also be printed in the WASMON console when you click the Print Buffer button in the first pane.

Print Buffer

Unless some data is flowing from WAS to WASMON, the buffer held in @BUFF is empty. Also, @BVAR and @DVAR might not be defined at this time unless you have configured the delegator as explained in the section "Considering the WASMON Helper Program: wasmonhelper." WASMON comes with a preconfigured set of dummy values so that you can test with the examples shown in this section.

Table 26-1 summarizes the statewide interaction between WASMON and its operator when the supervisor enters in parole.

State	WASMON	Operator maxou@node1
Starting WASMON	WASMON started in supervisor mode	-
Listen	WASMON listening but no WAS data; therefore, supervisor entered	-
Evaluate logical expression	Supervisor evaluates expression to true, PAROLE specified, and e-mail sent	Received e-mail
In parole	Monitoring continues	Read e-mail, identified from supervisor TK00
In parole	Monitoring continues	Reply back with id_0004_R:65:3
Exit in parole wait state and enter in standby	Detect e-mail from operator, process request, and enter in standby mode	Waiting for report
In standby but monitoring continues	Process request: WASMON in auto-buffer mode switches buffer on to 3; triggers 0004. Maybe new data flow from WAS due to the trigger	Waiting for report
Past 65 seconds, out of standby	Send e-mail to operator, e-mail contains report, and close in parole	Received e-mail
-	Continue monitoring	Read e-mailed report

Table 26-1   *Statewide Interaction Between WASMON and Its Operator*

Checking on the WAS Web Container

While the expressions (0) or (1) are inherently logical, an expression such as (!(@BOOL_URL_node1.tcnd.com_/wasbook/dumpenv)) is definitely more interesting because this expression evaluates to true only if the request http://node1.tcnd.com/wasbook/dumpenv fails. The exclamation point (!) is here to negate the evaluated expression.

This section mentions the Boolean variable @BOOL_URL prematurely. The idea is to introduce you to the WASMON supervisor and its logical expression in a practical way before going into detail about WASMON internal variables. You will learn how to set and configure these variables in the section "WASMON Delegation with the Helper Program: wasmonhelper."

Consider the following SUPERVISOR definition entered in the wasmon.conf instead of that shown in the previous section:

```
1.    WASMON MAIL FILE: /var/spool/mail/wasmon
2.    SUPERVISOR:ON,300, 1,1, 0003, maxou@node1, SUPERVISOR ALERT,,
          PAROLE(!(@BOOL_URL_node1.tcnd.com_/wasbook/dumpenv))
```

The supervisor is turned on; if data does not flow from WASMON in 300 seconds, then the logical expression is evaluated. The evaluation of the logical expression is equivalent to both checking the web container of WAS and checking the HTTP server service. If the variable @BOOL_URL_node1.tcnd.com_/wasbook/dumpenv returns 0, then the logical expression is evaluated to 1 (due to the negation with the exclamation point), in which case, the WASMON supervisor sends an alert and enters in parole.

The variable BOOL_URL_node1.tcnd.com_/wasbook/dumpenv is one of WASMON internal b-var variables. You will learn how to set such a b-var in the following section. To make use of this variable, you must know how to configure and run the delegator.

WASMON's Four Types of Internal Variables

The WASMON internal variables are separated into four categories—s-var, b-var, d-var, and g-var—denoting string, Boolean, differential, and glob variables.

- ▶ **s-var**   Internal variables that return a string as a value. The s-var variables are static and their values known a priori when WASMON is started.

- ▶ **b-var**   Boolean variables that return 0 for false and 1 for true. These variables are set periodically by the delegator, which makes them dynamic because their values may change with time.

- ▶ **d-var**   Differential variables that return Boolean (0 or 1) and the associated change between two different instances in time. These variables are set by the delagator, which makes them dynamic like the b-var variable.

- ▶ **g-var**   Glob variables that return a string. They are useful for checking on the status of WASMON. They are not static because they glob all variables, including those of type b-var and d-var.

All WASMON internal variables start with the at (@) character. These variables can be specified in the wasmon.conf file to be part of the following elements: logical expression, argument list of a trigger, e-mail subject, and e-mail body. Recall from Chapter 24 the comma-separated record that follows each directive (except the SUPERVISOR) in the wasmon.conf file:

```
n1,n2,DDDD,trigger-options, e-mail-address, cc-e-mail-address,
e-mail-subject,e-mail-body, logical-expression,
filter1[,filter2[...][,filterN]]
```

Table 26-2 summarizes each category of internal variables and where they may appear. The letter *Y* specifies the validity of an internal variable occurrence within the field of a configuration directive (in wasmon.conf) listed in the column.

The logical expression is similar to the one used with the Logical Alert directive and the SUPERVISOR directive. Only b-var and d-var can be specified within these logical expressions because their values are either 0 or 1.

When you pass one or more variables in the argument list of a trigger (trigger options), the whole list is being sent as one single argument, so you need to have your script splitting the list apart.

Var	Logical Expression	Argument List	E-Mail Subject	E-Mail Body
s-var @<svar>		Y	Y	Y
b-bar @BOOL_<v>	Y			
d-var @DVAR_<v>	Y			
g-var @BUFF @BVAR @DVAR		Y	Y	Y

Table 26-2   *List of Internal Variables*

The following sections discuss each of the four internal variable categories and the way the programmer can use them to logically program WASMON. The word "program" is used because as you will see, few of these variables allow you to logically program WASMON.

Static Variables: s-vars

The basic set of WASMON internal variables is called s-var, as shown in Table 26-3. Because these variables do not depend on the delegator, they are called static variables, or s-var. They are usually string.

Boolean Variables: b-vars

Boolean variables evaluate to true (1) or false (0). Usually, you need to negate a b-var to detect if what it refers to is at fault. You can specify b-var in the logical expression to be evaluated by WASMON while processing Logical Alert directives or when entering supervisor mode. Table 26-4 list the b-var currently supported with WASMON version 1.2.

Differential Variables: d-vars

A *differential variable* is an object that holds a Boolean value, a data-value1 at time t1, and a data-value2 at time t1+n* delta. When the Boolean value is true (or set to 1), this implies that the data-value1 at time t1 is different than the data-value2 at time t1+n* delta. The number *n* is initially set to 0; then it is incremented every time the data-value2 is evaluated.

The routine, known as the procedure, and its arguments executed by d-var, are also used to identify the d-var variables. The section "Understanding Differential Variables" explains in more detail how differential variables work.

There are currently five d-var variables, which are listed in Table 26-5.

Name of s-var	Variable Content
@BODY	The body of the e-mail.
@CC	A carbon copy of the e-mail or cc.
@E-MAIL	The e-mail address.
@FILTER	The filter or the list of filters.
@HTTP_ALTERNATE	The name of an auxiliary server that WASMON can rsh to. In case the HTTP server goes down, WASMON can start this server to masquerade the hostname and/or IP address of the dead server. This is a static value read from wasmon.conf, and set using the HTTP ALTERNATE directive.
@HTTP_SERVER	The name of the HTTP server that has been plugged in using the WAS module. This is a static value read from wasmon.conf, and set using the HTTP SERVER directive.
@LOGICAL	The logical expression being evaluated. This applies only to the Logical Alert directive and the SUPERVISOR directive.
@NUMMAIL	The number of e-mails to be sent. When used with SUPERVISOR, this variable returns either 0 or 1.
@NUMTRIG	The amount of time to trigger a script. When used with SUPERVISOR, this variable returns either 0 or 1.
@SUBJECT	The e-mail subject.
@TICKET	The ticket number that is opened for the corresponding assertion.
@TRIGARG	The arguments to be passed to the trigger.
@TRIGNUM	The number of triggers to be executed.
@TRIGURI	The fully qualified name of the script being triggered. This variable refers to the trigger URI of the script being triggered as it is defined relative to the WASMON root directory.
@WAS_ALTERNATE	The name of an auxiliary server that WASMON can rsh to it. Usually this is used in risk management to extract the latest WAS image of an interrogated server (a server that might have trouble and that has been interrogated by WASMON). You can design a trigger to extract the former image to the alternate server and then redirect the HTTP server to it by script editing (sed) the plug-in and restarting the HTTP server (@HTTP_SERVER).
@WAS_HOSTNAME	The WAS server machine being monitored originating the log file.
@WAS_NODE	The WAS node name (which is coincidentally the same as the server hostname on which WAS is installed).
@WAS_URI	The fully qualified name of the server where WAS is installed. For example, if WAS is installed in the directory /opt/WebSphere/AppServer on a Linux server whose hostname is node3.tcnd.com, then @WAS_URI returns node3.tcnd.com:/opt/WebSphere/AppServer, which is also equivalent to $WAS_NODE:/$WAS_HOME.

Table 26-3   *List of s-var or Static Variables*

Name of b-var	Explanation
@BOOL_ACTIVEPORT	Checks whether a server port is active, for example, whether UDB port 50000 is active. Checking whether a port is active also implies checking whether the server is reachable.
@BOOL_JNDILOOKUP	Looks up a JNDI by name on a particular server.
@BOOL_JNDISERVER	Checks whether the JNDI service is available on a particular server.
@BOOL_LOOKFILE	Checks for the occurrence of a string in a specified file.
@BOOL_LOOKPROCESS	Checks whether a process is running on a server.
@BOOL_PING	Pings a server.
@BOOL_RSHLOOKFILE	rsh to a server and checks for the occurrence of a string in a specified file.
@BOOL_RSHLOOKPROCESS	rsh to a server and checks whether the process is running on a server.
@BOOL_RSHURI	rsh to a server and checks for a fully qualified file name.
@BOOL_URI	Checks for a fully qualified filename.
@BOOL_URL	Checks whether a URL is resolvable.

Table 26-4   *List of b-var or Boolean Variables*

Name of d-var	Explanation
@DVAR_CHECKSUM	Differentiates the checksum of a file on the local machine.
@DVAL1_CHECKSUM	Contains the corresponding data-value1 at time t1.
@DVAL2_CHECKSUM	Contains the corresponding data-value2 at time t1 + n*delta.
@DVAR_RSHCHECKSUM	Differentiates the checksum of a file on a remote machine.
@DVAL1_RSHCHECKSUM	Contains the corresponding data-value at time t1.
@DVAL2_RSHCHECKSUM	Contains the corresponding data-value at time t1 + n*delta.
@DVAR_LOOKPROCESS	Differentiates the processnumber on the local machine.
@DVAL1_LOOKPROCESS	Contains the corresponding data-value1 at time t1.
@DVAL2_LOOKPROCESS	Contains the corresponding data-value2 at time t1 + n*delta.
@DVAR_RSHLOOKPROCESS	Differentiates the processnumber on a remote machine.
@DVAL1_RSHLOOKPROCESS	Contains the corresponding data-value1 at time t1.
@DVAL2_RSHLOOKPROCESS	Contains the corresponding data-value2 at time t1 + n*delta.
@DVAR_LOOKWASMONMAIL	Differentiates the existence of an identifier in the e-mail of a specified user (default wasmon user).
@DVAL1_LOOKWASMONMAIL	Contains the corresponding data-value1 at time t1.
@DVAL2_LOOKWASMONMAIL	Contains the corresponding data-value2 at time t1 + n*delta.

Table 26-5   *List of d-var or Differential Variables*

One of the purposes of differential variables is to either capture vital data that usually must not be changed (for example, the checksum of a web.xml file, a jar archive, or some .xmi file) or to detect any change in the state of an entity (for example, a process, a thread, and so on). The future release of WASMON supports differential variables that work on the boundaries of memory usage and threads consumption.

Glob Variables: g-vars

There are three glob variables: @BUFF, @BVAR, and @DVAR. These variables glob the buffer, the b-var variable, and the d-var variable, respectively. Table 26-6 describes these three variables.

Preparing the Internal Variables

Appendix E lists the directives used in wasmonhelper.conf. These directives are used mostly to prepare WASMON internal variables. Tables 26-7 and 26-8 list some of the internal variables and their corresponding directives and arguments as they are used in the wasmonhelper.conf file. A variable such as @BOOL_ACTIVEPORT_<hostname>_<portnumber> is used in the wasmon.conf file; however, this variable has a directive that needs to be specified in wasmonhelper.conf as shown in the following section.

The (1) that appears after each directive in the second column of table 8 stands for the d-vars refresh rate. You should usually specify this as 1. This value depicts the number of times to differentiate the d-var variable after the first difference occurred. Usually, you need to detect the first difference, and setting this value to 0 or 1 is appropriate. Setting the value to 0 will detect only the first difference. A d-var always returns 0 as long as there is no difference; however, once the first difference is detected the d-var returns 1. Because the difference is between the initial instance and any subsequent instance run in the future, the d-var will return 0 if any condition is restored to the initial instance.

NaList of g-var or Glob Variablesme of g-var	VariabList of g-var or Glob Variablesle Content
@BUFF	WASMON internally keeps some of the data processed in a buffer. The buffer size is limited, and its size is roughly defined by the line number. You enable the buffer by enabling its check box in the first pane and by typing a number for the number of lines to be held in the buffer. The WASMON supervisor may automatically switch this buffer on when it enters in parole with an operator.
@BVAR	Glob all b-vars.
@DVAR	Glob all d-vars.

Table 26-6   *List of g-var or Glob Variables*

Name of b-var	Directive and Arguments
@BOOL_ACTIVEPORT	BOOL ACTIVEPORT: *hostname portnumber*
@BOOL_JNDILOOKUP	BOOL JNDILOOKUP: *hostname portnumber name*
@BOOL_JNDISERVER	BOOL JNDISERVER: *hostname portnumber regularexpression*
@BOOL_LOOKFILE	BOOL LOOKFILE: *filename string*
@BOOL_LOOKPROCESS	BOOL LOOKPROCESS: *processnumber*
@BOOL_PING	BOOL PING: *hostname*
@BOOL_RSHLOOKFILE	BOOL RSHLOOKFILE: *hostname filename string*
@BOOL_RSHLOOKPROCESS	BOOL RSHLOOKPROCESS: *hostname processnumber*
@BOOL_RSHURI	BOOL RSHURI: *hostname fullyqualifiedfilename*
@BOOL_URI	BOOL URI: *fullyqualifiedfilename*
@BOOL_URL	BOOL URL: *hostname[:portnumber] uri*

Table 26-7   *The b-vars Variables (in wasmon.conf) to Directives Correspondence (in wasmonhelper.conf)*

WASMON Delegation with the Helper Program: wasmonhelper

The WASMON application comes with a wasmonhelper program that is located in the same directory as wasmon. The wasmonhelper program reads its configuration from wasmonhelper.conf. You need to edit the wasmonhelper.conf to enter monitoring directives that will eventually be returned as variables. Listing 26-6 shows a typical wasmonhelper.conf file.

Name of d-var	Directive and Arguments
@DVAR_CHECKSUM	DVAR CHECKSUM: (1) filename
@DVAR_RSHCHECKSUM	DVAR RSH CHEKSUM: (1) hostname filename
@DVAR_LOOKPROCESS	DVAR LOOKPROCESS: (1) processnumber
@DVAR_RSHLOOKPROCESS	DVAR RSHLOOKPROCESS: (1) hostname processnumber
@DVAR_LOOKWASMONMAIL	DVAR LOOKWASMONMAIL: (1) mailuserid numberedidentifier

Table 26-8   *The d-vars Variables (in wasmon.conf) to Directive Correspondence*

Listing 26-6 *wasmonhelper.conf*

```
1.   #
2.   #
3.   # WASLED(tm)/WASMON(tm)
4.   # (C) COPYRIGHT TOTAL COMPUTING & NETWORK DESIGN Corp. 2002
5.   #
6.   # wasmonhelper.conf contains the configuration for the wasmonhelper
       program.
7.   # Blank lines or lines starting with a hash (#) are not processed
8.   #
9.
10.  # wasmonhelper will refresh the data every 600 seconds (10 minutes)
11.  DELTA: 600
12.
13.  # BOOL
14.  BOOL ACTIVEPORT: node2 50000
15.

16.  # A known pattern must follow and be expressed as a regular expression
       without any space
17.  BOOL JNDISERVER: node1 900
       Leave(.)*com.ibm.rmi.iiop.CDRInputStream(.)*:IOR:
18.
19.  BOOL JNDILOOKUP: node1 900 WSsamples/AccountHome
20.
21.  BOOL PING: node2
22.
23.  BOOL URL: node1.tcnd.com   /wasbook/dumpenv
24.
25.  BOOL URL: node1.tcnd.com:9080   /wasbook/dumpenv
26.
27.  BOOL URL: node1.tcnd.com:9090 /admin
28.
29.  BOOL URI:
       /opt/WebSphere/AppServer/installedApps/wasdg.ear/webapp/WEB-INF/web.xml
30.
31.  BOOL RSHURI: node2
       /opt/WebSphere/AppServer/installedApps/wasdg.ear/webapp/WEB-INF/web.xml
32.
33.  BOOL LOOKFILE:
       /opt/WebSphere/AppServer/installedApps/wasdg.ear/webapp/WEB-INF/ibm-web-
ext.xmi
       reloadingEnabled=\"true\"
34.
35.  BOOL RSHLOOKFILE: node2
       /opt/WebSphere/AppServer/installedApps/wasdg.ear/webapp/WEB-INF/ibm-web-ext.xm
i
       reloadingEnabled=\"true\"
36.
37.  BOOL RSHLOOKFILE: node2 /etc/hosts wasdb.tcnd.com
38.
39.  BOOL LOOKPROCESS: 18056
40.
41.  BOOL RSHLOOKPROCESS: node2 17061
42.
43.  # DVAR
```

```
44.    DVAR CHECKSUM: (1)
           /opt/WebSphere/AppServer/installedApps/wasdg.ear/webapp/WEB-INF/web.xml
45.
46.    DVAR RSHCHECKSUM: (1) node2
           /opt/WebSphere/AppServer/installedApps/wasdg.ear/webapp/WEB-INF/web.xml
47.
48.    DVAR LOOKPROCESS: (1) 18056
49
50.    DVAR RSHLOOKPROCESS: (1) node2 17061
51.
```

On line 11, the DELTA directive specifies the iteration time frequency of the wasmonhelper program. Here, it is set to 600 seconds, which means that wasmonhelper will evaluate its variables every 10 minutes. The b-var and d-var[2] variables are evaluated every 10 minutes.

All the directives are self-explanatory. Each directive will map to a variable that you can reveal by running `wasmonhelper view`, which is explained in the next section.

The wasmonhelper program writes the b-vars and d-vars variables to the wasmon.delegate file. WASMON reads this file to resolve the b-var and d-var variables internally to its monitoring routines. Also, these are the values that WASMON globs and sends in a report when it comes out of the in parole mode and the standby mode.

Using the Internal Variables in wasmon.conf

You can find out what the internal variables are by running wasmonhelper with the view or ideal option:

```
# wasmonhelper view
```

This option allows the operator to print a list of the variables to the console. These variables are shown with their *ideal* values, where all b-vars are set to 1 and all d-vars are set to 0.

```
File  Sessions  Settings  Help

[root@node1 DB]# ./wasmonhelper view
BOOL_ACTIVEPORT_node2_50000      : 1
BOOL_JNDISERVER_node1_900        : 1
BOOL_JNDILOOKUP_node1_900_WSsamples/AccountHome : 1
BOOL_PING_node2                  : 1
BOOL_URL_node1.tcnd.com_/wasbook/dumpenv : 1
BOOL_URL_node1.tcnd.com:9080_/wasbook/dumpenv : 1
BOOL_URL_node1.tcnd.com:9090_/admin : 1
BOOL_URI_/opt/WebSphere/AppServer/installedApps/wasdg.ear/webapp/WEB-INF/web.xml : 1
BOOL_RSHURI_node2_/opt/WebSphere/AppServer/installedApps/wasdg.ear/webapp/WEB-INF/web.xml : 1
BOOL_LOOKFILE/opt/WebSphere/AppServer/installedApps/wasdg.ear/webapp/WEB-INF/ibm-web-ext.xmi_reloadingEnabled
=\"true\" : 1
BOOL_RSHLOOKFILE_node2_/opt/WebSphere/AppServer/installedApps/wasdg.ear/webapp/WEB-INF/ibm-web-ext.xmi_reloadi
ngEnabled=\"true\" : 1
BOOL_RSHLOOKFILE_node2_/etc/hosts_wasdb.tcnd.com : 1
BOOL_LOOKPROCESS_18056           : 1
DVAR_CHECKSUM_/opt/WebSphere/AppServer/installedApps/wasdg.ear/webapp/WEB-INF/web.xml : 0
DVAR_RSHCHECKSUM_node2_/opt/WebSphere/AppServer/installedApps/wasdg.ear/webapp/WEB-INF/web.xml : 0
DVAR_LOOKPROCESS_18056           : 0
DVAR_RSHLOOKPROCESS_node2_17061 : 0
[root@node1 DB]#
[root@node1 DB]# ./wasmonhelper view > wasmon.delegate
[root@node1 DB]# █

  New   Konsole
```

---

[2]   You may have to consider how d-var variables are updated because only one part of a d-var variable is being updated.

For testing purposes, you can generate the ideal set of internal variables and write it (pipe it) to the wasmon.delegate file:

```
# wasmonhelper ideal > wasmon.delegate
```

Then you can run WASMON and click the B-VAR and D-VAR buttons to print the contents of these variables.

| Send Email | Exec Command | Print Buffer | B-VAR | D-VAR | Reset Tk | Reset Smart |

Do not write to the wasmon.delegate file while wasmonhelper is running.

```
14:55:33 14/06/02 : B-VAR: BOOL_RSHURI_node2_/opt/WebSphere/AppServer/installedApps/wasdg.ear/webapp/WEB-
14:55:33 14/06/02 : B-VAR: BOOL_URI_/opt/WebSphere/AppServer/installedApps/wasdg.ear/webapp/WEB-INF/web.x
14:55:33 14/06/02 : B-VAR: BOOL_URL_node1.tcnd.com:9080_/wasbook/dumpenv 1
14:55:33 14/06/02 : B-VAR: BOOL_URL_node1.tcnd.com:9090_/admin 1
14:55:33 14/06/02 : B-VAR: BOOL_URL_node1.tcnd.com_/wasbook/dumpenv 1
14:55:35 14/06/02 : D-VAR: DVAR_CHECKSUM_/opt/WebSphere/AppServer/installedApps/wasdg.ear/webapp/WEB-INF/
14:55:35 14/06/02 : D-VAR: DVAR_LOOKPROCESS_18056 0
14:55:35 14/06/02 : D-VAR: DVAR_RSHCHECKSUM_node2_/opt/WebSphere/AppServer/installedApps/wasdg.ear/webapp
14:55:35 14/06/02 : D-VAR: DVAR_RSHLOOKPROCESS_node2_17061 0
```
'WASLED(tm)/WASMON(tm) Total Computing & Network Design, Inc.'

Printing the internal variables from within the WASMON console means that these variables have been defined in wasmonhelper. To make use of these variables, specify them in the wasmon.conf. (See the following section.)

When you run wasmonhelper, the program starts its cycle, updating the variables every 600 seconds and writing them to the wasmon.delegate file. On the other hand, WASMON reads this file to update its internal variables. For this reason, when using the delegator, you need to specify the refresh interval that dictates the periodicity for WASMON to read the wasmon.delegate file. In the wasmon.conf file, you can use the directive REFRESH INTERVAL to set the number of seconds in which the wasmon program refreshes its internal variables. If the supervisor is set to true (ON,) then the directive value set to the refresh-interval is ignored and the the delta time of the supervisor will take priority.

Using b-vars and d-vars in Logical Expressions

Logical expressions can be specified for Logical Alert directives and the SUPERVISOR directive. You can use b-bar and d-var in the logical expression of these directives. Consider Listing 26-7 as an example of the wasmon.conf file.

Listing 26-7   *Example of the wasmon.conf file*

```
1.    #
2.    # WASLED(tm)/WASMON(tm)
3.    # (C) COPYRIGHT TOTAL COMPUTING & NETWORK DESIGN, Inc. 2002
4.    #
5.    # wasmon.conf contains the additional configuration for the wasmon
        program.
6.    # Blank lines or lines starting with a hash (#) are not processed
7.    #
8.
```

```
9.    ### STATIC DATA ###
10.   HTTP SERVER:node1.tcnd.com
11.   HTTP ALTERNATE:node2.tcnd.com
12.   WAS HOSTNAME:node1.tcnd.com
13.   WAS NODE:node1
14.   WAS URI:/opt/WebSphere/AppServer
15.   WAS ALTERNATE:node2.tcnd.com
16.
17.   REFRESH INTERVAL:8
18.   WASMON MAIL FILE: /var/spool/mail/wasmon
19.   SUPERVISOR:ON,12, 1,1, 0002,maxou@node1,SUPERVISOR ALERT,,PAROLE((1==0)
         || !(@BOOL_ACTIVEPORT_node2_50000) ||
         !(@BOOL_URL_node1.tcnd.com_/wasbook/dumpenv) )
20.
21.   ALERT ON COMPONENT FAULT: 1,1,0012,Hello
         there,root@node1,admin@node3,ALERT:EJB CONTAINER ERROR, @BUFF,,CNTR
22.
23.   LOGICAL ALERT ON COMPONENT LIST:
         1,1,0002,restart node3,maxou@ibmsos.com,,ALERT:SOMETHING IS
         WRONG,@BUFF @TRIGURI,
         PAROLE(!(@BOOL_URL_node3.tcnd.com/wasbook/dumpenv)) && (c1 ||
         c2)),SRVE-E,CNTR-W
24.
25.   LOGICAL ALERT ON LIST FILTERS: 1,1,0002, @DVAR_CHECKSUM_/etc/hosts
         @DVAL1_CHECKSUM_/etc/hosts    ,maxou@node1,,ALERT:SOMETHING
         FILTERED,,PAROLE(@DVAR_RSHLOOKPROCESS_node2_15574 && c1 &&
         !(@BOOL_URL_node1.tcnd.com/wasbook/dumpenv)) && (( c2 || c3 || c4) &&
         c5),SRVE[0-9][0-9][0-9][0-9]W,SRVE[0-9][0-9][0-9][0-9],connection
         pool(.)*source,CONM6007I,CNTR[0-9][0-9][0-9][0-9]
26.
```

Here is how you can use WASMON to detect an error in the web container. On line 23 of Listing 26-7, the b-var requests the DumpEnv servlet, in which case it is expected to return 1 for a successful response from the web container (via the HTTP server). If this b-var returns a 0, then negating it with "!" is true, if WAS component SRVE is in error, or CNTR is in warning. Therefore, WASMON will enter in parole with maxou@ibmsos.com. Remember, too, from Chapter 24, that whether or not WASMON will enter in parole, the user maxou@ibmsos.com will receive a first ticket as an initial e-mail notification in which the body contains WASMON internal buffer (@BUFF) and the script URI that is being executed (@TRIGURI). WASMON executes the trigger 0002 and passes to it the argument "restart node2."

Considering the WASMON Helper Program: wasmonhelper

WASMON's internal variables can detect conditions of the surrounding environment in a WebSphere region. Conditions include the network connectivity to a server, the activity of a port, the state of a file (for example, web.xml file), a JNDI lookup by name, the HTTP serving status, the web container status, and so on. To collect all this data, WASMON delegates a data collection activity to its delegator: the wasmonhelper program. When using this extra capability of WASMON, you need to start the wasmonhelper first.

WASMON delegates such data collection to wasmonhelper for three reasons. First, WASMON does not compile the systemic data collection itself; it delegates it to wasmonhelper. The data to be collected might require a few to several seconds, and WASMON is busy monitoring the incoming data from a running WAS. Because the wasmonhelper program runs separately from WASMON, there is no delay caused by systemic data assessment.

Second, WASMON can run without the wasmonhelper. By adding the helper program separately, it is possible to have it configured separately by a system administrator.

Third, the data collected might refer to *differential variables,* each of which involves a time factor that is not appropriate for a run-time sensitive application (such as WASMON) to evaluate. Differential variables are further explained in the next section.

Understanding Differential Variables: d-var

The d-vars variables are called differential variables because they work on differentiating data collected for a particular function $F(x)$ between two instances. The function $F(x)$ can be a routine such that x is the argument passed to it. The difference result is returned as a Boolean in the @DVAR_F_x variable; data-set1 and data-set2 are returned in @DVAL1_F_x and @DVAL2_F_x; and the time when data-set1 and data-set2 are being collected is returned in @DVTM1_F_x and @DVTM2_F_x, respectively.

Unlike usual computational variables known to hold a value or an object, differential variables are functional variables that hold a Boolean value at the top level. They are functional because the Boolean value is dynamically updated due to a function that is held within the differential variable itself. Differential variables are objects that hold real-time data of a life system.

For example, a function can be a routine that gathers information about a process on a particular workstation, such as a routine rshlookprocess. The rshlookprocess is a function that is initially executed by the differential variable at time t1, and its returned value is held internally to the differential variable. Every 5 minutes, the differential variable executes the rshlookprocess and saves the returned value internally; in addition, it compares the saved value of rshlookprocess_v1(t1) with the most current value returned by rshlookprocess_v2(t1+n*delta). If the value is different,[3] then the top-level Boolean value of the differential variable is set to true. A program uses d-var to detect such a change and acts accordingly. In addition, a program can request to fetch the data of the returned value of the rshlookprocess at instant t1 and t1+n* delta, because these values are held inside the d-var variable in DVAL1_F_x and DVAL2_F_x.

In addition, a d-var variable holds a freeze attribute that you can set to a positive integer requesting a number of times to differentiate the values of the d-var after the first difference has been detected. Usually the d-var keeps on differentiating the values as long as they are equal.

---

[3]   This is a simple explanation about the differentiation made by a d-var. In reality, a d-var differentiation is more complex, for example, a comparison can be made at the object and its associated attributes level because a function can return more descriptive values that can be held in a record or an object.)

A unique number is needed to identify a d-var; however, because d-vars are functional and require a routine and its associated arguments, you identify a d-var by the function name and the arguments instead of the unique number to identify the variable.

Generic Monitoring with WASMON

You can use WASMON to monitor networked servers and any application that generates a log file. First, you can monitor networked servers because the WASMON supervisor runs periodically independently from WASLED whenever no data is flowing from WAS. You can elect not to run wasmoncl so that no WAS data flows to WASMON.

Because wasmonhelper uses many directives that can take different hostnames and different port numbers, you can monitor multiple servers and many different ports. Each monitored server and each monitored port will map to a different b-var or d-var variable that you can then use in the logical expression of the SUPERVISOR directive (defined in wasmon.conf).

Second, you can monitor any applications that generate a log file because WASMON does not enforce that the data to be filtered must be generated specifically from a WAS node. You can use generic filtering by specifying any of the four directives:

- ▶ Alert On Filter
- ▶ Alert On List Filters
- ▶ Logical Alert On List Filters
- ▶ Supervisor

It is also possible to replace the LEDs file with another file that is specific to any other application or application server if such an application generates well-defined messages such as WAS v4 in its log file.

One possibility of generic monitoring is to monitor when WAS is low on memory. In this particular case, you will have to monitor the stderr log file generated by WAS by redirecting its content to WASMON:

```
# tail -f $WAS_HOME/logs/default_server_stderr.log | wasmoncl 12345 pleiade
```

You can then use either the online filter or the generic filtering directives mentioned previously to look for particular strings that imply that WAS is going low on memory.

Monitoring Web Applications with WASLED/WASMON

In Chapter 23, we discussed the programming of the exception handler, WasdgException. The programming makes use of the bundle manager (BundleManager) to specify web application specific mnemonics. These mnemonics are grouped by components implemented and used by the web application, and are further described by English sentences. There are three properties files that fully provide the mapping of the mnemonics. Refer to Chapter 23 for a description of these properties files.

Using these properties files, we can generate two files: wasdg_components_r100.rec and wasdg_leddb_s_r100.rec. The first file, shown in Listing 26-8, maps a component acronym to a component explicit name. The second file, shown in Listing 26-9, maps mnemonics to severity levels and to their corresponding messages. The file nomination is immaterial.

Listing 26-8   *wasdg_components_r100.rec*

```
DATA:Data Access Component
UREG:User Registration
SESS:Session Containment
```

Listing 26-9   *wasdg_leddb_s_r100.rec*

```
DATA0001E:5: Database error: There is no connection to the remote database.
Make sure that you can access the remote database from the current server
DATA0001I:2: Using default settings for DBGUIDE database in dbguide.properties
DATA0002W:4: Cannot update database
UREG0001I:2: Updating database with new user registration
UREG0002I:2: Validating user registration
UREG0003W:4: Last name is required for user registration
UREG0004E:5: User has been denied access. User cannot login!
UREG0005W:4: User already registered
SESS0001I:2: Invalidating user session
SESS0002E:5: User logins or sessions are in excess than permitted!
```

In Listing 26-9, when mapping a mnemonic to severity level, consider the following numbering-to-color correspondence: 0 for black, 1 for blue, 2 for green, 3 for yellow, 4 for orange, and 5 for red. Usually black is used when the severity is of an unrecognized type; blue is used when the severity is not specified.

WASMON can then be started to monitor the web application that generates exceptions and messages using the mnemonics (or LEDs) described previously.

1. Start WASMON using the following command:

   ```
   # wasmon -xwasled -wc wasdg_components_r100.rec  -wl  wasdg_leddb_s_r100.rec
   ```

2. Start the web application and forward the log file to the exception being written to the server:socket where WASMON is listening:

   ```
   # tail -f /tmp/wasdg.log  |  wasmoncl  12345  node1
   ```

The first command monitors the WASDG application. The option -xwasled excludes the processing of all WAS exceptions and messages; the option -wc specifies the file that contains the description of the web components; and the option -wl specifies the file that contains the descriptions of the LEDs.

Figure 26-3 shows the WASMON when started monitoring the WASDG application. The second pane shows the mnemonics as being processed as LEDs.

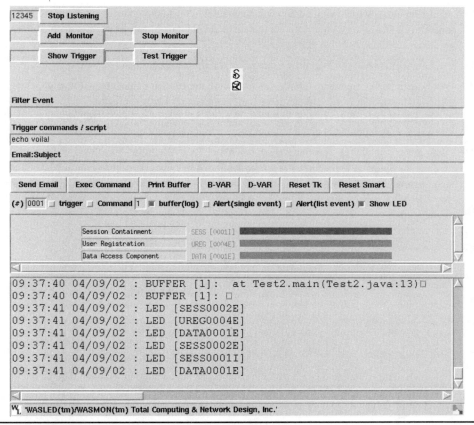

Figure 26-3   *WASMON monitoring the WASDG application*

The throbs in the first pane of the WASMON console will not be active unless you have defined a component whose acronym is SRVE (top throb) and another component whose acronym is CNTR (bottom throb).

Special Considerations When Running WASMON

This final section contains important points that a WASMON operator needs to consider:

▶ WASMON monitoring is based on the basic and advanced logging mode of WAS AE, WAS AE v4, or WAS AEs v5.

▶ Online filters must be eight or more characters.

▶ If more than one option is specified in the trigger argument, then the options sent to a trigger are sent as a single argument.

▶   Running WASMON on a RAM disk can make WASMON run faster. Although some operations require writing data on the disk, this is still minimal compared to the activity of Java serialization on an active server.

▶   It is recommended to define the e-mail file for the wasmon user account on a RAM disk.

▶   WAS activities might be minimal because of the nature of servlets loading, which initially takes place the first time a servlet is loaded. Therefore, the servlet container probe (in the first pane of the WASMON console) might not be changing state when the same servlet is loaded.

▶   You must redirect the standard output of WAS to a file other than the standard log file, because a programmer can write to the standard out messages that can put WASMON in a different state. Refer to Chapter 23 on how to write a web application to a specific log file. Chapter 23 discusses the implementation of an exception handler class and log writer class.

You can awaken WAS to start logging activity in several ways:

▶   You can request the SessionFairy servlet (Chapter 16) that will recreate the JSP file, SessionFairy.jsp, that you can then request.

▶   In the supervisor's logical expression, you can have a b-var that reactivates WAS, for example, calling a custom servlet called awake:
    `@BOOL_URL_node1.tcnd.com/wasbook/awake`

▶   You can trigger a shell script to restart WAS.

Wrapping Up

WASMON is a light application that is able to monitor to WAS standard output data, WAS' processes or any other processes, the networking state of the server on which WAS is running, any changing state in the file system or any changing state in the processes, and any privileged e-mail and its associated commands.

WASMON might lose contact with WAS if no data is being sent from the latter. Because WASMON monitoring occurs while WAS data is received, WASMON will not be able to decide on the state of WAS or the server on which WAS is running. Therefore, WASMON uses an internal supervisor that you must enable so that WASMON can check on the state of WAS and the corresponding systems in a WAS region.

The supervisor is disabled by default. However, it can be easily activated and configured by editing the wasmon.conf and setting the SUPERVISOR directive as follows:

```
WASMON SUPERVISOR:ON,600, 1,1, 0002,maxou@auream.tcnd.com,
    SUPERVISOR ALERT,,PAROLE(!(@BOOL_ACTIVEPORT_node2:50000)
        || !(@BOOL_URL_node1.tcnd.com/wasbook/dumpenv))
```

If WAS data does not flow to WASMON for a period of 600 seconds, then the supervisor is entered to evaluate its logical expression given in its configuration. The supervisor regularly continues performing such a check periodically as long as no WAS activity is detected. This means that WASMON in supervisor mode can monitor networked servers independently from WAS.

When the supervisor is activated, its delta time takes precedence over the refresh interval. However, if the data flows during the time that falls within this delta time, then the supervisor will not evaluate its logical expression because WASMON assumes that WAS is active.

WASMON uses a helper program called wasmonhelper to assess systemic data from the surrounding system. The data collected is common to any developer or administrator (for example, data that results from the `ping` command). WASMON delegates such activity to wasmonhelper because it is busy monitoring the WAS activity in real time and will try to avoid forking processes from within to collect the systemic data. Keep in mind that some data to be collected might take a couple of seconds, and wasmonhelper will make it available with a timestamp. WASMON uses the timestamp with the returned value to decide on a d-var.

The supervisor depends totally on the delegator, and the time given to gather the information is usually several seconds. In reality, the time spent to gather information depends on whether your networked environment is busy.

WASMON can also be started to monitor any client web application that throws exceptions similar to WAS exceptions (refer to Chapter 23). To monitor such a web application, you need to provide WASMON with two customized files: the web application components mapping, and the web application mnemonics mapping.

PART

VI

Appendixes

OBJECTIVES

Retrieving Information and Code Distribution

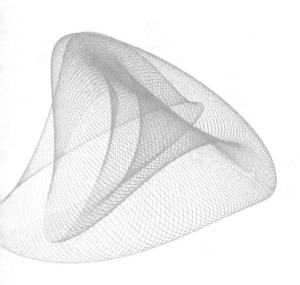

T his appendix explains how to download the applications and code distribution used in this book. It also shows how to access relevant documentation about the software.

The advantage of having the code distributed on the Internet is to provide fixes and last-minute updates whenever it is made available on the Web.

This appendix also explains how to install the code distribution, the Gramercy Toolkit, and the application WASLED/WASMON.

Essential Code Distribution Web Site

The following table lists software and documentation. Each cell contains four lines, generally followed by a few more lines of miscellaneous comments.

► The first line (in bold) is the name of the software or documentation.

► The second line is the web site where you can find the software or documentation.

► The third line contains a comment about licensing and/or requisite to download the code.

► The fourth line contains a suggested expression or keywords that you can enter in Google (www.google.com) to find out more about the software or documentation.

WAS AEs v4: WebSphere Application Server Advanced Edition Single Server v4
http://www-3.ibm.com/software/webservers/appserv
Fully functional trial version, but registration is required before downloading.
Google: "WebSphere Application Server" trial linux
Note: After accessing this site, select Download from the left pane, and you can select specific versions of WAS for different platforms.

WAS AE v3.5: WebSphere Application Server Advanced Edition v3.5
(See the previous cell.)

WebSphere Infocenter:
http:www-3.ibm.com/software/webservers/appserv/infocenter.html
Free of charge.
Google: Websphere infocenter download

IBM UDB v7.1 or v7.2: IBM Universal Database (previously called IBM DB2)
http://www6.software.ibm.com/devcon/devcon/docs/dbee3x72.htm
Fully functional trial version, but registration is required before downloading.
Google: "IBM Universal Database 7.2" download trial

WASDG code v1: The distribution code for the first edition of this text
www.osborne.com or www.tcnd.com
Free when you purchase this book.
Google: websphere jamaleddine

GTK v1: Gramercy Toolkit v1
www.osborne.com or www.tcnd.com
Fully functional trial version. Registration is required. License waved for educational institution.
Google: "Gramercy Toolkit"

WASLED/WASMON v1.2.1: WAS' LEDs monitoring and WAS Supervisor console
www.osborne.com or www.tcnd.com
Fully functional trial version. Registration is required. License waved for educational institution.
Google: "WASLED WASMON"

Unicode files: Unicode files provided by the Unicode Consortium
ftp://ftp.unicode.org/Public/
Free of charge.
Google: "unicode consortium" mappings

Apache SOAP User's Guide:
http://xml.apache.org/soap/docs/guide/
Free of charge.
Google: SOAP Apache deployment descriptor

Perl and Perl modules: Perl interpreter and modules as provided on CPAN
www.cpan.org or the cpan shell `cpan` >
Free of charge.
Google: libwww-perl Perl module
Note: Download the libwww-perl and DBI modules and install them. Alternatively, if connected to
the Internet, run the `cpan` command to start an interactive session at a cpan shell prompt: `cpan` >
Use www.cpan.org to search the CPAN organization web site for specific modules.

Linux RedHat v7.2: A fully functional Linux operating system
www.redhat.com
Free of charge.
Google: Linux RedHat 7.2 download ftp

Installing the Distribution Code

The distribution code for this book is available as a single file: wasbook-edition1.tar.gz,
which you can download from the Osborne web site. Download the code to the temporary
directory and extract the archive simply by invoking `gzip` followed by the `tar` command:

```
# gzip -d wasbook-edition1.tar
# tar xvf wasbook-edition1.tar
```

or you can directly use the `tar` command, whenever this command supports the gzip
compression with the t -z option:

```
# tar xfz wasbook-edition1.tar.gz
```

If you have extracted the archive in the /tmp directory, you will have the directory /tmp/BOOK,
which contains a list of directories that reflect the chapters and appendixes of this book. For
UNIX users, it is recommended to set up the BOOK directory relative to the root: /BOOK.
This is to simplify the editing of a few of the files of certain chapters that refer to other files
(such as properties files) found in other chapters. You do not need to extract the archive in the
root directory because it is possible to make a symbolic link to point to the directory where
the archive has been extracted:

```
# ln -s  /tmp/BOOK  /BOOK
```

The code of each chapter is contained in its own directory. Read the README.TXT to install and practice with the code. Be sure to read the chapter before testing its code.

Installing the Gramercy Toolkit

The Gramercy Toolkit is distributed as a compressed archive that you can download from the Osborne web site or from www.tcnd.com. Download the archive and extract it to a temporary directory. For example, if you downloaded the gramercy-toolkit_e1.tar.gz to the directory /tmp, then you extract its contents to /tmp/gtk-e1 simply by invoking `gzip` followed by the `tar` command:

```
# gzip -d gramercy-toolkit_e1.tar.gz
# tar xvf gramercy-toolkit_e1.tar
```

Or you can directly use the `tar` command, whenever this command supports the gzip compression with the -z option:

```
# tar xvfz gramercy-toolkit_e1.tar
```

First, change directory to /tmp/gtk-e1 and read the license agreement found in the LICENSE.TXT file. By continuing the installation you thereby agree to the terms and conditions as outlined in the LICENSE.TXT file. Instructions for continuing installation are briefly outlined here and can be found in the README file. Copy the files found in the /tmp/GTK-el-0 to the shared directory in your search PATH; for example, tools. Throughout the book, the directory /tools is used as a commonly shared directory. A quick way to copy the files from /tmp/GTK-el.0 to /tools is to use the `tar` command:

```
# cd /tools; tar cf - -C /tmp/gtk-e1 . | tar xf -
```

Make sure the program's bit mode is set to executable. For example, (assuming that the MrUnicode program is installed in /tools) to make sure the program can be executed by the owner, his or her group, and all others, issue this command:

```
# chmod 555 /tools/MrUnicode
```

Setting the GRAMERCY_DIR Environment Variable

Make sure the environment variable GRAMERCY_DIR is set to /tools:

```
# export GRAMERCY_DIR=/tools
```

You can also set the GRAMERCY_DIR variable in the system or user profile. Chapter 3 explains how to modify the system and user profile.

You must set the environment variable so that the utilities can find dependency libraries needed for their run time.

Getting the Version Number of the Tools

The *e1.0* in the suffix of the name of the gramercy-toolkit_e1.0 file refers to the distribution number of the toolkit. There is no version number for the toolkit.

You can obtain the version number of any of the tools by running the tool followed by the option -V.

Appendix D lists the programs provided by the Gramercy Toolkit and the chapters where they have been used. The README file contains the most recently updated information about the toolkit.

Installing WASLED/WASMON

WASLED/WASMON is an application that is started with a single program called wasmon. For this reason, the application is also called WASMON.[1]

WASMON is distributed free of charge when you purchase this book. Licensing is waved solely for academic use. However, you must read the license agreement before installing and running the product on your computer.

WASMON is distributed as the compressed file wasled-wasmon_v1.2.1.tar.gz, which you can download from the Osborne web site or from www.tcnd.com. The suffix of the file reflects the version number of WASMON.

Download the archive to a temporary directory and extract it using this command:

```
# tar xfz wasled-wasmon_v1.2.1.tar.gz
```

The directory WASMON is created. Locate the LICENSE.TXT file and read it. By continuing the installation, you thereby agree to the terms and conditions as outlined in the LICENSE.TXT file. Instructions for continuing installation are outlined in the README file. Refer to Chapter 24 and Appendix E for starting and using the WASMON console.

Because WASMON uses some of the Gramercy Toolkit's libraries, you also need to install the Gramercy Toolkit, as explained in the section "Installing the Gramercy Toolkit." For the latest version of WASLED/WASMON and its support of WAS v5, refer to Total Computing and Network Design, Inc. at its web site, www.tcnd.com.

Using This Book in Academic Disciplines

The five parts of this book have been written so that they can be split into three modules to be used in academic courses.

Students who would like to use Part III, "WAS Programming," do not need to read Parts I and II. A system administrator can set up the WAS computing environment as explained in Part I. Part IV can also be supplemented by Part III in a single course—in which case, the

---

[1] An additional program called WASLED, which is started with the command "wasled as a UNIX daemon, has not been released yet. The program wasled prints online information about WAS' LEDs and offers an applet that views the LED similar to the second pane of the WASMON console.

use of the stress-tester is highlighted in Chapter 22, and Chapter 23 contains the essential programming for logging and exception handling. Chapter 23 has been separated from Part III for two reasons: so that students will not be distracted by the mechanism of throwing exceptions and to enforce a discipline in a premature optimization by making students avoid throwing exceptions unnecessarily. The performance of web applications deployed under WAS can drastically suffer from such surplus in coding.

To use Parts III and IV independently of the rest of the text, you need to set up the WASDG development environment as outlined in the README file of chapters 3 and 4.

Generalizing J2EE Application Deployment Under WAS AEs

This section is useful after you have completed Chapter 11.

The scripts jtree, genwebxml, refreshear, and svlbuild that were presented in Chapter 11, build and deploy the WASDG application wasdg.ear with one web application: webapp.

The enterprise application display name, "The WASDG Application", is explicitly hard coded in the application.xml.

The document wasbook-jtree.pdf shows the altered code for the scripts of Chapter 11 so that you can deploy generic J2EE application under WAS AEs. The document also shows how to apply the modified scripts to build a generic enterprise application, UniBook.ear, which comprises Unicode mappings. The document wasbook-jtree.pdf and the modified code are part of the distribution code of this appendix.

Backing Up and Restoring

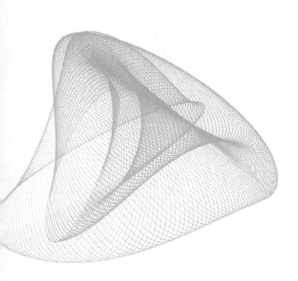

Hardware can fail, leaving an application in an unpredictable state. Therefore, management should instigate not only the quality assurance of a successful deployment, but also the possibility of its recovery. This appendix explains what to do in case unexpected hazardous events cripple your computer systems. The topics are general and apply to all platforms covered in this book.

Backing Up Your WAS Configuration Data

The backup strategy for configuration data differs depending on the version of WAS. WAS AEs v4 can be backed up using a simple UNIX command, such as the `cpio` or the `tar` command, whereas WAS AE requires the use of XMLConfig.sh, which is available in its binary distribution. In addition, because WAS AE saves its configuration data in a database repository, for safety[1], it is necessary that the database also be backed up.

Backing Up and Restoring WAS AEs

Because WAS AEs resides on a single server, you can perform its backup in two steps. First, stop the WAS server with $WASSTOP; then use the `tar` command to save the WAS AEs tree. If you want to save some storage space, then exclude the java directory. Here is a simple command to back up WAS AEs installed on node1:

```
# tar czf $COMMON_DIR/backup/wasaesNode1.tar -C $WAS_HOME   .
```

The archive is written to a commonly mounted directory $COMMON_DIR to all server machines. The czf options following the command direct `tar` to copy (c) and compress (z) the archive in a file (f) named wasaesNode1.tar.

To extract the archive, make sure the workstation on which you plan to restore WAS AEs is properly configured with its network resources: the same hostname as the original machine on which you have installed and then backed up WAS. The following commands will restore the wasaesNode1.tar to its initial directory:

```
# mkdir -p $WAS_HOME
# cd $WAS_HOME
# tar xzf $COMMON_DIR/backup/wasaesNode1.tar
```

It is also advisable to back up and restore the Java base installation directory and any JDBC driver used by the application server.

---

[1] You need to back up the configuration database in case the database server fails. You should not employ the backup and recovery method to migrate WAS configuration data from one server machine to another.

Backing Up WAS AE

There are three steps to backing up WAS AE:

▶ Back up the base installation image, which includes the installed WAS binary.

▶ Back up the WAS configuration data locally saved on the node itself.

▶ Back up the WAS repository data defined on the database server.

The following procedure applies to backing up WAS AE installed on node1. The WAS configuration data is assumed to be saved to the UDB database WASREP.

1. Back up the installation image. When you first install WAS and its fixpack, after setting the WebSphere domain and the WAS resources (such as virtual hosting and the JDBC driver), and before you install any enterprise application and its associated web applications, you need to make a backup image of this base installation to a reliable media. This can be done with the `tar` command:

```
# tar cvf /common/backup/WAS4AE-BASEIMG.tar -C $WAS_HOME  .
```

The archive image created here is the base image of the installed WAS binary. After saving this archive, you can start deploying enterprise applications in your WebSphere bailiwick.

2. Perform periodical backup of the configuration data using the XMLConfig:

```
#$XMLCONFIG -adminNodeName node1 -export
    $COMMON_DIR/backup/wasnode1.xml
```

3. Stop the node using WSCP:

```
wscp> Node stop /Node:node1/
```

4. Back up the local configuration data of WAS and the enterprise application data:

```
# tar cvf $COMMON_DIR/backup/wasnode1.tar -C $WAS_HOME
    bin/admin.config properties etc config installedApps
    installableApps
```

5. Back up the database repository. Log in with the UDB instance and make sure all applications have disconnected from the WAS database. You can use the `db2 list active` databases command to find out about the state of your database. Next, back up the database using this command:

```
db2 backup database WASREP to $COMMON_DIR/backup/WASREPnode1
```

Restoring WAS AE

The restore operation order is the same as the backup order. To restore a WebSphere domain to its previous state, follow these steps:

1. Ensure that the newly available server on which you will restore the WebSphere domain has the same network configuration as the one that failed. In particular, make sure the TCP/IP setting, the name resolution order through /etc/hosts and DNS, the ports defined

in its /etc/services, and the UDB client are properly installed. Restore the base image of the installed WAS binary:

```
# mkdir -p $WAS_HOME
# cd   $WAS_HOME
# tar xvf /common/backup/WAS4AE-BASEIMG.tar
```

2. Restore the local configuration data of the WAS in question:

```
cd $WAS_HOME; tar xvf $COMMON_DIR/backup/wasnode1.tar bin/
  admin.config properties etc installedApps installableApps
```

3. Re-create the UDB database repository and import the configuration data:

   ▶ Locate the createdb.sh script (or createdb.bat on Windows NT) and execute it on the node to be recovered.

   ▶ Edit the $WAS_HOME/bin/admin.config file and set the properties:

   ```
   install.initial.config=false
   com.ibm.ejs.sm.adminServer.createTables=true
   ```

4. Start the application server: $WASSTART.

5. Import the previously saved data:

```
$XMLCONFIG -adminNodeName yournode -import
    $COMMON_DIR/backup/wasnode1.xml
```

This should populate the WASREP database. However, you can use the DB2 `restore` command instead:

```
# db2 restore database WASREP from
    $COMMON_DIR/backup/WASREPnode1
```

Be aware that you should restore the database with this explicit command only after you stop the application server and make sure that the database is not active. (Use db2 list active databases to check on it.)

   ▶ Use the WSCP to stop the node: wscp> Node stop /Node:node1/.

NOTE

Backing up and restoring an IBM application is usually not that straightforward if the application is set up (and locked) with IBM License Use Management (LUM); this is not the case with WebSphere Application Server products, whose run time does not depend on LUM.

Migration Considerations

In Chapter 5, we used XMLConfig as a tool to migrate an enterprise application code from one WAS version to another. Such a migration is only administrative and is not contextual; that is, it does not take into consideration the change of the symbols in the programs.

Although Java code is meant to be portable to save corporations the cost of rewriting platform-independent modules, its migration from one version of WAS to another is not straightforward. In fact, some of the code must be rewritten when changing the version of WAS because the version of the Java machine is changed, resulting in deprecated Java methods.

The changes in code from one version of WAS to another is manifested in three areas: a newer Java version, different WAS libraries, and changes in J2EE specs.

It is recommended that you go over the migration thoroughly to examine each piece of code. You can use one of the following methods:

1. Cross references
2. Scripts to preprocess programs and make the change
3. Specification sheets

For the first two methods, you need to use a language that is rich enough in its regular expressions and can handle hash. Perl is such a language. This book provided enough scripts and UNIX commands so that you can package and migrate web applications from one version of WAS to another.

Demystifying Java 2's Internationalization with MrUnicode

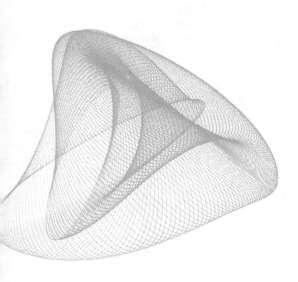

I nstead of listing the character sets and their corresponding Unicode mappings, the graphical representation of the Unicode, and the language codes, this appendix shows you how to use a utility script that can address any of these language encoding issues. MrUnicode (Mister Unicode) is distributed as part of the Gramercy Toolkit. (Refer to Appendix A.) Use MrUnicode in the following situations:[1]

▶   To view the Unicode tables provided by the Unicode Consortium. A table is viewed from the perspective of a servlet loaded in a web container and then shipped out to a browser.

▶   To print information about the supported converters and character sets in Sun Microsystems and IBM distributions of Java 2 v1.3 and v1.4.

▶   To print information about the languages, their corresponding codes, and their supported character sets.

MrUnicode is mostly used to view the Unicode tables provided by the Unicode Consortium. It is then used as a command that takes a Unicode file as input and generates a Java servlet as output. The servlet writes an HTML-formatted table and ships it out to a browser to reveal the Unicode mappings. The table shows the one-to-one mapping between a character set and the Unicode as it is listed by the Unicode Consortium.

MrUnicode's ability to print information about converters, charsets, and languages assists you to resolve the differences between the many converters supported by a specific vendor's Java 2 release.

Using MrUnicode for Internationalization and Unicode

Internationalization is a topic that is usually covered with servlets because it is a servlet that can write and ship out characters to a browser. Yet the browser should be able to interpret and perform the proper mapping of the character set, also called *Unicode*: the standardization of symbols that pertain to a particular language and that are mapped into a table. The Java Virtual Machine (JVM) stores everything internally, including all string data, as 2-byte Unicode. This section discusses how to use MrUnicode to generate servlets that map the Unicode.

In its standard usage, MrUnicode takes as input a Unicode file provided as is by Unicode, Inc. (the Unicode Consortium), and it takes as output a Java servlet that can be requested in a browser so that you can view the corresponding character set mapping. The syntax of MrUnicode follows:

```
MrUnicode -t unicodeTable [-s unicodeServlet] [-l locale | -c
     charset] [-clg contentLanguage] [-index] [-V] [-v]
```

---

[1]   Make sure that you have MrUnicode in your search path, and that the files mrunicode_s14_i14.map and mrunicode_lang_r1.map are in a common directory. The environment variable $GRAMERCY_DIR must be set and exported to point to the directory where these .map files are.

▶   **-t unicodeTable**   The text file that contains the data mapping as provided by the Unicode Consortium on how a particular character set maps into Unicode. The character set is usually identified with some name (or compound name) formed with an acronym and numbering schema, and each entry in the table has three tab-separated columns:

  ▶   Column 1 is the hex code of the character identified in the set.

  ▶   Column 2 is the hex number of the Unicode.

  ▶   Column 3 is the Unicode name, but it is given as a comment following the pound sign (#).

▶   **-s unicodeServlet**   The servlet name to be output by MrUnicode. If the unicodeServlet is not specified, then TabulateUnicode_<unicodeTable>.java is set as the generated servlet name. Notice that any hyphen (-) in the resulting filename for the unicodeServlet is substituted with an underscore (_).

▶   **-c charset**   The character set to be used by the servlet writer. If charset is not specified, then the charset is the same as the specified unicodeTable. For example, save the Unicode table for the character set ISO 8859-1 to the text file ISO-8859-1 so that you can use implicit processing with MrUnicode. An example is given at the end of this section. Use this option with the -clg option so that you can specify the "Content-Language in the HTML header.

▶   **-clg contentLanguage**   The content language to be set in the HTML header's "Content-Language.

▶   **-l locale**   If the locale is specified, then the -c charset and -clg contentLanguage are ignored and the servlet will use the implicit charset by setting the locale (using the HttpServletResponse.setLocale() method) before calling the HttpServletResponse. getWriter(). MrUnicode does not check on the validity of the named locale and will generate the servlet whatever named locale is given. This is done so that MrUnicode will work with new releases of the Java Virtual Machine that support new locales. Also note that the use of -l locale is recommended over the use of -c charset and -clg because the Content-Language is set properly when -l locale is specified.

▶   **-index**   The option that generates an index for these long Unicode mapping that will span three or more tables.

▶   **-v**   The option that specifies verbose mode to print statistics while generating the tables. The statistics printed show the number of characters defined in each table.

▶   **-V**   The option that prints the version number of MrUnicode.

All Unicode tables can be downloaded from ftp://ftp.unicode.org/Public/MAPPINGS. For example, from the Unicode, Inc., web site, download the tables for the ISO 8859-1 and for the Japanese Windows version and save them to the files ISO-8859-1 and Shift-JIS, respectively. The distribution code contains several tables with which you can practice using MrUnicode.

Invoke MrUnicode to get the servlet mapping as follows:

```
# MrUnicode -t ISO-8859-1 -v
TABLE 0 0 -- 256
```

Only one table is generated with 256 characters being mapped in it. The command generates the servlet source code TabulateUnicode_ISO_8859_1.java with a clause setting the response content type to ISO-8859-1:

```
res.setContentType("text/html; charset=ISO-8859-1");
```

Alternatively, if you have saved the ISO 8859-1 to the file ISO-8859-1.TXT, then the following command generates the servlet source code Uni88591.java, using the character set ISO-8859-1:

```
# MrUnicode -t ISO-8859-1.TXT -s Uni88591.java -c ISO-8859-1
```

Note that you need to explicitly specify the character set using the -c option.

You can also specify the Content-Language using the -clg option. For example, for Swedish, use this command:

```
# MrUnicode -t ISO-8859-1.TXT -s Uni88591.java -c ISO-8859-1 -clg sw
```

You should not rely on the response.setHeader() to set the Content-Language. (See the discussion on using Lynx at the end of this section.) However, the use of -l to specify the locale as a language type is more coherent in that it will use the response.setLocale() to set up the Content-Language:

```
# MrUnicode -t Shift-JIS -s Uni_Jap.java -l ja -index -v
```

This command creates the servlet Uni_Jap that you can compile and request in a browser. The page will include an index for the tables generated. Figure C-1 shows the Unicode mapping for the Japanese language for these symbols in Table 8E.

Use Lynx to view what is being sent from the servlet (server) in the HTML header:

```
# lynx http://node1/wasbook/unijap -mime_header | more
```

Locate the Content-Language to ensure that the language code is not automatically overridden by the HTTP server. If it is reverted to a different code than expected, use the locale option -l to set the language.

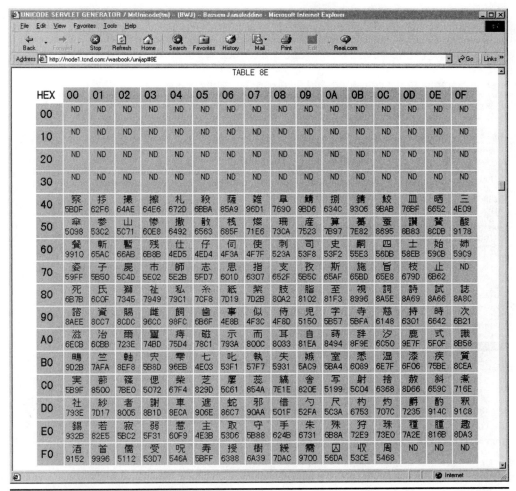

Figure C-1   *Table 8E for the Japanese language*

Printing Information about Converters and Character Sets

You can also use MrUnicode to print information about converters supported by Java 2 versions 1.3 and 1.4. The information MrUnicode provides is based on the latest data provided on the Sun Microsystems and IBM web sites.

Use the option -info with MrUnicode to print converter and charsets information:

```
MrUnicode -info [-list] [-conv convName] [-likeconv rexp] [-charset
    rexp] [-desc rexp] [-about converter] [-abouts converters]
```

For example, to list converters and their corresponding charsets

```
# MrUnicode -info -list
```

```
File Sessions Settings Help

[root@node1 UNICODE]# MrUnicode -info -list | more
   Converter            Charset Sun          Charset IBM                        Note
-------------------   -------------------   -------------------   ------------------------------------
ASCII                 US-ASCII              US-ASCII              Sun:Yes IBM:Yes
BIG5                  Big5                                        Sun:Yes IBM:No
BIG5_HKSCS            Big5-HKSCS                                  Sun:Yes IBM:No
BIG5_SOLARIS                                                      Sun:Yes IBM:No
CESU8                                       CESU-8                Sun:No  IBM:Yes Other:ibm14 nio
CP037                                       IBM-037               Sun:Yes IBM:Yes
CP1006                                       IBM-1006              Sun:Yes IBM:Yes
CP1025                                       IBM-1025              Sun:Yes IBM:Yes
CP1026                                       IBM-1026              Sun:Yes IBM:Yes
CP1027                                       IBM-1027              Sun:No  IBM:Yes Other:ibm13
CP1041                                       IBM-1041              Sun:No  IBM:Yes Other:ibm13
CP1043                                       IBM-1043              Sun:No  IBM:Yes Other:ibm13
CP1046                                       IBM-1046              Sun:Yes IBM:Yes
CP1046S                                      IBM-1046S             Sun:No  IBM:Yes Other:ibm12
CP1047                                       IBM-1047              Sun:No  IBM:Yes Other:ibm12
CP1088                                       IBM-1088              Sun:No  IBM:Yes Other:ibm13
CP1097                                       IBM-1097              Sun:Yes IBM:Yes
--More--
 New  Konsole
```

The commands in this section use information retrieval using MrUnicode -info. Most of the command results shown in this section are reflected in Figure C-2.

To show these converters with a regular expression "cp(.)*56" and their corresponding charsets, use this command:

```
# MrUnicode -info -conv "cp(.)*56"
```

To print these converters whose corresponding charsets contain "jis" (these are probably the Japanese charsets), use this command:

```
# MrUnicode -info -charset jis
```

To get the Arabic converters assuming that 1256 is in the charset, use this command:

```
# MrUnicode -info -charset 1256
```

To print information about a specific converter, such as the cp1256, use this command:

```
# MrUnicode -info -about cp1256
```

```
File Sessions Settings Help

[root@node1 UNICODE]# MrUnicode -info -conv "cp(.)*56"
(i14.CP1256S.windows-1256S) (i14.CP856.IBM-856) (s141.CP1256.windows-1256) (i14.CP1256.windows-
1256)
[root@node1 UNICODE]# MrUnicode -info -charset jis
(i14.JIS0212.JIS0212) (s141.SJIS.Shift_JIS) (i14.MS932.<csshiftjis cswindows31j ms_kanji shift_
jis s-jis sjis windows-31j x-sjis>) (i14.JIS0201.JIS0201) (i14.JIS0208.JIS0208)
[root@node1 UNICODE]# MrUnicode -info -charset 1256
(i14.CP1256S.windows-1256S) (i14.CP1256S.<Cp1256s ibm-1256s>) (s141.CP1256.windows-1256) (i14.C
P1256.windows-1256) (i14.CP1256.<ibm-1256>)
[root@node1 UNICODE]# MrUnicode -info -about cp1256
Result for the converter CP1256:
        Sun's J2SE 1.3.1 library i18n.jar with charset name (alias) [windows-1256]
        Sun's J2SE 1.4.1 library charsets.jar with charset name [windows-1256]
        IBM Java 2 version 1.4 with java.nio with charset name [windows-1256] and other aliases
<ibm-1256>
        Sun's description: Windows Arabic
        Sun's description: Windows Arabic
        IBM's description: Windows Arabic
[root@node1 UNICODE]# MrUnicode -info -likeconv "(.)*j(.)*"
UTF8J JIS0212 EUC_JP JOHAB SJIS ISO2022JP JIS0201 JIS0208 JISAUTODETECT EUC_JP_LINUX
[root@node1 UNICODE]# MrUnicode -info -charset "(.)*j(.)*"
(i14.UTF8J.UTF-8J) (i14.JIS0212.JIS0212) (i14.CP954C.<Cp954c ibm-eucjp>) (s141.EUC_JP.EUC-JP) (
i14.EUC_JP.EUC-JP) (i14.EUC_JP.<euc_jp euc_jp_linux eucjp euc-jp-linux x-euc_jp x-eucjp>) (s141
.SJIS.Shift_JIS) (s141.MS932.windows-31j) (i14.MS932.<csshiftjis cswindows31j ms_kanji shift_ji
s s-jis sjis windows-31j x-sjis>) (s141.ISO2022JP.ISO-2022-JP) (i14.MS949.<Cp1361 ibm-1361 ibm1
361 johab ksc5601-1992 ms1361>) (i14.JIS0201.JIS0201) (i14.JIS0208.JIS0208) (s141.EUC_JP_LINUX.
EUC-JP-LINUX)
[root@node1 UNICODE]# MrUnicode -info -desc japan
JIS0212 CP954C EUC_JP SJIS CP1351 CP930 MS932 CP939 ISO2022JP CP290 CP942C CP942 CP943 CP33722
CP943C CP954 CP300 CP301 CP1027 CP33722C CP897 CP1390 CP1399 JIS0201 JIS0208 CP1041 EUC_JP_LINU
X

 New    Konsole
```

Figure C-2   *Using MrUnicode for information retrieval*

To look for Japanese converters, you assume that each converter may contain the letter *J* or *j*. To get a list of converters whose names contain the letter *J* or *j*, use the regular expression (.)*j(.)* after the -likeconv option:

```
# MrUnicode -info -likeconv "(.)*j(.)*"
```

Or if you think the charsets for the Japanese language contain the letter *J* or *j*, then you can list all these charsets supported by the IBM and Sun Java 2 versions with this command:

```
# MrUnicode -info -charset "(.)*j(.)*"
```

This command can help you fetch these converters by searching their descriptions. For instance, to look for all converters where the expression "japan" occurs

```
# MrUnicode -info -desc "japan"
```

To look for traditional Chinese, use the expression "trad(.)*chin", etc.

Once you get a list of converters, you can look them up using the option -abouts:

```
# MrUnicode -info -abouts jis0212 cp954c euc_jp sjis cp1351
```

The options -conv and -charset can further refine the search by preceding any of these two options with one of the following: -sun131, -sun141, and -ibm141. This makes the retrieval of information specific to a version of Java 2.

Sun Microsystems vs. IBM Nomenclature in Java 2 Encoding

The previous section discussed how to use MrUnicode to print information about converters and character sets (known as charsets). This section takes the opposite tack to explain the nomenclature used for the encoding supported by Java 2. Such explanation is easy due to the practical use of MrUnicode shown previously.

The following converters and character sets are listed by MrUnicode:

▶ Sun's Java 2 SDK, Standard Edition, v1.3.1 (s131)

▶ Sun's Java 2 SDK, Standard Edition, v1.4.1 (s141)

▶ IBM's Java 2 v1.4 (i14) or earlier

The information MrUnicode prints shows the version of Java 2 where a converter is used. These are currently s131, s141, and i14. Typically, with Java 2 SDK v1.3, some classes in the packages java.lang and java.io are used to handle conversion between Unicode and a number of character encodings: java.io.InputStreamReader, java.io.OutputStreamWriter, and java.lang.String. Java 2 SDK v1.4 introduced the additional package java.nio.charset to handle such conversion. Java 2 v1.4 introduced the class java.nio.charset.Charset, which lists the encodings supported by all implementations of the Java 2 platform. IBM has added to this encoding many other character sets.

Although the Unicode Consortium is organizing and unifying the code mappings for characters, it is not unifying the nomination of converters.

Sun Microsystems refers to the names used for the encoding sets as *canonical names*. With J2SE 1.3.1, Sun used an alias to refer the character set mappings to these canonical names. With J2SE 1.4.1, the java.nio is introduced, and what used to be called alias under v1.3.1 is now called *canonical names for java.nio*. Therefore, for each canonical name for java.io and java.lang, a corresponding canonical name might be used in java.nio.

To complicate the inconsistent nomenclature adopted by both IBM and Sun Microsystems, IBM refers to a particular character's encoding and its corresponding character set(s) with the words "converter" and "charset(s)." MrUnicode uses IBM nomenclature because it shows natural correspondence between converters and charsets. The character set used in an HTML page is usually the charset name set in the mime's header Content-Type.

The information supplied by IBM and Sun is sometimes confusing: both IBM and Sun recognize the converter MS950 to have a corresponding charset windows-950, but IBM also uses the alias big5 as a charset. Sun recognizes Big5 as being a converter (canonical name) on its own, and IBM does not. Refer to the information about ms950 and Big5 by issuing these commands:

```
# MrUnicode -info -abouts Big5 ms950
```

Let's hope the differences between IBM and Sun will be resolved with future releases. You will most likely deal with only a few characters' encodings at once, and the simplest way to ensure that you are using the proper charset for a particular converter is to view it through a servlet. Use the MrUnicode servlet generator to view the graphical representation of a charset, as discussed in the section "Using MrUnicode for Internationalization and Unicode."

Printing Language Code with MrUnicode

Each language is represented by a language code. The language code is set in the mime's header Content-Language so that the browser can identify the language used while printing the page content.

Use MrUnicode to print information about a particular language, or to print a table showing the language codes and their suggested character sets. To print such language information, use the -langinfo option:

```
MrUnicode -langinfo [-list] [-lang language]
```

To list all languages, issue this command:

```
# MrUnicode -langinfo -list
```

```
File Sessions Settings Help

[root@node1 UNICODE]# MrUnicode -langinfo -list | more
        Language            Language Code          Suggested Charsets
-----------------------     -------------     ------------------------------
Albanian                    sq                ISO-8859-2
Arabic                      ar                ISO-8859-6,Cp-1256
Bulgarian                   bg                ISO-8859-5
Byelorussian                be                ISO-8859-5
Catalan Spanish             ca                ISO-8859-1
Chinese Simplified,Mai      zh                GB2312
Chinese Traditional,Ta      zh-TW             Big5
Croatian                    hr                ISO-8859-2
Czech                       cs                ISO-8859-2
Danish                      da                ISO-8859-1
Dutch                       nl                ISO-8859-1
English                     en                ISO-8859-1
Estonian                    et                ISO-8859-1
Finnish                     fi                ISO-8859-1
French                      fr                ISO-8859-1
German                      de                ISO-8859-1
Greek                       el                ISO-8859-7
--More--

 New   Konsole
```

To retrieve information about a specific language, you can follow the -lang option with a regular expression. For example, the following command finds the Arabic language:

```
# MrUnicode -langinfo -lang ara
(Arabic,ar,ISO-8859-6,Cp-1256)
```

D

Gramercy Toolkit Scripts and the WASDG Environment

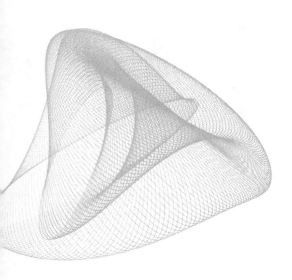

T he WASDG environment discussed in Chapters 3 and 4 set many environment variables to prepare a programmer's development environment. The environment is set with the setj.sh script. A programmer's environment parallels the specific version of WAS being used by the developer. This appendix explains how to use the chekenv script to verify the validity of the WASDG environment. In addition, it shows the syntax of some of the scripts that are provided by Gramercy Toolkit, and which were used earlier in this book.

Checking the WASDG Environment

The chekenv script prints your current environment variables. This script is available in the distribution code. Copy chekenv to a directory available in your search path, such as /tools, and execute it as a command. Figure D-1 shows the result of chekenv.

Listing D-1 shows the chekenv script.

Listing D-1   *chekenv*

```
1.    #!/usr/bin/perl
2.    ...
3.    @EL = (
4.    'ADMINPORT',
5.    'ASSEMBLY',
6.    'BASE_CLASSPATH',
7.    'BASE_DEV',
8.    'CLASSPATH',
9.    'CLASSPATHMORE',
10.   'CLIENTCONFIG',
11.   'COMMON_CLASSES',
12.   'DB2_CLASSPATH',
13.   'DRADMIN',
14.   'DRADMINPORT',
15.   'DUMPNAMESPACE',
16.   'EAREXPANDER',
17.   'INSTALLABLEAPPS',
18.   'INSTALLEDAPPS',
19.   'JAVA_EXE',
20.   'JAVA_HOME',
21.   'JSPCOMPILER',
22.   'LAUNCHCLIENT',
23.   'LD_LIBRARY_PATH',
```

```
24.    'LOGANALYZER',
25.    'PATH',
26.    'SEAPPINSTALL',
27.    'SOAPENABLER',
28.    'STARTWAS',
29.    'STOPWAS',
30.    'WASCFG',
31.    'WASCOMMANDS',
32.    'WASDOMAIN',
33.    'WASLOG_STDOUT',
34.    'WASLOG_STDERR',
35.    'WASLOG_ACTIVITY',
36.    'WAS_HOME',
37.    'WAS_NODE',
38.    'WAS_HOSTNAME',
39.    'WSCP',
40.    'WSCP_CL',
41.    );
42.    foreach $e (@EL) {
43.       $$e = $ENV{$e};    $env = $e; $value = $$e; write;
44.    }
```

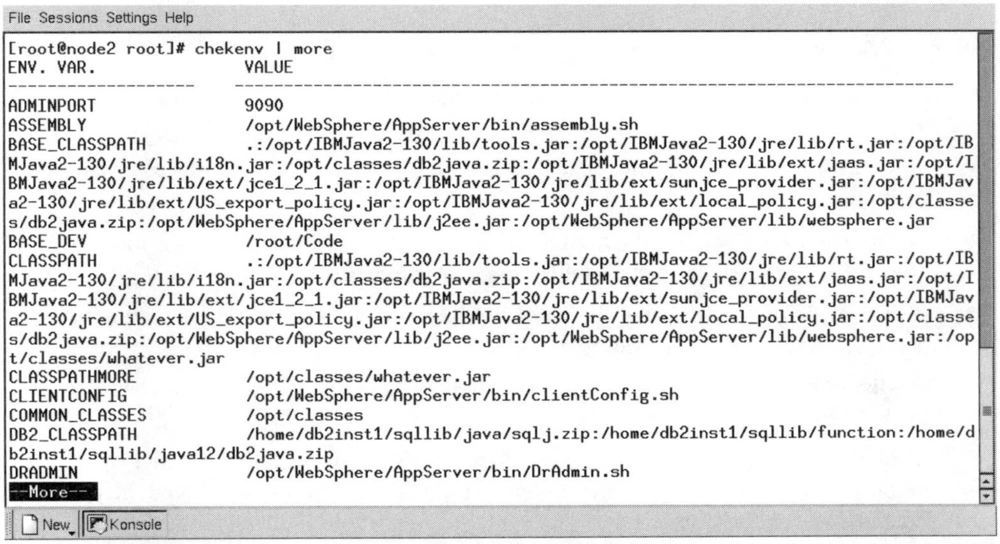

Figure D-1   *The chekenv script, which prints the WASDG environment*

Gramercy Toolkit Scripts

Some chapters used the scripts that are provided with the Gramercy Toolkit. (Appendix A describes how to download and install the toolkit.) Table D-1 lists the tools and the chapters where they have been used in the course of this text. This section summarizes the syntax of some of the tools that were not explained in the chapter—namely, BwjSort and cpfl, and modjar.

BwjSort

Use BwjSort to sort a comma- or tab-delimited report according to a specific criterion. The sorting is quickly accomplished by using this simple command at the command prompt. BwjSort is used in Chapter 22 to sort the stress-tester reports, and in Chapter 25 to sort the threads resulting with the use of MrThread.

The script BwjSort requires the Perl library inc_sort_subs. If you have the /tools directory in your search PATH, then copy inc_sort_subs and BwjSort to the /tools directory. Then you need to export the environment variable GRAMERCY_DIR=/tools so that BwjSort can find the required library inc_sort_subs. The syntax of BwjSort follows:

```
BwjSort -in <inputfile> -n <number> -f <list of fields> -o <list of
sort criteria> -d <list describing the fields type> -1 <comma | tab>
-2 <comma | tab>
```

The BwjSort options are the following:

- ▶ **-in <inputfile>** Specifies the input file to be processed

- ▶ **-1 <comma | tab>** Specifies whether the input file is comma delimited or tab delimited.

- ▶ **-2 <comma | tab>** Specifies whether the output file is comma delimited or tab delimited.

- ▶ **-n <number>** Specifies the number of fields to show in the output file; must be less or equal to the total number of fields. Starts counting at 1.

- ▶ **-f <list of fields>** Specifies the list of fields to sort by. The priority is maintained from left to right. Starts counting at 0.

- ▶ **-o <list of sort criteria>** Specifies how to sort the fields specified previously. Uses *a* for ascending, and uses *d* for descending.

- ▶ **-d <list describing the field's type>** Currently supports only integer and string. All fields must be described going from left to right. Uses *i* for a field of type integer or float and uses *s* for string.

Tool	Description	Reference
BwjSort	Works as a sort utility	Chapters 22 and 25
cpfl	Copies named files from a source directory to a destination directory	Chapter 18
modjar	Adds named files to a .jar file such as a web module or EJB module	Chapter 19
MrUnicode	Provides converters, charsets, and Unicode mappings	Appendix B
SharkUrl	Works as a stress tester	Chapter 22
MrThread	Monitors AIX threads	Chapter 25
MrTop	Monitors Linux processes or threads	Chapter 25

Table D-1   *Tools Distributed with Gramercy Toolkit*

cpfl

Use cpfl to copy a set of files from a source directory to a destination directory while preserving the directory path where a thought file is found. This script has the following syntax:

```
cpfl -name namedFiles -from fromDir -to toDir [-v] [-i] [-u] [-V]
```

The options of cpfl are as follows:

▶ **-name namedFiles**   Specifies the name of the files; this is the name as it is processed by the UNIX command: `find` when using the option `-name`.

▶ **-from fromDir**   Specifies the source directory.

▶ **-to toDir**   Specifies the destination directory.

▶ **-v verbose**

▶ **-i interactive**   Prompts before overwriting an existing file.

▶ **-u updates**   Copies source files that are newer than their corresponding destination files, or when they are missing.

▶ **-V**   Prints version information.

modjar

Use modjar to modify a Jar archive file and add to it these named files found in a source directory. modjar will preserve the directory path of each of the thought files to be added. The script modjar has the following syntax:

```
modjar -arc jarFile -from fromDir -name namedFiles [-scratch
scratchDir][-keep] [-v][-i][-u][-V]
```

The options of modjar are as follows:

► **-arc jarFile**   Specifies the Jar file to be modified

► **-from fromDir**   Specifies the source directory

► **-name namedFiles**   Specifies the name of the files; this is the name as it is processed by the UNIX command "find when using the option "-name

► **-scratch scratchDir**   Specifies a scratch directory. A scratch directory name is expected to have a name that matches the regular expression __(.)*_jarFile-without-extension_(.)*__. When the scratchDir is not specified the scratch directory is derived from the jarFile name and the process number; the directory is then created in /tmp.

► **-keep**   After modifying the Jar archive, keep the temporary tree and do not delete it. If not specified, the temporary directory is deleted.

► For the other options, **-v -i -u -V**   Refer to cpfl syntax shown previously.

When modjar runs, the jarFile is backed up to a file by the same name but suffixed with the process number.

WASLED/WASMON
Quick Reference

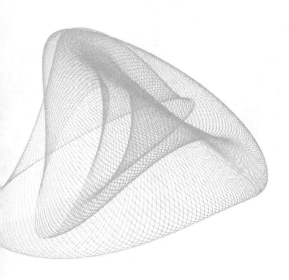

This appendix summarizes the use of the WASLED/WASMON applications and lists the configuration directives used in wasmon.conf and wasmonhelper.conf.

For further documentation on WASMON, download the wasmon121_ref.pdf from the Osborne web site or from www.tcnd.com. You can obtain the latest information about the application and its support for WAS v5 from www.tcnd.com.

Starting and Configuring WASMON

WASMON is started with the wasmon program. The syntax for wasmon follows:

```
wasmon [-was4] [-was5] [-xwasled] [-wc webappComponents] [-wl webappLeds] [--Version]
```

For WAS v4 monitoring, start wasmon at the command prompt without any option:

```
# wasmon
```

Currently, WASMON can monitor WAS v4 and v5. However, when monitoring WAS v5, not all mnemonics (symbolic messages) can be filtered directly as components. To monitor WAS v5, use the filtering capability that allows you to specify regular expressions. The -was4 and -was5 options are currently ignored, but they will be used whenever WAS v5 is officially released. The options –xwasled, -wc webappComponents, and -wl webappLeds are used to monitor web applications, as explained in Chapter 26.

Use the option -V or --Version to print the version of WASMON and its current state of WAS support:

```
# wasmon -V
 WASLED(tm)/WASMON(tm) v1.2.1 --(Compatibility: Perl Tk, UNIX and Windows)
 (C) COPYRIGHT TOTAL COMPUTING & NETWORK DESIGN Inc. 2002

 Support: WAS v4 components, WAS v5 limited to filters
 wasmon [-xwasled][-wc webappComponents][-wl webappLeds][--Version]
```

Table E-1 summarizes the important files and directories of the WASMON application. WASMON reads its configuration from wasmon.conf. In wasmon.conf, you can use Direct Alert directives and Logical Alert directives, which are followed by nine fields and a list of filters:

```
f1, f2, ... f9, [filter1[,filter2[,...[,filterN]]]]
```

Refer to Chapter 24 for the positional meaning of each field.
Table E-2 lists the directives that are currently used in wasmon.conf (version 1.2.1).

File or Directory	Description
wasmon	The WASMON program. To print version: `wasmon -V`.
wasmon.conf	The configuration file read by the wasmon program.
wasmontkt	The program to print the ticket. Use it to parse the wasmon.conf.
wasmoncl	The client program to forward log files to WASMON.
wasmonhelper	The helper program to assess WASMON variables: b-var and d-var.
wasmonhelper.conf	The configuration file read by wasmonhelper.
wasmon.delegate	The file used as a postboard; wasmonhelper writes its output to it, and wasmon reads it to update its b-var and d-var.
wasleddb_s_r402.rec	The LEDs database for WAS v4.
wasleddb_components_r402.rec	The components for WAS v4. Not used with WASMON v1.2.1.
wasleddb_s_r500.rec	The LEDs database for WAS v5. Not available yet.
wasleddb_components_r500.rec	The components for WAS v5. Not available yet.
wasmon.delegate	This file is created by the program wasmonhelper, and it is read by the program wasmon.
TriggersPool	The directory that holds the scripts used by WASMON. Usually triggers are numbered scripts that are deposited in this directory.

Table E-1   *Files and Directories Used in WASMON v1.2.1 Distribution*

Directive	Purpose
Direct Alert directives—Work with WAS v4 components	
ALERT ON COMPONENT FAULT	Alerts when a component error (E) is detected.
ALERT ON COMPONENT WARN	Alerts when a component warning (W) is detected.
ALERT ON COMPONENT LIST FAULTS	Alerts when one or many components' errors (E) are detected.
ALERT ON COMPONENT LIST WARNS	Alerts when one or many components' warnings (W) are detected.
Direct Alert directives—Work with filter(s) specified as a regular expression	
ALERT ON FILTER	Alerts when a user-defined filter is detected.
ALERT ON LIST FILTERS	Alerts when a list of user-defined filters are all detected. Filters are regular expressions.

Table E-2   *Directives Used in the WASMON v1.2.1 Configuration File*

Directive	Purpose
Logical Alert directives — Support the use of logical expressions	
LOGICAL ALERT ON COMPONENT LIST	Filters components of WAS based on their severity criteria. This directive accepts logical expressions for evaluation and can enter in parole. Refer to the keyword PAROLE in Chapter 26.
LOGICAL ALERT ON LIST FILTERS	Filters are regular expressions. This directive accepts logical expressions for evaluation and can enter in parole. Refer to the keyword PAROLE in Chapter 26.
Supervisor Mode directive — Can supervise systems independently from WAS	
SUPERVISOR	Enables the WASMON supervisor to check on the systems in a WebSphere region whenever no more data is received from WAS. The keyword PAROLE is also supported in supervisor mode.
Refresh Interval directive — Has a lower priority then the SUPERVISOR delta time	
REFRESH INTERVAL	Because the b-var and d-var are also used within the Logical Expression directives, you need to specify a refresh interval to update these variables. When SUPERVISOR is enabled, the refresh interval is ignored, and the delta time specified in the SUPERVISOR is used instead as the refresh rate to update these variables.

Table E-2   *Directives Used in the WASMON v1.2.1 Configuration File* (continued)

For examples on the use of Direct Alert directives and the Logical Alert directive, refer to Chapter 24. For an example of putting WASMON in supervisor mode using the SUPERVISOR directive, refer to Chapter 26.

Using Logical Expressions

Logical expressions can be used within the Logical Alert directives and within the SUPERVISOR directive. Wherever a logical expression is used, it can be prefixed with the PAROLE keyword to enter an operator in parole with WASMON: an operator enters in conversation with WASMON via e-mail.

Using Logical Expressions in a Logical Alert Directive

Logical expressions can be used within a Logical Alert directive. You need to specify two parts to make use of a logical expression from within such a directive:

▶   The expression itself, in which c1, ..., *cn* are used as a placeholder for the variables

▶   The variable mappings for these c1, ..., *cn*

In the expression mentioned in the first bullet, you can specify any of the logical variables: b-var or d-var. The following shows an example that is derived from Chapter 24, in the section "Conditional Monitoring with the Logical Alert Directives:"

```
(c1 && @BOOL_URL_node1.tcnd.com/wasbook/dumpenv) && (( c2||c3||c4) &&c5),
SRVE[0-9][0-9][0-9][0-9]W,SRVE[0-9][0-9][0-9][0-9],connection
     pool(.)*source,CONM6007I,CNTR[0-9][0-9][0-9][0-9]
```

In the previous example,

▶   c1 is true if `SRVE[0-9][0-9][0-9][0-9]W` is found in the message sent to WASMON.

▶   c2 is true if `SRVE[0-9][0-9][0-9][0-9]` is found in the message sent to WASMON.

▶   c3 is true if `connection pool(.)*source` is found in the message sent to WASMON.

▶   c4 is true if `CONM6007I` is found in the message sent to WASMON.

▶   c5 is true if `CNTR[0-9][0-9][0-9][0-9]` is found in the message sent to WASMON.

The variable @BOOL_URL_node1.tcnd.com/wasbook/dumpenv is a b-var and is true if http://node1.tcnd.com/wasbook/dumpenv cannot be resolved.

This b-var is assigned by wasmonhelper and is written to an intermediary file: wasmon.delegate. In wasmonhelper.conf, you will have the following directive:

```
BOOL URL: node1.tcnd.com  /wasbook/dumpenv
```

In addition, to use b-var and d-var, you need to have the wasmon program read the wasmon.delegate file. This is done periodically at an interval set by REFRESH INTERVAL, which is overridden by the delta time of the SUPERVISOR (second field) whenever the SUPERVISOR is set to ON.

Using Logical Expressions in the SUPERVISOR Directive

Logical expressions can be used within the SUPERVISOR directive, which is followed by nine fields, as shown here:

```
SUPERVISOR: ON|OFF,delta-time,0|1,0|1,trigger-number,operator-email,
email-subject,email-body,logical-expression|PAROLE(logical-expression)
```

NOTE

The delta time overrides the refresh interval whenever the SUPERVISOR is set to ON.

An example of the SUPERVISOR directive follows:

```
SUPERVISOR:ON,600, 1,1, 0002,maxou@auream.tcnd.com, SUPERVISOR
ALERT,,PAROLE(!(@BOOL_ACTIVEPORT_node2:50000) ||
!(@BOOL_URL_node1.tcnd.com/wasbook/dumpenv))
```

For a full description of this example, refer to Chapter 26.

WASMON Internal Variables

WASMON internal variables are of four types: s-var, b-var, d-bar, and g-var. Refer to Chapter 26 for the definitions of these variables. Table E-3 summarizes the b-var and d-var directives and their corresponding variable mappings. In the left column, the directive is shown first as it must appear in the wasmonhelper.conf file; it is then followed by its corresponding name (the italics within the parenthesis) as it will be used in wasmon.conf. Recall from Chapter 26 that all d-vars are followed by (1) as a first argument, and it is called the refresh rate; this parenthetical argument's listing is reserved internally for WASMON.

Directive and Variable Mapping	Purpose
b-var — Boolean variables	
BOOL ACTIVEPORT: hostname portnumber	Checks whether a server port is active; for example, if the UDB port 50000 is active. Checking if a port is active also implies checking if the server is reachable.
(@BOOL_ACTIVEPORT_<hostname>_<port>)	
BOOL JNDILOOKUP: hostname portnumber name	Looks up a JNDI by name on a particular server.
(@BOOL_JNDILOOKUP_<hostname>_<portnumber>_<name>)	
BOOL JNDISERVER: hostname portnumber regularexpression	Checks whether JNDI service is available on a particular server.
(@BOOL_JNDISERVER_<hostname>_<portnumber>)	
BOOL LOOKFILE: filename string	Checks for the occurrence of a string in a specified file.
(@BOOL_LOOKFILE_<filename>_<string>)	
BOOL LOOKPROCESS: processnumber	Checks whether the process is running on a server.
(@BOOL_LOOKPROCESS_<processnumber>)	

Table E-3   *Directives Used in wasmonhelper.conf Mapped to Their Corresponding Variable Names*

Directive and Variable Mapping	Purpose
b-var — Boolean variables	
BOOL PING: hostname	Pings a server.
(@BOOL_PING_<hostname>)	
BOOL RSHLOOKFILE: hostname filename string	rsh to a server and checks for the occurrence of a string in a specified file.
(@BOOL_RSHLOOKFILE_<hostname>_<filename>_<string>)	
BOOL RSHLOOKPROCESS: hostname processnumber	rsh to a server and checks if the process is running on a server.
(@BOOL_RSHLOOKPROCESS_<hostname>_<processnumber>)	
BOOL RSHURI: hostname fullyqualifiedfilename	rsh to a server and checks for a fully qualified filename.
(@BOOL_RSHURI_<hostname>_<fullyqualifiedfilename>)	
b-var — Boolean variables	
BOOL URI: fullyqualifiedfilename	Checks for a fully qualified filename.
(@BOOL_URI_<fullyqualifiedfilename>)	
BOOL URL: hostname[:portnumber] uri	Checks whether a URL is resolvable.
(@BOOL_URL_<hostname[:portnumber]_<uri>)	
d-var — Differential variables	
DVAR CHECKSUM: (1) fullyqualifiedfilename	Differentiates the checksum of a file on the local machine.
(@DVAR_CHECKSUM_<fullyqualifiedfilename>)	
DVAR RSHCHECKSUM: (1) hostname fullyqualifiedfilename	Differentiates the checksum of a file on a remote machine.
(@DVAR_RSHCHECKSUM_<hostname>_<fullyqualifiedfilename>)	
DVAR LOOKPROCESS: (1) processnumber	Differentiates the process number on the local machine.
(@DVAR_LOOKPROCESS_<processnumber>)	
DVAR RSHLOOKPROCESS: (1) hostname processnumber	Differentiates the process number on a remote machine.
(@DVAR_RSHLOOKPROCESS_<hostname>_<processnumber>)	
DVAR LOOKWASMONMAIL*: (1) mailuserid numberedidentifier	Differentiates the existence of an identifier in the e-mail of a specified user (default wasmon user).
(@DVAR_LOOKWASMONMAIL_<mailuserid>_<numberedidentifier>)	

*   Used internally only. This is not supported publicly yet.

Table E-3   *Directives Used in wasmonhelper.conf Mapped to Their Corresponding Variable Names* (continued)

Metacharacter	Action
\	Escapes the character immediately following it
.	Matches any character except newline (unless /s is used)
^	Matches at the beginning of a string
$	Matches at the end of the string
*	Matches zero or more preceding elements
+	Matches one or more preceding elements
?	Matches zero or one preceding element
{...}	Matches range of instances for the preceding element
[...]	Matches one from a set
(...)	Groups regular expressions
|	Matches either the expression preceding or following it

Table E-4   *Metacharacters Used in Perl and Mostly Native to UNIX*

A b-var returns 1 when the condition is satisfied. A d-var returns 1 when the condition has changed.

The regular expression used in WASMON's filters is specific to Perl. Table E-4 shows metacharacters used in Perl, and Table E-5 shows the Perl short coding scheme to match word- and number-based strings.

Code	Match
\d	A digit, equivalent to [0–9]
\D	A nondigit, equivalent to [^0–9]
\w	An alphanumeric word, equivalent to [a–zA–Z_0–9]
\W	A nonword
\s	A whitespace, equivalent to [\t\n\r\f]
\S	A nonwhitepsace

Table E-5   *Perl Short Coding Scheme*

A Quick Monitoring Scenario

Assume that the wasmonhelper.conf has the directive DELTA set to 300 seconds (5 minutes):

```
DELTA: 300
```

and the wasmon.conf has the directive REFRESH INTERVAL set to 420 seconds (7 minutes):

```
REFRESH INTERVAL: 420
```

Table E-6 summarizes the activities the wasmon and wasmonhelper programs undertake over time.

Now assume that the SUPERVISOR is ON, and the delta time (second field) is set to 480 seconds (8 minutes). In this case, the REFRESH INTERVAL is ignored, and the value of the delta time = 480 seconds is taken as the periodicity for the wasmon program to read the wasmon.delegate file. In this second case, the information in Table E-6 does not hold unless the periodicity is set properly in the first column. For instance, +0, +5, +8, and +16 are the values to be used in the first column.

Time in Minutes	Program	wasmon.delegate	Description
+0	wasmonhelper (started first) wasmon (started second)	Initiated with the ideal* values by wasmonhelper; then read by wasmon	All b-vars are set to 1, and all d-vars are set to 0
+5	wasmonhelper	Updated by wasmonhelper	b-vars and d-vars are updated
+7	wasmon	Read by wasmon	WASMON's logical expressions are evaluated with the updated b-vars and d-vars variables
+10	wasmonhelper	Updated by wasmonhelper	b-vars and d-vars are updated
+14	wasmon	Read by wasmon	WASMON's logical expressions are evaluated with the updated b-vars and d-vars variables

* The ideal value for a b-var is 1 and for a d-var is 0. Use the command `wasmonhelper ideal` to view these initial values.

Table E-6 *b-vars and d-vars Are Updated by the wasmonhelper Program and Read by the wasmon Program*

Support for WAS v5

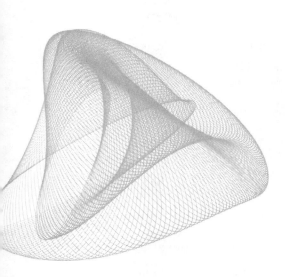

IBM has recently announced the impending release of WebSphere Application Server version 5.0. This appendix explains how to determine the level of support, known in WAS v4 and v5, for the many J2EE components. This appendix also discusses the changes you may need to implement in the scripts introduced in this book to make them applicable to WAS v5.

Although WAS v4 loads and uses Java 2 v1.3.0, you should not draw a conclusion about the level of WebSphere from the Java machine version that it uses; rather, you should look explicitly at the document type definitions (DTDs) in the version of WAS being installed. The next section shows how to retrieve such information.

The following table shows WAS v4 and v5 support for the Java 2 version and IHS version.

WAS v4	Java 2 v1.3.0	IBM HTTP Server 1.3.19
WAS v5	Java 2 v1.3.1	IBM HTTP Server 1.3.24

Determining WAS' Support Through the DTDs

To determine WAS' level of support for J2EE standard applications and other Java 2 components, look at its support for the DTDs. You can explicitly find the DTDs WAS supports in the following two places:

▶ The directory $WAS_HOME/deploytool/itp/plugins/com.ibm.etools.j2ee/dtds/

▶ The file $WAS_HOME/deploytool/itp/plugins/com.ibm.etools.j2ee/plugin.xml

You can quickly determine which applications and components WAS v5 supports by using the grep command as follows:

```
# grep "\-\- [A-Z]" $WAS_HOME/deploytool/itp/plugins/com.ibm.etools.j2ee/plugin.xml
```

The output of this command consists of several lines that reveal what is supported by WAS v5. A few of these lines are shown here:

```
<!-- Application Client J2EE 1.2 Nature         -->
<!-- Application Client J2EE 1.3 Nature         -->
<!-- EJB 1.1 Nature          -->
<!-- EJB 2.0 Nature          -->
```

Table F-1 contrasts the support of WAS v4 to v5 for many of the Java 2 components. As you can see in the table, code that has been written for WAS v4 using a prior level of support for a particular DTD is compatible with WAS v5. The code used in this book and the utility scripts are compatible with WAS v5.[1]

---

[1] With the exception of WSCP used in Chapter 7, WAS v5 replaced the wscp with wsadmin which uses Bean Scripting Framework (BSF) that is based on Java Management (JMX). Both WSCP and wsadmin can be programmed using the JACL (Java implementation of Tcl). The method explained in Chapter 7 to extrapolate WAS reports uses the Perl's pipe and Perl's formatting, and it does not depend on any framework. Therefore, you can apply the method (in the section "Practical reports extrapolation with Perl/WSCP" in Chapter 7) to WAS v5 to extrapolate WAS v5 reports using Perl and wsadmin.

Java Technology	WAS v4	WAS v5	DTD
J2EE v1.2	Y	Y	application_1_2 application-client_1_2
J2EE v1.3	N	Y	application_1_3 application-client_1_3
J2EE API 2.2	Y	Y	web-app_2_2
J2EE API 2.3	N	Y	web-app_2_3
Connector 1.0	Y	Y	connector_1_0
EJB 1.1	Y	Y	ejb-jar_1_1
EJB 2.0	N	Y	ejb-jar_2_0
JSP Tag Library 1.1	Y	Y	web-jsptaglibrary_1_1
JSP Tag Library 1.2	N	Y	web-jsptaglibrary_1_2

Table F-1   *Java 2 Components Support in WAS v4 Versus WAS v5*

You can locate the DTDs in the directory $WAS_HOME/deploytool/itp/plugins/ com.ibm.etools.j2ee/dtds/.

You can also locate the level of support of WAS' current version by editing the file $WAS_HOME/deploytool/itp/plugins/com.ibm.etools.j2ee/plugin.xml and looking for the DTD contribution segment. Such a segment is shown in Listing F-1 for WAS v5.

Listing F-1   *DTD contribution in WAS v5*

```
1.    <!--==========================================-->
2.    <!-- DTD Contributions                        -->
3.    <!-- Register known J2EE DTDs for XML editor  -->
4.    <!--==========================================-->
5.    <extension point = "com.ibm.etools.xmlutility.catalogContributor">
6.      <catalogContributor catalogId="default">
7.        <mappingInfo key="-//Sun Microsystems, Inc.//DTD Web Application
      2.2//EN" uri="dtds/web-app_2_2.dtd"/>
...
18.     </catalogContributor>
19.   </extension>
```

You can obtain additional libraries of information supported in WAS v5 by locating the segment for the class path entry contributions shown in Listing F-2.

Listing F-2   *Class path entry contributions in WAS v5*

```
<!--==================================-->
<!-- Version 5.0 WAS Class Path Entry Contributions -->
<!--==================================-->
```

```
<extension-point
id="EJB20ClassPathEntries"name="EJB20ClassPathEntries"/>
  <extension id="classpath_entry" point="EJB20ClassPathEntries">
...
  </extension>
```

WAS v5 Supports J2EE API 2.3

The web-app element is the root of the deployment descriptor for a web application. The web-app for J2EE API 2.3 supports extra elements that were not available in API v2.2 (WAS v4). The boldface elements in Listing F-3 are supported in WAS v5.

Listing F-3   *Elements describing the web application for J2EE API 2.3*

```
<!ELEMENT web-app (icon?, display-name?, description?, distributable?,
context-param*, filter*, filter-mapping*, listener*, servlet*,
servlet-mapping*, session-config?, mime-mapping*, welcome-file-list?,
error-page*, taglib*, resource-env-ref*, resource-ref*, security-constraint*,
login-config?, security-role*, env-entry*, ejb-ref*, ejb-local-ref*)>
```

In Chapter 13, servlet chaining was not discussed because in WAS v5, you can use the more adequate approach to filter servlet I/O. In WAS v5, the servlet filtering introduced with J2EE API 2.3 is supported.

The <ejb-local-ref> element is needed in EJB 2.0 to declare a local enterprise bean reference through the JNDI ENC. The <resource-env-ref> element is used in EJB 2.0 to declare additional administered objects required by the resource.

Reconsidering Scripts with WAS v5

At any time, you can reconsider the scripts used in this book that generate the enterprise application and its descriptor application.xml, the web application and its descriptor web.xml, and the EJB module descriptor ejb-jar.xml. For instance, among the scripts presented in this book, the following ones need to be changed: j2tree, genwebxml, and j2ejb.

The j2tree, from Chapter 11, generates the following:

▶ An enterprise application descriptor specific to J2EE v1.2

▶ A web application descriptor specific to J2EE API 2.2

This will still work with WAS v5, yet you can easily make the change to support the later level of the J2EE and its API.

Edit the j2tree from Chapter 11. Locate this first line

```
<!DOCTYPE application PUBLIC "-//Sun Microsystems, Inc.//DTD J2EE Application
1.2//EN" "http://java.sun.com/j2ee/dtds/application_1_2.dtd">
```

and change it to

```
<!DOCTYPE application PUBLIC "-//Sun Microsystems, Inc.//DTD J2EE Application
1.3//EN" "http://java.sun.com/dtd/application_1_3.dtd">
```

Also in the same j2tree, locate this second line

```
<!DOCTYPE web-app PUBLIC "-//Sun Microsystems, Inc.//DTD Web Application 2.2//EN"
"http://java.sun.com/j2ee/dtds/web-app_2_2.dtd">
```

and change it to

```
<!DOCTYPE web-app PUBLIC "-//Sun Microsystems, Inc.//DTD Web Application 2.3//EN"
"http://java.sun.com/dtd/web-app_2_3.dtd">
```

You must make a similar change to the second line in the genwebxml script.

EJB 2.0 is supported by WAS v5. Here, you will make the change to the script j2ejb of Chapter 18. Edit the j2ejb, and locate the line

```
<!DOCTYPE ejb-jar PUBLIC "-//Sun Microsystems, Inc.//DTD Enterprise
JavaBeans 1.1//EN" "http://java.sun.com/j2ee/dtds/ejb-jar_1_1.dtd">
```

and change it to

```
<!DOCTYPE ejb-jar PUBLIC "-//Sun Microsystems, Inc.//DTD Enterprise
JavaBeans 2.0//EN" "http://java.sun.com/dtd/ejb-jar_2_0.dtd">
```

Finally, you can also change the gentagtld script from Chapter 13 to support EJB 2.0. Currently, WAS v5 is still beta, and such a change cannot be verified until the official release of WAS v5.

Index

H

INTERNATIONAL CONTACT INFORMATION

AUSTRALIA
McGraw-Hill Book Company Australia Pty. Ltd.
TEL +61-2-9900-1800
FAX +61-2-9878-8881
http://www.mcgraw-hill.com.au
books-it_sydney@mcgraw-hill.com

CANADA
McGraw-Hill Ryerson Ltd.
TEL +905-430-5000
FAX +905-430-5020
http://www.mcgraw-hill.ca

GREECE, MIDDLE EAST, & AFRICA
(Excluding South Africa)
McGraw-Hill Hellas
TEL +30-1-656-0990-3-4
FAX +30-1-654-5525

MEXICO (Also serving Latin America)
McGraw-Hill Interamericana Editores S.A. de C.V.
TEL +525-117-1583
FAX +525-117-1589
http://www.mcgraw-hill.com.mx
fernando_castellanos@mcgraw-hill.com

SINGAPORE (Serving Asia)
McGraw-Hill Book Company
TEL +65-863-1580
FAX +65-862-3354
http://www.mcgraw-hill.com.sg
mghasia@mcgraw-hill.com

SOUTH AFRICA
McGraw-Hill South Africa
TEL +27-11-622-7512
FAX +27-11-622-9045
robyn_swanepoel@mcgraw-hill.com

SPAIN
McGraw-Hill/Interamericana de España, S.A.U.
TEL +34-91-180-3000
FAX +34-91-372-8513
http://www.mcgraw-hill.es
professional@mcgraw-hill.es

UNITED KINGDOM, NORTHERN,
EASTERN, & CENTRAL EUROPE
McGraw-Hill Education Europe
TEL +44-1-628-502500
FAX +44-1-628-770224
http://www.mcgraw-hill.co.uk
computing_neurope@mcgraw-hill.com

ALL OTHER INQUIRIES Contact:
Osborne/McGraw-Hill
TEL +1-510-549-6600
FAX +1-510-883-7600
http://www.osborne.com
omg_international@mcgraw-hill.com